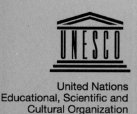

UNESCO

United Nations
Educational, Scientific and
Cultural Organization

UNESCO World Report

Investing in Cultural Diversity and Intercultural Dialogue

 *Azerbaijan performance at UNESCO Headquarters*

Foreword

Culture plays a very special role within UNESCO's mandate. Not only does it represent a specific field of activities, encompassing the safeguarding and promoting heritage in all its forms (both tangible and intangible), encouraging creativity (particularly in the cultural industries), and facilitating mutual understanding through intercultural dialogue, it also permeates all UNESCO's fields of competence. It is therefore a source of satisfaction that this cross-cutting relevance of culture should be underlined with the publication of this second volume in the series of UNESCO intersectoral world reports, devoted to cultural diversity.

In keeping with its function of stimulating international reflection, UNESCO has enlisted the help of many experts, thinkers, practitioners and decision-makers in the preparation of this World Report. Following landmarks such as the 1982 Mexico City World Conference on Cultural Policies, the 1996 publication of the report *Our Creative Diversity* by the World Commission on Culture and Development chaired by Javier Pérez de Cuéllar, former United Nations Secretary-General, and the 1998 Stockholm Intergovernmental Conference on Cultural Policies for Development, the UNESCO World Report *Investing in Cultural Diversity and Intercultural Dialogue* extends the reflection on culture to cultural change itself, highlighting the dynamic nature of cultural diversity and its capacity to renew our approaches to sustainable development, the effective exercise of universally recognized human rights, social cohesion and democratic governance.

Accelerating globalization processes place a premium on intercultural competencies, both individual and collective, which enable us to manage cultural diversity more effectively and monitor cultural change. Without such competencies, misunderstandings rooted in identity issues are liable to proliferate. A strengthening of these competencies is central to the recommendations of the present report, which governments, governmental and non-governmental organizations, the private sector and civil society should seek to implement as a matter of priority.

Through this World Report, UNESCO wishes to build on the advances of recent years and in particular to emphasize that cultural diversity has as its corollary intercultural dialogue, which implies a need to move beyond a focus on differences that can only be a source of conflict, ignorance and misunderstanding. Cultural diversity is related to the dynamic process whereby cultures change while remaining themselves, in a state of permanent openness to one another. At the individual level, this is reflected in multiple and changing cultural identities, which are not easily reducible to definite categories and which represent opportunities for dialogue based on sharing what we have in common beyond those differences.

The value of this new approach to cultural diversity is evident not only in UNESCO's activities in the cultural sphere; it also helps to renew the Organization's strategies in all its other fields of competence. On questions as important as multilingualism, realizing the education for all goals, developing quality media and stimulating creativity in the service of development, new solutions are emerging that need to be explored in greater depth if the international community is to prove equal to its own ambitions.

With this World Report, UNESCO reaffirms the continuing relevance of the United Nations approach based on universally proclaimed human rights and the principles of democratic governance. Better knowledge and recognition of our respective differences leads ultimately to better mutual understanding, with particular regard to those objectives we hold in common. Since the adoption of our Organization's Constitution in 1945, this truth has been inscribed at the heart of UNESCO's action.

Koïchiro Matsuura,
Director-General of UNESCO

The Moai of Peace

Preface

The publication of the UNESCO World Report *Investing in Cultural Diversity and Intercultural Dialogue* is particularly timely in light of the current world events. The financial crisis and its consequences for the economy, labour markets, social policies and international cooperation risk to show that culture often remains the first adjustment variable to be sacrificed when the drying up of financial resources imposes a drastic choice between a number of competing priorities. Yet this is a very short-term view. For at this crossroad, where some are urging us to think in terms of a new world in which human disasters of this kind would no longer be possible, greater acknowledgement of cultural diversity is proving a particularly promising avenue of approach.

This World Report seeks to show that acknowledging cultural diversity helps to renew the international community's strategies in a series of areas so as to further its ambitious objectives, with the support and involvement of local populations. For culture is not simply another sector of activity, a mass consumption product or an asset to be preserved. Culture is the very substratum of all human activities, which derive their meaning and value from it. This is why the recognition of cultural diversity can help to ensure that ownership of development and peace initiatives is vested in the populations concerned.

With regard to development initiatives, it has long been known that their success depends significantly on the extent to which they incorporate the cultural factor. But the message of sustainable development is that the planet is essentially finite, and that the resources humanity hoped to discover in its environment must now be found within itself, in its very diversity. Diversity must henceforth be considered a starting point rather than an obstacle to be overcome. Cultural diversity invites us to think in terms of a plural humanity, embodying a creative potential that precludes any prescribed model of development.

With regard to peace, we are convinced that its sustainability depends upon universally proclaimed human rights, which are the main token of our common humanity. The acknowledgement of cultural diversity and intercultural dialogue help to defuse the tensions that can arise in multicultural societies when a majority and minorities confront each other over recognition of their rights. What favours cultural diversity, which is in no way opposed to the universality of human rights, is a governance of reconciliation, which is the surest guarantee of peace.

This approach has a bearing on international reflection on the 'post-crisis' world and the new mechanisms needed for its construction. While the 'traditional' cultural sectors (such as book sales or cinema, theatre, and concert attendance) seem for the moment to be spared by the 'crisis', it is worth underlining that culture can serve as an 'anti-crisis' weapon by encouraging us to think in terms of alternative modes of development. In this connection, it should not be overlooked that economic actors are increasingly acknowledging the importance of cultural diversity, not only in public policy — with regard to education, languages, media content and the arts and culture — but also in the activities of the private sector. We are witnessing the rediscovery of the virtues of a diversified work environment, in which creativity and innovation derive less from competition than from mutual receptiveness, from the sharing and exchange of knowledge. New areas of encounter between public and private decision-makers are emerging, and UNESCO has a leading role to play in this regard.

A genuine acknowledgement of cultural diversity is thus essential to attain the Millennium Development Goals. The belated recognition of this truth at the 2005 World Summit must now be translated into practical action.

Campaigning for the acknowledgement of cultural diversity in fields not immediately identified with culture does not mean lessening our vigilance in the cultural field proper. Safeguarding our tangible and intangible cultural heritage, stimulating creativity and furthering the discovery of new cultural horizons will necessarily remain formidable challenges. While such goals may be seen by many as a pointless luxury, they are in fact of the essence, as those who possess little, or nothing, are only too aware.

Francoise Rivière
Assistant Director-General for Culture

Acknowledgements

This World Report would not have been possible without the generous and varied contributions of many individuals and organizations from around the world. The team expresses its sincere gratitude to Georges Kutukdjian and John Corbett who, from January to September 2009, finalized the drafting of the World Report.

Under the supervision of Françoise Rivière	**Assistant Director-General for Culture**
Georges Kutukdjian and John Corbett	General Editors

Team for the preparation of the UNESCO World Report

Core team

Frédéric Sampson	Editorial and Research Coordinator
Janine Treves-Habar	Project Editor and Production Coordinator
Michael Millward	Director of the World Reports Unit (effective until July 2007)

Principal consultants

Cristina Amescua Chávez	Research assistant (intangible heritage)
Berta de Sancristóbal	Research assistant (languages and education)
Maria Ejarque	Research assistant (communication and information)
Alessandro Giacone	Research assistant (social and human sciences)
Lucie Assumpta Guéguen	Research assistant (intercultural management)
Arian Hassani	Research assistant (cultural industries)
Sophia Labadi	Research assistant (heritage and governance)
Chantal Lyard	Research assistant (sciences)
Maria José Miñana	Research assistant (translations)

Statistics

Lydia Deloumeaux, Simon Ellis and Jose Pessoa	Senior statisticians, UNESCO Institute for statistics
Frédéric Payeur, Hind Aït Iken and Constantine Yannelis	Consultants for statistics
Akif Altundaş	Graphics and figures

Many thanks also to John Pritchard, who generously allowed us to use cartograms from www.worldmapper.org and to Philippe Rekacewicz. The team is also grateful for the help provided by Guiomar Alonso Cano, programme specialist.

Production team

Andrew Esson, Baseline Arts Ltd	Iconography
Marcus Brainard	Copyeditor
Alison McKelvey Clayson and Brian Smith	Proofreaders
Susan Curran	Indexer

Secretariat

Latifa Ouazany	Senior assistant
Janet Boulmer	Secretarial assistant

Advisory Committee for the World Report on Cultural Diversity

The World Report benefited greatly from intellectual advice and guidance provided by an external advisory panel of eminent experts, including:

Neville Alexander (South Africa)
Arjun Appadurai (India)
Lourdes Arizpe (Mexico)
Lina Attel (Jordan)
Tyler Cowen (USA)
Biserka Cvjetičanin (Croatia)
Philippe Descola (France)
Sakiko Fukuda-Parr (Japan)
Jean-Pierre Guingané (Burkina Faso)
Luis Enrique López (Peru)
Tony Pigott (Canada)
Ralph Regenvanu (Tuvalu)
Anatoly G. Vishnevsky (Russian Federation)
Mohammed Zayani (Tunisia)
Benigna Zimba (Mozambique)

The Advisory Committee accompanied the progression of the preparation of the World Report and was formally gathered on three occasions, in September 2006 (UNESCO Headquarters), for a preliminary brainstorming, in April 2007 (UNESCO Venice Office) for the examination of a first table of contents and the identification of possible contributors and in January 2008 (UNESCO Headquarters), for the examination of a first draft of the World Report.

Intersectoral Working Group

Intersectoral cooperation in the preparation of the World Report was ensured by an informal intersectoral working group constituted for the follow-up of the recommendations of the Advisory Committee and for the discussion of drafts submitted for consideration. The team expresses its sincere gratitude to the following individuals, who accepted to coordinate in Spring 2007 a review of existing literature on several topics: John Crowley on poverty, Moufida Goucha on cultural and religious identities, Linda King on education, Douglas Nakashima on the environment, Carmen Piñan on creativity, Mauro Rosi on languages, Alexander Schischlik on cultural consumption, Ann-Belinda Preis on migration, and Susanne Schnuttgen on knowledge diversity. In 2008, the guidance of Cécile Duvelle, Paola Leoncini-Bartoli, Ann-Belinda Preis and Mogens Schmidt, under the supervision of Françoise Rivière, was very helpful for the second redrafting of the World Report. In 2009, in the final phase of redrafting supervised by Georges Kutukdjian and John Corbett, the World Report received important inputs from Salvatore Arico and Ana Persic on biodiversity issues, Aaron Benavot on curricula issues, Maritza Formisano on human rights, Rosa Gonzales, Vijayananda Jayaweera, George Papagiannis and Mogens Schmidt on communication and information as well as Chifa Tekaya on poverty eradication. The work of the Intersectoral Working Group also benefited of contributions from: Abdelaziz Abid, Feriel Aït-Ouyahia, Claude Akpabie, Frances Albernaz, Massimo Amadio, Sandrine Amiel, Noro Andriamiseza, Francesco Bandarin, Hervé Barré, Peter Bates, Denise Bax, Jovanni Boccardi, Alice Bosquillon de Jenlis, Mounir Bouchenaki, Andrea Cairola, Alisa Cherepanova, Pilar Chiang-Joo, Moe Chiba, Bernard Combes, Monique Couratier, Timothy Curtis, Paul de Guchteneire, Vincent Defourny, Ian Denison, Helena Drobna, Ana Dumitrescu, Richard Engelhard, Majda Fahim, Vladimir Gai, Rosa Guerreiro, Heide Hackmann, Amina Hamshari, Nao Hayashi, Maria-Helena Henriques-Mueller, Klara Issak, Jing Feng, Marcel Kabanda, Ali Kazancigil, Lina Khamis, Anthony Krause, Sabine Kube, François Langlois, Jean-Yves Le Saux, Doyun Lee, Anne Lemaistre, Laurent Lévi-Strauss, Nicole

Lorin, Saorla McCabe, Ana-Luiza Machado, Anahit Minasyan, Edgar Montiel, Edmond Moukala, Ali Moussa Iye, Mary Murebwaire, Ayeh Naraghi, Hugue Ngandeu Ngatta, Thu Huong Nguyen Duy, Folarim Osotimehin, Antoine Pecoud, Georges Poussin, Frank Proschan, Philippe Ratte, Clinton Robinson, Mary Rosset, Mechtild Rössler, Galia Saouma-Forero, Susan Schneegans, Onno Seroo, Rieks Smeets, Germán Solinís, Katerina Stenou, Konstantinos Tararas, Petya Totcharova, Saori Terada, Marius Tukaj, Indrasen Vencatachellum, Reiko Yoshida, René Zapata, as well the members of the College of ADGs (to whom the draft report was presented in may 2009), notably Marcio Barbosa, Patricio Bernal, Nicholas Burnett, Hans d'Orville, Walter Erdelen, Abdul Waheed Khan, Amine Khene, Elizabeth Longworth, Saturnino Muñoz-Gómez and Pierre Sané. Carlotta Aiello from UNDP, Florian Forster from IOM and Emmanuel Kattan from the UN Alliance of Civilizations were also resourceful contacts for interagency cooperation.

External contributions

Several contributions were solicited from experts all around the world in the different phases of preparation of the World Report. In the preliminary phase (early 2006), institutional consultations were undertaken with civil society and academic communities, which benefited from valuable inputs from: the European Research Institute for Culture and the Arts (ERICarts), especially Danielle Cliche and Andreas Wiesand; George Mason University, especially Stefan Toepler; la Organización de Estados Iberoamericanos para la Educación, la Ciencia y la Cultura (OEI), especially Francesco Rueda and Néstor Garcia Canclíni; the Observatory for Cultural Policies in Africa (OCPA), especially Lupwishi Mbuyamba and Máté Kovács; the Middle East Center for Culture and Development (MECCAD), especially Iman al-Hindawi; the Asian Media Information Center (AMIC), especially Indrajit Banerjee and Madanmohan Rao; the International Music Council, especially Silja Fischer and Richard Letts; and the Institut de Cultura, Barcelona City Council (as chair of United Cities and Local Governments' Working Group on Culture), especially Jordi Pascual. In a later phase of the project (May 2007), a conceptual workshop was organized at UNESCO Headquarters, to which took part Barbara Cassin, Philippe Descola, Masahiro Hamashita, Paul Nchoji Nkwi, Victoria Tauli-Corpuz and Mourad Wahba. In

summer and fall 2007, several background papers were commissioned to the following experts: Abdullahi An-Na'im on 'Human rights and cultural diversity'; Pernilla Askerud on 'Cultural industries: mapping a new world'; Esther Benbassa on 'Diversity and national culture'; Annie Brisset on 'World translation flows and practices'; Peter Brosius on 'Cultural diversity and conservation'; Linda Caldwell on 'Boundaries and divides faced by young people'; Monica Caluser on 'Good governance and consideration of the human dimension in different cultural contexts'; Manuela Carneiro da Cunha on 'The future of cultures'; Johnson Cerda on 'Cultural diversity in a changing climate'; Antonio Damasio on 'Cultural diversity, neuroscience and education'; Jasleen Dhamija on 'Crafts, cultural diversity and development'; Doudou Diène on 'Nouvelles formes de racisme et de stigmatization culturelle contemporaines: de l'intolérance à la propagation de stéréotypes'; Marina Djabbarzade on 'Cultural diversity: an operational perspective'; Yvonne Donders on 'Human rights and cultural diversity'; Mahdi Elmandjra on 'Diversité culturelle : clé de la survie de l'humanité'; Okwui Enwezor and Jean Fisher on 'Artists in contemporary societies: national or global citizenships?'; Munir Fasheh on 'Cultural diversity in formal and non formal education systems'; Elfriede Fürsich on 'Media, and the representation of Others'; Amareswar Galla on 'Cultural diversity in human development'; Chérif Khaznadar on 'Performing artists, cultural diversity and creativity'; Will Kymlicka on 'The rise and fall of multiculturalism? New debates on inclusion and accommodation in diverse societies'; Michèle Lamont and Mario Small on 'Cultural diversity and poverty eradication'; Alain Le Diberder on 'Cultural industries, cultural diversity and the development of South countries'; Danilo Leonardi on 'Media law reform and policies in transitions countries'; Joseph Lo Bianco on 'The importance of language policies and multilingualism for cultural diversity'; Pierre Maranda on 'Paramètres cognitifs de l'ouverture à la diversité culturelle : une perspective anthropologique'; Carolina Ödman (Universe Awareness) on 'Diversity of knowledge and creativity for sustainable human development in the contexts of science and education'; Catherine Odora-Hoppers on 'Cultural diversity, traditions and modernities: complexity and opportunities in the 21st century'; Marc Raboy on 'Media pluralism and the promotion of cultural diversity'; Mike Robinson on 'Discovering and negotiating and cultural diversity through tourism texts'; Suzanne Romaine on 'Languages and cultural identities'; Carlo Severi on 'La communication interculturelle : une approche anthropologique et cognitive'; Daryush Shayegan on 'La diversité culturelle et la civilisation planétaire'; Crain Soudien on 'Multiple cultural identities and cultural fictions: cultural makeshifts and metissages'; Victoria Tauli-Corpuz on 'Indigenous peoples' voice in a globalised world'; Hermann Tillmann and Maria Salas on 'Cultural diversity, a key component of sustainability'; Victor Toledo on 'Cultural diversity, a key component of sustainability'; John Tomlinson on 'Cultural globalization and the representation of Otherness through the media'; Jorge Vala and Rui Costa-Lopes on 'Youth, intolerance and diversity'; Steven Vertovec on 'Towards post-multiculturalism? Changing communities, conditions and contexts of diversity'; Anatoly Vishnevsky on 'Diversité culturelle et transitions démographiques'; Jean-Pierre Warnier and Francis Nyamnjoh on 'La mondialisation culturelle: réelle ou imaginaire?'; Ben Wiesner on 'Climate change and cultural diversity' and Zhao Tingyang on 'The Clash of Civilizations from a Chinese perspective'. Important contributions were also received on the occasion of an International Meeting of Experts on Cultural Diversity and Education organized in Barcelona in early 2008 with the generous support of the UNESCO Centre for Catalunya and the Generalitat de Catalunya, to which participated: Magda Abu-Fadil, Mohammed Arkoun, Akira Arimoto, Christopher Drake, Mamoussé Diagne, Christoph Eberhard, Munir Fasheh, Vigdís Finnbogadóttir, José Antonio Flores Farfán, Sakiko Fukuda-Parr, Angeline Kamba, Grimaldo Rengifo, Madhu Suri Prakash, Tove Skutnabb-Kangas, Wole Soyinka, Marietta Stepanyants, Janusz Symonides, Joseph Tsang Mang Kin and Billy Wapotro. The preparation team also greatly benefited from exchange and consultations with the following individuals: Leif Almö, Helmut Anheier, Maurice Aymard, Anthony Kwame Appiah, Pascal Bello, Seyla Benhabib, Janet Bennett, Jean-Godefroy Bidima, Lise Boily, Mary Yoko Brannen, Marita Carballo, Joji Cariño, Isaac Chiva, Nigel Crawhall, Milagros Del Corral, Vladimir Donn, Erica Eyrich, Isabelle Ferin, Delia Ferri, Colette Grinevald, Jagdish Gundara, Yudhishthir Raj Isar, Jafar Jafari, François Jullien, Carme Junyent, Eleni Kampanellou, David Kessler, Gloria López-Morales, Luisa Maffi, Alexander Marc, Colin Mercer, John Paolillo, W. James Potter, Heritiana Ranaivoson, Raymond Ranjeva, Leila Rezk, Noella Richard, Irene Rodgers, Ghassan Salamé, Adama Samassékou, Daniel Sibony, Dan Sperber, Charles Taylor, David Throsby, Neil Van der Linden, Laure Veirier, Antonella Verdiani, Princess Wijdan Ali, Joseph Yacoub. Homi Bhabha's comments and encouragements were very helpful in the several phases of the project.

↻ 'Korean Fantasy', a performance of two Korean intangible heritage expressions at UNESCO Headquarters, 2004

Contents

Foreword — **Koïchiro Matsuura** *(Director-General of UNESCO)* — iii

Preface — **Françoise Rivière** *(Assistant Director-General for Culture)* — v

Acknowledgements — vi

General Introduction — 1

PART I. Cultural Diversity: What is at Stake? — 9

Chapter 1 **Cultural diversity** — 11
1.1 Cultural diversity in a globalizing world — 13
1.2 National, religious, cultural and multiple identities — 19
1.3 Regional and international initiatives on cultural diversity — 23
Conclusion and recommendations — 28
In focus: Standard-setting instruments adopted by UNESCO — 29
References and websites — 32

Chapter 2 **Intercultural dialogue** — 37
2.1 Cultural interactions — 39
2.2 Cultural stereotypes and intolerance — 41
2.3 The challenges of dialogue in a multicultural world — 45
2.4 Empowerment — 51
Conclusion and recommendations — 54
In focus: The history of dialogue at UNESCO and institutional initiatives on intercultural dialogue — 56
References and websites — 61

PART II. Key Vectors of Cultural Diversity — 65

Chapter 3 **Languages** — 67
3.1 Language dynamics today — 69
3.2 Languages and identities — 73
3.3 The challenges of language assessment and revitalization — 76
3.4 Multilingualism, translation and intercultural dialogue — 80
Conclusion and recommendations — 85
In focus: The key facets of language planning and policy-making — 87
References and websites — 90

Chapter 4 **Education** — 95
4.1 The relevance of educational methods and contents — 97
4.2 Learning societies and the right to education — 108
4.3 Participatory learning and intercultural competencies — 114
Conclusion and recommendations — 118
In focus: UNESCO's guidelines on intercultural education — 119
References and websites — 123

Chapter 5 **Communication and cultural contents** — 129
5.1 Globalization and new media trends — 131
5.2 Impacts of communication and cultural products — 137
5.3 Policies fostering cultural diversity — 144
Conclusion and recommendations — 150
In focus: Media toolkits for cultural diversity in broadcasting — 152
References and websites — 157

Chapter 6	**Creativity and the marketplace**	**161**
	6.1 Artistic creation and the creative economy	163
	6.2 Crafts and international tourism	167
	6.3 Cultural diversity and the business world	172
	Conclusion and recommendations	179
	In focus: Tools and approaches for increasing the relevance of cultural diversity to corporate audiences	181
	References and websites	183

PART III. Renewing International Strategies related to Development and Peace 187

Chapter 7	**Cultural diversity: A key dimension of sustainable development**	**189**
	7.1 The cultural approach to development	191
	7.2 Perceptions of poverty and poverty eradication	196
	7.3 Cultural diversity and environmental sustainability	203
	Conclusion and recommendations	209
	In focus: The Cultural Diversity Programming Lens: A tool for monitoring development projects	211
	References and websites	215

Chapter 8	**Cultural diversity, human rights and democratic governance**	**221**
	8.1 Cultural diversity and universally recognized human rights	223
	8.2 Cultural diversity: A parameter of social cohesion	231
	8.3 The challenge of cultural diversity for democratic governance	238
	Conclusion and recommendations	242
	In focus: Three examples of traditional mechanisms and intangible heritage in the service of democratic governance	243
	References and websites	246

| **General Conclusion** | | **251** |

| **Recommendations** | | **256** |

Statistical Annex		259
	Introduction to the Statistical Annex	260
	Methodological explorations of the measurement of culture and cultural diversity	261
	Reader's guide	276
	Table 1. Ratifications of the seven cultural conventions of UNESCO	277
	Table 2. World Heritage sites and Intangible Cultural Heritage of Humanity	281
	Table 3. Demographic context	286
	Table 4. Telecommunication access	294
	Table 5. Gender	298
	Table 6. Highlights of the World Values Survey	302
	Table 7. Languages	304
	Table 8. Translations	308
	Table 9. Education and literacy	312
	Table 10. Education and curricula	320
	Table 11. International flows of mobile students at the tertiary level	328
	Table 12. Newspapers	332
	Table 13. Broadcast content	340
	Table 14. Movies	344
	Table 15. Recorded music: Sales and repertoire	348
	Table 16. International flows of selected cultural goods and services	352

Table 17.   Tourism flows   360
Table 18.   Environment, biodiversity and habitat   364
Table 19.   Economic development and innovation   368
Glossary   372

List of abbreviations   382

Photographic credits   386

Index   387

Boxes

Chapter 1   Cultural diversity   11
             Box 1.1   The migration factor   15
             Box 1.2   Globalization and indigenous populations   17
             Box 1.3   Digital cultures and new diversity   18
             Box 1.4   Reconstructing Central Asian identities in the post-Soviet era   21

Chapter 2   Intercultural dialogue   37
             Box 2.1   UNESCO Slave Route Project: Celebrating the cultural expressions generated through
                        enforced dialogue   40
             Box 2.2   'What went wrong with the dialogue between cultures?' 44
             Box 2.3   Intercultural competencies: The basics   45
             Box 2.4   Reconciliation through common narrative: Revised history textbook initiatives   49
             Box 2.5   Through the eyes of hunters-gatherers: Participatory 3D modelling among
                        the Ogiek indigenous peoples in Kenya   52

Chapter 3   Languages   67
             Box 3.1   Languages in cyberspace   71
             Box 3.2   Monitoring linguistic diversity for biodiversity   74
             Box 3.3   Assessing language vitality   77
             Box 3.4   Minority indigenous languages in translation in South America   83

Chapter 4   Education   95
             Box 4.1   Data on educational curricula from UNESCO's International Bureau of Education   99
             Box 4.2   The evolution of indigenous bilingual education in Latin America   105
             Box 4.3   Education in Auroville, India   109
             Box 4.4   Museums as a space for intercultural learning   117

Chapter 5   Communication and cultural contents   129
             Box 5.1   The emergence of international and pan-regional news services   134
             Box 5.2   The Power of Peace Network (PPN)   139
             Box 5.3   Little Mosque on the Prairie   143
             Box 5.4   Implementing media literacy programmes   145
             Box 5.5   Aboriginal Peoples Television Network (APTN)   148

Chapter 6   Creativity and the marketplace   161
             Box 6.1   Towards the legal protection of folklore?   169
             Box 6.2   Religious tourism   170
             Box 6.3   Consumer values analysis in the BRICs   173
             Box 6.4   Adapting management practices to local contexts: Danone Mexico   176

Fantasia, on the occasion of a Berber festival in the Sahara Desert of southern Morocco

	Box 6.5	A correlation between diversity and economic performance?	178
Chapter 7		**Cultural diversity: A key dimension of sustainable development**	189
	Box 7.1	Population and development action programmes	194
	Box 7.2	The Fair Trade movement	200
	Box 7.3	Ecomuseums and poverty alleviation in Viet Nam	201
	Box 7.4	Sustainable development assistance for displaced populations and refugees	206
	Box 7.5	Local management of natural resources and biodiversity	208
Chapter 8		**Cultural diversity, human rights and democratic governance**	221
	Box 8.1	International case law highlighting cultural aspects of human rights	227
	Box 8.2	Individual and collective dimensions of cultural rights	229
	Box 8.3	The challenges of social cohesion in Africa: From colonial empire to African nationhood	234

Maps

Map 3.1	Living languages in the world according to Ethnologue	69
Map 3.2	Linguistic Diversity Index	81
Map 6.1	Innovation scores, 2008	172
Map 7.1a	Population living below the income poverty line (US$1.25 per day), 2006	196
Map 7.1b	Population living below the income poverty line (US$2 per day), 2006	196
Map 7.2	Protected terrestrial and marine areas, 2005	205
Map 8.1	Government policies on immigration, 2005	231
Map 8.2	Percentage of political positions in Parliaments held by women, 2007	239

Figures

Figure 1.1	Urban and rural population growth	13
Figure 1.2	Ratifications of the seven cultural conventions of UNESCO, per region	26
Figure 2.1	World Values Surveys on geographical belonging	43
Figure 3.1	Percentage of target-language translations	82
Figure 4.1	Type of language taught for selected countries, 2000, In grades 1-6, In grades 7-8	104
Figure 5.1	Percentage of exports by region, 2006	131
Figure 5.2	Exports and imports of audiovisual services and copyrights, 2006	132
Figure 5.3	Percentage of countries by type of domestic music piracy levels in 2006 (physical piracy only)	132
Figure 5.4	Public radio programming for selected countries in 2005	132
Figure 5.5	Origin of top movies exhibited in 2006	133
Figure 5.6	Public television programming for selected countries in 2005	133
Figure 5.7	Recorded music repertoire for selected countries in 2006	133
Figure 6.1	Share of International market for visual and plastic arts	166
Figure 7.1	Cultural Diversity Programming Lens (CDPL) general framework	214
Figure A.1	French labour force in cultural sector by type of activities in 2005	264
Figure A.2	The culture cycle	267
Figure A.3	Domains and activities	268
Figure A.4	Types of dichotomy useful to assess diversity	270
Figure A.5	Population of adults by ethnic group experiencing Taonga Tuku Iho activity during the last 12 months	271
Figure A.6	Share of foreign literature in French book publishing and in bestselling novels	272

A monk in Osaka, Japan

General Introduction

Cultural diversity has emerged as a key concern at the turn of a new century. Some predict that globalization and the liberalization of the goods and services market will lead to cultural standardization, reinforcing existing imbalances between cultures. Others claim that the end of the bipolar world of the Cold War and the eclipse of political ideologies will result in new religious, cultural and even ethnic fault lines, preluding a possible 'clash of civilizations'. Scientists warn of the threats to the Earth's environment posed by human activity, drawing parallels between the erosion of biodiversity and the disappearance of traditional modes of life as a result of a scarcity of resources and the spread of modern lifestyles. 'Diversity' is becoming a rallying call among those who denounce persistent socio-economic inequalities in developed societies. Cultural diversity is similarly posing a challenge to the principles of international cooperation: it is invoked by some to contest universally recognized human rights, while others — like UNESCO — hold firmly to the view that full and unqualified recognition of cultural diversity strengthens the universality of human rights and ensures their effective exercise.

Kihnu Island, Estonia

Yet the meanings attached to this catch-all term are as varied as they are shifting. Some see cultural diversity as inherently positive, insofar as it points to a sharing of the wealth embodied in each of the world's cultures and, accordingly, to the links uniting us all in processes of exchange and dialogue. For others, cultural differences are what cause us to lose sight of our common humanity and are therefore at the root of numerous conflicts. This second diagnosis is today all the more plausible since globalization has increased the points of interaction and friction between cultures, giving rise to identity-linked tensions, withdrawals and claims, particularly of a religious nature, which can become potential sources of dispute.

Underlying the intuition that all these phenomena are in practice linked and relate, each in its own way, to a particular understanding of cultural diversity, the essential challenge would be to propose a coherent vision of cultural diversity so as to clarify how, far from being a threat, it can become beneficial to the actions of the international community. This is the essential purpose of the present report.

From the start, UNESCO has been convinced of the inherent value and necessity of cultural diversity. With reference to the independence and integrity of its Member States, its Constitution (1945) speaks of the 'fruitful diversity' of the world's cultures. As the only United Nations agency responsible for culture, UNESCO promotes the process of mutual receptiveness among peoples with the purpose of contributing to the 'intellectual and moral solidarity' of humankind by combating ignorance and prejudice and thereby helping to build the 'defences of peace in the minds of men'. This project is as relevant today as ever, even if the definition of culture has become much broader since the 1982 World Conference on Cultural Policies in Mexico City, encompassing 'the whole complex of distinctive spiritual, material, intellectual and emotional features that characterize a society or social group, not limited to the arts and letters, and including

... the essential challenge would be to propose a coherent vision of cultural diversity so as to clarify how, far from being a threat, it can become beneficial to the actions of the international community

modes of life, the fundamental rights of the human being, value systems, traditions and beliefs'.

A UNESCO World Report

This report reflects UNESCO's new policy regarding the publication of its world reports, as decided by its Executive Board at its 160th session.

UNESCO's practice in the 1990s was to publish sectoral reports, usually consisting of a collection of opinion pieces or scholarly articles signed by leading academic experts or practitioners in the field. What was lacking was a report by the Organization as a whole, based on close cooperation between its different programme sectors (education, natural sciences, social sciences, culture, communication and information) and combining UNESCO's 'intellectual watch' function with the adoption of policy positions on the major issues within its remit. Such a report would have the advantage of expressing a viewpoint representative of the Organization as a whole, whereas sectoral specialization can result in a fragmentation of standpoints. It could also help to make the Organization more 'visible' by underlining the relevance and topicality of its analyses and work, even if it should not take the form of an activity report, this role being fulfilled by other reports of the governing bodies (Executive Board and General Conference).

Following the publication of a first intersectoral UNESCO World Report on the theme of 'knowledge societies' (2005), which formed part of the second phase of the World Summit on the Information Society (Tunis, 2005), the topic chosen for this second World Report was endorsed by the General Conference in October 2005, and the task of preparing the World Report on Cultural Diversity was formalized with the establishment of a World Reports Unit in May 2006. The work of the World Reports Unit has been guided by the in-house contributions of an informal intersectoral working group and by the recommendations of an advisory committee established in the summer of 2006 and consisting of experts from a variety of specialist and geographical backgrounds. Both have been particularly useful in identifying the topics to be covered, as well as the experts to be consulted, whose written contributions have provided valuable input to the chapters that follow.

The objectives of the World Report on Cultural Diversity are:

- to analyze cultural diversity in all its aspects, by attempting to show the complexity of the processes at work while at the same time identifying a main thread among the wide range of possible interpretations;

- to show the importance of cultural diversity in different areas (languages, education, communication and creativity), which, their intrinsic functions apart, may be seen as essential for the safeguarding and promotion of cultural diversity;

- to convince decision-makers and the various stakeholders of the importance of investing in cultural diversity as an essential dimension of intercultural dialogue, since it can renew our approaches to sustainable development, is a prerequisite for the exercise of universally recognized human rights and freedoms, and can serve to strengthen social cohesion and democratic governance.

The front of a small shop in Naivasha, Kenya

The World Report aims in this way to take account of the new perspectives opened up by reflection on the challenges of cultural diversity and, in so doing, to map out new approaches to monitoring and shaping the changes that are taking place. Thus, the World Report does not seek to provide ready-made solutions to the problems liable to confront decision-makers. Rather, it aims to underline the complexity of these problems, which cannot be solved by political will alone, but call for better understanding of the underlying phenomena and greater international cooperation, particularly through the exchange of good practices and the adoption of common guidelines.

It should also be stressed that the World Report does not claim to offer a global inventory of cultural diversity, established on the basis of available indicators in the manner of the Education for All (EFA) Global Monitoring Report. In the field of cultural diversity, the development of indicators is only just beginning. For the purposes of such an inventory, it would have been necessary to carry out, with the agreement of UNESCO's Member States, a truly global enquiry into cultural diversity — a task that would have required much greater resources than those allocated to the present report, but that could one day be undertaken by a World Observatory on Cultural Diversity, whose creation this report recommends. In the current state of research, the examples chosen serve mainly to illustrate the relevance of the arguments advanced. They have been selected on the basis of the materials available and in an effort to vary their geographical origin.

UNESCO hopes in this way to play a part in the recent renewal of thinking on cultural diversity, in keeping with its work in the 1950s and the conclusions of *Our Creative Diversity*, the report of the World Commission on Culture and Development (1996), chaired by former United Nations Secretary-General Javier Pérez de Cuéllar. In the text entitled *Race and History* written in 1952 for UNESCO, the French anthropologist Claude Lévi-Strauss argued that the protection of cultural diversity should not be confined to preservation of the status quo: it is 'diversity itself which must be saved, not the outward and visible form in which each period has clothed that diversity'. Protecting cultural diversity thus meant ensuring that diversity continued to exist, not that a given state of diversity should perpetuate itself indefinitely. This presupposed a capacity to accept and sustain cultural change, while not regarding it as an edict of fate. The report of the World Commission on

Culture and Development had argued along similar lines that cultural diversity is not simply an asset to be preserved but a resource to be promoted, with particular regard to its potential benefits, including in areas relatively distant from culture in the strict sense. The present report seeks to build upon the earlier report's main conclusions.

In recent years the arguments UNESCO has developed in its thinking on cultural diversity have been taken up by a significant number of programmes and agencies in the United Nations and Bretton Woods institutions. The World Bank, for example, has on several occasions followed UNESCO's lead in the context of the World Decade on Culture and Development (1988-1997) in its enquiries into the links between culture and development, notably at the international conferences 'Culture Counts' in Florence in 1999 and 'New Frontiers of Social Policies' held in Arusha, Tanzania, in 2005 (see Marc, 2005). The United Nations Development Programme (UNDP) and the United Nations Environment Programme (UNEP) have likewise published, respectively, a Human Development Report entitled *Cultural Liberty in Today's Diverse World* (2004) and a collection of articles on natural resource management entitled *Cultural and Spiritual Values of Biodiversity* (Posey, 1999). Subsequently, the Report of the High-level Group for the Alliance of Civilizations (2006) has given unprecedented prominence to initiatives promoting dialogue between peoples, cultures and civilizations. The present report is

⋒ *French anthropologist Claude Lévi-Strauss and René Maheu, Director-General of UNESCO, 1971*

A performance of the Burundi drums at UNESCO Headquarters, 1996

Cultural diversity should be defined as the capacity to maintain the dynamic of change in all of us, whether individuals or groups

also intended to contribute to the thinking and studies of UNESCO's partner programmes and agencies, particularly with regard to development.

What is cultural diversity?
The topic covered by this World Report is complex, and some preliminary clarifications are necessary in order to avoid misunderstandings.

Cultural diversity is above all a fact: there exists a wide range of distinct cultures, even if the contours delimiting a particular culture prove more difficult to establish than might at first sight appear. Moreover, awareness of this diversity has today become relatively commonplace, being facilitated by the globalization of exchanges and the greater receptiveness of societies to one another. While this greater awareness in no way guarantees the preservation of cultural diversity, it has helped to give the topic greater visibility.

Cultural diversity has moreover become a major social concern, linked to the growing variety of social codes within and between societies. It is increasingly clear that lifestyles, social representations, value systems, codes of conduct, social relations (inter-generational, between men and women, etc.), the linguistic forms and registers within a particular language, cognitive processes, artistic expressions, notions of public and private space (with particular reference to urban planning and the living

environment), forms of learning and expression, modes of communication and even systems of thought, can no longer be reduced to a single model or conceived in terms of fixed representations. The emergence on the political stage of local communities, indigenous peoples, deprived or vulnerable groups and those excluded on grounds of ethnic origin, social affiliation, age or gender, has led to the discovery, within societies, of new forms of diversity. The political establishment has in this way found itself challenged, and cultural diversity has taken its place on the political agenda in most countries of the world.

Confronted by this diversity of codes and outlooks, States sometimes find themselves at a loss to know how to respond, often as a matter of urgency, or how to address cultural diversity in the common interest. To contribute to the devising of specific responses to this situation, this report seeks to provide a framework for renewed understanding of the challenges inherent in cultural diversity. It will be necessary for that purpose to identify, beyond the mere fact of diversity, some of the theoretical and political difficulties it inevitably poses.

A first difficulty has to do with the specifically *cultural* nature of this form of diversity. Societies have recourse to various proxies, particularly ethnic or linguistic characterizations, to take account of their cultural heterogeneity. For example, examination of the population classification systems used in national censuses in different countries reveals wide divergences of approach to cultural categorization (ethnic origin, religious affiliation, skin colour, etc.). The first challenge will therefore be to examine the different policies pursued without losing sight of our topic, which is cultural diversity and not the proxies to which it is sometimes reduced. One solution would be to adopt the broadest possible definition of culture, along the lines of the consensus embodied in UNESCO's 1982 Mexico City Declaration on Cultural Policies, which has the merit of not restricting the definition of culture or focusing on a particular aspect (e.g. religion) in order to define a culture.

Another difficulty concerns the identification of the *constituents* of cultural diversity. In this connection, the terms 'culture', 'civilization' and 'peoples' have different connotations depending on context, for example scientific or political (Descola, 2005). Whereas 'cultures' refers to entities that tend to define themselves in relation to one another, the term 'civilization' refers to cultures that affirm their values or world views as universal and adopt an expansionist approach towards those who do not (or do not yet) share them. It is therefore a very real challenge to attempt to persuade the different centres of civilization to coexist peacefully. As conceived by UNESCO — a conception remote from those ideological constructions that predict a 'clash of civilizations' — civilization is to be understood as 'work in progress', as the accommodation of each of the world's cultures, on the basis of equality, in an ongoing universal project.

A third difficulty that needs to be provisionally identified concerns the relationship of cultures to change. For, as noted by Manuela Carneiro da Cunha, almost seven decades of the 20th century were to pass before cultures started to be understood as shifting entities. Previously, there was a tendency to view them as essentially fixed, their content being 'transmitted' between generations through a variety of channels, such as education or initiatory practices of various kinds. Today culture is increasingly understood as a process whereby societies evolve along pathways that are specific to them. 'What is truly specific in a society is not so much people's values, beliefs, feelings, habits, languages, knowledge, lifestyles etc. as the way in which all these characteristics change' (Cunha, 2007).

These considerations argue in favour of a new approach to cultural diversity — one that takes account of its dynamic nature and the challenges of identity associated with the permanence of cultural change. This necessarily entails changes to UNESCO's role in this context. For, whereas the Organization's longstanding concern has been with the conservation and safeguarding of endangered cultural sites, practices and expressions, it must now also learn to sustain cultural change in order to help individuals and groups to manage diversity more effectively — for this ultimately is the major challenge: *managing cultural diversity*.

The challenge inherent in cultural diversity is not posed simply at the international level (between nation-states) or at the infra-national level (within increasingly multicultural societies); it also concerns us as individuals through those multiple identities whereby we learn to be receptive to difference while remaining ourselves. Thus cultural diversity has important political implications: it prescribes the aim of freeing ourselves of stereotypes and prejudices in order to accept others with their differences and

complexities. In this way, it becomes possible to rediscover our common humanity through our very diversity. Cultural diversity thereby becomes a resource, benefitting cultural intellectual and scientific cooperation for development and the culture of peace.

The structure of the World Report

Given the essential ambition of the World Report, which is to shed light on the ways in which cultural diversity can serve the actions of the international community, the first requirement is to agree on what cultural diversity is, and what it is not. This is the aim of the report's first two chapters.

This is, of course, an old problem, one with which UNESCO has grappled since its establishment in 1945. But in recent times globalization seems to have radically altered the stakes, lending greater urgency to certain conceptual changes long in gestation. It has become clear that cultural diversity should be defined as the capacity to maintain the dynamic of change in all of us, whether individuals or groups. This dynamic is today inseparable from the search for pathways to an authentic intercultural dialogue. In this regard, it is important to analyze the causes (stereotypes, misunderstandings, identity-based tensions) that make intercultural dialogue a complex task. It is also necessary to explore the potential benefits of novel approaches, paying particular attention to new actors (women, young people) and the creation of new networks at all levels.

Part II of the report examines four key areas — languages, education, communication and cultural content, and creativity and the marketplace — with respect to the future of cultural diversity. In each of these areas, cultural diversity can be promoted and nurtured, for its own sake and for the benefit of the corresponding sectoral policies. Of course, virtually all activities can have an impact on cultural diversity, and vice versa. However, the fields in question are particularly relevant in the sense that cultural diversity both depends on and significantly influences their evolution.

Languages doubtless constitute the most immediate manifestation of cultural diversity. Today they are facing new challenges and steps must be taken both to revitalize endangered languages and promote receptiveness to others through a command of several languages — mother tongue, national language and an international language — and through the development of translation capacity.

These considerations argue in favour of a new approach to cultural diversity — one that takes account of its dynamic nature and the challenges of identity associated with the permanence of cultural change

In the field of education, we must seek to strike a balance between the requirements of education for all and the integration of cultural diversity in educational strategies through the diversification of educational contents and methods, and a new emphasis on the development of intercultural competencies conducive to dialogue. More generally, there is a need to promote practices involving out-of-school learning and value transmission, notably in the informal sector and through the arts, as developed by societies worldwide.

Concerning communication and cultural content, the focus is on the importance of overcoming certain obstacles that, by hampering the free circulation of ideas by word and image, can impair our responses to cultural diversity. Persistent stereotypes and major disparities in the capacity to produce cultural contents are a particular concern and call for greater efforts to promote media literacy and information skills, particularly through the information and communication technologies (ICTs).

Finally, we shall highlight the continuum that exists between artistic creativity and social creativity, ranging from cultural creation (including the arts) through commercialized sectors such as handicrafts and tourism, to the broader impacts of culture on business and the economy. In a globalized world, cultural diversity assumes new importance as a potentially significant factor in economic growth strategies.

The report's last two chapters (Part III) attempt to analyze how cultural diversity can help to renew the international community's approaches to a series of problems that have existed since the founding of the United Nations: development on the one hand, and peace-building on the other, in particular the promotion of universally recognized human rights.

It is well known that effective development policies must take account of the different cultural settings in which they are to be deployed. Cultural diversity can be instrumental in the empowerment of communities, populations and groups. It can be the linchpin of innovative strategies for protecting the environment and combating poverty and inequality.

Furthermore, to the extent that we are successful in encouraging an approach to cultural diversity based on the promotion of intercultural dialogue and the

development of unity in diversity, diversity can no longer be seen as being at odds with or opposed to the universally shared principles on which our common humanity is based. Cultural diversity accordingly becomes a key instrument for the effective exercise of universal human rights and for the renewal of strategies aimed at strengthening social cohesion through the development of new and more participatory forms of governance.

In each of the chapters, boxes containing examples and case studies — including views that UNESCO does not necessarily endorse — serve to illustrate different facets of the arguments presented. Most serve to promote 'good practices' and may prove useful to decision-makers confronted by similar challenges. At the end of each chapter, an 'In focus' section provides more detailed information on a potentially valuable topic, tool or reference in the field in question.

The eight chapters of the World Report are followed by a 'General Conclusion and Recommendations', and by a 'Statistical Annex', produced in collaboration with the UNESCO Institute of Statistics (UIS). The annex is divided into two parts: the first consists of a methodological chapter, which explores some of the many challenges inherent in the measurement of cultural domains and introduces the 2009 UIS Framework of Cultural Statistics; the second part presents 19 statistical tables, illustrating current coverage across a wide range of topics and more than 200 countries and territories.

⮫ *The Rabinal Achí dance drama of the Mayas, Guatemala*

References and websites

Background documents and UNESCO sources

Carneiro da Cunha, M. 2007. The future of cultures. Background paper.

UNESCO. 2005. *Towards Knowledge Societies*. Intersectoral World Report. Paris, UNESCO. http://unesdoc.unesco. org/images/0014/001418/141843e.pdf

UNESCO. 1982. *Mexico City Declaration on Cultural Policies*. World Conference on Cultural Policies, Mexico City, 26 July – 6 August. http://portal.unesco.org/culture/en/ files/12762/11295421661mexico_en.pdf/mexico_en.pdf

Websites

The Constitution of UNESCO (1945): http://unesdoc.unesco. org/images/0012/001255/125590e.pdf#constitution

UNESCO Culture Portal: http://portal.unesco.org/culture/en/ ev.php-URL_ID=34603&URL_DO=DO_TOPIC&URL_ SECTION=201.html

UNESCO Institute for Statistics: http://www.uis.unesco.org/ ev.php?ID=2867_201&ID2=DO_TOPIC

References

Alliance of Civilizations. 2006. *Report of the High-level Group*. 13 November. New York, United Nations. http://www. aocistanbul.org/data/HLG_Report.pdf

Bhabha, H. K. 1994. *The Location of Culture*. London, Routledge.

Descola, P. 2005. *Par-delà Nature et Culture*. Paris, Gallimard.

Elias, N. 2000. *The Civilizing Process: Sociogenetic and Psychogenetic Investigations*. Translated by E. Jephcott with some notes and corrections by the author. Edited by E. Dunning, J. Goudsblom and S. Mennell. Oxford, Blackwell.

Lévi-Strauss, C. 1952. *Race and History*. Paris, UNESCO.

Marc, A. 2005. Cultural diversity and service delivery: where do we stand? Draft working paper for the World Bank conference 'New Frontiers of Social Policy: Development in a Globalizing World', in Arusha, Tanzania, 12–15 December. http://siteresources. worldbank.org/INTRANETSOCIALDEVELOPMENT/ Resources/Marcpaper.rev.pdf

Posey, D. A. (ed.). 1999. *Cultural and Spiritual Values of Biodiversity: A Complementary Contribution to the Global Biodiversity Assessment*. London, Intermediate Technology Publications for the United Nations Environment Programme (UNEP).

United Nations Development Programme (UNDP). *Human Development Report 2004: Cultural Liberty in Today's World*. New York, UNDP. http://hdr.undp.org/en/media/ hdr04_complete.pdf

World Commission on Cultural and Development. 1996. *Our Creative Diversity*. Paris, UNESCO. http://unesdoc.unesco. org/images/0010/001055/105586e.pdf

South Pacific man

Women practising a traditional
dance in Shanghai, China

PART I.
CULTURAL DIVERSITY: WHAT IS AT STAKE?

The diversity of human cultures — the wealth of languages, ideas, beliefs, kinship systems, customs, tools, artistic works, rituals and other expressions they collectively embody —admits of many explanations and interpretations. These range from philosophical considerations, through an emphasis on cultures as emergent systems or in terms of intercultural contacts, to approaches that highlight the complex interactions between cultures and the human habitat. A current consensus regards cultures as systems that continually evolve through internal processes and in contact with the environment and other cultures. What is certain is that no society has ever been frozen in its history, even if some cultures have been viewed as 'timeless' from the perspective of others characterized by rapid change.

Cultural diversity, beyond the mere fact of its existence, has aesthetic, moral and instrumental value as the expression of human creativity, the embodiment of human strivings and the sum of humanity's collective experience. In the contemporary world — characterized as it is by space-time compression linked to the speed of new communication and transportation technologies, and by the growing complexity of social interactions and the increasing overlap of individual and collective identities — cultural diversity has become a key concern, amid accelerating globalization processes, as a resource to be preserved and as a lever for sustainable development.

In the context of the threats to cultural diversity, the international community has adopted a panoply of binding and non-binding instruments covering a wide range of cultural forms, including monuments and natural sites, tangible and intangible heritage, cultural expressions, and intellectual and artistic heritage. These instruments are dedicated to preserving and promoting such testimonies to human creativity as expressions of the common heritage of humankind. Part I of this report reviews some of these safeguarding mechanisms, with reference to the most recent developments. However, its main concern is with the wider phenomenon and multiple aspects of cultural diversity and with the related issue of intercultural dialogue. Indeed, cultural diversity and dialogue are mutually reinforcing, such that the maintenance of cultural diversity is intimately linked to the ability to establish dialogue and the ultimate challenge of cultural diversity is that of intercultural dialogue.

CHAPTER 1 **Cultural diversity**

Chapter 1 analyzes the nature and manifestations of cultural diversity in relation to globalization, considers the relationship between national, cultural, religious and multiple identities, and summarizes normative and other measures adopted at regional and international levels to preserve and promote the many facets of cultural diversity.

CHAPTER 2 **Intercultural dialogue**

Chapter 2 examines the interrelationship between cultural diversity and intercultural dialogue, and identifies stereotypes and stigmatization as major obstacles to intercultural understanding. It stresses the link between the diversity existing *between* individuals and groups and present *within* each individual and group, and indicates new pathways for dialogue in a multicultural world.

Two men on a bicycle
near Arusha, Tanzania

Cultural diversity

Globalization is not a wholly new phenomenon. Empires throughout history have sought to extend their dominion and influence beyond their immediate horizons. European colonialism reflected a similar imperialist impulse, inaugurating political, social, economic and cultural imbalances that have persisted into the new millennium. Yet contemporary globalization is of a different order to such historical anticipations. Recent decades have witnessed an unprecedented enmeshment of national economies and cultural expressions, giving rise to new challenges and opportunities. Communication networks have shrunk or abolished distance, to the benefit of some and the exclusion of others. Travel has never been so rapid and convenient, while remaining beyond the reach of many. In a world in which the possibilities of intercultural contact have multiplied, linguistic diversity and many other forms of cultural expression are in decline. How then is globalization to be viewed in terms of its impacts on cultural diversity?

Globalization is often conceived as potentially antithetical to cultural diversity, in the sense of leading to the homogenization of cultural models, values, aspirations and lifestyles, to the standardization of tastes, the impoverishment of creativity, uniformity of cultural expressions and so forth. The reality, however, is more complex. While it is true that globalization induces forms of homogenization and standardization, it cannot be regarded as inimical to human creativity, which continues to engender new forms of diversity, constituting a perennial challenge to featureless uniformity.

Opera dei Pupi, Sicilian Puppet Theatre, Italy

Cultural Diversity

1

1.1 Cultural diversity in a globalizing world ... 13
Figure 1.1 Urban and rural population growth 13
Box 1.1 The migration factor 15
Box 1.2 Globalization and indigenous
populations 17
Box 1.3 Digital cultures and new diversity 18

**1.2 National, religious, cultural and multiple
identities... 19**
Box 1.4 Reconstructing Central Asian
identities in the post-Soviet era...................................21

**1.3 Regional and international initiatives
on cultural diversity...................................... 23**
Figure 1.2 Ratifications of the seven cultural
conventions of UNESCO, per region 26

Conclusion... 28

Recommendations... 28

**In focus: Standard-setting instruments
adopted by UNESCO 29**

References and websites.................................. 32

*A billboard advertising a mobile
telephone operator in Nigeria*

1.1 Cultural diversity in a globalizing world

Globalization is often seen as a *unidirectional* and *unidimensional* process, driven by a Western-dominated global market economy and tending to standardize, streamline and transnationalize in ways inimical to cultural diversity. The focus is on the threat posed to local cultural products and practices by globalized consumer goods and services — on how television and video productions are tending to eclipse traditional forms of entertainment, how pop and rock music are drowning out indigenous music, or how convenience food is blunting the appetite for local cuisine. Some forms of cultural diversity are clearly more vulnerable than others. Vernacular languages are recognized as being particularly at risk, notably from the continuing expansion of English but also from the advance of vehicular languages such as Arabic, Hindi, Spanish and Swahili (see chapter 3). This process tends to be exponential — as illustrated by the emphasis placed by many parents on schooling their children in vehicular languages at the expense of mastery of their mother tongue.

A multidirectional and multidimensional process

Through the media, globalization conveys an often seductive image of modernity and provides a template for collective ambitions: salaried employment, the nuclear family, personalized transport, pre-packaged leisure, conspicuous consumption. Most local communities worldwide have been exposed to some extent to the images and consumer practices typical of this Western paradigm, which has now impacted on almost all countries, irrespective of culture, religion, social system and political regime (Nyamjoh and Warnier, 2007). The adoption of many of its facets is closely linked to rapidly expanding urban living, which now involves some 50 percent of the world's population (see Figure 1.1). Cultural erosion has accordingly become an issue of increasing concern since numerous modes of life are being lost and many cultural forms and expressions are disappearing. There is a widespread sense that globalization is leading to pervasive cultural homogenization, not to say hegemonization by stealth (see Barber, 1996; Tardif and Farchy, 2006).

There can be no doubt that the development of transnational markets, linked to the rise of consumerism promoted by skilful advertising, is impacting significantly on local cultures, which are finding it difficult to compete in an increasingly global marketplace. In this context, the tendency of enterprises to delocalize to the developing world as part of the liberalization of world trade is creating new consumer patterns in which the juxtaposition of contrasting lifestyles can serve to accelerate cultural change that may be neither welcome nor desirable. When, for example, a multinational corporation decides to transfer its production to a country in the South because of its lower labour costs, the products of Western consumer society begin to circulate domestically, sometimes to the detriment of local cultural models. In these circumstances, local cultures that find it difficult to compete in the global marketplace — but whose value is incommensurable with any market valuation — tend to be the losers, along with the diversity of the cultural manifestations they embody.

This said, the association of globalization with standardization and commodification is often overstated. The assertion that 'whatever [the] market touches turns into a consumer commodity; including the things that

Figure 1.1 Urban and rural population growth

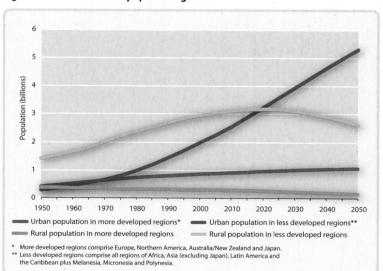

- Urban population in more developed regions*
- Urban population in less developed regions**
- Rural population in more developed regions
- Rural population in less developed regions

* More developed regions comprise Europe, Northern America, Australia/New Zealand and Japan.
** Less developed regions comprise all regions of Africa, Asia (excluding Japan), Latin America and the Caribbean plus Melanesia, Micronesia and Polynesia.

Source: Population Division of the Department of Economic and Social Affairs of the United Nations Secretariat, *World Population Prospects: The 2006 Revision and World Urbanization Prospects: The 2007 Revision*, http://esa.un.org/unup

try to escape its grip' (Bauman, 2005) fails to take account of the complexities inherent in the integration of cultural borrowings. Movements between geo-cultural areas invariably involve translation, mutation and adaptation on the part of the receiving culture, and cultural transfer does not usually take place unilaterally (Tomlinson, 1991; Lull, 2000). Globalized media, for instance, are increasingly being appropriated by marginalized and previously voiceless groups in order to advance their social, economic and political claims (see chapter 5). Furthermore, many areas of everyday cultural experience prove beyond the reach of the globalized market, such as our deeply rooted sense of national or ethnic identities, our religious or spiritual ties, our community interests, activities and attachments, not to mention our environments and social relationships. Most importantly, cultural commerce is to an ever greater extent a two-way process that takes place in an increasingly complex and interactive international context.

For all these reasons, globalization is best understood as a *multidirectional* and *multidimensional* process, evolving simultaneously within the economic, social, political, technological and cultural spheres. It is a complex and rapidly developing network of connections and interdependencies that operate within and between these spheres and exert increasing influence on material, social, economic and cultural life in today's world. Globalization can be described in terms of the increasing 'flows' of virtually everything that characterizes contemporary life: capital, commodities, knowledge, information, ideas, people, beliefs and so on. These flows — transiting essentially through the media, communication networks and commerce — consist of an ever-increasing volume of cultural goods, services and communications, including language and educational content. While this cultural traffic has tended to move along a mainly North-South axis, the rise of powerful new economies (in particular, the BRICs, i.e. Brazil, Russia, India and China) is diversifying or reversing the direction of these flows (see chapter 6).

One of the most far-reaching effects of globalization is a weakening of the usual connection between a cultural event and its geographical location as a result of the dematerialization or deterritorialization processes facilitated by information and communication technologies (Tomlinson, 2007). Indeed, globalization transports distant events, influences and experiences into our immediate vicinity, notably through visual and audio media. This weakening of the traditional ties between cultural experience and geographical location brings new influences and experiences into people's everyday lives. Digital cultures, for example, are having a considerable impact on cultural identities, especially among young people. In this way, an attitude of *cosmopolitanism* is developing, especially in the world's megalopolises (Sassen, 2001; Appiah, 2006). In some cases, this attenuation of ties to place may be experienced as a source of opportunity; in other cases, as a source of anxiety, loss of certainty and marginalization, leading on occasion to identity backlashes (see chapter 2). Still, as our identities are inextricably bound to the environments in which we grew up and those in which we live, the effect does not generally amount to a radical break with our cultural background or to cultural homogenization.

International migration has become a significant factor in intercultural dynamics (see Box 1.1). In countries of emigration, the drain on human resources — tending among other things to skew the relationship between the sexes and generations — inevitably entails some weakening of the socio-cultural fabric. In the receiving countries, migrants face the challenge of reconciling a traditional system of values, cultural norms and social codes with the often very different customs of the host countries. Among the possible responses to this challenge, most immigrants avoid the extremes of complete assimilation or outright rejection in favour of a partial adaptation to their new cultural environment while preserving their ties with their cultures of origin, notably through family connections or the media. The influx of sizeable numbers of migrant workers and the development of de facto multicultural communities prompts a complex range of responses, mirroring to some degree those of the immigrant population itself. The outcome of the implicit negotiations between these communities is usually some measure of pluralism, ranging from institutional recognition to tolerance of difference. In these circumstances, conviviality may put down roots if it is not thwarted by ideologies of exclusion. These roots may in turn nurture new cultural expressions, since diversity is always potentially in the making.

| Box 1.1 | **The migration factor** |

Major labour migration movements

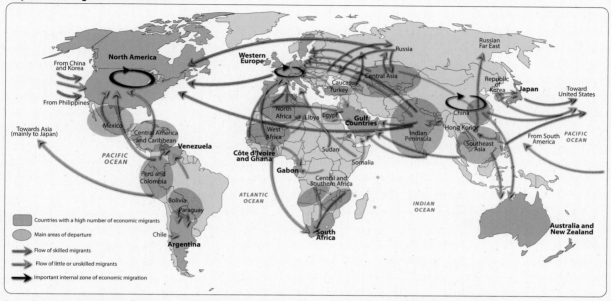

Source: Simon 1995; UNESCO 1998; CNRS-Université de Poitiers, Migrinter; Agence France Presse, Reuters and Philippe Rekacewicz (*Le Monde Diplomatique*).
Updated in December 2005.

Migrations are as old as human history, but took on new forms from the 1600s with the emergence of European mercantile interests and the conquest of the 'New World'. Slaves and indentured workers were shipped between continents to work plantations, mines and construction projects in the Americas, Asia and Africa. Industrialization in Western Europe and North America in the 19th century saw new movements of settlers to build railways, ports and cities, and work in new factories. Between 1860 and 1920, some 30 million people sailed to the United States.

However, globalization has brought about a dramatic increase in the volume and scope of international migration. In 2005, the world stock of migrants was estimated at 190 million people (see Table 3 in Annex). This mobility is transforming societies and cultures, creating diasporas and developing transnational identities — the feeling of belonging to two or more societies at once. Community links are forming between peoples across the globe. Migrant social networks span

the globe, thus facilitating further migration. The cities of North America, Europe and Oceania have become multicultural, while new immigration areas in Asia, Africa and Latin America are rapidly following the same path. Formerly homogenous populations now experience a bewildering diversity of languages, religions and cultural practices.

Many people do not move by choice: in 2006, the United Nations High Commissioner for Refugees (UNHCR) counted about 14.3 million of refugees throughout the world. The vast majority move in search of work and a better life. However, climate change is increasingly recognized as a factor that will force people to migrate (see chapter 7). Most of the world's migrants and refugees begin their journey as internal rural-urban migrants in developing countries, before moving on to other places where opportunities seem better.

A key development in recent years has been the feminization of migration. About 1.5 million Asian women, for example, worked abroad by

the end of the 1990s, most in jobs regarded as 'typically female': domestic workers, entertainers (often a euphemism for prostitution), restaurant and hotel staff, assembly-line workers in clothing and electronics. Domestic service may lead to isolation and vulnerability for young women migrants, who often have little protection against the demands of their employers. In 1995, the execution of Flor Contemplación, a Filipina maid in Singapore who was convicted of murder, made world headlines and highlighted the vulnerability of Overseas Contract Workers (OCWs).

However, few migrant-sending countries would be willing to hobble what has become an important commodity. Estimates of migrant workers' remittances have been placed at more than US$225 billion in 2004 (making labour second only to oil in global trade), and US$318 billion in 2007, of which US$240 billion went to developing countries. However, 'brain drain' is another consequence of migration, especially in recent years with the adoption by some receiving countries of

Box 1.1	The migration factor

new immigration policies looking for highly qualified migrants to meet the needs of their labour markets (see also chapter 8 and map 8.1).

While economic globalization has made labour more mobile, it has also made the available work more temporary. The era of permanent settlement that characterized post-war migrations from Europe is over. Labour markets in many countries now look for workers, both skilled and unskilled, to occupy specific jobs with a fixed duration rather than invite them to participate in the economy and infrastructure of a country. This is partly due to the difficulties migrant-receiving countries have in coping with permanent settlement by workers or refugees. The unplanned shift from temporary sojourn to new ethnic diversity places in question traditional ideas about culture and identity. Thus, developed countries with democratic traditions founded on individual freedoms are redefining who can and cannot belong.

Citizenship is now a prized possession as it means access not just to the economy but to broader social institutions that determine rights and freedoms. Post-colonial states, such as Malaysia, Indonesia, Singapore and the Republic of Korea, find it difficult to reconcile immigration and growing cultural diversity with the formation of their own national identity. Deportation campaigns, stricter border controls and measures to prevent permanent settlement are increasingly the norm. However, closing borders usually only makes a legal movement illegal. Trafficking of migrants has become a lucrative trade, with private agencies providing everything from information and travel assistance to forged documentation and direct smuggling of people across borders. The rapid internationalization of economics and culture virtually guarantees that migration will continue to grow in the years ahead. The pressure for long-term solutions remains. Encouraging the mobility of labour to fit the needs of a globalized world is one thing. Managing immigration to admit only those who are 'economically desirable' is something else altogether.

Source: UNESCO, 1998 updated in 2009.

International tourism is another phenomenon with a potentially significant impact on cultural diversity. Its growth in recent decades is suggested by comparing the number of international tourists in 1950, estimated at 25.3 million, with the 800 million recorded tourists in 2005 (see Statistical Annex, Table 17) and the World Tourism Organization's forecast of a global tourist flow of almost 1 billion in 2010. A significant trend has been the increase in tourism to the developing world, reflected in the average annual growth in tourist arrivals in the Middle East (9 percent), East Africa and the Pacific (7 percent) and Africa (5 percent) (Teller and Sharpley, 2008). The *qualitative* — as distinct from the *quantitative* — impact of this increase in the volume of intercultural contacts is obviously difficult to gauge. On the one hand, international tourism is to some extent self-contained and can generate new sources of income for local populations within the tourism industry and positively contribute to greater knowledge and understanding of different cultural environments and practices. On the other hand, the sheer volume of exchanges, even if in large part functional and transitory, carries with it with the risk of culturally 'freezing' local populations as objects of tourism. Such cultural fixity further marginalizes these populations 'since it is their marginality that they exhibit and sell for profit' (Azarya, 2004). While the immediate prospects for tourism growth remain unpredictable, it seems clear that intercultural contacts, including substantive exchanges, will continue to grow as a result of increased — and increasingly multidirectional — tourist flows, both real and virtual.

Both positive and negative impacts

Within a broader international context, the globalization of international exchanges is leading to the integration of a diversity of multicultural services and expressions in many countries. An obvious example is the expanding range of foreign restaurants found throughout the industrialized world, catering for immigrant and local populations alike. Reproduced in a wide variety of contexts, notably in the worlds of fashion and entertainment, this juxtaposition of cultural expressions and experiences is leading to a greater interaction and merging of cultural forms. Such examples, reflecting a more general intensification of transnational flows, are consistent with a trend towards multiple cultural affiliations and a 'complexification' of cultural identities. These new and growing intercultural phenomena reflect the dynamic character of cultural diversity, which cannot be assimilated into fixed repertoires of cultural manifestations and is constantly assuming new forms within evolving cultural settings.

Yet such positive outcomes should not lead us to underestimate the negative impacts of globalizing trends on the diversity of cultural expressions and on those for whom these expressions are intrinsic to their ways of life and very being (see Box 1.2). What is at stake for them is existential loss, not simply the disappearance of manifestations of human diversity. UNESCO's action in safeguarding intangible cultural heritage has highlighted some of the threats to traditional cultural expressions posed by what many see as the juggernaut of globalization. The supporters of the Carnaval de Oruro in Bolivia, for example, complain of the 'ill-conceived globalization trends that impose common rules and behaviour, disregarding cultural particularities' and the 'neoliberal tendency to analyze human activities from a cost-benefit perspective, without considering the magical and spiritual aspects of the Carnaval'. For the epic storytellers of Kyrgyzstan, it is the rise of the modern entertainment market that explains why the younger generations in their country are ceasing to identify with ancient cultural performances. These clashes between 'tradition' and 'modernity' are ubiquitous and problematic in terms of how they are to be perceived and addressed.

Over the last decade, a wide range of threats to traditional cultural expressions have been brought to the attention of UNESCO as the United Nations agency mainly responsible for protection of the world's cultural heritage in its tangible and intangible expressions (Amescua, 2007). They include:

- The development of sedentary lifestyles, reflected in increasing urbanization: this is the case, for example, with the indigenous Záparas people in Ecuador and Peru. In Morocco, the strong urbanizing tendencies in the Sahara have brought about a progressive disappearance of the nomadic lifestyle, together with whole segments of cultural life, such as traditional handicrafts and poetry.

- Religious intolerance: the defenders of Maya Achi identity in Guatemala stress the grave harm that can be done to their culture by the influence of fundamentalist Christian sects that view their traditional customs as pagan — if not 'diabolic' — activities to be eliminated.

The Samba de Roda of Recôncavo of Bahia, Brazil

Box 1.2   Globalization and indigenous populations

Among the negative impacts of globalization on indigenous populations, Victoria Tauli-Corpuz, Chairperson of the UN Permanent Forum on Indigenous Issues (UNPFII), has highlighted the following:

- Violation of rights to ancestral lands, territories and resources, including forced eviction and displacement of indigenous peoples by governments or by the private sector; competing claims and increased conflicts over lands, territories and resources; erosion and destruction of indigenous subsistence economic systems and other traditional livelihoods, such as pastoralism, trapping, hunting and gathering, in favour of cash-crop mono-production for the global market (flowers, agro-fuels, paper and pulp, etc.); massive extraction of natural resources in indigenous territories without prior informed consent of indigenous peoples, leading to environmental devastation,

expropriation of indigenous peoples' land and water, increased conflicts, over exploitation of forests, marine and mineral resources; militarization of indigenous territories; increased out-migration to urban areas and overseas, including increased numbers of indigenous women becoming domestic helpers, prostitutes or victims of trafficking.

- Weakened enforcement by states and multilateral institutions of laws, policies and international instruments that promote indigenous peoples' rights and autonomous development, resulting in the displacement of populations, commercialization of their cultural artefacts and appropriation of traditional knowledge.

- Reduced access to education, health and other social services for indigenous peoples, leading to deteriorating

health conditions, rising illiteracy rates and degeneration of quality of life:

- Increased use of forests and fertile agriculture lands for cash crops and livestock (agriculture, plantation crops and cattle breeding) and poorer land for food crops, thereby reducing food production and increasing food insecurity.

- Cultural homogenization through the influence of globalized multimedia, universalization of mainstream development paradigms, disappearance of indigenous languages.

- Undermining of indigenous governance and political systems.

- Commercialization of culture through the promotion of tourism.

Source: Tauli-Corpuz, 2007.

■ Lack of respect for forms of knowledge transmission in certain traditional societies: thus, in Nigeria, the Isa see the introduction of free primary education in the west of the country, dating from 1955, as the reason for a growing lack of interest among younger generations in their culture, particularly since Christian and Islamic doctrines are taught in school to the exclusion of traditional African religions. In Vanuatu, the time young children spend at school and in school activities are said to have kept them from learning the traditional practice of sand drawing, which is in decline.

■ The world culture relayed by the media: in India, defenders of the art of Kutiyattam say that they are unable to compete with the mass media, especially radio and television programmes. This complaint is echoed in China by the practitioners of the Guqin, a seven-string musical instrument related to the zither.

■ Failure to respect the sacred or devotional character of certain ceremonies: this is emphasized by the defenders of the Mask Dance of the Drums from Drametse, who deplore the growing lack of interest among the young generation in the deep spirituality of these practices.

■ The 'museification' of practices that were previously forms of collective leisure serving to preserve and strengthen social bonds, as in the case of the Opera dei Puppi in Sicily (Italy).

■ The replacement of ancient forms of cultural expression by new communication technologies: thus portable telephones and e-mails in Jamaica have rendered virtually obsolete the traditional means of communication in the form of the drum and abeng (conch shell), undermining the ancient musical traditions.

■ The impact of global distribution networks on local cinema productions: one example among many is French-speaking African cinema, which, following a splendid decade in the 1980s, has experienced a period of crisis mainly attributable to a decline in local demand; local viewers are influenced by foreign television and film as a result of the proliferation of parabolic antennae and low-cost access to recent films through DVDs.

To meet these threats to cultural diversity — to its expressions in word, sound, image, print and artistic works and activities — the international community

---

| Box 1.3 | **Digital cultures and new diversity** |

The rise of new information and communication technologies (ICTs) in the context of globalization has broadened the scope of possible interactions and experiments with personal identity, particularly among young people:

A July 2006 survey found that 100 million video clips are viewed daily on YouTube — a video-sharing website developed in February 2005 and bought by Google in November 2006 — with an additional 65,000 new videos uploaded every 24 hours. The website averages nearly 20 million visitors per month, according to Nielsen/ NetRatings, of which 44 percent are female, 56 percent male, and the 12- to 17-year-old age group is dominant. In July 2008, 258 million users were reported, including almost 100 million in the United States alone.

Facebook was launched in February 2004, and as of July 2009 could claim 250 million users, of whom over 120 million log on at least once a day. The largest user group appears to be Euro-Americans; the fastest growing age-group consists of those 35 years old and above.

Founded in August 2003, MySpace had 230 million accounts as of April 2008.

Second Life (SL) is an Internet-based virtual world — developed by Linden Lab and launched in 2003 (but not popularized by the media until late 2006) — that offers a 'virtual' environment in which people can interact, work, play and learn.

In these and many other ways, the Internet offers new possibilities to experiment with personal identity in an entirely anonymous, disembodied and synchronous way (chat,

blogging, etc.). By enabling virtual selves to be superimposed on real selves, the Internet opens up a new realm of self-expression. According to some experts, it thereby functions as an indicator of the hidden forces and trends at work in the societies in which it operates.

The access or exposure to a virtually infinite range of content on the web (including hoaxes, rumours and false information) may provoke unexpected encounters and cultural hybridization. However, some maintain that the overload of information on the Internet, and the massive use of filters and search engines, encourages Internet users to limit their contacts to peers with similar tastes, leading to self-enclosure and the rejection of differences (Sunstein, 2004).

Source: Caldwell, 2007; statistics updated using data from Social Media Statistics.

adopted, in 2003, the UNESCO *Convention for the Safeguarding of the Intangible Cultural Heritage* and, in 2005, the UNESCO *Convention on the Protection and Promotion of the Diversity of Cultural Expressions*.

It would be a mistake, however, to see the effects of globalization on cultural diversity as wholly negative, if only because there is nothing inevitable about the general trend towards cultural homogenization. As Claude Lévi-Strauss (2007) noted in a recent communication to UNESCO: 'Time does not always move in the same direction. Periods of pervasive uniformity can be followed by unexpected reversals. This has happened in the past, and there are grounds for hoping that at the heart of the globalization process itself new forms of diversity whose nature we do not suspect may be in gestation'. The rapid growth of digital cultures, for example, has given rise to new forms of cultural diversity, particularly among the young. Computer-mediated interactions through Internet sites, such as YouTube, Teen Second Life, FaceBook or MySpace, are means whereby people today 'live' increasingly in more than one reality. The innumerable possible combinations of the new media for cultural expressions and cultural practices creates a whole host of 'do-it-yourself cultures', which open the way to a broad range of new forms of cultural diversity.

Rather than attempting to evaluate the overall effect of globalization, to draw up a balance sheet of the forms of diversity that are disappearing compared with those coming into existence, it is more important to focus on the dynamic character of cultural diversity and to devise approaches to better managing the impact of cultural change on our individual and collective identities. Such efforts must also be complemented by the awareness that we cannot hope to preserve everything that is threatened with disappearance. As Claude Lévi-Strauss has observed, it is 'diversity itself which must be saved, not the outward and visible form in which each period has clothed that diversity'. It is important, then, to envisage new strategies for revitalizing cultural expressions and practices while helping vulnerable populations to acquire the tools necessary to 'manage' cultural change more effectively. A dynamic conception of this kind leads us to question a number of inoperative dichotomies and received categories, such as the opposition between tradition and modernity. Every living tradition is susceptible to continual reinvention, which makes it relevant to the present. Tradition is no more reducible to the past than is modernity to the present or future. For tradition, like memory or culture, is inscribed within a process of becoming. Cultural diversity, like cultural identity, is about innovation, creativity and receptiveness to new cultural forms and relationships.

Cultural diversity, like cultural identity, is about innovation, creativity and receptiveness to new cultural forms and relationships

1.2 National, religious, cultural and multiple identities

The contemporary world is marked by strong attachments to national, religious, ethnic, linguistic, social, cultural and/or even 'brand' or consumer-based identities. Such identities have become the refuge for many individuals and groups who see globalization and cultural change as a threat to their ways of life and standards of living. In this context, we witness the culturization of political claims, which run counter to the essentially dynamic and multifaceted nature of identities.

A resurgence of the question of identities
Culture and religion can be seen to be intimately linked in this often conflictual affirmation of separate identities. Religions have a collective dimension involving religious authorities and sometimes embodying religious dogma that is non-negotiable. Allied to political activism, religious affiliations can be a powerful marker of identity and a potential source of conflict. While in democratic

societies religious views can play an active role in shaping public policy on health, education and social services, religions run the risk of being instrumentalized for other purposes, for example, as vehicles for the promotion of ideological, political and/or economic agendas (Dallmayr, 2007). In such cases, religious differences, while not inherently incompatible, can potentially lead to violent clashes between religious groups (as recently played out, for example, between Muslims and Christians in Nigeria, Catholics and Protestants in Ireland, or Hindus and Muslims in India) or between secularism and religious belief and practice (such as in Malaysia and Australia, but also in Europe), between those who wish to confine religious identification to the 'private sphere', apart from the public and civic spheres, and those who see secularism as another committed value-standpoint with its own (declared or undeclared) presuppositions, biases and prejudices.

🎧 *Woman smoking, Lao People's Democratic Republic, 2006*

Religion is but one factor among others constitutive of individual and collective identities, to which we may add race, gender, and language

Generally speaking, this resurgence of religion has brought the issue of identities back into the civic and public arenas, as countries across the globe vigorously debate the question of abortion (especially in countries with a strong Catholic tradition), of the Islamic scarf (in France and the United States), or the legality of conversion from Islam to another religion (in Malaysia). Religion, however, is but one factor among others constitutive of individual and collective identities, to which we may add race, gender, and language, as noted by Bahjat Rizk (2009), who makes a parallel with the UNESCO Constitution that emphasizes that no distinction shall be made along the lines of race, sex, language and religion.

Until quite recently cultural diversity has been equated with the diversity of national cultures. Even within UNESCO's Constitution (1945), reference to cultural diversity appears in a domestic jurisdiction clause intended to guarantee respect for national sovereignty, with a view to 'preserving the independence, integrity and fruitful diversity of cultures and educational systems of [Member States]' (Art. 1, para. 3). Throughout the period of decolonization and the rise to independence of new nations, *culturalism* referred to a conception of cultural identities that served to legitimate the emergence of new national pathways. It may be that the resurgence of the religious factor is directly linked to the retreat of the nation as the source of cultural identity.

From monolithic to multiple identities

National identities are not monoliths: they are constructions, reflecting a multitude of collective experiences, memories and references, and encompassing differences of gender, class, race and religion. They evolve constantly, along a path prescribed by a sometimes mythical past towards a future dependent on adaptive change (see Box 1.4). In a globalizing world, which tends to blur national boundaries and re-energize cultural identities, it makes less and less sense to equate cultural identities with national identities.

This said, national identity plays a central role in providing a focus for our sense of commonality. The nation is a key principle of identification, operating through a shared set of collective memories, as narrated through popular culture, school curricula, the media and so forth (Benedict, 1948; Geertz, 1973). Ideas about the continuity of nations are often conveyed through a cultural perspective that emphasizes traditions and cultures as a set of fixed and repetitive practices, as a means of forging identity and combating the indeterminacy of changing events (Hobsbawm and Ranger, 1984). Like any work of memory, the concept of nation is selective and, in the case of official national identity, often reflects the interests of dominant elites. National identity can also be constructed around the myth of ethnic superiority, as the history of human conflict all too often and tragically attests.

Yet while national symbols and traditions tend to persist, the realities they represent do not stand still. For cultures are ever-changing and self-transforming in a process that is not linear. Culture is like a river, flowing 'through vast areas giving life to people. It changes all the time, although we go on referring to it as if it were the same river' (Fasheh, 2007). It has been suggested that we need to understand culture not as a substantive but as a verb: 'The most important issue is to avoid reification, to move along the grammatical continuum from substantives towards verbs. The "problem" with reification is that it tends to consolidate what is, to mask what is becoming' (Alexander, 2007). Some have even claimed that cultural identity is an 'illusion' (Bayart, 1997). Others have said that culture should be conceived less in terms of a past inheritance than in terms of a future project (Appadurai, 2004). In short, cultural identity — like culture — should be regarded as a process and envisaged in terms of creative growth.

In a world made more complex by the unprecedented reach, intensity and immediacy of human interchanges, national identities no longer represent the sole dimension of cultural identity. Reflecting a reality defined and constructed in response to projects of a political nature, the foundation of national identity is typically overlaid with a multiplicity of other affiliations. We increasingly define ourselves, as individuals and societies, in terms of *multiple identities*. The point is well made by Amartya Sen (2006a) when he says:

The very odd presumption that people of the world can be uniquely categorized by single and overarching systems of partitioning does not work anymore. [...] In everyday life, human beings do not belong only to one group. [...] In our normal lives, we see ourselves as members of a variety of groups—we belong to all of them. The same person can be, without any contradiction, an American citizen, of Caribbean origin, with African ancestry, a Christian, a liberal, a woman, a vegetarian, a long-distance runner, a historian, a schoolteacher, a novelist, a feminist, a heterosexual, a believer in gay and lesbian rights, a theater lover, an environmental activist, a tennis fan, a jazz musician [. . .]. None of them can be taken to be the person's only identity or singular membership category.

This plasticity of cultural identities mirrors the growing complexity of the globalized flows of people, goods and information and the increasing interdependence of economic systems and frames of governance.

Each individual exposed to this multiplicity of potential identities lives or manages it differently. Some affirm their right to dispense with old identities and choose new ones as a distinct phase in a process of identity construction. Others — and this is particularly true

Each individual exposed to this multiplicity of potential identities lives or manages it differently

---

Box 1.4   Reconstructing Central Asian identities in the post-Soviet era

The Central Asian Republics (Kazakhstan, Kyrgyzstan, Tajikistan, Turkmenistan and Uzbekistan), which gained independence from the Soviet Union in 1991, all face the same dilemma: how to legitimize the borders of a geo-political entity inherited from the recent Soviet past while the only available and functioning identity reference points are those dating from the medieval period? The shifts in identity that have emerged from the redefinition of the national identities of these young republics continue to be an uncommon phenomenon with serious political consequences.

According to many specialists, the five new republics of Central Asia were the least prepared for political independence when the Soviet Union was suddenly dissolved in 1991. This imposed freedom forced the peoples of Central Asia to reflect on their origins, who they are and what they wish to become. Owing to its history, Central Asia is a region of sharp contrasts, its nomadic northern areas (Kazakhstan, Kyrgyzstan) differing from those of the more sedentary south (Tajikistan, Uzbekistan).

This north-south opposition strongly influenced the way Islam spread and mingled with regional identities over the centuries of Islamization. While Uzbekistan was profoundly Islamized between the eighth and tenth centuries (the first mosque was built in Bukhara in 712), the nomadic peoples of Kazakhstan and Kyrgyzstan did not embrace Islam until about the 10th century. Moreover, this process occurred in a sporadic and uneven manner.

The rapid Islamization of the sedentary southern regions of Central Asia was propitious to the emergence of identities firmly rooted in the religion. By contrast, the gradual encounter of Islam and pagan and shamanistic beliefs in the northern nomadic regions paved the way for the emergence of the present-day Sufi communities whose identities continue to be nourished by pre-Islamic traditions. The Russian conquest and the settlement of many groups of Christian origin in northern Central Asia have contributed to further blurring the map of identities in the region, where, comparatively speaking, identity reference points remain considerably less religious.

The region's religious identities were profoundly influenced by the atheistic policies of the Soviet Union as well as by the creation of national identities to the detriment of religious identities. All 'citizens' found themselves endowed with a 'nationality' associated with an assumed ethnic belonging and superimposed on the borders of the State to which they were supposed to belong. Yet, even though the religious practice and cultural presence of Islam have suffered, Islam often remained the principal identification reference point. The de-Stalinization process and the 1960s and 1970s enabled the Central Asian Republics to 'relive', to a certain extent, their identities and to reclaim their historic Islamic heritage, which was used to reflect a shared and unifying heritage.

After independence, Islam became the requisite identity reference point on which the elites based their new legitimacy. At

the same time, Islam was strictly controlled and secularism explicitly affirmed in the constitutions of Turkmenistan and Kazakhstan.

In an attempt to reconstruct national identities without calling into question the borders inherited from the Soviet Union, the region's medieval and Islamic past were re-evaluated and exploited as a new component of identity, thereby making it possible to overcome ethnic and group divisions.

In Uzbekistan, for example, Tamerlane was rehabilitated and then elevated to the status of hero symbolizing the new-found Uzbek conscience and identity. In Tajikistan, national history now relies on the idealization of the resistance of Persian culture to the unrelenting spread of Turkish influence in Central Asia.

The politicization of cultural reference has gone hand-and-hand with the elimination of numerous Russian words from the vocabularies of national languages. They have been replaced by words of Arabic — or in the case of Tajikistan — Persian origin. In the 1990s, there was a noteworthy renewed interest in Islam with an overall increase in religious practices even though the latter remain largely a personal matter limited to the private or family sphere.

Nonetheless, the traditional ethnic, group and regional divisions have been perpetuated, and they sometime surface as a threat to regional stability. The sense of ethnic identity is strengthened along with tribal and regional identity, particularly in Uzbekistan and Tajikistan.

Source: UNESCO.

in the case of migrants confronted by a new cultural environment — can exist in contradictory or ambivalent modes (Bhabha, 1994). Still others, confronted by a context of cultural mixity, decide to live in it as if this state were a genuine choice involving the exercise of their cultural freedom, creating for themselves an original cultural profile by combining elements borrowed from a diversity of different cultural contexts (UNDP, 2004). It is

Aboriginal elder uses mobile phone, central Australia

significant in this connection that a number of prominent contemporary novelists, including Salman Rushdie, Gabriel García Márquez, Milan Kundera and J. M. Coetzee, have been drawn to this topic of migrants confronted with new cultural environments and obliged to construct new cultural identities.

The notion of *hybridity* is widely used to designate this latter form of cultural mixing. The term 'draws attention towards individuals or cultural forms that are reflexively — self-consciously — mixed, [comprising] syntheses of cultural forms or fragments of diverse origin' (Eriksen, 2007). A more general, and less self-conscious, form of hybridity with deeper historical roots is the kind of continuous cultural intermingling that took place, for example, between migrants, colonizers and first nations, giving rise to new hybrid identities regarded as typical of Latin American cultures (Canclini, 1992). A distinction is often made between the concept of hybridity and that of creolization. The latter term has somewhat different connotations depending on language and locale, but generally refers to 'the intermingling and mixing of two or several formerly discrete traditions and cultures' (Eriksen, 2007). While the reference here is mainly to the distinctive mix of linguistic and cultural elements in the French Afro-Caribbean territories, 'creolization' has tended to be used more generally to describe various processes of cultural mixing involving the aggregation rather than the fusion of disparate elements. Many other examples of syncretic cultural forms show the phenomenon of mixing to be a constant feature of cultural diversification.

One of the effects of globalization has been a paradoxical loosening of the grip of modernity through a reconstitution of the relationship between individuals and their communities of allegiance, thereby inaugurating new conceptions of identity (Appadurai, 1996). In this context, individuals are called upon to act, respond and create in the process of negotiating a new sense of identity. While often reduced to a possession or an inheritance, identity is revealed through such examples as fluid, permeable and evolving. It is essentially an experience in the making. Individual and collective identities, while deriving from the past, are to some extent the creation of time and place, developing out of a complex articulation of social determinants and individual agency (Giddens, 1984; Long and Long, 1992). In this way, the blurring of frontiers and the partial disenmeshment of the individual in the context of globalization have favoured the emergence of a *nomadic spirit*, which some regard as the new horizon of contemporary cultural experimentation (Clifford, 1997).

As information and communication technologies (ICTs) reach into the remotest corners of the planet, paving the way for a world of multiple cultural affiliations in which hybrid and multicultural identities become ever more widespread, the challenge posed to the international community is to manage these far-reaching changes so as to safeguard the manifestations of cultural diversity while at the same time recognizing the opportunities offered by cultural diversity to further the ability to adapt to different social and political contexts and circumstances and to favour innovation and a cross-fertilization of cultural expressions and practices.

The challenge posed to the international community is to safeguard the manifestations of cultural diversity while at the same time recognizing the opportunities offered by cultural diversity to further the ability to adapt to different social and political contexts and circumstances

1.3 Regional and international initiatives on cultural diversity

In a world marked increasingly by the intermingling of cultures, efforts to safeguard the manifestations of cultural diversity assume particular importance for national governments, as well as for the international community as a whole. Political and economic interests, as well as concerns linked to heritage, inform a wide variety of initiatives — governmental and non-governmental — which converge at national, regional and international levels. From the standpoint of sustainable development, the tangible and intangible expressions of cultural heritage — as markers of cultural identity and tokens of cultural diversity — are the cornerstone in the construction of a more harmonious, polyphonic and pluralistic world.

While impossible to review here, myriad country-specific initiatives support cultural diversity, many of which are referred to throughout this report. It is equally difficult to do justice to the many programmes undertaken in a non-governmental context. Suffice it to say that all the projects, actions and activities pursued at the inter-governmental level rely considerably on the activities of a vast number of non-governmental bodies operating at all levels throughout the membership of the United Nations. A few of these organizations may be singled out here, however, for their close cooperation and significant contributions to the promotion of cultural diversity within the framework of the United Nations system: the International Council on Monuments and Sites (ICOMOS), the International Music Council (IMC), the International Network for Cultural Diversity (INCD) and MEDIACULT.

The following sections sketch in broad outline first the regional and then the international initiatives taken to protect and promote cultural diversity, including the various strategies adopted in support of regional integration in the cultural field. In keeping with its mandate, UNESCO has played a leading role in the formulation, promotion and implementation of these international instruments — in fields as varied as cultural, physical and intangible heritage, cultural expressions, cultural exchanges and the illicit traffic in cultural goods and intellectual property — in an effort to safeguard and promote various facets of the complex reality encapsulated in the term 'cultural diversity'. These different initiatives and agreements represent a collective response by the international community to the challenges inherent in the preservation of our creative diversity.

Regional initiatives

National projects and international standard-setting activities and related programmes are often reflected in regional action plans for the promotion of cultural diversity, contingent upon a broad convergence of views. Such plans correspond to the wish of many states for a greater pooling of resources and exchange of best practices and experiences at the regional level, or are framed in response to specifically regional problems, which can be properly addressed only at that level.

In Africa the *Charter for African Cultural Renaissance*, adopted in Khartoum in January 2006 by the Member States of the African Union, affirms that 'African cultural diversity and unity are a factor of equilibrium, strength in African economic development, conflict resolution and reducing inequality and injustice to promote national integration'. It underlines in particular the urgent need 'to edify educational systems which embody the African and universal values', 'to resolutely ensure the promotion of African languages', and 'to carry out a systematic inventory with a view to preserving and promoting tangible and intangible cultural heritage, in particular in

A fantasia, during the Moussem of Tan Tan, a festival of nomad tribes, Morocco

Children with the sacred balafon instrument known as the Sosso-Bala, Guinea

Declaration (UNESCO, 1994), in particular, prepared the ground for the drafting of an *Iberoamerican Cultural Charter* (OEI, 2006), 'placing priority [. . .] on cultural rights, the cultural and natural, tangible and intangible cultural heritage, cultural industries and links between culture and development, education and training, innovation, the economy, employment, the environment, tourism, science, technology and communications media'. The growing awareness of the continent's cultural diversity has led not only to a rediscovery of the indigenous cultures threatened by large-scale deforestation and growing impoverishment, but also to reflection on the specificity of cultural identities born of the encounter between the Old and the New Worlds and on the need to ensure that cultural mixing and multiple identities, as part of the colonial legacy, do not lead to splits that are difficult to reconcile. Moreover, political recognition of the rights of indigenous peoples in countries such as Bolivia, Ecuador and Peru have led some younger members of traditional societies to reclaim an indigenous status bestowing rights — the reforms underway having in some cases made land redistribution and other social advantages dependent on mastery of an indigenous language.

In Southeast Asia the 2003 *Bali Concord II* (*Declaration of ASEAN Concord II*) reaffirmed that ASEAN 'is a concert of Southeast Asian nations, bonded together in partnership in dynamic development and in a community of caring societies, committed to upholding cultural diversity and social harmony'. The 2005 ASEAN Ministerial Meeting endorsed the aim 'to increase the capabilities and competitiveness of Asian countries by maximizing on cultural diversity and abundant resources'. Mention should also be made of the Jodhpur Initiatives, a specific regional initiative for the development of creative industries, launched in February 2005. In Southeast Asia, the harmonious coexistence of extremely modern and highly traditional societies is not always easily achieved. A large gap separates the rural world, which is relatively shielded from the effects of globalization, from the large urban centres, which have undergone considerable modernization in recent decades (an example being the construction of the Petronas Towers in Kuala Lumpur). The scale of the rural exodus is creating potentially conflictual situations, exacerbated by mutual misunderstanding, mistrust and indifference.

the spheres of History, Traditions, Arts and Handicrafts, Knowledge and Know-how'. A growing awareness of Africa's exceptionally rich heritage — represented by the diversity of cultures, languages and historical trajectories of its different societies — is reflected in the resolve to preserve and manage that heritage. Thus, to prevent the resurgence of inter-ethnic conflicts linked to adverse economic conditions (such as the xenophobic riots in South Africa at the start of 2008) or to processes of political transition (as in Kenya at the end of 2007), the issue of reconciliation in post-conflict situations (as in Botswana, Côte d'Ivoire and Rwanda) has become a focus of attention. A similar concern with the challenges posed by cultural diversity for social governance is reflected in the activities of the African Academy of Languages (ACALAN), which, in addition to seeking to preserve the continent's linguistic diversity, proposes to transform that diversity into a principle of harmonious coexistence through the promotion of multilingualism.

In Latin America various declarations have been adopted in recent years at Ibero-American conferences of high-level cultural officials (Santo Domingo, Dominican Republic, May 2006), Ministers of Culture (Córdova, Spain, June 2005) and Heads of State and Government (Salamanca, Spain, October 2005). The *Salamanca*

In the case of the Arab States, the *Riyadh Declaration* of the League of Arab States (2007) expresses the determination to

act diligently to protect the Arab identity, boost its components and bases, and strengthen belonging to it in the hearts and minds of children, adolescents and young men and women, since Arabism is not a racist or ethnic concept but rather a unified cultural identity, with the Arabic language as its means of expression and preservation of its heritage, and a common cultural framework based on spiritual, moral and humanistic values, enriched by diversity and plurality, by openness to other human cultures, and by corresponding to accelerating scientific and technological advances.

Reflection on Arab identity and on ways to combat cultural isolationism (one of the essential dimensions of fundamentalism) is linked to questions concerning the relationship between the 'Arab world' and the 'West', particularly around the Mediterranean Basin. As underlined by recent events, the failure to resolve the Israeli-Arab conflict in Palestine and the West Bank continues to fuel deep resentment, which contributes to problems involving issues of identity in the region. Another prominent issue is the so-called 'colonization of minds', which is prompting large numbers of young people to chance their luck in Europe or North America.

In Europe the European Commission's 2007 *Communication on a European Agenda for Culture in a Globalizing World* states,

The originality and success of the European Union is in its ability to respect Member States' varied and intertwined history, languages and cultures, while forging common understanding and rules which have guaranteed peace, stability, prosperity and solidarity — and with them, a huge richness of cultural heritage and creativity to which successive enlargements have added more and more.

It specifies the role of the European Union's internal policies and programmes, with particular reference to 'facilitating mutual understanding, stimulating creativity, and contributing to the mutual enrichment of our cultures'. It notes in that connection the contribution

of a number of initiatives in the sphere of exchanges (Erasmus programme) and in the audiovisual sector (MEDIA programme), and reaffirms objective of a 'European Agenda for Culture'.

The Council of Europe has also played an important role in recognizing the importance of cultural diversity between and within the European States. The December 2000 *Declaration on Cultural Diversity* recognizes that 'respect for cultural diversity is an essential condition of human society' and that 'cultural diversity has always been a dominant European characteristic and a fundamental political objective in the process of European construction'. It stresses that cultural diversity, 'expressed in the co-existence and exchange of culturally different practices and in the provision and consumption of culturally different services and products [. . .] cannot be expressed without the conditions for free creative expression, and freedom of information existing in all forms of cultural exchange, notably with respect to audiovisual services'. It reaffirms the links between cultural diversity and sustainable development and invites the members of the Council of Europe to support and promote cultural and linguistic diversity, particularly through cultural, linguistic and audiovisual policies. Finally, a White Paper on Intercultural Dialogue, entitled *Living Together as Equals in Dignity*, was adopted in May 2008 within the framework of the Council of Europe.

A broad convergence of views on the safeguarding of cultural diversity is thus apparent at the regional level. A similar convergence is observable between the different regional approaches, despite the diversity of historical and political contexts and the variable impacts of globalization. These varied approaches testify to the common concern to identify ways of adequately addressing the wide-ranging challenges inherent in the protection and promotion of a common cultural heritage.

International initiatives
International initiatives in the field of cultural diversity correspond to a number of evolving concerns relating to the protection and promotion of cultural heritage and, later on, creativity. UNESCO has played a leading role in this respect, as the only organization within the United Nations system possessing a mandate in the field of culture, including a standard-setting function.

A new er with th the c dive a and of cultur although flu and transitory in nature, must be valued in their own right

. has begun
exploration of
ncept of cultural
sity, representing
rowing concern
f the international
community, affirming
the simultaneous need
for the recognition of
cultural differences
and the promotion of
intercultural dialogue

In order to contribute to the 'intellectual and moral solidarity of mankind' and to combat ignorance and prejudice, UNESCO is called upon, under its Constitution (1945), to 'give fresh impulse to the spread of culture' and to promote 'the fruitful diversity' of the world's cultures, implying both their interaction and the preservation of their independence and integrity. Cultural diversity is thus understood in terms of both heritage (tangible and intangible) and creativity. It is on this basis, influenced by changing perspectives on culture, that the institutional content of the notion of cultural diversity has been forged and furthered at UNESCO since its creation in 1945, and has led to the adoption of a range of standard-setting instruments in the spheres of artistic creation, the movable and immovable heritage, intangible cultural heritage and, most recently, the diversity of cultural expressions (see Figure 1.2).

Following the adoption of the *Universal Declaration of Human Rights* in 1948, UNESCO responded to its task of increasing the circulation of educational, scientific and cultural materials and protecting scientific, literary and artistic property through the successive adoption of the *Beirut Agreement for Facilitating the International Circulation of Visual and Auditory Materials of an Educational, Scientific and Cultural Character* (1948), the *Florence Agreement on the Importation of Educational, Scientific and Cultural Materials* (1950) and the *Universal*

Copyright Convention (1952). The concept of 'cultural property' was consecrated internationally with the adoption of the 1954 *Hague Convention for the Protection of Cultural Property in the Event of Armed Conflict*. This Convention laid the basis for the concepts of 'common heritage' and 'global' commons, which later found resonance in the UNESCO-led campaign to safeguard the Nubian Monuments threatened by the rising waters behind the newly constructed Aswan Dam. This major project served to highlight the universal significance of manifestations of cultural heritage, which the international community had a duty to safeguard as expressions of a common human inheritance.

In 1966 the UNESCO General Conference outlined this philosophy in the *Declaration on Principles of International Cultural Co-operation*. This Declaration states that each 'culture has a dignity and value which must be protected and preserved' and that every 'people has the right and the duty to develop its culture' before going on to affirm that 'all cultures form part of the common heritage belonging to all mankind'. While this Declaration may in some instances have served to justify certain *culturalist* or localist tendencies, UNESCO always sought to correct such imbalances by underlining that the Declaration is designed to facilitate the relations between cultures *by emphasizing their unity in diversity and fostering the capacity for shared enjoyment of a universal culture constituted by the*

Figure 1.2 Ratifications of the seven cultural conventions of UNESCO, per region*

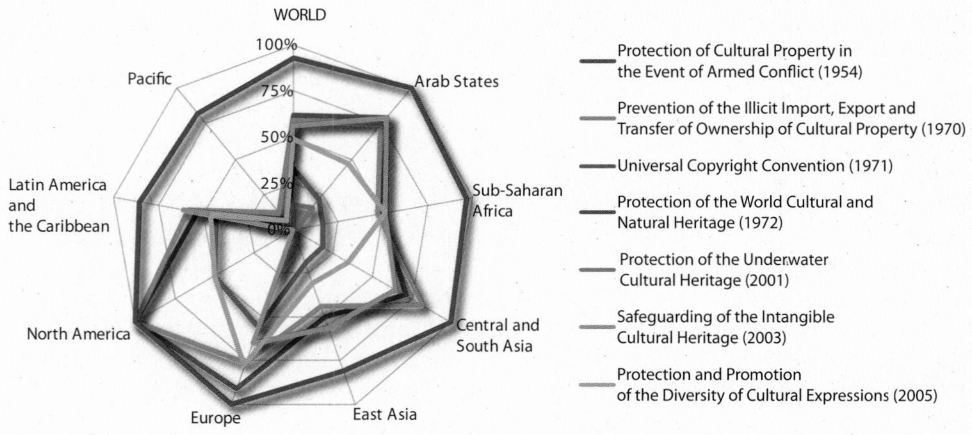

Protection of Cultural Property in the Event of Armed Conflict (1954)

Prevention of the Illicit Import, Export and Transfer of Ownership of Cultural Property (1970)

Universal Copyright Convention (1971)

Protection of the World Cultural and Natural Heritage (1972)

Protection of the Underwater Cultural Heritage (2001)

Safeguarding of the Intangible Cultural Heritage (2003)

Protection and Promotion of the Diversity of Cultural Expressions (2005)

* Calculated by summing the number of UNESCO Member States per region (non member are excluded from calculation).

Source: Data from UNESCO, Standard-Setting Instruments, 2009.

creations representing the common heritage of humanity. Subsequently, at the 1972 Stockholm Conference on the Human Environment, the international community recognized that the planet as a whole constitutes an inheritance held in trust for future generations. The concepts of cultural and natural heritage were formally united in 1972 with UNESCO's adoption of an instrument that would become a landmark in the heritage field, namely the *Convention Concerning the Protection of the World Cultural and Natural Heritage.*

At each successive stage in the debate on globalization and its positive and negative effects, it became increasingly obvious that cultures identify themselves not only with their material expressions in stone, wood, metal, cloth, paper, etc., and with their permanence in defiance of time, but also with a vision of the world embodied in beliefs, representations, celebrations, customs and social relations that are by nature intangible, fluctuating and transitory. These cultural manifestations — including oral traditions, performing arts and traditional know-how with respect to crafts or nature — are the ferment of cultures. Conscious that cultural heritage as defined in the 1972 Convention covered only one aspect of cultural creation, UNESCO adopted in 2003 the *Convention for the Safeguarding of the Intangible Cultural Heritage.* The concept of 'outstanding universal value' is not employed in this Convention, which considers all those expressions and traditions recognized as important by a given community to be equally valuable, without hierarchical distinction. What matters for the international recognition of this living heritage is its importance for the sense of identity and continuity of the communities in which it is created, transmitted and re-created rather than any implicit valuation of the practices concerned.

This progressive development in the concept of cultural heritage, and the shift of emphasis with respect to its connection with identity and continuity, reflect a dual movement: one leads to the recognition of a 'common heritage' that the international community has a duty to safeguard as the expression of a shared human inheritance; the other leads to the recognition of the specificities of cultures, which, although fluctuating and transitory in nature, must be valued in their own right.

A new era has begun with the exploration of the concept of cultural diversity, representing a growing concern of the international community. A long process of reflection during the 1980s and 1990s was to lead eventually to the adoption in 2001 of the *Universal Declaration on Cultural Diversity*. Key moments in this process included: the Declaration of World Conference on Cultural Policies (MONDIACULT, Mexico City, 1982), which in defining culture as 'the whole complex of distinctive spiritual, material, intellectual and emotional features that characterize a society or social group [including] not only the arts and letters, but also modes of life, the fundamental rights of the human being, value systems, traditions and beliefs' reconciled the universal dimension of culture with its particular constituents; the 1996 report of the World Commission on Culture and Development, entitled *Our Creative Diversity*; and the conclusions of the 1998 Stockholm Intergovernmental Conference on Cultural Policies for Development, which affirmed the simultaneous need for the recognition of cultural differences and the promotion of intercultural dialogue The 2001 *Universal Declaration*, developing the earlier Mexico City Declaration, identifies culture as 'the set of distinctive spiritual, material, intellectual and emotional features of society or a social group, [that] encompasses, in addition to art and literature, lifestyles, ways of living together, value systems, traditions and beliefs' (Preamble) and reminds us that 'culture takes diverse forms across time and space', that '[t]his diversity is embodied in the uniqueness and plurality of the identities of the groups and societies making up humankind' and that 'cultural diversity is as necessary for humankind as biodiversity is for nature' (Art. 1).

While the 2003 Convention focuses primarily on the processes of transmission of knowledge within the communities and groups that are the bearers of this heritage, the goal of the 2005 *Convention on the Protection and Promotion of the Diversity of Cultural Expressions* is to create the conditions in which the diversity of cultural expressions can flourish and freely interact in a mutually beneficial manner. It recognizes the distinctive character of cultural activities, goods and services, aims to stimulate cultural diversity, and is committed to sustainable development and international

⊃   *Traditional Japanese puppet theatre, Ningyo Johruri Bunraku*

Cultural diversity and intercultural dialogue are essentially linked, diversity being both the product and precondition of dialogue

cooperation. In addressing the exchanges between the cultures that constitute our universal heritage, the 2005 Convention marks the dawn of a new era in standard-setting instruments in which those instruments are aimed at preserving the specificities of cultures while promoting their development on a global scale through exchange and commercialization. Indeed, culture has two meanings, which are different yet wholly complementary. Firstly, culture is the creative diversity embodied in particular 'cultures', each with its own traditions and tangible and intangible expressions. Secondly, culture (in the singular) refers to the creative impulse at the source of that realized diversity. These two meanings of culture — one self-referential, the other self-transcending — are indissociable and the key to the fruitful interaction of all peoples in the context of globalization.

Through its normative apparatuses, UNESCO promotes these two approaches simultaneously: encouraging the world's cultures to affirm themselves in their infinite diversity, while furthering recognition of the universality of their expressions. By awakening a shared sense of wonder at the myriad manifestations of cultural creativity, it seeks to highlight the common sources of our humanity.

Conclusion

Often seen as a threat to cultural diversity, globalization is in practice far more diverse in its effects, for while it may in some respects deplete cultural diversity it also serves to reconfigure certain of its forms, not least in association with the development of digital technologies. The challenge is thus to limit the negative consequences of globalization for cultural diversity, which calls in the first instance for a more informed and nuanced understanding of its impacts. The establishment of a World Observatory on Cultural Diversity, as proposed in this report, could play a significant role in this regard.

It is also important to recognize that national — as distinct from cultural — identity is always to some extent an historical construction. Like any work of memory, the concept of nation is selective. No culture is ever wholly fixed or isolated, and national identity is always the product of processes of evolution and interaction. In a globalizing world, such changes are pervasive and make for the increased complexity of individual and group identities. Indeed, the recognition — and even affirmation — of multiple identities is a characteristic feature of our time. One of the paradoxical effects of globalization is thus to provoke forms of diversification conducive to innovation of all kinds and at all levels.

Yet cultures are not equal in the face of globalization processes, and every effort must be made to safeguard cultural expressions struggling to survive. However, safeguarding measures by themselves will not be enough: we must also find ways to help the communities in question to better manage cultural change within a context of intercultural dialogue. For cultural diversity and intercultural dialogue are essentially linked, diversity being both the product and precondition of dialogue.

Chapter 1 Recommendations

Consideration should be given to establishing a World Observatory on Cultural Diversity to monitor the impacts of globalization on cultural diversity and to serve as a source of information and data for comparative research with a forward-looking function.

To this end, action should be taken to:

a. Collect, compile and widely disseminate data and statistics on cultural diversity, building *inter alia* on the revised 2009 UNESCO Framework for Cultural Statistics (FCS).

b. Develop methodologies and tools for assessing, measuring and monitoring cultural diversity that are adaptable to national or local conditions by governments and public and private institutions.

c. Establish national observatories to monitor policies and advise on appropriate measures for the promotion of cultural diversity.

Standard-setting instruments adopted by UNESCO

The Universal Copyright Convention, which was adopted in 1952 and entered into force in 1955, introduced the idea that culture (literary, scientific and artistic works) embodies universal values requiring common protection and accordingltty a shared responsibility of the international community. Among its essential features are the preferential provisions for developing countries (introduced by the Paris *Act of the Convention* in 1971) to take account of the role of works of the mind in the general context of development and the economic, social and cultural needs of developing countries. After establishing international copyright protection worldwide, the *Universal Copyright Convention* began to lose ground in the 1980s, with many countries preferring to adhere to the stronger standards of the *Berne Convention for the rotection of Literary and Artistic Works* (1886, completed in 1896, revised in 1908, completed in 1914, revised in 1928, 1948, 1967, 1971 and amended in 1979).

At the same time, reflecting dramatically heightened awareness of the need to protect heritage in times of war, the Convention for the Protection of Cultural Properties in the Event of Armed Conflict was adopted in The Hague, Netherlands, in 1954. This international treaty, together with its *First Protocol* adopted the same year, introduced the expression 'cultural property' as a comprehensive and homogenous category of movable and immovable property deemed worthy of protection due to their unique cultural value — such as architectural, artistic or historical monuments and centres, archaeological sites, *museums, large libraries and archive depositories,* works of art, manuscripts, books, and other objects of artistic, historical or archaeological interest. The 1954 *Convention,* now complemented by *the Second Protocol* of 1999, laid the foundation for the concepts of common heritage and the common good of humanity.

In 1966 the UNESCO General Conference adopted the *Declaration on the Principles of International Cultural Co-operation.* The Declaration established the essential features of UNESCO's cooperation policies in the field of culture by stating that 'each culture has a dignity and value which must be respected and preserved', and that 'every people has the right and duty to develop its culture and that all cultures form part of the common heritage belonging to all mankind', thereby positing the notion that humanity as a whole constitutes a foundation shared by all individuals and that it possesses rights superseding those of nations.

In 1972 the General Conference adopted the Convention Concerning the Protection of the Cultural and Natural Heritage of the World. Like the 1954 *Hague Convention*, this landmark instrument focuses on immovable cultural property (in this case 'of outstanding universal value') but introduces the key notion of 'heritage of mankind'. With its programmatic approach, based on a listing system and the use of operational guidelines for its implementation, the 1972 Convention strengthened heritage conservation policies and became the standard reference for including conservation policies as a means of development, with particular emphasis on tourism. At the present time, 890 cultural, natural or mixed sites have been inscribed on the World Heritage List. These sites are located across the globe, enabling developed and developing countries alike to benefit from the opportunities associated with this Convention. The World Heritage label carries with it great prestige and is much coveted by the signatories to the Convention to gain recognition for their heritage, protect sensitive sites, landscapes and species, and attract tourism. More generally, World Heritage sites serve to sensitize and educate people to the need to protect the heritage for future generations, and to foster intercultural respect and understanding through appreciation of the diversity and wealth of expressions forming part of humanity's common patrimony.

The purpose of the *Convention on the Means of Prohibiting and Preventing the Illicit Import, Export and Transfer of Ownership of Cultural Property*, adopted in 1970, is quite different. It does not aim to protect cultural property in the name of its universal value but rather to recognize the national ownership of that property. The issue of the looting of cultural objects (or property) and the illicit trafficking of such property were also addressed in 1995 by the complementary *UNIDROIT Convention on Stolen or Illegally Exported Cultural Objects* and by the *Convention on the Protection of the Underwater Cultural Heritage*, adopted by the General Conference of UNESCO in 2001. This Convention established a standard for the protection of archaeological sites underwater comparable to that granted by other UNESCO Conventions to land-based cultural heritage. Its regulations are linked to the 1970 UNESCO Convention and the 1995 UNIDROIT Convention insofar as it contains detailed provisions concerning the prevention of the illicit trafficking of cultural property recovered from the sea. However, it is not intended to arbitrate quarrels or claims to ownership and does not contain a restitution clause.

The 2001 *Universal Declaration on Cultural Diversity*, unanimously adopted at the 31st session of UNESCO's General Conference, broke new ground in its specific reference to cultural diversity as 'the common heritage of humanity', which is to be 'recognized and affirmed for the benefit of present and future generations' and whose defence is deemed to be 'an ethical imperative, inseparable from respect for human dignity'. Such recognition is also seen to embody the practical imperative that 'care should be exercised that all cultures can express themselves and make themselves known', with implications for freedom of expression, media pluralism, multilingualism, and equal access to art and scientific and technical knowledge. The *Universal Declaration on Cultural Diversity* states that 'respect for the diversity of cultures, tolerance, dialogue and cooperation, in a climate of mutual trust and understanding' is one of 'the best guarantees of international peace and security' and affirms the need for 'international cooperation and solidarity' based on partnerships between the public sector, the private sector and civil society.

The 2003 *Convention for the Safeguarding of the Intangible Cultural Heritage* grew out of UNESCO's programme on the *Proclamation of Masterpieces of the Oral and Intangible Heritage of Humanity*, launched in 1997, with proclamations in 2001, 2003 and 2005. Intangible cultural heritage, which this Convention calls a 'mainspring of cultural diversity', is widely recognized as a key element in the protection of cultural identity, the promotion of creativity and the preservation of traditional cultural expressions. The definition of intangible heritage contained in the 2003 Convention — comprising a non-exhaustive list of domains, such as oral traditions and expressions (including language), performing arts, social practices, rituals and festive events, knowledge and practices concerning nature and the universe, and traditional craftsmanship — constitutes an important contribution towards the recognition of the multifaceted nature of cultural diversity. It aims to safeguard a heritage that is living, constantly evolving and embodied in human practices. In the 2003 Convention, the role assigned to communities and groups of tradition-bearers is therefore considerable. International recognition — for example, through inclusion of intangible heritage elements in the *List of Intangible Cultural Heritage in Need of Urgent Safeguarding* (UNESCO, 2003, Art. 17) and the *Representative List of the Intangible Cultural Heritage of Humanity* — is based on inventories drawn up by State Parties and on criteria adopted in June 2008 by the Assembly of State Parties to the Convention.

The *Convention on the Protection and Promotion of the Diversity of Cultural Expressions*, adopted in 2005, deals more specifically with cultural expressions produced, circulated and shared by contemporary means. Cultural diversity is innovatively defined as 'the manifold ways in which the cultures of groups and societies find expression. These expressions are passed on within and among groups and societies. Cultural diversity is made manifest not only through the varied ways in which the cultural heritage of humanity is expressed, augmented and transmitted through the variety of cultural expressions, but also through diverse modes of artistic creation, production, dissemination, distribution and enjoyment, whatever the means and technologies used' (Art. 4).

The 2005 Convention also includes the important statement that 'cultural diversity is strengthened by the free flow of ideas, and [. . .] is nurtured by constant exchanges and interaction between cultures', that 'linguistic diversity is a fundamental element of cultural diversity', that 'while the processes of globalization [. . .] afford unprecedented conditions for enhanced interaction between cultures, they also represent a challenge for cultural diversity, namely in view of risks of imbalances between rich and poor countries' (Preamble), as well as that 'equitable access to a rich and diversified range of cultural expressions from all over the world and access of cultures to the means of expressions and dissemination constitute important elements for enhancing cultural diversity and encouraging mutual understanding' (Art. 2.7).

The 2005 Convention recognizes the distinctive role of cultural activities, goods and services as vehicles of identity and values, aims at stimulating creative diversity and is committed to sustainable development and international cooperation. It establishes rights for contracting parties: each state party may adopt measures aimed at protecting and promoting the diversity of cultural expressions within its territory. In turn, State Parties have a number of duties, notably to ensure, within their territory, an environment that encourages individuals and groups to create, produce, disseminate and distribute their cultural expressions and have access to them. They also are required to pay particular attention to the special situation of minority and/ or marginalized individuals and groups and to commit themselves to international cooperation. Parties are likewise requested to raise awareness and foster public understanding of the importance of the diversity of cultural expressions and to encourage the active participation of civil society in efforts by parties to achieve the Convention's objectives.

In the field of cultural policies, UNESCO's work pertaining to cultural diversity also includes a series of Recommendations, notably the *Recommendation concerning the Most Effective Means of Rendering Museums Accessible to Everyone* (1960), the *Recommendation concerning the Preservation of Cultural Property Endangered by Public or Private Works* (1968), the *Recommendation concerning the Safeguarding and Contemporary Role of Historic Areas* (1976), the *Recommendation concerning the International Exchange of Cultural Property* (1976), the *Recommendation for the Protection of Movable Cultural Property* (1978), the *Recommendation for the Safeguarding and Preservation of Moving Images* (1980), the *Recommendation concerning the Status of the Artist* (1980) and the *Recommendation on the Safeguarding of Traditional Culture and Folklore* (1989).

Outside the field of cultural policies, other significant UNESCO instruments related to cultural diversity include the following:

a. **In the field of the fight against racism, the:**
- 1978 *Declaration on Race and Racial Prejudice*, which reaffirms the 'right to be different', significantly making reference to the complexity of cultural identities as irreducible to identity of origin;
- 1995 *Declaration of Principles on Tolerance*, which re-situates the issue of living together with our differences, in view of the new challenges arising from globalization and the emergence of worldwide networks.

b. **In the field of freedoms and rights, the:**
- 1976 *Recommendation on Participation by the People at Large in Cultural Life and Their Contribution to It*, which includes provisions related to diversity in the media, bearing in mind the 'extreme diversity of audiences, in order to 'enhance the cultural quality of programmes intended for the public at large';
- 1997 *Declaration on the Responsibilities of the Present Generations towards Future Generations*, which states that 'it is important to make every effort to ensure [. . .] that future as well as present generations enjoy full freedom of choice [. . .] and are able to preserve their cultural and religious diversity'.

c. **In the field of information and communication technologies (ICTs), the:**
- 2003 *Charter on the Preservation of Digital Heritage*, which — building on the Memory of the World programme launched by UNESCO in 1992 and dedicated to increasing worldwide awareness of the existence and significance of documentary heritage by drawing up international inventories — advocates the development of strategies and policies for the protection and promotion of digital heritage;
- 2003 *Recommendation on the Promotion and Use of Multilingualism and Universal Access to Cyberspace*, which notes that 'linguistic diversity in the global information networks and universal access to information in cyberspace are at the core of contemporary debates'.

d. **In the field of education, the:**
- 1960 *Convention against Discrimination in Education*, which refers in its Preamble to the objective of 'respecting the diversity of national educational systems';
- 1974 *Recommendation concerning Education for International Understanding, Cooperation and Peace and Education relating to Human Rights and Fundamental Freedoms* and the 1993 *Recommendation on the Recognition of Studies and Qualifications in Higher Education*, which are aimed at promoting better understanding between cultures and peoples, including mutual respect for their diversity.

⌒ *UNESCO Headquarters, Paris*

References and websites

Background documents and UNESCO sources

Alexander, N. 2007. Rethinking culture, linking tradition and modernity. Paper presented at the second meeting of the Advisory Committee of Experts, Venice, 2–3 April.

Amescua, C. 2007. An analysis of the nomination files for masterpieces of the oral and intangible heritage of humanity. Background paper.

Bouma, G. 2007. Religious identity and cultural identity. Background paper.

Cowen, T. 2006. Cultural diversity and globalization. Background paper.

Dallmayr, F. 2007. Cultural identity and religious identity. Background paper.

Fasheh, M. 2007. Cultural diversity in formal and non-formal educational systems. Background paper.

Langlois, F. 2007. Distorsions identitaires en Asie Centrale post-soviétique. Background paper.

Nyamnjoh, F. and Warnier, J. P. 2007. Cultural globalization: real or imaginary? Background paper.

Soudien, C. 2007. Multiple cultural identities and cultural fictions: cultural makeshifts and metissages. Background paper.

Tauli-Corpuz, V. 2007. Indigenous people's voice in a globalized world. Background paper.

Tomlison, J. 2007. Cultural globalization and the representation of otherness through the media. Background paper.

UNESCO. 2009. UNESCO Framework for Cultural Statistics: Task Force Meeting Summary. May. Paris. http://www.uis.unesco.org/template/pdf/cscl/framework/TFM_Summary_EN.pdf

—. 2007. *Standard-Setting in UNESCO II: Conventions, Recommendations, Declarations and Charters adopted by UNESCO (1948–2006)*. Paris, UNESCO.

—. 2005. *Convention on the Protection and Promotion of the Diversity of Cultural Expressions*. Paris, UNESCO. http://unesdoc.unesco.org/images/0014/001429/142919e.pdf

—. 2003a. *Charter on the Preservation of Digital Heritage*. 17 October. http://portal.unesco.org/ci/en/files/13367/10700115911Charter_en.pdf/Charter_en.pdf

—. 2003b. *Recommendation on the Promotion and Use of Multilingualism and Universal Access to Cyberspace*. 15 October. http://portal.unesco.org/ci/en/files/13475/10697584791Recommendation-Eng.pdf/Recommendation-Eng.pdf

—. 2003c. *Convention for the Safeguarding of the Intangible Cultural Heritage*. Paris, UNESCO. http://unesdoc.unesco.org/images/0013/001325/132540e.pdf

—. 2001a. *Universal Declaration on Cultural Diversity*. Paris, UNESCO. http://unesdoc.unesco.org/images/0012/001271/127160m.pdf

—. 2001b. *Convention on the Protection of the Underwater Cultural Heritage. 2 November. Paris, UNESCO. http://unesdoc.unesco.org/images/0012/001260/126065e.pdf*

—. 2001c. *Proclamation of Masterpieces of the Oral and Intangible Heritage of Humanity*. 18 May. http://www.unesco.org/bpi/intangible_heritage/index.htm

—. 1998. Making the Most of Globalization. *Sources*, No. 97, pp. 7-8.

—. 1997. *Declaration on the Responsibilities of the Present Generations towards Future Generations*. 12 November. http://portal.unesco.org/en/ev.php-URL_ID=13178&URL_DO=DO_PRINTPAGE&URL_SECTION=201.html

—. 1995. *Declaration of Principles on Tolerance*. 16 November. http://www.unesco.org/webworld/peace_library/UNESCO/HRIGHTS/124-129.HTM

—. 1994. *Salamanca Declaration and Framework of Action*. World Conference on Special Needs Education: Access and Quality, Salamanca, Spain, 7–10 June. Paris, UNESCO. http://www.ecdgroup.com/download/gn1ssfai.pdf

—. 1993. *Recommendation on the Recognition of Studies and Qualifications in Higher Education*. 16 November. http://portal.unesco.org/en/ev.php-URL_ID=13142&URL_DO=DO_PRINTPAGE&URL_SECTION=201.html

—. 1989. *Recommendation on the Safeguarding of Traditional Culture and Folklore*. 16 November. http://portal.unesco.org/en/ev.php-URL_ID=13141&URL_DO=DO_PRINTPAGE&URL_SECTION=201.html

—. 1982. *Mexico City Declaration on Cultural Policies*. World Conference on Cultural Policies (MONDIACULT), Mexico City, 26 July — 6 August. http://portal.unesco.org/culture/en/files/12762/11295421661mexico_en.pdf/mexico_en.pdf

—. 1980a. *Recommendation concerning the Status of the Artist*. 27 October. http://portal.unesco.org/en/ev.php-URL_ID=13138&URL_DO=DO_TOPIC&URL_SECTION=201.html

—. 1980b. *Recommendation for the Safeguarding and Preservation of Moving Images*. 27 October. http://portal.unesco.org/en/ev.php-URL_ID=13139&URL_DO=DO_TOPIC&URL_SECTION=201.html

—. 1978a. *Recommendation for the Protection of Movable Cultural Property*. 28 November. http://portal.unesco.org/en/ev.php-URL_ID=13137&URL_DO=DO_TOPIC&URL_SECTION=201.html

—. 1978b. *Declaration on Race and Racial Prejudice*. 27 November. http://www.unesco.org/webworld/peace_library/UNESCO/HRIGHTS/107-116.HTM

—. 1976a. *Recommendation concerning the International Exchange of Cultural Property*. 30 November. http://portal.unesco.org/en/ev.php-URL_ID=13132&URL_DO=DO_PRINTPAGE&URL_SECTION=201.html

—. 1976b. *Recommendation concerning the Safeguarding and Contemporary Role of Historic Areas*. 26 November. http://portal.unesco.org/en/ev.php-URL_ID=13133&URL_DO=DO_TOPIC&URL_SECTION=201.html

—. 1976c. *Recommendation on Participation by the People at Large in Cultural Life and Their Contribution to It*. 26 November. http://portal.unesco.org/en/ev.php-URL_ID=13097&URL_DO=DO_TOPIC&URL_SECTION=201.html

—. 1974. *Recommendation concerning Education for International Understanding, Cooperation and Peace and Education relating to Human Rights and Fundamental Freedoms*. 19 November. http://www.unesco.org/education/nfsunesco/pdf/Peace_e.pdf

—. 1972. *Convention Concerning the Protection of the World Cultural and Natural Heritage*. Adopted by the General Conference at its seventeenth session, Paris, 16 November. Paris, UNESCO. http://whc.unesco.org/archive/convention-en.pdf

—. 1968. *Recommendation concerning the Preservation of Cultural Property Endangered by Public or Private Works*. 19 November. http://portal.unesco.org/en/ev.php-URL_ID=13085&URL_DO=DO_TOPIC&URL_SECTION=201.html

—. 1966. *Declaration of the Principles of International Cultural Co-operation*. 4 November. http://portal.unesco.org/en/ev.php-URL_ID=13147&URL_DO=DO_TOPIC&URL_SECTION=201.html

—. 1960a. *Recommendation concerning the Most Effective Means of Rendering Museums Accessible to Everyone*. 14 December. http://portal.unesco.org/en/ev.php-URL_ID=13063&URL_DO=DO_TOPIC&URL_SECTION=201.html

—. 1960b. *Convention against Discrimination in Education*. 14 December. http://portal.unesco.org/en/ev.php-URL_ID=12949&URL_DO=DO_TOPIC&URL_SECTION=201.html

—. 1954. *Convention for the Protection of Cultural Property in the Event of Armed Conflict*. The Hague, 14 May. http://portal.unesco.org/en/ev.php-URL_ID=13637&URL_DO=DO_TOPIC&URL_SECTION=201.html

—. 1952. *Universal Copyright Convention*. Geneva, 6 September. http://portal.unesco.org/en/ev.php-URL_ID=15381&URL_DO=DO_TOPIC&URL_SECTION=201.html

—. 1950. *Agreement on the Importation of Educational, Scientific and Cultural Materials*. Florence, 17 June. http://portal.unesco.org/en/ev.php-URL_ID=12074&URL_DO=DO_TOPIC&URL_SECTION=201.html

—. 1948. *Agreement For Facilitating the International Circulation of Visual and Auditory Materials of an Educational, Scientific and Cultural Character*. Beirut, 10 December. http://portal.unesco.org/en/ev.php-URL_ID=12064&URL_DO=DO_TOPIC&URL_SECTION=201.html

—. 1945. *The Constitution of UNESCO*. Paris, UNESCO. http://unesdoc.unesco.org/images/0012/001255/125590e.pdf#constitution

Vishnevski, A. 2007. Cultural diversity and demographic transitions. Background paper.

World Intellectual Property Organization (WIPO). _. *Berne Convention for the Protection of Literary and Artistic Works*. http://www.wipo.int/export/sites/www/treaties/en/ip/berne/pdf/trtdocs_wo001.pdf

Websites

African Academy of Languages (ACALAN): http://www.acalan.org

Council of Europe, Committee of Ministers. 2000. *Declaration on Cultural Diversity*. https://wcd.coe.int/ViewDoc.jsp?id=389843

Council of Europe, Diversity: http://www.coe.int/t/dg4/cultureheritage/topics/diversity_en.asp#

Erasmus Programme: http://ec.europa.eu/education/lifelong-learning-programme/doc80_en.htm

European Commission, Culture: Cultural diversity and intercultural dialogue: http://ec.europa.eu/culture/our-policy-development/doc401_en.htm

International Council on Monuments and Sites (ICOMOS): http://www.icomos.org

International Music Council (IMC): http://www.imc-cim.org

International Network for Cultural Diversity (INCD): http://www.incd.net

International Research Institute for Media, Communication and Cultural Development (MEDIACULT): http://www.mediacult.at

League of Arab States. 2007. *Riyadh Declaration*. 29 March. http://www.pij.org/documents/Riyadh%20Declaration.pdf

MEDIA Programme: http://ec.europa.eu/information_society/media/index_en.htm

Organización de Estados Iberoamericanos para la Educación, la Ciencia y la Cultura (OEI): http://www.oei.es/cultura.htm

Second life, Wikipedia: http://en.wikipedia.org/wiki/Second_Life#Teen_Second_Life

Social Media Statistics: http://socialmediastatistics.wikidot.com

UNESCO, Culture portal: portal.unesco.org/culture/en/ev.php-URL_ID=34603&URL_DO=DO_TOPIC&URL_SECTION=201.html

UNESCO, Culture: Diversity of cultural expressions: http://portal.unesco.org/culture/en/ev.php-URL_ID=33014&URL_DO=DO_TOPIC&URL_SECTION=201.html

UNESCO, Culture: Intangible cultural heritage (ICH): http://portal.unesco.org/culture/en/ev.php-URL_ID=34325&URL_DO=DO_TOPIC&URL_SECTION=201.html

UNESCO, Representative List of the Intangible Cultural Heritage of Humanity: http://www.unesco.org/culture/ich/index.php?pg=00173

UNESCO, The Stockholm Conference: http://portal.unesco.org/culture/en/ev.php-URL_ID=18717&URL_DO=DO_TOPIC&URL_SECTION=201.html

UNIDROIT. 1995. *UNIDROIT Convention on Stolen or Illegally Exported Cultural Objects*. Rome. http://www.unidroit.org/english/conventions/1995culturalproperty/1995culturalproperty-e.htm

United Nations Conference on the Human Environment (Stockholm, 1972): http://www.unep.org/Documents.Multilingual/Default.asp?DocumentID=97

United Nations Permanent Forum on Indigenous Issues (UNPFII): http://www.un.org/esa/socdev/unpfii

United Nations. 1948. *Universal Declaration of Human Rights*. 10 December. http://www.un.org/en/documents/udhr

World Heritage Centre: http://whc.unesco.org

World Heritage List: http://whc.unesco.org/en/list

World Tourism Organization (UNWTO): http://www.unwto.org/index.php

References

Association of Southeast Asian Nations (ASEAN). 2005. *Joint Communiqué of the 38th ASEAN Ministerial Meeting.* Vientiane, 26 July 2005. http://www.aseansec.org/17592.htm

Association of Southeast Asian Nations (ASEAN). 2003. *Declaration of ASEAN Concord II (Bali Concord II).* Bali, Indonesia, 7 October. http://www.aseansec.org/15159.htm

African Union. 2006. *Charter for African Cultural Renaissance.* Addis Ababa, Ethiopia: African Union. http://www.africa-union.org/root/au/Documents/Treaties/text/Charter%20-%20African%20Cultural%20Renaissance_EN.pdf

Appadurai, A. 2004. The capacity to aspire: Culture and the terms of recognition. V. Rao and M. Walton (eds.), *Culture and Public Action.* Stanford, Calif., Stanford University Press.

—. 1996. *Modernity at Large: Cultural Dimensions of Globalization.* Minneapolis, Minn., University of Minnesota Press.

Appiah, K. A. 2006. *Cosmopolitanism: Ethics in a World of Strangers.* New York, W. W. Norton.

Azarya, V. 2004. Globalization and international tourism in developing countries: Marginality as a commercial commodity. *Current Sociology,* Vol. 52, No. 6, pp. 949–67.

Barber, B. R. 1996. *Jihad vs. McWorld: How Globalism and Tribalism Are Reshaping the World.* New York, Ballantine Books.

Bauman, Z. 2005. *Liquid Life.* Cambridge, Polity.

—. 2001. *The Individualized Society.* Cambridge, Polity.

Bayart, J.-F. 1997. *L'illusion identitaire.* Paris, Fayard.

Benedict, R. 1948. The study of cultural continuities in the civilized world. Lecture given to UNESCO, Seminar on Childhood Education, Podebrady (Czechoslovakia), 15 September. SEM.III/Lec.10. http://unesdoc.unesco.org/images/0015/001556/155613eb.pdf

Bhabha, H. K. 1994. *The Location of Culture.* London: Routledge.

Cicero, M. T. 1853. *Tusculan Disputations.* In *The Academic Questions, Treatise De Finibus, and Tusculan Disputations, of M. T. Cicero.* Translated by C. D. Yonge. London, H. G. Bohn.

Clifford, J. 1997. *Routes: Travel and Translation in the Late Twentieth Century.* Cambridge, Mass., Harvard University Press.

European Commission. 2007. *Communication from the Commission to the European Parliament, the Council, the European Economic and Social Committee and the Committee of the Regions on a European Agenda for Culture in a Globalizing World.* COM(2007) 242 final. 10 May. http://eur-lex.europa.eu/LexUriServ/LexUriServ.do?uri=COM:2007:0242:FIN:EN:PDF

A mosque in the Dubai airport

Council of Europe. 2008. *White Paper on Intercultural Dialogue: Living Together as Equals in Dignity.* Strasbourg, Council of Europe. http://www.coe.int/t/dg4/intercultural/Source/Pub_White_Paper/White%20Paper_final_revised_EN.pdf

Eriksen, T. H. 2007. *Globalization: The Key Concepts.* Oxford, Berg.

García Canclini, N. 1995. *Hybrid Cultures: Strategies for Entering and Leaving Modernity.* Translated by C. L. Chiappari and S. L. López. Minneapolis, Minn., University of Minnesota Press.

Geertz, C. 1973. *The Interpretation of Cultures: Selected Essays.* New York, Basic Books.

Giddens, A. 1984. *The Constitution of Society: Outline of the Theory of Structuration.* Berkeley, Calif., University of California Press.

Hobsbawm, E. and Ranger, T. (eds.). 1984. *The Invention of Tradition.* Cambridge, Cambridge University Press.

Kass, J. D., Friedman, R., Lesserman, J., Zuttermeister, P. and Benson, H. 1991. Health outcomes and a new index of spiritual experiences. *Journal for the Scientific Study of Religion,* Vol. 30, No. 2, pp. 203–11.

Lévi-Strauss, C. 2005. Réflexion. *60 ans d'histoire de l'UNESCO. Actes due colloque international, Paris, 16–18 novembre.* Paris, UNESCO, pp. 31–35. http://unesdoc.unesco.org/images/0015/001541/154122f.pdf#31

—. 1952. *Race et histoire.* Paris, UNESCO.

Long, N. and Long, A. (eds.). 1992. *Battlefields of Knowledge: The Interlocking of Theory and Practice in Social Research and Development*. London, Routledge.

Lull, J. 2000. *Media, Communication, Culture: A Global Approach*. New York, Columbia University Press.

Maalouf, A. 1998. *Les identités meurtrières*. Paris, Grasset.

Organización de Estados Iberoamericanos para la Educación, la Ciencia y la Cultura (OEI). 2006. *Iberoamerican Cultural Charter*. Adopted at the Ninth Iberoamerican Conference on Culture, Montevideo, 13–14 July. http://www.oei.es/cultura/Montevideo-ing.pdf

Organización de Estados Iberoamericanos para la Educación, la Ciencia y la Cultura (OEI). 2005. *Para una Carta Cultural Iberoamericana*. Eighth Ibero-American Conference on Culture, in Córdoba, Span, 13–15 June. http://www.oei.es/CARTACULTURALIBEROAMERICANA1.pdf

Ranger, T. 1984. The invention of tradition in Colonial Africa. E. Hobsbawm and T. Ranger (eds.), *The Invention of Tradition*. Cambridge, Cambridge University Press.

Rizk, B., *Les paramètres d'Hérodote ou les identités culturelles collectives*. Paris, L'Orient Le Jour, 2009.

Sassen, S. 2001. *The Global City: New York, London, Tokyo*. Princeton, N.J., Princeton University Press.

Sen, A. 2006a. *Identity and Violence: The Illusion of Destiny*. New York, W. W. Norton.

—. 2006b. The illusion of identity. IRDC lecture, 12 April. http://www.idrc.ca/fr/ev-96559-201-1-DO_TOPIC.html.

Simon, G. 1998. *Geodynamics of international migrations in the World*. Paris, Presses Universitaires de France (PUF).

Sunstein, C. 2001. *Republic.com*. Princeton, N.J., Princeton University Press.

Tardif, J. and Farchy, J. 2006. *Les Enjeux de la mondialisation culturelle*. Paris, Éditions Hors Commerce.

Teller, D. J. and Sharpley, R. 2007. *Tourism and Development in the Developing World*. London, Routledge.

Tomlinson, J. 1991. *Cultural Imperialism: A Critical Introduction*. London, Pinter.

United Nations Development Programme (UNDP). 2004. *Human Development Report 2004: Cultural Liberty in Today's World*. New York, UNDP. http://hdr.undp.org/en/media/hdr04_complete.pdf

World Commission on Culture and Development. 1996. *Our Creative Diversity*. Paris, UNESCO. http://unesdoc.unesco.org/images/0010/001055/105586e.pdf

The Mostar Bridge was rebuilt
after the war in Bosnia

Intercultural dialogue

Human beings relate to one another through society, and express that relationship through culture. All of our actions, thoughts, behaviour, attitudes and material or intellectual creations imply a cultural relationship. Even the natural world that we name, describe and analyze may be said to be informed by human culture, to be invested with 'inward meaning'. In this fundamental sense, our similarities are more profound than our cultural differences. These differences, moreover, embody a positive potential, for it is through them that we complement one another in devising novel solutions for living together in our social and natural settings. Cultural diversity represents the sum of these solutions, and dialogue is the bridge between them.

If we are to respond to the challenges inherent in a culturally diverse world, we must develop new approaches to intercultural dialogue, approaches that go beyond the limitations of the 'dialogue among civilizations' paradigm. The prerequisites for such a dialogue include consideration of the ways in which cultures relate to one another, awareness of cultural commonalities and shared goals, and identification of the challenges to be met in reconciling cultural differences and identities.

A caravan of camels at Mingsha Shan in Dunhuang, China

Intercultural Dialogue

2.1 Cultural interactions **39**
Box 2.1 UNESCO Slave Route Project:
Celebrating the cultural expressions
generated through enforced dialogue 40

2.2. Cultural stereotypes and intolerance **41**
Figure 2.1 World Values Survey on
geographical belonging 43
Box 2.2 'What went wrong with the dialogue
between cultures?' 44

**2.3 The challenges of dialogue
in a multicultural world** **45**
Box 2.3 Intercultural competencies:
The basics 45
Box 2.4 Reconciliation through common
narrative: Revised history textbook initiatives 49

2.4 Empowerment **51**
Box 2.5 Through the eyes of hunters-gatherers:
Participatory 3D modelling among the Ogiek
indigenous peoples in Kenya 52

Conclusion **54**

Recommendations **55**

**In focus: The history of dialogue at UNESCO
and institutional initiatives
on intercultural dialogue** **56**

References and websites **61**

A young boy in Kihnu Island, Estonia

2.1 Cultural interactions

Cultures are not self-enclosed or static entities. They overlap and interact, if only to distinguish themselves from one another. 'Cultures are like clouds, their confines ever changing, coming together or moving apart [. . .] and sometimes merging to produce new forms arising from those that preceded them yet differing from them entirely' (Droit in UNESCO, 2007). Even cultures long regarded as isolated or hermetic can be shown to have had contacts with other cultures in the form of economic or proto-political exchanges. One of the fundamental obstacles to intercultural dialogue is our propensity to hypostasize other cultures, to conceive of them as fixed entities, as if fault lines separated them. Where such fault lines are seen as absolute, often as a result of totalitarian ideologies or beliefs, we pass into the realm of confrontation or conflict. One of the main objections to Huntington's thesis of a 'clash of civilizations', apart from the risk that it could become a self-fulfilling prophecy, is that it presupposes singular rather than multiple affiliations between human communities and fails to take account of cultural interdependency and interaction (Huntington, 1996). To describe as fault lines the differences between cultures — even those characterized by divergent or opposing beliefs — is to overlook the porosity of cultural boundaries and the creative potential of the individuals they encompass.

Civilizations, societies and cultures, like individuals, exist in relation to one another. As one historian has noted, 'consciously or otherwise [. . .] civilizations observe one another, seek each other out, influence one another, mutually define one another. Their founding texts may endure, but they themselves do not remain static' (Baubérot, 2003). Culture, it has been said, is contagious. Down through the centuries, exchanges and interactions of all kinds — through travel, trade and trespass — have acted as *translations* between cultures. 'Translation cannot be reduced to a technique practised spontaneously by travellers, traders, ambassadors, smugglers and traitors, and elevated to a professional discipline by translators and interpreters. It constitutes a paradigm for all exchanges, not only between languages but also between cultures' (Ricoeur, 2004). These translations merge with endogenous features to give rise to new traditions as part of the complex tectonics of cultures and civilizations.

This intermingling of cultures through the ages has found expression in a multitude of cultural forms and human practices. Some of these are reflected in the Representative List of the intangible cultural heritage of Humanity, created under the 2003 Convention — a repository of oral traditions, social practices, performing arts and traditional knowledge and crafts, transmitted from generation to generation, constantly recreated and providing communities with a sense of identity and continuity (see Table 1 in the Statistical Annex). Underlying this multifarious heritage, it is possible to distinguish three main modes of cultural interaction: cultural borrowings, cultural exchanges and cultural impositions. While ethically distinctive, all these forms of interaction have impacted very significantly, and in many cases very fruitfully, on forms of cultural expression.

⌒ *The Samba de Roda of Recôncavo of Bahia, Brazil*

Cultural *borrowing* occurs when the cultural practice of one population is assimilated by another in recognition of its perceived advantages over the one it has previously employed. Populations may be prepared to abandon even very ancient customs when enabling mechanisms are found to facilitate the integration of new practices. An example is the use of snow scooters by the Sami people in Finland, who, while remaining attached to their traditions and beliefs, have adapted to a harsh environment by embracing modern technology. The 'borrowing' of practices or customs can become the basis for entirely new forms or modalities through adaptation to their new setting or divorce from their original meaning. In the rainbow cultures characteristic of many modern societies, borrowing has sometimes become so pervasive as to challenge the distinction between endogenous and exogenous cultural elements.

Cultural *exchanges* can become generalized between neighbouring and mutually dependent cultures. The Silk Roads represented a common trading framework that ensured relatively peaceful relations between neighbouring peoples and fostered a genuine receptiveness to difference, which benefited the cultural development of the populations concerned and enabled significant cultural transfers to take place across large geographical areas. Generally speaking, trade between different cultural regions has contributed

Box 2.1 **UNESCO Slave Route Project: Celebrating the cultural expressions generated through enforced dialogue**

The slave trade and slavery constitute one of the darkest chapters in human history. This dehumanizing enterprise, which challenged the very basis of universal values and has been roundly condemned by the international community, has nonetheless contributed to the development of some of the most valuable forms of cultural human resistance to domination.

Beyond its economic impact, the slave trade has also given rise to significant interactions among the peoples of Africa, Europe, the Americas, the Indian Ocean, the Arab-Muslim world and Asia, which have profoundly and lastingly transformed their cultures, knowledge, beliefs and behaviour. The intercultural process that began with the slave trade is still going on and continues to transform humanity. Hence, the concept of 'route' was chosen to illustrate this flow of exchanges among peoples, cultures and civilizations, which transformed the geographical areas affected by slavery — a unique interaction generating forms of intercultural dialogue of considerable importance to the building of modern societies.

Zoungbodji Memorial commemorating the slave route in Ouidah, Benin

By retracing these cultural interactions brought about by the slave trade, which transported so many African men and women far from their birthlands, the Slave Route Project is contributing to a better understanding of cultural traditions, forms of ingenuity, technical and scientific knowledge, skills and spirituality which were transferred from Africa to the Americas, the Caribbean, Asia, the Indian Ocean and the Arab-Muslim world. It draws attention to the major imprint of African cultures on the formation of the world's identities, cultures and civilizations, the African contribution to the world's rich diversity as expressed through Creole cultures, languages, religions, music and dance.

The influence of African art and particularly music is widely acknowledged today. Jazz and other styles of Afro-American music, such as the blues, appeared in the 1890s, over a quarter century after the abolition of slavery in the United States. The syncopated rhythms of this music fused traits of African folk music with European popular music, but also Native American music, and reflected the mores and social situations of the first generation of African Americans born outside of slavery.

African heritage is also a primary basis of Brazilian samba, Cuban rumba and Trinidadian calypso. Combining the skills of African storytelling, singing and instrument making, calypso usually involves some social commentary, typically in the form of satire, with an infectious beat. It has since been influenced by European, North American and other Caribbean cultures to produce reggae and the latest creation of black music today: rap.

Rooted in Bantu traditions of Angola, Capoeira was used by Africans enslaved in Brazil to practice their fighting skills, unbeknownst to their enslavers. When colonial authorities discovered its real purpose, it was banned on penalty of death. Capoeira continued to be practiced by fugitive slaves who set up independent settlements, known as Quilombos, although it remained illegal in Brazil until the 1930s, when it finally

received national recognition as a martial art. In recent years, Capoeira has spread beyond Brazil and continues to grow in popularity. According to the International Capoeira Angola Foundation, it is now practiced in 74 countries, and over 1,000 Capoeira schools are listed on the Internet.

Enslaved Africans also carried spiritual traditions to the New World, where they were modified to meet the conditions of slavery. While many believe that Voodoo hails from Haiti, it in fact originated in West Africa (*voodoo* means 'spirit') and took on new forms in Haiti, including elements of Roman Catholicism, as a means of survival and resistance to slavery. A Voodoo temple in Cotonou, run by a Haitian-born priest, features candles, bells and a cross, and the gods are identified with Roman Catholic saints.

Africans enslaved in America blended African musical forms with European Christian hymns to create spirituals, which developed into gospel music. Gospel and blues merged in America to produce yet another popular genre known as soul, which also gives its name to a cuisine commonly associated with African Americans in the southern United States. Soul food reflects gastronomic responses to racial discrimination and economic oppression and makes creative use of African products, such as yams, peanuts, okra, black-eyed peas and rice.

While the diversity of cultural expressions generated through the slave trade and slavery continues to influence our societies beyond the regions in which slavery was practiced, the added values of such cultural enrichment still need to be properly acknowledged as part of Africa's contribution to the world's cultural heritage. This is a one of the major objectives of the Slave Route Project launched by UNESCO in 1994 and the new strategy for highlighting the African presence throughout the world.

Source: UNESCO.

to the mutual enrichment of humanity and to the interconnectedness between cultures for the benefit of all. What would the scientific revolution of Renaissance Europe have been without the contribution of the Arab sciences, which themselves drew on the intellectual heritage of the ancient world? Cultural exchanges refer to the many collective developments and are at the origin of most human achievements and tend to invalidate claims to exclusivity for any one civilization.

Cultural *imposition* through war and conquest has constituted a major form of cultural interaction down through the ages. More recently, processes of colonization imposed Western culture with little regard for the value and meaning of the cultures of the populations 'discovered' or conquered. Yet even in the extreme condition of slavery, discreet processes of reverse enculturation take place and the cultural practices of the dominated populations come to be assimilated by the dominating culture (Bhabha, 1994). The resulting cultural interactions are today exemplified in all those parts of the world touched by the African diaspora (see Box 2.1). Of course, past legacies continue to weigh heavily on many cultures, and globalization processes have in many cases compounded inequalities in the cultural field. Yet the achievement of independence by subjugated populations, the progress of the human sciences (in particular, ethnography), and the recognition of the cultural dimension of human rights have made it increasingly possible to arrive at fairer valuations of previously misunderstood cultures and to think in terms of genuine exchanges between all cultures.

Today globalization, international trade and the rise of information and communication technologies (ICTs) and the media are making for more systematic encounters, borrowings, juxtapositions and cultural exchanges. Yet this new degree of mutual receptiveness among cultures will not place them on an equal footing if we do not begin to rethink our shared cultural categories. The transcultural ties that manifest themselves across the complex interplay of multiple identities are potentially powerful facilitators of intercultural dialogue. Irrespective of the stances adopted by the various parties, or their identification with the particular culture of which they believe themselves to be the 'representatives', the acceptance of multiple identities shifts the focus away from 'differences' and towards our shared capacity to interact and to accept encounters, coexistence and even cohabitation between different cultures.

Knowledge of the forms of cultural interaction in a country, subregion or region is an asset for identifying ways and means of facilitating intercultural dialogue. Even where such interaction has been marked by imposition or oppression, recognition and discussion of past grievances can help, paradoxically, to ensure that the focus of such dialogue does not remain negative. All this implies historical awareness and the capacity to engage in the critical examination of different cultural frames of reference. Knowledge of cultural interactions should also include the resources employed by societies and individuals to build dialogue, even in situations of tension. Observing these as conventions is an important step towards overcoming cultural stereotypes on the path to intercultural dialogue.

Stereotyping is a way of demarcating one group from an alien 'other' and implicitly asserting its superiority. Stereotypes carry with them the danger that dialogue may stop short at difference and that difference may engender intolerance

⋂   *A Central Asian performer at UNESCO Headquarters*

2.2. Cultural stereotypes and intolerance

Cultural stereotypes are ubiquitous. In the workplace, the classroom, the press and the media, they are perpetuated through jokes, anecdotes, songs and images. While the degree to which they intend or not to give offence varies, these reductive simplifications of the 'outsider' contain the seeds of prejudice. Stereotyping is a way of demarcating one group from an alien 'other' and implicitly asserting its superiority. Stereotypes carry with them the danger that dialogue may stop short at difference and that difference may engender intolerance.

In many ways, the emergence of information and communication networks is facilitating contacts between

different cultures and multiplying the possibilities for mutual knowledge. Yet it would be a mistake to underestimate the tenacity of prejudice, the depth of the reflex that prompts us to define our identity in opposition to others. Intercultural dialogue is necessary as a permanent corrective to the diversity of our cultural allegiances. Cultures belonging to different traditions are particularly prone to mutual stereotyping. With reference to Western attitudes towards the non-Western world, Edward Said (1978) has argued, for example, that 'Orientalism is fundamentally a political doctrine willed over the Orient because the Orient was weaker than the West, which elided the Orient's difference with

Intercultural encounters between individuals, communities and peoples invariably involve a certain cultural tension... Within a multicultural society, the two main axes involved are those of memory and values

its weakness. [. . .] As a cultural apparatus, Orientalism is all aggression, activity, judgment, will-to-truth, and knowledge'. If this is the case, then it can equally well be asserted that 'Occidentalism' is no less reductive of Western cultural identity. Human beings are all too ready to define themselves in opposition to one another, to have recourse to reflex stereotyping.

Several methods exist for measuring the stereotypes prevalent in a given society. Public opinion surveys conducted in different countries involve interviewing people and asking them to categorize others according to various criteria — from nationality to standardized attributes (such as 'hardworking', 'brave', 'intelligent', 'cruel'). Yet here too a danger of stereotyping lurks: the underlying biases of such approaches (through choice of categorization, terms used, etc.) must themselves be questioned, since the same traits may refer to different realities in different languages, and the very choice of a given list of attributes is already a way of influencing the answer. Other methods for measuring stereotypes and prejudices include, for example, the 'serial reproduction investigation technique', according to which a person is shown a picture and asked to describe

it to someone else, who is in turn asked to describe it to a third person, and so on. The serial reproduction amplifies the stereotype so as to make it more apparent. On another level, national census classifications can also be interesting with regard to the different ways in which difference is categorized.

Intercultural encounters between individuals, communities and peoples invariably involve a certain cultural tension, whose terms depend on the context in which they occur and the value systems brought into play. Within a multicultural society, the two main axes involved are those of *memory* and *values* (Diène, 2007). The particular memories of different groups, communities or peoples make up the collective memory of a multicultural society. Competing memories may stem from or provoke open or latent conflict — such as between the constitution of a national memory by a dominant group and the demands by other groups that their own memories be taken into account. This applies *a fortiori* to the competing memories of the colonizer and the colonized. National memory, formalized and legitimized by its place in national history texts and transmitted by national and civic educational systems, often leads to the denial, omission or

Figure 2.1 World Values Survey on geographical belonging

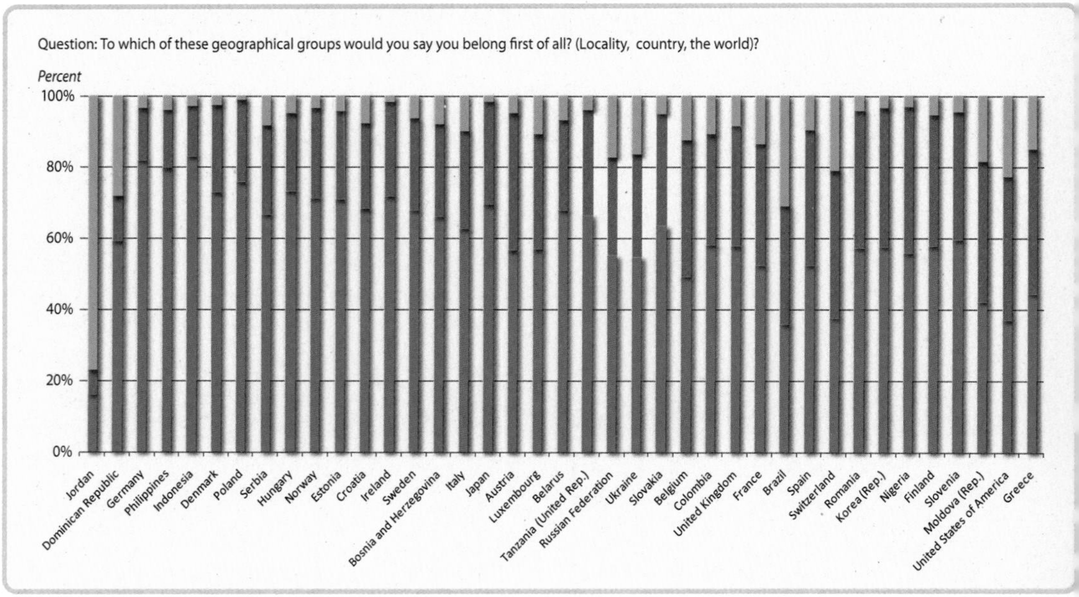

Source: World Values Survey database, 2008.

perversion of the specific memories of certain minority groups or communities.

It is often in the realm of cultural, spiritual or religious values that the identity of each group, community or people has its deepest roots. The search for one's identity can be open and dynamic, oriented towards a definition of the self always in the making. It can be backward-looking or fixed according to ethnic or even genetic differences, as illustrated by the new market of genetic ancestry.[1] In the multicultural process, identity strain occurs, according to historical circumstance and political context, when a group or a community intentionally or otherwise imposes its cultural and spiritual values on other minority groups, or when a group or community tries to ignore or deny the values of other groups or communities. Such identity strain can insidiously play itself out generations later, as sometimes happens in the suburbs of megacities in former colonial countries in which forms of discrimination going back to the colonial era are perpetuated with regard to certain population groups (Diène, 2007). The civilizing and proselytizing discourse of colonialism — which is still echoed in some conceptions of cultural and scientific progress — is a particularly egregious example of the kind of ideological-cum-political hegemony that is inimical to cultural diversity.

If diversity is not to be experienced as a restriction of identity or unbridgeable difference, and if it is to favour dynamic interactions between ethnic, cultural and religious communities, it is essential to promote intercultural dialogue within each society, as well as at the international level, as the only enduring response to identity-based and racial tensions. The cultural challenge that faces each multicultural society is to reconcile the recognition and protection of, and respect for, cultural particularities with the affirmation and promotion of universally shared values emerging from the interplay of these cultural specificities. Indeed, as illustrated by opinion surveys such as the World Values Survey (see Table 6 in the Statistical Annex), when individuals are asked to which geographical groups they feel they belong, in many countries in the world they declare multiple identities (see Figure 2.1). But the tension between different identities can become the driving force for a renewal of national unity based on an understanding of social cohesion which integrates the diversity of its cultural components.

The tension between different identities can become the driving force for a renewal of national unity based on an understanding of social cohesion which integrates the diversity of its cultural components

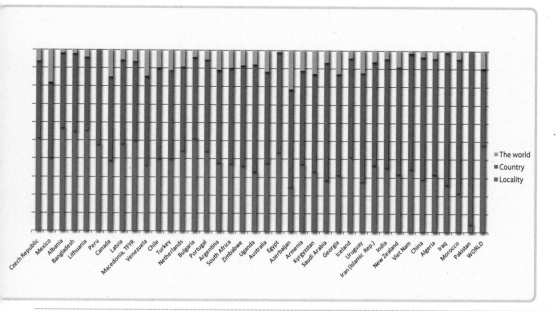

1. Genetic ancestry involves the analysis of an individual's DNA in order to determine its historical pattern based on comparison with participants from around the world and thereby to ascertain the individual's genetic roots. See the Genographic Project's website.

○ *'Korean Fantasy', two Korean intangible heritage expressions at UNESCO Headquarters*

Box 2.2   **'What went wrong with the dialogue between cultures?'**

The last two decades, with their increasing numbers of events for a Dialogue between Cultures and Civilizations, are lost decades. Most efforts were invested in a much too limited concept of dialogue, which remained within the logic of Huntington's 'clash' scenario even while contradicting his conclusions. This scenario was never a cause of problems; it is just one example of an almost omnipresent limited understanding of culture as heritage alone rather than also as a space for human creativity and liberty. To be sure, cultural forces shape attitudes and behaviour; but this is only one side of the coin. Such a passive view of culture has its roots in 19th century traditions of nation-building. The related concept of 'national cultures' reduces the creative dimension of culture to a collective instrument for national cohesion and identity. This definition is at the expense of the right to cultural self-determination, which is among the core values enshrined in all international human rights conventions and agreements.

To contain and resolve the present crisis in cultural relations, a number of key arguments need to be communicated among actors already involved or interested in organizing the dialogue between cultures. The following six arguments are considered particularly important:

1. Traditional modalities of dialogue between cultures, developed over the past decade, have largely failed because of their almost exclusive focus on what cultures and religions have in common. The present crisis calls for dialogue on differences and diversity.

2. The lack of mutual knowledge about sensitive issues linked to religions and any other belief is obvious. This gap needs to be filled as a matter of urgency. Information on religious pluralism needs to be provided at all levels of formal and non-formal education, in a terminology that is not faith-loaded but accessible to people maintaining diversified beliefs and opinions. This information must include difficult concepts, such as what is 'sacred', 'holy' or 'insulting'.

3. Too often, dialogue events have stressed collective identities (national, ethnic, religious) rather than identities of individuals or social groups. Dialogue fora composed of 'representatives' of religious or ethnic groups are counter-productive and contribute to the clash of civilizations scenario rather than preventing it. Dialogue between cultures must create space for mutual perception and appreciation of overlapping, multiple and dynamic cultural identities of every individual and social or cultural group.

4. There is urgent need for strengthening the human-rights-based dimension of dialogue. Rather than seeking values common to all religions and cultures, the core values of the *Universal Declaration of Human Rights* need to be stressed. No discrimination based on origin, race, colour, gender, language, religion or any other belief or opinion has been agreed upon by the international community 60 years ago. In line with recent UN terminology, all cultures must be considered having equal dignity.

5. Active tolerance, involving mutual respect, needs to be promoted rather than mere acceptance of diversity.

Calls for boycotting a whole people are an alarm signal. They are an indicator of tendencies towards deepening stereotypes, of desires to balance perceived discrimination with discrimination against others, and of perceived double standards regarding their application to others.

What we need now is to develop a common language for understanding and respecting cultural differences, without doing harm to our universal values. Many elements of such common language have been developed over the past decade. The following five elements of such a common language are of particular importance:

1. Cultural diversity between as well as within countries is as essential for humankind as biodiversity is for nature.

2. The right to be different is a core element of a rights-based understanding of culture.

3. Overlap between cognitive and emotional elements of intercultural relations is the rule and not the exception.

4. Deconstructing self-referential systems of belief and knowledge is essential.

5. Freedom of opinion or any other belief is not only a basic human right; it is also intrinsic to any human understanding of religion. Enforcing belief would be a contradiction in and of itself, as much as imposing values 'comes down in the end to negating them' (Jacques Delors).

Much more needs to be done to enable citizens of the increasingly multicultural world of the 21st century to know about, understand and respect their differences in cultural and religious expression.
Source: Schoefthaler, 2006.

2.3 The challenges of dialogue in a multicultural world

Just as it can provoke a retreat into separate identities, cultural diversity can also be experienced as an invitation to discover the other. It is somewhat misleading to speak of *cultures* in this context, however, for, in reality, it is not so much cultures as *people* — individuals and groups, with their complexities and multiple allegiances — who are engaged in the process of dialogue. To be effective, intercultural dialogue must free itself of the concept of exclusive and fixed identities and embrace a worldview predicated on pluralism and multiple affiliations. It is not enough simply to acknowledge our differences: genuine dialogue presupposes a reciprocal effort to identify and inhabit a common ground on which encounter can take place.

In practice this calls for capacities of negotiation and compromise, allied to a commitment to mutual understanding and deployed in a wide range of cultural contexts, including the fields and sectors discussed in Part II of this report. A further requirement for meaningful dialogue is a level playing field and the strict equality of status for all participants in intercultural initiatives. In this respect, particular attention must be paid to the needs and expectations of vulnerable and marginalized groups, including indigenous peoples, the very poor and women (see Box 2.2). It is essential that provisions be made for the empowerment of all participants in intercultural dialogue through capacity-building and inclusive projects that permit interaction without loss of personal or collective identity. Building intercultural competencies, promoting interfaith dialogue, and reconciling conflicting memories may be seen as the three major challenges of dialogue in a multicultural world.

Intercultural competencies

Intercultural dialogue is dependent to an important extent on intercultural competencies. Defined as the 'complex of abilities needed to perform effectively and appropriately when interacting with those who are linguistically and culturally different from oneself' (Fantini, 2007), these abilities are essentially communicative in nature, but they also involve reconfiguring our perspectives and understandings of the world (see Box 2.3). They are the means whereby a shift can occur away from a 'clash' and towards an 'alliance' of civilizations.

Various strategies exist for acquiring intercultural competencies and facilitating cultural encounters in the promotion of intercultural dialogue (Bennett, 2009). Many of these have been formalized by intercultural management and communication teams on the basis of the lived experiences of migrant workers and their families, who have had to adjust to the realities of living in and/or between two cultures (UNESCO, 1982; Hoffman, 1989). The ultimate goal would be that intercultural competencies become an indispensable element of school curricula within a larger framework of cultural literacy training (see chapter 4).

| Box 2.3 | **Intercultural competencies: The basics** |

In an intercultural encounter, basic capacities include the ability to listen, dialogue and wonder:

- *Listening* is understood here in the sense of 'resonating with an experience', similar to the 'participant observation' required of an anthropologist in a field study (Sperber, 1985). Robert Vachon (1998) has put it as follows:

Interculturalism [. . .] is to experience another culture, to accept the truth of the other culture. It is therefore allowing the other culture and its truth to affect me directly, to penetrate me, to change me, to transform me, not only in my answers to a question, but in my very questions, my presuppositions, my myths. It is therefore a meeting in myself of two convictions. The place of that meeting is the heart (not the head) of a person, within a personal synthesis which can be intellectually more or less perfect. There is no co-existence possible without a co-insistence, i.e. without their penetrating into each other's heart. It is therefore a matter of approaching the other from inside. It is contemplative listening to the other where one begins to see the possibilities not only of solutions, but of radically different fundamental questions.

- *Dialogue* is born from the resonance with others and within ourselves, in the process of which we realize our own untapped dimensions, potentials other than those we have developed (making us feel either comfortable or uncomfortable), and we begin a process of 'understanding from within'. As Raimon Panikkar (1979) has said: 'I shall never be able to meet the other as he meets and understands himself if I do not meet and understand him in and as

Box 2.3	Intercultural competencies: The basics

myself. To understand the other as "other" is, at the least, not to understand him.'

■ *Wonder* is the capacity to be touched by difference, a state of mind that has to be continuously trained, especially in the information society where, paradoxically, we believe we already know everything (because we know it exists or we saw it on TV or in newspapers).

Wonder is a form of 'active openness', in which the other is not simply positioned on a scale of differences/resemblances with us. Too often, we fail to recognize the originality of others and simply reduce them to an inverted image of ourselves and fall into the trap of essentialism. When we start to think that we have developed intercultural competences, it is very likely that we have in fact started to close ourselves off from what is actually going on and that we are 'losing' it. Interculturality is an ongoing discovery, a perpetual wondering, the recognition that the other is not a void to be filled but a plenitude to be discovered.

The intercultural encounter thus reveals our own rootedness at the same time as it unveils that of our counterpart. There cannot be *intercultural* competency without a *cultural* competency that allows us to realize where we speak from, our bias, what makes our point of view different from the other's point of view. It is then through critical distance from oneself that one may open oneself to encounter the other. The intercultural encounter is very much about overcoming one's own resistances, becoming aware of one's ethnocentrism or even racism, and starting to discover the possibility of radically different existential choices. It is only after the first cultural shock is over, and one starts to gain some understanding of another culture, that a more complex picture of the other and of oneself arises.

Source: Eberhard, 2008.

It is not so much knowledge of others that conditions the success of intercultural dialogue; rather, it is cognitive flexibility, empathy, anxiety reduction and the capacity to shift between different frames of reference. Humility and hospitality are also crucial

The most obvious way to reduce intergroup conflict and prejudice is to increase contacts between members of different groups in such a way as to break down boundaries and build bridges between self-enclosed communities, thereby fostering more complex and personalized views of others' worlds through knowledge. Such strategies are successful when they meet certain conditions — an equivalent social status, a positive context, an equal knowledge-base and reasonable objectives — while not seeking to solve all social-isolation issues at once (Allport, 1954). While more ambitious goals for reducing social gaps should not be abandoned, the strategy should begin by overcoming cultural boundaries by focusing on the concrete goals at hand. Since the aim is to foster authentic encounter between human beings who, beyond their differences, share common expectations, the contact should involve a more intimate dimension and not be seen as merely functional or circumstantial. For it is not so much knowledge of others that conditions the success of intercultural dialogue; rather, it is cognitive flexibility, empathy, anxiety reduction and the capacity to shift between different frames of reference (Pettigrew, 1998). Humility and hospitality are also crucial: 'humility because it is impossible to understand another culture totally; and hospitality because one needs to treat other cultures like many traditional societies treat strangers, i.e. with open arms, open minds and open hearts' (Fasheh, 2007).

Numerous initiatives aimed at fostering dialogue and empathy between young people from different cultures are being initiated, from school projects and educational programmes (such as the Children International Summer Village and AMIDEAST programmes) to exchange programmes that bring together participants from diverse cultural backgrounds for semester-long study trips (such as the EU's Erasmus and the Scholar Ship programmes). Projects and initiatives involving participatory cultural, artistic and sports activities are a particularly powerful means for providing intercultural dialogue incentives, particularly to underprivileged children in conflict-ridden countries. Indeed, the arts and creativity testify to the depths and plasticity of intercultural relations and the forms of mutual enrichment they embody. By the same token, they help to combat closed identities and promote cultural pluralism. Notable examples can be gleaned from the experiences of the DREAM programme; established in 2003, it has implemented projects in Afghanistan (Kabul), Cambodia (Phnom Penh), East Jerusalem (Pétion-ville) and Liberia (Monrovia) to help street children express themselves freely in a safe and culturally aware environment. Art, painting, drawing, dancing, music, theatre, photography, crafts and sports are seen as the means for addressing the basic needs and rights of children, building creativity and self-esteem, helping them to work on personal issues and traumas (UNESCO-Felissimo, 2008).

In the 'global cities' existing in many parts of the world, which serve as hubs or networks for multiculturalism, cultural festivals have emerged that enable the intermingling of different cultures and transcend the barriers between them — whether linguistic, religious or otherwise — in order to share moments of urban communion and entertainment. In this way, public spaces become spheres of pluralism, conviviality and interaction. As noted by United Cities and Local Governments (Pigem, 2006), carnivals that had been ignored if not scorned between 1960 and 1980 have today been recognized as genuine cultural activities in which heritage and contemporary creation can meet and evolve.

Through the founding and fostering of intercultural relationships, a gradual shift has occurred among long-established ethnic and cultural festivals; they have become less mono-ethnic and more pluralistic celebrations. The Vancouver Chinese New Year's Festival is a good illustration of this phenomenon: while it initially celebrated specifically Chinese culture, it now also showcases Brazilian, Afro-Canadian, Japanese, and Aboriginal cultures. While the 'ownership' of spaces or venues by specific cultural communities

remains an extremely contentious issue, some cities have provided spaces in which ethnic communities can interact, such as Clissold Park (Northeast London) and Cannon Hill Park (Birmingham) in the UK. On the other hand, some cities have found it necessary to create physical spaces for members of specific cultural communities, such as in Helsinki, where a new space, a 'cultural living room', called 'The Veranda' was built for cultural events in Swedish. Whatever the specific circumstances, effective intercultural dialogue entails promoting dialogue between individuals in all the complexities of their multiple identities and ensuring the necessary conditions of equality among them. Since the latter involves recognition, by all parties, of the dignity and value of all cultures involved, we need to reflect on the specific circumstances confronting vulnerable and marginalized groups.

In all these ways, the promotion of intercultural dialogue converges significantly with the 'multiple identities' approach. This refers not only to the possibility of coexisting allegiances but also to the potential of these allegiances to evolve without loss of our sense of rootedness. Dialogue is openness, but it is not self-loss. As Raimon Panikkar (1979) has said:

> *Dialogue is fundamentally opening myself to another so that he might speak and reveal my myth that I cannot know myself because it is transparent to me, self-evident. Dialogue is a way of knowing myself and of disentangling my own point of view from other viewpoints and from me, because it is grounded so deeply in my own roots as to be utterly hidden from me [. . .]. Dialogue sees the other not as an extrinsic, accidental aid, but as the indispensable, personal element in our search for truth, because I am not a self-evident, autonomous individual [. . .]. Dialogue seeks truth by trusting the other, just as dialectics pursues truth by trusting the order of things, the value of reason and weighty arguments.*

When we cease to perceive others in fixed and unilateral terms, the potential for authentic dialogue increases significantly: we open up the possibility of moving from mere compromise between fixed positions towards mutual enrichment upon newly discovered common ground.

When we cease to perceive others in fixed and unilateral terms, the potential for authentic dialogue increases significantly: we open up the possibility of moving from mere compromise between fixed positions towards mutual enrichment upon newly discovered common ground

↻ *Processional Giants in Belgium*

The teaching of different religions, belief systems and spiritual traditions is essential to breaking down the walls of ignorance, which are often buttressed by pseudo-knowledge that encloses the different communities within hermetic universes

◉ *Woman in prayer, Lao People's Democratic Republic*

◉ *The Ifa divination system, practiced among Yoruba communities (and by the African diaspora in the Americas and the Caribbean), Nigeria*

Interfaith dialogue

Interfaith dialogue — understood to encompass spiritual and animistic traditions, as well as religions — is a crucial dimension of international understanding, and thus of conflict resolution; it is indissociable from a critical debate on the rights of all stakeholders to freedom of conviction and conscience (see chapter 8 on religious mediation for social cohesion). Religious and spiritual convictions invariably inform cultural affiliations, even if they rarely define a culture in its totality. Thus, religion is now on the agenda of the international community, which has realized that misunderstanding and ignorance of religion only heighten tensions and revive communitarianism. The lack of instruction in schools about the historical and sociological aspects of religion or the predominance of religious instruction in only one faith may also lead to a lack of understanding among individuals and groups belonging to different faiths or having non-religious convictions. Such a lack of understanding may also give rise to a lack of sensitivity with regard to religious expressions and events and religious symbols and signs, which may then be misused (UNESCO, 2007b).

Some view interfaith dialogue as inherently problematic. This is however to overlook the myriad interactions between religions and other philosophical and cultural traditions that have taken place over four millennia. For example, Israeli archaeologists date the Bible from the 7th century BCE and link it to specific historical events. Mithraism shows intriguing similarities with Christianity, and Parmenides' thought may have been nurtured by contacts with Tibetan monks (Hulin, 2001). Such interactions are often concealed from a sectarian standpoint, as if a religion were somehow diminished by being set in an historical context, shown to reflect the state of knowledge at a particular time or shown to have benefited from exchanges with other belief systems. In fact, openness to dialogue is a mark of the resilience of a belief, showing that it does not shrink from confronting opposing viewpoints and even from questioning its own basic tenets. This is why interfaith dialogue should not be restricted to institutional exchanges between authoritative or representative figures. Insofar as interfaith dialogue is understood as dialogue between representative authorities of the major religions, difficulties will arise for not all major religions necessarily have representative authorities and it is not religions themselves that engage in dialogue but the people

who belong to the various religions who interact and eventually engage in dialogue (UNESCOCat, 2008).

Informal networks, at the local or community level, can play a valuable role in reconciling different viewpoints, particularly when they involve people who have previously been excluded in some cases from interfaith dialogue, including women and young people. The teaching of different religions, belief systems and spiritual traditions is essential to breaking down the walls of ignorance, which are often buttressed by pseudo-knowledge that encloses the different communities within hermetic universes. While the teaching of the history of religions will inevitably take place in a particular cultural context, the approach adopted should be inclusive and ideally not confined to the monotheistic traditions. In this sense, there is a need to foster competences and skills in interfaith dialogue in the wider context of furthering intercultural understanding. In this spirit, UNESCO places emphasis on capacity-building, which involves developing pedagogical materials related to inter-religious dialogue in partnership with the regional UNESCO Chairs, the Oslo Coalition and the Central Asian Women's Cultural Network (training of trainers, diffusion of the proceedings of the various conferences organized on that issue, preparation and publication of teaching materials, etc.). Strengthening of the knowledge-base for the promotion of interfaith dialogue is also important. For example, an adult-education course has been developed at the University of Geneva; while initially intended for journalists, it has been open for the past three years to individuals who are in contact with other cultures and confessions. In the same vein, a manual for young people on the cultural and ritual aspects of Christianity and Islam which offers an objective and detailed description of each religion and explains their symbology and meaning has been developed in Lebanon.

Reconciling conflicting memories

Divergent memories have been the source of many conflicts throughout history. The different forms of institutional memory preservation and transmission (state archives, museums, media, school textbooks) tend to embody alternative views of the past, each with its own logic, protocols and perspectives. States often hold an historical monopoly on such records and testimonies, which often tend to be reductive of other cultures. Traditional cultures in particular have been subject to such appropriation of their history. The path to reconciliation — which may involve acts of repentance and even compensation — lies in a process of active dialogue, which requires that the interlocutors contemplate other points of view in order to assess the plausibility of competing claims. Some international initiatives, such as UNESCO's Slave Route project, are committed to facilitating such forms of reconciliation. In some cases, States themselves have initiated these procedures through recognition of the suffering of a particular population group, as did Australia and Canada with respect to their indigenous communities. A key element of intercultural dialogue is the building of a common, shared memory base, recognized and accepted by all parties involved. Engaging in such dialogue may require participants to admit faults, openly debate about competing memories and make compromises in the interests of reconciliation and social harmony.

At a time when memory conflicts in numerous multicultural environments undermine social cohesion, there is an urgent need to place divergent histories in perspective. A number of attempts have been made to transcend competing memories by framing a common historical narrative in situations where the conflict has been resolved but also where the conflict has just ended or is ongoing (see Box 2.4).

| **Box 2.4** | **Reconciliation through common narrative: Revised history textbook initiatives** |

When the passage of time has blurred the memory of war, it becomes possible to envisage the drafting of a shared history. In this way, some States have launched bi- or multilateral initiatives aimed at integrating the viewpoint of their erstwhile enemies into school textbooks and reducing prejudices caused by mutual ignorance.

A novel experiment took place in East Asia between China, the Republic of Korea and Japan in 2002, when the three countries established the 'Forum for Historical Knowledge and Peace in Central Asia' bringing together a number of public or para-public research institutions, historians and secondary-school teachers from the three countries in order to draft a joint history textbook. The chapters were divided up among three authors, one from each of the three countries; each author was free to express national viewpoints and disagreements before the introduction of modifications necessary for the establishment of a joint text. Three international meetings were convened in the process: one in Nanjing in 2002, one in Tokyo in 2003 and one in Seoul in 2004. In the interest of East Asian integration, national histories and the major phases of international history (such as the 'Korean War' or the role of the US or the USSR) were generally excluded from the undertaking. Conceived as a school textbook, the volume devotes space to the problem of memory, citing the testimony of many victims and instancing a number of memorial places (museums, monuments, commemorations). Published in 2005, the textbook has met with great popular success: the initial print run of 20,000 copies sold out in two days; and a year after publication, 110,000 revised manuals had been sold in China, 50,000 in the Republic of Korea and 70,000 in Japan.

A similar initiative was launched in Europe in 2003 between France and Germany, on the occasion of the 40th anniversary of the French-German Elysée Treaty, and was strongly promoted by the educational institutions in both countries. In September 2006, French and German schools were given the opportunity to use a common manual, jointly published in the two languages and drafted, over a period of about ten months, by a Franco-German team of about ten history professors. Each chapter is made up of intersecting French and German perspectives, on which consensus was reached through multiple discussions and critical terminology analyses. Following the success of the 2006 textbook, which sold more than 75,000 copies on both sides of the Rhine, a second volume was released in 2008.

Even where conflict is still ongoing, progress towards dual-history textbooks is being made in different parts of the world, as illustrated by the work of the Peace Research Institute in the Middle East (PRIME), established in 1998 following the Oslo Accords. Since 2002, a group involving Israeli and Palestinian history teachers, under the supervision of two historians from the Universities of Jerusalem and Bethlehem, has produced three booklets for use in Palestinian and Israeli high schools that present the two groups' contradictory visions of history. Each page is divided into three parts: one section each for the Palestinian and the Israeli narratives and a blank third section, which is for the pupil, Israeli or Palestinian, to fill in. As explained by Sami Adwan, co-founder with Dan Bar-On of PRIME, while 'the dates may be the same, the interpretation of each side is very different' (Chen, 2007). Entitled *Learning Each Other's Historical Narratives*, the booklet has been translated into English, French, Spanish, German, Italian, Catalan and Basque, and has sold over 23,000 copies in France alone.

This model has also been followed in other conflict-ridden societies, notably by the Centre for Human Rights and Conflict Resolution at Skopje University in Macedonia, which has published parallel Macedonian-Albanian narratives. Such initiatives are crucial first steps in the process of reconciliation.

Source: Giacone, 2007.

Showcasing 'places of memory', as physical sites for dialogue between communities with opposing memories, can also contribute to post-conflict reconciliation

We need to think carefully about ways in which intercultural dialogue can be integrated into conflict prevention strategies or employed in post-conflict situations. Without proper attention, painful memories — of a 'past that is still present' — can lead to the resumption or exacerbation of conflict. As pointed out by Paul Ricoeur (2003), the obscuring of a crime or a conflict (*amnesia*) ultimately leads to a return of memory (*anamnesis*), and care must be taken to ensure this does not result in the crystallization of memory conflicts (*hypermnesis*). Conflicting memories of the same event by people who have experienced a dispute from opposing sides can sometimes be reconciled through the presence of a *mediator*, even in cases where the differing positions seems unbridgeable. This issue assumes particular importance in cases where memory fractures occur within the same country.

In the 1990s, South Africa invented a new model for dealing with the traumas caused by apartheid, the Truth and Reconciliation Commissions. They were designed to re-establish the new South African State on the basis of a shared memory while allowing repressed memories to resurface. Reconciliation thus became a collective enterprise in which no community or group was able to represent itself as totally innocent. This model, although it did not entail any reparation by former perpetrators of torture, has been followed in other States emerging from civil war, including some countries in Central America. In the wake of the civil wars and ethnic massacres in Rwanda, national reconciliation processes (as distinct from international initiatives for judging those responsible for the genocide) have included the removal of references to the Hutu and Tutsi ethnic groups on identity cards, the celebration of a national commemoration day (7 April) and the introduction in 2002 of *gacacas*, or ancestral courts, aimed at promoting reconciliation and justice by trying the accused in the presence of family and neighbours (Anheier and Isar, 2007).

Showcasing 'places of memory', as physical sites for dialogue between communities with opposing memories, can also contribute to post-conflict reconciliation. The Robben Island Prison in South Africa, where most of the leaders of the African National Congress, including Nelson Mandela, were held and which was named a UNESCO World Heritage Site in 1999, demonstrates the educational potential of

➲ *A man from the 'cultural space of the Sosso Bala', Guinea*

such sites. Too often, because it is regarded as enemy heritage, a site or monument can become threatened by destruction, as happened with the Mostar Bridge in Bosnia and the Buddhas of Bamyan in Afghanistan. In this context, the concept of the 'common natural and cultural heritage' embodied in the 1972 World Heritage Convention (UNESCO, 1972) retains all its relevance. It demonstrates that what distinguishes us can also become what unites us, and that a community of experience in contemplation of the achievements of very different cultures and civilizations can strengthen the sense of our common humanity.

2.4 Empowerment

Ensuring a level playing field for cultural encounters and guaranteeing equality of status and dignity between all participants in initiatives to promote intercultural dialogue involve recognizing the ethnocentric ways in which certain cultures have hitherto proceeded. Central to the many problems arising in this context is the Western ideology of knowledge transparency, which cannot do justice to systems of thought recognizing both 'exoteric' and 'esoteric' knowledge and embodying initiatory processes for crossing the boundaries between them. This recently became an issue, for example, in the field of museography in connection with the public exhibition of ritual objects from Vanuatu at the Musée du Quai Branly in Paris. Before the exhibition opening, it was found necessary to construct separate viewing areas for male and female visitors in order to safeguard the 'power' of certain sacred objects, as traditionally required in their place of origin (Huffman, 2007). This highlighted the particular sensitivities associated with cultural resources and the need for dialogue to take account of the value systems embedded in the practices surrounding them.

Cultural or community mapping (which began with Inuit indigenous populations in the 1970s) can significantly contribute to this dual objective of making the intangible heritage and local/indigenous knowledge of different communities visible, and ensuring that it is appropriate and relevant by allowing knowledge bearers to express themselves in confidence, without fear of being dispossessed of the knowledge in question. Typically used when communities need to negotiate about territories and rights (such as access to, control over and use of natural resources), cultural mapping allows

The 1972 World Heritage Convention demonstrates that what distinguishes us can also become what unites us, and that a community of experience in contemplation of the achievements of very different cultures and civilizations can strengthen the sense of our common humanity

non-dominant or marginalized cultural groups to be fully represented in a context of intercultural dialogue and mutual respect. Various forms of cultural mapping and methodologies have evolved around the world (more so in Latin America and South and Southeast Asia than in Africa) which serve to express the myriad levels of relationship between the natural, mental and spiritual worlds: a wide array of techniques and activities ranging from community-based participatory approaches in identifying and documenting local cultural resources and activities, to the use of innovative and sophisticated information tools like Geographic Information Systems (GIS) and 3D-modelling (see Box 2.5). The resulting 'map' can be of an anthropological, sociological, archaeological, genealogical, linguistic, topographical, musicological and/or botanical nature and often represents a matrix combining a number of these elements simultaneously.[2]

As an exercise in dialogue across generations or among subgroups within a community, participatory mapping exercises also provide an opportunity to reinforce communicative participation and collaborative processes in spatial problem analysis and decision-making to produce stand-alone scale relief models, which have

---

| Box 2.5 | Through the eyes of hunters-gatherers: Participatory 3D modelling among the Ogiek indigenous peoples in Kenya |

As part of a 2006–2008 project aimed at 'Strengthening the East African Regional Mapping and Information Systems Network' (ERMIS-Africa), a participatory three-dimensional modelling (P3DM) exercise took place in the village of Nessuit (Nakuru District, Kenya) in August 2006, following a ten-month preparation period involving the Ogiek, traditionally one of the larger hunter-gatherer communities in Eastern Africa. Using a fully participatory method and drawing on P3DM experiences in other regions of the world, particularly Southeast Asia and the Pacific, this was the first exercise of its kind in Africa.

During the 11 days of the mapping exercise, members of the local communities (including schoolchildren, teachers and about 120 Ogiek elders, men and women delegated by the 21 clans), facilitators, and national and international trainees discussed facilitation techniques and P3DM practices, constructed a scaled and geo-referenced 3D model, composed the map legend and extracted these data via digital photography. On-screen digitizing, ground-truthing and thematic map generation took place in the following months. The exercise led to the construction of a solid three-dimensional, 1:10,000-scale model of the Eastern Mau Forest Complex which covered a total land area of 576 km^2 and depicted the local bio-physical and cultural environments as they had been in the 1920s, with a highly dense forest cover, a permanent river network flowing from the upper water catchments and a dense population of beehives, among other characteristics. It was decided to visualize the 1920s landscape because it was during that period that Nessuit became a site of both colonial missionary activity and industrial forestry, compounded thereafter by overtly or tacitly accepted logging practices on the Mau Forest Complex, which have led to serious ecological disasters, forest and related biodiversity depletion, and consequently the destruction of the Ogiek natural and cultural landscapes.

While community mapping exercises have many interesting components, it has been argued that the collaborative development of the map legend is the key process on which the quality of such an exercise and its outputs depend, allowing local spatial knowledge to be expressed in an objective manner but in contrast to the dominant intellectual framework of 'official' maps. The making of the legend involved intense discussions among elders, reaching agreements among clans on the naming and description of 'the way the Ogiek traditionally discern the territory and its eco-cultural-systems', in order to define and code culturally acceptable land units. This process benefited from skilled facilitation, beginning with individual consultations and followed by focused group discussions, including storytelling, in order to redress the shortcomings resulting from differing categorizations of land units. A matrix was used to provide elders from different clans with the opportunity to achieve consensus, or at least common understanding, about the terminology and categorization of areas. New legend items were added, updated and reworded, and new paints and pin codes were invented to capture the full diversity of the Ogiek worldview.

The final model features hundreds of labels, which locate place names, names of watercourses and water bodies, and clan classifications. The 3D mapmaking exercise proved to be an excellent way to enable people of all ages to engage with their landscape and heritage in an inspiring and motivating collegial environment, as well as to become a catalyst in stimulating memory and creating visible and tangible representations of natural landscapes for the transmission of crucial knowledge, wisdom and values.

Source: Rambaldi et al., 2007.

---

2. UNESCO has supported many participatory mapping initiatives, including: the South African San Institute's project with the Khomani San community; PROCED's project with the Pygmies of Gabon; the Research Institute for Mindanao Culture's project with Philippine indigenous cultures (the Mamanua, the Higaunon, the Manobo, the Eastern Manobo, the Banwaon and the Subanen); the Buffalo Trust's project with the Kiowa people of Oklahoma; and the project with Bolivia's Iruitu community.

proven to be particularly user-friendly. This both facilitates a community's reflection on its specific cultural traditions, resources and institutions, as well as their forms of intergenerational transmission, and helps to better equip the community to defend its rights and interests, thereby revitalizing its identities and cultural resources.

A specific task of intercultural dialogue is to be sensitive to the fact that all communities do not experience and respond to phenomena such as globalization in the same way. Indigenous peoples, for example, are likely to see it as an exacerbation of certain trends — such as the encroachment of extractive industries on their territories — that are eroding their traditional ways of life and livelihoods. At the same time, globalization and global networks favour the emergence of indigenous movements at the international level, enabling the collective memory of domination and struggle to serve as an 'ideological weapon' in support of claims regarding ancestral land and resources and self-determined development (see chapter 1). Thus, indigenous activists have become strongly engaged with the United Nations Conference on Environment and Development and the *Convention on Biological Diversity* and the United Nations *Framework Convention on Climate Change*, and have helped to secured the adoption, on 13 September 2007, of the *United Nations Declaration on the Rights of Indigenous Peoples*, which now serves as a primary reference in the formulation of policies and national laws concerning the rights of indigenous peoples (an example being the Philippines' 1997

Indigenous Peoples' Rights Act). It is likewise being used as a framework for the UNDP's principles of engagement with indigenous peoples (UNDP, 2001), the World Bank's *Operational Policy on Indigenous Peoples* (2006) and the Asian Development Bank's *Policy on Indigenous Peoples* (1998). Furthermore, since the adoption of the *United Nations Declaration on the Rights of Indigenous Peoples*, it has been cited in a judgement by the Supreme Court of Belize, in a case filed by the Maya against the Government of Belize, and has served in Bolivia as the basis for its *National Law 3760 on the Rights of Indigenous Peoples*, as

◊ *Mbende Jerusarema Dance, a popular dance style practiced by the Zezuru Shona people living in eastern Zimbabwe*

◊ *Kutiyattam, a form of sacred theatre from Kerala, India*

◊ *Traditional ceremonies of the Kallawaya, Bolivia*

◊ *A performer of Kun Qu Opera*

The key to successful intercultural dialogue lies in the acknowledgement of the equal dignity of the participants... based on the premise that all cultures are in continual evolution and are the result of multiple influences throughout history

announced by President Evo Morales on 7 November 2007 (Tauli-Corpuz, 2007).

In many social contexts, women can also be counted among the 'new voices' that have a distinctive role to play in the promotion of cultural diversity. Women are identifiable agents for cultural change since they are often the ones engaged in processes involving the validation and reinterpretation of cultural meaning and practices. The role of women as 'value carriers' in the transmission of language, ethical codes, value systems, religious beliefs and behavioural patterns to their children is increasingly augmented by their role as 'value creators' (feminist theory having contributed to this development). Recognition of the multiple identities of groups and individuals enables women not only to contest mainstream or dominant views from within but also to belong to other groups and even voluntarily to exit their communities of origin. Cultural diversity is to this extent bound up with recognition of women as autonomous agents in the construction of their identities.

A major obstacle still to be overcome is the pervasive gender discrimination and stereotyping that subordinate women to male-dominated interpretations of cultural traditions and religion. Demands by women for access to the public sphere and to full enjoyment of civil and political rights are increasingly widespread and insistent. Other demands concern gender equality in the private sphere, where women have often been subject to legal discrimination, since family law has assumed either implicitly or explicitly that the traditional male-headed family is the natural household unit. Gender inequality is multidimensional and manifests itself in all areas of social life (the household, the labour market, property ownership, etc.) and interacts with other forms of inequality (racial, social, economic, age-based, etc.). Issues relating to the promotion of women's role in opening up new avenues of intercultural dialogue have been highlighted in the *Dushanbe Declaration* on 'the Role of Women in Intercultural Dialogue in Central Asia' (UNESCO, 2003) and in the *Baku Declaration* on 'Expanding the Role of Women in Cross-cultural Dialogue' (UNESCO/ISESCO, 2008).

Tension can arise between the advocacy of gender equality and claims made in the name of cultural

diversity. While it is possible in general terms to argue for accommodating 'contexts of choice', there are cases in which 'there are clear disparities of power balance between the sexes, such that the more powerful [. . .] are those who are generally in a position to determine and articulate the group's beliefs, practices and interests. In such circumstances, group rights are potentially, and in many cases actually, anti-feminist' (Benhabib, 2002; Song, 2005). In such cases, to accept the 'group' claims would be to do injustice to the women concerned, who could well be contesting the values and ways of life of the group and, more specifically, the status, roles and rights accorded to them. In short, group rights adduced in the name of cultural diversity cannot claim precedence over fundamental human rights, as sometimes occurs in connection with the dramatic examples of female genital mutilation (FGM) or female infanticide.

The key to successful intercultural dialogue lies in the acknowledgement of the equal dignity of the participants. This presupposes recognition of — and respect for — the diverse forms of knowledge and their modes of expression, the customs and traditions of participants and efforts to establish, if not a culture-neutral context for dialogue, then at least a culturally neutralized context that enable communities to express themselves freely. Although intercultural dialogue cannot hope to settle on its own all the unresolved conflicts in the political, economic, social and historical spheres — as there are divergences in moral premises that individuals and groups are not prepared to discuss — no effort should be spared in the endeavour.

Conclusion

Any effort towards intercultural dialogue must be based upon the premise that all cultures are — and have always been — in continual evolution and are the result of multiple influences throughout history, both external and internal. From this perspective, the perceived fixed traits or identities that seem to isolate us from one another and plant the seeds of stereotype, discrimination or stigmatism should be seen not as barriers to dialogue but as the very ground upon which such dialogue can begin. New initiatives for intercultural dialogue have been launched in recent years, including the UN General Assembly's proclamation of 2010 as the International Year for the Rapprochement of Cultures and its proposed designation of 2011–2020 as the United Nations Decade of Interreligious Dialogue and Cooperation for Peace.

Intercultural capacities can be developed as tools to help level the ground of encounter between people from different cultures, on the basis of a strict equality of rights and an awareness that it is not so much cultures but *people* — individuals and groups, with their complexities and multiple allegiances — who are engaged in the process of dialogue. What conditions the success of intercultural dialogue is not so much knowledge of others but rather the basic abilities to listen, dialogue and wonder. These prompt cognitive flexibility, empathy and the capacity to shift between different frames of reference, humility and hospitality. Informal networks, at the local or community level, and the arts and creativity generally speaking, must not be underestimated as valuable means by which to combat closed identities and promote cultural pluralism. Hence the need for continued reflection on ways to establish genuine intercultural dialogue today, including the development of appropriate skills (based on respect for others, receptiveness, learning to listen), support for initiatives and networks of all kinds (including those convinced of and those sceptical about the value of dialogue) and the involvement of many new actors (women, young people) and so on.

↻ *Muslims praying in Jakarta, Indonesia*

Support should continue to be given to networks and initiatives for intercultural and interfaith dialogue at all levels, while ensuring the full involvement of new partners, especially women and young people.

To this end, action should be taken to:

a. Develop measures to enable members of communities and groups subject to discrimination and stigmatization to participate in the framing of projects designed to counter cultural stereotyping.

b. Support initiatives aimed at developing real and virtual spaces and provide facilities for cultural interaction, especially in countries where inter-community conflict exists.

c. Showcase 'places of memory' that serve to symbolize and promote reconciliation between communities within an overall process of cultural rapprochement.

The history of dialogue at UNESCO and institutional initiatives on intercultural dialogue

UNESCO and the United Nations have long been at the forefront of international efforts to strengthen dialogue among civilizations and cultures. Over the past decade, in opposition to the different currents of thought epitomized in the notion of a 'clash of civilizations', they have sought to propose alternative visions and frameworks for cultural encounters and exchanges.

From its inception, under its programme for easing tensions and conflicts throughout the world, UNESCO has been concerned with institutional initiatives for promoting 'dialogue' as a means to the peaceful resolution of disputes. The second session of its Executive Board in 1947 saw the adoption of an educational programme for international understanding, formalized by a resolution of the General Conference in 1949, which subsequently gave rise to a whole series of studies on tensions and national stereotypes as related to international understanding (e.g. research studies by Otto Klineberg, Margaret Mead and Jean Stoetzel). The inauguration in 1948 of the *UNESCO Collection of Representative Works* likewise reflected this concern to help revitalize international cultural exchanges and mutual understanding, as did the creation in 1949 of the *UNESCO*

Catalogue of Reproductions and in 1961 of the *UNESCO Collection of Traditional Music*. From 1948 to 1983, over 900 titles deriving from over 90 national literatures were translated and published by UNESCO, including the works of 11 Nobel Laureates or future Laureates in Literature.

UNESCO has also launched a number of projects aimed at providing new bases for studying interactions between cultures and civilizations, including the establishment in 1953 of the collection entitled *Cultural Unity and Diversity*, the first volume of which consisted of an opinion poll on the 'current conception of cultures, which are native to the different countries of the world and their relationships with one another' (Stenou, 2003). From 1957 to 1966, the *Major Project* on *Mutual Appreciation of Eastern and Western Cultural Values* contributed to a better knowledge of the civilizations of Southern Asia and the Far East, under the direction of Jacques Havet and the supervision of the Assistant Director-General for Culture, Jean Thomas. Over 250 works were published under the Programme for the Translation of Oriental Literatures, including the works of Yasunari Kawabata, which led to his being awarded the Nobel Prize for Literature in 1968.

➲ *Maranao women, expressing their history and beliefs through the Daragen epic, Philippines*

Other major projects followed, including studies on Islamic civilization and the major project on the Silk Roads, which was launched in 1988 under the title 'Integral Study of the Silk Roads: Roads of Dialogue' and which, by its completion in 1997, had benefited from the contributions of over 2,000 scholars from more than 30 countries and from five international scientific expeditions (the 'Desert Route' from Xi'an to Kashgar, the 'Maritime Routes' from Venice to Osaka, the 'Steppe Route' in Central Asia, the 'Nomad Route' in Mongolia and the 'Buddhist Route' in Nepal). The aim of the Silk Roads Project was to recreate the context for their renewal by rediscovering the extraordinary fertility of the cultural exchanges along the Silk Roads. The passing expeditions prompted the creation or establishment in several countries of research institutes or international institutes working in fields closely linked to the Silk Roads, with particular reference to nomadic and Buddhist cultures. The Silk Roads were followed by other routes, including the Slave Route (to end the silence that had long surrounded the question of the slave trade), the Iron Route, the Routes of Al-Andalus and the Chocolate Route.

UNESCO's series 'General and Regional Histories' and 'History of Humanity', the outcome of a project going back to 1952, were likewise aimed at mobilizing scholars worldwide around an ambitious agenda, concerning a critical challenge of our time. The History of Humanity series is concerned in particular with highlighting the common inheritance, the reciprocal influences and the contributions of the different peoples and cultures to the progress of Humanity. From 1968 onwards, the five other multi-volume regional histories (*General History of Africa, General History of Latin America, General History of the Caribbean, History of the Civilizations of Central Asia,* and *The Different Aspects of Islamic Culture*) have attempted to 'decolonize' the history of those regions by giving a voice to local historians while encouraging the exchange of viewpoints and intellectual discussion on a particular regional historical context. Over 1,600 historians and other specialists have participated in the drafting of these histories, which comprise some 50 volumes. The challenge now is to improve the spread of the historical knowledge thereby gained so as to reach the widest possible public and to strengthen mutual understanding among peoples. This should involve, in particular, the inclusion of these histories in educational curricula and the drafting of textbooks that adapt their content for school learners.

☜ *Girls at the nakamal dancing place after a ceremony, hills of Tanna, Vanuatu*

The term 'dialogue of civilizations' first appeared on the international scene in 1961 during a symposium organized by the European Centre of Culture. According to Denis de Rougemont, he coined the term in response to the first wave of globalization induced by Western 'technologies of production, transportation and information' and the 'coming into contact of all regions of the earth ineluctably, irreversibly and literally superficially' (cited in de Libera, 2003). The theme of dialogue — previously a largely intellectual exercise — took on a new political dimension as of the end of 1993, when Samuel Huntington published his thesis of the conflict of civilizations in the review *Foreign Affairs*.

⊙ *Women in burkas, Kandahar, Afghanistan*

Following the proposal of President Khatami of the Islamic Republic of Iran, the year 2001 was proclaimed the 'United Nations Year of Dialogue Among Civilizations', and in November of that year the General Assembly adopted the 'Global Agenda for Dialogue among Civilizations'. UNESCO was assigned the lead role within the United Nations system for the 'Dialogue among Civilizations', adopting for the purpose a multi-stakeholder approach with a special focus on youth and women and involving the mobilization of its existing networks, such as the UNESCO Associated Schools Network, UNESCO Chairs, UNESCO Institutes, Centres and Clubs.

Key dates and documents in framing the Organization's contribution to reflection on the dialogue among civilizations

over the current decade have included the *New Perspectives in UNESCO's Activities Pertaining to the Dialogue among Civilizations and Cultures* adopted by the General Conference in 2003, the *Rabat Commitment* adopted in June 2005 (which identified a series of concrete and practical actions in UNESCO programme-related areas) and the 2006 intersectoral *Plan of Action for the Promotion of the Dialogue among Peoples and UNESCO's Contribution to International Action against Terrorism*. International, regional and national conferences were also held in order to raise awareness among decision-makers and civil societies about the value and potential of intercultural dialogue, as well as to debunk myths arising from prejudice and contributing to the ignorance of other people's histories, languages, heritage and religions.

Along with other system agencies and programmes, UNESCO is also contributing to the United Nations Alliance of Civilizations (AoC) initiative, which was launched following the release in November 2006 of the latter's *Report of the High-Level Group*. The AoC focuses on the challenges of the 'relations between Western and Muslim societies'.

UNESCO's Interreligious Dialogue programme aims to highlight the dynamics of interaction between spiritual traditions and their specific cultures by emphasizing the borrowings that have taken place between them. This programme's landmark achievements include the:

■ *Tashkent* and *Bishkek Declarations* (of 1998 and 1999, respectively), which prepared the way for the development of consultative mechanisms and processes between religious communities and governments as a means of resolving disputes and drawing on religious capacities; and

■ Philippine Initiative, based on the outcome of the first Informal Summit of Leaders and Interfaith Leaders on Cooperation for Peace in 2005.

Discussions concerning the establishment of a Religious Advisory Council under the United Nations or UNESCO are ongoing. Other UNESCO initiatives in the field of interreligious dialogue include combating defamation of religions, investigating the role of religions as mediators for social cohesion and hosting interreligious meetings, such as the third World Congress of Imams and Rabbis for Peace in December 2008.

In November 2005, the United Nations General Assembly recognized that 'mutual understanding and interreligious dialogue constitute important dimensions of the dialogue among civilizations and of the culture of peace' and expressed its appreciation of UNESCO's work in this area and 'its focus on concrete action at the global, regional and subregional levels and its flagship project on the promotion of interfaith dialogue' (UN, 2005). Discussions are ongoing about the possible celebration of a United Nations Decade of Interreligious Dialogue and Cooperation for Peace in 2011–2020.

Other regional institutions pursuing initiatives for the strengthening of dialogue among civilizations include:

- The Council of Europe, whose White Paper on Intercultural Dialogue (2008), representing the outcome of a process launched in 2005 at the Summit of Heads of State and Government (*Faro Declaration*), is aimed at identifying 'how to promote intensified intercultural dialogue within and between societies in Europe and dialogue between Europe and its neighbours'. This initiative pursues a longstanding commitment on the part of the Council of Europe to support intercultural dialogue. Its key dates include: the First Summit of Heads of State and Government of Member States in 1993, which affirmed that 'the diversity of traditions and cultures has for centuries been one of Europe's riches and that the principle of tolerance is the guarantee of the maintenance in Europe of an open society' (*Vienna Declaration*); the *Framework Convention for the Protection of National Minorities* (1995); and the European Youth Campaign against racism, anti-Semitism, xenophobia and intolerance ('All Different — All Equal').

- ALECSO, ISESCO and other regional institutions and NGOs active in the field of international cooperation, such as the Anna Lindh Euro-Mediterranean Foundation for the Dialogue between Cultures, regularly participate in expert meetings on intercultural dialogue, in particular those organized by UNESCO.

↻ *Gelede ceremony, performed by the Yoruba-Nago community spread over Benin, Nigeria and Togo*

References and websites

Background documents and UNESCO sources

Benbessa, E. 2007. Diversité et culture nationale. Background paper.

Bennett, J. 2009. Cultivating intercultural competences. Training for UNESCO staff, Intercultural Communication Institute.

Diène, D. 2007. Nouvelles formes de racismes et de stigmatisation culturelle à notre époque : de l'intolérance à la propagation de stéréotype. Background paper.

—. (ed.). 2001. *From Chains to Bonds: The Slave Trade Revisited.* Paris, UNESCO/New York, Berghann Books.

Eberhard, C. 2008. Rediscovering education through intercultural dialogue. Background paper. http://www.dhdi.free.fr/recherches/horizonsinterculturels/articles/eberhardeducation.pdf

Elmandjra, M. 2007. Diversité culturelle: clé de la survie de l'humanité. Background paper.

Fasheh, M. 2007. Cultural diversity in formal and non-formal educational systems. Background paper.

Giacone, A. 2007. Note on 'Conflicts and Memory'. Background paper.

Maranda, P. 2007. Paramètres cognitifs de l'ouverture à la diversité culturelle: une perspective anthropologique. Background paper.

Pigem, J. 2006. Local policies for cultural diversity. Background paper.

Severi, C. 2008 Formes et contenus de la communication interculturelle: une approche anthropologique et cognitive. Background paper.

Shayegan, D. 2007. La diversité culturelle et la civilisation planétaire. Background paper.

Tauli-Corpuz, V. 2007. Indigenous people's voice in a globalized world. Background paper.

UNESCO. 2007a. *Mainstreaming Principles of Cultural Diversity and Intercultural Dialogue in Policies for Sustainable Development.* Final Communiqué of the Meeting of Experts, Paris, 21–23 May. Paris, UNESCO. http://acl.arts.usyd.edu.au/threecities/images/interieur%20(3final%20communique%20may%20meeting.pdf

—. 2007b. *Report to the Executive Board on the Place of Religion in the Programme on Interfaith and Interreligious Dialogue and Activities Designed to Promote Respect for Dialogue among Cultures.* 176 EX/19. 5 April. Paris, UNESCO. http://unesdoc.unesco.org/images/0015/001503/150328e.pdf

—. 2006a. *Cultural Diversity and Transversal Values: East-West Dialogue on Spiritual and Secular Dynamics.* Paris, UNESCO.

—. 2006b. *New Stakes for Intercultural Dialogue.* Acts of the international seminar, Paris, 6–7 June. Paris, UNESCO. http://unesdoc.unesco.org/images/0015/001583/158389e.pdf

—. 2006c. *Plan of Action for the Promotion of the Dialogue among Peoples and UNESCO's Contribution to International Action against Terrorism.* 174 EX/5 Add.2. http://unesdoc.unesco.org/images/0014/001441/144164e.pdf#page=11

—. 2005a. *Fostering Dialogue among Cultures and Civilizations through Concrete and Sustainable Initiatives.* Proceedings of the international conference, Rabat, Morocco, 14–16 June. http://unesdoc.unesco.org/images/0015/001541/154100E.pdf

—. 2005b. *The Rabat Commitment.* Conclusions and recommendations of the Rabat Conference on Dialogue among Cultures and Civilizations through Concrete and Sustained Initiatives, Rabat, Morocco, 14–16 June 2005. http://www.unesco.org/dialogue/rabat/Rabat_Commitment.pdf

—. 2004. *Cultural Diversity and Globalization: The Arab-Japanese Experience.* Proceedings of the international symposium, 'Cultural Diversity and Globalization: The Arab-Japanese Experience — A Cross-Regional Dialogue', Paris, 6–7 May. http://unesdoc.unesco.org/images/0013/001393/139318e.pdf

—. 2003a. *Dushanbe Declaration.* Adopted by the international conference 'The Role of Women in Intercultural Dialogue in Central Asia', Dushanbe, Tajikistan, 11–13 June. CLT/CPD/DIA/2008/RP/50. http://unesdoc.unesco.org/images/0015/001587/158762E.pdf

—. 2003b. *New Perspectives in UNESCO's Activities Pertaining to the Dialogue among Civilizations and Cultures.* 32 C/INF.15. Paris, UNESCO. http://unesdoc.unesco.org/images/0013/001320/132074e.pdf

—. 2003c. *The Political Aspects of the Dialogue of Civilizations.* Paris, UNESCO. http://unesdoc.unesco.org/images/0013/001316/131631eo.pdf

—. 2001. *Dialogue among Civilizations: The Round Table on the Eve of the United Nations Millennium Summit.* Paris, UNESCO.

—. 1999a. *Bishkek Declaration*. Adopted at the international forum 'Culture and Religion in Central Asia', Kyrgyz Republic, 13–18 September. http://portal.unesco.org/culture/es/files/25653/11089829755Bishkek_declaration.pdf/Bishkek+declaration.pdf

—. 1999b. *Towards a Constructive Pluralism*. Report. Paris, UNESCO. http://unesdoc.unesco.org/images/0012/001211/121144eo.pdf

—. 1998. *Tashkent Declaration*. Adopted by the Executive Board of UNESCO at its 155th Session, Tashkent, Uzbekistan, 6 November. http://www.unesco.org/cpp/uk/declarations/tashkent.pdf

—. 1997. *Integral Study of the Silk Roads: Roads of Dialogue*. Paris, UNESCO. http://unesdoc.unesco.org/images/0015/001592/159291eo.pdf

—. 1982. *Living in Two Cultures: The Socio-Cultural Situation of Migrant Workers and Their Families*. Aldershot, Gower/Paris, UNESCO.

—. 1972. *Convention Concerning the Protection of the World Cultural and Natural Heritage*. http://whc.unesco.org/archive/convention-en.pdf

UNESCO Centre of Catalonia (UNESCOCat). 2007a. *Final Report of the International Congress on Religions and Cultural Diversity: Mediation towards Social Cohesion in Urban Areas*. Barcelona, Unescocat. http://www.unescocat.org/religions-mediacio/publicacions/revista_eng.pdf

UNESCO Centre of Catalonia (UNESCOCat). 2007b. *Religious Diversity and Social Cohesion: A Contribution to the UNESCO World Report on Cultural Diversity*. http://www.unescocat.org/religions-mediacio/publicacions/world_report_on_cultural_diversity.pdf

UNESCO and Islamic Educational, Scientific and Cultural Organization (ISESCO). 2008. *Baku Declaration*. Adopted by the international conference, 'Expanding the Role of Women in Cross-cultural Dialogue', Baku, Azerbaijan, 11 June. http://www.isesco.org.ma/english/confSpec/documents/declarationBaku2008.pdf

UNESCO-Felissimo. 2008. The DREAM Programme: Key achievements and lessons learned, 2004–2007.

Vala, J. and Costa-Lopes, R. 2007. Youth, intolerance and diversity. Background paper.

Zhao, T. 2008. Knowledge diversity, diversity of worldviews and pitfalls of Huntingtonian claim of clash of civilizations: a Chinese point of view. Background paper.

UNESCO. 2004. Message from the Director-General of UNESCO on the occasion of the International Year to Commemorate the Struggle against Slavery and its Abolition, December 2003. *New Courier*, December. See http://unesdoc.unesco.org/images/0013/001312/131242e.pdf

Websites

America-Mideast Educational and Training Services (AMIDEAST): http://www.amideast.org

Anna Lindh Euro-Mediterranean Foundation for the Dialogue between Cultures: http://www.euromedalex.org

Arab League Educational, Cultural and Scientific Organization (ALECSO): http://www.alecso.org.tn

Children International Summer Village (CSIV): http://www.cisv.org

Convention on Biological Diversity (CBD): http://www.cbd.int and http://www.cbd.int/doc/legal/cbd-un-en.pdf

Erasmus Programme: http://ec.europa.eu/education/lifelong-learning-programme/doc80_en.htm

European Commission, European Culture Portal: http://ec.europa.eu/culture/portal/action/dialogue/dial_en.htm

Genographic Project: https://genographic.nationalgeographic.com/genographic/index.html

International Capoeira Angola Foundation: http://www.capoeira-angola.org

Ministère de l'éducation nationale: http://eduscol.education.fr/DO156/all-manuel-franco-allemand.htm

Oslo Coalition: http://www.oslocoalition.org

Peace Research Institute in the Middle East (PRIME): http://vispo.com/PRIME

Research Institute for Mindanao Culture (RIMCU): http://rimcu.elizaga.net

Scholar Ship Programme: http://www.thescholarship.com

South African San Institute (SASI): http://www.sanculture.org.za

UNESCO Associated Schools Network (ASPnet): http://portal.unesco.org/education/en/ev.php-URL_ID=7366&URL_DO=DO_TOPIC&URL_SECTION=201.html

UNESCO Beirut Project: http://www.unesco.org/en/beirut/single-view/news/teachers_train_on_teaching_cultral_aspects_of_christianity_and_islam_at_schools_in_lebanon/back/9437

UNESCO Chairs: http://portal.unesco.org/education/en/ev.php-URL_ID=41557&URL_DO=DO_TOPIC&URL_SECTION=201.html

UNESCO, Culture Portal: Dialogue: http://portal.unesco.org/culture/en/ev.php-URL_ID=34327&URL_DO=DO_TOPIC&URL_SECTION=201.html

UNESCO, Interreligious Dialogue programme: http://portal.unesco.org/culture/en/ev.php-URL_ID=35270&URL_DO=DO_PRINTPAGE&URL_SECTION=201.html

UNESCO, Representative List of Intangible Cultural Heritage of Humanity: http://www.unesco.org/culture/ich/index.php?pg=00173

UNESCO, Strategic Planning: Dialogue among civilizations: http://portal.unesco.org/en/ev.php-URL_ID=37084&URL_DO=DO_TOPIC&URL_SECTION=201.html

UNESCO, The Slave Route Project: http://portal.unesco.org/culture/en/ev.php-URL_ID=25659&URL_DO=DO_TOPIC&URL_SECTION=201.html

United Cities and Local Governments (UCLG): http://www.cities-localgovernments.org/uclg

United Nations Alliance of Civilizations: http://www.unaoc.org

United Nations Conference on Environment and Development (UNCED): http://www.un.org/geninfo/bp/enviro.html

United Nations Declaration on the Rights of Indigenous Peoples, 13 September 2007: http://www.un.org/esa/socdev/unpfii/en/drip.html

United Nations Environment Programme (UNEP): http://www.unep.org

United Nations Framework Convention on Climate Change (UNFCCC): http://unfccc.int

United Nations Permanent Forum on Indigenous Issues (UNPFII): http://www.un.org/esa/socdev/unpfii

United Nations Year of Dialogue Among Civilizations: http://www.un.org/Dialogue

University of Geneva: http://portal.unesco.org/es/ev.php-URL_ID=18249&URL_DO=DO_TOPIC&URL_SECTION=201.html

World Congress of Imams and Rabbis for Peace: http://www.imamsrabbis.org/en/congresses/detail/1/10/96

References

Allport, G. W. 1954. *The Nature of Prejudice*. Cambridge, Mass., Addison-Wesley.

Anheier, H. and Isar, Y. R. (eds.). 2007. *Conflict and Tensions*. (Cultures and Globalization Series, Vol. 1.) Thousand Oaks, Calif., Sage.

Asian Development Bank (ADB). 1998. *The Bank's Policy on Indigenous Peoples*. April. Manila, ADB. http://www.adb.org/documents/policies/indigenous_peoples/ADB-1998-Policy-on-IP.pdf

Baubérot, J. et al. (eds.). 2003. *Les civilisations dans le regard de l'autre II. Actes du colloque international Unesco-EPHE, Paris, 30 janvier*. Paris, UNESCO. http://unesdoc.unesco.org/images/0013/001329/132906fo.pdf

Benhabib, S. 2002. *The Claims of Culture: Equality and Diversity in the Global Era*. Princeton, N.J., Princeton University Press.

Bhabha, H. K. 1994. *The Location of Culture*. London, Routledge.

Chen, J. 2007. To get on the same page. *Newsweek*, 13 August. http://vispo.com/PRIME/newsweek.htm

Council of Europe. 2008. *White Paper on Intercultural Dialogue: Living Together as Equals in Dignity*. Strasbourg, Council of Europe. http://www.coe.int/t/dg4/intercultural/Source/Pub_White_Paper/White%20Paper_final_revised_EN.pdf

—. 2005. *Faro Declaration on the Council of Europe's Strategy for Developing Intercultural Dialogue*. CM(2005)164. 7 November. https://wcd.coe.int/ViewDoc.jsp?id=927109

—. 1995. *Framework Convention for the Protection of National Minorities*. 1 February. http://conventions.coe.int/Treaty/en/Treaties/Html/157.htm

—. 1993. *Vienna Declaration*. 9 October. https://wcd.coe.int/ViewDoc.jsp?id=621771&BackColorInternet=9999CC&BackColorIntranet=FFBB55&BackColorLogged=FFAC75

de Libera, A. 2003. De l'invective au dialogue. Essai de typologie. J. Baubérot et al. (eds.), *Les civilisations dans le regard de l'autre II. Actes du colloque international Unesco-EPHE, Paris, 30 janvier*. Paris, UNESCO, pp. 179–89. http://unesdoc.unesco.org/images/0013/001329/132906fo.pdf

Delissen, A. 2007. La nouvelle bataille des falaises rouges? à propos du manuel commun 'Chine-Corée-Japon'. *Vingtième Siècle: Revue d'histoire*, Vol. 94, pp. 57–72.

Fantini, A. 2007. *Exploring Intercultural Competence: Developing, Measuring, and Monitoring*. Research Report 07-01. St. Louis, Center for Social Development, Washington University. http://csd.wustl.edu/Publications/Documents/RP07-01.pdf and http://proposals.nafsa.org/Abstract_Uploads/118.61212.GS049.pdf

Hoffman, E. 1989. *Lost in Translation: A Life in a New Language*. New York, Penguin.

Huffman, K. 2007. Synthèse. B. Latour (ed.), *Le Dialogue des cultures: Actes des Rencontres inaugurales du musée du Quai Branly (21 juin 2006)*. Paris, Actes Sud, pp. 380-381.

Hulin, M. 2001. *Sankara et la non-dualité*. Paris, Bayard.

Huntington, Samuel P. 1996. *The Clash of Civilizations and the Remaking of World Order*. New York, Simon & Schuster.

—. 1993. The clash of civilizations? *Foreign Affairs*, Vol. 72, No. 3, pp. 22–49.

Klineberg, O. 1951. The scientific study of national stereotypes. *International Social Science Bulletin*, Vol. 3, pp. 505–15.

Okin, S. M. 1999. Is multiculturalism bad for women? J. Cohen, M. Howard and M. C. Nussbaum (eds.), *Is Multiculturalism Bad for Women?* Princeton, N.J., Princeton University Press, pp. 7–26.

Panikkar, R. 1979. *Myth, Faith and Hermeneutics: Cross-Cultural Studies*. New York, Paulist Press.

Pettigrew, T. F. 2008. Future directions for intergroup contact research. *International Journal of Intercultural Relations*, Vol. 32, No. 3, pp. 187–99.

—. 1998. Intergroup contact theory. *Annual Review of Psychology*, Vol. 49, pp. 65–85.

Philippines. 1997. *The Indigenous Peoples Rights Act of 1997*. Republic Act 8371. *Official Gazette*, Vol. 94, No. 13 (1998). http://www.glin.gov/download.action?fulltextId=54141&documentId=61555&glinID=61555

Rambaldi, G., Muchemi, J., Crawhall N. and Monaci, L. 2007. Through the eyes of hunter-gatherers: participatory 3D modelling among Ogiek indigenous peoples in Kenya. *Information Development*, Vol. 23, No. 2–3, pp. 113–28.

Ricoeur, P. 2006. *Memory, History, Forgetting*. Translated by K. Blamey and D. Pellauer. Chicago, Ill., University of Chicago Press.

—. 2004. Universal project, multiple heritages. J. Bindé (ed.), *The Future of Values: 21st Century Talks*. Paris, UNESCO/ New York, Berghann Books.

Said, E. 1978. *Orientalism*. London, Routledge.

Schoefthaler, T. 2006. Challenges in assuring dialogue between cultures. Edited version of keynote address to the forum 'Europe in Dialogue and Interaction between Cultures', Helsinki, Finland, 5 April. http://portal.unesco.org/education/en/files/53755/11840807615Schoefthaler.pdf/Schoefthaler.pdf. Also published in *Adventures in Diversity: New Avenues for the dialogue between cultures*. Bonn, German Commission to UNESCO, 2007.

Song, S. 2005. Majority norms, multiculturalism, and gender equality. *American Political Science Review*, Vol. 99, No. 4, pp. 473–89.

Sperber, D. 1985. *On Anthropological Knowledge*. Cambridge, Cambridge University Press.

Stenou, K. 2003. The World Policy of UNESCO. *Internet-Zeitschrift für Kulturwissenschaften*, Vol. 15. http://www.inst.at/trans/15Nr/plenum/stenou15EN.htm

United Nations Alliance of Civilizations (AoC). 2006. *Report of the High-level Group*. 13 November. New York, United Nations. http://www.aocistanbul.org/data/HLG_Report.pdf

United Nations Development Programme (UNDP). 2001. *UNDP and Indigenous Peoples: A Policy of Engagement*. http://www.undp.org/partners/cso/indigenous/docs/ipp_policy_english.doc

United Nations. 2005. *Promotion of Interreligious Dialogue and Cooperation for Peace*. A/RES/60/10. 3 November. http://www.un-documents.net/a60r10.htm

—. 2001. *Global Agenda for Dialogue among Civilizations*. A/RES/56/6. New York, United Nations. http://www.un.org/documents/ares566e.pdf

Vachon, R. 1998. IIM and its journal: An intercultural alternative and an alternative interculturalism. *Interculture*, Vol. 135, pp. 4–74.

World Bank. 2006. *Operational Policy on Indigenous Peoples*. Washington, D.C.: World Bank.

◑ *Old believers from the cultural space of the Semeiskie, Russia*

A man in Niamey, Niger

PART II.
KEY VECTORS OF CULTURAL DIVERSITY

Faced with the challenges of rethinking intercultural dialogue, countering stereotypes as well as tendencies towards withdrawal into closed identities, a deeper examination of the implications of cultural diversity in areas outside of culture in its restricted sense is equally important to public policy-making today. While virtually all human activities are shaped by and in turn help to shape cultural diversity, the prospects for the continued vitality of diversity are crucially bound up with the future of languages, education, the communication of cultural content, and the complex interface between creativity and the marketplace.

From the most immediate manifestation of cultural diversity — languages — to its pervasiveness across the entire social and economic fabric — the marketplace — including its role in education, media and communication policies, Part II explores these often overlapping fields — all central to UNESCO's mandate — with a view to identifying trends and factors that impact on the state of cultural diversity and refining our political agendas for its preservation and promotion in keeping with the complex realities of today's world.

CHAPTER 3 – **Languages**

Chapter 3 addresses the need to safeguard linguistic diversity in the wider context of managing cultural change, while facilitating dialogue and mutual understanding through the promotion of multilingualism and translation capacities.

CHAPTER 4 – **Education**

Chapter 4 argues the case for broadening the compass of educational systems to take account of informal learning environments and learning needs in culturally diverse settings, with a view to enhancing the quality of education and preparing us to live together with our differences through the development of intercultural competencies.

CHAPTER 5 – **Communication and cultural contents**

Chapter 5 analyzes recent trends in the communication of cultural contents, highlighting the challenge of ensuring that the expansion of media diversity and outreach is matched by efforts to redress the imbalances inherent in the digital divide so as to further processes of cultural exchange and mutual understanding.

CHAPTER 6 – **Creativity and the marketplace**

Chapter 6 explores the continuum across artistic creativity, social innovation and economic growth, highlighting the added-value of cultural diversity in key sectors ranging from contemporary art practices, crafts and tourism to corporate activities ranging from management and human resources to marketing and 'cultural intelligence'.

A translation and typing service in Hyderabad, India

Languages

Languages mediate our experiences, our intellectual and cultural environments, our modes of encounter with others, our value systems, social codes and sense of belonging, both collectively and individually. From the perspective of cultural diversity, linguistic diversity reflects the creative adaptation of groups to their changing physical and social environments. In this sense, languages are not just a means of communication but represent the very fabric of cultural expressions; they are the carriers of identity, values and worldviews.

While languages have always been susceptible to the political, socio-economic and cultural pressures of more influential language communities (as in the case of the marginalization or eclipse of vernacular languages in the context of European colonialism), today's pressures are impacting with increasing force on all communities as a consequence of globalization and the far-reaching communication developments accompanying it. In opening up previously self-enclosed societies and subjecting some minority languages to increasing competition, globalization and urbanization are major factors in contemporary patterns of linguistic erosion — the bulk of today's languages being far from equal in the face of these developments and the most vulnerable among them being threatened with rapid extinction. Yet, the effects of globalization on languages are complex and multidirectional (see chapter 1), and new linguistic practices are appearing among different social groups, especially young people. These practices are opening up a broad range of new forms of cultural diversity.

The importance of languages as identity markers becomes evident when dealing with issues relating to language loss and the emergence of new linguistic practices. From the perspective of intercultural relations, safeguarding linguistic diversity goes hand-in-hand with promoting multilingualism and must be matched by efforts to ensure that languages serve as a bridge between cultures, as a means to promoting the 'fruitful diversity' of the world's cultures.

A sign outside a school in Dar Es Salaam, Tanzania

Languages

3.1 Language dynamics today **69**
Map 3.1 Living languages in the World according to Ethnologue 69
Box 3.1 Languages in cyberspace............................71

3.2 Languages and identities **73**
Box 3.2 Monitoring linguistic diversity for biodiversity 74

3.3 The challenges of language assessment and revitalization **76**
Box 3.3 Assessing language vitality 77

3.4 Multilingualism, translation and intercultural dialogue................................. **80**

Map 3.2 Linguistic Diversity Index............................81
Figure 3. 1 Percentage of target-language translations 82
Box 3.4 Minority indigenous languages in translation in South America 83

Conclusion.. **85**

Recommendations... **86**

In focus: The key facets of language planning and policy-making....................... **87**

References and websites................................... **90**

A calligrapher in Hangzhou, China

3.1 Language dynamics today

Linguists believe that a large percentage of the world's languages are likely to disappear in the course of the 21st century. While the precise number of languages spoken in the world today is disputed, inventories such as the *Ethnologue* and *Linguasphere* put the total at somewhere between 6,000 and 8,000. Half of the existing languages are spoken by fewer than 10,000 people, and one such language is said to be disappearing every two weeks (Crystal, 2000). The prospects for language communities that are small in number or economically weak are particularly bleak. One study has calculated — on the assumption that languages with less than 150 speakers are in grave danger — that 600 (or 11.5 percent) of the world's languages are on the brink of extinction. If the threshold of viability is set at 10,000 speakers, language loss in the medium term will amount to some 60 percent. If the threshold is set at 100,000 speakers, over 80 percent of the world's languages will be lost, including most of the indigenous tongues in Australia and the Pacific. If one assumes a medium-term threshold of 1 million speakers, then '95.2 percent of all languages will be lost, including every single language indigenous to North America, Central America, Australia, New Guinea and the Pacific, plus almost all of those in South America' (Nettle, 1999).

A language under pressure is often a language whose speakers shift to a different, dominant language in response to political, social, economic and cultural pressures. The failure of the intergenerational transmission of a language can be likened to the reproductive failure of a species (Krauss, 1992). If such pressures persist across generations, such languages will be endangered (UNESCO Ad Hoc Expert Group on Endangered Languages, 2003a), a language being considered moribund when its speaking community no longer passes it on to younger generations. The point at which a language can be said to be critically endangered varies from language to language — for example, a language with 500 speakers may be in trouble in parts of Africa but not in the Pacific because of differing social and political conditions (Grimes, 1995). Likewise, many other conditions related to linguistic extinction cannot be inferred from the number of speakers alone (see section 3.3). Such conditions include the community's own attitudes towards its language and other sociolinguistic factors, as well as governmental attitudes and policies towards minority languages, and the presence or absence of programmes to preserve or perpetuate languages (Maffi and Skutnabb-Kangas, 1999).

Map 3.1 Living languages in the World according to Ethnologue

The countries and territories are re-sized according to the number of indigenous living languages identified by Ethnologue.

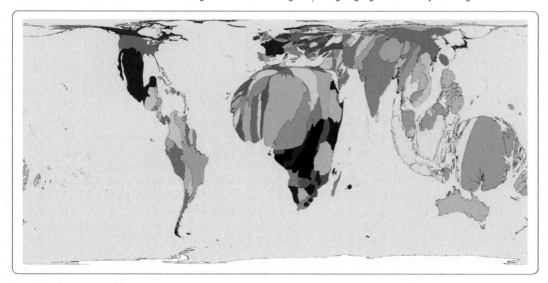

Source: Ethnologue, 2005; worldmapper.org

Globalization seems to be affecting the linguistic make-up of countries throughout the world in varied and often contradictory ways

Linguistic homogenization typically accompanied the creation of nation-states in the wake of decolonization and, more recently, the collapse of the Soviet Union and its affiliated satellites. Nation-states can constitutionally define the status of languages spoken in their territory and decide on the spheres in which they are to be used. A language that is given official status is generally that used in the educational system, public media, courts and public administration. In addition to official languages, some countries explicitly nominate a number of national languages in their constitution (in Senegal, for example, the official language is French and the national languages include Diola, Malinke, Pular, Serer, Soninke, Wolof 'and all codified languages'), yet this rarely influences their use in public domains. In most countries, official languages are associated with modernization and economic progress, the rest (usually local languages) tend to be restricted to the private domain, compounding the social and political marginalization of their speakers.

While its full impact is difficult to estimate, globalization seems to be affecting the linguistic make-up of countries throughout the world in varied and often contradictory ways. With more than 1 billion (first- and second-language) speakers, English is undeniably the most widespread language of communication. It is the official or main language in almost 60 countries (nearly one-third of the Member States of the United Nations), is present in another 75 countries, and is also the matrix language of more than 40 creole and pidgin languages. English has been described as 'the only shared medium across the vast Asian region' (Kachru, 2005), home to the world's largest population, and remains the dominant language across cultural industries, the Internet and media, as well as in diplomacy (Crystal, 2000; Camdenton, 2001). Two billion people — one-third of the world's population — could be learning English by 2010–2015, with as many as 3 billion people, or half the world's population, speaking the language in the near future (Graddol, 2006), leading to the oft-stated conclusion that the world has already adopted a de facto international auxiliary language. This trend is further confirmed by translation statistics, with most translations being from English as source language and comparatively little of the work published around the world in other languages being translated into English — somewhere between 2 and 4 percent of total books published in the US and the UK (see Venuti, 1995, and section 3.4 below). One need look no further than cyberspace to note the preponderance of a handful of the most widespread written languages, which is having detrimental impacts on the representation of other languages and on the viability of non-written languages (see Box 3.1).

While it has fore-grounded the expanding role of English, the effects of globalization on languages are nonetheless multidirectional, making it hard it to predict the impact of the expansion of English on multilingualism. While English appears to occupy a unique position as a convenient vehicular code across the world in tandem with the rise of information and communication technologies (ICTs), further technological innovation promises to make electronically mediated communication better able to support character-based languages (without romanization or alphabetization)[3] and oral-based communication (through voice recognition, for example) in the future (Lo Bianco, 2007). It may also be that the widespread use of English will be limited to specific purposes, such as transactions and functional communication. Globalization has also encouraged more plural and hybrid approaches to English, notably in India and Nigeria (Kachru and Smith, 2008; Kachru, Kachru and Nelson, 2006; Kachru, 1992, 2005; Kirkpatrick, 2007), which reveal the immensely complex modes in which language, identity and relationships interact and in which speakers adapt inherited forms of language to new cultural contexts and for new purposes.[4] Furthermore, in many instances of language loss, transfer away from minority languages is not towards English but towards other rival languages and regional dialects, such as Bangla (Bengali) in Bangladesh and India, and Kiswahili in Eastern Africa. Indeed, across Africa, Europe, Asia, the Americas and the Pacific, a range of widely spoken regional languages serve as vehicular languages or lingua francas (Giddens, 1999; Miller, 2003).

---

3. On internationalized domain names (IDNs), see ICANN (2001) and the corresponding Wikipedia entry.

4. For more information on the diversity of World Englishes, see also the following scientific journals: *English World-Wide: A Journal of Varieties of English,* *World Englishes: Journal of English as an International and Intranational Language,* and *English Today: The International Review of the English Language.*

| Box 3.1 | **Languages in cyberspace[1]** |

Few studies have undertaken large-scale quantitative analyses of the languages used on the Internet, and those that haven done so have tended to focus on the World Wide Web to the exclusion of other communication modes, such as email and chat, because the Web is more directly observable and easier to survey than other forms of Internet communication.

Languages on the Web, 2003

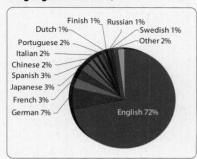

Source: O'Neill, Lavoie and Bennett, 2003.

Studies from the Online Computer Library Center (OCLC) (Lavoie and O'Neill 2000 and 2003), for example, have used a random sample of available websites on the Internet as the basis of an initial survey conducted at two different times, one year apart, in order to assess trends in the use of different languages. The 1998–1999 survey suggested that some international expansion of the Web was taking place (some 29 identifiable languages in the 1999 sample of some 2,229 random websites), and that the use of different languages was closely correlated with the domain in which each website originated. As expected, English was clearly dominant, representing 72 percent of the total websites surveyed. The 2002 follow-up survey showed the proportion of English on the web to be fairly constant in relation to the previous study, although small differences appeared for other languages.

Overall, the conclusion was that linguistic diversity of the web, while approaching that of many multilingual countries, is a poor reflection of linguistic diversity worldwide.

The 1999 OCLC survey also determined the proportions of Web pages that are multilingual from each domain of origin, and noted which language pairs are used. If a website used more than one language, English was always one of these. In total, 100% of the 156 multilingual sites surveyed used English (and 30% of these also used French, German, Italian and Spanish), even though 87% of the multilingual websites originated in domains outside major English-speaking countries (Australia, Canada, the United Kingdom and the United States). This finding directly contradicts the popular notion that the web somehow promotes linguistic diversity.

The most direct effort to estimate the linguistic diversity of Internet users comes from the translation services company Global Reach,

which produced yearly estimates between 1996 and 2004 based on International Telecommunication Union (ITU) estimates of user populations in each country. They define a 'user' as someone who has used the Internet in the past three months, and have divided 'user populations' into language populations calculated from *Ethnologue* estimates and adjusted with UN population data. Another set of estimates, from Internet World Stats, was used for the period from March 2004 through March 2009.

The findings resulting for the compilation of estimates are consistent with those of the OCLC studies: English, with an estimated 464 million users in March of 2009, is the most used language on the Internet, followed by Chinese, with approximately 321 million users. A remarkable trend is the dynamism of Spanish, which since 2006 is the third most frequently used language on the web, followed by Japanese, French and Portuguese. Thus, while English-speaking users represented

Estimated language populations of Internet users (millions)

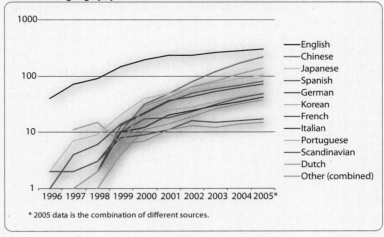

* 2005 data is the combination of different sources.

Source: Global Reach, 2004.

---

1. For a regional overview, see the website 'Recent Experiences on Measuring Languages in Cyberspace'.

Box 3.1   Languages in cyberspace

Estimated linguistic diversity of Internet users

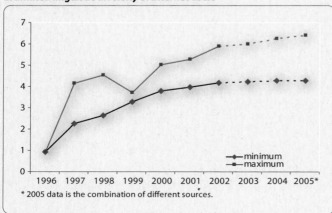

* 2005 data is the combination of different sources.

Source: Global Reach, 2004.

Internet users by region (in millions)

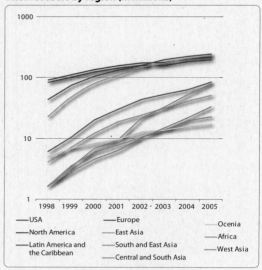

Source: International Telecommunication Union, 2008.

approximately 53 percent of total Internet users in 2000, by 2009 they represented only 29 percent of total Internet users.

Linguistic-diversity indices for the global population of Internet users can be calculated using Global Reach estimates. Minimum and maximum values for the index have been calculated based on the assumption of single-language representations (the minimum diversity) and a uniform distribution across 6,000 languages (the maximum diversity).

Yet linguistic diversity on the Internet is nowhere near as large as the index of any other region of the world as a whole (perhaps because Internet hosts remain concentrated in North America and Europe), the Internet cannot be said to embrace linguistic diversity.

The prevalence of English in cyberspace, while difficult to quantify, can largely be explained by computer-systems development

and the effects of the digital divide. In the mid-1990s, for example, Microsoft chose not to develop non-roman versions of its products, despite the availability of commercial technological solutions (such as Apple Computer's WorldScript), seemingly because non-roman markets were too small to justify creating a new version of their product.

When correlated with the existing imbalances in global access to the Internet per region, the link between lower linguistic-diversity areas (such as in North America, Latin America and the Caribbean, Europe and East Asia) and higher Internet usage is striking.

According to some, low linguistic diversity facilitates the provision of Internet access based on the small number of standardized technological solutions needed to target each of the major language populations. Regions and countries with greater linguistic diversity typically require more complex arrangements

for Internet access, and resource customization for each of a large number of minority languages. This situation appears in the extreme in India, where even large languages like Hindi have a plethora of duplicate solutions, such that almost every Hindi website has its own Hindi font set, which is incompatible with other Hindi font sets. People who wish to read Hindi material on these websites must separately install the fonts required by each site; this renders searching across different sites extremely difficult, since words do not match up in the different representations (Information Sciences Institute, 2003). Furthermore, regions such as Africa remain serious challenges, as even some of the larger languages in some countries are not yet in use on the Internet. Significant technological work remains to be done before the goal of reaching these language groups can be realized.[2]

Source: Based on Paolillo and Das, 2006.

2. UNESCO is highly committed to improving linguistic diversity in cyberspace, as expressed in the *Recommendation on the Promotion and Use of Multilingualism and Universal Access to Cyberspace* (2003) and the outcomes of the 2005 World Summit on the Information Society. See the UNESCO webpage 'Multilingualism in Cyberspace'.

Through migration, colonial expansion, refugee displacement or professional mobility, many language communities are now dispersed across the world. As connections between language and place are becoming increasingly multiple, communication patterns also become highly variegated, characterized by code-switching, multilingualism, different receptive and productive competencies in different languages or dialects, and are marked by mixtures of full, partial and specialized proficiencies. Just as globalization contributes to cultural hybridization (see chapter 1), it also favours the emergence of new linguistic forms and practices, especially among young people. In this way, continuously expanding networks based on mobile phones, broad-band Internet and other ICTs are creating new forms of human association of unprecedented scale and flexibility, spanning cities, nations and cultures. These are in turn forging new cultural identities that are broadening and redefining existing boundaries, extending them across public/private domains and social, cultural and educational contexts (Ito et al., 2008). A special case of this phenomenon are 'third culture kids' (TCK), transcultural youth who live with their parents but grow up in a culture different from their parents' originating culture and are thus faced with creating new ethnic and/or national identities (some of which may be at odds with one another) and innovative cultural systems (Fail, Thompson and Walker, 2004).

While the impacts of digital communication on languages and forms of social identity and organization have yet to be fully understood, it is nonetheless clear that the assumption that 'language equals culture equals identity' is too simple to account for the intricate linkages between languages and cultural identities. Consequently, today's policy-makers must take very many factors into account when devising language policies, including advances in linguistics, the human, social and political sciences, and market economics.

3.2 Languages and identities

People tend to hold strong beliefs when it comes to their language, which has the important function of marking boundaries between groups; these beliefs play a key role in the construction and maintenance of distinctive human identities, both between different and within same-language communities. For even within linguistic communities, distinctive features will distinguish speakers' origins: the English spoken in England is different from that spoken in the United States, New Zealand and South Africa; and even within a country locally distinct varieties tied to specific areas or social status will arise, so that the English spoken in New York City is different from that spoken in New Orleans or Boston, and Cockney English is distinct from that spoken by the British upper middle class. Like human cultures and species, languages adapt to specific ecological niches, and like cultural artefacts, they have historicity, and express the worldviews, values and belief systems inherent in a given culture. Even today, despite the complexity of the modern world in which languages have come to reflect many identities, histories, cultures, sources and places, the majority of the world's languages are 'narrow-niched', that is to say, they are confined to a single group, village or territory.

A language's vocabulary is an organized catalogue of a given culture's essential concepts and elements. Taking the case of indigenous cultures, the requirements of Pacific Island cultures differ from those of Siberian reindeer-herding cultures. The language traditionally associated with a culture is in general the language that relates to that culture's environment and local ecosystem, the plants and animals it uses for food, medicine and other purposes, and expresses local value systems and worldviews (Fishman, 1991). The naming of geographic features of the landscape ensures a sense of connection to place and the histories linked to it. The Apache language in the southwestern United States, for example, includes descriptively specific place names, which often consist of complete sentences ('water flows down on a succession of flat rocks') and are essential to the genealogies of Apache clans since place names are also associated with kin groups. Thus, native claims about symbolic links to land and personal relationships tied to environment may not be so readily interpretable.

From this perspective, the displacement of indigenous peoples from their traditional lands and the loss of key cultural sites is likely to involve far more than physical dislocation: it can represent a break in the historical

Languages are not just a means of communication but represent the very fabric of cultural expressions, the carriers of identity, values and worldviews

| Box 3.2 | Monitoring linguistic diversity for biodiversity |

Research on the relationship between cultural and biological diversity is becoming increasingly pertinent. Findings point to the remarkable correlations between the world's areas with high biological richness and those with high diversity of languages (the single best indicator of a distinct culture). Based on the comparative analysis of eight main biological groups (mammals, birds, reptiles, amphibians, freshwater fishes, butterflies, tiger-beetles and flowering plants), 12 'mega-diversity' countries (hosting the largest numbers of species and endemic species) can be identified, nine of which represent the countries with the highest number of languages: Australia, Brazil, China, Colombia, Ecuador, India, Indonesia, Madagascar, Mexico, Peru, Philippines and Venezuela. Thus, nine of the countries with the highest species richness and endemism are also in the list of the 25 nations with the highest number of endemic languages (Toledo, 2001).

To exhibit such a correlation between the richness of some groups of organisms and the number of languages worldwide, an *Index of Biocultural Diversity* (IBCD) was created. It represents the first attempt to quantify global biocultural diversity by means of a country-level index. The IBCD uses five indicators: the number of languages, religions and ethnic groups (for cultural diversity), and the number of bird/mammal and plant species (for biological diversity). The application of this index revealed three 'core regions' of exceptional biocultural diversity.

UNESCO recently addressed the biocultural diversity paradigm at an operational level, through its Main Line of Action on 'Enhancing linkages between cultural and biological diversity as a key basis for sustainable development,' including activities focused on traditional knowledge and indigenous languages. Of note are the efforts to develop an indicator of the status of and trends in linguistic diversity and the numbers of speakers of indigenous languages. The indicator is being developed within the framework of the 2010 Biodiversity Target, adopted in 2004

by the Conference of States Parties to the 1992 *Convention on Biological Diversity* (CBD), which aims 'to achieve by 2010 a significant reduction of the current rate of biodiversity loss at the global, regional and national level as a contribution to poverty alleviation and to the benefit of all life on Earth' (CBD, 2005).

This indicator will serve as a proxy for measuring the status and trends in 'traditional knowledge, innovations and practices', one of the seven focal areas identified for 70 the 2010 Target (CBD, 2005; see UNESCO webpage on 'Linguistic diversity in relation to

 A local flower market in Antananarivo, Madagascar

biodiversity'). Two parallel approaches have been used in developing this indicator:

- An informant-based survey of language vitality and endangerment was conducted through a Standardized Tool for primary data collection operationalized as a questionnaire entitled *Linguistic Vitality and Diversity*. The questionnaire was based on the framework developed by the UNESCO Ad Hoc Expert Group on Endangered Languages (2003b) to assess the degree of language vitality/endangerment (see Box 3.3).

- A desk study was conducted on the numbers of speakers of indigenous languages using national censuses and secondary sources. However, the low quality of available data

on numbers of speakers and the lack of comparability among different sources made it difficult to develop an indicator at the global level. UNESCO is currently conducting a comprehensive study on the variables and phrasing of the questions used in national censuses to collect data on languages. The aim thereby is to develop a set of guidelines that will increase the reliability and international comparability of census data on languages.

This newly developed methodology aims to establish a baseline for identifying and

tracking trends on the numbers of speakers of indigenous languages in the coming years. Data from the third edition of UNESCO's *Atlas of the World's Languages in Danger* (2009) are also complementary to the data collected through the *Linguistic Vitality and Diversity* questionnaire and the information provided by national censuses.

Increasingly, alliances are being established along these lines by non-governmental organizations (NGOs), foundations, academic institutions and scholars to support language policies for indigenous languages, thereby linking language preservation to ecological conservation (see also chapter 7).

Source: UNESCO.

continuity of a community's consciousness of its distinct identity and culture. When people are forced to move or resettle on land that differs from that on which they traditionally lived (e.g. Gaelic speakers displaced from the Scottish Highlands), the links between language, culture and the environment are weakened. Languages are thus in large part culture-specific: they carry with them extensive indexical and symbolic content, which comes to represent the particular ethnic, cultural and/or national groups that speak them. When a language is lost, it is far more difficult to recover it than other identity markers.

Furthermore it is increasingly obvious that the anticipated loss of the majority of languages will have a detrimental impact on all kinds of diversity — not only on cultural diversity in terms of the richness of worldviews and philosophical systems but also on diversity in environmental and ecological terms, for research is making increasingly clear the link between the erosion of linguistic diversity and that of the knowledge of biological diversity (Harmon and Loh, 2008; see Box 3.2). It is precisely the awareness of this link between biological diversity and cultural diversity — most distinctively represented by the loss of languages (Skutnabb-Kangas, Maffi and Harmon, 2003) and the related loss of knowledge of nature, history, memory, cultural knowledge, practices, norms and values (Mühlhäusler, 1996; Grenoble and Whaley, 1998; Diamond, 2001) — that led to the International Society of Ethnobiologists' 1988 *Declaration of Belem* on cultural diversity and biological diversity. The conclusions of a study on a number of small languages that had remained stable over time and their relations with the biological richness of these areas highlight the extent to which knowledge is encoded in a given language, such that cultural systems can be said to co-evolve in small-scale groups with local ecosystems (Nettle and Romaine, 2000). Stated differently, 'Life in a particular human environment is [. . .] dependent on people's ability to talk about it' (Mühlhäusler, 1996). In this sense, the magnitude of the threat to the world's linguistic

diversity and the serious implications of its loss plead strongly for the identification and the adoption of best practices in this area.

Of course, no systematic or necessary correlation exists between language and culture: languages are in constant flux, and socio-economic, political or other factors have continuously played a role in language shifts. Where there is ethnic or cultural stigmatization, a language may be abandoned as an act of survival or self-defence; some parents, for example, do not speak their native language at home so as to prepare their children for school in the dominant language. In some places where traditional languages have disappeared, people may vest their identity in a new language — in some cases in a distinctive form of the dominant language; in other cases, a creole language.[5] In large parts of Australia, many Aboriginal people speak Aboriginal English, Torres Strait Creole, or Kriol as their first language. In other parts of the world, many speak English or another language as a second or additional language. Although European colonial encounters have produced the best known and most studied indigenous pidgins and creoles, there are examples predating European contact, such as Sango in the Central African Republic and Hiri Motu in Papua New Guinea. Such languages may spring up wherever speakers of different languages have to work out a common means of communication (Romaine, 2006). Most creoles coexist with the original language with which they share most of their vocabulary; often, negative attitudes have prevented pidgins and creoles from receiving official recognition or being used in education, even where the majority of a population speaks them. Even in the few countries where pidgins and creoles have received some token recognition as an official or national language, they have not been widely integrated in schools. In the few instances in which they have been, results have generally been positive (e.g. Tok Pisin and Hiri Motu in Papua New Guinea, Sango in the Central African Republic, Seselwa in the Seychelles, Papiamentu

The Moussem of Tan Tan, a festival of nomad tribes, Morocco

5. A *pidgin* is a contact language restricted in form and function and native to no one, formed by members of at least two (and usually more) groups of different linguistic backgrounds. Tok Pisin ['talk pidgin'], for example, is spoken by millions of people in Papua New Guinea. A *creole* is a nativized pidgin, expanded in form and function to meet the communicative needs of a community of native speakers (e.g. Creole French in Haiti). While some creole speakers will use the term 'creole' to refer to their languages (e.g. Kriol in Australia, Krio in Sierra Leone, Kreyòl in Haiti), in other places it is unknown as such to its speakers. The term *patois* is used throughout much of the Anglophone Caribbean. Other names are also used, in some cases pejoratively, e.g. Broken (i.e. broken English) for Torres Strait Creole English, spoken by about 5,000 people in the Torres Strait Islands of Australia, and Papiamento (from Spanish *papear*, 'to jabber/chat') spoken by around 250,000 in the Netherlands Antilles (Brown, 2005).

A guiding principle of cultural diversity is therefore to continue to strengthen and maintain the diversity of languages, all the while supporting international languages that offer access to global communication and exchange of information

in the Netherlands Antilles) and have led to increased motivation and academic performance (Eckkramer, 2003; see chapter 4 below).

People who speak two or more languages will often index more than one identity, and even avoid aligning themselves with only one identity. In 1997, a heated debate took place in Hong Kong over a speech to be delivered by the first new chief executive, Tung Chee Wah, in the handover ceremony to China: Should it be delivered in Putonghua or Cantonese, each being symbolic of different alignments and identities? Tung finally delivered it in Putonghua, the official language of mainland China, but he delivered his first policy address in Cantonese, which has always been the lingua franca for Chinese ethnic groups in Hong Kong and is the spoken medium of instruction in primary schools and Chinese-medium secondary schools there (Tsui, 2007). Obviously, choice of language use suggests that languages and forms of speech may not enjoy equal status or be regarded as equally appropriate or adequate in all circumstances. The emotional strength of words spoken in a local language as opposed to those spoken in the language of a former colonizer will not be the same for the bilingual speaker and are not interchangeable. Through such selection processes, we display what may be called 'acts of identity'

(Le Page and Tabouret-Keller, 1985) and throughout our lives we develop allegiances to a variety of groups, based on the values and attitudes in our surrounding community and then extended to broader society, defined in the different ways (cultural, ethnic, religious, national) that shape and influence who we are and how we perceive ourselves (see chapter 2).

Thus the idea of fixed identities, cultures and languages must yield to a view of them as constructed and dynamic, subject to change in endless processes of symbolic reconstruction and negotiation. At the same time, even as we increasingly engage with both local and global cultural systems (through mass communication, technology, tourism, migration), the link between racial, ethnic and religious affiliations and cultural and linguistic identity remains very strong. Local and national languages therefore remain crucial, even if global languages are a necessary tool of communication for expressing our identities as citizens of the world. A guiding principle of cultural diversity is therefore to continue to strengthen and maintain the diversity of languages (including those of nomadic or scattered populations), *all the while* supporting international languages that offer access to global communication and exchange of information.

3.3 The challenges of language assessment and revitalization

For many, language vitality is a benchmark for cultural diversity because virtually every major aspect of human culture, from kinship classification to religion, is dependent on language for its transmission (Haarmann, 2004). Yet, as we have seen, language is not equivalent to culture. There are numerous instances in which the same language is spoken by groups with otherwise radically different cultural practices and worldviews. When ethnic identification is in question, the complex relationship between an individual and a group may occur along with language affiliation, but this is not always the case.

Traditional approaches to documenting and assessing language shifts have focused mainly on linguistics and have tended to neglect socio-economic realities and

political contexts. Yet language loss is a late onset form of cultural attrition, indicating an already advanced process of cultural decline (Fishman, 2001). The variety of circumstances surrounding language health and its prospects for revitalization when threatened by erosion depend upon the specific socio-cultural, economic, political and historical configurations that apply uniquely to each language, and thus language health tends to defy generalization and broad analysis (see Box 3.3). While many of today's approaches to minority language revitalization and preservation recognize and integrate these factors,[6] the process remains profoundly political (Walsh, 2005). Indeed, active preservation of an eroded language can be perceived as competing with the instrumental value of the dominant language (e.g. as it affects economic opportunity and social status),

6. The ecological approach focuses on the communication context to which languages belong, their role in the economy and processes of communication

(see Mühlhäusler, 1996); the socio-linguistic approach addresses the issue of specialization of languages (see Fishman, 2001).

Box 3.3   Assessing language vitality

Documentation is an essential component for counteracting the seemingly inexorable loss of the world's linguistic resources, and UNESCO has long sought to alert the international community to the chain reaction resulting from language loss. Since the publication of the 1994 *Red Book of Languages in Danger of Disappearing*, which already at that time claimed that 90 percent of all languages were in danger of disappearing within two generations, UNESCO has supported many studies on language endangerment. At the invitation of Tokyo University, an International Clearing House for Endangered Languages was established in 1995, and in 1996 the first edition of its *Atlas of the World's Languages in Danger* was published. The second updated edition was produced in 2001, listing by region some 900 endangered languages and their degrees of endangerment. The third, fully revised and updated edition, prepared within the framework of the United Nations International Year of Languages (2008) and recently released in both print and online interactive versions (2,500 endangered languages listed on a revisable basis), uses more subtle and sensitive indicators of language endangerment, based on a multi-factorial schema adopted by the UNESCO Ad Hoc Expert Group on Endangered Languages (2003a). It identifies five degrees of endangerment: i) vulnerable (607 languages), ii) endangered (652 languages), iii) severely endangered (530 languages), iv) critically endangered (573), and v) extinct (242 languages).

According to the Expert group, nine factors can be identified for assessing the vitality of a language. Since a language that has a favourable situation in terms of one or more factors may have a very unfavourable situation with regard to others, a combination of these nine factors is the best guide to a language's overall sociolinguistic situation.

Other methodologies exist for assessing a language's vitality. In a quantitative study, Statistics Canada used 1996 census responses

to calculate an 'index of continuity' and an 'index of ability' for the country's indigenous languages (Norris, 1998). The *index of continuity* measures a language's vitality by comparing the number of people who speak it at home with the number who learned it as their original mother tongue. In this index, a 1:1 ratio is scored at 100 and represents a perfect maintenance situation in which every mother-tongue speaker keeps the language as a home language. Any score lower than 100 indicates a decline in the language's strength. The *index of ability* compares the number of those who report being able to speak the language (at a conversational level) with the number of mother-tongue speakers. Here, a score of over 100 indicates that an increment of people have learned it as a second language and may suggest some degree of language revival.

The report found that only three of the country's 50 native languages have speaking populations large enough to keep them secure over the long term, and the index of continuity for all native languages declined almost 15 percent between 1981 and 1996 (Norris, 1998). The vast majority of indigenous languages in North America is in trouble and up to 80 percent are moribund in Canada and in the United States jointly (Krauss, 1992). If current trends continue, the general outlook

for the continued survival of these languages is very poor (Robins and Uhlenbeck, 1991).

A review of the native languages of California paints a similar picture: of the 50 contemporary languages in the State (some 50 having already been lost following European contact), more than 15 have recently become extinct and many others have fewer than 10 speakers (all elders), and only 2 or 3 have as many as 150 or 200 speakers (Hinton, 1994). Along the temperate rainforest coast, stretching from northern California to Alaska, 26 languages of the 68 native language groups present at European contact are now extinct, 18 are spoken by fewer than 10 people, and only 8 are spoken by more than 100 individuals (Wolf, Mitchell and Schoonmaker, 1995). In Mexico, the danger of extinction exists in every area where indigenous languages are found (Garza Cuarón and Lastra, 1991). Most endangerment information comes from anecdotal reports that young people no longer speak the language in certain social situations, or that they have given it up altogether.

Still, current indicators and indices, including the linguistic diversity index (see Map 7.1 and Table 7 in the Statistical Annex), cannot for the moment fully account for the vitality of languages, since it varies widely depending on the different

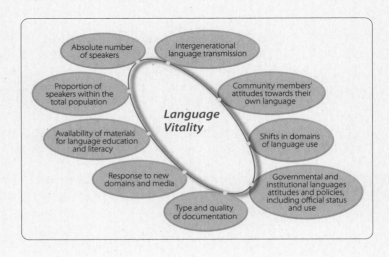

Box 3.3	Assessing language vitality

situations of speech communities and since societies are endowed with a complex array of language competencies among their members (Beacco, 2007). And while it may be possible to aggregate language statistics on a global basis, we are a long way from having highly accurate figures on global language use: indeed, our capacities for language census cannot capture the nuances of language use, let alone those of cultural affiliation (on the limitations of *Ethnologue* data, see Harmon, 1995; Paolillo and Das, 2006). Experts even disagree about what constitutes a language or a mother tongue. While the 14th edition of *Ethnologue* (2000) cites some 41,000 distinct languages based on native speakers throughout the world, linguists and anthropologists tend to regroup languages into families and count approximately 7,000 languages. Such divergences indicate the degree of subjectivity inherent in assessment of the state of linguistic diversity.

Source: UNESCO.

giving rise to a situation in which advocates of language preservation may be regarded as backward-looking and parochial or, even worse, as biased against national unity and cohesion.

The survival of many indigenous peoples is often dependent on modern means of production. Many appreciate that there are benefits to be derived from increased interaction with the dominant society, but wish to preserve a certain cultural autonomy and have a say in determining their own future, with particular reference to the right to educate their children in their own way and to safeguard their language and culture (see the 2007 *Declaration on the Rights of Indigenous Peoples*). However, to preserve their distinctive identities, what is needed is access to economic resources available in the marketplace. Today, the preservation of Inuktitut in the Eastern Canadian Arctic is partly a product of its integration into the dominant linguistic market and political economy, where it has been standardized and promoted in education, government publications, and other written forms. This process has been further strengthened by the development of an Inuktitut version of the Windows operating system. Despite modern paradoxes and lifestyle transformations, indigenous peoples seek to maintain their language and culture. Driving snowmobiles, wearing jeans and listening to pop music are not inherently incompatible with cultural and linguistic continuity and indigenous identity any more than speaking English need be at odds with speaking Inuktitut or Navajo. According to the 2001 Canadian Census, however, overall only 15 percent of the country's Aboriginal children learn an indigenous mother tongue, and fewer still are spoken to in such a language at home.

The prestige of the dominant language and its predominance in public institutions lead communities to undermine the value of their own language in a process of symbolic domination

The reasons behind endangerment may be either external (e.g. effects of globalization, political or other pressures) or internal (e.g. a negative community attitude to the language). The dominant languages of nation-states, and colonial languages, which prevail in all areas of public and official life (government, school and media), often hamper the ability of speakers of other languages to preserve them as the domains of usage become increasingly restricted. The prestige of the dominant language and its predominance in public institutions lead communities to undermine the value of their own language in a process of symbolic domination. This has been the case in almost all countries of Francophone Africa, where the newly independent States chose French as their official language (to be used in schools, public media, courts and administration), leaving the many African languages spoken as mother tongues restricted to private usage. In Latin America, Quechua speakers, numbering some 7–10 million in the Andean regions of Argentina, Bolivia, Colombia, Ecuador and Peru have largely succumbed to the assimilative pressures of Spanish over the last century.

Language revitalization, which is often the key to recovering cultural identity, depends first and foremost on a community's reassertion of the value of its own cultural identity. Even where a language has not been transmitted over a long period of time (the case of so-called 'sleeping languages'), it is possible for them to be reclaimed through the mobilization of identities. Two examples come from Australia and the United States. First, Kaurna, once used by Aboriginal people around Adelaide in South Australia but not spoken for over a century, is today being reclaimed through greetings, songs and activities relying on earlier documents and records of the language (Amery, 2001). Another example of a language linguists thought to be extinct since the 1960s is that of an Algonquian Miami tribe in Oklahoma; it is currently being reclaimed by families that have incorporated the language into their daily household activities, and young children are now acquiring conversational proficiency in it (Baldwin, 2003). Although such reappropriated languages are likely to be substantially different from the languages historically spoken — and some have dismissed these less-than-fluent uses — they clearly have the potential to serve important community and cultural functions for many native groups throughout Australia, North and South America and other parts of the world. Such efforts will become increasingly important wherever people claim a link to a linguistic heritage that is no longer actively transmitted.

New ICTs may have a positive impact on revitalization, especially when digital technologies are utilized to collect documentation on languages or when computers are used to transcribe and translate endangered languages into languages of wider communication. In some cases, revitalization would imply the development of writing systems (Austin, 2008). Such initiatives are particularly fruitful in the case of unwritten languages, whose native speakers are usually unable to benefit from all the advantages that would be offered by written communication. But opting for a system of transcription should be made only in close consultation with the concerned communities, since it is not without its political dimensions. Thanks to Unicode, an initiative involving several companies in the information technology sector (programmers, research institutions and users associations) and facilitating the encoding of more than 65,000 different characters, some minority languages are now in a position to reach a much larger public on the Internet. But such ICT-based initiatives of language revitalization are most successful in combination with wider media efforts. In the Canadian Province of Nunavut, efforts for the revitalization of Inuktitut (made compulsory at school and for the recruitment of civil servants) have been supported by the development of an Inuktitut version of the Windows operating system. In New South Wales (Australia), the Gamilaraay language, which was almost extinct at the end of the 1970s, has been revived thanks to a clear commitment by the State and concrete initiatives involving the release of a paper and online dictionary, the teaching of the language at school, and the production of textbooks, books and CDs.

In general there is a great need for communication across minority and majority communities. Preservation of all languages, especially those small and endangered, is in everybody's interest, members of 'majority' and 'minority' communities alike. While positive measures to protect the variety and diversity of languages are implicit in many existing international instruments, the question of language rights remains contentious, as illustrated by the debates over the 1996 Barcelona Draft of the *Universal Declaration on Linguistic Rights*. The adoption in September 2007 of the *United Nations Declaration on the Rights of Indigenous Peoples*, though a non-binding instrument, may yield the most immediate effects on the preservation, revitalization and perpetuation of linguistic diversity among indigenous and minority peoples. UNESCO's Executive Board is currently debating the feasibility of a new standard-setting instrument on languages, including the issue of whether it should be focused on the safeguarding of linguistic diversity generally or on the protection of the linguistic rights of certain vulnerable groups (see chapter 8). What is clear is that effective language policies for marginalized populations must integrate knowledge of community practices and relationships, taking into account the specificity of each setting, and stress the need to conduct the functional activities of everyday life in ways that are culturally appropriate (Fettes, 1997).

◑ *Playing the duduk, an Armenian oboe*

There is a need to both preserve global linguistic diversity as a prerequisite for cultural diversity and to promote multilingualism and translation in order to foster intercultural dialogue

3.4 Multilingualism, translation and intercultural dialogue

Multilingualism and translation have necessary and complementary roles in the promotion of intercultural dialogue. Multilingualism fulfils the dual function of facilitating communication between individuals of different cultures and contributing to the survival of endangered languages. Translation for its part serves as a necessary bridge over the many linguistic divides that multilingualism is not able or available to fill. Both multilingualism and translation are essential components of a pluralistic society.

Multilingualism as a resource

In a world in which we all have overlapping and intersecting identities, it is no longer possible to classify people on the basis of a single language, religion or culture. While distinctive food, dress, song, etc. are often accepted and integrated into mainstream culture, this is much less true of language diversity. Despite claims that multilingualism is socially disruptive, there is no necessary connection between linguistic variety in a given society and difficulties of cross-group communication. In fact, social cohesion and citizenship require shared forms of communication and comprehension, not monolingualism.

A common criticism levelled at language policies promoting multilingualism in schools is that they usually involve invidious choices, since it is not possible for all minority languages to be supported. From this standpoint, it is preferable to choose a single foreign or international language of prestige or a trade language, or even to refrain from offering other languages altogether. Many examples around the world prove the fallacy of this argument.

Multilingualism in schools is now practised in many countries, though the world is still far from the objective of trilingual education (see Table 7 in the Statistical Annex and chapter 4 below). In Australia for example, following years of ambivalent or hostile attitudes towards the inclusion and transmission of indigenous and immigrant languages, some school systems today offer as many as 47 languages, though not necessarily all during normal school hours. Some are supported by radio broadcasts, digital media or after-hours community providers integrated into the schools' examination and assessment system; others are simply acknowledged formally within mainstream education proper, thereby validating community language preservation efforts. Australia's adoption in 1987 of a comprehensive *National Policy on Languages* (Lo Bianco, 1987) — the first explicitly multilingual national policy in an English-speaking nation — links sub-national multilingualism with national economic interests and social cohesion (rather than seeing these as being in competition with one another) and highlights the potentially powerful effects of collaboration across diverse language interests. Significant progress towards a comprehensive language policy was made possible when the policy voices of immigrant and indigenous groups were combined with those of professional academic and teacher communities and business and political elites (Clyne, 2005; Lo Bianco, 1987).

Similar creative solutions in favour of multilingualism exist in many countries where national educational objectives have made unity, citizenship and intra-national communication (including the support of language minorities and multilingualism) the first priority of public investment in education (García, Skutnabb-Kagas and Torres Guzmán, 2006). Papua New Guinea, a small, developing society with a high degree of multilingualism, is a case in point. With the world's highest Linguistic Diversity Index (LDI), representing about 820 living indigenous languages, the country has set up an integrated educational system based on local languages (in the earliest years of schooling) linked to regional creole languages of wider communication, and the national language, English, which has global reach. While critics and opponents of multilingualism often stress the administrative and economic inefficiency of multilingual provision, the case of Papua New Guinea highlights the importance of locally based language planning and policy, its administrative feasibility and educational effectiveness, notably increased attendance and participation rates, including among girls (for additional case studies, see Lo Bianco, 2007; and UNESCO, 2003, 2004, 2005, 2007a–b).

Because languages are highly complex and flexible sets of practices that interact with all aspects of people's social and personal lives, they are problematic objects of policy-making. Yet language policies that support multilingualism, language learning and endangered languages are indispensable to the long-term sustainability of cultural diversity. Such policies moreover have the potential to bring to the learner's attention the culturally specific ways in which knowledge is organized and appreciated in distinct traditions, in terms of thought, belief, values and as unique histories of human experience. This in turn promotes understanding, insight, perspective and appreciation, enabling cultural gaps to be bridged through processes of translation, encounter, imagination, narration, art, faith and dialogue.

Yet the growth and patterns of multilingualism still do not receive the attention they should, nor has multilingualism been duly recognized as an intellectual and a cultural asset, as well as a resource for participatory citizenship and the effective exercise of human rights (see Ruiz, 1984).

To ensure the continued viability of the world's languages, we must find ways both to safeguard linguistic diversity by protecting and revitalizing languages and to promote multilingualism by developing policies at the national level that foster the functional use of all languages within a given society. These two objectives are intertwined, since the promotion of a multilingualism that includes mother-tongue-based education also constitutes a means of safeguarding indigenous and endangered

languages. At the international level, this translates into a two-pronged approach: 1) to preserve and enrich global linguistic diversity as a prerequisite for cultural diversity and 2) to promote multilingualism and translation (including in administration, education, the media and cyberspace) in order to foster intercultural dialogue.

Translation as a tool for dialogue

The study of contemporary translation flows highlights a number of issues concerning the status of languages in the world. These flows reflect a global asymmetry in the representation of cultures, peoples, ethnic groups and languages, and the unequal circulation of cultural goods. At the institutional and symbolic levels, translation can potentially help to redress such asymmetry and is slowly regaining importance in the new communication networks of contemporary society.

A census based on data compiled between 1979 and 2007, undertaken by the *Index Translationum*, confirms the dominant position of English as a reference language: 55 percent of book translations are from English as the source language as compared to only 6.5 percent into English. In addition, 96 percent of all translations are limited to about 20 source languages, of which 16 are European (constituting 93 percent of the total), the four other languages most translated

Map 3.2 Linguistic Diversity Index

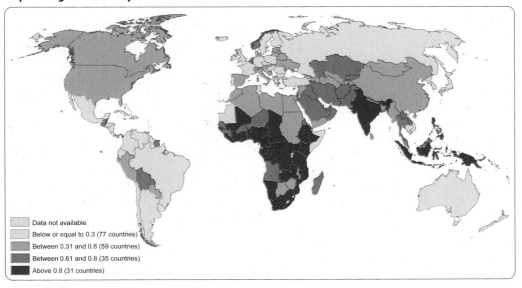

Data not available
Below or equal to 0.3 (77 countries)
Between 0.31 and 0.6 (59 countries)
Between 0.61 and 0.8 (35 countries)
Above 0.8 (31 countries)

The Linguistic Diversity Index (LDI) represents the probability that in a given country any two people selected at random would have different mother tongues. The LDI ranges from 0 (least diversity) to 1 (greatest diversity). The computation of the index is based on the population of each language as a proportion of the total population (Ethnologue, 2005). Countries with the highest LDI include Papua New Guinea, India, Nigeria and Indonesia (see Table 7 in the Statistical Annex).

Source: UNESCO Institute for Statistics, based on Ethnologue data (SIL International), 2005.

Given that translation plays an important role in the promotion of cultural diversity, there is a case for the development of a translation policy on a global scale, with an emphasis where possible on reciprocity

being Japanese (0.67 percent), Arabic (0.54 percent), Hebrew (0.46 percent) and Chinese (0.4 percent). Seventy-five percent of all published books are translated from only three languages: English, French and German.

As for target-language translations, some 20 languages account for 90 percent of all registered translations. The breakdown is as follows: German (15.27 percent), Spanish (11.41 percent) and French (10.86 percent) lead the way, followed by English (6.45 percent), Japanese (6.14 percent), Dutch (5.83 percent), Portuguese (4.10 percent), Russian (3.63 percent), Polish (3.52 percent) and Italian (3.41 percent), with the next 10 languages somewhere between 1 and 3 percent:

Figure 3.1 Percentage of target-language translations

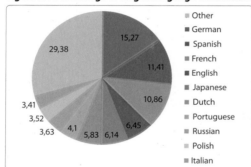

Legend: Other, German, Spanish, French, English, Japanese, Dutch, Portuguese, Russian, Polish, Italian

Values shown: 29,38 · 15,27 · 11,41 · 10,86 · 6,45 · 6,14 · 5,83 · 4,1 · 3,63 · 3,52 · 3,41

Source: Brisset, 2007.

Again, most are European languages. The hierarchy between majority and minority languages determines translation flows; translations into or from indigenous populations hardly exist.

Economic integration worldwide has spurred the development of technical and audiovisual translations linked to product development and services for multilingual markets, especially in the fields of software development, multimedia, the Internet, film and video games. While there is a decline in the less profitable enterprise of literary translation, technical translation in the most industrialized countries is estimated to be increasing at a rate of 25–30 percent per annum. The fields in greatest demand include aerospace science, biotechnology and pharmaceutical products, energy

(petrol, natural gas, hydroelectricity, nuclear power and renewable energies), transport and ICTs. The banking and finance sector and the commercial services sector (marketing, advertising and Internet sites) are also large consumers of translation. Since 80 percent of localization activities concern software produced in the United States, English is the predominant language source of multimedia translations. The target languages are mainly Asian, with 40 percent of US software being sold in the Asia-Pacific region, where Japanese is the main target translation language together with Chinese and Korean (Gamas and Knowlden, 1999).

The global expansion of the audiovisual industry, with increasingly diversified products and marketing strategies, has entailed the application of new translation parameters. Screen translation methods differ widely from country to country: subtitling reigns in Scandinavian and Dutch-speaking countries, as well as in most Western European speech communities with less than 25 million speakers. This is not the case, however, in Spain, Italy and German-speaking regions, where subtitling tends to be less used. Given that many subtitling tracks are commercialized together on the same DVD and can be accessed by anyone anywhere, the tendency is to use the same conventions in all languages, even though in some cases they might be at odds with domestic

⤴ *J.K. Rowling's Harry Potter books in Italian, German, Spanish, Catalan and Czech translations*

practice. This relatively new development raises questions about the balance among languages and cultures in the audiovisual world, since not only are the vast majority of programmes and films produced in English, but their translations are also being done and decided in the country of origin (see chapter 5). Generally speaking, anglophone media products carry about the same weight as national products in nearly all countries, in terms of both penetration and prestige, and English continues to be regarded as the lingua franca of the media world.

With the progress in computer technology, automatic translation systems (involving little or no human intervention) and computer-assisted translation (employing various forms of integrated or non-integrated software for different operations, such as terminological management, documentary research or pre-translation) are becoming increasingly sophisticated and widespread. Wholly or partially automated procedures make it possible to increase the volume of texts translated and, above all, to translate a larger number of languages at lower cost. Automatic translations have an identifying function, and enable administrators to grasp content immediately, particularly useful in the case of internal documents with a very limited effective lifespan.[7] Mostly developed for use by large public or private corporations, these systems enable hundreds of thousands of pages to be translated into several dozen languages simultaneously. This is the case in particular with the European Commission where automatic

translation, introduced in 1970, enables documents to be translated into 28 language pairs, to which will eventually be added 11 other languages corresponding to the new Member Countries. In 2005, the volume of translations produced automatically in EU bodies amounted to over 860,000 pages.

However, languages for which automatic translation systems have been developed remain very few in number. They typically correspond to the languages that are most translated or those into which most translation takes place (English, French, German, Portuguese, Italian and Spanish). Japanese and Korean also boast powerful systems for translation from or into English, but this is not yet the case for Chinese. Other systems also exist for the combinations Laotian-French, Thai-English/German and French/English-Vietnamese. In India, research on automatic translation is very active. Systems exist for translating between the country's main languages and from these languages into English and vice versa. One of these systems is used to translate official documents automatically from Hindi into English. Apart from one or two systems, African languages remain relatively ignored. Automatic translation systems for some Amerindian languages (Aymara, Huao, Inpiaq, Mapudungun, Quechua, Siona) have been developed under Carnegie Mellon University's AVENUE project or financed by the Organization of American States (OAS). The dearth of automatic translation systems for minority languages reflects the difficulty of devising

---

| Box 3.4 | **Minority indigenous languages in translation in South America** |

A case study conducted from 1979 to 2001 on international translations between Spanish/Portuguese and the indigenous languages of Argentina, Brazil, Chile, Guatemala and Peru showed that these were — in most cases — almost non-existent: Argentina registered 4 internal translations, Chile registered 3, and Brazil 11. Judging from the available data, neither the creation of MERCOSUR in 1991 nor that of the Community of Andean Nations (CAN) in 1989 seem to have had

an impact on translation flows from or to indigenous languages in these countries.

Things were quite different in the cases of Peru and Guatemala, however. Peru registered a total of 77 internal translations from and into aboriginal languages, almost all published after 1993 when the Peruvian Constitution officially recognized indigenous languages — primarily Quechua and Aymara, the most widely spoken.

In Guatemala, even with Spanish as the only official language and despite a total number of 28 intranslations in the Index, 22 internal translations were conducted for indigenous languages. In proportion with the number of intranslations, the number of internal translations is quite significant, and most probably related to the fact that 43 percent of Guatemala's population is Mayan.

Source: Brisset, 2007.

---

7. Directorate General for Translation (DGC): ‹http://www.ec.europa.eu/dgs/translation/index_en.htm›; Commission européenne (EC): http://www.ec.europa.eu/index_en.htm. See the study undertaken by Drugan (2008) on the use of automatic translation tools in the framework of an expanded European Union in 2004. For their application in private enterprise, see Austermühl (2001).

systems that are effective for pairs of languages with very different structures. Automatic translation between two languages requires, first of all, that they be codified and that a sufficient volume of texts exists in the two languages. Among the innovative organizations that are making strides towards reducing the divide in assisted translation, noteworthy is Translation.org.za, an NGO

○ *Advertisement in the streets of Hangzhou, China*

created to develop hardware and software able to process South Africa's 11 official languages.

Alongside automatic translation where human intervention is non-existent or limited, computer tools have been developed to enable translators to translate more quickly and reliably. They include pre-translation systems, such as the *MultiTrans* system employed at UNESCO, which exploit language pairings among large corpora of translated texts, and a wide variety of terminology data banks, such as UNTERM and UNESCOTERM within the United Nations system, IATE in the European Union, and Canadian Translation Bureau's *Termium*. The development of linguistically inclusive automatic translation services — as is pursued, for example, by UNESCO's Initiative B@bel programme — has become particularly important for the purpose of reducing the disparities between languages and narrowing the information and knowledge divides (and not simply the digital divide) between human groups.

As migration flows have intensified with globalization, they have significantly modified the ethno-linguistic makeup of a number of countries and have created new linguistic and translation needs, especially in administrative, legal and medical circuits worldwide. In the United States, for example, the translation profession has skyrocketed with the demographic evolution of the country, where, at the end of the 1990s, one citizen in ten was of foreign origin and 14 percent of residents spoke a language other than English. In 2000, the US Congress passed *An Act Requiring Competent Interpreter Services in the Delivery of Certain Acute Health Care Services* to ensure that American clinics and hospitals act in a legally responsible manner towards non-English-speaking patients, an act based on the 1964 civil-rights law that prohibits any discrimination based on race or country of origin (of which language is a defining trait according to recent jurisprudence). Thus, public medical or hospital services are required to ensure competent interpretation services, 24 hours per day, 7 days per week, in any given language (by phone or teleconference if needed), including sign languages, under the *Americans with Disabilities Act* of 1990.

The importance of translation, including its socio-economic repercussions, is often neglected.

Where translation policies are integrated in linguistic policies, they usually relate to specific historical circumstances in a particular country. Thus Paraguay's return to democracy was accompanied by a new constitution, which guaranteed linguistic equality between Spanish and Guarani; while post-Apartheid South Africa promotes its nine most spoken languages, in addition to English and Afrikaans. In most other cases, translation and interpretation provision, including training, is often left to private initiatives or associations, without sufficient regard, for example, to socio-cultural makeup, communications development, globalization of trade, or migration flows.

Given that translation plays an important role in the promotion of cultural diversity, there is a case for the development of a translation policy on a global scale, with an emphasis where possible on *reciprocity*. Translating and disseminating works from unfamiliar or endangered cultures is precisely the aim of the *Words Without Borders* movement and of the literary translators, authors and publishers signatory to the *Manifesto on Behalf of Cultural Diversity from Literary Translators, Publishers and Writers* sponsored by the International Federation of Translators (2002). In the field of international cooperation, several projects have been initiated to enhance the promotion of indigenous languages in translation, including the 1998 cooperation agreement between the Ministry of Culture of the Basque Government (Spain) and Chile's National Corporation for Indigenous Development (CONADI), which seeks to promote aboriginal languages and design language policies.

Given that effective language policy and planning must respond to local situations, there is a need to foster discussion forums and encourage alliances across language-interest communities in support of multilingualism and cultural diversity. Effective language policy and planning require processes of deliberation, negotiation, problem-definition and the participation of all stakeholders, backed by specialist expertise (see 'In focus' below). Data to inform policy-making in deliberative processes is crucial for the identification of alternative approaches, the establishment of reliable evaluation and monitoring procedures, and the assessment of likely costs and consequences.

Conclusion

Languages are a critical marker of the vitality of cultural diversity, for they are — above and beyond tools of communication — the prism through which individuals and communities apprehend and give meaning to their relationships and environment. From this perspective, any form of linguistic decline has to be taken as a sign of cultural impoverishment, and the disappearance of any language as an irreplaceable loss for the common cultural heritage of humankind.

While globalization, characterized by the dominance of a few so-called international languages over the rest, may indeed be negatively impacting on the vitality of smaller languages of more restricted currency, paradoxically the extension of digital networks has sometimes helped to revive dying or dead languages. In reality, language decline is the consequence of a language's political, social, administrative and cultural status. Thus, while Icelandic, which is the mother tongue of 350,000 people, is threatened neither by English nor by a lack of inter-generational transmission, Pulaar (also called Fulfulde) spoken by four times as many people throughout Africa, is threatened in these ways.

The demand that all languages be treated equally is a call for recognition of the dignity of all individuals, irrespective of their language. In many parts of the world, people are speaking up on behalf of endangered mother tongues or the reconstitution of languages (e.g. Amerindian languages) that died out over half a century ago. This is a significant trend, which is linked to the phenomenon of multiple identities, since individuals now find fulfilment in their diversity and not only in their singularity.

Multilingualism (understood as the ability to master several languages) has today become necessary for knowing where one comes from (one's mother tongue) and for knowing others (national or vernacular languages and international languages); it is a fundamental means of receptiveness to others and a constituent of intercultural skills. Translation, for its part, permits access to other systems of thought and the discoveries born of them. Equally important as a tool of dialogue, it serves as a bridge between different languages.

The demand that all languages be treated equally is a call for the recognition of the dignity of all individuals... Multilingualism has today become necessary for knowing where one comes from and for knowing others

Chapter 3
Languages

 *Boy selling newspapers in Costa Rica*

Chapter 3 Recommendations

National language policies should be implemented with a view to safeguarding linguistic diversity and promoting multilingual competencies.

To this end, action should be taken to:

a. Facilitate language use through appropriate measures, be they educational, editorial, administrative or other.

b. Make provision — as appropriate — for the learning, alongside mother tongues, of a national and an international language.

c. Encourage the translation, by all possible means, of written and audiovisual materials in order to promote the international circulation of ideas and artistic works, including through the use of new technologies.

d. Develop reliable and internationally comparable indicators for assessing the impact of language policies on linguistic diversity, and promote good practices in this regard.

The key facets of language planning and policy-making

Attempts to direct and influence the forms and uses of languages are probably as old as language itself. Whether overt or implicit within educational systems, social organization, cultural norms, economic relations, etc., language planning has historically aimed at changes both *within* and *across* languages in relation to the communication patterns of a community. The social transformations of the last decades of the 20th century began altering language policy and planning beyond the formation and strengthening of States. Economics, social and human sciences and digital communication increasingly began to impact on language policies and planning.

But different States face different linguistic challenges. In East Asia, multiple script literacies and bi- or trilingualism have long been an issue (Gottleib and Chen, 2001), as is illustrated by China, whose linguistic diversity today involves some 55 formally recognized sub-national communities, representing 80–120 languages and more than 106 million people, among whom there is even greater diversity. Since 1954, mainland China's national official institution for language, renamed the State Language and Script Commission (*Guojia Yuyan Wenzi Gongzuo Weiyuanhui*) in 1986, has been actively dealing with script and writing reform (Rohsenow, 2004). In the Republic of Korea, standardization was the central issue, for reasons related to economic development (Gottleib and Chen, 2001; Song, 2001). In Latin America, the coexistence of European languages with indigenous languages posed a considerable challenge. Paraguay, with close to 90 percent of the non-indigenous population speaking the indigenous language Guaraní, offers the unprecedented example of an indigenous language that participates in national public life in the sense that it is being widely learned. In the Arab States, translation has become an important issue.

Language policy is linked to governance, the distribution of resources and therefore vested interests, but it proceeds most efficiently when it is decided and implemented on the basis of informed public debate. Thus, language policies in support of multilingualism and plurilingualism[8] are not protocols or formulae, but matters of governance to be deliberated, and accompanied by legislative and regulatory texts.

Through public texts (e.g. laws, regulations), public discourse (e.g. statements, debate and public attitudes accompanying the latter), actions (by prominent individuals or institutions) and facilitated deliberations (combining experts, concerned populations and interested authorities), debate takes place around language policy-making. They reflect the dynamic character of policy formulation, its enactment and implications, with respect to a number of key facets, including the status of languages, aspects of their corpus, aspects of learning and acquisition, the usage of languages, the esteem or prestige attached to languages, and the discourse and attitudes that surround given languages.

The status of languages

The formal status of a language is its legal standing and public functions as envisaged by the constitutional arrangements in particular countries. That status is typically ascribed via public texts, such as constitutional provisions, and is upheld within the realm of sovereignty of State authorities. However, sub-national groupings, such as regions or provinces operating under autonomy statutes, can modify, elaborate or even contradict public texts and laws issued by authorities with overlapping sovereignty. Supranational groupings, such as the European Union and the Council of Europe, can also attribute and formalize status to languages. This occurred in 1992 with the *European Charter of Regional and Minority Languages* (ECRML; Council of Europe, 1992). The Association of South East Asian Nations (ASEAN) has designated English as its sole operating language, but this is a jurisdictional rather than a sovereign sphere of activity and applies only to the ASEAN's operating arrangements. The African Union, when it was still known as the Organization of African States, issued a Language Plan, but the Organization's lack of both sovereignty and jurisdiction made it impossible to implement the Plan.

Many countries have both exclusive sovereignty and jurisdiction and include statements in their national constitutions about national or official language(s), thereby also determining the status of other languages. This legal recognition can be very simple, such as the formal nomination of the designated official language, or more elaborate, specifying roles of languages or prescribing functions and jurisdictional domains within which they can

---

8. The Council of Europe distinguishes between *multilingualism* as a characteristic of societies, and *plurilingualism* as a characteristic of individuals.

operate. For instance, South Africa's Constitution recognizes 11 languages: Afrikaans, English, Ndebele, Northern Sotho, Southern Sotho, Swati, Tsonga, Tswana, Venda, Xhosa and Zulu. Australia's Constitution, on the other hand, makes no mention of an official language. Ethiopia's constitutional provisions are closely tied to a transfer of administrative authority, and therefore jurisdiction, to a range of numbered *kilil*, which are in turn mostly language-based and have considerable language autonomy.

Each country makes use of the legal provisions available to it to organize the national linguistic resources under the sovereignty and the administrative scope provided or limited by its constitution. Canada, for example, recognizes two official languages and declares their equality across the country; thus, although English is economically and socially dominant, English and French enjoy equal legal status. However, a series of laws in the Province of Quebec has modified the application of this legal equality in some of the Province's domains of jurisdiction, such as immigrant selection, public signage and education. India's Constitution recognizes Hindi and English as official national languages, but takes account of 13 more languages in somes states and additionally recognizes a large number of minority languages for sub-national, regional or other jurisdictionally defined functions.

In Europe, where language planning has classically been a state enterprise aimed at national unity through communication in a single, standardized, written language (Lo Bianco, 2005), the emergence of international organizations, such as the Council of Europe and the European Union, has recently enabled support to be given to minority languages that had previously been neglected in the process of nationalistic language planning.

The corpus of a language

The activity of corpus planning involves modifications in a language's internal meaning-making resources. This can include devising an orthographic system for a language that lacks a writing system, or modifying an existing orthography. Extensions to the terminological range of languages, including standardizing translation, codifying expression, and disseminating the use and adoption of new norms, are part of the corpus planning activity. The work of linguists to develop writing systems for indigenous languages or to develop terminology and expressions for both indigenous and national languages is ongoing. Dictionary writing

and prestige literature also impact on the corpus of a language, as do social movements. Major changes in English expression since the 1970s have resulted, for example, from the success of feminists who have argued for the removal of masculine orientations in English, in both written and spoken expression. A major objective of corpus planning for small indigenous languages has been to enhance the prospects of intergenerational language maintenance or to reverse language shift (Fishman, 2001) in order to ensure that public education, or secondary socialization, can support intra-family language transfers.

Language learning and the acquisition of literacy

This occurs within the remit of public education institutions and is consequently dependent on jurisdictional authority. Often action occurs at the level of local curriculum implementation rather than in overarching policies issued to promote language acquisition or the expansion of literacy. A variety of agents undertakes actions to facilitate learning of new, additional or extended language skills or literacy, actions that involve interaction among experts, researchers, curriculum writers, assessment agencies, credentializing authorities and learners and their families. As far as literacy is concerned, NGOs have been extremely active in developing countries, as have the aid and assistance programmes of international organizations. Since the early 1990s and the emergence of human capital theories of education, developed countries have focused on increasing standards and levels of literacy in the belief that the more competitive economies are those that invest in strengthening their workforce's human capital skills. Human rights thinking, as well as improvements in health, rural development and social progress (particularly for marginalized populations, the poor and rural women), has animated the majority of literacy campaigns in developing countries.

Foreign language teaching — typically within the exclusive jurisdiction of education ministries but sometimes given prominence in national language policies — also belongs in this category of actions. Historically, there have been several strands or types of foreign language teaching policy, which have reflected social hierarchies, positions and interests. Social elites have favoured the acquisition of prestige languages, especially the languages of admired cultural or intellectual traditions. Human capital and economics planning authorities, as well as national security agencies, have favoured the acquisition of languages of strategic importance for trade, diplomatic, security or foreign relations.

Chapter 3
Languages

Religious-oriented curricula, or movements, have favoured the acquisition of literacy, less often of spoken skills, in languages of sacred texts and associated with the canon of belief at the heart of the particular religious tradition.

The domains and usage of a language

More recently, actions taken to extend the settings and domains in which a language is spoken have proved to make that language stronger and longer lasting. An example is the work of the Welsh Language Board in Wales, which has had considerable success in revitalizing a language that had been seriously endangered. Through child-rearing practices and early socialization (i.e. primary schooling) in Welsh, more young children are being raised speaking the language. Usage planning depends on significant individuals behaving linguistically in supportive ways. Sustaining the desirability and encouraging positive identification with the marked language through appropriate actions are crucial to the success of this kind of language policy and planning. Usage planning requires integrated action to modify communication practices — across businesses, broadcast and publicity industries, employment practices and sporting and recreational activities — to create naturalized spaces for the use of the target language. Usage planning in the Spanish region of Catalonia has also been successful; one instance involved shopkeepers who cooperated in a campaign to encourage consumers (particularly young people) to prefer interaction in Catalan in daily life and thereby extend the perceived utility of the language. As a result, today Catalan is a more vibrant language than it was a few decades ago.

The prestige and esteem of a language

This refers to how social prestige affects the reputation of a language. Historically speaking, the esteem associated with important works of literature has been conferred onto the languages in which they have been produced. Language dialects have in the same way gained status over time through the work of authoritative poets, novelists or scientists. Official academies support literature in the national language, especially if it is a language that has been suppressed in the past. However, increasingly today other forms of expression, beyond literature — alternative modes of speech, music and performance genres of all kinds and multi-modal digital communications — are finding their way towards esteem and recognition through their importance in community and identity creation.

Discourses and attitudes

These depend mostly on spheres of influence and action and have little to do with jurisdiction or sovereignty. Discourse planning has a range of meanings, which include training people to develop persuasive ways to express themselves so that they can participate in society and accomplish their goals by effective use of written or oral communication.

Action to support multilingualism in language policy and planning will require making use of arguments that are able to persuade diverse audiences. To promote multilingualism in the interest of traditional languages, and at the sub-national, intra-national and extra-national levels, language planners will have to persuade public administrators, education officials, government agents and other stakeholders that it is in their national interest to develop a comprehensive national policy. This is best achieved by focusing on the practical communication problems that societies face and providing evidence that comprehensive language planning can aid in solving communication problems. In this connection, a recent, innovative project by the European Centre for Modern Languages called *Valuing All Languages in Europe* (or VALEUR) is instructive. This project sought to support plurilingualism. In response to the proliferation of community languages, it mapped the provision and needs of young European users of these languages between 2004 and 2007). While provision was found to vary greatly, examples of good practices were identified, and, overall, bilingual and trilingual provision is on the rise.

The cultural space of the Sosso-Bala, Guinea

References and websites

Background documents and UNESCO sources

Brisset, A. 2007. World translation flows and practices. Background paper.

Lo Bianco, J. 2007. The importance of language policies and multilingualism for cultural diversity. Background paper.

Paolillo, J. 2005. Language diversity on the internet: Examining linguistic bias. UNESCO Institute for Statistics (ed.), *Measuring Linguistic Diversity on the Internet*. Paris, UNESCO, pp. 43–89. http://www.uis.unesco.org/template/pdf/cscl/MeasuringLinguisticDiversity_En.pdf

Paolillo, J. and Das, A. 2006. *Evaluating Language Statistics: The Ethnologue and Beyond*. A report prepared for the UNESCO Institute for Statistics. 31 March. http://indiana.academia.edu/documents/0009/2975/UNESCO_report_Paolillo_Das.pdf

Romaine, S. 2007. Languages and cultural identities. Background paper.

UNESCO. 2007a. *Advocacy Kit for Promoting Multilingual Education: Including the Excluded*. Bangkok: UNESCO Bangkok. http://www2.unescobkk.org/elib/publications/110/Advocacy_kit.pdf

—. 2007b. *Mother Tongue-based Literacy Programmes: Case Studies of Good Practice in Asia*. Bangkok: UNESCO Bangkok. http://www2.unescobkk.org/elib/publications/113/mother-tonque-based.pdf

—. 2005. *First Language First: Community-based Literacy Programmes for Minority Language Contexts in Asia*. Bangkok: UNESCO Bangkok. http://www2.unescobkk.org/elib/publications/first_language/first_language.pdf

—. 2004. *Manual for Developing Literacy and Adult Education Programmes in Minority Language Communities*. Bangkok: UNESCO Bangkok. http://unesdoc.unesco.org/images/0013/001351/135164e.pdf

—. 2003a. *Education in a Multilingual World*. UNESCO Education position paper. Paris, UNESCO. http://unesdoc.unesco.org/images/0012/001297/129728e.pdf

—. 2003b. *Recommendation on the Promotion and Use of Multilingualism and Universal Access to Cyberspace*. 15 October. http://portal.unesco.org/ci/en/files/13475/10697584791Recommendation-Eng.pdf/Recommendation-Eng.pdf

—. 2001. *Universal Declaration on Cultural Diversity*. Paris, UNESCO. http://unesdoc.unesco.org/images/0012/001271/127160m.pdf

—. 1996. *Universal Declaration on Linguistic Rights*. Barcelona, Spain, 6 June. http://www.unesco.org/most/lnngo11.htm

—. 1994. *Red Book of Languages in Danger of Disappearing*. http://portal.unesco.org/ci/en/ev.php-URL_ID=16721&URL_DO=DO_TOPIC&URL_SECTION=201.html

UNESCO Ad Hoc Expert Group on Endangered Language. 2003a. *Language Vitality and Endangerment*. Document submitted to the 'International Expert Meeting on UNESCO Programme Safeguarding of Endangered Languages', Paris, 10–12 March. http://www.unesco.org/culture/ich/doc/src/00120-EN.pdf

UNESCO Ad Hoc Expert Group on Endangered Language. 2003b. *UNESCO Survey: Linguistic Vitality and Diversity*. Paris. http://www.eva.mpg.de/lingua/tools-at-lingboard/pdf/Unesco_Vitality_Diversity_%20Questionnaire1.pdf

Websites

'International Doman Name', Wikipedia: http://en.wikipedia.org/wiki/Internationalized_domain_name

2010 Biodiversity Target: http://www.cbd.int/2010-target

AVENUE (Language Technologies Institute, Carnegie Mellon University): http://www.cs.cmu.edu/~avenue

Community of Andean Nations (CAN): http://www.comunidadandina.org/endex.htm

Convention on Biological Diversity (CBD): http://www.cbd.int and http://www.cbd.int/doc/legal/cbd-un-en.pdf

Council of Europe. 1992. European Charter for Regional and Minority Languages (ECRML). 5 November. Strasbourg: Council of Europe. http://conventions.coe.int/treaty/en/Treaties/Html/148.htm

Directorate General for Translation (DGC): http://www.ec.europa.eu/dgs/translation/index_en.htm

Ethnologue: Languages of the World: http://www.ethnologue.com/web.asp

Global Reach: http://web.archive.org/web/20041020045128/global-reach.biz

IATE (Inter-Active Terminology for Europe): http://iate.europa.eu

Index of Biocultural Diversity (IBCD): http://www.terralingua.org/projects/ibcd/ibcd.html

Initiative B@bel: http://portal.unesco.org/ci/en/ev.php-URL_ID=16540&URL_DO=DO_TOPIC&URL_SECTION=201.html

International Clearing House for Endangered Languages: http://www.tooyoo.l.u-tokyo.ac.jp/archive/ichel/ichel.html

International Telecommunication Union (ITU): http://www.itu.int

Internet World Stats: http://www.internetworldstats.com

Linguasphere Observatory Register: http://www.linguasphere.com

MERCOSUR: http://www.mercosur.int

Multilingualism in Cyberspace: http://portal.unesco.org/ci/en/ev.php-URL_ID=16539&URL_DO=DO_TOPIC&URL_SECTION=201.html

Online Computer Library Center (OCLC): http://www.oclc.org

Organization of American States (OAS): http://www.oas.org

Recent Experiences on Measuring Languages in Cyberspace (2007): http://portal.unesco.org/ci/en/ev.php-URL_ID=23943&URL_DO=DO_TOPIC&URL_SECTION=201.html

Statistics Canada: http://www.statcan.gc.ca

Termium: http://www.termiumplus.gc.ca

Chapter 3
Languages

Translate.org.za: http://translate.org.za

UNESCO case studies featuring multilingual education in Papua New Guinea, Mali and Peru, see Bühmann and Trudell (2008); in India, see URL_ID=41355&URL_DO=DO_TOPIC&URL_SECTION=201.html; in Africa, see the 2005 ADEA study http://www.adeanet.org/adeaPortal; for Asia, the collected papers of the 2003 and 2008 major Conferences on Language Development, Language Revitalization and Multilingual Education at http://www.sil.org/asia/ldc/plenary_presentations.html and http://www.seameo.org/_ld2008/document.html

UNESCO Interactive Atlas of the World's Languages in Danger: http://www.unesco.org/culture/ich/index.php?pg=00206

UNESCO MOST Clearing House on Linguistic Rights: http://www.unesco.org/most/ln1.htm

UNESCO, Endangered Languages: Linguistic diversity in relation to biodiversity: http://www.unesco.org/culture/ich/index.php?pg=00144

Unicode: http://www.unicode.org/standard/WhatIsUnicode.html

United Nations Declaration on the Rights of Indigenous Peoples, 13 September 2007: http://www.un.org/esa/socdev/unpfii/en/drip.html

United Nations International Year of Languages (2008): http://www.un.org/events/iyl

UNTERM: http://unterm.un.org

VALEUR (Valuing All Languages in Europe): http://www.ecml.at/mtp2/Valeur/html/Valeur_E_Results.htm

Welsh Language Board: http://www.byig-wlb.org.uk

World Summit on the Information Society (WSIS): http://www.itu.int/wsis

References

Amery, R. 2000. *Warrabarna Kaurna! Reclaiming an Australian Language*. Lisse: Swets & Zeitlinger.

Austin, P. 2008. Comment les linguistes et les communautés autochtones documentent et revitalisent les langues en danger. Chirac Foundation Conference, Musee du quai Branly, Paris, 9 June. A video of the talk may be viewed at: http://www.fondationchirac.eu/videos-discours-peter-austin

Austermühl, F. 2001. *Electronic Tools for Translators*. (Translation Practices Explained 2.) Manchester, St. Jerome.

Baldwin, D. 2003. *Miami Language Reclamation: From Ground Zero*. Minneapolis, Minn., Center for Writing, University of Minnesota. http://writing.umn.edu/docs/speakerseries_pubs/baldwin.pdf

Beacco, J.-C. 2007. *From Linguistic Diversity to Plurilingual Education: Guide for the Development of Language Education Policies in Europe*. Main version. Strasbourg, Language Policy Division, Council of Europe. http://www.coe.int/T/DG4/Linguistic/Source/Guide_Main_Beacco2007_EN.doc

Benveniste, E. 1966. Catégories de langue et catégories de pensée. *Problèmes de linguistique générale*. Paris, Gallimard.

Bühmann, D. and Trudell, B. 2008. *Mother Tongue Matters: Local Language as a Key to Effective Learning*. Paris, UNESCO. http://unesdoc.unesco.org/images/0016/001611/161121e.pdf

Brown, Keith (ed.). 2005. *Encyclopaedia of Language and Linguistics*. 2nd ed. Amsterdam, Elsevier.

Chaudenson, R. 2001. *Creolization of Language and Culture*. London, Routlege.

Clyne, M. 2005. *Australia's Language Potential*. Sydney, University of New South Wales Press.

Convention on Biological Diveristy (CBD). 2005. *Handbook of the Convention on Biological Diversity Including its Cartagena Protocol on Biosafety*. 3rd ed. Montreal, CBD. http://www.cbd.int/doc/handbook/cbd-hb-all-en.pdf

Council of Europe. 1992. *European Charter for Regional and Minority Languages* (ECRML). 5 November. Strasbourg: Council of Europe. http://conventions.coe.int/treaty/en/Treaties/Html/148.htm (Accessed 21 July 2009.)

Crystal, D. 1997. *English as a Global Language*. Cambridge, Cambridge University Press. [2nd ed. 2003]

Crystal, D. 2000. *Language Death*. Cambridge, Cambridge University Press.

Diamond, J. 2001. Deaths of languages. *Natural History*, Vol. 110, No. 3, pp. 30–38.

Drugan, J. 2008. Intervention through computer-assisted translation: the case of the EU. J. Munday (ed.), Translation as Intervention. London, Continuum.

Eckkramer, E. M. 2003. On the perception of 'creole' language and identity in the Netherlands Antilles. G. Collier and U. Fleischmann (eds.), *A Pepper-Pot of Cultures: Aspects of Creolization in the Caribbean*. Amsterdam, Rodopi.

Fail, H., Thompson, J. and Walker, G. 2004. Belonging, identity and Third Culture Kids: life histories of former international school students. *Journal of Research in International Education*, Vol. 3, No. 3, pp. 319–38.

Fettes, M. 1997. Stabilizing what? An ecological approach to language renewal. J. Reyhner (ed.), *Teaching Indigenous Languages*. Flagstaff, Ariz.: Northern Arizona University, pp. 301–18. http://jan.ucc.nau.edu/~jar/TIL_25.html

Fishman, J. A. 1991. *Reversing Language Shift: Theoretical and Empirical Foundations of Assistance to Threatened Languages*. Bristol, UK, Multilingual Matters.

Fishman, J. A. (ed.). 2001. *Can Threatened Languages Be Saved? Reversing Language Shift, Revisited: A 21st Century Perspective*. Bristol, UK, Multilingual Matters.

Gamas, G. and Knowlden, B. 1999. *L'industrie canadienne de la traduction. Stratégie de développement des ressources humaines et d'exportation*. Rapport final. Ottawa, Comité sectoriel de l'industrie canadienne de la traduction. http://www.uottawa.ca/associations/csict/stratf.pdf

García, O., Skutnabb-Kangas, T. and Torres Guzmán, M. (eds.). 2006. *Imagining Multilingual Schools: Language in Education and Glocalization*. Bristol, UK, Multilingual Matters.

Garza Cuarón, B. and Lastra, Y. 1991. Endangered languages in Mexico. R. H. Robins and E. M. Uhlenbeck (eds.), *Endangered Languages*. Oxford, Berg.

Giddens, A. 1999. *Runaway World: How Globalization is Reshaping Our Lives*. London, Profile.

Gordon, R. G. (ed.). 2005. *Ethnologue: Languages of the World*. 15th edn. Dallas, Tex.: SIL International. [16th edn. available at: http://www.ethnologue.com]

Gottleib, N. and Chen, P. (eds.). 2001. *Language Planning and Language Policy: East Asian Perspectives*. London, Curzon.

Graddol, D. 2006. *English Next*. London, The British Council. http://www.britishcouncil.org/learning-research-english-next.pdf

Grenoble, L. A. and Whaley, L. J. (eds.). 1998. *Endangered Languages: Language Loss and Community Response*. Cambridge, Cambridge University Press.

Grimes, J. E. 1995. Language endangerment in the Pacific. *Oceanic Linguistics*, Vol. 34, No. 1, pp. 1–12.

Grinevald, C. 2008. Comment penser la diversité linguistique: de quoi est-elle faite et pourquoi la préserver? Fondation Chirac, 9 June. http://www.fondationchirac.eu/discours-de-colette-grinevald

Grin, F. 2003. *Language Policy Evaluation and the European Charter for Regional and Minority Languages*. London, Palgrave MacMillan.

Haarmann, H. 2004. Evolution, language, and the construction of culture. F. M. Wuketits and C. Antweiler (eds.), *Handbook of Evolution: The Evolution of Human Societies and Cultures*. Weinheim, Wiley-VCH.

Loh, J. and Harmon, D. 2005. A global index of biocultural diversity. *Ecological Indicators*, Vol. 5, pp. 231–41. http://www.csin-rcid.ca/downloads/loh_harmon_ei.pdf (Accessed 21 July 2009.)

Harmon, D. and Loh, J. et al. 2008. Measuring and monitoring state and trends in biodiversity and culture. Background paper presented at the symposium 'Sustaining Cultural and Biological Diversity in a Rapidly Changing World: Lessons for Global Policy', American Museum of Natural History, New York City, 2–5 April. http://symposia.cbc.amnh.org/archives/biocultural/pdf-docs/measuring.pdf

Harmon, D. 1995. The status of the world's languages as reported in 'Ethnologue'. *Southwest Journal of Linguistics*, Vol. 14, No. 1–2, pp. 1–28.

Hinton, L. 1994. *Flutes of Fire: Essays on California Indian Languages*. Berkeley, Calif.: Heyday Books.

Information Sciences Institute. 2003. USC Researchers Build Machine Translation System — and More — for Hindi in Less than a Month. http://www.usc.edu/isinews/ stories/98.html

Internet Corporation for Assigned Names and Numbers (ICANN). 2001. ICANN Melbourne Meeting Topic: Introduction of Internationalized Domain Names. http://www.icann.org/en/meetings/melbourne/idn-topic.htm

International Federation of Translators (FIT). 2002. *Manifesto on Behalf of Cultural Diversity from Literary Translators, Publishers and Writers*. Montreal, FIT. http://www.alafrangaltd.com/mak6_manifesto.pdf

Public library in the Cuenca municipal building, Ecuador

International Society of Ethnobiology (ISE). 1988. *Declaration of Belem*. First International Congress of Ethnobiology. July. http://ise.arts.ubc.ca/_common/docs/DeclarationofBelem.pdf

Ito, M. et al. 2008. *Living and Learning with New Media: Summary of Findings from the Digital Youth Project*. John D. and Catherine T. MacArthur Foundation Reports on Digital Media and Learning, November. http://digitalyouth.ischool.berkeley.edu/files/report/digitalyouth-WhitePaper.pdf

Jiang, Q., Liu, Q., Quan, X. and Ma, C. 2007. EFL education in ethnic minority areas in Northwest China: an investigational study in Gansu Province. A. Feng (ed.), *Bilingual Education in China, Practices, Policies and Concepts*. Bristol, UK: Multilingual Matters.

Kachru, B. B. 2005. *Asian Englishes: Beyond the Canon*. Hong Kong: Hong Kong University Press.

Kachru, B. B. (ed.). 1992. *The Other Tongue: English across Cultures*. 2nd ed. Champaign, Ill., University of Illinois Press.

Kachru, B. B., Kachru, Y. and Nelson, C. (eds.). 2006. *Handbook of World Englishes*. Oxford, Wiley-Blackwell.

Kachru, Y. and Smith, L. E. 2008. *Cultures, Contexts, and World Englishes*. New York, Routledge.

Kinkade, M. D. 1991. The decline of native languages in Canada. R. H. Robins and E. M. Uhlenbeck (eds.), *Endangered Languages*. Oxford, Berg.

Kirkpatrick, A. 2007. *World Englishes: Implications for International Communication and English Language Teaching*. Cambridge, Cambridge University Press.

Krauss, M. 1992. The world's languages in crisis. *Language*, Vol. 68, No. 1, pp. 1–42.

Lavoie, B. F. and O'Neill, E. T. 2000. How 'world wide' is the web? Trends in the internationalization of web sites. *Annual Review of OCLC Research 1999*. http://worldcat.org:80/arcviewer/1/OCC/2003/03/18/0000002655/viewer/file40.html

Le Page, R. B. and Tabouret-Keller, A. 1985. *Acts of Identity: Creole-based Approaches to Language and Ethnicity*. Cambridge, Cambridge University Press.

Lo Bianco, J. 2005. Globalization and national communities of communication. *Language Problems and Language Planning*, Vol. 29, No. 2, pp 109–33.

—. 1987. *National Policy on Languages*. Canberra, Australian Government Publishing Service. http://www.multiculturalaustralia.edu.au/doc/lobianco_2.pdf

Maffi, L. and Skutnabb-Kangas, T. 1999. Language maintenance and revitalization. D. A. Posey (ed.), *Cultural and Spiritual Values of Biodiversity: A Complementary Contribution to the Global Biodiversity Assessment*. London, Intermediate Technology Publications for the United Nations Environment Programme (UNEP).

McArthur, T. 1998. *The English Languages*. 3rd ed. Cambridge, Cambridge University Press.

Miller, M. J. 2003. *The Age of Migration: International Population Movements in the Modern World*. 3rd ed. Basingstoke, Palgrave Macmillan.

Mühlhäusler, P. 1996. *Linguistic Ecology: Language Change and Linguistic Imperialism in the Pacific Region*. London, Routledge.

Nettle, D. 1999. *Linguistic Diversity*. Oxford, Oxford University Press.

Nettle, D. and Romaine, S. 2000. *Vanishing Voices: The Extinction of the World's Languages*. Oxford, Oxford University Press.

Norris, M. J. 1998. Canada's aboriginal languages. *Canadian Social Trends*, Winter, pp. 9–16.

Robins, R. H. and Uhlenbeck, E. M. (eds.). 1991. *Endangered Languages*. Oxford, Berg.

Rohsenow, J. S. 2004. Fifty years of script and written language reform in the P.R.C.: the Genesis of the Language Law of 2001. M. Zhou and H. Sun (eds.), *Language Policy in the People's Republic of China: Theory and Practice Since 1949*. Dordecht: Kluwer.

Romaine, S. 2005. Pidgins and Creoles. K. Brown (ed.), *Encyclopaedia of Language and Linguistic*. 2nd ed. Amsterdam, Elsevier. Vol. 9.

Ruiz, R. 1984. Orientations in language planning. *National Association for Bilingual Education Journal*, Vol. 8, No. 2, pp. 15–34.

Skutnabb-Kangas, T., Maffi, L. and Harmon, D. 2003. *Sharing a World of Difference: The Earth's Linguistic, Cultural and Biological Diversity*. Paris, UNESCO.

Song, J. J. 2001. North and South Korea: Language policies of divergence and convergence. N. Gottlieb and P. Chen (eds.), *Language Planning and Language Policy: East Asian Perspectives*. London, Curzon.

Toledo, V. M. 2001. Biocultural diversity and local power in Mexico: challenging globalization. L. Maffi (ed.), *On Biocultural Diversity: Linking Language, Knowledge, and the Environment*. Washington, D.C., Smithsonian Institution Press.

Tsui, A. B. M. 2007. Language policy and the social construction of identity. A. B. M. Tsui and J. W. Tollefson (eds.), *Language Policy, Culture, and Identity in Asian Contexts*. Mahwah, N.J.: Lawrence Erlbaum Associates.

United States Congress. 1990. *Americans with Disabilities Act*. http://www.ada.gov/archive/adastat91.htm

United Nations Development Programme (UNDP). 2004. *Human Development Report 2004: Cultural Liberty in Today's World*. New York, UNDP. http://hdr.undp.org/en/media/hdr04_complete.pdf

Venuti, L. 1995. *The Translator's Invisibility: A History of Translation*. London, Routledge.

Walsh, M. 2005. Will indigenous languages survive? *Annual Review of Anthropology*, Vol. 34, pp. 293–315.

Wolf, E. C., Mitchell, A. P. and Schoonmaker, P. K. 1995. *The Rain Forests of Home: An Atlas of People and Place. Part 1: Natural Forests and Native Languages of the Coastal Temperate Rain Forest*. Portland, Ore., and Washington, D.C.: Ecotrust, Pacific GIS, and Conservation International. http://www.ecotrust.org/publications/Rainforests_of_Home.pdf

Zepeda, O. and Hill, J. H. 1991. The condition of Native American languages in the United States. R. H. Robins and E. M. Uhlenbeck (eds.), *Endangered Languages*. Oxford, Berg.

A young indigenous girl in a classroom in High Orenoque, Venezuela

Education

Following decades of emphasis on educational standard-setting throughout the world, there is growing awareness of the linkages between cultural diversity and education, as well as of the importance of integrating the diversity of learners' needs and a diversity of methods and contents into educational practices. A major advance in international thinking on education was the recognition of its multiple layers, which consist of not only *knowledge* transmission but also *values* transmission, including social and cultural factors as they are bound up with experiences and memory, creativity and imagination (Faure et al., 1972; Delors et al., 1996). 'Lifelong learning', 'learning societies' and 'knowledge societies' are all notions that attempt to capture the cultural dimension of learning processes as they play themselves out within and between generations and across cultures.

Education is a fundamental human right to which *all* children and adults should have access, contributing as it does to individual freedom and empowerment, and to human development. For the past two decades, the international community has been committed to ensuring basic education and the advancement of the right to education for all, as stated in the 1990 *Jomtien Declaration* and reiterated in the 2000 *Dakar Framework for Action*, according to which Education for All (EFA) should be achieved by the year 2015. Cultural diversity can play a vital role in attaining this objective, especially in improving enrolment, retention and achievement and enhancing the nexus between formal, non-formal and informal educational frameworks.

With the advent of increasingly multicultural societies, educational systems are faced with new challenges that require the development of more flexible, appropriate and inclusive forms of education. Living together with our differences will involve the strengthening of multicultural education — for majority groups as well as for ethnic-linguistic minorities and indigenous and other vulnerable groups — so as to inculcate critical intercultural competencies and skills. This will be possible only to the extent that policies in the field of education seek to educate *through* and *for* diversity.

Class of a secondary school in Hanoi, Viet Nam

Education

4.1 The relevance of educational methods and contents.................................. **97**

Box 4.1 Data on educational curricula from UNESCO's International Bureau of Education......99

Figure 4.1 Type of language taught for selected countries, 2000 (In grades 1-6, In grades 7-8)....................................104

Box 4.2 The evolution of indigenous bilingual education in Latin America....................105

4.2 Learning societies and the right to education................................. **108**

Box 4.3 Education in Auroville, India....................109

4.3 Participatory learning and intercultural competencies............................. **114**

Box 4.4 Museums as a space for intercultural learning.......................................117

Conclusion..**118**

Recommendations.................................**118**

In focus: UNESCO's Guidelines on Intercultural Education....................................**119**

References and websites..................................**123**

A pupil at Ferdeusi school in Kabul, Afghanistan

4.1 The relevance of educational methods and contents

In 1990 the *World Declaration on Education for All* (EFA) — also known as the *Jomtien Declaration* (UNESCO, 1990) — adopted at the World Conference on Education for All in Jomtien, Thailand, emphasized the need to make education both universally available and more relevant, identifying 'quality' as a prerequisite for achieving the fundamental goal of equity. The discussion about quality was linked to the two primary objectives of education: to ensure the cognitive development of learners and to nurture their creative and emotional growth so that they are able to acquire the values and attitudes for responsible citizenship.

A decade later, the *Dakar Framework for Action* (UNESCO, 2000a) re-emphasized that quality lies 'at the heart of education' as a fundamental determinant of enrolment, retention and achievement, declaring access to quality education to be the right of every child. In 2005, the *EFA Global Monitoring Report* highlighted the role of quality education as a new approach to inclusive education and the achievement of EFA by 2015, expanding the definition of quality education to include 'the desirable characteristics of learners (healthy, motivated students), processes (competent teachers using active pedagogies), content (relevant curricula) and systems (good governance and equitable resource allocation).' Thus, it identified the need for more relevant education as one of the three key components of quality education, together with greater equity of access and outcome and proper observance of individual rights.

This new emphasis was prompted by the recognition that imported or inherited curricula were often considered, especially by developing countries, to be insufficiently sensitive to the local context and to learners' socio-cultural circumstances.[1] The emergent issue of indigenous education also contributed to this shift in educational strategies: the lack of relevance of mainstream approaches imported from Europe leant support to the local design of curriculum content, pedagogies and assessment, with increased participation of learners in defining their own educational strategies. Cultural diversity can be a powerful lever for ensuring the contextual relevance of educational methods and content, and it reminds us that education is never a culturally neutral process: teaching and classroom learning do not take place in a vacuum, in isolation from their social and cultural contexts, nor are facilitators (teachers) and learners free of specific cultural orientations. The goal must therefore be to become aware of and embrace cultural diversity and thereby to help learners to develop their capacities, which are themselves culturally rooted.

Thus, a curriculum based on the standardization of learning processes and contents — a 'one size fits all' approach — is not desirable, since it does not serve learners' needs in the context of their lives. Indeed, national models of school education, and the very notion of standardized learning processes, have sometimes created immense gaps between what pupils learn and what they live. Although inspired to some extent by the principle of universality, which prescribes equal educational opportunities for all, in practice such an approach results in unacceptably high

Children in class in Adwa, Ethiopia

---

1. See *Convention on the Rights of the Child*, Art. 29.1a, which stresses the importance of a child-centred approach to teaching and learning, which takes due account of the child's social, cultural, environmental and economic context.

*Cultural diversity
can be a powerful
lever for ensuring the
contextual relevance
of educational
methods and content
... it reminds us that
education is never
a culturally neutral
process*

levels of educational failure, particularly among pupils from deprived or disadvantaged backgrounds, for whom school education is seen as being disconnected from their own experiences and concerns.

In this sense, the core objectives of Education for All — ensuring quality basic education for all, especially in literacy, numeracy and essential life skills — cannot be realized without contextually adapted pedagogies, appropriate teacher training and diversified support mechanisms, nor can they be realized without the contributions of diverse stakeholders, including civil society and the private sector, to lifelong learning. This is becoming increasingly obvious to a growing number of countries which are seeking alternative pathways within formal educational systems and 'planning for cultural diversity' (Inglis, 2008). The adoption in January 2006 of the *Charter for African Cultural Renaissance* by the member states of the African Union expresses this point in its proclamation that 'it is imperative to edify educational systems which embody the African and universal values, so as to ensure the rooting of youth in African culture, their exposure to the values of other civilizations, and mobilize the social forces in the context of a sustainable, endogenous participatory development (Preamble).

Curriculum development and inclusive education

Schooling plays an instrumental role in helping individuals to achieve their own economic, social and cultural objectives and in helping to ensure social cohesion and strong governance. These intrinsic social benefits are highly dependent on the quality of the teaching-learning process. How well students are taught and what they learn have a crucial impact on the value and the duration of their schooling. As explained in the *EFA Global Monitoring Report 2005*, while there is no general theory as to how to improve learning outcomes, 'many approaches in the economic tradition have assumed there is a workable analogy between schools and industrial production, in the sense that a set of inputs to schooling is transformed by teachers and pupils into a set of products, or outputs, in a fairly uniform way.' Regardless of the approach used, it has to take due account of the cultural dimensions of the learning process.

Sensitivity to cultural diversity encourages us to reflect on the *content* and *methods* of educational systems.

Since its creation, UNESCO has given major importance to the issue of textbooks, based on its 'Model Plan for the Analysis and Improvement of Textbooks and Teaching Materials as Aids to International Understanding' (1949). Indeed, both the content and the design of textbooks are key factors in supporting learning processes that are relevant, engaging and responsive to multiple intelligences and learning styles. Among the most recent achievements in this area, the production of the *Comprehensive Strategy for Textbooks and Other Learning Materials* (2005) aims at responding to the needs of a changing world by adopting a rights-based approach to guide programmatic work in the areas of policy development, quality enhancement and availability. However, little information is available about the kinds of education people are actually receiving across the globe and how education differs across (and sometimes within) countries. Apart from certain data on literacy and on enrolment and recruitment within educational systems (see Table 9 in the Statistical Annex), available data on curricula is incomplete and restricted to tabulation of the number of hours devoted to the main school disciplines, by age-group, within the different national systems (see Box 4.1 and Table 10 in the Statistical Annex). Broader inquiries into learning content and methods, informed by local, regional and global perspectives, are needed.

While the field of curriculum studies is still 'strongly rooted in the notion that educational contents reflect national policies and dominant cultural priorities, and are almost exclusively informed by shifting national interests and stakeholder pressure' (Benavot and Braslavsky, 2007), national models of school education are facing a number of challenges, including the need to:

1. adjust learning processes, curriculum content and school management to both the learner's circumstances (local culture, ways of life and local languages) and the opportunities related to instrumental knowledge and professional qualifications at local scales, in cities or abroad;

2. stress democratic citizenship and respect for human rights (including cultural rights) as the overarching values of education, taking measures within school and other learning environments to address issues related to discrimination and exclusion;

> **Box 4.1** **Data on educational curricula from UNESCO's International Bureau of Education**

One of the major challenges for assessing the diversity of educational systems is the lack of comparable data that could be used as a proxy to capture the qualitative differences of in-school education programmes among countries. Household surveys — such as those conducted by the Education Policy and Data Center — are expensive and not free from bias (e.g. with respect to the terminology or the categories used to identify the cultural specificities of a given context). National assessments prepared within the framework of the EFA global strategy could provide clues of a more qualitative nature regarding educational systems, but such elements are not necessarily comparable.

Global curricula surveys based on the timetables collected by UNESCO's International Bureau of Education (IBE) are an interesting proxy of the diversity of educational content, since they provide information about the relative emphasis placed on certain subject matters — even though they do not say much about the content taught in classes (e.g. in history or moral education classes). Moreover, while official curricula tell us something about policy-makers' intentions, those intentions are not necessarily reflected in actual practice within schools. For a description of what happens on the ground, the assessments of learning outcomes conducted in some 60 countries are more relevant. In this

connection, see the OECD Programme for International Student Assessment (PISA), the two surveys of the International Association for the Evaluation of Education Achievement (IAE), TIMSS (Trends in International Mathematics and Science Study), and PIRLS (Progress in International Reading Literacy Study).

A per-country analysis of IBE data on the time devoted to curriculum categories (e.g. 'languages', 'mathematics', 'science, computer and technology', 'social sciences', 'religion', 'moral education', 'arts', 'sports') as a percentage of average yearly instructional hours provides interesting results regarding the respective emphasis on different subject matters across different contexts between 1980 and 2000.

Grades 1–6 (primary education)

There has been a general increase in the number of hours devoted to language education and mathematics since the 1980s, at the expense of moral education, religious education, the social sciences, the arts, and skills and competencies (i.e. the human capital that individuals need in order to lead successful and responsible lives in society).

Regionally, however, there are large disparities: in South and West Asia, as well as in Central and Eastern Europe, the teaching of arts is on the rise. In South and West Asia, the teaching of social sciences is decreasing, contrary to trends in East Asia and the Pacific.

Percentage of annual instructional time allocated to each subject area in primary education (grades 1-6), world average, circa 1985 and 2000

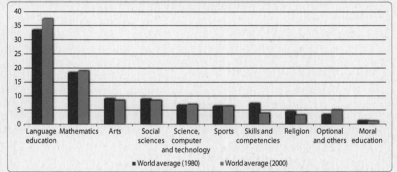

Percentage of total instructional time allocated to subject area in primary education (grades 1-6), circa 1985 by EFA region

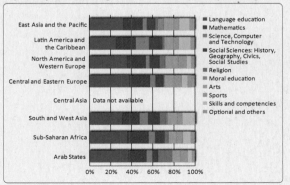

Percentage of total instructional time allocated to subject area in primary education (grades 1-6), circa 2000 by EFA region

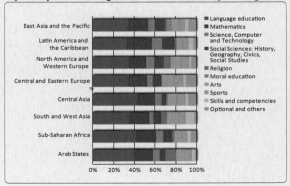

Box 4.1 Data on educational curricula from UNESCO's International Bureau of Education

Grades 7–8 (lower secondary education)

A similar global trend can be observed for grades 7-8, though the teaching of the social sciences is slightly on the rise. Regional disparities, however, are even greater.

Generally speaking, language education is the subject matter allocated the largest amount of time per given school year worldwide, but all other subject matters vary considerably across regions: for instance, the percentage of time allocated to religious education is relatively high in North America and Western Europe, the Arab States and South and West Asia, whereas skills and competencies are given more time in South and West Asia in primary education.

Percentage of annual instructional time allocated to each subject area in lower secondary education (grades 7-8), world average, circa 1985 and 2000

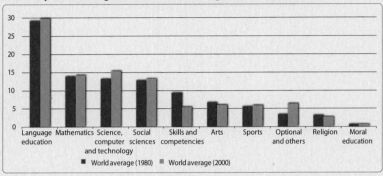

Percentage of total instructional time allocated to subject area in lower secondary education (grades 7-8), circa 1985 by EFA region

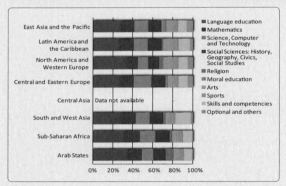

Percentage of total instructional time allocated to subject area in lower secondary education (grades 7-8), circa 2000 by EFA region

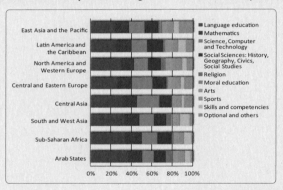

Source: IBE, Benavot, 2008.

3. emphasize sustainable development as the desired social outcome of education, and to link this to curriculum development and teacher training;

4. take special measures to reach vulnerable and marginalized groups, which may include school food programmes, itinerant teachers, health support, including education on HIV and STI, materials and instruction in minority languages, and measures for the disabled;

5. improve school and educational environments, paying special attention to the needs of girls regarding safety, sanitation and teacher attitudes.

Indeed, more *relevant* education means finding more *flexible* and *socially responsive* solutions (i.e. adapted to changing societies and responding to the needs of students within their *diverse social and cultural settings*) and ensuring the *appropriateness* of education (i.e. culturally acceptable).

Quality education is thus essentially about learning rooted in local environments and focused on broader knowledge and competencies applicable to learners' lives. It also opens up new horizons and enables learners to bring local knowledge into creative contact with knowledge from other cultures. In terms of curriculum development, 'bringing the real world into schools' applies to both content and form, which entails the development of multicultural and multilingual curricula, based on multiple perspectives and voices and on the histories and cultures of all groups in a given society, including minorities. Placing educational objectives within local development dynamics favours a *non-centric approach* to knowledge and values, which spans multiple frames of reference. Such a non-centric approach is indispensible for enabling teachers to develop the inclusive and shared values necessary in order to respond to the multiplicity of learner's needs in multicultural contexts. This is illustrated — in keeping also with the goals of the United Nations Decade of Education for Sustainable Development (DESD, 2005-2014) — by many projects initiated by the UNESCO Associated Schools Project Network (ASPnet), according to which 'each school is different, each place is unique and each culture has its own specific characteristics' and there is a need to 'strengthen the link between school and society' (ASPnet, 2009).

The challenges of inequality in education can best be met through *inclusive education*, which is understood as 'a process of addressing and responding to the diversity of needs of all learners through increasing participation in learning, cultures and communities, and reducing exclusion within and from education' (UNESCO, 2005a). For children with diverse backgrounds and abilities, attending schools increases their opportunities to learn because they are able to interact with other children. They learn respect and to value each other's abilities, no matter what they are, as well as patience, tolerance, and understanding. They come to realize that each person is 'special' and to embrace diversity and cherish it (UNESCO Bangkok, 2004; see Dutcher, 2004).

It is particularly important that such environments ensure that prejudice and discrimination are not reflected, even unintentionally, in curriculum and learning materials, especially with regard to girls, children affected by HIV and AIDS, children with disabilities and children from diverse cultural backgrounds. Equity in curriculum design and adapted teaching methods are thus the keys to inclusiveness in the classroom.

Diversified teaching methods

Developing flexible and culturally sensitive education calls for teachers who are knowledgeable about and

sensitive to cultural differences (see 'In Focus' section). This indicates that the teaching-learning relationship is *the* crucial variable for improving learning outcomes and increasing the relevance of education (UNESCO, 2004). In an influential study, James S. Coleman (1966, quoted in Gauthier and Dembélé, 2004) identified teacher characteristics as having a pronounced effect on school achievement among pupils from modest socio-economic backgrounds and ethnic minorities. More recent meta-analyses designed to assess the factors that are most likely to help children learn has confirmed the significance of the teacher effect. In a rigorous study of 28 such factors, for example, the two most prominent ('classroom management' and 'metacognitive processes') were found to be directly related to the teacher (Wang, Haertel and Walberg, 1993). A synthesis of 134 meta-analyses (Hattie, 1992) reached similar conclusions, indicating that even when there are significant differences in learners' backgrounds, teachers can exert a powerful influence in raising levels of achievement (Crahay, 2000).

Efforts must be made to address the entire range of teaching and learning activities, from memorization and repetition to problem-solving and creative thinking, as well as analytic and synthetic activities and diversified teaching methods. The Toolkit developed by UNESCO's Bangkok office (2004) suggests several activities in this connection, including: using blocks, models and other object which tap into children's visual understanding; asking children to draw pictures for the stories read to them; and linking their experience of movement in space to visual and mathematical concepts. When children survey their community, identify problems within it and use their skills cooperatively to suggest solutions to these problems, they are learning how to apply what they learn in school to the world beyond. Apart from being good education, this process helps the community to understand the school's work.

Teachers are currently ill-equipped to take on the increasingly complex task of confronting racist and discriminatory attitudes and behaviour — not to mention religious divides — among students and peer-group cultures, for which a high level of cultural skills and professionalism, in addition to policies and institutional support, are necessary within schools. The teaching of cultural skills should include expertise in interpersonal

Teachers are currently ill-equipped to take on the increasingly complex task of confronting racist and discriminatory attitudes and behaviour — not to mention religious divides — among students and peer-group cultures

relations, particularly in how to conduct conversations, moderate difficult debates, deal with conflicts and work with parents. Moreover, as education is not limited to teachers but encompasses school personnel (headmasters, administrators, etc.) as well as the children's learning environment, the entire teaching community should be involved in this effort, including parents and the larger community. All too often, the organizational weaknesses of schools are cited as a major cause of low learning achievement.

Opening the classroom to the real world is thus a promising pathway towards greater recognition of the cultural diversity of learners. New categories of teachers and contributors, such as local storytellers, foreign language assistants and foreign pupils from associated schools, may contribute to the diversification of the teaching staff and to the achievement of high standards of professionalism and competence. The concern to promote relevant teaching methods for the whole range of educational publics also requires the diversification of educational media and methods, especially with the assistance of the private sector and in partnership with NGOs. ICTs have facilitated the emergence of new educational tools (the Internet, videogames, multimedia programmes), which can open up the classroom to the real world by exploring tangible instances of cultural diversity — an example being *Dora the Explorer*, which, like other role playing games, can help to actively raise children's awareness of cultural issues (Maranda, 2006; King, 2002).

Bilingual and multilingual education

Mother-tongue-based multilingual approaches[2] in formal and non-formal education greatly enhance the relevance of education and help to expand educational opportunities for marginalized and underserved groups, including immigrant populations. This is one of UNESCO's long-standing concerns, as expressed in a number of its normative instruments on education, including: the 1960 *Convention against Discrimination in Education* (especially Art. 5, on the respective roles of mother-tongue and majority languages), the 1976 *Recommendation on the Development of Adult Education* (especially Art. 22, which

...many countries still provide essentially monolingual education, prescribing the use of only one language in their schools. This amounts to exclusion for many children...

explicitly recommends mother-tongue instruction), the 1993 *Delhi Declaration and Framework for Action* (which supports 'initial instruction in the mother tongue, even if it may in some cases be necessary for the students to subsequently master a national language or other language of wider usage if they are to participate effectively in the broader society of which they are part'), as well as the 1996 *Amman Affirmation* and the 1997 *Hamburg Declaration on Adult Learning* (Art. 15). The 1998 *World Declaration on Higher Education for the Twenty-first Century: Vision and Action* outlines the importance of multilingualism in higher education to furthering international understanding, as does the Article 6 of the Action Plan accompanying the 2001 *Universal Declaration on Cultural Diversity*.

Despite UNESCO's efforts in this regard, many countries still provide essentially monolingual education, prescribing the use of only one language in their schools. This amounts to exclusion for many children and has been shown to contribute to high levels of repetition and/or dropout rates. Indeed, when a multilingual country uses only one primary language in public schools, as well as in the administration of government services and activities, only those who use the chosen language as a primary language benefit, while those who have either lower or no proficiency in that language are penalized, exacerbated by the fact that they are denied the benefit of using and identifying with their primary language (Romaine, 2007). This is true even in the case of officially bilingual societies, as illustrated by the paradoxical case of Paraguay, where 80 percent of the population speaks both Guarani and Spanish. The paradox lies in the fact that, while Paraguayans need not be indigenous to speak Guarani, Paraguayan society's appropriation of Guarani as a national identity symbol has given rise to a linguistic divide between the variety of Guarani (Jopará) spoken nationally and the other indigenous varieties, a divide that has limited access to education for people speaking one of the other 19 indigenous varieties of Guarani — despite the fact that Paraguay officially recognizes Guarani-Spanish bilingual education (López, 2009).

---

2. Bilingual and multilingual education refers to the use of two or more languages as mediums of instruction. In much of the specialized literature, these two types are subsumed under the term bilingual education. However, UNESCO adopted the term 'multilingual education' in 1999 (General Conference, Resolution 12; UNESCO, 2000b) to refer to the use of at least three languages in education: the mother tongue, a regional or national language and an international language Resolution 12; UNESCO, 2000b).

The drafting of education laws and policies frequently involves intense debate on the issue of a primary language of education, which has important consequences for linguistic diversity. Education as a cultural right often seems to be overshadowed by the political dimensions of decisions regarding official languages and languages of instruction, their financial implications, and the varied experiences in responding to the learners' needs (Tomasevski, 2001). Schools, together with the family circle, are often the primary sites in which the fate of endangered languages is decided, and a long history of socio-linguistic research shows that schools can be unreliable allies of language preservation (Fishman, 1967), even though school is but one factor in the broader socio-political and cultural landscape (see chapter 3). Official language policies in education can facilitate or inhibit multi-linguistic vitality.

While many countries have still a long way to go in promoting mother-tongue-based multilingual approaches, progress is nevertheless being made. For example, among other good practices, Cambodia has introduced several minority languages as media of instruction in pilot projects. Zambia's Primary Reading Programme uses mother tongues for the first three years of schooling as the main medium of instruction. India strongly upholds the principle of mother-tongue teaching. In some instance, the access to mother languages can be facilitated through switches between different scripts, as illustrated by research in Hong Kong and Singapore on the different kinds of literacy demands arising from different writing systems. In these countries, bilingual and multilingual education has been shown to significantly improve learning. A necessary prerequisite for such improvement is that teachers be proficient in the mother tongue and that teaching resources in various languages be made widely available (UNESCO, 2007).

The benefits of mother-tongue multilingual education are illustrated by a number of UNESCO case studies (on Mali, Papua New Guinea, Peru and the US) collected in 2007 (Bühmann and Trudell, 2008) which suggest that the implementation of mother-tongue-based bilingual education programmes can enhance learners' outcomes and raise academic achievements when compared to monolingual second-language systems. Developing community support is also crucial for implementing sustainable bilingual education programmes. On

the other hand, if the overall quality of an education programme remains poor, a change in the language of instruction is not likely to yield significant results. Without adequate teacher training and the availability of appropriate learning materials, and without the support of educational professionals for the implementation of reform programmes, learning outcomes can remain poor. Furthermore, with sound financial planning, bilingual education is more cost effective than educational systems that use learners' second language as the medium of instruction since student learning improves significantly when a mother tongue is used in tandem with the official language.

Bilingual education programmes may also be directed at immigrant populations whose languages differ from the language of public education or at regional minorities who are trying to preserve their first language. These children speak a minority language at home — often a mother tongue that is rarely supported in the wider community and is often a language that the children's parents are struggling to preserve — and learn the mainstream language in school. The path to bilingualism for these children in school would ideally involve the preservation of their first language (through which their basic communication and thinking skills would have been developed) combined with the learning of the second (mainstreamed national) language. However, efforts,

Early childhood reading education in Dublin, Ireland

time and resources to preserve minority languages are often challenging to pin down, especially since most bilingual children in standard educational systems are 'immersed' in the second majority language and, as a result, ultimately lose their initial minority language or mother tongue.

Decades of research across the globe (especially from North America, Canada in particular, and Nordic countries) have shed light on how language teaching and learning can most effectively support cultural diversity, noting the significant differences between *academic* and *conversational language*. Children can appear to be conversationally fluent in a language quite quickly, sometimes in six to eight months. However, it takes five to seven years on average for a minority child coming into a new system to reach *academic* levels in the main language of instruction. In this respect, bilingual programmes that are not maintained for five

or more years do not make the most of the potential advantages they offer to minority children. Of course, one-to-three-year programmes can still be culturally valuable, especially in instances of early language transition: they help children to meet the challenge of initial literacy and make initial concepts in education clearer so that children can grasp them more easily. Academically speaking, however, it is best that a bilingual programme last longer in order to maximize the intellectual benefits for learners.

Countries around the world are still far from attaining the objective of teaching national, local/regional and international languages in their official curricula (see UNESCO, 2000b). As highlighted by an analysis of timetables collected by IBE on language education (see Table 7 in the Statistical Annex and Figure 4.1), lower primary grades continue to focus largely on the teaching of one national language or in some cases on several official languages (in South Africa for example, where Afrikaans, English, IsiNdebele, IsiXhosa, IsiZulu, Sepedi, Sesotho, Setswana, SiSwati, Tshivenda and Xitsonga are all official languages). Most countries introduce an international language in the upper primary grades, but few countries allocate time to local languages. These policies not only undermine the preservation of linguistic diversity, but also reduce the impact of multilingualism, which can improve intellectual functioning and intercultural dialogue (see chapter 3 above and section 4.3 below).

Figure 4.1 Type of language taught for selected countries, 2000

In grades 1-6

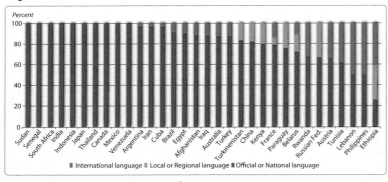

In grades 7-8

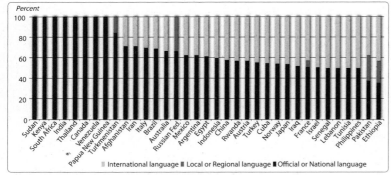

Source: International Bureau of Education and Aaron Benavot, 2009.

Strategies for marginalized groups

Negative attitudes towards children with diverse backgrounds and abilities — especially girls and children from indigenous groups — are a major barrier to including these children in school. Negative attitudes can stem both from the school and the community and from marginalized children themselves. Fears, taboos, shame, ignorance and misinformation all contribute to negative attitudes towards such children and their situations (King and Schielmann, 2004). Discrimination plays itself out in complex and sometimes insidious ways and creates vulnerabilities for marginalized children that often lead to their exclusion from school. If educational opportunities are to be made available to all groups and thereby contribute to the enhancement of both democratic citizenship and respect for human rights, then obstacles to access must be identified and programmes must be organized to cater for vulnerable and marginalized groups (ICAE, 2003).

All too often, education neither enhances social mobility nor contributes to the elimination of discrimination. As a result, children from indigenous groups and ethnic minorities tend to be less likely to enrol in primary school and more likely to repeat grades or drop out of school. They also tend to be the last to benefit from school creation and expansion. Data from Latin American countries show that disparities in educational attainment between indigenous and non-indigenous populations are more marked than disparities based on gender or area of residence. Language of instruction

also plays a key role: bilingual education programmes in Guatemala and Mexico have been able to improve the schooling outcomes of children from indigenous communities (see Box 4.2). Children belonging to pastoralist or nomadic communities face immense challenges, to which governments in several countries, such as Mongolia and Ethiopia, have attempted to respond by providing schools with boarding and hostel facilities — though important concerns about the quality of education still remain. In the EU, Roma children, among other groups exposed to discrimination at school, are no longer subjected to systematic segregation but face other forms of exclusion due to the lack of appropriate structures. As a result, UNESCO

| Box 4.2 | **The evolution of indigenous bilingual education in Latin America** |

In Latin America the historical denial of the right to one's language and culture in schools has impacted negatively on the educational situation of indigenous children and adolescents; though initially completely excluded from education systems, indigenous children and adolescents were eventually made to assimilate within 'modern', industry-based Christian systems (see Hamel, 2007; López and Sichra, 2008; López and Küper, 2000). In a recent comparative survey of youth and adult indigenous literacy (López and Hanemann, 2009) in six Latin American countries (Bolivia, Ecuador, Guatemala, Mexico, Nicaragua and Peru), indigenous illiteracy among people aged 15 years and over ranged from 12.9 percent (Nicaragua) to 47.7 percent (Guatemala), while national averages ranged between 7.2 percent (Peru) and 23.97 percent (Guatemala). Educational inequalities are also systematic, even in primary education: over 20 percent of indigenous children aged 6–11 years do not enjoy their right to education. Paraguay offers the most severe example of exclusion, since 38 percent of indigenous children are out of school, and only 21 percent complete primary schooling.

As a response to these challenges, indigenous bilingual education began developing in the 1940s, when rural teachers and indigenous leaders took it upon themselves to introduce local indigenous languages in youth and adult literacy programmes. This was the case

in Ecuador, Mexico and Peru. The history of indigenous bilingual education in Latin America is heavily marked by the application of linguistics to education, and particularly of phonetics and phonology to the design of alphabets and to second-language teaching. Mexico was among the first to undertake this process, when, for political reasons, the State and the Protestant Summer Institute of Linguistics (SIL) became allies in the development of indigenous bilingual education (Schmelkes et al, 2009). The methodologies developed during this early period were then transferred to other countries on the continent through the meetings of the Inter-American Indigenist Congress promoted by Mexico (Marzal, 1993). Special emphasis was placed on the language issue, as it was clear that education had to effect a profound cultural change among the indigenous population (Townsend, 1949).

In the late 1970s and early 1980s, a shift in the aims and objectives of bilingual education took place as a result of the increasing demands and active participation of indigenous leaders, intellectuals and teachers, particularly in South America (see López and Sichra, 2008). 'State indigenism' — which aimed at cultural assimilation — was partially abandoned and replaced by 'critical indigenism' (Marzal, 1993), with the rise of cultural pluralism in theory and practice. Indigenous leaders, some of whom were former transitional bilingual education students, demanded greater and improved

attention to their cultures and languages, and strategically regarded indigenous culture as a political resource by which to gain more visibility for and to increase the participation of indigenous people in the countries in which they lived. The adoption of strategic development orientations and of intercultural demands resulted from this ideological shift. Thus, indigenous bilingual education became a unifying cause for interventions in indigenous areas. Informed by this new perspective, governments, NGOs and indigenous organizations committed themselves to education programmes and projects in indigenous territories. As a result, people in the region began to modify their views on indigenous languages and cultures, and new laws and regulations were enacted that recognized the right of indigenous peoples to education in their own languages.

As of the mid-1990s, the embrace of interculturalism for all has led to another change in emphasis: from a focus on problems to one on rights and the recognition of indigenous languages and cultures as a resource (see Ruiz, 1984). Against this backdrop, indigenous bilingual education has been implemented in some countries as a national policy, while in others it remains the target of compensatory programmes and projects.

Source: López, 2009.

Children from indigenous groups and ethnic minorities tend to be less likely to enrol in primary school and more likely to repeat grades or drop out of school

and the Council of Europe are preparing guidelines on Early Childhood Education for Roma and Traveller Children, based on the *Curriculum Framework for Romani* developed by the Language Policy Division of the Council of Europe (see Council of Europe, 2007; UNESCO and Council of Europe, 2007).

While the *Universal Declaration of Human Rights* (UN, 1948: Art. 26) and the *International Covenant on Economic, Social and Cultural Rights* (UN, 1966: Art. 13 and 14) underline the right to education for all, this has largely come to be understood in terms of the right to *receive* education and not the right to *choose* one's education — the latter of which the promotion of cultural diversity is highly committed. Frameworks exist for the extension of quality education to minorities and vulnerable groups, a notable example being Article 13.1 of the Council of Europe's 1995 *Framework Convention for the Protection of National Minorities*, which recognizes the right of persons belonging to a national minority to set up and manage their own private educational and training establishments. In accordance with this provision, government strategies in Central and Eastern Europe have included financial incentives for schools and learners, as well as the appointment of classroom mediators to support children and their families (UNESCO, 2007). Indigenous peoples across the world are also demanding that education be both linguistically and culturally appropriate to their needs

while not excluding them from broader access to national education systems. Examples of good practices in this regard can be found in Botswana, Brazil, Cambodia, Guatemala, India, Malaysia, Mexico, New Zealand, Peru, the Russian Federation and the United States (King and Schielmann, 2004).

To fulfil the goals of EFA with regard to indigenous education, it will be necessary to address a number of issues in curriculum development. In addition to prioritizing students' learning about indigenous culture and values, the curriculum will also have to provide them with the practical skills they will need to participate fully in national society. To achieve both, the curriculum should:

- reinforce community-based practices of early childhood care;

- use local languages for initial literacy;

- create culturally responsive programmes of bilingual or multilingual education for children and adults;

- increase the number of teachers from indigenous groups and ethnic minorities who could act as role models;

- provide skills specific to indigenous cultures, such as hunting, trapping and weaving, as well as more general skills, knowledge, attitudes, values and beliefs;

- provide equal opportunities for further learning;

⊃ *Pupils of Bombali school, Sierra Leone*

- develop self esteem and esteem for one's culture;

- develop appropriate learning materials;

- use methods such as distance education, radio-broadcasting and e-learning, as well as the development of in-situ programmes and training and employing local teachers to meet the needs of remote communities;

- link education to other aspects of a learner's life, such as health, nutrition, safe water and the natural environment;

- use and integrate formal and non-formal learning styles and teaching methods as a means of recognizing indigenous ways of generating and transmitting knowledge and of giving value to the oral wisdom of indigenous peoples and non-verbal communication in education.

In formal education systems, the study of traditional life and culture must be placed on equal footing with the study of standard subjects, such as math, science and natural history (see section 4.2 below).

New normative frameworks are being developed expressly for the purpose of facilitating the progress of indigenous education. As early as 1989, Articles 26 and 27.1 of the International Labour Organization's *Convention Concerning Indigenous and Tribal Peoples in Independent Countries* stipulated that members of indigenous communities should have the opportunity to acquire education at all levels on at least an equal footing with the rest of the national community:

> *Education programmes and services for the peoples concerned shall be developed and implemented in co-operation with them and address their special needs, and shall incorporate their histories, their knowledge and technologies, their value systems and their further social, economic and cultural aspirations (…) such measures also include the provision of financial resources as an important factor for the success and sustainability of quality education (Art. 27.1, ILO, 1989).*

More recently, the UN *Declaration on the Rights of Indigenous Peoples* (2007) recognized the right of indigenous families and communities to retain shared responsibility for the upbringing, training, education and well-being of their children, consistent with the rights of the child. Article 14 establishes the right of indigenous people to establish and control their educational systems and institutions, providing education in their own languages, in a manner appropriate to their cultural methods of teaching and learning. And Article 15.1 states that indigenous peoples have the right to the dignity and diversity of their cultures, traditions and histories, all of which are to be appropriately reflected in education and public information.

Among the policies devised for eliminating discrimination in education towards indigenous, immigrant, disadvantaged, minority or disabled children, some have privileged mechanisms that favour one or another group within the mainstream system using an *affirmative action* approach. While this can yield some concrete results, others contend that such policies may also induce counterproductive side effects, since they sometimes help to solidify the uniqueness of identities and thereby exacerbate differences and obscure points of commonality among different groups (Gundara, 2008). Looking at experiences of grassroot communities may inspire policy-makers to develop a deeper understanding of people's educational needs so as to respond to them appropriately, for such an understanding is essential to ensuring pluralistic education (Delors et al., 1996).

The promotion and protection of cultural diversity contributes to the effective advancement of the right to education along these lines. It is therefore important that the diversity of knowledge and learning contexts be integrated both in formal education systems and schooling *and* in informal educational settings. Indeed, neither inclusive formal education nor multilingualism will be sufficient in and of themselves for realizing EFA; they will be successful in this regard only if they are coupled with an exploration of non-mainstream and non-formal education, and even informal education[3].

The right to education for all has largely come to be understood in terms of the right to receive education and not the right to choose one's education…

Chapter 4
Education

---

3. 'Informal learning' refers to learning events as they may arise in the contexts of the family, the workplace and the daily life of every person, in self-directed, family-directed or socially-directed ways (UNESCO, 1996).

4.2 Learning societies and the right to education

Education is typically assumed to be a process that takes place only in schools and within the public education system, and thus enrolment ratios are often used as a means to monitor progress in achieving EFA goals. Yet increased funding for new schools worldwide has not been sufficient to increase enrolment or attendance. Indeed, despite the international community's sustained efforts, in 2006 some 75 million children (55 percent of whom were girls) did not attend school (most of them from cultural minorities and indigenous or nomadic populations) and 776 million adults worldwide (16 percent of the world's adult population) lacked basic literacy skills — almost two-thirds of whom were women, a share that has remained virtually unchanged since the early 1990s (UNESCO, 2008a). These results would seem to imply that other learning methods and content should be recognized as providing important learning opportunities both for in-school children and for out-of-school children, youth and adults, whom the formal system, at present, hardly ever reaches (Pimparé, 2002).

There are serious and multiple reasons why children are not in school, ranging from family chores to poor economic conditions and lack of schooling facilities, poor teaching standards, hostile school environments or distance from school, not to mention inappropriate educational methods and content coupled with a lack of awareness among parents about the necessity for education (especially for girls). The lack of recognition of the importance of other, out-of-school learning environments is not helping the situation.

The paradigm of 'learning societies' put forward in the Delors report advocates the combination of conventional teaching and out-of-school approaches which 'enable children to experience the three dimensions of education: the ethical and cultural, the scientific and technological, and the economic and social' (Delors et al., 1996). Such a strategy stems from the *Jomtien Declaration*, which emphasizes that serving 'the basic learning needs of all requires more than a recommitment to basic education as it now exists. What is needed is an expanded vision that surpasses present resource levels, institutional structures, curricula, and conventional delivery systems while building on the best in current practices' (UNESCO, 1990). This expanded vision of basic

Education should be seen not as confined to formal schooling but as taking place through a variety of learning systems, including non-formal education, informal education and the transmission of local and indigenous knowledge and values

education, which emphasizes the role that learners can play in defining their own educational needs, including through non-formal and lifelong learning activities, calls on us to expand our ideas about educational delivery systems, in accordance with UNESCO's position that 'issues involving values education in multilingual and multicultural societies' should be included in EFA action plans (UNESCO, 2002).

This requires broadening the means and scope of education to focus on the cultural environment of learning and knowledge acquisition, and a shift in emphasis that does not restrict education to a question of enrolment, attendance in organized programmes and certification requirements in formal schooling systems. Following this line of thought, education and addressing learning needs should be seen not as confined to formal schooling but as taking place through a variety of learning systems, including non-formal education, informal education and the transmission of local and indigenous knowledge and values. The notion of a *learning environment* would thus require further development to enable linkages and synergies between various learning systems. The aim of education, as a lifelong pursuit, is to increase our autonomy and our capacity to adapt to both the constraints of the job market and our cultural environment. Accordingly, a new relationship with learning should be cultivated, one that harnesses each learner's cultural background, in a participatory manner, so as to favour the 'full development of human personality', that is, a creative, artistic, ethical, spiritual and social development, to which the promotion of cultural diversity strongly contributes: for *empowerment* lies at the crossroads of life experience, work experience and schooling (Ardoino, 2000).

Learning communities

The increasing instability of today's world raises the question of the ability of any pre-determined programme of learning in childhood to prepare children fully for their adult lives (Miller, 2001). The concept of *learning communities* or *learning societies* has arisen of late to emphasize the value of self-learning and innovative learning in the context of adapting to needs and shaping one's desired future. Every society is a learning society with specific cultural patterns and embedded learning mechanisms through which the inter- or intra-generational exchange of knowledge, know-how, values, beliefs or worldviews takes place and within which individuals should be free to choose their learning path, without prejudice to the paths others have chosen.

When schooling runs counter to these culturally embedded learning environments, it will not necessarily yield positive outcomes for learners. Research undertaken at the end of the 1990s showed that educational systems do not always have an empowering effect on learners. Indeed, as an organizational structure, it creates filtration mechanisms according to which children have to 'compete for the limited goodies waiting at the top of the pyramid' (PROBE, 1999). This can act as a disincentive for children, especially if the way in which school knowledge is structured and articulated leads to the stigmatization of rural or indigenous children (as opposed to the 'privileged' urban ones) through representations in textbooks or ambiguous and problematic depictions that cause a sense of alienation among these children or lower their self-esteem. Children who are also engaged in labour activities — agriculture, animal husbandry, small industry

or petty commerce — participate in equally crucial learning environments, which cannot be systematically reduced to issues relating to 'child labour' when these are not forced activities and constitute genuine learning spaces linked to the functional framework of their communities. In those spaces, there is much to be learned about which schools do not teach, for example about local medicine, forest skills or traditional harvesting. In the same spirit, efforts should be made to preserve other learning spaces that also have a positive role to play in children's development (see Box 4.3).

Case studies from India indicate that decisions relating to educational and learning options are usually taken within families, who evaluate the relative importance of literacy in their lives and whether to send one child or all of them to school (Pimparé, 2002, 2005). The benefit of this approach is that it underlines the extent to which schooling is to be reintegrated in its cultural environment and does not develop in isolation from it. It also reintegrates schooling into a holistic perspective that highlights schooling as one learning space among others that should also have their place in educational

---

Box 4.3   Education in Auroville, India

The Auroville Charter sets forth an educational philosophy within the very functioning of its society, which it views as a place 'of an unending education, of constant progress and a youth that never ages', dedicated to 'a living embodiment of an actual human unity'. In today's world many children grow up without a true sense of belonging, herded into conventional merit-oriented school systems that do not allow for exploration of who they really are and growth into fully realized beings where mind, body, and spirit flow as one. They have lost that deep sense of community that was once so important in traditional societies. And as a result more and more children are alienated from the learning process.

In Auroville the aim is promote the integral development of the multifaceted personality of each individual. Education is not a matter of skills acquisition so much as one of awakening to a process of self-discovery, self-becoming and self-perfection. This is the only way to foster creative individuals who can work

in a dedicated manner without 'burning themselves out': whatever excellence they may have comes from the development of their inner personality and not from the pressure of a competitive environment that exhausts their faculties without enriching them.

Nearly 50 different nations and about 80 linguistic groups co-create in Auroville, which may make Auroville, which counts more than two thousand residents, one of the most diverse intercultural communities on Earth. This in itself is an immense challenge. About a dozen schools are experimenting with the philosophy of integral education, the ideas of Maria Montessori and the Rishi School, as well as more conventional methods. Children and youth from all races, ethnic groups, and classes study together in English, French, Tamil and Sanskrit, as well. Because there is a large cultural diversity from the outset, children are much more tolerant of each other from an early age. The emphasis is on learning to be in

community together. Service to others is an important part of the code of life.

Integral education focuses on the global development of the child. Singing and sports are as important as math and physics. Martial art techniques and breathing exercises develop psychic and physical equilibrium. Awareness of one's surroundings and the flow of conscious energy are emphasized to balance the body-mind relationship. Children are given an opportunity to manifest their talents in an environment that recognizes that each child has a capacity to develop multiple aspects of being. The emphasis is not career development but rather on learning to engage with life; sharing is stressed; competition is discouraged as concepts of success and failure are relative. What is important is that a child develops according to their true potential. Leadership is seen more in terms of helping others than in terms of personal gain.

Source: Verdiani, based on De Pezeral, 2007; SAIIER, 2008; Verdiani, 2008.

strategies. It thus allows for the recognition of the value of other learning spaces that may arise in the family, the community, the workplace, the place of worship, the market place, as well as other learning forms that may be embedded in traditions, festivals, art, song, music, prayers, radio, television and newspapers, or simply in human exchanges that facilitate its transmission. The *motivation* of individuals is a decisive factor in their involvement in any learning space at any given moment of their lives.

Alternative ways of learning are embedded in the social fabric of people's lives; they place value on knowledge transmission and skills acquisition based on the cultural context of learners — a very different perspective from formal schooling, where children and communities are often viewed as 'blank slates' or 'empty vessels' (Freire, 2000). Learning related to agricultural activities takes place in the fields or at home: all children, whether attending school or not, learn about soil conditions, seed quality, field preparation or sowing time through practical activities and observation. For children involved in animal husbandry, all the required learning (grazing, grass identification, hygiene of cattle, animal disease and cures) takes place outside school. As for labour (paid ploughing, house construction, firewood chopping, artisan craftwork), the place of work is also an important learning space, where survival depends on what one learns (Pimparé, 2002). Learning likewise takes place through the intergenerational transmission of knowledge, but it also relies on a 'collection of discrete items of information, extracted from both the local context and people who *know* them' and has to do with a knowledge directly tied to personal experience (Bates, 2009). Within Inuit communities, for example, knowledge and learning are grounded in a context of practices that enable community members to gain survival skills and to adapt rapidly to the environment in which they live. Far from being incompatible with contemporary knowledge, the specificity and utility of contextualized learning drives home the message that what is learned is not necessarily determined by the way in which it is learned.

Governments, ministries or other bodies usually respond to the learning needs of youth and adults by expanding formal secondary and tertiary education and the certification of knowledge through exams. Yet in doing so, they do not necessarily consider that skills acquisition often takes place through informal means and in non-formal settings. Improved monitoring of supply and demand for non-formal education is urgently needed at national levels. While we are still far from a systematic survey of learning communities and traditional modes of transmission, methodologies have been developed in order to collect them without cultural bias. Action research in particular emphasizes the need to further participatory methods and conceptualization approaches (Carr et al., 1986; Barbier, 1996). It seeks to respect local peoples' ability to conceptualize their lives and take responsibility for their own empowerment and development through self-organizing dialogue initiatives. Participatory approaches

An open-air school in the South Omo, Ethiopia

provide a powerful lever for learners to take ownership and regenerate their learning spaces from a pluralistic perspective. As illustrated by cases in Mexico and Peru, such approaches help local communities to engage in a constructive, critical examination of 'cultural imports' (UNESCO, 2006a).

Harnessing diverse ways of learning for revitalizing EFA

The report of the International Commission on Education for the Twenty-first Century (Delors et al., 1996) notes that the misalignment between local learning spaces and mainstream forms of education results from an outgrowth of historical trajectories:

> All too often, the inherited colonial systems of education have been preserved more or less intact, generally with the rationale of 'preserving standards', although these so-called standards were more illusory than real, with a very small élite enjoying exactly the same education as in the metropolitan country and the vast majority being deprived of any form of modern education at all.

Increasingly, however, the international community is recognizing that traditional and pragmatic ways of learning can be as efficient as Western didactic ways of learning and that complementarities may exist between all forms of education, especially when a recognition of alternative learning environments can help mitigate a shortage of financial resources for realizing EFA. While, for example, literacy strategies may create an undesired devaluation of oral cultures, the introduction into schools of storytellers, as previously noted, may contribute to the revitalization of oral cultures. A rapprochement emerging between different educational cultures from both mainstream education and non-formal communities is beginning to yield a new emphasis on the diversity of ways of learning. UNESCO's Bangkok office (2004) has identified seven such pathways by which children learn:

- *Verbal or linguistic*, where some children think and learn through written and spoken words, memory and recall.

- *Logical or mathematical*, where some children think and learn though reasoning and calculation. They can easily use numbers, recognize abstract patterns and take precise measurements.

- *Visual or spatial*, where some children learn through art, such as drawing, painting or sculpture. They can easily read maps, charts and diagrams.

- *Bodily or kinaesthetic*, where some children learn through body movement, games and drama.

- *Musical or rhythmic*, where some children learn best through sounds, rhyme, rhythm and repetition.

- *Interpersonal*, where some children learn easily in groups through cooperative work. They enjoy group activities, easily understand social situations and can easily develop relationships with others.

- *Intra-personal*, where some children learn best through personal concentration and self-reflection. They can work alone, are aware of their own feelings and know their own strengths and weaknesses.

Not all of these pathways are recognized in mainstream education, but their rediscovery is one of the benefits that may result from a stronger dialogue between mainstream education and alternative learning spaces.

Greater attention is now being given to the 'educational culture' of communities — which, in many cases, refers to the diversity of modes of intergenerational knowledge transmission (Ishizawa and Rengifo, 2009). While the specific aspects of knowledge transmission are to be respected and safeguarded (e.g. oral modes of transmission), other aspects of traditional education — images and sounds, analogies and metaphors — and local methods and strategies of knowledge acquisition can easily be supported by 'modern' tools. Similarly, formal education can use elements of the local culture in educational strategies.

Combining local practices and knowledge with curricular subjects in a contextual way (e.g. by incorporating methods in school that parents use at home to teach their children about food preparation or housekeeping, or by making excursions to learn about the cultural significance of places and associated stories, rituals or usages) strengthens the link between the community and the school and provides a foundation for the community's further integral development. Decontextualized approaches to

The failure to take account of non-mainstream forms of learning risks further marginalizing those populations that education should seek to empower

learning have everything to gain from contextualized approaches, since, through relating instructional contents to the specific contexts of learners, which increases motivation to learn, a greater ownership of education can be developed (Dirkx and Prenger, 1997).

As Luis Enrique López (2009) has underlined, a deeper understanding of the differences and similarities between indigenous community 'informal' education and formal education may give rise to the development of richer curricular content in indigenous schools, varied learning styles and pedagogical strategies, contextualized language learning and transmission. New trends are emerging in the development of indigenous educational strategies (López, 2009), which emphasize the involvement of community elders and leaders, the observance of socialization processes, the revitalization of indigenous languages, cooperative learning and the revival of indigenous ancestral orality. Education has much to gain from a consideration of multiple perspectives and pluralistic approaches to ways of learning, understanding and explaining the world.

Knowledge diversity

The 1999 World Conference on Science in Budapest, co-organized by UNESCO and the International Council for Science (ICSU), brought the relationship between science and other systems of knowledge to the fore, as noted in the *Declaration on Science and the Use of Scientific Knowledge* (UNESCO, 1999a: para. 26) which emphasizes the valuable contribution to science and technology made by traditional and local knowledge systems. This is further highlighted in its *Framework for Action* (UNESCO, 1999b: para. 36):

> *Traditional societies (…) have nurtured and refined systems of knowledge of their own, relating to such diverse domains as astronomy, meteorology, geology, ecology, botany, agriculture, physiology, psychology and health. Such knowledge systems represent an enormous wealth. Not only do they harbour information as yet unknown to modern science, but they are also expressions of other ways of living in the world, other relationships between society and nature, and other approaches to the acquisition and construction of knowledge.*

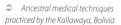 *Ancestral medical techniques practiced by the Kallawaya, Bolivia*

However, despite such statements, there remains a widespread belief about neutral and value-free theories and conceptualizations, which are unrelated to the social settings in which they arose. In many ways, the call for the building of 'knowledge societies' — based on universal access and knowledge-sharing — may have unwittingly contributed to the assimilation of all knowledge to scientific knowledge.

There is no shortage of literature maintaining that the sciences are also socially and culturally constructed, meaning that the learning of science is itself a form of socialization and enculturation (see, e.g., Kuhn, 1996; Woolgar and Latour, 1979; Bourdieu, 2001). Insofar as mainstream educational discourse considers science to be universal, this leads to the reductive compartmentalization of 'traditional' knowledge. Yet such knowledge, when recognized and valued, can actually enrich scientific research: as stated on the occasion of the launch of the International Year of Astronomy (2009), the use of astronomical data or mythological beliefs can contribute to the historical record of celestial events; and knowledge of the medicinal qualities of plants can lead to the discovery of curative molecules (Ödman, 2007).

The history and philosophy of science today recognize that societies have constructed different logical systems and visions of the world to explain the relationship of human beings to nature, the universe and the world of thought and emotion. These logical systems serve to organize the knowledge stemming from this relationship, in particular on the basis of observations and experience. Knowledge is meaningful only within the logical system within which it is embedded. A wide range of logical systems exists throughout the world, which Philippe Descola has attempted to classify in four categories — naturalism, animism, totemism, and analogy — according to the type of relationship between nature and culture they involve (Descola, 2006).

The scientific system developed in the West from the 16th century CE onwards has tended to eclipse other systems of knowledge and other visions of the world. It should be remembered, however, that this system drew substantially on a wide range of sources. These included Arab, Jewish and Persian medical traditions (and later that of Timbuktu), dating from the 6th to the 12th centuries CE, which were based largely on fairly advanced knowledge of human anatomy and the practice of dissection of the human body taught in the universities. Christian medicine came much later as a result of the religious prohibition on dissection. Western science and technology in general also has roots in the traditions of China and India, as well as in the navigation, transport and other technical achievements of the Arabic Golden Age. The diversity of these sources is a reminder that other visions of the world and logical systems should not be dismissed, since doing so would not only impoverish cultural diversity but exclude the possibility that Western science might derive enrichment from non-Western sources.

Recognition of the diversity of knowledge must be placed on equal footing with recognition of the dignity of each knowledge system as a whole (see UNESCO's LINKS Programme) — which is not the case when the value of indigenous knowledge as a resource for development and environmental conservation leads, for example, to the creation of databases in which 'useful' knowledge is separated from the other knowledge, practices, milieus, contexts and cultural beliefs with which it exists (Agrawal, 2002). Mutual respect among diverse knowledge systems fosters intercultural dialogue and mutual understanding, which in turn contribute to empowerment and self-development and a renewal of strategies for the enhancement of our ability to live together with our differences. Intercultural education has become all the more relevant today with the development of multicultural societies in which up to 190 million people live outside their countries of origin (a figure that would be even higher if undocumented migrants were included). Thus, multicultural education must be complemented by intercultural education,[4] and education *through* cultural diversity must go hand-in-hand with education *for* cultural diversity.

---

4. 'Interculturalism in education' refers to learning that is rooted in one's own culture, language, values, worldview and system of knowledge but that is, at the same time, receptive, open to and appreciative of other forms of knowledge, values, cultures and languages. The ultimate aim of intercultural education is learning to live together, since systems of knowledge, civilizational patterns, cultures and languages are seen in complementary distribution rather than from the perspective of segregation or opposition (López, 2009).

In increasingly complex multicultural societies, education must enable us to acquire the intercultural competencies that will permit us to live together with — and not despite — our cultural differences

4.3 Participatory learning and intercultural competencies

One of the major challenges facing lifelong education involves our capacities to *learn to live together* by 'developing an understanding of others and their history, traditions and spiritual values and, on this basis, creating a new spirit which, guided by recognition of our growing interdependences and a common analysis of the risks and challenges of the future, would induce people to implement common projects or to manage the inevitable conflicts in an intelligent and peaceful way' (Delors et al., 1996).

Education today must come to grips with the realities of multicultural populations and ensure both the inclusion of minorities through social integration (see section 4.1 above) and the social cohesion of multicultural societies through mutual understanding and dialogue. If not, as demonstrated in conflict or post-conflict contexts, education can be a basis for cultural misunderstanding, animosity, ethnic conflict or violence (see Davies and Talbot, 2008). Adapting educational content within textbooks and curricula and the teaching of foreign languages contribute to the improvement of our knowledge of ourselves and others and therefore help to prevent clashes born of ignorance. But overcoming the obstacles to intercultural dialogue (including distrust, stereotypes and misunderstanding) is equally important. Educating *through* diversity must be complemented with educating *for* cultural diversity.

A number of strategies, formal and non-formal alike, have been elaborated for developing intercultural competencies and raising awareness of the challenges involved in interacting with 'cultural' others. Within the existing frameworks, UNESCO's 1974 *Recommendation Concerning Education for International Understanding, Cooperation and Peace* and the 2005 *Rabat Commitment* are particularly noteworthy. The *Rabat Commitment* (adopted as the outcome document of the expert-level conference on 'Dialogue among Cultures and Civilizations through Concrete and Sustained Initiatives') emphasizes the need for intercultural education to become an integral part of quality education, from preschool education up through ongoing adult education, as well as in non-formal educational contexts, literacy campaigns and extracurricular activities. The importance of

this endeavour was recently reaffirmed at the Copenhagen Conference on 'Education for Intercultural Understanding and Dialogue' (see UNESCO, 2008b).

Arts and humanities education, multimedia activities, museums, travel and discovery activities all help to develop the critical capacities — curiosity, humility and hospitality — that are indispensable to combating unilateral points of view and building confidence, both in oneself and in others. These are basic competencies that allow people to adapt to a culturally diverse social environment, even when it is not always possible to fully understand the other.

Sensitizing people to cultural diversity is more a matter of approaches and methods than of the assimilation of content. Tolerance must be practised before it can become a habitual response. Intercultural skills and cultural diversity cannot really be meaningfully taught in a mechanical way, as add-ons to standard curricula: they are developed through other subject matters, methods or activities that are already part of educational curricula. Pluralistic education and participatory approaches to learning can be of great importance to the development of intercultural competencies, becoming aware of the relative nature of one's own culture, and learning to distinguish what unites rather than what separates us. Such competencies go beyond the mere capacity to 'live together', since they involve, besides the tolerance that makes us capable of living in peace alongside one another, a true capacity to open up to differences, to transcend what makes us who we are so as to meet others as they are.

Intercultural competencies and pedagogies
The founding principles of UNESCO enshrined in its Constitution (1945) are based on the conviction that education is fundamental to addressing the ignorance and the mistrust that are the source of human conflict. Since prejudice is based, among other things, on what we do not know or on false preconceptions, facilitating cultural openness through the development of intercultural competencies in schools and out of school is the key to fostering intercultural dialogue and winning the fight against a 'clash of ignorances' (see section 2.3 in chapter 2).

The issue of intercultural competencies (or skills) is riddled with difficulties and has spurred many debates (see for example Benavot and Braslavsky, 2007). It has been extensively argued that such competencies relate to each society's context and situation, and thus vary widely depending on one's particular lifestyle or value system. Some anthropologists even claim that certain societies are more open than others (Maranda, 2007). The challenge here is to identify a strategy that the international community could implement for promoting the development of intercultural competencies, without falling prey to a 'one size fits all' approach to education and furthering the homogenization of educational systems. In each society, specific procedures, as well as competencies, exist through which its members apprehend and manage intercultural situations. In some societies, cultural differences are managed through healing rites and songs (Severi, 2008). We would make a major step towards identifying intercultural competencies if we were to discover what is common to different societal approaches in dealing with what is alien to them. Some of these practices are not necessarily recognized at first sight as explicitly relating to intercultural situations, but a thorough inventory of some of them, using mechanisms such as those provided in UNESCO's 2003 *Convention on the Safeguarding of Intangible Cultural Heritage*, could benefit a pluralistic approach to intercultural dialogue.

It is generally admitted that the teaching of intercultural competencies should start as early as possible and last throughout life as an adaptive strategy. As illustrated by social distance indicators available in World Values Surveys 1999–2000 (see Inglehart et al., 2004), research into the extent to which people are willing to embrace the existence of individuals or groups perceived as different in everyday life, namely within neighbourhoods, shows that youth tend to be more tolerant than adults (Vala and Costa-Lopes, 2008). Educational strategies for the development of intercultural competencies can benefit from this finding: young people's basic curiosity, their capacity to listen and their willingness to engage in role-play tend to override any sense of threat in the face of difference. From this perspective, the benefits of diverse classrooms for the flourishing of intercultural competencies are obvious. The more children encounter differences, especially in the facilitated environment of a classroom, the more they can possibly learn that diversity is a gift, not a liability (UNESCO Bangkok, 2004).

Building intercultural awareness through the humanities and social sciences

The importance of the humanities and social sciences for the development of intercultural competencies relates to their contribution to the discovery of multiple knowledge systems that do not necessarily conform to the learners' cultural backgrounds. History, geography, social studies, philosophy, languages and the like are therefore crucial for the teaching of cultural diversity and the discovery of cultural differences. In some countries, moral education also plays an important role. In this respect, as underlined by the High-Level Group for the Alliance of Civilizations, formal schooling can be 'a major avenue' for the development of intercultural competencies, 'because existing infrastructure and policies make attendance compulsory in most countries, and because there is already a place for studying human history and other relevant subjects in public-sector and private schools' (Alliance of Civilizations, 2006).

The study of history and geography brings learners into contact with different times and different places, encouraging them to become aware of their own biases and to re-examine their assumptions. The same occurs in the study of different artistic traditions, religious beliefs and performance genres. Ideally, this increases *intercultural*

The humanities and the arts provide powerful incentives to explore the rootedness and interrelatedness of all things, situations, concepts and values. In this way, they make a major contribution to critical thinking

awareness and produces a disposition to *world-mindedness*, a way of thinking and an attitude that extends knowledge of difference and acceptance of its naturalness to groups and traditions beyond those the individual has directly studied and known. To this end, subjects like history and social sciences need to be contextualized in accordance with the contemporary needs of societies. To demonstrate how cultures have always been enriched by each other and have evolved through contact, exchange and dialogue with each other, it is necessary to develop fair, accurate and balanced educational materials that fuel learners' curiosity. Learning about world or regional history, geography and contemporary societies in today's interconnected world is especially important and should be allocated sufficient place in national school systems, alongside local and national (or sub-national) histories. With its General and Regional Histories (*General History of Africa, General History of Latin America, General History of the Caribbean, History of Civilizations of Central Asia, The Different Aspects of Islamic Culture*, and *History of Humanity*), one of UNESCO's ambitions has been to contribute to such contextualization and increase the relevance of the teaching of history.

Since our understanding of cultural diversity relies as much on our knowledge of others as on our knowledge of the group to which we belong, civic education — which specifically aims at facilitating our learning to live together — is vital. Moreover, at a time when many misunderstandings about world religions are arising which become grounds for cultural sensitivities and clashes, it may be time to examine the possibility of including world religions and faiths (their origins, beliefs, practices and traditions) in curricula in order to nurture respect for our deepest differences while approaching them through the diversity of cultural experiences and expressions that accompany them (arts, rituals, customs).

Intercultural education through the arts
The arts can help foster attitudes favouring intercultural openness. Arts education can also help to address issues such as ethnocentrism, relativity of tastes, bias, stereotyping, prejudice, discrimination and racism.

In keeping with the recommendations of the International Commission on Education for the Twenty-first Century about learning in all areas of cultural life (Delors et al., 1996), the arts can be a strong and universal tool for developing mutual understanding and competencies.

Indeed, arts education, in the broadest sense possible, is a critical means for teaching about the diversity of approaches and cultivating an awareness of cultural diversity. The 2006 Lisbon World Conference on Arts Education highlighted in particular the diversity of practices that contribute to the development of individual capacities through art, and how the encounter with cultural differences in a given context helps individuals to develop sensitivity to the diversity of the world's cultures. From the perspective of the cognitive sciences, the teaching of the arts, like the teaching of humanities, helps to reconnect scientific and emotional processes with intuition, a key factor of intercultural openness (Damasio and Dornsife, 2007; Lehrer, 2008). Practising the arts is also a powerful way of socializing with others. In formal education, arts education generally includes dance, music, painting (and other forms of visual arts), theatre and crafts.

Thus arts education is not a mere luxury in school curricula, where the ultimate objective is to instil openness and encourage innovation. In arts education, the opportunities for wonder are multiplied through aesthetic experience; it is particularly effective with young children, as arts education taps into children's natural curiosity and desire for discovery, while also teaching them to accept and appreciate culturally different forms of expression (see chapter 2, DREAM Centres). This in turn helps to enhance self-esteem and identify strengths, weaknesses, values, aspirations and goals. Arts education therefore offers a powerful approach to addressing such issues as ethnocentrism, relativity of tastes, bias, stereotyping, prejudice, discrimination, and racism (Witte, 2006). All these skills, which have a long-term impact on youth, can be carried over into many culturally diverse circumstances and situations, thereby enhancing communication and cooperation, problem-solving and resolution skills.

A cultural-diversity approach to arts education is not about aesthetic enculturation but about respecting cultures. One way is to begin with similarities. For instance, if a North American teacher wants to introduce a koto (Japanese musical instrument) to a class, he or she could start by describing the commonly shared appreciation of music among all cultures, and then draw comparisons with other instruments that may be more familiar to the class; the idea being that different music is still equally valuable and carries value in another culture. There is a pathway in cultural attitudes that leads from awareness to curiosity to discovery and then to tolerance and eventually appreciation. Arts education allows for a channel of creative and emotional expression that might otherwise be suppressed, or expressed in the form of negative emotions and attitudes directed against others. A practical application of such an approach is the Peace through Art programme of the International Child Art Foundation (ICAF), which organized a three-week programme in 2002, in which ten Greek-Cypriots and ten Turkish-Cypriots learned about their respective prejudices and stereotypes via artistic expressions. In this way, arts education can help to counter prejudice while contributing to more balanced personal and social development.

Intercultural education beyond the classroom

Since the education process that harnesses cultural diversity is a lifelong process, the development of intercultural competencies is not — and indeed cannot be — limited to the classroom but must extend to the 'university of life'. To this end, greater use could be made of cultural institutions — art galleries, museums and archives, under the guidance of the curators and oral historians, who can help to re-contextualize the objects exhibited (Kamba, 2006).

Such institutions must, of course, guarantee an unbiased, pluralistic and participatory approach, providing concerned parties with information (including scientific information) about cultural issues. Museums in this vein have been emerging as places for encountering cultural diversity through the social interaction of multiple voices and viewpoints of represented communities. In going beyond a purely folklore-based approach, these new means of representation have the potential to arouse the public's interest in the significance of the object or form of cultural expression set before them, giving equal value to all the cultural expressions presented. What is more, museums, cultural centres and other places of memory can also play a special role in reconciliation and in post-conflict situations. Reference to a common artistic or cultural heritage often helps to restore the cohesion of the national community after years of conflict (see Box 4.4 and chapter 2).

The humanities and the arts, generally speaking, provide the means for seeing cultural differences as equal and equally respectable, and provide powerful incentives to explore the rootedness and interrelatedness of all things, situations, concepts and values. In this way, they make a major contribution to critical thinking, since, without becoming aware of the multiplicity of ways of living, ways of learning and the 'thickness' and complexity of life, assumptions that hinder intercultural awareness and dialogue cannot be swept aside. As stated in the *Rabat Commitment*, awareness of the positive value of cultural diversity goes hand in hand with intercultural education and awareness-building (see UNESCO *Guidelines*

| Box 4.4 | **Museums as a space for intercultural learning** |

The Luanda National Museum of Anthropology in Angola provides a remarkable example of the key role museums can play in promoting tolerance and cultural diversity. Following the 1975–2002 civil war, which ripped apart the country's social fabric, the reorganization of the museum's collections helped to bring to the fore the common Bantu cultural basis shared by Angola's various ethnic groups (Kongo, Cokwe, Ambundu, Nyaneka, Ambo, Ovimbundu, etc.), despite the diversity of political and religious customs. The exhibition also helped to convey a message of unity and break down cultural barriers between ethnic groups by representing the unifying rather than differentiating factors.

Using such an approach, museums and other types of institutions can exercise their central educational function and foster intercultural awareness and restore a sense of dignity to minority and marginalized communities. But even here these institutions must be sensitive to the views of others. For example, for some indigenous communities, the direct ownership of sacred objects is taboo, an attitude that runs counter to the very principle of permanent collections of works of art. As a consequence, some cultural centres, such as the *Uma Fukun* (meeting place) cultural centre in Timor-Leste, have respected this tradition by leaving such sacred objects in the hands of the indigenous populations themselves and having them displayed in a place of safekeeping, that is, 'a place set aside for everything that is unique, venerated, respected, protected and celebrated'. Responses such as this must be encouraged and widely disseminated as models for how to adapt different understandings of art and history to the world's varied social and/or traditional contexts.
Source: UNESCO.

on *Intercultural Education* in 'In focus' and UNESCO, 2006b). Inclusiveness must be fostered not only in the classroom (as a professional responsibility of teachers) or school administration but in the educational system and the learning environment as a whole. Indeed, inclusiveness can take hold only if parents and communities become involved in these processes in a participatory and empowering way, facilitated by a pluralistic approach to education.

Conclusion

The quest for quality education is today inextricably linked to the challenges of providing inclusive and pluralistic educational strategies, adapted to the contexts of learners' lives in both content and form. Indeed, the ambitions of Education for All (EFA) cannot be realized if the right to education is understood in terms of imposed curricula or if learning is restricted to formal schooling to the detriment of overall empowerment and appropriate and fruitful development. The universal ambition of education for all is synonymous with lifelong learning for all and must allow for the diversity of culturally embedded learning environments that exist throughout the world.

As underlined at the Geneva International Conference on Education (2004), the principal challenge for education in the 21st century is to *learn to live together*, which requires improving our ability to equip people with capacities to deal with cultural differences and cultural change within increasingly multicultural societies. This is a new kind of literacy, on a par with the importance of reading and writing skills or numeracy: *cultural literacy* has become the lifeline for today's world, a fundamental resource for harnessing the multiple venues education can take (from family and tradition to the media, both old and new, and to informal groups and activities) and an indispensible tool for transcending the 'clash of ignorances'. It can be seen as part of a broad toolkit of worldviews, attitudes and competences that young people acquire for their lifelong journey. The advocacy for linguistic and cultural diversity within education is an awareness-raising campaign in need of holistic and official recognition at the highest possible levels in order to convince all parties of its benefits and relevance.

Chapter 4 Recommendations

In order to further the process of learning to live together, there is a need to promote intercultural competencies, including those embedded in the everyday practices of communities, with a view to improving pedagogical approaches to intercultural relations.

To this end, action should be taken to:

a. Undertake a global comparative survey of educational content and methods, including traditional modes of transmission, with particular reference to the recognition and accommodation of cultural diversity.

b. Support efforts to identify and/or create opportunities and facilities for culture-specific learning in each educational system, making use of existing instruments such as EFA National Assessment Reports.

c. Adapt teaching methods to the requirements of the everyday life of learners, with the necessary support of educational policy-makers, educational professionals at all levels and local communities, recognizing the cultural dimension as a central pillar of Education for Sustainable Development.

d. Develop international guidelines for the promotion of intercultural dialogue through the arts, based on the identification of good practices in arts education.

In focus:

UNESCO's Guidelines on Intercultural Education

These Guidelines represent the outcome of an Expert Meeting on Intercultural Education held at UNESCO in March 2006. They aim to address the key issues arising in increasingly multicultural societies as they relate to: culture and identities, culture and education, culture and language, culture and religion, cultural diversity and cultural heritage, majority and minority cultures, and multiculturalism and interculturalism. Within the general framework of the four pillars of education identified by the International Commission on Education for the Twenty-first Century (Delors et al., 1996) — 'learning to be', 'learning to know', 'learning to do' and 'learning to live together' — these key issues have been developed with reference to the whole set of existing international standard-setting instruments (the *Universal Declaration of Human Rights*, treaties, conventions and covenants, declarations and recommendations) as well as to the existing outcomes from international conferences.

The issues are articulated around three basic principles, which serve as frameworks for the identification of concrete strategies to be pursued.

Principle 1: Intercultural education respects the cultural identity of the learner through the provision of culturally appropriate and responsive quality education for all.

This principle can be achieved through:

1.1. The use of curricula and teaching and learning materials that:
- build upon the diverse systems of knowledge and experiences of the learners;
- incorporate their histories, knowledge and technologies, value systems and further social, economic and cultural aspirations;
- introduce the learners to an understanding and an appreciation of their cultural heritage;
- aim at developing respect for the learners' cultural identity, language and values;
- make use of local resources.

1.2. The development of teaching methods that:
- are culturally appropriate, for example through the integration of traditional pedagogies and the use of traditional forms of media, such as story-telling, drama, poetry and song;
- are based on practical, participatory and contextualized learning techniques that include: activities resulting from collaboration with cultural institutions; study trips and visits to sites and monuments; and productive activities that are linked to the community's social, cultural and economic needs.

1.3. The development of culturally appropriate methods of assessment.

1.4. The choice of a language of instruction which includes, where possible, the mother tongue of the learners.

1.5. Appropriate teacher training that aims at:
- familiarizing teachers with the cultural heritage of their country;
- familiarizing teachers with practical, participatory and contextualized teaching methods;
- raising awareness of the educational and cultural needs of minority groups;
- imparting the ability to adapt educational contents, methods and materials to the needs of groups whose cultures diverge from the majority group;
- facilitating the application of diversity as a tool in the classroom to benefit the learner.

1.6. The promotion of learning environments that are respectful of cultural diversity through, for example, awareness of dietary requirements; respect for dress codes; and the designation of areas for prayer or meditation.

1.7. Interaction between the school and the community and the involvement of the learners and/or their communities in the educational processes through the:

- use of the school as a centre for social and cultural activities, both for educational purposes and for the community;
- participation of traditional artisans and performers as instructors;
- recognition of the role of learners as vehicles of culture;
- decentralization for the development of contents and methods to take into account cultural and institutional differences from one region to another; and
- participation of learners, parents and other community members, teachers and administrators from different cultural backgrounds in school management, supervision and control, decision-making, planning and the implementation of education programmes, and the development of curricula and learning and teaching materials.

Principle 2: Intercultural education provides every learner with the cultural knowledge, attitudes and skills necessary to achieve active and full participation in society.

This principle can be achieved through:

2.1. The guaranteeing of equal and equitable opportunities in education via the:

- provision of equal access to all forms of education for all cultural groups of the population;
- elimination of all forms of discrimination in the education system;
- provision of educational qualifications to ensure equal access to secondary and postsecondary education and vocational training;
- adoption of measures that facilitate the integration in the education system of groups with special cultural needs, such as the children of migrant workers;
- provision of equal opportunities for participation in the learning process;
- provision of learning environments that are non-discriminatory, safe and peaceful;
- implementation of special measures to address contexts where historical backlogs limit the ability of learners and teachers to participate as equals with everyone else in society.

2.2. The use of curricula and teaching and learning materials that:

- impart knowledge about the history, traditions, language and culture of existing minorities to majority groups;
- impart knowledge about society as a whole to minorities;
- aim at eliminating prejudices about culturally distinct population groups within a country;
- involve various cultural systems through the presentation of knowledge from different cultural perspectives;
- create a comprehensive grasp of reading, writing and the spoken word, enabling citizens to gain access to information, to understand clearly the situation in which they are living, to express their needs, and to take part in social activities.

2.3. Appropriate teaching methods that:

- promote the learners' active participation in the education process;
- integrate formal and non-formal, traditional and modern teaching methods;

- promote an active learning environment, for example through the conduct of concrete projects, in order to demystify book-based knowledge and to give people a sense of confidence and to acquire cultural skills, such as the ability to communicate or to cooperate with others.

2.4. A clear definition and accurate assessment of learning outcomes, including knowledge, skills, attitudes and values.

2.5. Appropriate language teaching: all learners should acquire the capacity to communicate, express themselves, listen and engage in dialogue in their mother tongue, the official or national language(s) of their country and in one or more foreign languages.

2.6. Appropriate teacher initial education and permanent professional training that provides teachers with:

- a profound comprehension of the intercultural paradigm in education and its implication for the transformation of everyday practice in classrooms, schools and communities;
- a critical awareness of the role education ought to play in combatting racism and discrimination;
- a rights-based approach to education and learning;
- the competencies to design, implement and evaluate locally determined school curricula based on the needs and aspirations of learners and the communities to which they belong;
- the skills to incorporate pupils from non-dominant cultures into the learning process;
- the skills to take into account the heterogeneity of the learners;
- a command of methods and techniques of observation, listening and intercultural communication; of more than one working language where appropriate and of some notions of anthropological analysis;
- a command of appropriate assessment procedures and open-mindedness to continual assessment, evaluation and redefinition of methods.

Principle 3: Intercultural education provides all learners with cultural knowledge, attitudes and skills that enable them to contribute to respect, understanding and solidarity among individuals, ethnic, social, cultural and religious groups and nations.

This principle can be achieved through:

3.1. The development of curricula that contribute to:

- discovery of cultural diversity, awareness of the positive value of cultural diversity and respect for cultural heritage;
- critical awareness of the struggle against racism and discrimination;
- knowledge about cultural heritage through the teaching of history, geography, literature, languages, artistic and aesthetic disciplines, scientific and technological subjects;
- understanding and respect for all peoples; their cultures, civilizations, values and ways of life; including domestic ethnic cultures and cultures of other nations;
- awareness of the increasing global interdependence between peoples and nations;
- awareness not only of rights but also of duties incumbent upon individuals, social groups and nations toward each other;
- understanding of the necessity for international solidarity and cooperation;
- awareness of one's own cultural values that underlie the interpretation of situations and problems as well as the ability to reflect on and review information enriched by the knowledge of different cultural perspectives;

- respect for differing patterns of thinking.

3.2. Adequate teaching and learning methods that:

- treat the heritages, experience, and contributions of different ethnic groups with comparable dignity, integrity, and significance;
- provide for learning in an egalitarian context;
- correspond to the values taught;
- provide for interdisciplinary projects.

3.3. The acquisition of skills to communicate and cooperate beyond cultural barriers and to share and cooperate with others through:

- direct contacts and regular exchanges between pupils, students, teachers and other educators in different countries or cultural environments;
- the implementation of joint projects between establishments and institutions from different countries, with a view to solving common problems;
- the setting up of international networks of pupils, students and researchers working towards the same objectives;
- the acquisition of abilities for conflict resolution and mediation.

3.4. The teaching and learning of foreign languages and the strengthening of the cultural component in language teaching.

3.5. Adequate teacher initial education and permanent professional development aiming at creating:

- awareness of the positive value of cultural diversity and of the right of the person to be different;
- a critical awareness of the role that local communities and local knowledge systems, languages and social practices play in the learning process and construction of the person in national, regional and global societies;
- knowledge of the history of civilization and anthropology so as to facilitate better understanding and the ability to convey the idea of the plural, dynamic, relative and complementary nature of cultures;
- the social and political competencies and the open-mindedness conducive to the permanent promotion of active social participation in school management and in the design, implementation and evaluation of school projects and programmes;
- development of an ability to make the best use of visits to museums and other institutions for effective intercultural teaching;
- open-mindedness and an ability to interest the student in learning about and understanding others;
- the acquisition of techniques of observation, sympathetic listening and intercultural communication.

Another outcome of the Expert Meeting on Intercultural Education was the discussion of a database on intercultural education (see UNESCO, 2006c).

Source: UNESCO, 2006b.

References and websites

Background documents and UNESCO sources

Bates, P., Chiba, M., Kube, S. and Nakashima, D. (eds.). 2009. *Learning and Knowing in Indigenous Societies Today*. Paris, UNESCO. http://unesdoc. unesco.org/images/0018/001807/180754e.pdf

Benavot, A. 2008. Background material for the compilation of IBE [International Bureau of Education] figures on timetables and curricula.

Bühmann, D. and Trudell, B. 2008. *Mother Tongue Matters: Local Language as a Key to Effective Learning*. Paris, UNESCO. http://unesdoc.unesco.org/images/0016/001611/161121e.pdf

Damasio, A. and Dornsife, D. 2007. Cultural diversity, neuroscience and education. Background paper.

Delors, J. et al. 1996. *Learning: The Treasure Within*. Report to UNESCO of the International Commission on Education for the Twenty-first Century. http://unesdoc.unesco.org/images/0010/001095/109590Eo.pdf

Diagne, M. 2008. Babel n'est pas une catastrophe. Contribution to the International Meeting of Experts on Cultural Diversity and Education, Barcelona, 14–16 January.

Eberhard, C. 2008. Rediscovering education through intercultural dialogue. Contribution to the International Meeting of Experts on Cultural Diversity and Education, Barcelona, 14–16 January.

Fasheh, M. 2007. Cultural diversity in formal and non-formal educational systems. Background paper.

Faure, E. et al. 1972. *Learning to Be: The World of Education Today and Tomorrow*. Report to UNESCO of the International Commission on the Development of Education. Paris, UNESCO. http://unesdoc.unesco.org/images/0000/000018/001801e.Pdf

Gauthier, C. and Dembélé, M. 2004. Qualité de l'enseignement et qualité de l'éducation. Revue des résultats de recherché. Background paper. http://unesdoc.unesco.org/images/0014/001466/146641f.pdf

Gundara, J. 2008. Some current intercultural issues in multicultural societies. Contribution to the International Meeting of Experts on Cultural Diversity and Education, Barcelona, 14–16 January.

Inglis, C. 2008. *Planning for Cultural Diversity*. Fundamentals of Educational Planning Series, No. 87. Paris, UNESCO.

Kamba, A. 2006. Festivals in Zimbabwe. Contribution to the regional consultation in Africa (Observatory of Cultural Policies in Africa).

King, L. and Schielmann, S. 2004. *The Challenge of Indigenous Education: Practice and Perspectives*. Paris, UNESCO.

Koenig, M. and Guchteneire, P. F. A. (eds.). 2007. *Democracy and Human Rights in Multicultural Societies*. Aldershot, Ashgate.

López, L. E. 2009. Reaching the unreached: indigenous intercultural bilingual education in Latin America. Background paper.

Maranda, P. 2006. Paramètres cognitifs de l'ouverture à la diversité culturelle: une perspective anthropologique. Background paper.

Ödman, C. 2007. Diversity of knowledge and creativity for sustainable human development in the contexts of science and education: intercultural aspects of knowledge, its creation, transmission and utilization. Background paper.

Pascual, J. 2006. *Local Policies for Cultural Diversity*. Barcelona, UNESCO and Working Group on Culture of the United Cities and Local Governments. http://www.cities-localgovernments.org/uclg/upload/newTempDoc/EN_332_report_local_policies_for_cultural_diversity_en.pdf

Pimparé, S. 2005. *Beyond Empowerment*. Developing Learning Communities Series, No. 2. Paris, UNESCO. http://unesdoc.unesco.org/images/0014/001421/142118e.pdf

—. 2002. *'Liberate School': A Case Study*. Developing Learning Communities Series, No 1. Paris, UNESCO. http://unesdoc.unesco.org/images/0013/001309/130927E.pdf

Rengifo, G. 2008. Educar en la diversidad. Aportes de la diversidad cultural a la educación. Contribution to the International Meeting of Experts on Cultural Diversity and Education, Barcelona, 14–16 January.

Severi, C. 2008. La communication interculturelle : formes et contenus. Une approche anthropologique et cognitive. Background paper.

Shikshantar (ed.). 2003. *If the Shoe Doesn't Fit? Footprints of Learning Societies in South Asia. Vimukt Shiksha*, Vol. 12. http://www.swaraj.org/shikshantar/vimukt_shoe.htm.

Stepanyants, M. 2008. Challenges for education in the age of globalization. Contribution to the International Meeting of Experts on Cultural Diversity and Education, Barcelona, 14–16 January.

UNESCO. 2008a. EFA Global Monitoring Report 2009. *Overcoming Inequality: Why Governance Matters*. Paris, UNESCO. http://unesdoc.unesco.org/images/0017/001776/177683e.pdf

—. 2008b. Closing Statement of the two co-chairs of the high-level inaugural segment of the Copenhagen Conference 'Education for Intercultural Understanding and Dialogue'. http://portal.unesco.org/es/ev.php-URL_ID=43799&URL_DO=DO_PRINTPAGE&URL_SECTION=201.html

—. 2007. EFA Global Monitoring Report 2008. *Education for All by 2015: Will we make it?* Paris, UNESCO. http://unesdoc.unesco.org/images/0015/001548/154820e.pdf

—. 2006a. *Emerging and Re-Emerging Learning Communities: Old Wisdoms and New Initiatives from Around the World*. Developing Learning Communities Series, No. 3. Paris, UNESCO. http://unesdoc.unesco.org/images/0014/001459/145997e.pdf

—. 2006b. *Guidelines on Intercultural Education*. Paris, UNESCO. http://unesdoc.unesco.org/images/0014/001478/147878e.pdf

—. 2006c. *Expert Meeting on Intercultural Education, Paris, 20–22 March. Report*. Paris, UNESCO. http://unesdoc.unesco.org/images/0014/001475/147539e.pdf

—. 2005a. *Guidelines for Inclusion: Ensuring Access to Education for All*. Paris, UNESCO. http://unesdoc.unesco.org/images/0014/001402/140224e.pdf

—. 2005b. *The Rabat Commitment*. http://www.unaoc.org/repository/rabat_commitment.pdf

—. 2004. EFA Global Monitoring Report 2005. *Education for All: The Quality Imperative*. Paris, UNESCO. http://unesdoc.unesco.org/images/0013/001373/137333e.pdf

—. 2003a. *Education in a Multilingual World*. UNESCO Education Position Paper. Paris, UNESCO. http://unesdoc.unesco.org/images/0012/001297/129728e.pdf

—. 2003b. *Convention on the Safeguarding of Intangible Cultural Heritage*. Paris, UNESCO. http://unesdoc.unesco.org/images/0013/001325/132540e.pdf

—. 2002. *Education and Cultural Diversity*. Paris, UNESCO. http://unesdoc.unesco.org/images/0012/001252/125205e.pdf

—. 2001. *Universal Declaration on Cultural Diversity*. Paris, UNESCO. http://unesdoc.unesco.org/images/0012/001271/127160m.pdf

—. 2000a. *Dakar Framework for Action — Education for All: Meeting Our Collective Commitments*. Paris, UNESCO. http://unesdoc.unesco.org/images/0012/001211/121147e.pdf

—. 2000b. General Conference Resolution 12: Implementation of a language policy for the world based on multilingualism. 30 C/Resolution 12. *Records of the General Conference, 30th Session, Paris, 26 October to 17 November 1999*. Volume 1: *Resolutions*. Paris, UNESCO, pp. 35–36. http://unesdoc.unesco.org/images/0011/001185/118514E.pdf

—. 1999a. *Declaration on Science and the Use of Scientific Knowledge*. http://www.unesco.org/science/wcs/eng/declaration_e.htm

—. 1999b. *Science Agenda: Framework for Action*. http://www.unesco.org/science/wcs/eng/framework.htm

—. 1997. *Hamburg Declaration on Adult Learning*. http://www.unesco.org/education/uie/confintea/pdf/con5eng.pdf

—. 1996a *Amman Affirmation*. http://www.unesco.org/education/efa/ed_for_all/background/amman_affirmation.shtml

—. 1996b. *Manual for Statistics on Non-Formal Education*. Paris, UNESCO.

—. 1993. *Delhi Declaration and Framework for Action*. http://www.mopme.gov.bd/DELHI.pdf

—. 1990. *World Declaration on Education for All: Meeting Basic Learning Needs* [= *Jomtien Declaration*]. http://www.unesco.org/education/efa/ed_for_all/background/jomtien_declaration.shtml

—. 1976. *Recommendation on the Development of Adult Education*. http://www.unesco.org/education/pdf/NAIROB_E.PDF

—. 1974. *Recommendation Concerning Education for International Understanding, Cooperation and Peace*. http://www.unesco.org/education/nfsunesco/pdf/Peace_e.pdf

—. 1960. *Convention against Discrimination in Education*. 14 December. http://portal.unesco.org/en/ev.php-URL_ID=12949&URL_DO=DO_TOPIC&URL_SECTION=201.html

UNESCO and Council of Europe. 2007. *Educating Roma Children in Europe: Towards Quality Education for Roma Children; Transition from Early Childhood to Primary Education*. Expert Meeting Final Report. http://unesdoc.unesco.org/images/0016/001611/161164e.pdf

UNESCO Associated Schools Project Network (ASPnet). 2009. *Good Practices in Education for Sustainable Development*. http://unesdoc.unesco.org/images/0018/001812/181270E.pdf

UNESCO Bangkok. 2004. *Embracing Diversity: Toolkit for Creating Inclusive, Learning-Friendly Environments*. Bangkok, UNESCO Bangkok. http://www2.unescobkk.org/elib/publications/032revised/EmbracingDiversity.pdf

United Nations. 2007. *Declaration on the Rights of Indigenous Peoples*. http://www.un.org/esa/socdev/unpfii/documents/DRIPS_en.pdf

—. 1966. *International Covenant on Economic, Social and Cultural Rights*. http://www2.ohchr.org/english/law/cescr.htm

—. 1948. *Universal Declaration of Human Rights*. http://www.un.org/en/documents/udhr

Vala, J. and Costa-Lopes, R. 2008. Youth, intolerance and diversity. Background paper.

Wapotro, B. 2008. La diversité de l'éducation: Comment traduire, en terme de programme éducatif la reconnaissance de la diversité culturelle. Contribution to the International Meeting of Experts on Cultural Diversity and Education, Barcelona, 14–16 January.

Websites

Auroville Charter: http://www.auroville.org/vision/charter.htm

Education Policy and Data Center: http://epdc.org

International Bureau of Education (IBE): http://www.ibe.unesco.org

International Child Art Foundation (ICAF): http://www.icaf.org

International Institute for Educational Planning (IIEP): http://www.iiep.unesco.org

LINKS Programme: http://portal.unesco.org/science/en/ev.php-URL_ID=1945&URL_DO=DO_TOPIC&URL_SECTION=201.html

OECD Definition and Selection of Competencies (DeSeCo): http://www.oecd.org/document/17/0,3343,en_2649_39263238_2669073_1_1_1_1,00.html

OECD Programme for International Student Assessment (PISA): http://www.pisa.oecd.org/pages/0,3417,en_32252351_32235731_1_1_1_1,00.html

Peace Through Art: http://www.icaf.org/programs/peacethroughart/default.html

TIMSS (Trends in International Mathematics and Science Study) & PIRLS (Progress in International Reading Literacy Study) International Study Center: http://timss.bc.edu

UNESCO Associated Schools Project Network (ASPnet): http://portal.unesco.org/education/en/ev.php-URL_ID=7366&URL_DO=DO_TOPIC&URL_SECTION=201.html

UNESCO, Education for All (EFA) International Coordination: http://www.unesco.org/en/efa-international-coordination

UNESCO, General and Regional Histories: http://portal.unesco.org/culture/en/ev.php-URL_ID=35021&URL_DO=DO_PRINTPAGE&URL_SECTION=201.html

UNESCO, Inclusive Education: http://www.unesco.org/en/inclusive-education

UNESCO, Indigenous People: http://www.unesco.org/en/inclusive-education/indigenous-people

UNESCO, Languages in Education: http://www.unesco.org/en/languages-in-education

United Nations Decade of Education for Sustainable Development (2005–2014): http://www.unesco.org/en/esd

United Nations Literacy Decade (2003–2012): http://www.unesco.org/en/literacy/un-literacy-decade

World Conference on Arts Education (Lisbon, 6-9 March 2006): http://portal.unesco.org/culture/en/ev.php-URL_ID=26967&URL_DO=DO_TOPIC&URL_SECTION=201.html

References

African Union. 2006. *Charter for African Cultural Renaissance*. Addis Ababa, Ethiopia: African Union. http://www.africa-union.org/root/au/Documents/Treaties/text/Charter%20-%20African%20Cultural%20Renaissance_EN.pdf

Agrawal, A. 2002. Indigenous knowledge and the politics of classification. *International Social Science Journal*, Vol. 173, pp. 287–97. http://www-personal.umich.edu/~arunagra/papers/Indigenous%20Knowledges.pdf

Anderson, B. 1991. *Imagined Communities: Reflections on the Origin and Spread of Nationalism*. 2nd ed. London, Verso.

Ardoino, J. 2000. *Les Avatars de l'éducation*. Paris, Presses Universitaires de France.

Barbier, J.-M. (ed.). 1996. *Les savoirs théoriques et les savoirs d'action*. Paris, Presses Universitaires de France.

Batelaan, P. and Coomans, F. (eds.). 1999. *The International Basis for Intercultural Education including Anti-Racist and Human Rights Education*. 2nd ed. Paris, International Association for Intercultural Education (IAIE) in co-operation with the International Bureau of Education (IBE) and the Council of Europe. http://www.ibe.unesco.org/fileadmin/user_upload/archive/publications/free_publications/batelaan.PDF

Bates, P. 2009. Learning and Inuit knowledge in Nunavut, Canada. P. Bates, M. Chiba, S. Kube and D. Nakashima (eds.), *Learning and Knowing in Indigenous Societies Today*. Paris, UNESCO. http://unesdoc.unesco.org/images/0018/001807/180754e.pdf

Benavot, A. and Braslavsky, C. (eds.). 2007. *School Knowledge in Comparative and Historical Perspective: Changing Curricula in Primary and Secondary Education*. Dordrecht, Springer.

Bialystok E., Luk G. and Kwan, E. 2005. Bilingualism, biliteracy, and learning to read: Interactions among languages and writing systems. *Scientific Studies of Reading*, Vol. 9, No. 1, pp. 43–61.

Bialystok, E. and Hakuta, K. 1994. *In Other Words: The Science and Psychology of Second-Language Acquisition*. New York, Basic Books.

Bourdieu, P. 2001. *Science de la science et réflexivité*. Paris, Raisons d'agir.

Campbell, J. (ed.). 2001. *Creating Our Common Future: Educating for Unity in Diversity*. Paris, UNESCO.

Carr, W. and Kemmis, S. 1986. *Becoming Critical: Education, Knowledge and Action Research*. Basingstoke, Falmer Press.

Coleman, J. S. 1966. *Equality of Educational Opportunity Study (EEOS)*. Washington, DC, U.S. Department of Health, Education, and Welfare, Office of Education/National Center for Education Statistics.

Coomans, F. 2007. Content and Scope of the Right to Education as a Human Right and Obstacles to Its Realization. Y. Donders and V. Volodin (eds.), *Human Rights in Education, Science and Culture: Legal Developments and Challenges*. Paris, UNESCO. http://www.unesco.org/library/Donders2007.pdf

Council of Europe. 2007. *A Curriculum Framework for Romani*. Strasbourg, Language Policy Division, Council of Europe. http://www.coe.int/t/dg3/romatravellers/documentation/education/CurriculumframeworkRomani.pdf

—. 1995. *Framework Convention for the Protection of National Minorities*. http://conventions.coe.int/Treaty/Commun/QueVoulezVous.asp?NT=157&CL=ENG

Crahay, M. 2000. *L'école peut-elle être juste et efficace? De l'égalité des chances à l'égalité des acquis*. Brussels, De Boeck Université.

Cummins, J. 1979. Cognitive/academic language proficiency, linguistic interdependence, the optimum age question and some other matters. Working Papers on Bilingualism, No. 19, pp. 198–205. http://www.eric.ed.gov/ERICDocs/data/ericdocs2sql/content_storage_01/0000019b/80/37/ad/8c.pdf

Davies, L. and Talbot, C. 2008. Learning in conflict and postconflict contexts. *Comparative Education Review*, Vol. 52, No. 4 (1 November 2008), pp. 509–518.

De Pezeral, M. 2007. Growing up in Community: The Auroville Experience. *Beyond you and me*. Hampshire, Permanent Publications.

Delors, J. and Draxler, A. 2001. From unity of purpose to diversity of expression and needs: A perspective from UNESCO. D. S. Rychen and L. H. Salganik (eds.), *Defining and Selecting Key Competencies*. Kirkland, Wash.: Hogrefe & Huber.

Descola, P. 2005a. On anthropological knowledge. *Social Anthropology*, Vol. 12, Pt. 1, pp. 65-74.

—. 2005b. *Par-delà Nature et Culture*. Paris, Gallimard.

Diagne, M. 2005. *Critique de la raison oral: les pratiques discursives en Afrique noire*. Paris, Karthala.

Diop, C. A. 1981. *Civilisation ou barbarie: anthropologie sans complaisance*. Paris, Société Nouvelle Présence Africaine.

Dirkx, J. M. and Prenger, S. M. 1997. *A Guide for Planning and Implementing Instruction for Adults: A Theme-Based Approach.* San Francisco, Calif., Jossey-Bass.

Dutcher, N. 2004. *Expanding Educational Opportunity in Linguistically Diverse Societies.* 2nd ed. Washington, DC, Center for Applied Linguistics. http://www.cal.org/resources/pubs/fordreport_040501.pdf

Fishman, J. A. 1972. *Language and Nationalism: Two Integrative Essays.* Rowley, Mass. Newbury House.

—. 1967. Bilingualism with and without diglossia; diglossia with and without bilingualism. *Journal of Social Issues,* Vol. 32, pp. 29–38.

Freire, P. 2000. *Pedagogy of the Oppressed.* Translated by M. Bergman Ramos. 30th anniversary ed. New York, Continuum.

Hamel, R. E. 2007. Bilingual education for indigenous communities in Mexico. J. Cummins and N. H. Hornberger (eds.), *Bilingual Education.* (Volume 5 of N. H. Hornberger (ed.), *Encyclopedia of Language and Education.*) 2nd ed. Dordrecht, Springer.

Hattie, J. 1992. *Self-concept.* Hillsdale, N.J., Lawrence Erlbaum Associates.

Hölscher, P. (ed.). 1994. *Interkulturelles Lernen. Projekte and Materialien für die Sekundarstufe I.* Frankfurt am Main, Cornelsen Scriptor.

Holt, J. C. 1995. *Escape from Childhood.* Wakefield, Mass, Holt Associates.

Illich, I. 1970. *Deschooling Society.* London, Marion Boyars.

Inglehart, R., Basanez, M., Diez-Medrano, J., Halman, L. and Luijkx, R. (eds.). 2004. *Human Beliefs and Values: A Cross-Cultural Sourcebook Based on the 1999–2002 Values Surveys.* Ann Arbor, Mich., World Values Survey.

Inglehart, R. et al. 2004. *World Values Surveys and European Values Surveys, 1999–2001. User Guide and Codebook.* First ICPSR version. Ann Arbor, Mich.: Institute for Social Research. http://prod.library.utoronto.ca:8090/datalib/codebooks/icpsr/3975/cb3975.pdf

International Council of Adult Education (ICAE). 2003. *Agenda for the Future: Six Years Later.* Montevideo, ICAE. http://www.icae.org.uy/eng/icaeCONFINTEA8.htm

International Labour Organization (ILO). 1989. *Convention Concerning Indigenous and Tribal Peoples in Independent Countries.* Convention No. 169. Geneva, ILO. http://www.ilo.org/ilolex/cgi-lex/convde.pl?C169

Ishizawa, J. and Rengifo, G. 2009. *Biodiversity regeneration and intercultural knowledge transmission in the Peruvian Andes.* P. Bates, M. Chiba, S. Kube and D. Nakashima (eds.), *Learning and Knowing in Indigenous Societies Today.* Paris, UNESCO. http://unesdoc.unesco.org/images/0018/001807/180754e.pdf

King, B. 2002. Online games go multicultural. *Wired,* 30 January. http://www.wired.com/gaming/gamingreviews/news/2002/01/50000

Kuhn, T. S. 1996. *The Structure of Scientific Revolutions.* 3rd ed. Chicago, Ill., University of Chicago Press.

Latour, B. 2005. *Nous n'avons jamais été modernes: essai d'anthropologie symétrique.* Paris, La Découverte.

Lehrer, J. 2008. *Proust Was a Neuroscientist.* New York, Houghton Mifflin Harcourt.

López, L. E. and Hanemann, U. (eds.). 2009. *Alfabetización y multiculturalidad. Miradas desde América Latina.* Guatemala, UNESCO and UIL-GTZ.

López, L. E. and Küper, W. 2000. *Intercultural Bilingual Education in Latin America: Balance and Perspectives.* Eschborn, GTZ. http://www2.gtz.de/dokumente/bib/00-1510.pdf

López, L. E. and Sichra, I. 2008. Intercultural bilingual education for indigenous peoples in Latin America. J. Cummins and N. H. Hornberger (eds.), *Bilingual Education.* (Volume 5 of N. H. Hornberger (ed.), *Encyclopedia of Language and Education.*) 2nd ed. Dordrecht, Springer.

Marzal, M. 1993. *Historia de la antropología indigenista. México y Perú.* Lima, PUCP.

Meyer, J. W., Kamens, D. H. and Benavot, A. 1992. *School Knowledge for the Masses: World Models and National Primary Curricular Categories in the Twentieth Century.* Washington, DC, Falmer Press.

Miller, V. 2001. A learning society retrospective. *Vimukt Shiksha,* Vol. 9. http://www.swaraj.org/shikshantar/ls2_miller.pdf

Page, N. and Czuba, C. E. 1999. Empowerment: What is it? *Journal of Extension,* Vol. 37, No. 5, pp. 1–6. http://www.joe.org/joe/1999october/comm1.php

Pedersen, P. B. and Carey, J. C. 2002. *Multicultural Counseling in Schools: A Practical Handbook.* 2nd ed. Boston, Allyn & Bacon.

PROBE. 1999. *Public Report on Basic Education in India (PROBE).* New Delhi, Oxford University Press.

Progler, Y. 2000. Contemplating an education system for decolonization and rejuvenation. *Muslimedia,* 1–15 February. http://www.muslimedia.com/archives/features00/edusys.htm

Rapport, J. 1984. Studies in empowerment: introduction to the issue. J. Rappaport and R. Hess (eds.), *Studies in Empowerment: Steps toward Understanding and Action.* London, Routledge.

Romaine, S. 2007. The impact of language policy on endangered languages. M. Koenig and P. F. A. Guchteneire (eds.), *Democracy and Human Rights in Multicultural Societies.* Aldershot, Ashgate. http://www.unesco.org/most/vl4n2romaine.pdf

Rychen, D. S. 2004. Key competencies for all: an overarching conceptual frame of reference. D. S. Rychen and A. Tiana, *Developing Key Competencies in Education: Some Lessons from International and National Experience.* Paris, UNESCO.

Schmelkes, S., Águila, G. and Núñez, M. A. 2009. Alfabetización de jóvenes y adultos indígenas en México". In L. E. López and U. Hanemann (eds.), *Alfabetización y multiculturalidad. Miradas desde América Latina.* Guatemala: UNESCO and UIL-GTZ.

Seelye, H. N. 1993. *Teaching Culture: Strategies for Intercultural Communication.* 3rd ed. Chicago, Ill., NTC.

Seelye, H. N. and Wasilewski, J. H. 1996. *Between Cultures: Developing Self-Identity in a World of Diversity.* Chicago, Ill., NTC.

Sperber, D. 1982. *Le savoir des anthropologues: trois essais.* Paris, Hermann.

Sri Aurobindo International Institute for Educational Research (SAIIER). 2008. An integral education for ever progressing human beings: An introduction to education in Auroville. Report presented at the UNESCO Round Table 'Auroville, an Emerging World', 10 October. http://www.auroville.org/education/Text_of_Report_to_UNESCO_on_Education_in_AV.htm

Tomasevski, K. 2001. *Annual Report of the Special Rapporteur on the Right to Education.* UN Doc. E/CN.4/2001/52. New York, United Nations. http://www.unhchr.ch/Huridocda/Huridoca.nsf/0/8774217173a3fde0c1256a10002ecb42/$FILE/G0110177.pdf

United Nations Alliance of Civilizations (UNAOC). 2006. *Research Base for the High-Level Group Report — Education: Analysis and Existing Initiatives.* New York, Alliance of Civilizations. http://www.unaoc.org/repository/thematic_education.pdf

United Nations. 2002. United Nations Literacy Decade: Education for All; International Plan of Action; Implementation of General Assembly Resolution 56/116. A/57/218. http://daccessdds.un.org/doc/UNDOC/GEN/N02/484/86/IMG/N0248486.pdf?OpenElement

Verdiani, A. 2008. *L'éducation à la joie : un exemple d'éducation intégrale dans les écoles d'Auroville (Inde).* PhD thesis. University of Paris 8.

Wang, M. C., Haertel, G. D. and Walberg, H. J. 1993. Toward a knowledge base for school learning. *Review of Educational Research,* Vol. 63, No. 3, pp. 249–94 and 365–76. http://www.eric.ed.gov:80/ERICDocs/data/ericdocs2sql/content_storage_01/0000019b/80/14/b1/46.pdf

Witte, R. 2006. Cultural Competency Record. Contribution to the World Conference on Arts Education (Lisbon, Portugal, 6-9 March 2006).

Woolgar, S. and Latour, B. 1986. *Laboratory Life: The Social Construction of Scientific Facts.* 2nd ed. Princeton, N.J., Princeton University Press.

Zimmerman, M. A. 1984. Taking aim on empowerment research: On the distinction between individuals and psychological conceptions. *American Journal of Community Psychology,* Vol. 18, No. 1, pp. 169–77. http://deepblue.lib.umich.edu/bitstream/2027.42/44024/1/10464_2004_Article_BF00922695.pdf

A 'dialogue school' in Kazakhstan

Television satellite dish outside a yurt in Mongolia

Communication and cultural contents

This chapter looks at the entire landscape of communication and cultural contents — understood to encompass the press, books, radio, recorded media, cinema and television, as well as more recent phenomena (new media or information and communication technologies) such as the Internet, CDs, DVDs, video games, chat rooms and the blogosphere — from the standpoint of cultural diversity. Because the media and cultural industries have become highly dynamic sectors in economic, social and political terms, they are increasingly shaping individual and collective identities, worldviews, values and tastes in ways that are challenging formal education systems. As a result, today's communication and cultural products are becoming powerful tools of non-formal education and cultural transmission with the potential to expand intercultural understanding — though only insofar as they translate the reality, complexity and dynamics of cultural diversity.

Yet the current situation is riddled with paradoxes relating to issues of media access and information and media literacy. While the new media and new forms of distribution facilitate greater access to content production and the dissemination of cultural content, thereby opening up more opportunities for intercultural dialogue, political and economic imbalances, the asymmetries implicit in the digital divide, continue to restrict the opportunities for genuine cultural exchange. Moreover, the very multiplicity of choices and the cultural challenges they embody can result in cultural isolation as well as a proliferation of stereotypes.

The first section of this chapter reviews the impacts of globalization and technological innovation on the ways in which communication (by word, sound and image) and cultural contents both shape and are shaped by cultural diversity. The second section looks at the messages conveyed by the media and cultural industries in terms of the perception of other cultures and peoples, and how new media consumption patterns — revolutionized by multichannel television access, films and DVDs, telecommunication services, user-generated content, mobile media content, diaspora media and social networks — are both favourable and detrimental to cultural diversity. The third and final section highlights the need to invest in media and information literacy initiatives and policies that can strengthen the media and cultural industries to the benefit of cultural diversity, by harnessing the capacities offered by digital technologies for user-generated content and non-linear production.

Communication and Cultural Contents

5.1 Globalization and new media trends 131

Figure 5.1 Percentage of exports by region, 2006 131

Figure 5.2 Exports and imports of audiovisual services and copyrights, 2006 132

Figure 5.3 Percentage of countries by type of domestic music piracy levels in 2006 (physical piracy only) 132

Figure 5.4 Public radio programming for selected countries in 2005 132

Figure 5.5 Origin of top movies exhibited in 2006 133

Figure 5.6 Public television programming for selected countries in 2005 133

Figure 5.7 Recorded music repertoire for selected countries in 2006 133

Box 5.1 The emergence of international and pan-regional news services 134

5.2 Impacts of communication and cultural products 137

Box 5.2 The Power of Peace Network (PPN) 139

Box 5.3 Little Mosque on the Prairie 143

5.3 Policies fostering cultural diversity 144

Box 5.4 Implementing media literacy programmes 145

Box 5.5 Aboriginal Peoples Television Network (APTN) 148

Conclusion 150

Recommendations 151

In focus: Media toolkits for cultural diversity in broadcasting 152

References and websites 157

A woman listening to radio in Namaacha, Mozambique

5.1 Globalization and new media trends

In the last two decades, cultural diversity has enjoyed unprecedented visibility through the expansion of increasingly visual communication and cultural products for definitions, which have been at the forefront of far-reaching changes in contemporary culture since the end of the 1980s.[1] While it is undeniable that globalization has played an integrative role as a 'window on the world', mostly to the profit of a few powerful international conglomerates, recent shifts prompted by technological innovation and new consumption patterns are spurring new forms of 'globalization from below' and creating a two-way flow of communication and cultural products.

Global flows and imbalances

The importance of the media and cultural industries in quantitative and economic terms may be gauged from the statistics on cross-border flows. In 2006, the sector generated about US$51 billion in commercial revenue and a significant part of worldwide exports. In terms of employment and economic growth, in developing and developed countries alike, surveys (KEA, 2006; UNCTAD, 2008) indicate that global cultural industries accounted for more than 7 percent of global GDP and were worth about US$1,300 billion in 2006, that is, nearly twice the total of international tourism receipts, estimated at US$680 billion (UNWTO, 2007). In the 1990s in OECD countries, the cultural industries economy (also known as the economy of cultural and creative sectors, e.g. in UNCTAD terminology) grew at an annual rate twice that of service industries and four times that of manufacturing. In the EU, for example, this sector (comprising television, cinema, music, performing arts and entertainment) generated €654 billion and contributed 2.6 percent of the EU's GDP in 2003 and employed at least 5.8 million people in 2004.

In 2006 the six largest multimedia and transnational 'cultural' corporations — Disney, Time Warner, General Electric, Sony, Vivendi and Bertelsman — generated about US$320 billion in annual revenue. Generally speaking, there has been a concentration of power in the hands of a few global media players, notably AOL, News Corporation, CNN, MTV and Google, in addition to those cited above. Of course, the overall figures for the trade of cultural goods and services mask wide regional disparities, especially between developed and developing countries, as evidenced by the following 2006 trends in printed and recorded media (see Figure 5.1):

For *printed media* (books, newspapers, periodicals and other printed matter), the world's top five exporters accounted for more than 56 percent of the world's exports: the US (16.7 percent), the UK (15.6 percent), Germany (13.6 percent), France (5.7 percent) and China (4.9 percent). Europe dominated the sector (64 percent), followed by North America (20 percent), East Asia (10.7 percent), Latin America and the Caribbean (2.7 percent), Central and South Asia (0.9 percent), the Pacific (0.87 percent), sub-Saharan Africa (0.35 percent) and the Arab States (0.23 percent). In 2006, the top five importers of printed media were Canada, the UK, France, Germany and Switzerland.

For *recorded media* (primarily music, sound recordings and related software), the top five exporters accounted for more than 62 percent of the world's exports: Ireland (14.2 percent), Germany (13.9 percent), the US (12.4 percent), the Netherlands (11.5 percent) and the UK (10.6 percent). Europe also dominated this sector (71 percent), followed by North America (15 percent), East Asia (6.7 percent), Central and South Asia (3.6 percent), Latin America and the Caribbean (2.2 percent), the Pacific (0.83 percent), sub-Saharan Africa (0.41 percent) and the Arab States (0.02 percent). In 2006, the top five importers of recorded media were Italy, Germany, the UK, France and Belgium.

... recent shifts prompted by technological innovation and new consumption patterns are spurring new forms of 'globalization from below' and creating a two-way flow of communication and cultural products

Chapter 5 Communication and cultural contents

Figure 5.1 Percentage of exports by region, 2006

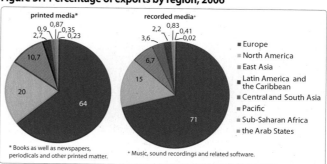

printed media*

recorded media+

- Europe
- North America
- East Asia
- Latin America and the Caribbean
- Central and South Asia
- Pacific
- Sub-Saharan Africa
- the Arab States

* Books as well as newspapers, periodicals and other printed matter.

+ Music, sound recordings and related software.

Source: UIS, 2008 based on data from UN Comtrade database, DESA/UNSD.

1. For UNESCO's definitions of communication and cultural products, please refer to the glossary pp 372-81.

Figure 5.2 provide percentages of exports and imports of cultural goods and services between OECD and non-OECD countries. They make it abundantly clear that a handful of countries dominate the marketplace (mainly Northern countries as opposed to developing countries from the South) and that the international trade in cultural goods and services is still rather weak in developing countries.

Yet, while international trade in creative goods and services experienced an unprecedented average annual growth rate of 8.7 percent between 2000 and 2005 and the value of world exports of creative goods and services reached US$424.4 billion in 2005 (representing 3.4 percent of total world trade), Africa's share in this global trade of creative products remains marginal at less than 1 percent of world exports, despite its abundance of creative talent (UNCTAD, 2008). Indeed, the vast majority of developing countries are not yet in a position to harness their creative capacities for development. Moreover, more than half the world's population is presently in danger of cultural and economic exclusion, as 90 percent of the world's languages are still not represented on the Internet (see chapter 3 above).

At the same time, these statistics on cross-border flows do not adequately capture the local consumption of cultural content or the impact of peer-to-peer (P2P) technologies and piracy (see Figure 5.3). This makes it difficult to calculate their extent and the relative importance of local and foreign production.

Figure 5.2 Exports and imports of audiovisual services and copyrights, 2006

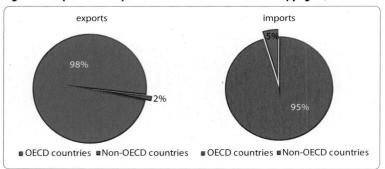

Source: UIS database 2008, based on data from UN Comtrade database, DESA/UNSD.

Figure 5.3 Percentage of countries by type of domestic music piracy levels in 2006 (physical piracy only)

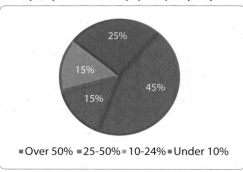

Source: UIS based on IFPI: Recording Industry in Numbers, 2007.

Figure 5.4 Public radio programming for selected countries in 2005

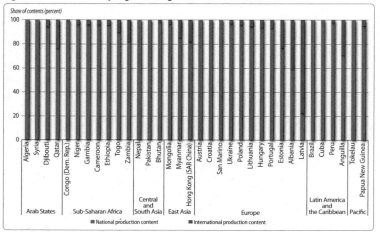

Source: UIS Culture & communication database, 2008.

In terms of origin of content production, radio, television and film broadcasting show similar global trends, although important disparities can be observed according to the media concerned. Indeed, radio programming, for linguistic and localization reasons, does not lend itself to internationalization in the same way as do cinema, television or music (see Figures 5.4–5.7). Television and music, while frequently influenced by international models and formats, are to some extent more adaptable to local realities.

As for cinema, national productions are generally struggling to compete with the blockbusters produced by large motion picture conglomerates. This is compounded by the fact that 88 countries out of

185 have never produced their own films (Nyamnjoh, 2007; see also Rourke, 2004; Oguibe, 2004). However, there are some notable exceptions. In France, for example, thanks to a strong national co-financing mechanism, the share of French films in domestic movie theatres (approximately 50 percent) is now higher than it was in the 1970s. One of the paradoxes of the development of local film conglomerates (e.g. India's Bollywood industry) is that they can actually restrict the diversity of productions at the local level, even if those conglomerates contribute positively to diversity at the international level.

Counter-flows, local and regional trends

While developed countries continue to dominate the global market for communication and cultural products, a recent move towards re-fragmentation and diversification on a global level can be observed. This move has permit the growth in recent years of 'counter-flows' that are modifying the global media landscape. A handful of developing countries are emerging both as exporters of cultural and media equipment and as content producers (UNCTAD, 2008). Developing countries' exports of cultural and media equipment increased rapidly over the period 1996–2005 from US$51 billion to US$274 billion as a result of strategies to increase global competitiveness and an expanding demand for communications equipment (including televisions, computer and video equipment, CD and DVD readers and recorders, game consoles and multifunction portable telephones). This trend, accompanied by increased piracy and a decrease in the levels of cinema attendance (with a few exceptions such as in India), has facilitated the emergence of local markets for media content, such as the Nigerian home video entertainment industry known as Nollywood. While they represent forms of 'globalization from below', these markets remain relatively localized due to technological limitations and distribution difficulties.

The emergence of counter-flows has led to a number of changes: the development of media exports from newly industrialized societies (e.g. the Republic of Korea; see Kim, 2007; Iwabuchi, 2007); the rise of new regional media hubs (e.g. the role of post-apartheid South Africa in Anglophone Africa; see Teer-Tommaselli, Wasserman and de Beer, 2007); the global significance of the Latin American audiovisual sector (the export

Figure 5.5 Origin of top movies exhibited in 2006

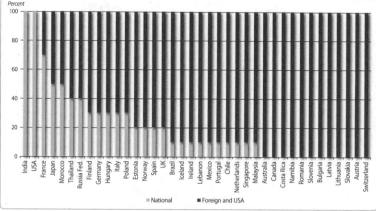

Source: UIS database, 2008.

Figure 5.6 Public television programming for selected countries in 2005

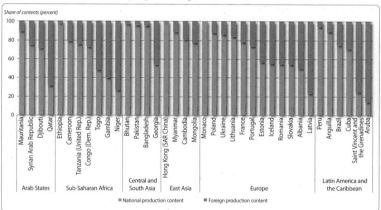

Source: UIS Culture & communication database, 2008.

Figure 5.7 Recorded music repertoire* for selected countries in 2006

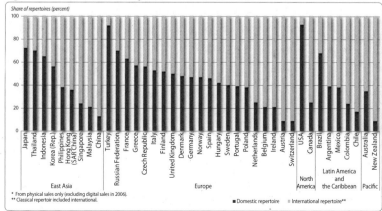

Source: International Federation of the Phonographic Industry, 2007.

of Brazilian *telenovelas* to Portugal, for example, or the rise of pan-regional news services, such as Al Jazeera or Nuevo Television del Sur; see Box 5.1). At the same time, international networks such as TV5, which targets the French-speaking world, and others mentioned above have been created to counterbalance the influence of networks such as CNN and BBC World.

Examples include the flow of Indian film and television programmes to British Asian communities and the above-mentioned Bollywood phenomenon (Thussu, 2005), as well as the ever larger audience for Chinese media products both in the Greater China cultural region (Chan, 2005) and across the Chinese global diaspora, 'the world's biggest audience' (Curtis, 2007).

Box 5.1	The emergence of international and pan-regional news services

The emergence of pan-regional and international news services (on television and online) on the global media scene has been depicted as a shift away from the monopoly long held by dominant, Western-based news media. News services such as Al Jazeera, and most recently Nuevo Television del Sur (commonly referred to as Telesur), attempt to provide news programming from a particular regional setting and in a region's primary language. Their presence reflects the prominence of news and current affairs programming in a globalized context, the diversity of the global media audience and the need to respond to this diversity.

Al Jazeera, the Arabic news channel, was launched in 1996 with a grant from the Qatari Government. Since then, it has grown considerably, expanding its programming to include sports, children's shows, documentaries and public interest shows. In 2006 it added an English-based international news station called Al Jazeera International. As part of its code of ethics, it aims to present a diversity of perspectives and recognize diversity among peoples and societies through the acknowledgment of differences in cultures, beliefs and values. Cultural diversity is also an active policy in its human resources management; substantial efforts to ensure representation of all Arab countries has yielded positive results. As Al Jazeera grows beyond its original regional focus to become an alternative news voice on the international scene, new questions arise about its position as a transnational mainstream news network and how suitably it can balance the needs of a pan-Arabian audience with those of a growing global audience (Iskandar, 2006). While it aims to 'present all colours of the spectrum', some have criticized it for its coverage of certain aspects of world politics.

A new addition to the global news media scene, Telesur, was established in 2005 with major financial support from the government of Venezuela, as well as support from the governments of Cuba, Argentina and Uruguay. Telesur has already expressed an interest in following Al Jazeera's example. In 2006, the two transnational news service providers signed a cooperation agreement to share content and expertise.

Source: Raboy, 2007.

In these ways, the development of new forms of media are producing a much more complex and fluid global media market, undermining older perceptions of a linear, unidirectional flow of media and facilitating the emergence of networks of all kinds (Warnier and Nyamnjoh, 2007). Some of these include: Reporters sans Frontières, Amnesty International, the World Free Press Institute, the International Freedom of Expression network, the European Audiovisual Observatory, and regional networks such as New Latino Spaces, the Bruno Manser Fund's *Tong Tana* and Africultures. Diasporic communities and indigenous, minority and other special-interest groups are also establishing media outlets that give a voice and provide information to their communities — through radio and satellite television and through increased access to computer-mediated communication (Dayan, 1999; Georgiu, 2006).

The innovations in ICTs are just beginning to have an impact on the structure and content of the mainstream media players and the possibilities they offer for alternative, small, local and community media. New practices and content — linked to the development of some of the newer cultural, informational and communication products accessible via the Internet, mobile phones or similar tools — are appearing. These permit the emergence of small production structures targeting micro-markets and new models of content creation and delivery. New technologies are having a major impact on the dissemination of media content, especially in the field of publishing, where the reduction of fixed costs associated with production and storage, the possibility of doing small print runs (print on demand) and selling online have favoured the emergence of small, artisanal publishing houses catering for niche markets (e.g. Traficante de Sueños).

Another interesting impact of new technologies is the substantial growth in the production of cultural and media equipment and related software and network operations, which have spurred a corresponding increase in the consumption of products conceived for this hardware, including video and CD players, computers, television receivers, consoles and mobile phones. The shift in consumer preferences has created substitution mechanisms. Thus, the stagnation of the print publishing sector in Western countries (including newspapers and magazines) is directly related to the emergence of online distribution systems (e.g. Amazon, news websites) and e-book formats (digital libraries, the Internet Archive, Google Books, etc.). The rise in home viewing of cultural products thanks to the flourishing of DVD production and distribution is inversely related to the decrease in cinema attendance (which, in some countries, may also be explained by the amount of piracy present there).

A changing media landscape

As access to the Internet widens and is appropriated by social, political and religious movements of all types and sizes across the globe, the World Wide Web has the potential to significantly redress not only imbalances in political and economic power between the local and the global but also divides between various groups in society. The Internet is in effect an ideal means of facilitating cross-border information streams and sustaining and promoting cultural diversity through content production. It is also engendering a boom in alternative media production and use.

The growth in number of Internet connections is a good indicator of the potential for development of alternative media in cyberspace. From 500 million users in 2000 the number shot up to 1.2 billion by 2007. In addition, the number of hours spent communicating via Internet, the number of connections and the volume of documents made available, consulted or downloaded show an equally tremendous increase in use (Esteban, 2006). This is true for all generations of Internet users. Market surveys show that, in the US, time spent online among children aged 2–11 increased 63 percent in the last five years, from nearly 7 hours

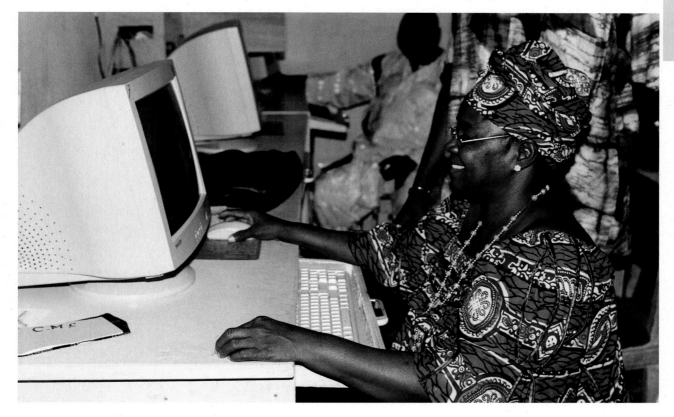

○ *A woman in front of a computer in Koutiala, Mali*

◎ *The roofs of a city in North Africa*

mobility. It also refers to the range of new anxieties and perplexities in contemporary life: from worries over climate change and fears of global influenza pandemics, to concerns about how fluctuations in the global economy may affect job security or interest payments locally. The dramatic increase in media connectivity in the late 20th and early 21st centuries embodies a dual potential for increased cultural interaction and greater cultural uniformity.

Interactivity refers to the audience shift from relatively passive recipients of pre-determined broadcast content to participants in the very production and dissemination of cultural and communication contents, which are increasingly user-generated. The ability to actively use the Internet — via blogs, chat rooms, bulletin boards, multi-user websites and so on — to express opinions, establish relationships and pursue individual and collective projects is undoubtedly changing the fundamental experience of media use. In particular, Web 2.0 technologies are causing many media companies to change their strategies; they are providing more and more tools for customers, partners and other interested parties to post content including text, video, and pictures.

Media convergence refers to the use of a single platform (e.g. a laptop computer or a mobile phone) to perform a range of functions — watching television, downloading videos or music, web-browsing, emailing, on-line shopping, telephoning — which until recently were distinct activities. It is significantly altering the practice and experience of using the media. The most striking example today is the cellular phone, which now enables one to consult the press, receive email, listen to music, watch television, take photos, consult street and road maps, shop, etc. It is also a means — in Africa for example — of communicating in oral languages, thereby helping to preserve linguistic diversity. This convergence involves a personalization of the traditional domestic media audience, since people can choose among a potentially unlimited range of sources of entertainment, information and cultural practice, and achieve greater mobility and interactivity. This last point is potentially the most significant for the promotion of cultural diversity. With the progressive replacement of VHS by DVD formats for videos, new avenues have opened up for the interactive use of media content (e.g. enabling the viewer to choose subtitles or even the

per month in May 2004 to more than 11 hours per month in May 2009 (Nielsen, 2009), in tandem with the rise of social networking technologies (e.g. Facebook, MySpace, YouTube; see chapter 1, Box 1.2). The Internet's scope, potential and versatility can serve the interests of the very big and the very small. The increasing multiplicity of actors is having a major impact on the nature and, potentially, the diversity of media content.

The changes taking place in the media landscape are fundamentally characterized by three factors: connectivity, interactivity and convergence. *Connectivity* refers to the growing interdependence between the networks and global flows associated with new communications technologies — email, the Internet, mobile phones — and the (increasingly urban) environments in which people live. Connectivity influences the way people across the globe earn their living, the sort of food they eat, the music, cinema and television they choose as entertainment, as well as their language of viewing). But the synergies between the Internet and the more classical media (such as a weekly newspaper) are more significant than often noticed. Increasingly, the media sector is becoming not only an 'enabler of globalization' but also a 'powerful agent' of social, cultural and political transformation (Siochrú, 2004). The Internet can also be a powerful tool for the conservation and dissemination of cultural diversity, as illustrated by UNESCO initiatives such as Memory of the World and the recent World Digital Library launched in April 2009 — a project in which UNESCO and the US Library of Congress have played a leading role.

Obviously the extent of the growth and the impact of alternative media, Internet development and accessibility in a given country will depend on the economic and political conditions prevailing there. In some countries, economic conditions or the political control exercised over the Internet do not favour their development. New physical and virtual spaces are emerging, often as a result of private initiatives ('citizen' cafés, forums, blogs), and satellite television is reconnecting diaspora audiences with their homelands while general audiences are able to discover broadcasts from other countries and new cultural horizons. The multiplicity of players and distribution channels has made public information generally more accessible, allowing its integration into different socio-economic frameworks and creating new opportunities for developing public and private enterprise models, all of which are greatly contributing to diversification. For example, digitization (of visual and written content) has resulted in a rapid, radical and permanent reduction in the cost of these systems, bringing them within the financial — if not the cultural — reach of the underprivileged (Le Diberder, 2008).

If today's media landscape is characterized by a number of interesting and paradoxical changes as we move towards increasingly interconnected and creative economies, it nevertheless remains marked by power imbalances (social, political and economic in nature) and driven by profit maximization, at the heart of which the struggle for identity and communication plays itself out. The emergence of counter-flows is a promising trend towards the reduction of those imbalances. In the framework of UNESCO's 2005 *Convention on the Protection and Promotion of the Diversity of Cultural Expressions*, the creation of an International Fund for Cultural Diversity — which, although not yet operational, has already received considerable financial support — is a sign that the international community is ready to implement mechanisms to redress existing imbalances in national production capacities and access to international markets. Of course, a precondition for this is the existence of national revenue-generating mechanisms, since without them creative industries cannot flourish. If optimized, however, globalization and technological innovations can contribute to the enhancement of cultural diversity in communication and cultural products worldwide.

5.2 Impacts of communication and cultural products

Researchers and experts in a wide range of fields, including cultural studies, communication and information sciences, economics, international law and political science, have sought to describe, account for and measure these new realities through a variety of approaches. User-generated media harbour the potential for diversifying voices, thereby creating new opportunities for interactive exchanges among participants from different cultural backgrounds. Furthermore, increased interconnectedness and interactivity make it possible to overcome the kind of 'passive learning' that has often burdened visual communication media. Yet if the growth of on-demand digital content on the Internet and the widespread availability of readily reproducible and exchangeable media (DVDs, streaming media, audio and video files) hold out new promise, they also pose new challenges for cultural diversity, particularly audience fragmentation and stereotyping. These can and must be addressed through appropriate information and media literacy initiatives.

Audience fragmentation and cultural prescription
Along with the changes it has brought about through the increased availability of media content, the digital era has also had a considerable impact on demand and how the public consumes such content. The 'long tail' effect refers to the increased possibility, created by digital media, of making available specialized or limited-audience works as a result of lower production and distribution costs (Anderson, 2006).

… the World Wide Web has the potential to significantly redress not only imbalances in political and economic power between the local and the global but also divides between various groups in society

The effect of the diversification of content on the range of consumer choices is more complex than it might seem at first glance. Digital recording has given rise to an overabundance of choices in media content, but also to increased piracy facilitated by the distribution of recordable CDs and DVDs and multiformat recorders, both in the North and in many urban centres in the countries of the South. While only one-fifth of humanity has access to the Internet, between two- and three-fifths have access to video copies or musical files (see also Figure 5.3).

The increased supply of media content is not necessarily reflected in greater diversity of consumption. Confronted by an excess of choice, some consumers prefer to confine themselves to a small number of familiar titles rather than explore unknown or different content (Benhamou, 2004). Cultural preferences are usually fed by interactions with others (e.g. talking about a puppet performance, borrowing or lending content, sharing activities like watching television, listening to radio with fellow workers), a phenomenon known as 'cultural prescription'. Interestingly, the enlargement of choice made possible by the digital revolution is also causing some to seek out prescription from their closest relations. A recent study in France by the National Film Centre (Centre national de la cinématographie) showed for example that in 60 percent of the cases, a person viewed a film at the cinema as the result of a recommendation from someone close to the person rather than due to advertising or a critic's review (Le Diberder, 2008).

At the same time, as the traditional agents of prescription — school, immediate family, local retailers

An increased supply of media content can lead to a 'false diversity', masking the fact that some people are communicating only with those who share the same cultural references

— are becoming overwhelmed by the sheer number of television channels and the seemingly endless range of programmes, a significant intergenerational gap is opening up, particularly due to the emergence of new practices of consumption of digital content linked to new forms of social networking (e.g. online services such as Facebook or Messenger). The existence of too many choices is thus fragmenting audiences and triggering closure and social isolation. More and more audiences are made up of 'fans' or 'sects' that have little contact with one another and tend to be exclusive of other modes of thinking (Sunstein, 2001). The danger of such a phenomenon is that it can lead to a 'false diversity', masking the fact that people are actually only communicating with those who share the same cultural frames of reference.

The rise of satellite channels today caters simultaneously to the consumer interested in travel, history, classical music, horses, old films, women's topics or children's programmes, and supplies foreign channels in their original languages. But if, for example, only women watch channels for women, if history enthusiasts do not watch geography channels, if foreign channels are watched only by immigrants who accordingly shun national channels in their country of adoption and simply nurture their attachment to the culture they have left behind, then the possibility of interculturality and dialogue is compromised. In some cases, the 'long tail' effect can lead to the 'tribalization' of cultural consumption, the dangers of which are obvious since they contravene any attempt to promote intercultural dialogue and mutual understanding. Moreover, this may also contribute to the reinforcement of stereotypes about others. Such diversity amounts to little more than a juxtaposition of parallel singularities.

The emergence of new viewing and listening practices linked to technological development thus has important implications for cultural diversity. In this connection, it is essential to bear in mind that the digital revolution's impact on diversity is asymetric and has differential effects depending on the regions and income categories under consideration. Thus, in the countries of the North and the South, its effects on cultural diversity are likely to differ according to the digital practices prevalent in a given location, and dependent upon Internet access and use, and piracy levels (Le Diberder, 2008).

For people in the North connected to the Internet, digital media expand existing provisions by catering to broader and more diversified tastes. On the other hand, for those in the North with only limited or no access to an Internet connection, advertising campaigns for the promotion of blockbuster movies probably impact negatively on cultural consumption. In the countries of the South, an Internet connection is more likely to provide access to what is most readily available, i.e. media content produced in the developed countries, to the detriment of local productions . For those in the South without an Internet connection, lack of access to digital technology is a major ongoing concern, the result of which is increased piracy. The impacts of digital media on local productions are, however, more ambiguous. While they face greater competition, local productions are beginning to secure support and networking facilities, both internationally and locally, as in the case of Nigerian audiovisual products.

As we shall see, to counter these undesirable effects of the new economy of prescription, it is necessary to increase initiatives that foster digital media literacy, with particular regard to providing the public with the tools it needs and the necessary critical distance to make more effective use of search engines. This is one of the aims of the UNESCO Power of Peace Network (PPN) programme (see Box 5.2).

Box 5.2   The Power of Peace Network (PPN)

Because the mass media have become a vital means of educating the general public about history and the world, there is a need for 'integrated documentary film projects aimed at improving knowledge among cultures [and] films that reflect both excellent scholarship, and a strong sense of contemporary relevance and visual impact' (UN Alliance of Civilizations, 2007). A number of ongoing projects are working towards this goal, including the productions of the Unity Productions Foundation (UPF), notably *Muhammad: Legacy of a Prophet* (and its companion website *The Islam Project*), or the documentary on the period of Muslim rule on the Iberian Peninsula. Other films funded by public-private initiatives for international audiences include *A Prince Among Slaves*, about Africans in the US, and the BBC series *Story of Africa, Connections* and *The Day the Universe Changed.*

The UNESCO Power of Peace Network (PPN) is an interactive platform that seeks to harness innovative mechanisms to promote peace through media and ICTs. PPN fosters global collaboration in the use of ICTs for cultural self-expression, mutual understanding, the reduction of conflict, and the promotion of sustainable living. PPN endeavours to bring young people to the forefront of this effort, drawing on their energy and often ground-breaking approaches to the challenges that lie ahead. Its goals include:

- Leading the ongoing debate on how to effectively promote mutual understanding by harnessing the Web 2.0 technologies, as well as television, newspapers and magazines, and how to bring youth to the vanguard of leadership, empower civil society and make the power of peace an agent of change.

- Providing an online environment for the sharing of ideas and content, including blogs, audio-visual and written materials that are educational, informative and support the PPN mission.

- Creating a strong network and bringing together stakeholders in the PPN initiative (including NGOs, youth organizations, media and ICT specialists, government and international agencies, private sector interests, religious and cultural institutions, universities and other educational institutions) in order to respond to new social and economic challenges in communities around the world.

- Contributing to sustainable development through knowledge-sharing and by finding practical ways to use the technologies at our disposal to encourage self-expression, achieve better understanding of ourselves and others, and ultimately enhance the human condition.

- Encouraging the formation of a global coalition of universities and other educational institutions to develop a collaborative program that incorporates media in peace and conflict studies for broad public education and for reaching out to young people on university campuses around the world.

- Facilitating a network of those engaged in the media and peace-building and identifying possible partnerships between those working on the ground (NGOs and other civil society organizations) and ICTs and media outlets, experts and trainers, supporters of content development, educators, researchers, business advisors and managers.

Generally speaking, PPN activities aim to serve as an interdisciplinary platform for dialogue among civilizations and as a clearing house for audiovisual content in the context of promoting peace, by providing support to educational institutions through curriculum development, training, and a focus on peace and conflict studies, and opportunities for lifelong learning among media professionals, especially in conflict-sensitive reporting.

Source: UNESCO, 2009.

Stereotypes and representations of cultural diversity

There is no question that the media exercise enormous power in shaping our perceptions of, attitudes towards and opinions about 'others'. As the strongest purveyors of globalization, and able to penetrate even the remotest corners of the planet, the media (television, radio, instant messaging, newspapers and magazines, advertising and the Internet) inundate us with representations of how other people look, feel, live, eat, dress and think (Appadurai, 1990).

The media's hold over attitudes, consumption patterns and creation, as well as over cultural expressions and cultural diversity, is all too real. They feed into processes of self-identification on individual and collective levels, and contribute to the formation of 'imagined communities' (Anderson, 1991). Appadurai (1990) uses the term 'mediascapes' to designate the 'imaginary landscapes of the media' that play a crucial role in the ways in which we conceive of our lives. Mediascapes may indeed be quite powerful and become insidious sources of conflict, tensions and even violence in societies.

Debates abound on the extent of the media's influence in constructing both individual and collective attitudes towards others and cultural diversity (Fürsich, 2008). While for some, the media have a direct and immediate effect on passive and easily manipulated audiences (often referred to as the 'Magic Bullet Theory'), others have claimed that media have no significant behavioural or attitudinal effects (the 'Limited Effects Paradigm', especially in US mass communication research from the 1940s into the 1970s). According to the latter, the media influence people only indirectly, with psychological predispositions, demographics, cognitive processes, interpersonal contacts and other such factors hindering their direct impact. 'Spiral of Silence' theorists argue that the media can contribute significantly to a climate of opinion that can obfuscate the real attitudes on an issue in the mainstream population while stopping people with dissenting views from speaking out. And 'Cultivation Theory' (Gerbner et al., 1986) argues that television influence should not be measured by way of significant short-term effects. Instead, lifelong exposure to television seems to lead especially heavy viewers to take television's constructed reality to be the actual social reality (e.g. viewers starting to see the world as a very violent and dangerous place).

While it is no longer assumed that individuals are purely passive receivers of media content, there is considerable research (by educational psychologists and across opinion surveys) that points to the extent to which the media can and do reinforce people's values, attitudes, opinions, beliefs and feelings, and therefore the ways in which individuals react to ethnic or cultural differences. The constructed realities of the media undeniably contribute to establishing the norms, communication and behavioural patterns towards people, groups and institutions, that is to say, the actual social realities of contemporary society. Benjamin Barber (1996) goes so far as to state: 'It is time to recognize that the true tutors of our children are no longer the school teachers and university professors, but the filmmakers, advertising executives and pop culture purveyors. Disney does more than Duke, Spielberg outweighs Stanford, MTV trumps MIT'. These representations of 'central signifying practices for producing shared meaning' are constitutive of culture, meaning and knowledge about ourselves and the world around us (Hall, 1997). In short, media representations normalize specific worldviews and contribute to perceived reality.

◑ *A young girl talks with a German journalist about life working in a garment factory in Bangladesh*

As is obvious from the limited range of representations in circulation, the media participate in the creation of stereotypes through what is often called the process of 'othering', namely the determination of what separates me from other individuals, groups and communities by cataloguing them as 'others'. Indeed, national media (whether commercial or public-service-oriented) usually cater to national audiences and can often depict both foreigners and minorities (whether ethnic, linguistic, racial, religious or gender minorities) in essentialized or stereotyped ways, thereby dehumanizing and caricaturizing them. The process of 'othering' can also be informed by contexts or situations, such as in accounts or depictions of international relations, conflicts and cultures. In an environment increasingly saturated by visual communication, imagery has the propensity to maintain, confirm and re-create such problematic representations of 'others' ad infinitum. Over the last 25 years, media specialists have explored the role the media play in maintaining problematic stereotypes (e.g. Dines and Humez, 2003; Castañeda and Campbell, 2006).

A similar trend is apparent in the way in which the media, particularly television, sometimes detach certain cultural phenomena from their context and transpose them into other contexts where they contribute to cultural change. This can lead in some cases to an 'unconscious Westernization' (Shayegan, 2008), with people purchasing the goods or wearing the clothes they have just seen on television or on the screen. An example of the kinds of cultural encounters that may occur through the media is provided by the impact in the Arab world of certain South American soap operas (or *telenovelas*), which have attracted a huge following and have had some surprising consequences, such as in Morocco, where the number of young Muslim girls being given the first name 'Guadalupe' (the name of their mother's favourite *telenovela* heroine), despite its strong Christian connotation, has soared to such an extent that the state registry of births and religious authorities have taken note of the situation (*Tel Quel*, 2008).

In Western societies in particular, as research on opinion surveys amply illustrates, the repertoire of representations of cultural diversity offered by contemporary media is often linked to historical constructions based on national and collective memory and racially based imagery (in the continuum of colonialism). There are three main reasons for the persistence of such representations:

1) the ubiquity, saturation and repetitiveness of mass media seem to reinforce the longevity of these representations; 2) profit-driven commercial media systems proved to have difficulties introducing more complex representations in order to undermine problematic ones; and 3) the media seem to be too closely aligned with the elites in societies to be interested in changing the status quo. Lately, a debate has begun on whether digital technology and the Internet can undermine traditional systems of representation by adding new outlets. And it may be that the increasing audience fragmentation caused by a growing number of media outlets available to audiences in nearly all countries of the world will help to diminish the impact of negative representations. However, since representation speaks to a sustained image delivered across media channels and outlets (and not exposure to an individual depiction in the media), long-established representations are bound to survive across genres and media platforms (Fürsich, 2007).

Since the invention of motion pictures or film over a century ago, visually based mass media have stockpiled forms of representation that are constantly recycled across a variety of media outlets and genres (e.g. the lack of character development in sitcoms), production practices (e.g. the use of script conventions) and economic pressures (e.g. the need to attract a large mainstream audience), (Entman and Rojecki, 2000, quoted in Fürsich, 2007). Even shows and media content that openly try to 'counter-stereotype', and thereby undermine negative representations, by presenting opposite roles and characters often have only a limited effect because they are bound up with the same problematic and often broadcast together (Gray, 1995). Television in general has an inherent tendency to fixate; its traditional logic of production and editing, as well as its narrative structure, forces closure. At the same time, postmodernism has opened up more flexible, albeit sometimes ambiguous, modes of representation (as in music videos), and the impacts of the Internet are certainly changing our modes and capacities for interaction and dialogue in interesting ways.

Television news broadcasting plays an important role in national integration and has often led to 'othering' anyone outside national borders and to the suppression of regional, local and minority audience interests.

Debates abound on the extent of the media's influence in constructing both individual and collective attitudes towards others and cultural diversity

Different strategies have been designed in order to eliminate stereotypes, distorted images and misperceptions transmitted and supported by communication and cultural products

Travel journalism also illustrates some of the ambiguities and paradoxes inherent in mediated images of cultural diversity: fundamentally structured by the search for difference (considered by some as the ultimate motivation of tourism), travel journalism often results in the perpetual cycle of manufacturing, celebrating and exoticizing difference (Robinson, 2007). Stressing individual pleasure and personalized travel, the narratives often neglect the broader political, social and economic problems of countries and communities. Travelogues can thereby reduce local communities and individuals to nameless and voiceless essentialized 'types', instead of 'unpacking cultures' by portraying and celebrating the multiple and very real aspects of the country or location covered.

In a media-saturated culture, lack of attention to entire segments of a population is a form of silencing — what cultural specialists call 'symbolic annihilation' — which is insidiously perpetuated in the power imbalances of the current media landscape and across today's media flows. A key issue in this regard is the phenomenon of 'global localization' or 'glocalization' — the attempt by global media industries to tailor cultural products to the tastes of local markets. As Koichi Iwabuchi (2002; 2005) has shown, glocalization produces a paradox:

> As multinational media corporations press ahead with global tie-ups and partnerships, they are also trying to raise their profits by tailoring this axis to every corner of the world while promoting cultural diversity in every market. The world is becoming more diverse through standardization and more standardized through diversification. [...] In fact, it is now almost impossible to imagine local cultural creativity outside the context of globalization and the profits cannot be sufficiently produced without 'respecting' local specificity [...].

One of the most important ways in which this paradox is enacted is via the use of standardized genres and formats for television programmes which can be attuned and adapted to different cultural contexts. Standardized game-show and reality-television formats are a case in point: such shows no longer originate only from the West (such as *Who Wants to Be a millionaire?* and *The Weakest Link*) but also from Japan, for example, where quiz shows like *Show by Shobai* and reality television shows like *Shiawase Kazoku Keikaku* (*Happy Family Plan*) are being widely distributed throughout East Asia and increasingly globally. Hence,

to reach new audiences, and capture and address local diversity and creativity, more diversity is introduced. The significance, for example, of the spectacularly successful *Super Girl Contest* staged by Hunan Satellite Television in China in 2005 is not so much in its having adapted the global *Pop Idol* format to a Chinese audience (Silverstone, 2007; Hewitt, 2007) but rather in its having thereby reproduced some of what Zygmunt Bauman (2005) calls the 'explicit and tacit assumptions about the ways of the world, visions of happiness and the ways to pursue them' that inform the 'consumer syndrome'. These include the cult of celebrity, an emphasis on popular glamour as something to which to aspire, an individualist approach to life goals based on eliminative competition, and the reduction of the expression of opinion to audience polls.

Many attempts have been made to combat stereotypes, distorted images and false perceptions. They are situated at different levels, depending on whether they involve information, games or fiction. Generally speaking, one of the most fruitful approaches is to present a community stigmatized by stereotypes in a positive light, by emphasizing the cultural traits that distinguish them from others. Such representations, in documentaries or geographical-historical programmes, can restore dignity to communities that feel themselves to be undervalued. Different strategies have been designed in order to eliminate stereotypes, distorted images and misperceptions transmitted and supported by communication and cultural products, which ultimately hinder our understanding of peoples and cultures and thus our capacity for dialogue:

■ A common approach to overcoming outright stereotyping has been to *counter-stereotype*, that is, to take a previously stereotyped minority and create media content that shows this minority in a positive light. For some media specialists, the internationally successful American situation comedy *The Cosby Show* is an example of such a strategy, while others maintain that this example shows that to be portrayed positively, minorities have to 'act white'. A difficulty with counter-stereotyping strategies is that they often refer back to negative representations and may come across as overly didactic or as inauthentic.

■ Another strategy for contesting the 'dominant regime of representation' is known as *trans-coding,* an audience-driven activity that permits 'taking an existing meaning and re-appropriating it for new meanings' (Hall, 1997). It is unclear, however, just how easily this strategy can be implemented in the media landscape, since it assumes that representations are readily identifiable. Nonetheless, 'some important avenues for trans-coding might be story-lines that open up representations and break stereotypes through the use of humour and exaggeration to present the dominant position in a new light (such as ethnicizing "whiteness" as opposed to constructing it as a latent and normalized category)' (Fürsich, 2008).

- Yet another approach is to make evident the concrete (most of the time hidden) conditions of production, emphasizing their construction and fixity, such that space can be provided for other voices. This approach is employed in strategies that seek to promote *information literacy*.

Whatever approach is used, it is imperative that media practitioners not retreat to a seemingly safe position of objectivity but rather actively embrace the role of 'go-between' and thereby become facilitators of intercultural dialogue (see Box 5.3). In determining their own position and then using it to challenge traditional modes of representation, they can help their audiences to build a capacity for openness. Ultimately, media professionals could aid in reflecting upon the 'in-between' situations in contact and conflict zones (Pratt, 1992).

Box 5.3 Little Mosque on the Prairie

The critically acclaimed Canadian television series *Little Mosque on the Prairie* presents a fresh approach to the promotion of cultural diversity through the media. Launched in January 2007 by the Canadian Broadcasting Corporation (CBC), the series unabashedly challenges in a humorous way the dominant stereotypes and misrepresentations of Muslims. The show's creator, Zarqa Nawaz, a Canadian Muslim woman originally from Pakistan, developed the series as a counterpoint to Western media images of Islam and Muslims.

Little Mosque focuses on a small Muslim community living in a fictional rural Canadian town. The show's writers entertainingly capture the mosaic of living together in a diverse environment, highlighting the everyday experiences of Muslims as they interact with each other and with non-Muslims. The show strives to heighten the viewer's exposure to issues of diversity and provoke them to consider previously unquestioned assumptions that are commonly held about Muslims and diversity within and between generations, cultures and communities. The sheer popularity and international appeal of the television series suggest that mainstream public broadcasting can be critical, provocative and entertaining while at the same time seeking to promote cultural diversity. The Canadian series premiere attracted an audience of 2.1 million viewers. Thereafter it drew a weekly viewing audience of 1.2 million viewers for the first season. Now in its third season, *Little Mosque* will be translated into French and is scheduled for broad international distribution and viewership. The show has already started airing in France, Switzerland and French-speaking African countries. Turkey, Finland and the United Arab Emirates recently signed distribution agreements to broadcast the series. Israeli television began distributing the series in English (with Hebrew subtitles) in October 2007. *Little Mosque* has also been made available for viewing in the West Bank and Gaza.

Notwithstanding its international popularity, the programme series is not without its critics, who decry the show's representation of Muslims. For example, the Muslim Canadian Congress has questioned the absence of secular Muslims in the community on which it is based, and whether the series truly captures the diverse spectrum of Canada's Muslim community (Fatah and Hassan, 2007). Nevertheless, the show has attracted unprecedented attention at a time when relations (perceived or real) between Muslims and non-Muslims remain vulnerable.

Among its many accolades, *Little Mosque* received the Academy of Canadian Cinema and Television's Canada Award in 2007, which recognizes excellence in mainstream television programming that reflects Canada's racial and cultural diversity. International awards from the 2007 RomaFictionFest, an international television festival, were also significant accomplishments. Most notable perhaps, *Little Mosque* was awarded the prestigious Common Ground Award in 2007 by the US human rights organization Search for Common Ground in recognition of the programme's promotion of collaboration as a viable alternative to conflict. In so doing, it joined the ranks of recipients such as former US President Jimmy Carter, Nobel Peace Laureate Archbishop Desmond Tutu and former heavyweight boxer Muhammad Ali.

Whether *Little Mosque on the Prairie* challenges 'Orientalist expectations' about Muslims (Taylor, Davis and Zine, 2007) and provides a meaningful articulation of diversity or, as some critics suggest, upholds stereotypical representations, it is nevertheless clear that it is no simple feat to address issues of cultural diversity in mainstream media. Since the show has generated positive worldwide attention, it may inspire new approaches to promoting cultural diversity that use the media as a vehicle for change. In the words of Zarqa Nawaz, the hit sitcom's creator: 'people are talking about it and it's opened up dialogue' (Taylor, Davis and Zine, 2007).

Source: Raboy, 2007.

Samburu near Maralal, Kenya

5.3 Policies fostering cultural diversity

Initiatives are needed to ensure that global audiences and cross-border programming contribute to the pluralism and the free flow of ideas that foster cultural diversity. To this end, more critical consumption of media, and increased awareness of the importance of understanding other cultures from within (Benson, 2005) — *media and information literacy* — are essential to countering audience fragmentation, isolation and stereotypes. In this sense, cultural diversity is not merely a supplement to but rather the very definition of quality media. Furthermore, despite the vital role played by the media in enhancing (or not) the plurality of perspectives, the entertainment, culture and news media tend to be considered separately from each other and from the policy discussions that aim to promote cultural diversity. While not diminishing the relevance of policies addressing the issues of 'older' media (television and radio for example), the recent move towards newer digital technologies requires enhanced regulatory and industry support mechanisms in order to accurately reflect the dynamics and the breadth of contemporary creation and content distribution in the promotion of cultural diversity.

Media and information literacy

This is the aim of media and information literacy, which must not only be made an integral part of non-formal education but also be recognized as a tool for empowerment and capacity-building in the production of local content. In practice, this form of literacy can take place through various means, including:

- *Contextualizing coverage as much as possible.* Indeed, the media tendency to narrow-cast makes it difficult to go beyond one person's story in order to shed light on underlying conditions that have made it possible (e.g. in the case of a migrant's story, the underlying global inequalities that cause migration). With hypertext links in digital media, an increasing number of print or broadcasting topics can be offered to interested audiences as background or supplementary material.

- *Taking critical distance.* Some visual anthropologists recommend adopting aesthetic strategies that break with viewers' expectations, such as journalistic narrative that makes obvious its production methods or showcases the underlying interests shaping the message or story.

- *Deconstructing representations.* The constructedness of some media productions and the power effects at stake can be exhibited through the juxtaposition of differing experiences. For example, a travel show could employ traditional, monolithic and essentialized images of a culture alongside the fluid, hybrid contemporary situation of that culture (Clifford, 1988).

- *Opening up meaning.* To show that there cannot be an 'objective' journalistic perspective on reality, some content producers and intermediaries leave it up to the audience to make sense of the story to which they have just been exposed. Of course, this approach should not contradict or nullify the 'explanatory' function of the media for the discovery of new forms of cultural expression (Rony, 1996).

Media literacy can foster critical capacities and promote multiple perspectives, thus protecting vulnerable cultures from what some experts have called the 'colonization of minds', such as when modes of consumption and ways of living from the 'centre' are uncritically adopted by communities or cultures on the 'periphery' (Alexander, 2007). Media literacy thus needs to move beyond the mere textual deciphering of media messages to an understanding of aspects of production and reception. From this perspective, media literacy should become a cornerstone of journalism and production education and training. Cultural Studies, as an interdisciplinary movement, is also an important factor in these media literacy efforts. Active audiences can then independently decode problematic representations (McLaren, Hammer, Sholle and Reilley, 1995).

Media literacy is also an important aspect of media access. Research on the digital divide has highlighted the problems of unequal distribution and use of digital media within and across nations. When one considers that only a minority of the world's population (less than 20 percent) actually use online media, it becomes clear that the issue of access is still a pressing one. In this context, stronger capacities to use nomad technologies combined with the recent boom of mobile telephony in the developing world provide a great opportunity. At the end of 2006, according to the GSM Association and the ITU, the total number of people with access to a mobile phone averaged about 2.7 billion, and 80 percent of the world population was covered by a GSM network. These figures illustrate the potential of mobile platforms to offer new solutions for services, in concert with other options, also increasingly available, such as low-cost laptops.

With this expansion of networks, media literacy efforts have increasingly branched out from individualistic pedagogical efforts to media-critical grassroots movements that attempt to translate media criticism into lobbying efforts to influence policy. Similar to the free radio and press cooperative movement of the 1970s, the past 15 years have seen a growing number of movements across the globe that are critically engaged in overcoming a limited media environment by using alternative networking strategies such as the Internet. Earlier

groups include the Cultural Environmental Movement (CEM) founded by George Gerbner in 1990. More recent groups include the umbrella organization Voices21 and Communication Rights in the Information Society (CRIS). Some of these groups use e-mail campaigns to inform politicians and media producers of their concerns; others try to engage in media literacy efforts, raise awareness and develop proposals for cultural policy.

Today new technologies challenge traditional approaches to media literacy as the media increasingly open up and allow audiences to become participants and creators in a digital world. Such developments have initiated an important new approach to media literacy that integrates production and reception situations (Livingstone, 2004). This also shows the importance of media literacy to ensuring that the media as a whole have a positive effect not only on the visibility of

Media literacy can foster critical capacities and promote multiple perspectives, thus protecting vulnerable cultures from what some experts have called the 'colonization of minds'

| Box 5.4 | **Implementing media literacy programmes** |

Media literacy programmes should not be restricted to children's education, but should be offered to the community at large and especially media professionals and university students in media studies. Recommendations for step-by-step implementation of media literacy programmes include:

a. **For parents and their school-age children:**

- Identify target audiences.

- Organize media literacy activities, such as 'media weeks' in different regions and in schools, talks, discussion groups, workshops and interactive presentations countrywide.

- Develop media literacy toolkits for parents and children.

- Organize a media literacy conference grouping parents, children, media practitioners, academics and others involved in the field.

- Evaluate various phases of the project.

a. **For university students and young media professionals:**

- Create media literacy programmes for students and journalists on both sides of the proverbial 'cultural divide' so that they learn each other's languages, cultural backgrounds, history, politics and traditions in a sustained and comprehensive way. Unfortunately, what we have today is very superficial and rather distorted. Parachute journalism and the use of translators can be more harmful than informative.

- Institute solid journalism programmes at universities that provide rich curricula that not only teach reporting, editing, photography and blogging, but that also emphasize media ethics and sensitivity training and require comprehensive language skills.

- Encourage exchange programmes between students and journalists (each category separately) so that they can appreciate the hardships faced by their colleagues in their respective countries.

- Encourage journalists to contribute to each other's media, whenever and wherever possible, to encourage the cross-pollination of ideas. An article, a feature, an audio report, an Internet posting, a television segment may help to alleviate tensions and foster understanding.

- Create networks that provide support and solidarity in times of crisis. Sometimes it is not what you know, but who you know that gets you out of trouble.

- Create an unofficial watchdog mechanism to monitor offensive media reporting and work to defuse tensions as soon as they emerge and before things get out of hand. Work cooperatively to promote genuine good relations.

- Very importantly, give more of a voice to women and youth so that they can contribute to the media dialogue and ensure that they are fully empowered and not marginalized or discredited.

Source: Abu-Fadil, 2008.

cultural diversity but also on the audiences' capacities to 'discover' the other and to open themselves to mutual understanding and intercultural dialogue. Of course, cultural diversity does not only concern the origin of cultural and communication content and the deciphering of their meanings and underlying messages. It also concerns public debates and the multiplicity of voices that can be heard in the public arena. In this respect, insofar as the media as a whole contribute to the flourishing of pluralism, they can make a strong contribution to cultural diversity.

Public initiatives

In the field of cultural industries, governments have progressively implemented a complex range of regulatory and industry support mechanisms to foster the development of more classical or 'analogue' content production and distribution industries, particularly in film, television, radio and publishing. These policies play a key role in protecting media practice and audience exposure; the operational tools range from self-regulation and codes of ethics to professional standards and public service broadcasting (PSB). Several regional organizations, from the EU to the Organization of American States (OAS) and the African Commission on Human and People's Rights (ACHPR), have highlighted the specific role of the media in the promotion of cultural diversity and have stressed the importance of a free media environment for the construction of democratic societies. This must be particularly borne in mind as new digital technologies create new challenges for regulatory and industry support mechanisms.

On a national level the past decade has been marked by a renewed policy interest in cultural industry development and the promotion of content diversity. In this regard, Australia took the lead in the early 1990s, and was soon followed by the UK, Finland and many other OECD countries, as well as Brazil, China, Colombia, India and other developing countries. Generally speaking, this flourishing of policy initiatives upholds a number of paramount principles, notably the importance of a solid industrial base to allow diversity to thrive and the recognition of the importance of the cultural industries as vehicles for the transmission of contemporary creativity and the diversity of expression. However, there is still no consensus on what the optimum package of policies on the cultural industries would entail. Experience has

shown that cross-sector policies (mixing cultural, media, telecommunications, industrial, foreign trade and labour policies) are most effective, as is taking account of the specificities of cultural identities within the competitive advantages of particular sectors, such as music, publishing or crafts.

Access to the public sphere through the media remains a very challenging issue in many cases (at the legislative level or in practice) and is still far from being universally guaranteed to all. Large segments of the population, especially marginalized groups and ethnic minorities, are often absent from (or inappropriately depicted in) the media partly because of their lack of access to editorial, managerial or gate-keeping positions inside media outlets. Fostering internal diversity in the newsroom and diversity of cultural backgrounds and gender within media structures are fundamental steps towards ensuring diversity in content production, as are support mechanisms for community-owned media and public-service media (UNESCO, 2006).

Equipped with user-friendly software, inexpensive technical devices and 24-hour connections, audiences participate increasingly in the transmission and creation of information and knowledge, and are fundamentally altering the nature of information production (Bowman and Willis, 2003). This is leading to new cultural patterns, new forms of transmission (broad- and web-casting), modification of work routines and flexible strategies in media and cultural production. With the development of *user-generated content*, a new system of definition of cultural demand has appeared, where traditional institutions, the media and formal education are complemented by a layer of social attitudes and behaviours facilitated by convergence. Innovative journalism practices are emerging, through mobile-device-based video-reporting and direct uploading onto platforms (such as YouTube) of fragments of reality that can dramatically impact on the daily headlines of the international press. New strategies for news production, which include different viewpoints and diversified reporting, are being used by professionals across the world; one such strategy involves the use of thematic blogs in which information, videos and pictures are exchanged and commented on, discussed and criticized. Hybrid reporting across ethnic, cultural and national boundaries — through co-production and

◑ *Boys reading books in Afghanistan*

◑ *Bilingual class at Footscray Primary School in Melbourne, Australia*

pool-production schemes or through national, regional and international networks of media professionals — are being tested and encouraged, as is reporting organized along interest groups.

The implications of such new approaches are considerable. As we have seen, the Internet offers the potential for communicational democracy and involvement at a local level in a range of progressive cultural initiatives: capacity for identity-building within diasporic communities (Chitty and Rattikalchalakorn, 2006); support structures for defending the interests of minority cultures; the establishment of online communities with shared cultural interests, lobbying and campaign groups (e.g. concerning environmental or human rights issues); and the possibility of bypassing mainstream information sources (Atton, 2002; Couldry and Curran, 2004). Of course, this potential varies greatly depending on the degree of connectivity and the local contexts for expression on the part of cultural groups, which may lead to favouring one kind of media over another. For instance, a detailed study of Internet technologies as understood and assimilated in Trinidad and by local and diasporic Trinidadians looked at some of the ways in which Trinidadians have come to appropriate various technical possibilities that add up to 'their Internet' (Miller and Slater, 2000). Trinidadians, it seems, have a 'natural affinity for the Internet', which corresponds to established social forms in Trinidad according to which 'being a family has long meant integrating over distances through any means of communication'. Given the intensity of migration to metropolitan areas,

> the Internet — specifically email — allows the kind of mundane, constant and taken-for-granted daily contact that enables Trinidadians to uphold their notion of family, to be involved in active parenting and mutual support, despite the diasporic conditions that had earlier been making this impossible.

In this sense, the

> Internet may have helped bring the potential for being Trini back to Trinidad: indeed, it worked both for Trinis at home (who could have direct access to global cultural flows, global markets, and world-class skills and technologies) and for Trinis 'away' (who could 'repair' other aspects of Trini-ness such

as national identity, 'liming', 'ole talk', family and friendships).

These interesting new usage patterns provide a glimpse into the potential environments of the future. However, it remains to be seen whether the current trend towards digital, global but fragmented media use will create a more globally mediated reality. The best-case scenario points to new media platforms in which diverse audiences can see themselves represented in terms of their unique experiences, concerns and achievements. The worst-case scenario involves the fragmentation of audiences along ethnic, religious, sexual or other cultural lines. While these new practices related to the production of communication and cultural contents admittedly hold great promise, they nevertheless are not a solution in and of themselves. Rather, important challenges remain which need to be addressed by decision-makers if they want the media as a whole to contribute to the promotion of cultural diversity.

The challenges to be addressed

Three challenges have to be met if communication and cultural contents are to contribute to cultural diversity: the production of innovative content, access (including to ICTs) and balanced representation.

The *production of innovative content* ensures the transposition of cultural diversity into communication and cultural products. Every country in the world can be the source of innovative content that aims to take account of the diversity of the communities concerned and highlight their histories, cultures, future orientations and projected roles in the concert of nations. This content can also be conceived to specifically counter approaches that are often overlooked or minimized, such as the gender perspective, the voice of young people, the discourse of the excluded and the viewpoint of the disabled. The challenge is to create the conditions for thinking otherwise: a way of thinking about the world based on fellowship and the responsibility of all to others and the planet.

Ensuring diversity in the media will require increased emphasis on the development and production of local content by local communities. While the media have sought to define and represent the nation-state and national identity since the advent of newspapers in the

Cultural diversity also concerns public debates and the multiplicity of voices that can be heard in the public arena. In this respect, insofar as the media as a whole contribute to the flourishing of pluralism, they can make a strong contribution to cultural diversity

19th century, their strong emphasis on national content has been detrimental to the vitality of local content. National monopolies of media content are now being challenged, particularly since 2002, with increasing recognition that cultural diversity is as much about internal diversity as it is about diversity among nations. On a macro-level, key drivers are to be identified for the development of content industries in parts of the world where cultural expressions are a long way away from finding viable markets and extended audiences. On a micro-level, this means developing programmes that support the production and dissemination of local content through both standard and new media in disadvantaged communities of the developing world by training content creators, supporting local content production and enhancing content distribution. Such approaches have proven very helpful in identifying ways to empower local communities and help them to express themselves.

UNESCO has facilitated the production of local content through its Creative Content programme and through the creation of multi-purpose community telecentres (MCTs), which enable rural and poor communities in many regions of the developing world to manage their own development through access to appropriate facilities, resources, training and services (from education and training to business, from health to local governance). It also focuses on identifying good practices concerning community media throughout

the world, especially in the domain of policy, legislation, management, code of practices, self-regulation, funding mechanisms and entrepreneurship options, programming, sustainability, access, participation and media literacy issues. Community media have increasingly become a source of empowerment and dialogue for excluded and marginalized groups and a central vehicle for participatory social and cultural development. The global community radio movement in particular has been steadily growing in importance as an instrument for social and political change and for the promotion of cultural and linguistic diversity (AMARC, 2007). Examples abound of community radio stations worldwide. They include: Radio Sagarmatha, the first independent community radio station in South Asia, established in 1997 in Kathmandu, Nepal, as a conduit for investigative and 'watchdog' public affairs programming; Radio Suara Perempuan (Women's Voice Radio) introduced in West Sumatra, Indonesia, as a means of curbing gender violence; Radio Jën Poj and Radio Uandarhi, the first indigenous community radio stations in Mexico, were granted their broadcasting licences in 2004 and focus on indigenous language and cultural preservation, as well as relevant social and economic issues. Community radio broadcasting is present throughout Africa where it fosters cultural transmission and social cohesion.

While donors and development agencies have often stressed the importance of local content at international

---

| Box 5.5 | **Aboriginal Peoples Television Network (APTN)** |

The story of national Aboriginal broadcasting in Canada represents a significant milestone for indigenous cultural preservation and promotion through the media. Launched in September 1999, the Aboriginal Peoples Television Network (APTN) was the world's first national Aboriginal television service. APTN promotes the diverse histories, cultures and languages of indigenous peoples in Canada and throughout the world, providing Aboriginal programming across a variety of genres, including national news, children's animation, youth programmes, and cultural and traditional

programming. APTN targets both Aboriginal and non-Aboriginal Canadian audiences.

Today APTN is broadcast to over 10 million Canadian households and businesses through various platforms, including cable, direct-to-home satellite and fixed wireless television services. The rich linguistic traditions of indigenous peoples is captured in APTN's diverse programming: while 56 percent of programmes are broadcast in English and 16 percent in French, a notable 28 percent is broadcast in various Aboriginal languages, such as Inuktitut, Cree, Inuinaqtuun, Ojibway,

Inuvialuktun, Mohawk, Dene, Gwich'in, Miqma'aq, Slavey, Dogrib, Chipweyan, Tlingit and Mechif (APTN, 2005).

No less than 70 percent of APTN programming is developed in Canada, offering various professional opportunities to Aboriginal writers, directors, producers, actors and news anchors. The network also broadcasts a small portion of indigenous programming from various other parts of the world, including Australia, New Zealand, the US and Central and South America.

Source: Raboy, 2007.

meetings, concrete initiatives in this area are still rare. Most content initiatives using ICTs tend to 'push' external content onto local communities, which contributes to the free flow of ideas and to intercultural dialogue, provided that local communities have the capacity to receive such foreign contents without losing their identities. With a few exceptions, new technologies are not used to strengthen the 'push' of local content from local people. When tested, such as with the project *Development of a National Strategy for the Jamaica Music Industry* (Global Alliance for Cultural Diversity, 2004), the results are rather mixed, due mainly to the complexity of intellectual property issues — that ensure revenues for local creators of music content — and the difficult conditions for e-trade in developing economies.

In other instances, pressure from audiences themselves has had a positive impact on decisions privileging local production, of which the Bollywood film industry in Mumbai is one of the most striking examples, producing as it does over 800 films per year (more than Hollywood), which are distributed throughout the world. In the UK, the BBC's Channel 4 recently stated its intention to buy fewer foreign dramas in order to spend more money on locally developed shows; home to shows like *Friends, Ugly Betty* and *Desperate Housewives*, the channel said it would spend 20 percent less on imports by 2013 (BBC News, 2008).

The development of local content is all the more important since the media's power to steer attention to and from public issues often determines which problems society will tackle and which it will ignore: only those issues that gain publicity and visibility have the potential to generate political interest and make people think about social and political ramifications that go beyond their immediate experience (see Box 5.5).

Access has to be approached from different angles. In the first place, it involves coherent measures to reduce the digital divide by providing equipment at affordable prices, training, maintenance, technology updates , etc. Secondly, production and distribution networks should be accessible to innovative content. For example, one of the major problems confronting film production in Africa is that, despite the creativity it has demonstrated (African films garnered three awards at the Cannes International Film Festival in 1987 and 1990, during a period when

A man filming an algebra lesson in Tunisia

the African film industry was able to finance its productions by means of an effective European aid system and the consolidation of distribution networks through the *Inter-African* Film Distribution *Consortium*), it still has limited access to the major production and distribution networks. Very talented filmmakers, with competent teams and promising subjects, are often unable to finance their film projects. Thirdly, access has also to do with the visibility of minorities, which could be facilitated by new mechanisms that ensure the representation of a gender perspective and opposing viewpoints in discussions on all subjects (many journals adopt this approach) or, where appropriate, the inclusion of members of different ethnic groups or religious communities. Policies on access, and especially access to technologies of production and to distribution channels, have to identify financially sound schemes that permit the talent of any country to create content of any kind and thereby contribute to cultural diversity.

Finally, a third challenge to be addressed is that of *balanced representation*. Whole segments of the population tend to be ignored or do not recognize themselves in the ways they are depicted in the media and cultural industries. As some researchers stress, members of the groups or communities concerned

The development of local content is all the more important since the media's power to steer attention to and from public issues often determines which problems society will tackle and which it will ignore

do not want to be represented as stereotypes, that is to say, in a manner that devalues them. But they are wholly in favour of being represented in ways that value their knowledge, culture and traditions. Cultural diversity here requires a balanced representation of the different communities that live together in a particular country, even though the mechanisms that would allow such balance have yet to be agreed upon (e.g. quotas, ombudsman mechanisms or rights of response). The same consideration naturally applies at the international level where balanced representation in and more equal access to the media and cultural industries are a continuing concern in accordance with the principles of freedom of expression and the free flow of ideas, which should always prevail.

At the professional level, strategies aiming at diversifying the workforce might help to promote cultural diversity. In fact, such diversity could contribute to overcoming the current representations of 'others' that prevail today in the media. Self-directed support organizations (such as, in the US, the organization Unity for Journalists of Color) act as important lobbying groups for a more diverse workforce. Increasingly, public broadcasters around the world are diversifying their hiring strategies: the French news network France24, for example, broadcasts its news in French, English and Arabic, and therefore has been recruiting multilingual and multicultural journalists and television presenters. Similarly, in the US, the percentage of 'minorities' working in journalism and media production has been growing over the years. In other cases, government authorities have sought to influence or even to require proportional representation within broadcasting or other media institutions: such a strategy, based on 'positive discrimination' (the rough equivalent of the US affirmative action policies) has sometimes led to complaints about government interference and the undermining of the neutrality mandates of public broadcasters.

While a more diverse workforce is in and of itself a worthwhile goal, it is less clear whether and to what extent a more diverse media workforce will automatically lead to more diverse media content, and research for the moment remains inconclusive on this issue. Given the intensely competitive environment of journalism, the recent rise in 'ethnic' coverage may reflect more an

economic necessity than a desire to promote cultural diversity. Nevertheless, a more diversified workforce is likely to facilitate the dissemination of diversified media contents and thereby help to keep the gates open.

Conclusion

Across the immense diversity of cultural expressions that are communicated, transmitted and transformed by the myriad means available today (from print to digital technology), the communication of cultural content has undeniably contributed to enhanced awareness and greater knowledge of cultural diversity. The new technologies associated with the rise of new media practices favour productions geared to export and thereby broaden markets for local cultural industries, which are beginning to counter the dominant flows that have been detrimental to traditional cultural expressions (storytelling, dance, traditional games) and voices of marginalized populations. In this sense, contrary to oft-held positions, globalization cannot be said to have had only a negative impact on the diversity of cultural content, for it has enlarged choice and stimulated the production of local content. User-generated technology has in turn the potential to empower individuals and groups that were previously marginalized by institutional and economic obstacles and help them to find a voice and the means to circulate their ideas and viewpoints to the public at large. Increased appropriation of methods and technologies — provided that there is sufficient media and information access and literacy — are essential for combating stereotypes and biases.

While media pluralism is a precondition of cultural diversity, it will not be sufficient if universal access to the media is not guaranteed; for only by guaranteeing such access will it be possible to enable full participation in the formulation, expression and dissemination of diverse viewpoints. This implies the implementation of measures to strengthen the capacities of all to take full advantage of the opportunities provided by the new technologies. Information and media literacy is not only an important aspect of media access but an essential part of ensuring quality media on the one hand and critically informed consumption on the other. In light of the sheer quantity of cultural representations and messages that characterize contemporary society, the risks of 'a false diversity' masking social isolation, identity fallback and stereotypical attitudes loom large; they threaten to block any real progress towards intercultural dialogue. The challenge of 'false diversity' should be taken all the more seriously since, beyond issues of access to the media, culture and entertainment, the role and responsibility of the media are to contribute to better mutual knowledge and understanding among people. Nothing would be gained in bridging the digital divide if it left in place a knowledge divide. Only if the latter is overcome will it be possible to achieve the goal of establishing inclusive knowledge societies.

↻ *An official campaign to promote school in Herat, Afghanistan*

Chapter 5
Communication and cultural contents

Chapter 5 Recommendations

There is a need to encourage cultural sensitivity in the production and consumption of communication and information contents, thereby facilitating access, empowerment and participation.

To this end, action should be taken to:

a. Support the production and distribution of innovative and diversified audiovisual materials, taking account of local needs, contents and actors, and having recourse as appropriate to public-private partnerships.

b. Assess the impact of ICT-driven changes on cultural diversity, with a view to highlighting good practices of multilingual access to written and audiovisual productions.

c. Promote media and information literacy for all age groups in order to increase the ability of media users to critically evaluate communication and cultural contents.

Media toolkits for cultural diversity in broadcasting

Several toolkits have been developed with an emphasis on cultural diversity and public broadcasting, both by UNESCO and by its partner institutions. Among UNESCO's contributions, *Public Service Broadcasting: A Best Practices Sourcebook* (Banerjee and Seneviratne, 2005) and *Media Development Indicators: A Framework for Assessing Media Development* (IPDC, 2008) have set out guidelines for the assessment and implementation of the factors that contribute to cultural diversity.

Public Service Broadcasting: A Best Practices Sourcebook identifies four factors to be taken into account in determining whether a public service broadcasting (PSB) system is 'playing the role it is expected to perform'. These are: *universality* (to ensure that public broadcasting is accessible to every citizen throughout the country), *independence* (to ensure that public broadcasting is a forum where ideas can be expressed freely, where information, opinions and criticisms can circulate), *distinctiveness* (to ensure that the public broadcasting services offered are distinguished from that of other broadcasting services) and *diversity*, which covers a wide range of criteria, including cultural diversity (with reference to the targeted audiences):

> *The services offered by public broadcasting should be diversified in at least three ways: the genres of programmes offered, the audiences targeted, and the subjects discussed. Public broadcasting must reflect the diversity of public interests by offering different types of programmes, from newscasts to light programmes. Some programmes may be aimed at only part of the public, whose expectations are varied. In the end, public broadcasting should reach everyone, not through each programme, but through all programmes and their variety. Finally, through the diversity of the subjects discussed, public broadcasting can also seek to respond to the varied interests of the public and so reflect the whole range of current issues in society. Diversity and universality are complementary in that producing programmes intended sometimes for youth, sometimes for older people and sometimes for other groups ultimately means that public broadcasting appeals to all.*

The importance of cultural diversity in broadcasting is emphasized with respect to comparability:

> *For the majority of the world population, particularly by those belonging to disadvantaged groups, radio and television remain the most accessible and widespread means of information and communication. [. . .] It is crucial that PSB serves all populations reflecting the needs, concerns, and expectations of the different audiences irrespective of their sizes. Public Service Broadcasting is an essential instrument to ensure plurality, social inclusion, and to strengthen the civil society.*

This commitment of PSB to diversity in broadcasting is explicitly made, for example, in the *African Charter on Broadcasting 2001* (UNESCO, 2001), adopted on the tenth anniversary of the adoption of the *Windhoek Declaration on the Development of an Independent and Pluralistic African Press* (UNESCO, 1991). Other national instruments are even more explicit in their reference to cultural diversity, such as the *Australian Broadcasting Corporation Act of 1983*, which sets out the Charter for the Australian Broadcasting Corporation (ABC), in which ABC is invited, among other things, 'to broadcast programmes that contribute to a sense of national identity and inform and entertain, and reflect the cultural diversity of, the Australian community'.

Indeed, cultural diversity has a special role to play both in 'building citizens' participation' (treated in chapter 4 of the *Sourcebook*), in keeping with the 'primary obligation of broadcasters to promote the public's right to know through a diversity of voices and perspectives in broadcasting', and in standard-setting for PSB (as treated in chapter 6 of the *Sourcebook*), especially when it comes to 'building national identity' and 'minority programming'. In this area, the *Sourcebook* underlines the major role of PSB in broadcasting for ethnic and religious minorities:

> *In most countries, programming for these sectors of the community is not commercially profitable for private broadcasters, especially when most of these communities may be in the lower socio-economic category.*

> *To address this problem, in some countries there are dedicated ethnic or religious radio and television channels. In some cases, these needs may be catered for through 'window' style programming on national or regional PSB channels.*

A bookshop in Dakar, Senegal, 1971

Last but not least, the *Sourcebook* (in chapter 8) also sheds light on the new opportunities offered by PSB in the digital age, especially for reaching out to migrant workers (with best practices from the Philippines and Fiji).

The concept of knowledge societies that UNESCO advocates offers a holistic and comprehensive vision — cutting across all of UNESCO's domains — with a clear development-oriented perspective that captures the complexity and dynamism of current global trends and prospects. Knowledge societies require an empowering social vision, which encompasses plurality, inclusion, solidarity and participation. Based on the principles of freedom of expression, universal access to information and knowledge, promotion of cultural diversity, and equal access to quality education, knowledge societies are increasingly recognized as essential for attaining major development goals.

The more recent *Media Development Indicators: A Framework for Assessing Media Development* (IPDC, 2008) focuses on the media's role as 'a vehicle for cultural expression and cultural cohesion within and between nations', in addition to their being 'a channel of information and education through which citizens can communicate with each other', 'a disseminator of stories, ideas and information', 'a corrective to the "natural asymmetry of information" between governors

and governed and between competing private agents', 'a facilitator of informed debate between diverse social actors, encouraging the resolution of disputes by democratic means', and 'a means by which a society learns about itself and builds a sense of community, and which shapes the understanding of values, customs and tradition'. Here cultural diversity is seen to play an important role in media development, especially with regard to the following issues:

- *Regulatory system for broadcasting.* According to the five UNESCO declarations on Promoting Independent and Pluralistic Media, as well as the texts adopted by other intergovernmental bodies and independent professional associations (see Article 19, 2002), the 'powers and responsibilities [of regulatory bodies] should be set out in law, including explicit legal requirements to promote freedom of expression, diversity, impartiality and the free flow of information'.

- *Media concentration.* The 'authorities responsible for implementing laws' against undue concentration of ownership 'must have the power divest media operations where plurality is threatened or unacceptable levels of concentration are reached, and to impose sanctions where required'.

- *Diverse mix of public, private and community media.* 'In general, a diverse mix of public, community and private media is best achieved through legal, financial and administrative measures, with specific provisions to encourage community media and, in the broadcasting sector, a fair and equitable allocation of the spectrum'.

- *Licensing.* 'Licensing is a way of achieving diversity — there is a need to take diversity into account when licensing broadcast outlets. It is also important not only to ensure the equitable allocation of licences between the different types of broadcasters but also a sufficient allocation of frequencies to broadcasting in the first place'.

- *Availability and use of technical resources by the media.* 'Meeting the information needs of marginalized groups may require diverse types of infrastructural and technical support in any given country. These may include the provision of digital media technology, production equipment, satellite technology or independent printing presses to allow for efficient news gathering, production and distribution. They may also include lower-tech interventions, such as the means for community-based media to produce and distribute cassette tapes'.

Of course the challenge is to promote a media environment characterized by freedom of expression, pluralism and diversity, with laws restricting media freedom being narrowly defined and limited to those necessary in a democracy, and with legal provisions that ensure a level economic playing field. This requires provisions for public and community-based media as well as private media.

Among the tools developed by UNESCO partners, the European Broadcasting Union's *A Diversity Toolkit for Factual Programmes in Public Service Television* (EBU, 2007) also highlights the importance of fostering cultural diversity in order 'to serve entire national populations and to reflect the cultural, racial and linguistically diverse character of society accurately in content and in the workforce', particularly since 'experience shows that all too often programmes can reinforce stereotypes and repeat misunderstandings about minorities'.[1]

The *Toolkit* offers examples of news programmes aimed at broadcast journalists, instructors and students of journalism, as well as producers, programme-makers and human-resource professionals, as well as trainers and managers in broadcasting organizations. In Part I, it lays out a series of questions concerning the portrayal of minority audiences, together with news clips illustrating their relevance, with the goal of bringing to the fore issues that are often overlooked. The issues include:

- *Balanced representations.* News stories 'often focus on the negative issues relating to immigration and minorities', not on positive ones. Moreover, minorities are 'all too often treated as issues, not as people, and even then, are hardly ever covered as consumers, employers, employees, parents, students or viewers'. Thus, it is necessary to be aware of the ways in which viewers will decode and retain stereotypes 'which, when repeated in the news, can easily become the reality'.

- *The necessity of checking facts.* Since 'each reporter is influenced by cultural assumptions and prejudices, and often unaware of them', there is a need for 'checks and balances [. . .] to make sure that adequate background information is given in a news report. The opinions should be counterbalanced by facts. The relevance of mentioning ethnic or religious identity should be well judged in the coverage of crimes or accidents'.

- *The uncertainties about 'who we are seeing'.* Diversity 'is not only being able to count the number of ethnically different faces on the screen. The important question is how they are portrayed, how they are part of the story' — thus, populations should be represented in all their variety.

- *'Who chooses the stories?'* Since television 'transmits a sense of belonging and of citizenship', it is important to give voice to all, including minorities.

1.UNESCO and the EBU co-sponsor the 'Boundless' Cultural Diversity Media Award for intercultural reporting.

'Viewers that never "see" themselves on the television screen can understandably feel irrelevant', and with potentially dire consequences.

- *The need to reflect the views of the audience in order to remain relevant and viable.* Since PSB is 'a creative opportunity to make interesting and engaging programmes featuring stories and perspectives from a wide range of viewpoints', it is important that PSB 'take risks, dare to try something new, dare to make programmes that aim at the minority audiences specifically, as well as the mainstream audience generally'.

- *How to 'tell it like it is'.* It is not necessary to 'approach the problems of living in a multicultural society only in a serious way'; humour can be 'a good way to communicate on delicate issues'.

A 'Diversity checklist' is also provided, which consists of the following questions:

1. Am I aware of my personal assumptions about the issues, the stories and the people I choose to report on?

2. Am I aware of the power of images, words, sounds and music?

3. Do I mention ethnicity if it is not relevant to the story?

4. Do I spend enough time checking the facts? Am I sure that I am using the correct terms?

5. Do I consult more experienced colleagues — and those from different backgrounds — when necessary?

6. Do I choose my interviewees because of their relevance to the story or because I expect them to attract the attention of the viewer?

7. Do I try to find a variety of opinions among the minority spokespeople and witnesses I interview?

8. Are the minority subjects presented in my story chosen for authentic reasons?

9. Do I find new angles and develop my stories a bit further?

10. Do I challenge myself to find new sources and to question the dominant discourse?

11. Do I reflect on whether my stories maintain stereotypes?

12. Do I consider the impact of my report not only on viewer opinion but also on the lives of the subjects portrayed?

13. Do I actively try to recruit colleagues who will bring a diversity of perspectives into the newsroom?

14. Am I interested in cultures other than my own and open to accepting proposals for stories from different cultural viewpoints?

Part II of the *Toolkit* presents useful practices, encompassing 'ideas that work', 'new ideas that could be tried', 'management policies', as well as 'individual actions that can be very effective without huge means, and that can be adapted'. It presents good practices in the newsroom and in the workplace. It concludes by proposing key indicators for measuring progress, including qualitative tools and processes that can indicate minority audience reactions to programmes.

Children running in the playground in Hanoi, Viet Nam

Chapter 5
Communication and cultural contents

References and websites

Background documents and UNESCO sources

Alexander, N. 2007. Rethinking culture, linking tradition and modernity. Background paper.

Banerjee, I. and Seneviratne, K. (eds.). 2005. *Public Service Broadcasting: A Best Practices Sourcebook*. Paris, UNESCO. http://unesdoc.unesco.org/images/0014/001415/141584e.pdf

Fürsich, E. 2007. Media and the representation of others. Background paper.

International Programme for the Development of Communication (IPDC). 2008. *Media Development Indicators: A Framework for Assessing Media Development*. Paris, UNESCO. http://portal.unesco.org/ci/en/files/26032/12058560693media_indicators_framework_en.pdf/media_indicators_framework_en.pdf

—. 2006. Defining indicators for media development. Background paper. http://portal.unesco.org/ci/en/files/21385/12058536053media_development_indicators_en.pdf/media_development_indicators_en.pdf

Le Diberder, A. 2008. Numérique, diversité culturelle et prescription. Background paper.

Leonardi, D. 2007. Media law reform and policies in transition countries: how legal frameworks condition the media environment. Background paper.

Nyamnjoh, F. and Warnier, J. P. 2007. 'Cultural globalization': Real or imaginary? The impact of the media and globalization on cultural diversity, traditional practices, living creation and consumption habits. Background paper.

Raboy, M. 2007. Media pluralism and the promotion of cultural diversity. Background paper,

Robinson, M. 2007. Discovering and negotiating and cultural diversity through tourism texts. Background paper.

Shayegan, D. 2008. La diversité culturelle et la civilisation planétaire. Background paper.

Tomlinson, J. 2007. Globalization, the media and cultural diversity. Background paper.

UNESCO. 2006. *Trends in Audiovisual Markets: Regional Perspectives from the South*. Paris, UNESCO. http://unesdoc.unesco.org/images/0014/001461/146192e.pdf

—. 2005. *Convention on the Protection and Promotion of the Diversity of Cultural Expressions*. Paris, UNESCO. http://unesdoc.unesco.org/images/0014/001429/142919e.pdf

—. 2001. *African Charter on Broadcasting 2001*. http://portal.unesco.org/ci/en/files/5628/10343523830african_charter.pdf/african%2Bcharter.pdf

—. 1991. *Windhoek Declaration on the Development of an Independent and Pluralistic African Press*. http://www.chr.up.ac.za/hr_docs/african/docs/other/other23.doc

—. 1982. *Living in Two Cultures: The Socio-Cultural Situation of Migrant Workers and Their Families*. Aldershot, Gower/Paris, UNESCO.

UNESCO Centre of Catalonia (UNESCOCat). 2007. *Religious Diversity and Social Cohesion: A Contribution to the UNESCO World Report on Cultural Diversity*. http://www.unescocat.org/religions-mediacio/publicacions/world_report_on_cultural_diversity.pdf

UNESCO Institute for Statistics (UIS). 2005. *International Flows of Selected Cultural Goods and Services, 1994–2003: Defining and Capturing the Flows of Global Cultural Trade*. Montreal, UIS. http://www.uis.unesco.org/template/pdf/cscl/IntlFlows_EN.pdf

Websites

Academy of Canadian Cinema and Television: http://www.academy.ca

African Commission on Human and People's Rights (ACHPR): http://www.achpr.org

Africultures: http://www.africultures.com

Amnesty International: http://www.amnesty.org

Article 19: Global Campaign for Free Expression: http://www.article19.org

Australian Broadcasting Corporation Act of 1983: http://www.austlii.edu.au/au/legis/cth/consol_act/abca1983361

Binger Filmlab: http://www.binger.nl

'Boundless' Cultural Diversity Media Award: http://portal.unesco.org/ci/en/ev.php-URL_ID=24682&URL_DO=DO_TOPIC&URL_SECTION=201.html

Bruno Manser Fund: http://www.bmf.ch

Centre national de la cinématographie (CNC): http://www.cnc.fr

Communication Rights in the Information Society (CRIS): http://www.crisinfo.org

European Audiovisual Observatory: http://www.obs.coe.int

GSMA: http://www.gsmworld.com

International Freedom of Expression Network: http://www.ifex.org

International Telecommunication Union (ITU): http://www.itu.int

Islam Project: http://www.islamproject.org

Little Mosque on the Prairie: http://www.cbc.ca/littlemosque

Media, Communication, Information: Celebrating 50 Years of Theories and Practices (international conference, Paris, 23–25 July): http://portal.unesco.org/ci/en/ev.php-URL_ID=24350&URL_DO=DO_TOPIC&URL_SECTION=201.html

Motion Picture Association of America (MPA): http://www.mpaa.org

Muhammad: Legacy of a Prophet: http://www.upf.tv/upf06/Projects/MuhammadLegacyofaProphet/tabid/75/Default.aspx

Muslim Canadian Congress: http://www.muslimcanadiancongress.org

National Film and Video Foundation: http://nfvf.co.za

New Latino Spaces (Nouveaux Espaces Latinos): http://www.espaces-latinos.org

Organization of American States (OAS): http://www.oas.org

Recording Industry Association of America (RIAA): http://www.riaa.com

Reporters sans Frontières: http://www.rsf.fr

RomaFictionFest: http://en.romafictionfest.it

Search for Common Ground (SFCG): http://www.sfcg.org

Traficante de Sueños: http://www.traficantes.net

UNESCO, Community Media programme: http://portal.unesco.org/ci/en/ev.php-URL_ID=1527&URL_DO=DO_TOPIC&URL_SECTION=201.html

UNESCO, Content Development: http://portal.unesco.org/ci/en/ev.php-URL_ID=19486&URL_DO=DO_TOPIC&URL_SECTION=201.html

UNESCO, Creative Content: Radio, TV, New Media: http://portal.unesco.org/ci/en/ev.php-URL_ID=3981&URL_DO=DO_TOPIC&URL_SECTION=201.html

UNESCO, Creative Industries: http://portal.unesco.org/culture/en/ev.php-URL_ID=35024&URL_DO=DO_TOPIC&URL_SECTION=201.html

UNESCO, Cultural Diversity in the Era of Globalization: http://portal.unesco.org/culture/en/ev.php-URL_ID=11605&URL_DO=DO_TOPIC&URL_SECTION=201.html

UNESCO, International Fund for Cultural Diversity: http://portal.unesco.org/culture/en/ev.php-URL_ID=38235&URL_DO=DO_PRINTPAGE&URL_SECTION=201.html

UNESCO, Memory of the World: http://portal.unesco.org/ci/en/ev.php-URL_ID=1538&URL_DO=DO_TOPIC&URL_SECTION=201.html

UNESCO, Power of Peace Network (PPN): http://portal.unesco.org/fr/ev.php-URL_ID=42589&URL_DO=DO_TOPIC&URL_SECTION=201.html

Unity for Journalists of Color Organization: http://www.unityjournalists.org

Unity Productions Foundation (UPF): http://upf.tv

Voices21: http://comunica.org/v21

World Digital Library: http://www.wdl.org

World Free Press Institute: http://www.pressfreedom.org

References

Aboriginal Peoples Television Network (APTN). 2005. Factsheet. http://www.aptn.ca/corporate/facts.php

Abu-Fadil, M. 2008. Fostering critical capacities and fighting against unilateral points of view: finding a common ground and the subject matters amenable to cultural diversity learning. UNESCO Meeting of Experts on 'Cultural Diversity and Education. Barcelona, Spain, 14–16 January.

AMARC (World Association of Community Radio Broadcasters). 2007. Proceedings of the Africa-MENA Conference held in Rabat, Morocco, 22–24 October. http://amarcwiki.amarc.org/?p=AMARC_Africa-MENA_Conference

Anderson, B. 1991. *Imagined Communities: Reflections on the Origin and Spread of Nationalism*. 2nd ed. London, Verso.

Anderson, C. 2006. *The Long Tail: Why the Future of Business is Selling Less of More*. New York, Hyperion.

Appadurai, A. 1996. Disjuncture and difference in the global cultural economy. *Modernity at Large: Cultural Dimensions of Globalization*. Minneapolis, Minn., University of Minnesota Press.

Article 19. 2002. *Access to the Airwaves: Principles on Freedom of Expression and Broadcast Regulation*. London, Article 19. http://www.article19.org/pdfs/standards/accessairwaves.pdf

Atton, C. 2002. *Alternative Media*. Thousand Oaks, Calif., Sage.

Barber, B. R. 1996. *Jihad vs. McWorld: How Globalism and Tribalism Are Reshaping the World*. New York, Ballantine Books.

Bauman, Z. 2005. *Liquid Life*. Cambridge, Polity.

BBC News. 2008. Channel 4 'will cut US imports'. 14 March. http://news.bbc.co.uk/2/hi/entertainment/7296229.stm

Benhamou, F. 2004. *L'économie de la culture*. 5th ed. Paris, La Découverte.

Benson, R. 2005. American journalism and the politics of diversity. *Media, Culture and Society*, Vol. 27, No. 1, pp. 5–20.

Bowman, S. and Willis, C. 2003. *We the Media: How Audiences Are Shaping the Future of News and Information*. Reston, Va., The Media Center and the American Press Institute. http://www.hypergene.net/wemedia/download/we_media.pdf

Castañeda, L. and Campbell, S. (eds.). 2006. *News and Sexuality: Media Portraits of Diversity*. Thousand Oaks, Calif., Sage.

Castells , M. 1996. *The Rise of the Network Society*. (The Information Age: Economy, Society and Culture, Vol. 1.) Oxford, Blackwell.

Chan, J. M. 2005. Trans-border broadcasters and TV regionalization in Greater China: processes and strategies. J. K. Chalaby (ed.), *Transnational Television Worldwide*. London, I. B. Tauris.

Chitty, N. and Rattikalchalakorn, S. (eds.). 2006. *Diasporic Communication*. Special Edition of *The Journal of International Communication*, Vol. 12, No. 6.

Clifford, J. 1988. *The Predicament of Culture: Twentieth-Century Ethnography, Literature, and Art*. Cambridge, Mass., Harvard University Press.

Couldry, N. and Curran, J. (eds.). 2004. *Contesting Media Power: Alternative Media in a Networked World*. Lanham, Md.: Rowman & Littlefield.

Curtin, M. 2007. *Playing to the World's Biggest Audience: The Globalization of Chinese Film and Television*. Berkeley, Calif., University of California Press.

Dayan, D. 1999. Media and diasporas. J. Gripsrud (ed.). 1999. *Television and Common Knowledge*. London, Routledge.

Dines, G. and Humez, J. M. (eds.). 2003. Gender, Race, and Class in Media: A Text-Reader. Thousands Oaks, Calif., Sage.

Entman, R. M. and Rojecki, A. 2000. *The Black Image in the White Mind: Media and Race in America*. Chicago, Ill., University of Chicago Press.

European Broadcasting Union (EBU). 2007. *A Diversity Toolkit for Factual Programmes in Public Service Television*. Vienna, European Union Agency for Fundamental Rights (FRA). http://www.ebu.ch/CMSimages/en/toolkit%20low_tcm6-56142.pdf

Fatah, T. and Hassan, F. 2007. Little masquerade on the prairie. *The Toronto Sun*, 12 February. http://www.muslimcanadiancongress.org/20070212.html

Fürsich, E. and Shrikhande, S. 2007. Development broadcasting in India and beyond: redefining an old mandate in an age of media globalization. *Journal of Broadcasting and Electronic Media*, Vol. 51, No. 1, pp. 110–28.

Georgiu, M. 2006. *Diaspora, Identity and the Media: Diasporic Transnationalism and Mediated Spatialities*. Cressskill, N.J., Hampton Press.

Gerbner, G., Gross, L., Morgan, M. and Signorielli, N. 1986. Living with television: The dynamics of the cultivation process. Bryant, J. and Zillman, D. (eds). Perspective on media effects. Hilldale, Lawrence Erlbaum Associates.

Global Alliance for Cultural Diversity. 2004. *Development of a National Strategy for the Jamaican Music Industry*. Project fact sheet. http://portal.unesco.org/culture/en/files/30661/11443338253jamaican_music_industry.pdf/jamaican_music_industry.pdf

Gray, H. 1995. *Watching Race: Television and the Struggle for 'Blackness'*. Minneapolis, Minn., University of Minnesota Press.

Hall, S. (ed.). 1997. *Representation: Cultural Representations and Signifying Practices*. Thousand Oaks, Calif., Sage.

Hewitt, D. 2007. In a world of their own. *China Review*, No. 40, pp. 12–14. http://www.gbcc.org.uk/files/documents/Chinareview40.pdf

Iskandar, A. 2006. Clashing perceptions? Al-Jazeera's challenge to Western media. Unpublished lecture at the University of Washington, DC, 15 August.

Iwabuchi, K. 2007. Contra-flows or the cultural logic of uneven globalization? Japanese media in the global agora. D. K. Thussu (ed.), *Media on the Move: Global Flow and Contra-Flow*. London, Routledge.

—. 2005. Transnational media culture and the possibility of transgressive dialogues. L. Wong (ed.), *Globalization and Intangible Cultural Heritage*. International conference, Tokyo, 26–27 August 2004. Paris, UNESCO, pp. 129–35. http://unesdoc.unesco.org/images/0014/001400/140090e.pdf

—. 2002. *Recentering Globalization: Popular Culture and Japanese Transnationalism*. Durham, N.C., Duke University Press.

KEA. 2006. *The Economy of Culture in Europe*. Study prepared for the European Commission. Brussels, KEA European Affairs. http://www.keanet.eu/Ecoculture/Study%20new.pdf

Kim, Y. 2007. The rising East Asian 'wave': Korean media go global. D. K. Thussu (ed.), *Media on the Move: Global Flow and Contra Flow*. London, Routledge.

Livingstone, S. 2004, Media literacy and the challenge of new information and communication technologies. *The Communication Review*, Vol. 7, pp. 3–14. http://www.lse.ac.uk/collections/media@lse/pdf/SLstaff_page/SL_94.pdf

McLaren, P., Hammer, R., Sholle, D. and Reilley, S. S. (eds.). 1995. *Rethinking Media Literacy: A Critical Pedagogy of Representation*. New York, Peter Lang.

Miller, D. and Slater, D. 2000. *The Internet: An Ethnographic Approach*. Oxford, Berg.

Mjwacu, T. 2003. Opportunities and challenges of the new technologies in media and communication: the Windhoek Declaration. A. Zegeye and R. L. Harris (eds.), *Media, Identity and the Public Sphere in Post-Apartheid South Africa*. Leiden, Brill.

ᕮ   *On the Bohicon market, Benin*

ᕮ   *A fisherman's wife in Aral Sea region, Kazakhstan*

ᕮ   *Kutiyattam, a form of sacred theatre from Kerala, India*

Nielsen. 2009. Time spent online among kids increases 63 percent in the last five years. *Nielsen Online Data Quick Take: Kids Online*, 6 July. http://en-us. nielsen.com/main/news/news_releases/2009/july/Nielsen_Online_ Data_Quick_Take__Kids_Online

Nyamnjoh, F. B. 2007. Cultures, conflict and globalization: Africa. H. Anheier and Y. R. Isar (eds.), *Conflict and Tensions*. (Cultures and Globalization Series, Vol. 1.) Thousand Oaks, Calif., Sage.

Oguibe, O. 2004. *The Culture Game*. Minneapolis, Minn., University of Minnesota Press.

Pratt, M. L. 1992. *Imperial Eyes: Travel Writing and Transculturation*. London, Routledge.

Rony, F. T. 1996. *The Third Eye: Race, Cinema, and Ethnographic Spectacle*. Durham, N.C., Duke University Press.

Rourke, J. T. 2004. *Taking Sides: Clashing Views on Controversial Issues in World Politics*. London, McGraw-Hill.

Silverstone, R. 2007. Media and Morality: On the Rise of the Mediapolis. Cambridge, Polity.

Siochrú, Seàn Ó. 2004. *Social Consequences of the Globalization of the Media and Communication Sector: Some Strategic Considerations*. International Labour Office Working Paper No. 36. Geneva, International Labour Office. http://papers.ssrn.com/sol3/papers.cfm?abstract_id=908237

Spurr, D. 1993. *The Rhetoric of Empire: Colonial Discourse in Journalism, Travel Writing, and Imperial Administration*. Durham, N.C., Duke University Press.

Sunstein, C. 2001. *Republic.com*. Princeton, N.J., Princeton University Press.

Taylor, L. K., Davis, H. E. and Zine, J. (eds.). 2007. *Contested Imaginaries: Reading Muslim Women and Muslim Women Reading Back: Transnational Feminist Reading Practices, Pedagogy and Ethical Concerns*. Special issue of *Intercultural Education*, Vol. 18, No. 4.

Teer-Tommaselli, R., Wasserman, H. and de Beer, A. S. 2007. South Africa as a regional media power. D. K. Thussu (ed.), *Media on the Move: Global Flow and Contra-Flow*. London, Routledge.

Tel Quel, N° 350, déc. 2008. Rabat, Morocco. http://www.telquel-online.com

Thussu, D. K. 2007. Mapping global media flow and contra-flow. D. K. Thussu (ed.), *Media on the Move: Global Flow and Contra-Flow*. London, Routledge, pp. 11–32.

—. 2005. The transnationalization of television: the Indian experience. J. K. Chalaby (ed.), *Transnational Television Worldwide*. London, I. B. Tauris.

United Nations Alliance of Civilizations (AoC). [2006]. *Research Base for the High-level Group Report Analysis on Media*. New York, Alliance of Civilizations. http://www.unaoc.org/repository/thematic_media.pdf

United Nations Conference on Trade and Development (UNCTAD). 2008. *Creative Economy Report 2008: The Challenge of Assessing the Creative Economy towards Informed Policy-making*. New York, United Nations. http://www.unctad.org/en/docs/ditc20082cer_en.pdf

World Tourism Organization (UNWTO). 2007. *Tourism Market Trends 2006*. Madrid, World Tourism Organization.

Chapter 5
Communication and
cultural contents

Roça Ribeira Peixe plantation in Sao Tome and Principe

Street art in Rio de Janeiro, Brazil

Creativity and the marketplace

While the previous chapter looked at the impacts of communication and cultural contents on cultural diversity, this chapter explores the interrelations between cultural diversity and a broad spectrum of activities extending from cultural creation and innovation through the commercialization of cultural expressions to the impact of culture in the business world.

Creativity is fundamental to cultural diversity, which is itself conducive to creativity. In a context of pervasive cross-border flows, cultural diversity can be preserved only if its roots are constantly nourished by creative responses to a rapidly changing environment. The creative impulse at the root of cultural diversity is essential when it comes to analyzing the present situation of the world's cultures and addressing the imbalances they reveal. As the World Commission on Culture and Development emphasized in its 1996 report, *Our Creative Diversity*: 'Today it is ever more necessary to cultivate human creativity, for in our climate of rapid change, individuals, communities and societies can adapt to the new and transform their reality only through creative imagination and initiative'. Creativity is understood here as applicable to the whole spectrum of human activities, from the arts and the sciences to the world of commerce, including invention and innovation both by individuals and by groups and their institutions.

As illustrated by current trends in the contemporary world of art, music and literature, diversity in the arts is facilitated by the growth of artistic exchanges worldwide. The same is true for the crafts and tourism industries, as well as in contemporary business practices. With the broadening of the boundaries of the arts and creativity to encompass the whole spectrum of human activity, cultural diversity has become increasingly pertinent as a source of invention and innovation and as a resource for sustainable economic development. Cultural policy at the national level, while rightly concerned with supporting endogenous creation, should ensure that tradition remains creative, implying responsiveness to a plethora of cross-cultural influences that guarantee its continuing vitality.

Russian matrioshka dolls

Creativity and the Marketplace

6.1 Artistic creation and the creative economy 163
Figure 6.1 Share of International market for visual and plastic arts 166

6.2 Crafts and international tourism 167
Box 6.1 Towards the legal protection of folklore? 169
Box 6.2 Religious tourism 170

6.3 Cultural diversity and the business world 172
Map 6.1 Innovation scores, 2008 172
Box 6.3 Consumer values analysis in the BRICs . 173

Box 6.4 Adapting management practices to local contexts: Danone Mexico 176
Box 6.5 A correlation between diversity and economic performance? 178

Conclusion 179

Recommendations 180

In focus: Tools and approaches for increasing the relevance of cultural diversity to corporate audiences 181

References and websites 183

A performance of the Carnival of Barranquilla (Colombia) at UNESCO Headquarters

6.1 Artistic creation and the creative economy

In approaching the subject of artistic diversity, it is important to avoid the trap of ethnocentrism, of confining ourselves to a culturally determined conception of the arts. As Le Thanh Khoi (2000) has asked:

Should we not apply the term 'art' to all the material productions by which human beings give meaning to their existence [...]? Over the course of millennia, art was not dissociated from life. All members of the community participated in its ritual, poetical and musical activities. Only the activities endowed with magical powers required the intervention of a specialist.

Today, reflecting expanded communication and travel, there is greater awareness and understanding of other cultures. Thus, one finds that the term 'primitive arts' is yielding to that of 'traditional arts', and a number of distinctions, such as between art and crafts or between fine arts and decorative arts, are being called into question. Nevertheless, the definition of what is artistic — and conceptions of art as a collective or individual activity — varies greatly from one culture to another. In Africa, for example, art encompasses ritual functions and everyday objects, which often have a strong symbolic charge. In China, the 'four arts' — music, poetry, painting and calligraphy — continue to mark Chinese culture, with painting and calligraphy focusing less on ornamentation than on the expression of life. In Islam, art is represented *par excellence* by the book arts, since writing is regarded as the vehicle of the word of God, with ornamentation playing an important role, particularly in architecture (Khoi, 2000).

The boundaries of art are prescribed not only by the divergent outlooks of social groups but also by the materials and techniques available to them. Ornamentation of the body is the most immediate form of plastic art surviving among peoples living close to nature, whereas others have clothed their nakedness under the influence of religious doctrine or philosophical belief. Because of their arid environment, the Aborigines of Australia express themselves more in painting than in sculpture, whereas the peoples of Oceania have created out of an abundant vegetation the most fantastic and exuberant of artistic universes. The Amerindians for their part are unsurpassed in the arts of weaving and gold working' (Khoi, 2000). In the realm of the arts, as with cultural expression more generally, creative diversity has its origins in both the natural and the social environments.

Contemporary art practices

The encounter with diversity in the arts is facilitated by the growth of artistic exchanges worldwide. Today 'cultural diversity' in the art world has come to mean more than the cosmopolitanism of early 20th century European modernity. The era of decolonization and subsequent worldwide liberation movements from the 1960s onwards were accompanied by changes in the field of contemporary art — including exhibitions, conditions of production, museums and markets — prefiguring the geopolitical realignments that were to mark the world of globalization. The 1990s saw a remarkable shift in the circuits of contemporary art owing to the slow rise to prominence of new venues for its display, increasingly receptive to previously excluded artistic expressions — that of Africans, Asians, Latin Americans, Chicanos, First Nation Peoples and women.

Towards the end of the 20th century, large exhibitions known as biennials began to emerge as the pre-eminent global forums for organizing the multiple positions of contemporary artistic practice. In 1984, the Havana Biennial and the Cairo Biennial were among the first to take place outside Europe and North America, followed by Istanbul in 1987 (which established a new network for artists working in the Middle East and Eastern Europe), then Dakar in 1992, Gwangju in 1995, and Johannesburg in 1995. Not only have the coordinates of art-making become scrambled due to changes in global networks but the narratives of artistic production now exist in often heterogeneous, competitive and mutually contradictory logics of production. Even in Europe, an early sign of the impact of the fall of the 'iron curtain' in 1989 was the establishment in 1995 of Manifesta, an itinerant pan-European biennial that moved every two years to a new city on the continent, from the Balkans to the Baltics, from the Mediterranean to the North Sea. By recognizing this very multiplicity of approaches, biennials became key sites after 1989 for the production of new discourses and the redrawing of a complex map of contemporary art.

The encounter with diversity in the arts is facilitated by the growth of artistic exchanges worldwide. Today 'cultural diversity' in the art world has come to mean more than the cosmopolitanism of early 20th century European modernity

From the perspective of contemporary art practices, 'the world can no longer be structured in terms of the centre/periphery relation'. There is a 'slow decentring of the West' in which, 'the constitution of lateral relations in which the West is an absolutely pivotal, powerful, hegemonic force, is no longer the only force within which creative energies, cultural flows and new ideas can be concerted'. This new face of the world 'has to be defined in terms of a set of interesting centres, which are both different from and related to one another', centres that function by means of cultural networks and in alignment with larger geopolitical shifts (Hall, 2001). This broadening of artistic outlooks, sympathies and expressions has contributed significantly to cultural diversity through processes of cross-fertilization that are increasingly germane to all forms of artistic creation.

However, the range and impact of such influences inherent in globalizing trends is not without its dangers to cultural diversity. The borrowings or hybrid forms to which cultural diversity gives rise can take the form of reductive syntheses that are little more than stereotypes. By the same token, the Western vogue for 'exotic' forms of expression can make for a confinement of local forms — for example, through their assimilation to categories such as 'primitive' art. It can pre-empt or radically alter the individual's ability to operate as an artist at all levels, since he or she is also presented as a member of a given 'minority' community. In this way, international markets in indigenous or 'exotic' art can function as exogenous forms of 'official' art, rewarding conformism with prestige and financial gain. The issue is complicated by the fact that the canon of originality is not equally applicable to all artistic traditions. The originality of art identified variously as 'primitive', 'indigenous', 'tribal' or even 'ethnographic' is necessarily relative to the standards of Western artistic traditions.

One way to counter the exoticization of non-Western forms of expression in the art market is to ensure a better balance in the representation of artists from the developing and developed countries in their mutual encounters with each other and in the ways in which they make themselves visible to the public. In this respect, the international community's commitment to guarantee the 'free flow of ideas through word or image', as enshrined in UNESCO's Constitution (1945), should be implemented in practice, including through the facilitation of travel for artists. As illustrated by the findings of the World Observatory on the Social Status of the Artist, there is no common approach on this matter within the international community. Discussions are ongoing about the possibility of facilitating the exchange and circulation of artists through the generalization of cultural visa mechanisms, such as those employed in Brazil or Japan.

A performance of traditional Japanese puppet theatre, Ningyo Johruri Bunraku, at UNESCO Headquarters

Trends in relation to cultural diversity

The diversification and interpenetration of artistic traditions observable in the visual and plastic arts are reflected in the performing arts through the international circulation of theatre productions and traditions. The discovery of Balinese theatre and Japanese Noh drama by European dramatists in the first half of the 20th century is an early example of the significant role of non-European artistic traditions in the renewal of European theatrical aesthetics. The scope of such exchanges has been very broad, extending from high art to all forms of entertainment, including ritual practices 'consumed' outside their place of origin as though they were artistic performances — as illustrated by the vogue for the performance of the *teyyam* or divine dance tradition of Kerala at European and Asian cultural festivals. Opera, while remaining primarily centred in Europe and the Americas, is increasingly international in appeal, finding enthusiastic audiences as well as a rich vein of performers in Asia (Japan and Korea in particular). Classical music in general, supported by a strong tradition of major orchestral tours between Europe, the US and Asia, has continued to expand its influence worldwide. In Latin America, where music has strong and diverse roots, an enlightened policy of musical education in Venezuela for example has revitalized the performance of classical music under the baton of the prodigy Gustavo Dudamel, 'the symbol of classical music oriented towards the future, open to a new world'.

In the field of popular music, diversity is everywhere. In the West, the range of often overlapping genres — including rock, pop, jazz, folk, Latin, blues, country, reggae and musical comedy — is virtually limitless. Musical traditions on all continents display a vast array of forms. Festivals offer great opportunities to sensitize the public to this diversity of expression. The 'world music' festival, where the audience is invited to move between performances representative of a variety of cultures and styles, is an especially good vehicle in this regard. In Australia, the WOMAD (World of Music and Dance) music festival franchise has greatly influenced the growth of interest in world music. Yet, while this expansion of musical tastes and encounters with often radically different musical traditions is to be welcomed, the potential drawbacks from the standpoint of cultural diversity should not be overlooked. As with the globalization of cultural exchanges more generally, the risk here lies in the commodification and commercialization of musical expressions at the expense of their authenticity and originality, leading to the creation of niche consumer markets, the reductive appropriation of exogenous cultural forms, and the substitution of a 'world culture' concept for the diversity of cultural expressions.

The challenge of preserving and promoting cultural diversity is situated precisely at this point of transition (or tension) between cultural creation and cultural commercialization, between the market valuation and the cultural values inherent in artistic creation. Virtually all cultural expressions, even intangible ones related to ways of life or identities, may be commodified, that is to say, given economic value and subsequently commercialized. The phenomenon is nothing new, of course: 'All cultures and all artists have felt the tension between [. . .] the self-forgetfulness of art and the self-aggrandizement of the merchant' (Hyde, 2007). However, globalization processes and technology have altered the stakes for the creative — or aspiring — artist, just as they have for the potential entrepreneur. They have posed with unprecedented force the 'perennial question of how to trade off pure artistic creativity against hard economic realities' (Thorsby, 2008). The financial rewards available within a globalized trading environment have tended to favour economic considerations, with important implications for cultural diversity and authenticity.

Popular music is arguably the field in which the pressures of commercialization make themselves most strongly felt. Their impact is twofold: on the one hand, the pressures constitute an inducement to local artists to exploit their creative talents in an increasingly global market; on the other, they serve as a vector of acculturation processes related to the asymmetry of global cultural flows. In the case of popular music, four out of five of the major music industry conglomerates are located in the US, the other being in the UK; and the music sales market is dominated by the Western countries together with Japan and the Republic of Korea — Brazil being the only developing country to figure among the top 20 commercial outlets (Anheier and Isar, 2008). As seen in chapter 5 similar huge imbalances in commodified cultural exchanges between developed and developing countries are found in all branches of printed, recorded and audiovisual media. New

The challenge of preserving and promoting cultural diversity is situated precisely at this point of transition (or tension) between cultural creation and cultural commercialization, between the market valuation and the cultural values inherent in artistic creation

technologies linked to the Internet, which are in the process of profoundly altering the way in which music is distributed and accessed, potentially offer the best prospects for the diversification of creative flows in this sector, depending on political will and economic constraints.

Similar trends are apparent in the visual and plastic arts, including painting, engraving, prints, original sculpture and statuary. For example, the top five exporting countries — namely, the UK (22.4 percent), China (20.4 percent), the US (18 percent), Switzerland (6.3 percent) and France (6 percent) — accounted for 73 percent of the world's exports in 2006. Europe's share of the international market (50.4 percent) was largest, followed by East Asia (26.2 percents), North America (18.5 percent), Central and South Asia (2.8 percent), Latin America and the Caribbean (0.82 percent), the Pacific (0.6 percent), sub-Saharan Africa (0.71 percent) and the Arab States (0.06 percent) (see Figure 6.1). The top five importers of visual arts were the UK, Switzerland, Germany, France and Japan. More recently, the number of buyers from Asia, Russia and the Middle East has risen significantly, but it is not yet clear how the recent crisis in the world's financial markets will impact on this trend and, more generally, on new or existing clients of the art market (Anheier and Isar, 2008).

Figure 6.1 Share of International market for visual and plastic arts

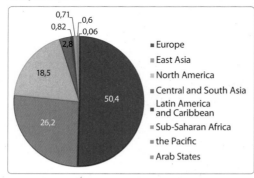

Source: UNESCO Institute for Statistics, 2008 based on data from UN Comtrade database, DESA/UNSD.

The contemporary art world remains entrenched in power hierarchies, even if counter-flows may have begun to emerge. In 2003, 39 percent of the 87 artists exhibited at the Centre Georges Pompidou in Paris were French and 61 percent were foreign (represented by 11 countries), broken down as follows: US 32 percent, Italy 23 percent, Germany 19 percent, Switzerland 7.5 percent, UK 5.7 percent, Belgium 3.8 percent, and Austria, Brazil, China, Israel and the Republic of Korea 1.9 percent each. A similar pattern is revealed in the analysis of the number of galleries per country selected to exhibit at the highly influential fair, Art Basel, where in 2000 and 2005 Germany, the US, Switzerland, France, the UK and Italy dominated. It is also reflected in *Kunstkompass*'s ranking of 100 internationally recognized artists per country for 1979, 1997, 2000, 2004, 2005 and 2007, in which the relative positions of the US, Germany, the UK, France, Italy and Switzerland periodically interchange but do not lose their places as the top six countries. As Okwui Enwezor and Jean Fischer (2007) have noted, while the discourse on globalization, cultural relativism and mixing has allowed for the emergence of artists from a wider variety of countries — the Third World in particular — their recognition by the market remains slight, the market being controlled largely by Westerners and favouring mainly artists living in the West.

Compared with the mutually intelligible, if stylistically distinct, languages of music and the visual and plastic arts, literature presents something of a barrier to acculturation. On the other hand, in an increasingly plurilingual world, literatures in the main vehicular languages have a clear advantage in terms of cultural diffusion, which is evident from the imbalance in the flow of translations into and out of the world's dominant languages. This historical imbalance is reflected in the roster of Nobel Laureates in Literature, some 75 percent having come from Western Europe or the US, as compared with less than 10 percent from Asia, Africa and the Middle East combined. A valuable corrective to this trend is provided by a number of literary prizes devoted to foreign works in translation, including the annual International Literature Awards of the US National Endowment for the Arts ('provid[ing] Americans with as direct a connection as possible to both the individual voice of the author and the heart of a culture'), the Arts Council England's Foreign Fiction Prize and the French Prix Médicis for foreign literature in translation. Mention should also be made of the Pen World Voices Festival of International Literature, whose 2009 meeting in New York hosted 160 writers from 40 countries.

In this context, the discontinuation of the UNESCO Collection of Representative Works, consisting of some 1,300 titles from more than 80 countries, translated from 100 or so different languages, is regrettable. The collection nonetheless remains a useful source of information on foreign classics in translation, as well as for publishers interested in publishing new editions of the texts. At the same time, the recently launched World Digital Library — a collaborative venture by UNESCO and the US Library of Congress — is making available significant primary materials in multilingual formats from cultures around the world (including manuscripts, maps, rare books, musical scores, recordings, films, prints, photographs, architectural drawings and other significant cultural materials). This online collection fosters intercultural awareness and understanding by providing resources to educators, expanding non-English and non-Western content on the Internet and supporting scholarly research.

It is a matter for conjecture how far globalization will nurture a process with deep historical roots to which Goethe refered when he wrote at the beginning of the 19th century: 'National literature is now a rather unmeaningful term; the epoch of world literature is at hand, and everyone must strive to hasten its approach.' Contemporary authors writing from an increasingly intercultural perspective — the names of Rushdie, Marquez, Coetzee spring to mind — may be seen as exemplars of new forms of world literature, representing, as it were, windows on a globalizing world. Some may see such globalizing trends as a threat to literary traditions in national languages. However, a case can be made for regarding such expressions not as inimical to cultural diversity but as modern avatars of diversity — 'locally inflected and translocally mobile' (Cooppan, cited in Damrosch, 2003) — of the continuing dialectic between cultural diversity and intercultural dialogue.

While literature in general may be influenced by globalizing trends affecting most aspects of cultural life, poetic expression may be more resistant to such trends. If globalization can be said to have less purchase on poetry than on any other literary form, it may be, on the one hand, because poetry expresses a propensity to the universal and, on the other, because poetry's singularity makes it non-commodifiable, inconvertible into any value other than itself. In the tradition of a Walt Whitman, Rabindranath Tagore, Saint-John Perse, Pablo Neruda, or Derek Walcott, poets inhabit universes of their own creation, which commend themselves to us as our own. In this sense, poetry remains a wellspring of diversity within a continuum that runs from culture to commerce.

Artistic creation and all forms of innovation spanning the spectrum of human activity may be seen as primary sources of cultural diversity

6.2 Crafts and international tourism

Cultural commerce and consumption today concern an increasingly broad public and encompass an expanding range of commodified cultural expressions and experiences. Crafts and international tourism are culturally and economically important in this regard: the former, by giving artistic shape to decorative or domestic objects; the latter, by providing access to the diversity of cultures in their natural settings. These two sectors — among many possible examples — illustrate the tension between authenticity and commercialization that is central to the preservation and promotion of cultural diversity.

Crafts and the commercialization of cultural objects
Despite the relative lack of data and research in the field, the economic importance of the craft sector is indicated by a number of examples highlighted in a recent UNESCO study (Richard, 2007). In Italy, for example, 24 percent of enterprises belong to this sector, which employs one-fifth of workers in the private domain. In Colombia, craft production represents an annual income of roughly US$400 million, including some US$40 million in exports, providing workers in the sector with an annual income ranging from US$140 to US$510. Tunisia's 300,000 craftworkers (two-thirds of whom work part-time) produce 3.8 percent of the country's annual GDP, or an annual income per family of US$2,400. In Morocco, crafts production represents 19 percent of its GDP, including exports estimated at US$63 million. In Thailand, the number of craftworkers is estimated at 2 million (out of the 20 million workers in the informal sector), almost half of whom can be regarded as full-time workers. In recent years, crafts have become a major means of income-generation and capacity-building for trade. Craft fairs are appearing in more and more countries, sometimes to raise funds for humanitarian causes but increasingly to sell products for utilitarian use, such as furnishing or decoration.

Crafts and international tourism ... illustrate the tension between authenticity and commercialization that is central to the preservation and promotion of cultural diversity

Crafts production is an important form of cultural expression, reflecting as it does the aesthetics, symbolism and worldviews of the producing communities. As tradable forms of cultural diversity, crafts have become a significant source of additional income and employment in many parts of the world. Major segments of the populations of the Kashmir Valley and Bali, for example, derive their income from handicrafts as well as tourism. In isolated areas of Myanmar, craftwork — such as the weaving of lungi (the traditional garment made from hand-spun cotton) — boosts household incomes, and in Central Asia where, following the collapse of the USSR, women employ their traditional skills in the processing of raw materials, such as local wool and silk cocoons. Highly skilled and labour-intensive craft-making is an important income-generating activity for women, especially in societies where their mobility is restricted. In Iran, Afghanistan, Central Asia, the Balkans, India and Pakistan, lace-making, embroidery skills and carpet weaving are important sources of income and access to credit.

As an increasingly high-growth industry, crafts have become part of a highly organized system of guilds, traders, organizations and banking systems. Industrialization and marketing, combined with the forces of globalization, are helping the traditional economy of crafts to adapt to the demands of the global marketplace. Yet craftwork that remains faithful to its traditions adapts an object or product to the materials at hand and to the symbolism of its context. Each product placed on the market embodies

a philosophy specific to the culture from which it derives. However, the pressures and opportunities of the global economy risk imposing a form of mass production excessively geared to commercial demands. Such mass production threatens to impoverish craftwork by cutting it off from its cultural roots and robbing it of all creativity.

Strong demand can also prompt price increases that place a product beyond the reach of local populations, inducing them to turn to cheap products manufactured in the countries of the North. The flooding of traditional markets with Western industrial products has had a serious impact on craft economies. The introduction of mill-made English cloth to the Indian market or machine-made goods in Indonesia are two examples. India, which has the largest number of independent, self-supporting craftworkers in the world, is currently operating a dual economy policy under which small-scale and cottage industries can develop alongside large-scale industry. In this way, it has been able to support a revival in craft activities, such that old markets that had been lost are being regained and new ones are being created. Increased demand for craft products should not lead to a decline in their quality or to the loss of ancient know-how. Ensuring fair returns on craft products and preserving traditional know-how are concerns that should carry equal weight. In this connection, a case can be made for ensuring the protection of craft manufacture through the legal protection of folklore (see Box 6.1).

Microfinance and micromarketing

The promotion of cultural diversity depends to large extent on support for commercial ventures adapted to cultural contexts and local economic constraints, which in turn calls for a more pluralistic and accessible marketplace. Microcredit — which consists in lending small sums (often under US$100) and charging competitive interest to very small business owners — has proven remarkably successful in this regard, especially in developing countries. The source of its success is based on the fact that the mechanisms of the commercial economy take into account the structures of cooperation specific to a given society, especially in contexts to which the traditional banking system cannot adapt. Microfinance has proven effective in reducing poverty and increasing self-empowerment throughout the developing world, particularly among women. The

⊃ *An Indonesian woman making a basket*

| Box 6.1 | **Towards the legal protection of folklore?** |

While the rise of globalization has enabled the recognition of the world's rich folklore tradition (including crafts, folktales, music, dances and designs), the pressures of the global marketplace have led to the unfair exploitation of folklore and other traditional cultural expressions (TCE), without regard for the interests of the communities in which they originate. The issue of their legal protection has been bogged down in international disagreements over the past 30 years.

The question was first raised at the international level in 1973, when the Bolivian Government invited UNESCO to examine the possibility of providing for the legal protection of folklore by means of an amendment to the *Universal Copyright Convention* (UNESCO, 1952), as well as an agreement concerning the conservation, promotion and distribution of folklore. Difficulties arose, however, regarding the protection of folklore under copyright since the notion of 'author' central to copyright law is inapplicable to the continuous and collective nature of the creative process underlying traditional folklore.

Attempts to arrive at a solution to the problem led, in 1982, to the formulation of model legal provisions, by the World Intellectual Property Organization (WIPO) and UNESCO, on the protection of expressions of folklore against illicit exploitation, prescribing intellectual-property-type protection for expressions of folklore at the national level. Following the adoption by many developing countries of domestic measures for the protection of folklore, attention turned to the need for international measures to protect folklore expressions beyond their countries of origin. The debate by joint WIPO/UNESCO committees continued without finding a solution until the end of the 1990s.

In 2000 WIPO established the Intergovernmental Committee on Intellectual Property and Genetic Resources, Traditional Knowledge and Folklore (GRTKF) as a forum for international policy debate and development of legal mechanisms and practical tools concerning the protection of traditional knowledge (TK) and TCE/folklore against misappropriation and misuse, and the

intellectual property (IP) aspects of access to and benefit-sharing in genetic resources. Despite efforts, little progress has been made in reaching consensus on an international norm on the protection of folklore.

Alongside these efforts, however, UNESCO has made some important strides towards standard setting in the preservation and safeguarding of TCE, notably through the 1989 *Recommendation on the Safeguarding of Traditional and Folklore* and the 2003 *Convention for the Safeguarding of the Intangible Cultural Heritage. While neither of these instruments contains any provisions on intellectual property rights or legal protection proper, they serve as benchmarks in the continuing efforts to secure such provisions.*

Source: UNESCO.

Nobel Peace Prize awarded to Muhammad Yunus in 2006 has focused attention on the virtues of such a system in combating poverty and stimulating local economies.

Microfinance and micromarketing have the potential to help small businesses from the developing world to innovate and compete within the marketplace. A recent survey (Light Years IP, 2008) estimates that by harnessing the intangible value of certain of their products (e.g. Ethiopian leather, Kenyan tea, Malian mudcloth, Namibian marula oil and Togolese black soap) sub-Saharan African countries can increase their export income by a factor of 2–3, rising to 80–200 solely for the television animation market, and 40–60 for the creative industries. UNESCO's 'Award of Excellence' programme, established in 2001 to encourage craftworkers to use traditional skills and materials to ensure the perpetuation of traditional knowledge and set quality standards, now operates in Asia, Western Africa, Latin America and the Caribbean, and thereby helps to raise international awareness about

handicraft products, as well as to enlarge and strengthen the markets for these products.

Tourism and the commercialization of intercultural experiences

In recent years tourism has enjoyed unprecedented growth, generating significant revenues for both developed and developing countries. With a growth factor of about 5 percent annually, it is predicted that tourism will double in size over the next 15 years. In 2004, it represented approximately 10 percent of the EU's GDP (compared with 2.6 percent for the cultural and creative sector). In Colombia, 650,000 tourists have brought in revenues totalling some US$800 million. In Morocco, the tourism industry represents about 6.5 percent of GDP (Richard, 2007). Some experts estimate that it could continue to develop, reaching the figure of 1.56 billion travellers by 2020 (1.2 billion intra-regional travellers and some 400 million long-distance, extra-regional tourists). Europe is forecast to be the top receiving region (with

Tourists standing with a South American Indian woman

717 million tourists), followed by East Asia and the Pacific (with 397 million), the Americas (with 282 million), and then Africa, the Middle East and South Asia. Above average growth is forecast for East Asia and the Pacific, South Asia, the Middle East and Africa. However, other experts foresee the approaching end of the low-cost flight boom — given the volatility of the price of petrol and the possibility of a longer-term rise in petrol prices in a context of scarcity — which would once again restrict cheap flight to a clientele able to afford increasingly costly journeys.

As illustrated by a recent ISTC and ATLAS survey on 'youth and travel' (Richards and Wilson, 2003), tourism is a key example of the contribution of profit-oriented initiatives to intercultural dialogue and better understanding among peoples. People engage in new cultures because they are curious. For 83 percent of the 2,300 young people and students interviewed from Canada, the Czech Republic, Hong Kong, Mexico, Slovenia, South Africa, Sweden and the UK, their main motivation was 'exploring

other cultures', followed by 'excitement' (74 percent) and 'increasing knowledge' (69 percent). The survey identifies the main benefits gained from travel as being an increased understanding and appreciation of other cultures linked to a thirst for more travel. The promotion of tourism plays an important role with respect to intercultural dialogue and the negotiation of difference, and special efforts should be made to involve local populations in tourism development, including vetting the information provided for tourists.

After decades of so-called mass tourism, there has been a resurgence of tourism in search of authenticity, motivated by the desire to discover other people in their natural, social and cultural settings. The World Tourism Organization (2008) estimates that cultural tourism represented about 40 percent of all travel in 2006, making it one of the highest growth sectors in the world. Whereas the major hotel groups previously tended to provide an international clientele with standards of comfort and cuisine akin to those found in the major

| Box 6.2 | Religious tourism |

An increasingly important segment of cultural tourism relates to 'faith travel', tourism motivated by religious or spiritual reasons or associated with religious heritage sites. Previously a largely domestic phenomenon, religious tourism has turned into a major international commercial service. Travel agencies offer extensive multi-faith journey packages to ancient places of worship, sacred destinations and pilgrimage sites associated with the mainstream faiths. In November 2008, the World Religious Travel Association (WRTA) held the first global trade and educational conference aimed at the 300 million potential faith travellers, with exhibitors from more than 30 countries drawn from ecumenical communities and travel agencies.

Thus globalization has opened up religious tourism to commercialization, transforming it into a marketable economic product serving overlapping markets: spirituality, physical and mental health, leisure activities, culture, short stays and city breaks. Given its considerable demographic base, this form of tourism holds enormous potential

for fostering interfaith and intercultural dialogue if it is harnessed. Indeed, if correctly conceived, tourism can be a tremendous development tool and an effective means of preserving and promoting cultural diversity. Part and parcel of this process is ensuring that such tourism remains sustainable, which means that it deals effectively with issues related to environmental, social and cultural conservation and preservation of local areas.

With regard to pilgrimage sites and destinations, sustainability entails taking steps to equip and maintain — often ancient — monuments that must be protected and restored, as well as providing environmental protection for natural sites using access ways and traffic corridors in order to prevent congestion and not exceed load capacities. Other issues relate to the management and promotion of these destinations, the development of sustainable local economies and respect for the traditions and customs of the host populations. In the case of large religious events and gatherings, challenges

include how best to manage flows and access in order to ensure that participants are received and accommodated under proper hygienic and public-health conditions (including the allocation of appropriate food services for participants who observe the dietary rules prescribed by their religion), guarantee the safety and security of persons and their property, provide assistance for the sick, the elderly and children who may get lost, and supply information on programming (times of ceremonies, meals, types of meals according to religion and dietary traditions). Pilgrimage routes and religious itineraries require well-coordinated partnerships and collaboration among all the host communities, tourism professionals and territorial development authorities involved. The World Tourism Organization (UNWTO) has developed objectives and guidelines specifically aimed at promoting the rise of sustainable religious tourism.

Source: UNWTO, 2008.

Western capitals, the focus today is increasingly on providing 'typical' experiences, a décor reflecting the local environment and customs and an opportunity to experience local cuisine. New forms of tourism have come into being, catering for the traveller anxious to explore what is different or inaccessible. Travel packages are becoming increasingly varied — combining, for example, trekking expeditions, lodging with local populations and learning different cultural expressions or traditional sports. Another new form of 'cultural' tourism is religious tourism (see Box 6.2), which has led to the creation of very sophisticated infrastructures in pilgrimage sites and varied tourist itineraries. In the case of the Muslim Hajj, which lasts up to 45 days, some tourist agencies propose a variety of cultural excursions in combination with visits to holy shrines.

The results of this new trend in local tourism are mixed: the authenticity of the experiences on offer inevitably becomes somewhat problematic, such as when some initiatives 'exoticize' cultural diversity. The sensationalizing of difference is taken to extremes when discriminatory or degrading practices to which particular groups (such as women) are subject are highlighted in order to satisfy tourists' curiosity. An egregious example is that of the 'giraffe women' of the Karen hilltribes in Burma: the practice of elongating their necks by means of a series of brass coils, supposedly to protect them from tiger attacks, has been turned into a tourist spectacle without regard to the dignity or possible dangers to the health of the women concerned. It is important that tourism avoid turning cultural practices and expressions into 'folklore spectacles', divorced from their true context and meaning. The risk inherent in cultural tourism is that it may reify others, reducing them to mere objects to be discovered — and 'consumed' — rather than permitting them to be subjects who may equally well discover us. The preservation of cultural diversity presupposes the promotion of its living expressions while avoiding any action or attitude that denigrates these by reducing them to imitations.

Tourism linked to UNESCO World Heritage sites plays an important role in the promotion of cultural diversity: by lending historical depth to other cultures, situating others in their natural setting, and highlighting the diversity of cultural expressions as a collective heritage to be preserved for present and future generations. The economic benefits from this form of tourism can also be substantial: they can

take the form of direct revenues from tourist visits, the sale of local crafts, music and other cultural products, and the promotion of longer-term development objectives. For these potential benefits to be realized in practice, it is necessary that the countries concerned fulfil their responsibilities to conserve and maintain the sites in question — which as World Heritage sites are held in trust for humanity as a whole. Another — albeit intangible — benefit from cultural tourism linked to World Heritage sites is that it can nurture a sense of pride, which is an essential factor in the dynamic of sustainable development intrinsic to the flourishing of cultural diversity.

Thus both crafts and tourism can function as effective levers for sustainable development, provided that the excessive 'culturalization' of such economic sectors is avoided in the interest of preserving cultural diversity. Today, an increasing number of enterprises highlight the 'cultural' nature of their products. In some cases, this reflects a genuine wish to promote local products, particular types of manufacture or gastronomic traditions. In other cases, it is no more than an artifice designed to boost the sales of the product concerned.

Statues of the Holy Virgin Mary in a souvenir shop in Lourdes, France

Today cultural diversity has a central role to play in the conception, brand image and marketing strategies of products that are successful in the global market. But cultural diversity is also beginning to be integrated into the internal functioning of businesses and to inform operational and development strategies

6.3 Cultural diversity and the business world[1]

The internationalization of markets has increased the importance of competitive advantage based on creativity and innovation. As illustrated in the map below, an assessment of innovation systems as measured by the World Bank — i.e. involving firms, research centres, universities, think tanks, consultants and other kinds of organizations — shows important disparities between Europe and North America, on the one hand, and the rest of the world's regions on the other. The map does not however show the creative potential that can result from capitalizing on cultural diversity in terms of culturally diverse forms of innovation. The business world is beginning to understand and respond to the challenges of cultural diversity as a key factor of economic success. In an increasingly global marketplace, the capacity to create a universe with which consumers can identify adds significantly to a product's value. Today cultural diversity has a central role to play in the conception,

brand image and marketing strategies of products that are successful in the global market. But cultural diversity is also beginning to be integrated into the internal functioning of businesses and to inform operational and development strategies. Indeed, corporate governance is becoming more and more multinational and diversified in order to satisfy a diverse range of partners, collaborators and clients. As a result, cultural diversity today figures as prominently on private-sector agendas as it does on those of political decision-makers at the national or international level.

Marketing, diversification and customization
Multinational corporations are becoming increasingly aware of the benefits of diversifying and customizing their products in order to penetrate new markets and meet the expectations of local consumers. Diversification runs parallel to a general standardization of tastes

Map 6.1 Innovation scores*, 2008

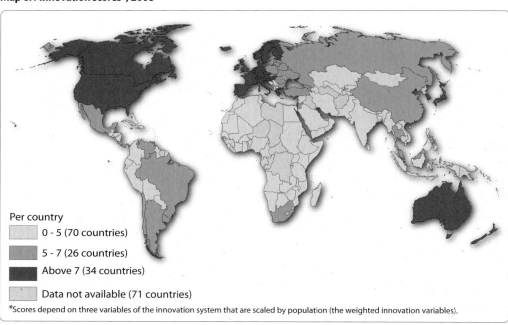

Per country

☐ 0 - 5 (70 countries)

☐ 5 - 7 (26 countries)

■ Above 7 (34 countries)

☐ Data not available (71 countries)

*Scores depend on three variables of the innovation system that are scaled by population (the weighted innovation variables).

Source: World Bank Institute, 2009.

1. In this section, reference to companies and brands has been limited to those companies that are members of the United Nations Global Compact. See the relevant website, listed below.

and lifestyles, especially in global cities (Sassen, 2001). The worldwide expansion of the Coca-Cola brand, for example, has been accompanied by the emergence of rival brands (in the Arab States, in Iran), which offer a similar product but under a different name with local associations. Its popularity has also spurred older products to evolve in keeping with local tastes and supply, an example being the Russian drink *Kvas*, made from black bread, which is sometimes labelled the 'Russian Coca-Cola'. Customizing or tailoring a product to a particular cultural context is a new strategic element in marketing policies worldwide.

Major global brands, such as Nike and Coca-Cola, spend millions of dollars advertising and promoting their products to align with the cultures, needs and aspirations of their consumers. Increasingly, global and national marketers are adapting universal brand positioning to the cultures and aspirations of the markets they are in, seeking to find more common ground and to reflect the full range of diversity that may be present in given market. One example is the corporate sponsorship of national athletes, teams and celebrities, such as Nike's support of cricket in India.

In the global economy, cultural diversity has the potential to become a more prominent factor in commercial strategy. An example in the banking sector is HSBC, which in 2004 mounted a global advertising campaign to illustrate its claim to be 'the world's local bank'. The campaign expressed the idea that individual and cultural differences are, in fact, the lifeblood of innovation and creativity, that knowledge of and sensitivity to these differences are at the heart

of successful relationships and mutual understanding. HSBC promoted these as crucial values in a global advertising campaign and on a website that invited visitors to explore different points of view. Another important group in retail clothing has also sought to capitalize on expressions of diversity through a focus in its communications strategy on global humanitarian concerns, such as peace and the struggle against racism and intolerance. In the manufacturing sector, it is now a general principle that a product must take specific account of local conditions and preferences, even if the brand itself is international. Thus, for example, as a consequence of Renault-Nissan's position that 'There is no such thing as a "world car"', the company is changing its approach to manufacturing: cars intended for Chinese consumers are built with vertical suspension and very elaborate interiors, while those intended for Japanese consumers have horizontal suspension and simpler and more sober interiors (FNSP, 2008; Smith, 2008). Diversity in the global commercial context is thus a protean concept, sometimes engineered into the product and sometimes underpinning a claim to universality.

The new consumer class arising in developing countries — especially the BRICs (Brazil, Russia, India and China) — is of particular interest to market specialists today, offering attractive potential markets that call for fresh observation, measurement and analysis. Consumer research based on measures of income, media habits and consumption patterns, gathered through extensive opinion studies paralleling the analytical tools developed by and used in Western consumer societies , is seeking to capture the complexity of cultural attitudes within a variety of national settings (see Box 6.3).

| Box 6.3 | Consumer values analysis in the BRICs |

A study issued by the Target Index Group (TGI), entitled *Brand Building in the BRICs* (Wicken and Lobl, 2006), focuses on the mainstream consumer market and the comparative examination and analyses related to adults aged 20–54 who live in one of the two or three largest urban areas in each country, which are considered a key target by many brand owners. These cities are 'leading the

charge' towards consumerism, offering the largest distribution networks and the greatest numbers of potential brand purchasers, many of whom are at the forefront of their countries' social and economic development.

These four countries have very different urbanization patterns: While more than 70 percent of Brazilians and Russians live in

cities, less than 40 percent of Indians and Chinese do. Thus, beyond the two or three major urban areas of these four countries — São Paulo and Rio de Janeiro in Brazil; Moscow and St. Petersburg in Russia; Mumbai, Delhi and Calcutta in India; and Beijing, Shanghai and Guangzhou in China — it would be extremely difficult to fix any criteria for the comparison of the four countries. Comparisons with

Box 6.3	Consumer values analysis in the BRICs

developed markets were made, based on four Western European countries (France, Germany, Spain and the UK), and the entire span of the 20- to 54-year-old populations were taken as the best comparative representation of the developed consumer populations. Data were compiled in three categories — universal values, specific values and divergent values — and were commented upon as follows:

Universal values, which show very similar levels of agreement among the BRICs and Western Europe, are related to the importance of the family and to conservative forms of behaviour.

Universal values: % agreement with statement: (age 20 to 54)	Brazil 2 cities	Russia 2 cities	India 2 cities	China 2 cities	Europe 4 countries	Average Deviation
How I spend my time is more important than the money I make	51	49	49	49	48	2%
It is important to keep young looking	67	62	62	n.a.	58	3%
In this day and age it is important to juggle various tasks at the same time	69	71	n.a.	76	68	4%
I enjoy spending time with my family	76	75	62	73	81	7%
I often do things on the spur of the moment	32	39	38	32	37	7%
I don't like the idea of being in debt	79	72	61	68	80	8%
I like to understand about nature	76	61	56	64	60	9%
I like to have control over people and resources	40	35	48	39	41	9%
I try to keep up with developments in technology	51	49	51	38	51	10%
I am worried about pollution and congestion caused by cars	76	68	56	n.a.	59	11%
If at first you do not succeed you must keep trying	90	80	65	n.a.	83	11%
I have a practical outlook on life	76	59	54	66	62	11%
Children should be allowed to express themselves freely	75	49	63	66	64	11%
I think its important to have a lasting relationship with one partner	90	80	63	72	81	11%
It is important to continue learning new things throughout your life	95	78	59	79	84	12%

Specific values not shared by Europeans basically related to how one is perceived by one's family or society. A desire to succeed, get rich ('Money is the best measure of success'), be recognized by one's family ('It's important my family thinks I'm doing well') and become an affluent consumer ('I really enjoy any kind of shopping') appears to be the driving force behind most of these. In another respect, however, we see less individualism in the BRICs markets than in their Western counterparts. There is a greater degree of acceptance of the view that individuals have to act within the collective framework of society ('It is more important to do your duty than to live for your own enjoyment'). This also reflects strong family structures. For instance, in each of the BRICs, children live at home well into adulthood. Looking after your parents is 'expected' behaviour.

Specific values: % agreement with statement: (age 20 to 54)	Brazil 2 cities	Russia 2 cities	India 2 cities	China 2 cities	Europe 4 countries	Average Deviation
I tend to spend money without thinking	30	29	28	n.a.	17	2%
I like to pursue a life of challenge, novelty and change	56	n.a.	51	53	37	3%
I ask people advice before buying new things	50	56	51	47	37	5%
I find it difficult to say no to my children	50	45	42	41	30	7%
It's important my family thinks I'm doing well	77	69	57	71	42	8%
I like to enjoy life and don't worry about the future	39	41	48	49	29	10%
There's little I can do to change my life	33	40	41	48	17	10%
Because of my busy lifestyle, I don't take care of myself as well as I	61	50	46	n.a.	37	11%
I really enjoy any kind of shopping	49	62	66	n.a.	29	11%
I would be prepared to pay more for environmentally friendly products	71	57	45	54	41	13%
It is more important to do your duty than to live for your own	50	46	58	70	35	14%
Money is the best measure of success	43	56	44	61	27	15%
People come to me for advice before buying new things	34	40	34	52	28	15%
I read the financial pages of my newspaper	24	28	36	n.a.	19	15%
I am willing to sacrifice my time with my family in order to get ahead	48	n.a.	40	61	25	15%

Box 6.3	Consumer values analysis in the BRICs

Divergent values are important because they indicate points of difference among BRICs. Fundamentally, these are reflected in statements that are related much more closely to local attitudes or values and are often controversial issues rooted in local culture. Faith, a woman's place, men crying and being attractive are very controversial areas, and the responses to statements bearing on such matters vary significantly, indicating that each country has its own views about them.

Divergent values: % agreement with statement: (age 20 to 54)	Brazil 2 cities	Russia 2 cities	India 2 cities	China 2 cities	Europe 4 countries	Average Deviation
My faith is really important to me	86	25*	74**	n.a.	29	40%
I am perfectly happy with my standard of living	48	19	72	n.a.	48	39%
I am very good at managing money	60	18	52	n.a.	53	39%
Real men don't cry	10	50	47	60	12	38%
I would like to set up my own business one day	84	34	44	n.a.	32	37%
I find I am easily swayed by other people's views	15	n.a.	47	34	19	35%
A woman's place is in the home	13	42	38	64	9	35%
I like taking risks	19	31	40	60	27	33%
I worry a lot about myself	61	21	44	n.a.	37	33%
I always look out for special offers	88	30	48	52	45	31%
It is important to be attractive to the opposite sex	80	74	46	40	63	28%
I like to stand out in a crowd	39	31	62	61	23	27%
I think we should strive for equality for all	94	49	58	n.a.	68	27%
Music is an important part of my life	74	37	39	46	48	26%

*R: Religion plays an important part in my life **I: I pray perform Pujas regularly

An interesting theme in this group is related to risk-taking: Brazilians seems to be the most conservative and least individualistic, in clear contrast to the Chinese, with Russia being closer to Brazil, and India to China. Status is a key personal driver in China and India, perhaps an outcome of the opening up of new economic opportunities and growing wealth. At this stage in China's development, especially among those living in the three largest cities, it is most important to convey status at the individual level. In Brazil however looking attractive, especially to the opposite sex, is much more important than status, thereby clearly contrasting with Chinese and Indians. Russians are much closer to Brazilians in this respect.

Source: Pigott, 2008, based on Wicken and Lobl, 2006.

Some have predicted that these emerging countries could become the largest economies in the world by 2050 (Wilson and Purushothaman, 2003). Earthwatch estimates that this consumer class now exceeds 300 million people in both China and India (Pigott, 2008). Fuelled by a US$400 billion advertising industry (combining print, radio, television, Internet, billboards), many of the brands promoted are endowed with emotional and cultural meanings that far exceed the functional benefits of the given product, whether it be a mobile phone, a soft drink, a beauty product, a car or fast food. Inevitably, these meanings will influence consumers' perceptions of and outlooks on dress, style, popularity and belonging, not to mention attitudes towards food, diet, health and exercise, significantly adding to the complexification of contemporary identities (see chapter 1). Indeed, it appears that the attraction, trust and interest in brands is significantly stronger in a number of developing countries than in the so-called developed world, underscoring the importance of this influence in countries with younger demographics. The omnipresence of commercial media in the streets creates an environment that is conducive to consumerism.

In this way, new products appear on the market, reconciling the values specific to a local context (or at least the perception of these values) with the efficiency of global trading instruments. This holds particularly in the case of commercial activities that could be thought to be incompatible with a particular cultural context due to religious proscriptions. Thus, in Muslim countries, Islamic banking services designed to be compatible with the prohibition on money lending (on the payment or receipt of interest) have been conceived as solutions to a specific cultural problem. Launched some 30 years ago, Islamic financial institutions now number more than 400

Managerial competencies now have to include the ability to work in very different cultural contexts. This has triggered a range of culturally sensitive human resources policies, which have in turn spurred the need for new corporate governance patterns

worldwide, spread over 70 countries and representing over US$800 billion in capital, corresponding to an average annual rate of increase of 15 percent (Les Dossiers, 2007). In Morocco, for example, three 'alternative' products entered the market in July 2007: one for trade financing, another for capital investment and a third resembling a form of leasing that is also applicable to equipment and property. Even in a country not predominantly Muslim, such as Kenya, Barclays Bank has launched a range of commercial products compatible with the Islamic banking system and aimed at the country's 8 million Muslims (afrik.com, 2005). However, these products are subject to the same uncertainties as traditional commercial products. In Morocco, for example, clients have been reticent to use these alternative products because of their significantly higher cost as compared with traditional banking services (Sqalli, 2007).

Diversity management and corporate culture

As the development of commercial strategies tailored to diverse cultural contexts becomes an increasingly important component of successful business strategies, the notion of corporate culture is beginning to change — internally in terms of human relations, resources and management, and externally in terms of corporate operations and governance practices. This has cast doubt on many of the assumptions underpinning mainstream business practices and has prompted a re-evaluation of 'good business practices' worldwide, inasmuch as national cultures will obviously have a bearing on local business cultures, as well as on the degree of adaptability of foreign corporate cultures (Bollinger and Hofstede, 1987; Hofstede, 2001; see also Box 6.4).

In a globalized business world, very different cultures are brought into professional contact across multinational partnerships, mergers and relocations. While many still experience 'cultural differences' more as 'a source of conflict rather than of synergy' (Hofstede, 2009), it is becoming increasingly clear that cultural misunderstandings can be avoided through awareness-raising aimed at reinforcing cooperation in multinational contexts (Gancel, Raynaud and Rodgers, 2002). In response to questions related to cultural mistakes that occurred when the SkyTeam Alliance of airlines started out, the president of a member company remarked that what is often underestimated is the importance of how people come to conclusions and the very different

| Box 6.4 | **Adapting management practices to local contexts: Danone Mexico** |

The Mexican subsidiary of the French group Danone represents an outstanding case of a highly successful company in an emerging country. Impressed by the subsidiary's superb technical performance and profitability, the group's executives attributed the success to its employees' high level of motivation. While the executives linked the motivation with the group's social policy of 'dual commitment' (associating business success with social progress), they were nonetheless intrigued by the enthusiastic response the policy inspired. They wondered to what extent the response stemmed from the fact that the group's policies were particularly well suited to the Mexican context. Further investigation revealed that the personnel saw the company as an entirely different social form, with ways of being and acting not found in ordinary Mexican companies. Unlike traditional companies, where considerable distance and indifference

exist between hierarchical levels and peers, the personnel of Danone Mexico felt that they belonged to a tightly knit and intensely supportive group of peers. This enabled them to feel as strong collectively as they are powerless individually. A combination of policies relating to social policy, labour organization, hierarchical levels and the company's actions towards local communities, has caused the relations typical of most Mexican companies to gradually give way to behaviour that is more familial in character.

Once outside the American context and vision of society, management practices based on the prevailing standards of American business no longer serve as an effective frame of reference. In Mexico, for example, the prevailing vision of good hierarchical relations is quite different from American contractual relations. Whereas a clear-cut definition of individual responsibilities as a means of judging personal achievements

and knowing unequivocally whether employees have fulfilled their contractual obligations are the norm in the US, the exact opposite is true in Mexico, where collective responsibility is the norm. It is, of course, necessary — as it is in the US and elsewhere — to identify precisely what functions more or less well in a company, so that problems can be corrected. This is simply a universal imperative for management. However, in Mexico one tends to do so without drawing a close connection between the evaluation of results and the judgement of individuals; rather, the aim is to locate and correct the faulty processes without necessarily seeking out the individuals responsible for these failings. Such differences between local conceptions and American conceptions of management practices can be found in all of the cases examined.

Source: d'Iribarne and Henry, 2007.

'logical structures' used by different populations to arrive at the same conclusion, thus underlining the necessity of making room for flexibility in thinking. Indeed, today's managers are increasingly aware of the need to take cultural factors into account in order to optimize both working conditions and company performance. Strategies range from adopting culturally neutral professional attitudes to emphasizing sensitivity to the specific origins or cultural backgrounds of colleagues.

In the 1990s diversity discourse shifted away from the affirmative action approaches that grew out of the civil rights movement in the 1960s, designed to overcome patterns of exclusion or discrimination and legally ensure fair employment practices (Thomas, 1991). Since then, corporations have come to recognize the added value of a diversified workforce for corporate operations (Kochan, 2003) and have 'discovered culture' (Gordon, 1995). Corporate culture[2] has sought increasingly to ensure that employees feel valued and respected by their colleagues, particularly regarding ethnicity and gender, in order to build organizations that are more fully integrated across occupations and hierarchical levels (Ely and Thomas, 2001). Recruitment and training campaigns have become more and more competitive internationally as companies attempt to attract or retain people with very different backgrounds who have themselves developed a stronger drive for self-fulfilment in the workplace. Managerial competencies now have to include the ability to work in very different cultural contexts. This has triggered a range of culturally sensitive human resources policies, which have in turn spurred the need for new corporate governance patterns able to bridge different corporate cultures, especially following a cross-boarder merger or acquisition (see 'In focus' below).

In the US, the non-profit organization Business Opportunities for Leadership Diversity (BOLD) launched an initiative in 1996 among industry chief executive officers (CEO) and human resource (HR) professionals to demonstrate the added value of a diversified workforce for corporate operations (Kochan, 2003). Since then, a number of surveys have sought to show the correlations between diversity and performance

○ A multinational business team joining hands

(Lagace, 2004), although the complexity of the issue and the sensitivity of the subject matter make this difficult to measure. Available literature and surveys suggest that not attending to diversity may jeopardize group processes (communications, conflict and cohesion) (Jehn, Northcraft and Neale, 1999) and point to the importance of the organizational context in which the work takes place, that is, human resources practices and corporate culture (Gomez-Mejiaf and Palich, 1997). In this context, the position of 'chief diversity officers' (CDO) has been created; CDOs are tasked with promoting and managing diversity within companies so as to prevent conflicts in daily operations which could be detrimental to the group's overall performance (Jehn, Northcraft and Neale, 1999). Indeed, if multinationals are to enhance the flow of technological know-how in transnational exchanges, spur innovation and promote activity-sharing among business units in the global landscape,

2. 'Corporate culture' is loosely defined as 'the pattern of shared beliefs and values that gives the members of an institution meaning, and provides them with the rules for behaviour in their organization' (Davis, 1984; Schein, 1999).

Recent research suggests the existence of a positive link between diversity and the financial and economic performance of multinational corporations

they have little choice but to tackle diversification and cultural diversity head-on.

As cultural diversity becomes an ever more prominent concern in corporate intercultural management studies, researchers are also seeking to assess the diversity-performance link in an increasingly competitive marketplace. Recent research indicates that there is a positive link between diversity and the financial and economic performance of multinational corporations (see Box 6.5).

In these ways, firms are putting themselves in a better position to overcome the impacts of greater cultural diversity through deliberate strategies related to: the potential benefits of employee diversity in terms of greater creativity and innovation and more successful marketing to different types of consumers; comprehensive decision-making as firms internationalize and become exposed to a variety of environments, and

careful employee selection and training (Kochan et al., 2003; Gomez-Mejiaf and Palich, 1997).

From social intelligence to cultural intelligence
In addition to other indicators of ability, such as *social intelligence* and *emotional intelligence*, employers are now paying more attention to the *cultural intelligence* of their staff as a way to synergize differences in international organizations and to build capacities adapted to the strategic outlook of markets (Earley, Ang and Tan, 2006). Cultural intelligence is a concept that is gaining currency in the corporate world, marking the potential engagement in support of cultural diversity as both a key business driver and a significant opportunity for innovation when leveraged. It involves *knowledge* of the importance of respecting and understanding cultures and the dynamics among those cultures, developing the *capacity* and a skills-set to create and promote programmes that are more mindful of cultural diversity, and the will and commitment to prioritize cultural diversity in individual

---

| Box 6.5 | A correlation between diversity and economic performance? |

UNESCO commissioned the extra-financial rating agency BMJ Ratings to conduct a survey of the 120 multinational corporations quote on the Paris Stock Exchange's SBF 120 index. The survey sought to determine whether there is a correlation between socio-cultural diversity and overall economic and financial performance. The results were plotted as follows:

This figure maps the coordinates of the 120 multinationals as measured according to correlations between a consolidated socio-cultural diversity indicator (perfDIV) and a consolidated overall economic performance indicator (perfECO). The perfDIV criteria were based on a qualitative and quantitative assessment of factors related to social cohesion (overall nationality, nationality of managers and directors, minority integration) and non-discrimination (gender parity at different levels of hierarchy, corporate social responsibility and recruitment policies concerning minorities). The perfECO indicator combines three partial indicators: 2007–2008 sales figures (perfCA), net results (perfRES) and stock-market values (perfB).

Correlation between cultural diversity and economic development for French stock market companies

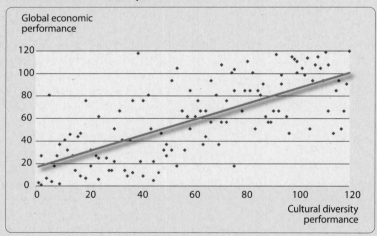

Source: UNESCO, PBC, Diversity and Performance Report, 2009.

While coefficient correlations reveal little or no causality between perfDIV and perfCA, perfRES or perfB taken individually, the analysis concluded that a causal link does exist between

diversity and global economic performance (perfECO) and found that socio-cultural diversity explains 49 percent of the variance.
Source: Bello, 2009.

and/or institutional spheres and translate them into *concrete actions and policies* that promote respect for and appreciation of diverse cultures (Pigott, 2008).

The benefits of developing cultural intelligence relate essentially to the notion of inclusion, understood as both a value and a process for creating an enabling corporate environment in order to establish clear metrics that support intelligent investment in cultural diversity. As a first step towards sizing up cultural intelligence, an international research team led by Simon Fraser University (Canada) created an online test to assess a variety of skills and traits, such as tolerance of uncertainty and adaptability, empathy and cultural knowledge (Leung, 2008). Anecdotal evidence linked to this project suggests that smart people with good social skills do not necessarily make a good showing when interacting with people of other cultures. On the other hand, individuals with high cultural intelligence are able to adapt quickly across cultures and are sharply attuned to nuances regardless of the country (see 'In focus' below).

Because an individual's cultural makeup is composed of a cross-section of traits and numerous allegiances corresponding to regional, national, social, religious, ethnic, sexual and many other kinds of affiliations, including personal history, choices and other commitments, the ability to think globally as well as locally and to apply cultural intelligence will enable global leaders and management to move beyond stereotypes. Inattentiveness to many of the assumptions embedded in our conceptions of others is evident in the research literature on international management, where the word 'culture' is often still used synonymously with 'nation', and national cultural traits tend to systematically be treated as indicative of predictable behavioural patterns (Brannen, 2009). Today, global business success increasingly depends not only on understanding different cultures but on being able to build bridges between them and negotiate within complex organizational structures and contexts.

Practical incentives exist for firms to develop the kind of *corporate social responsibility* (CSR) on which achievement of the UN's environmental and political goals largely depend. Indeed, this is the central purpose of the United Nations Global Compact, a voluntary international corporate network initiated in 2000 to

The Santa Fe International Folk Art Market

encourage both the private sector and other social actors to participate in promoting the advancement of responsible corporate citizenship and universal social and environmental principles in order to meet the challenges of globalization. This global initiative, with over 6,000 participants, spans some 130 countries. While it is but a small step towards integration of the UN goals in the world of commerce, it may nevertheless yield significant benefits in terms of the safeguarding and furtherance of cultural diversity if the notion of sustainable development becomes anchored ethically as well as strategically in business practices and outlooks. As CSR and sustainability become significant strategic aspects of business, it is important that cultural diversity, identity and cultural recognition are understood as key factors in dealings with all stakeholders.

Conclusion

Creativity is fundamental to cultural diversity, which is itself conducive to creativity at all levels of society and in all spheres of action, whether cultural, scientific, social or political. The crafts and tourism industries highlight the extent to which the cultural dimension can stimulate the vitality of culture-related sectors. As diversity becomes a cornerstone in the business world, from marketing to corporate management, it will be important to develop tools and capacity-building mechanisms that emphasize the benefits of *cultural* diversity together with other forms of diversity (e.g. ethnic or gender diversity). Cultural diversity must thus be considered an asset, whose added value is coming to be recognized in more and more areas of economic development, notably through the rise of the creative sector, which, according to recent surveys, accounted for up to 7.8 percent of GDP in the US in 2001 and 6.7 percent of GDP in Brazil in 1998 (Anheier and Isar, 2008; UNCTAD, 2008). There is a need to promote new initiatives favouring the diversification of exchanges so as to ensure a better balance in the circulation of cultural products between the countries of the North and the South.

What matters is that the social, economic and political conditions governing the production, distribution and exploitation of ideas and expressions in knowledge societies be conducive to creativity and innovation (Venturelli, 2001). Policies that contribute to the harnessing of cultural diversity for the benefit of creativity and innovation, such as Creative Clusters, Creative Cities and the Global Alliance for Cultural Diversity, must be furthered. Such policies may help to stimulate public-private partnerships for the sharing of know-how and experiences, as well as for the development of suitable sector policies and legislative frameworks. These include promoting international respect for and enforcement of intellectual property rights, which help to protect artistic works and turn creativity into viable sources of income.

It goes without saying that turning cultural diversity to economic account must be compatible with the principles of *sustainable development*, thereby ensuring the protection of the environment and the social fabric. As will be seen in Part III, cultural diversity also has a crucial role to play in renewing the international community's strategies for achieving sustainable development and peace.

Monks waiting for the ferry to take them across the Chao Phraya River to Pak Cret island in Bangkok, Thailand

Chapter 6 Recommendations

Creativity being a source of social and technological innovation, there is a need to invest in its development, both in the cultural sector and in the business sector, within which cultural diversity is to be understood as a source of profit and enhanced performance, conducive to corporate 'cultural intelligence'.

To this end, action should be taken to:

a. Facilitate the exchange of artistic productions and the circulation of artists, including through a system of cultural visas.

b. Develop appropriate systems for the protection of traditional know-how in the crafts sector, as well as ways and means of compensating the communities concerned for the commercial exploitation of such know-how.

c. Draw up and widely disseminate good practices in relation to tourism development with a view to maximizing its positive impacts on cultural diversity.

d. Develop 'cultural intelligence' in the business and marketing world through the establishment of real and virtual forums and the production of relevant research on the profitability of cultural diversity, not limited only to ethnic or gender difference.

Tools and approaches for increasing the relevance of cultural diversity to corporate audiences

As Nancy Adler (2002) has pointed out, 'the importance of world business has created a demand for managers sophisticated in global management and skilled at working with people from other countries'. She says further:

Cross-cultural management describes the behaviour of people within countries and cultures; compares the behaviour of people across countries and cultures; and, perhaps, most important, seeks to improve the interaction among colleagues, managers, executives, clients, suppliers, and alliance partners from countries and cultures around the world. Cross-cultural management thus expands the scope of domestic management practice to encompass multicultural and global dynamics.

With the goal of predicting the behaviour of counterparts with differing cultural backgrounds, cross-cultural management has tended to reduce cultural differences to national differences, as illustrated by André Laurent's (1986) typology of managers, which aims to provide some indicative trends across a typology of diverse management styles throughout Europe:

German managers, more than others, believe that creativity is essential for career success. In their minds, successful managers must have the right individual characteristics. German managers' outlook is rational: they view the organization as a coordinated network of individuals who make appropriate decisions based on their professional competence and knowledge.

British managers hold a more interpersonal and subjective view of the organizational world. According to them, the ability to create the right image and to get noticed for what they do is essential for career success. British managers view organizations primarily as a network of relationships among individuals who get things done by influencing each other using communication and negotiation.

French managers look at organizations as an authority network where the power to organize and control members stems from their position in the hierarchy. French managers focus on the organization as a pyramid of differentiated levels of power to be acquired or dealt with. They perceive the ability to manage

power relationships effectively and to 'work the system' as critical to their career success.

The risk of such generalizations, however, is that one will fall prey to stereotypes. Today's research, in tandem with the rise of global operations and a diversified workforce, has accordingly come to deal more with the cross-cultural skills that managers need to develop to maximize their firm's global operations (intercultural management).

Based on cultural audits in large multinational corporations, some specialized consulting firms (e.g. Aperian Global, Berlitz Cultural Consulting, and ICM Associates) have designed specific toolkits for managing complex multicultural corporate situations, exploring skill-sets related to being a good manager, refining appropriate communication, developing curiosity and openness, being aware of one's cultural bias or being able to adapt and to develop empathy with others. In talking about the way to deal most efficiently with mergers or acquisitions, Torben Laustsen, Corporate Head of Group Identity and Communications at Nordea, advises that 'it is very important to allocate enough time in the first phase to investigate the cultural differences and test existing opinions and values. Do this together with your new partners so that you can formulate, together, the values and vision for the new company' (Gancel, Raynaud and Rodgers, 2002).

In response to company needs, most intercultural management consultancy firms changed their emphasis in the 1990s: seminars and workshops aimed at sensitizing the participants to cultural differences and conceived almost wholly in terms of nationality were progressively replaced by training courses concerned with the differences between business cultures so as to optimize mergers and acquisitions. Ivar Hafsett, Strategic Advisor of Hydro Aluminium, notes that his company 'goes beyond language and national differences and acknowledges that ways of doing things and managing business are different within companies, even from the same country or in the same business' (Gancel, Raynaud and Rodgers, 2002). Some CEOs even recognize that when they claim that their company's culture is based on diversity, it is because they think that there is not only one way to do things and that diversity should be part of the corporate culture. Such a dynamic approach to diversity, as opposed to fixed approaches to diversity (e.g. solely in terms

Ecuadorean blankets

of ethnic or gender differences), makes the case for better taking account of cultural diversity.

Peter Isackson, director of the consultancy firm ICBM, is currently writing an educational handbook for the global network, Cultural Detective, on the topic of 'corporate cultures', in order to accompany the process of mergers and acquisitions. The Cultural Detective network encourages the practice of observation in intercultural contexts and helps readers and trainees 'to acquire detective reflexes', that is, 'to look at what is the case rather than coming with one's mind made up'. A handbook on 'global diversity and inclusion' written by Rui-ling King, Alan Richter and Jeremy Solomons, consultants in intercultural management working around the globe, is due to be published shortly. The advertising copy for their book states: '"Global Diversity" has become something of a buzzword in recent years as organizations and individuals try to grapple with all the ways people are different and similar across the world. In the USA, differences might focus on race and gender. In Latin America, heritage and socio-economic status. In India, religion, language and caste' (Cultural Detective, 2009).

To take advantage of the opportunities that diversity has to offer in the of building an organizational culture, human resources practices and managerial/group process skills need to translate diversity into positive managerial results at both group and individual levels. This can be achieved by adopting a more analytical approach, supporting experimentation and evaluation, and providing training for the desired skills. In this spirit, a leading microelectronics company created its own 'Diversity Council' in 2003, chaired by its CEO, to ensure that it visibly encourages and values the contributions and differences of employees from various backgrounds. Its chief objectives are to heighten employee and management awareness and encourage the effective use of a diverse workforce through key initiatives, such as developing attraction and recruiting strategies along with retention and awareness strategies. Under the guidance of the Diversity Council, a series of cultural diversity employee roundtables have been held to gather more face-to-face feedback and ideas from staff. These meetings have generated some practical ideas for increasing awareness of cultural diversity within the company. Some, like the suggestion of a cross-cultural communications course, were simple ideas that became pilots for full-fledged diversity training initiatives. Other ideas, such as a networking and 'cultural evening', were one-off events.

In the end, it is the diversity of experiences observable within a single context that makes the company a remarkable laboratory for studying the relationship between forms of governance and cultural context. This diversity leaves room for both successes and failures. Comparing the two makes it possible to shed light on those management methods that benefit most from capitalizing on the cultural context, and clearly to discern what distinguishes them from less effective approaches. In this way, intelligence can be developed about the phenomena that come into play during the implementation of a form of management that has been tailored to a particular cultural context.

As operational guidelines, Tony Pigott (2008), CEO of J. W. Thompson (JWT) Canada, suggests a clear, accessible approach to reframing and advancing cultural diversity in and through the corporate sector. The approach has three main components: respect, rapport and return. He sketches these as follows:

Respect

- Respect for cultural traditions and values.

- Respect for the impact that culture has on business in all its facets — from manufacturing to labour to marketing.

- Conscious inclusion of diverse cultures and backgrounds throughout business operations.

Rapport

- Rapport with and among cultures and communities.

- Enhanced rapport with and inclusion of key stakeholder groups through knowledge and appreciation of cultural factors.

Return

- Return on investment in cultural diversity and understanding.

- Establishment of clear metrics that support and encourage more intelligent investment in cultural diversity.

References and websites

Background documents and UNESCO sources

Askerud, P. 2007. Cultural and creative industries: Mapping a new world. Background paper.

Bello, P. 2009. Quand la diversité des effectifs sert l'efficacité collective de l'entreprise. Background paper.

Enwezor, E. and Fisher, J. 2007. Artists in contemporary societies: National or global citizenships? Background paper.

Khaznadar, C. 2007. Performing artists, cultural diversity and creativity. Background paper.

Pigott, T. 2008. The culture lab: Reframing and advancing cultural diversity in and through the corporate sector. Background paper.

Robinson, M. 2007. Discovering and negotiating and cultural diversity through tourism texts. Background paper.

UNESCO. 2003. *Convention on the Safeguarding of Intangible Cultural Heritage*. Paris, UNESCO. http://unesdoc.unesco.org/images/0013/001325/132540e.pdf

—. 1998. *World Culture Report: Culture, Creativity and Markets*. Paris, UNESCO.

—. 1989. *Recommendation on the Safeguarding of Traditional Culture and Folklore*. 16 November. http://portal.unesco.org/en/ev.php-URL_ID=13141&URL_DO=DO_PRINTPAGE&URL_SECTION=201.html

—. 1952. *Universal Copyright Convention*. Geneva, 6 September. http://portal.unesco.org/en/ev.php-URL_ID=15381&URL_DO=DO_TOPIC&URL_SECTION=201.html

—. 1945. *The Constitution of UNESCO*. Paris, UNESCO. http://unesdoc.unesco.org/images/0012/001255/125590e.pdf#constitution

World Commission on Culture and Development. 1996. *Our Creative Diversity*. Paris, UNESCO. http://unesdoc.unesco.org/images/0010/001055/105586e.pdf

Websites

Aperian Global: http://www.aperianglobal.com

Art Basel: http://www.artbasel.com

Berlitz Cultural Consulting: http://www.berlitzculturalconsulting.com

Creative Cities: http://www.creativecities.com

Creative Clusters: http://www.creativeclusters.com

Cultural Detective: http://www.culturaldetective.com

Earthwatch Institute: http://www.earthwatch.org

Global Alliance for Cultural Diversity: http://portal.unesco.org/culture/en/ev.php-URL_ID=24504&URL_DO=DO_TOPIC&URL_SECTION=201.html

ICM Associates: http://www.icmassociates.com

Intergovernmental Committee on Intellectual Property and Genetic Resources, Traditional Knowledge and Folklore (GRTKF): http://www.wipo.int/tk/en/igc

International Communication for Business Management (ICBM): http://www.icbm.fr

Manifesta: http://www.manifesta.org/index1.html

Religious Tourism: http://www.religious-tourism.com/religoustourism.htm

SkyTeam Alliance: http://www.skyteam.com

UNESCO Catalogue of Representative Works: http://www.unesco.org/unesdi/index.php/eng/biblio/tous.185

UNESCO Power of Peace Network: http://www.unesco.org/webworld/powerofpeace

UNESCO Award of Excellence for Handicrafts: http://portal.unesco.org/culture/en/ev.php-URL_ID=37649&URL_DO=DO_TOPIC&URL_SECTION=201.html

United Nations Global Compact, Participants and Stakeholders: http://www.unglobalcompact.org/ParticipantsAndStakeholders

United Nations Global Compact: http://www.unglobalcompact.org

World Digital Library: http://www.wdl.org/en

World Intellectual Property Organization (WIPO): http://www.wipo.int

World Observatory on the Social Status of the Artist: http://portal.unesco.org/culture/en/ev.php-URL_ID=32056&URL_DO=DO_TOPIC&URL_SECTION=201.html

World of Music and Dance (WOMAD): http://womad.org

World Religious Travel Association (WRTA): http://www.wrtareligioustravel.com/WRTA

World Tourism Organization (UNWTO): http://www.unwto.org

References

Adler, N. J. 2002. *From Boston to Beijing: Managing with a World View.* Cincinnati, Oh., Thomson Learning.

afrik.com. 2005. La Barclays introduit le système bancaire islamique au Kenya. 22 December. http://www.afrik.com/article9221.html

Anheier, H. and Isar, Y. R. (eds.). 2008. *The Cultural Economy.* (Cultures and Globalization Series, Vol. 2.) Thousand Oaks, Calif., Sage.

Bollinger, D. and Hofstede, G. 1987. *Les différences culturelles dans le management: comment chaque pays gère t'il ses hommes.* Paris, Editions d'Organisation.

Brannen, M.-Y. 2009. Reflexive culture's consequences. C. Nakata (ed.), *Beyond Hofstede: Cultural Frameworks for Global Marketing and Management.* London, Palgrave Macmillan.

Cooppan, V. 2001. World literature and global theory: comparative literature for the new millennium. *Symploke,* Vol. 9, No. 1–2, pp. 15–43.

Cultural Detective. 2009. [Advertising copy for R. L. King, A. Richter and J. Solomons, *Cultural Detective: Global Diversity and Inclusion*]. http://www.culturaldetective.com/package.html#DIV

d'Iribarne, P. and Henry, A. 2007. *Successful Companies in the Developing World: Managing in Synergy with Cultures*. Translated by G. Gladstone, J. Graham and E. O'Keeffe. AFD Notes and Documents No. 36. Paris, Agence Française de Développement (AFD). http://www.afd.fr/jahia/webdav/site/afd/users/administrateur/public/publications/notesetdocuments/ND36-ven.pdf

Damrosch, D. 2003. *What Is World Literature?* Princeton, N.J., Princeton University Press.

Davis, S. M. 1984. *Managing Corporate Culture*. Cambridge, Mass., Ballinger.

Earley, P. C., Ang, S. and Tan, J.-S. 2006. CQ: Developing Cultural Intelligence at Work. Stanford, Calif., Stanford University Press.

Ely, R. J. and Thomas, D. A. 2001. Cultural diversity at work: The effects of diversity perspectives on work group processes and outcomes. *Administrative Science Quarterly*, Vol. 46, No. 2, pp. 229–73.

FNSP. 2008. Diversity: A reality check in a global world. A conference organized by Sciences Po and Renault on the occasion of the French Corporate Diversity Day. Paris, 29 May. http://www.admin.renaultcomv5.aw.atosorigin.com/SiteCollectionDocuments/Communiqué%20de%20presse/en-EN/Pieces%20jointes/16925_PROGRAMME_GB.pdf

Gancel, C., Raynaud, M. and Rodgers, I. 2002. *Mergers, Acquisitions and Strategic Alliances: How to Bridge Corporate Cultures*. New York, McGraw-Hill. http://www.icmassociates.com

Gomez-Mejiaf, L. R. and Palich, L. 1997. Cultural diversity and the performance of multinational firms. *Journal of International Business Studies*, Vol. 28, No. 2, pp. 309–35.

Gordon, A. 1995. The work of corporate culture: diversity management. *Social Text*, No. 44, pp. 3–30. http://leeds-faculty.colorado.edu/selto/CURISES%202007%20Cost%20Mgt/Readings/diversity%20mgmt.pdf

Hall, S. 2001. Museums of modern art and the end of history. *Annotations 6: Modernity and Difference*. London, Institute of International Visual Arts (INIVA), pp. 8–23. http://www.iniva.org/library/archive/people/h/hall_stuart/museums_of_modern_art_and_the_end_of_history

Hofstede, G. 2001. *Culture's Consequences: Comparing Values, Behaviors, Institutions, and Organizations Across Nations*. 2nd ed. Thousand Oaks, Calif., Sage,

Hofstede, G. 2009. Geert Hofstede cultural dimensions. Itim international. http://www.geert-hofstede.com

Hyde, L. 2007. *The Gift: Creativity and the Artist in the Modern World*. 2nd ed. New York, Vintage Books.

Jehn, K. A., Northcraft, G. A. and Neale, M. A. 1999. Why differences make a difference: A field study of diversity, conflict and performance in workgroups. *Administrative Science Quarterly*, Vol. 44, No. 4, pp. 741–63.

Khoi, L. T. 2000. *A Desire for Beauty*. Paris, Horizons du Monde.

King, R. L., Richter, A. and Solomons, J. Forthcoming. *Cultural Detective: Global Diversity and Inclusion*.

Kochan, T. et al. 2003. The effects of diversity on business performance: report of the Diversity Research Network. *Human Resource Management*, Vol. 42, No. 1, pp. 3–21. http://www.chrs.rutgers.edu/pub_documents/38.pdf

Lagace, M. 2004. Racial diversity pays off. *Harvard Business School Working Knowledge*, 21 June. http://hbswk.hbs.edu/item/4207.html

Laurent, A. 1986. The cross-cultural puzzle of international human resource management. *Human Resource Management*, Vol. 25 No. 1, pp. 91–102.

Les Dossiers. 2007. Vues de presse internationale: La finance Islamique. *Les Dossiers* No. 6 (May). http://www.dipacint.com/content/download/1580/7765/version/1/file/Dossier+6+-+2007-06+-+FINANCE+ISLAMIQUE.pdf

Leung, W. 2008. Low cultural IQ could hijack your career. *The Globe and Mail*, 25 February. http://www.theglobeandmail.com/life/article669060.ece

Light Years IP. 2008. *Distinctive Values in African Exports: How Intellectual Property Can Raise Export Income and Alleviate Poverty*. Washington, DC, Light Years IP. http://www.lightyearsip.net/downloads/Distinctive_values_in_African_exports.pdf

Lobl, R., Carter, P. and Wicken, G. 2006. Building in the BRICs: Market understanding and strategic development for international brands. *Global Diversity 2006*. Amsterdam, ESOMAR.

Richard, N. 2007. *Handicrafts and Employment Generation for the Poorest Youth and Women*. UNESCO Policy Paper No. 17. Paris, UNESCO. http://unesdoc.unesco.org/images/0015/001567/156772e.pdf

Richards, G. and Wilson, J. 2003. *Today's Youth Travellers, Tomorrow's Global Nomads: New Horizons in Independent Youth and Student Travel*. A report for the International Student Travel Confederation (ISTC) and the Association of Tourism and Leisure Education (ATLAS). 2nd ed. Amsterdam, (ISTC). http://www.wysetc.org/Docs/ISTC_ATLAS_Full%20Report.pdf

Sassen, S. 2001. *The Global City: New York, London, Tokyo*. Princeton, N.J., Princeton University Press.

Schein, E. H. 1999. *The Corporate Culture Survival Guide: Sense and Nonsense About Culture Change*. San Francisco, Calif., Jossey-Bass.

Smith, R. M. 2008. In the driver's Seat: The CEO of Nissan and Renault on turnarounds. *Newsweek*, 30 June. http://www.newsweek.com/id/142411

Sqalli, N. 2007. Produits bancaires islamiques: Attijariwafa bank révèle son offre. *L'economiste*, 5 October. http://www.leconomiste.com/article.html?a=81274

Thomas, R. R. 1992. *Beyond Race and Gender: Unleashing the Power of Your Total Workforce by Managing Diversity*. New York, AMACOM.

Thorsby, D. 2008. *Economics and Culture*. Cambridge, Cambridge University Press.

United Nations Alliance of Civilizations and the United Nations Global Compact Office. 2009. *Doing Business in a Multicultural World: Challenges and Opportunities*. New York, United Nations. http://www.unglobalcompact.org/docs/news_events/9.1_news_archives/2009_04_07/DBMW_Final_Web.pdf

United Nations Conference on Trade and Development (UNCTAD). 2008. *Creative Economy Report 2008: The Challenge of Assessing the Creative Economy towards Informed Policy-making*. New York, United Nations. http://www.unctad.org/en/docs/ditc20082cer_en.pdf

Venturelli, S. 2001. From the Information Economy to the Creative Economy: Moving Culture to the Center of International Public Policy. Washington, DC, Center for Arts and Culture. http://www.culturalpolicy.org/pdf/venturelli.pdf

Wicken, G. and Lobl, R. 2006. *Brand Building in the BRICs: Market Understanding and Strategic Development for International Brands*. New York, TGI (Target Group Index). http://www.tgisurveys.com/knowledgehub/reports/BRICs_Global%20TGI.pdf

Wilson, D. and Purushothaman, R. 2003. *Dreaming with BRICs: The Path to 2050*. Goldman Sachs Global Economics Paper No. 99. October. New York, Goldman Sachs. http://www2.goldmansachs.com/ideas/brics/book/99-dreaming.pdf

World Tourism Organization (UNWTO). 2008. *International Conference on Tourism, Religions and Dialogue of Cultures*. Cordoba, Spain, 29–31 October 2007. Madrid, World Tourism Organization.

◗ *A beggar passing a street advertisement in Athens, Greece*

Chapter 6
Creativity and
the marketplace

PART III.

Renewing International Strategies related to Development and Peace

Cultural diversity — understood as a dynamic process within which cultural change can best be managed through intercultural dialogue — can become a powerful lever for renewing the international community's strategies towards development and peace, based on respect for universally recognized human rights. Sometimes construed as being of secondary importance, cultural diversity needs to be placed at the heart of policies for the furtherance of international cooperation and cohesion. Recognition of its enabling role is necessary for attaining the UN Millennium Development Goals.

Within the framework of a broader commitment to universalism and international cooperation, cultural diversity offers a new approach that highlights the cultural dimension of all areas of policy formulation and stresses the insufficiency of 'one-size-fits-all' approaches insensitive to the diversity of cultural contexts. This approach rests on the empowerment of individuals and communities and takes us beyond notions of fixed and isolated identities, furthering openness to others and dialogue within and between groups, and promoting a plurality of possible ways for achieving overarching objectives. As a source of artistic, intellectual, scientific and material creativity, cultural diversity represents an engine of social transformation and renewal.

CHAPTER 7 — **Cultural diversity: A key dimension of sustainable development**

Chapter 7 examines the cultural assumptions underlying conceptions of socio-economic development increasingly confronted by their own limitations, argues the case for reviewing poverty alleviation strategies and environmental issues through the lens of cultural diversity, favouring the support and active participation of local populations.

CHAPTER 8 – **Cultural diversity, human rights and democratic governance**

Faced with the tendency of individuals or groups to fall back upon singularities, chapter 8 shows that cultural diversity, when properly understood, contributes to the appropriation and hence to the effective exercise of universally recognized human rights and freedoms. In so doing, it facilitates social cohesion in multicultural societies and points towards renewed approaches of democratic governance.

Two young children playing at a local waste dump in Maputo, Mozambique

Cultural diversity: A key dimension of sustainable development

Despite widespread assumptions to the contrary, there is no prescribed pathway for the development of a society, no single model on which development strategies should be based. The Western model of development, conceived as a linear process involving largely economic factors, is often incompatible with the complex social, cultural and political dimensions of societies pursuing different goals, reflecting their own values. The ideology of development has all too often tended to damage the social fabric and foundations — often rooted in traditions of communal solidarity — of the communities that have received 'development aid'.

Just as no development strategy can be said to be culturally neutral, a culturally sensitive approach to development is the key to addressing the interlinked social, economic and environmental problems confronting the planet as a whole. Cultural diversity — which emphasizes the dynamic interactions between cultures *and* sensitivity to cultural contexts — thus becomes a key lever for ensuring sustainable, holistic development strategies. While the international community, in its attempts to operationalize the concept of sustainable development over the last two decades, has begun to acknowledge the role of culture in the development process, the cultural factor has yet to be fully integrated into the development equation.

The 1987 Bruntland Report of the UN Commission on Environment and Development (UNCED), entitled *Our Common Future*, was seminal in its assertion that genuine development must be sustainable — denoting a form of growth 'that meets the needs of the present without compromising the ability of future generations to meet their own needs'. At the 1992 Earth Summit in Rio de Janeiro, sustainability was conceived in terms of the three pillars of economic viability, social responsiveness and respect for the environment. These pillars have since served as the basis for important standard-setting instruments, including the *Convention on Biological Diversity* (CBD) and the *United Nations Framework Convention on Climate Change* (UNFCCC). The 2002 World Summit on Sustainable Development in Johannesburg went further by recognizing cultural diversity as a significant cross-cutting factor in sustainable development. Cultural diversity must be seen as a cross-cutting dimension (rather than as a separate, fourth pillar of sustainability), with an important role to play in all development projects, from poverty eradication and the safeguarding of biodiversity to resource management and climate change.

Cultural diversity: A key dimension of sustainable development

7.1 The cultural approach to development ..191
Box 7.1 Population and development action programmes...194
Map 7.1a Population living below the income poverty line (US$1.25 per day), 2006 196
Map 7.1b Population living below the income poverty line (US$2 per day), 2006........................196

7.2 Perceptions of poverty and poverty eradication 196
Box 7.2 The Fair trade movement 200
Box 7.3 Ecomuseums and poverty alleviation in Viet Nam..201

7.3 Cultural diversity and environmental sustainability... 203
Map 7.2 Protected terrestrial and marine areas, 2005..205

Box 7.4 Sustainable development assistance for displaced populations and refugees..............206
Box 7.5 Local management of natural resources and biodiversity 208

Conclusion...209

Recommendations...210

In focus: The Cultural Diversity Programming Lens: A tool for monitoring development projects 211
Figure 7.1 Cultural Diversity Programming Lens (CDPL) general framework 212

References and websites...................................215

Lake in China

7.1 The cultural approach to development

A widely held view in the industrialized world rests on the tacit assumption of a causal relationship between 'culture' and 'underdevelopment' holding that individuals either are or remain poor because cultural beliefs and attitudes impede their development. It has been argued, for example, that some countries in Latin America and the Caribbean remain underdeveloped due to a lack of social cohesion, sense of social justice and commitment to self-realization (Harrison, 1985; Harrison and Huntington, 2000). The Chairman of the UN Permanent Forum on Indigenous Issues (UNPFII) has traced the notion of underdevelopment back to European colonialism and its aftermath, and to the sometimes misguided, if well-intentioned, efforts of the North to aid the poor countries of the South. Significant in this regard is said to have been US President Harry S. Truman's 1949 call to Western countries to make the benefits of their scientific, technological and industrial progress available for 'the growth and improvement of underdeveloped areas' (quoted in Tauli-Corpuz, 2008). The effect of Truman's speech has been summed up as follows:

> On that day, two billion people became underdeveloped. In a real sense, from that time on, they ceased being what they were, in all their diversity, and were transmogrified into an inverted mirror of the others' reality: a mirror that belittles them and sends them off to the end of the queue, a mirror that defines their identity, which is really that of a heterogeneous and diverse majority, simply in the terms of a homogenizing and narrow minority (Gustavo Esteva, 1991).

In this way culture came to be seen in development thinking as a barrier to growth. The free-market and trade liberalization policies advocated in the 1990s were accordingly rooted in the idea that the policies that had successfully spurred the economic growth of Western countries would produce growth elsewhere, regardless of cultural context.

In recent decades, various international conferences and initiatives have attempted to situate the development process within a broader cultural framework. Following the Accra Intergovernmental Conference on Cultural Policy in Africa (1975), where culture was identified as 'a *conditio sine qua non* of endogenous, compatible

and balanced development' (Obuljen, 2002), the theme was taken up at the 1982 Mexico World Conference on Cultural Policy (Mondiacult) in Mexico City (UNESCO, 2000) and led to the United Nations World Decade for Cultural Development (1988–1997) and the 1988 Stockholm proceedings of the Intergovernmental Conference on Cultural Policy for Development. Meanwhile, the 1996 publication of *Our Creative Diversity*, the landmark report of the World Commission on Culture and Development, made the case for placing culture at the centre of development thinking, since culture is precisely the medium through which individuals express their ability to fulfil themselves and is therefore an integral part of development. In the same spirit, the UNDP's 2004 Human Development Report, *Cultural Liberty in Today's Diverse World*, stressed the importance of culture and multiculturalism in human development strategies.

These key dates reflect the emergence of a broader and more nuanced conception of development, which considers that, while the existence of different value systems can account for different business attitudes and practices, successful economic performance does not necessarily entail a cultural conversion to Western-style values based on individualism and competition (Weber, 2002). In a Japanese context, for example, the Samurai's code of honour and the *Kaitokudo* educational institution may be seen to play a role in an economy based on group responsibility, company loyalty, interpersonal trust and implicit contracts (Sen, 2001). Some countries, such as the Republic of Korea, draw on a strong Confucian tradition in their corporate practices. Other cultural traditions, characterized by a social rather than a mercantile conception of trade, implicitly challenge the association of development with the maximization of profit and the accumulation of material goods (see chapter 6).

What is striking in most theories of development — e.g. the modernization theories (Rostow, 1960; Deutsch, 1961; Inkeles and Smith, 1974), the dependency theories (Cardoso and Faletto, 1979), the world systems theories (Wallerstein, 1974), and the economic growth theories (Domar, 1946; Harrod, 1939; Solow, 1957; Arrow, 1962; Lucas, 1988; Romer, 1990) — is the assumption that development refers to a process that is *linear* (i.e. moving

A child is vaccinated against polio in Afghanistan

A man fishing in the French Antilles

on a straight path from point A to point B) and *evolutionary* (i.e. progressing from a less developed or lower, 'primitive' or 'traditional', level to a more developed and higher, 'advanced' or 'modern', level). Thus, applying the term 'development' in cross-cultural contexts is problematic. The term brings with it assumptions about the status of the persons targeted in development policies and the purpose of development. Yet culture is often left out of the equation, wheras it can become the very facilitator of development. Experience has repeatedly demonstrated that when 'development' is imposed upon a society from the outside, this invariably leads to ecological and societal dislocation. Furthermore, when inadequate consideration is given to social factors and cultural contexts, the receiving community's rejection of the development project is almost inevitable, with culture acting, so to speak, as a society's 'immune system' (Odora-Hopper, 2007).

The cultural dimension of development

The role of culture in shaping the development of individuals and groups calls into question the so-called *cultural neutrality* of development aid projects. It has been argued that certain development policies have impaired the capacity of local cultures to contribute to the well-being of their communities by imposing a vision of the world dictated by economic productivity and by contributing to the dissemination of a psychology of 'cultural inferiority' (Regenvanu, 2007). Indeed, development strategies 'are heavily impregnated with their culture of origin, what one might call the subconscious component of development. [. . .] This cultural bias is rooted in the donor agency's inability to imagine models other than those within which it is accustomed to work, to which it subscribes and whose legitimacy is, for the agency at least, indisputable' (UNESCO, 2000).

Examples abound of well-intended but inappropriate development responses by international NGOs that fail to integrate cultural parameters into the project design — from collective facilities (for freshwater, sanitation, medicine and agriculture) built in symbolically unsuitable village locations where no villager would be willing to use them (Guingané, 2007), to inappropriate concrete classrooms situated in places where school lessons are typically held outdoors. The consequences of poorly conceived development strategies can be dramatic. The replacement of domestic farming with industrial-type monoculture production of cash crops has not only undermined

indigenous and traditional modes of living and endangered the management of natural resources (Shiva, 2005) but may have contributed to the world food crisis in 2008. Other examples of actions with unanticipated consequences include the forced sedentarization of nomadic peoples, the rapid loss of local languages, cultural practices and values when an external formal education system is put in place, or the distribution of relief supplies during famines or natural disasters which do not take account of the social and cultural dynamics of the societies in question.

Insufficient cultural awareness among international organizations and national governments concerning the local groups scheduled to receive aid can have particularly tragic consequences in conflict-ridden and crisis situations. Simon Harragin (2004) argues compellingly that the distribution of famine relief in Sudan in 1998 was hampered by the failure of international organizations to take proper account of local culture. Not only were early signs of imminent famine ignored by relief organizations, but the community response to aid was misunderstood. Among the Dinka in southern Sudan, the allocation of resources, status and local authority is based on the kinship system, and all resources (aid included) are thus to be evenly distributed among the population. Food reallocation mechanisms among the community are precisely the means by which the Dinka prevent famine. However, relief agencies perceived aid redistribution of this type as a form of political corruption and patronage, such that by 1998 the age-old system of self-support had long been severely strained.

Mainstream development programmes often fail to recognize that societies hastily labelled as 'underdeveloped' have in fact been living sustainably for generations. The application of external recipes for development — as if these societies had never developed on their own — must today be seriously challenged. Greater awareness, at the local level, of the importance of the human dimension — notably 'cultural' and 'diversity' factors — is undoubtedly the key to any development that can be deemed entirely sustainable. This implies genuine efforts to understand and respect cultural specificities, identities, values and worldviews. As former World Bank president James Wolfensohn has said (quoted in Gould, 2007):

> *We are realizing that building development solutions on local forms of social interchange, values,*

traditions and knowledge reinforces the social fabric. We are starting to understand that development effectiveness depends, in part, on 'solutions' that resonate with a community's sense of who it is.

Global development policies arose in response to the plight of newly decolonized countries and 'development' became an extremely attractive option as governments sought to transform countries devastated by the effects of colonization into modern nation-states as rapidly as possible. Yet the question of how development was to be implemented gave rise to differences of approach in a multilateral context in which the developing countries were widely coveted as sources of natural resources, new markets for expanding economies and as bases for geopolitical ambitions. The unanticipated result, as Majid Rahnema (1997) has pointed out, was often to create new forms of poverty:

> *the virtues of simplicity and conviviality, [. . .] of the wisdom of relying on each other, and the arts of suffering, were derided as signs of underdevelopment. A culture of 'individual' success [. . .] led younger men to depart their villages, leaving behind dislocated families of women, children and older men who had no one to rely on but the promises of often unattainable 'goods' and 'services'.*

Lack of consideration of the cultural relevance of development projects has sometimes led to downright resistance to their implementation and to communities vigorously defending practices on which they might have been ready to negotiate. In some regions of Africa, for example, where slash-and-burn cultivation has been traditionally linked to ancestor worship, efforts on the part of development agencies to prohibit it — stemming from the false assumption that *all* types of slash-and-burn agriculture are environmentally destructive (the practices of the Karen peoples in northern Thailand actually serve to increase biodiversity) — have often resulted in a withdrawal into local identity, which has in turn nurtured a stronger attachment to these practices on the part of those communities. Clearly, more respectful solutions that make room for symbolic attachments need to be found, as well as strategies in which participatory mechanisms are an integral part of the design and implementation of development projects (see 'In focus' section).

Towards a dynamic approach to development thinking

In acknowledging 'the cultural traits of a human society or group as core elements, as the most complete manifestations of its economic, social, political, ethical, spiritual, intellectual and ideological operation, and as representing all those processes by which society is able to solve its own problems' (UNESCO, 2000), the cultural approach to development facilitates an understanding of development in terms of adaptation. Every human group, faced by a specific and changing environment (natural, political, social, economic), must adapt its responses and strategies to achieve overall well-being. But this adaptation is not a one-way relationship: societies shape their environments, which in turn shape them. The dynamic perspective of cultural diversity is a useful prism through which to view this two-way and reflexive relationship, in which cultures are constantly in contact with other cultures and are continually readjusted and adapted to the new environments in which they evolve. When applied to development processes, cultural diversity reveals itself as a 'mainspring for sustainable development for communities, peoples and nations', as stated in the Preamble of the *Convention on the Protection and Promotion of the Diversity of Cultural Expressions* (UNESCO, 2005).

Following the UNDP's elaboration in the 1990s of the human development model, a shift of focus began to take place marked by growing acknowledgment of dimensions of development other than strictly economic ones. However, it was not until the 2002 Johannesburg Summit that the cultural approach to development began to find reflection in the international strategies, such as those implemented under the auspices of the Spanish MDG Achievement Fund.[1] Indeed, it is impossible to negotiate any level of human change without confronting culture. Development cannot ignore the 'webs of significance' — as Clifford Geertz (1973) defined 'culture' — through which people develop their values, relationships, behaviour and social and political structures: 'A cultural approach sets out to systematically engage with the "webs of significance" that people create; it takes account of the cultural context in which communities and groups exist; it negotiates with local social hierarchies and living patterns; and it draws on local forms of communication and expression to engage people' (Gould, 2007).

The dynamic perspective of cultural diversity is a useful prism through which to view this two-way and reflexive relationship, in which cultures are constantly in contact with other cultures and are continually readjusted and adapted to the new environments in which they evolve

1. In the framework of the MDG Fund created in 2006, 18 national programmes have been implemented in the past 3 years reflecting the contribution of culture to the MDGs and the joint action of a dozen UN bodies. UNESCO plays a leading role in the inter-agency coordination and in the implementation of projects.

Chapter 7
Cultural diversity:
A key dimension of
sustainable development

Increasingly, donors are looking at how they can work within these cultural webs to improve the impact of work on the ground. The United Nations Population Fund (UNFPA), for example, has sought to integrate the cultural factor in its programme strategies, as illustrated in case studies involving a range of countries and focusing on improving the status of women. UNFPA has found that its broader cultural approach (culture as content) has helped it to achieve programme goals more effectively and with greater transparency and satisfaction by the donor, which has in turn built trust, greater community involvement and sense of ownership,

thereby helping to create a virtuous circle that serves to expand opportunities for all parties (see Box 7.1).

Regarding HIV and AIDS prevention, for example, better results have been achieved when projects were adapted to their specific socio-cultural contexts. Health-related attitudes are often hard to dissociate from worldviews, ancestral beliefs and practices, and trust in traditional doctors and medicine. Ann Swidler (2007) has found that governments and NGOs were more effective in reducing HIV and AIDS infection in Uganda and Botswana when they mobilized local meaning systems

---

Box 7.1   Population and development action programmes

Case studies from Brazil, Ghana, Guatemala, India, the Islamic Republic of Iran, Uganda and Yemen provide good examples of UNFPA's country-level strategy to serve as a 'facilitator' of change in contexts of long-standing 'hardening of positions' on sensitive issues. In all these countries, through an understanding of local context networks, 'local change actors' were identified who had the capacity and the leadership to tap local resources and launch effective action to promote International Conference on Population and Development (ICPD) action programmes. Once engaged, leadership could be taken on the ground, with UNFPA continuing to facilitate the process as requested and providing technical assistance as needed. UNFPA's role as a facilitator was complex in these cases, in that it required Country Offices to build a strong in-house capacity to 'manage diversity' by bringing together political leaders, civil society organizations, local power structures, religious and faith-based institutions, and the private sector concerning key issues — in the case of Guatemala, for example, an reproductive health and rights issues.

As a facilitator UNFPA had to bring about, to the extent possible, the convergence of the various interests of diverse groups by building on commonalities in their respective agendas. The case studies on Guatemala, India and the Islamic Republic of Iran concluded that 'consensus on culturally sensitive issues can be created

through interventions based on ICPD respect for cultural diversity, in conformity with universally recognized human rights.' Project reviews also demonstrated that participatory approaches should be adapted to the specific cultural context. In some cases (Guatemala, the Islamic Republic of Iran, Uganda and Yemen), it was necessary to engage the leaders of local power structures and religious and faith-based institutions *before* involving grassroots communities in project design and implementation. Facilitating those leaders' participation in the initial stages of the programme then led to their call for grassroots participation.

The case studies indicate that developing a *culturally sensitive language* 'is an invaluable negotiating and programming tool. If the language used is loaded with negative judgements on the community or its values, it creates unnecessary tensions and constructs a wall between the community and the programme.' For example, when a community has practised female genital cutting for centuries, it might perceive the phrase 'female genital mutilation' as value-loaded. This perception may lead to the community's resistance, at least in the project-launching phase, to any advocacy campaigns to terminate the practice. By contrast, the phrase 'female genital cutting' describes the practice in neutral language that allows discussions of the practice and its negative impact on the health and rights of women.

Language sensitivity also applies to the choice of project titles and the messages they convey to the target community, especially in areas where reproductive health and rights projects have not previously existed. Interviews in some countries indicate that when reproductive health projects were established for the first time, it was better to give titles that frame reproductive health in the broader context of health, and then to move gradually to the more specific issues of reproductive health and rights. This is not a matter of semantics but an approach that increases inclusivity. In the initial phases of projects, it offers wide latitude for diverse partners to engage, participate and provide support.

Interviews in the course of the case studies indicated that it is important to clarify the distinction between 'cultures as broad ethical and value systems' and certain 'traditional practices' that are harmful to the individual and the community. In sensitization processes during the pre-project implementation phase, it was also essential to underline UNFPA's position: that it does not make value judgements on cultures, even though it stands firm on specific traditional practices that are considered harmful to women's health and violate their human rights, such as early marriage and female genital mutilation.

Source: UNFPA, 2004.

and social solidarities.[2] Any health policy that seeks to be sustainable must take account of the deep roots of traditional medicine in population lifestyles. Increasingly, we are seeing a symbiosis between traditional and modern medicine, notably in Cameroon, Mali, Nigeria, Tanzania and Zambia.

In 2002 the World Health Organization (WHO) set up its first traditional medicine strategy, thereby acknowledging the critical importance of local knowledge and know-how with regard to prevention: in Africa, for example, 80 percent of the population uses traditional medicine; in China, it represents 40 percent of delivered healthcare; in Malaysia, an estimated US$500 million is spent annually on traditional healthcare as compared to about US$300 million on allopathic medicine; and in Ghana, Mali, Nigeria and Zambia, the first line of treatment for 60 percent of children with malaria is the use of herbal medicines at home. The popularity of traditional medicine in these contexts is explained by its efficacy, accessibility and affordability, in comparison with Western medicine, as well as the fact that it is embedded in wider belief systems. Yet still today only 25 of the 191 WHO Member States have developed policies on the use of traditional medicine (see World Bank, 2006), and bio-prospecting (and bio-piracy) by the pharmaceutical industry has expanded, sometimes to the detriment of local knowledge and local ownership of traditional medicines.

Recognition of the cultural specificity of lifestyles, modes of production and forms of governance is thus necessary for the viability of any sustainable development project. The sustainability agenda is applicable in many different cultural and religious traditions (Hasan, 2006). In this respect, acknowledgement of the cultural factor adds a crucial dimension to projects in terms of relevance and appropriation. Indigenous groups have for many years been calling for 'self-determined development' (Tauli-Corpuz, 2008), especially where poverty-eradication strategies have been concerned. It highlights, in particular, how perceptions of the poor tend to relegate them to situations of inferiority, which constitute major obstacles to their empowerment. Taking account of the

diversity of cultural contexts and making provision for local participation can in this way become crucial levers for overcoming poverty.

⚲ *A camp of nomad tribes in Southern Morocco*

Chapter 7
Cultural diversity:
A key dimension of
sustainable development

7.2 Perceptions of poverty and poverty eradication

Since the 1993 Vienna World Conference on Human Rights, poverty has come to be recognized as a denial of basic human rights, a violation of human dignity. Yet despite the endorsement of this position by the UN General Assembly and UN specialized agencies (such as WHO with regard to the right to health, FAO with regard to the right to food, UNESCO with regard to the right to education), this remains a political statement that needs to be operationalized at all levels, based on the indivisibility of human rights (see chapter 8). Poverty is not just about the denial of access to basic social services (going to school, receiving medical treatment, benefiting

Map 7.1a Population living below the income poverty line (US$1.25 per day), 2006

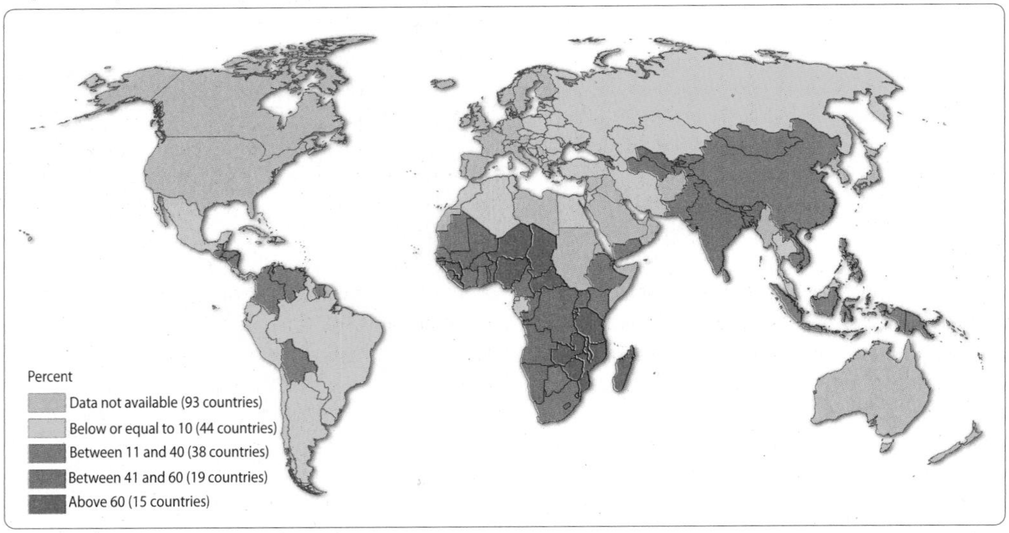

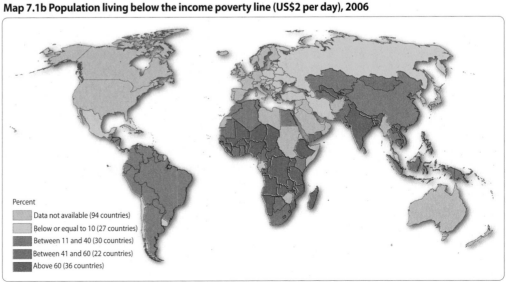

Percent
- Data not available (93 countries)
- Below or equal to 10 (44 countries)
- Between 11 and 40 (38 countries)
- Between 41 and 60 (19 countries)
- Above 60 (15 countries)

Source: UNESCO Institute for Statistics, based on the World Bank indicators database, 2007.

Map 7.1b Population living below the income poverty line (US$2 per day), 2006

Percent
- Data not available (94 countries)
- Below or equal to 10 (27 countries)
- Between 11 and 40 (30 countries)
- Between 41 and 60 (22 countries)
- Above 60 (36 countries)

Source: UNESCO Institute for Statistics, based on the World Bank indicators database, 2007.

from housing facilities, exercising civil and political rights); it has cultural dimensions that are often left unattended. We must re-examine the very definition of poverty, with a view both to revising the strategies for poverty eradication devised in the 1950s and ensuring better participation of those concerned. Cultural diversity can play an important role in addressing these challenges and in facilitating the implementation of policies for poverty eradication according to the will of the societies concerned.

Defining poverty

It is obvious that economic poverty measures do not provide a satisfactory understanding of the complexity of this multifaceted phenomenon. Those of the World Bank, for example, define poverty in terms of a threshold of income or consumption (since 2005, US$1.25 a day per person measured in 'purchasing power parity' — absolute poverty line — or a median poverty level of US$2 a day; see maps) below which people are 'poor' regardless of standard of living. Other poverty lines are determined nationally in terms of food minima and non-food. While these approaches have the merit of providing comparable information, they tend to exclude the effects of poverty in human terms, as well as the possibility of qualifying development in non-quantitative terms. The examples of Vanuatu and the Solomon Islands, which are classed among the least developed countries in terms of GDP per capita, amply illustrate that both the nature of poverty and what qualifies as the fulfilment of basic needs must be assessed on a case-by-case basis. These relate, in the cases of Vanuatu and the Solomon Islands, to customary land ownership systems, clan-based social networks and subsistence food production. Poverty must be looked at from the inside and with a clear commitment to a human rights-based approach to eradication, so that local solutions may be found in concert with the communities involved, who can thereby contribute to finding their own way out of poverty.

In reaction to the World Bank and IMF donor frameworks for intervention which enforced 'stabilization packages' and 'structural adjustments' upon the national economic policies of poor countries as a precondition for receiving loans, alternative paradigms to dealing with poverty began emerging in the 1990s. These led in turn to new political approaches and development strategies (Riddell, 2004), notably UNDP's work on human development that takes account of the multi-dimensional aspect

of poverty. In 2007, President Abdoulaye Wade of the Republic of Senegal suggested that poverty should be expressed not so much in terms of income but rather 'a set of deficits in terms of individual needs and basic social services'. He proposed that poverty be defined as 'as a cluster of unsatisfied human needs, in particular those seven wounds of the modern age where the majority of the world's population is concerned', which are 'lack of access to basic housing, to clothing, to drinking water, to an adequate supply and quality of food, to health care, to literacy and children's education, and to a healthy environment' (Wade, 2007).

In the social sciences alone, poverty has at least 12 different meanings (Spicker, 2007). Dozens of economic poverty lines, poverty gaps, poverty orderings and the like have been proposed, each shedding light on a different aspect of the phenomenon (see Sen, 1976; Atkinson, 1987; Jenkins and Lambert, 1993). The definition put forward by the UN Committee on Social, Economic, and Cultural Rights (CESCR, 2001) states that poverty is 'a human condition characterized by sustained or chronic deprivation of the resources, capabilities, choices, security and power necessary for the enjoyment of an adequate standard of living and other civil, cultural, economic, political and social rights.' The challenge of a broad and comprehensive definition, however, is not to lose sight of the specific issues in need of attention so as to distinguish between poverty and other human and social problems (OHCHR, 2004). Indeed, not all social problems are related to poverty, nor are all forms of denial of human rights, social exclusion or deprivation.

The understanding of poverty as a denial of basic human rights follows on the work of such influential thinkers as Amartya Sen (1999) and Thomas Pogge (2002) and from international reflection and research, consultations and dialogue initiatives, such as those by UNESCO (see Pogge, 2007). This perspective is important for poverty eradication because it can draw on fundamental freedoms and human rights as engines of social change, including with respect to the institutions that may have a causal role in the generation and persistence of poverty. During the same period, greater attention began to be paid to the idea that the perception of poverty is culturally based and that its meaning is as diverse as the cultural perspectives within which it is experienced. Indeed, in a culture that values detachment from material goods rather than

Poverty must be looked at from the inside and with a clear commitment to a human rights-based approach to eradication, so that local solutions may be found in concert with the communities involved, who can thereby contribute to finding their own way out of poverty

Ultimately, what the poor are denied is their human fulfilment. They are denied the freedom to fulfil themselves, as human beings and as citizens; they are blocked in their access to options and in their freedom of choice

monetary wealth, the Western conception of 'being poor' is untenable. Culture shapes how people understand and experience poverty: historical background, lifestyles and systems of belief condition how poverty is conceived and should therefore dictate the strategies needed to combat it (Appadurai, 2004).

Sociological definitions of poverty are often quite helpful for grasping the complexity of the phenomenon, for they take as their perspective the overall organization and functioning of societies (Bruto da Costa, 2008). Sociologists describe how power structures (political, economic, cultural, social) emerging from economic systems actually force out segments of the population – sometimes the great majority of their citizens – and keep them from participating in the collective actions of a society. These factors may function as obstacles to poverty eradication (e.g. resistance to change) or even as causes of poverty. The solutions lie in social change, based on the principles of social justice, solidarity and the common good.

In this respect, a powerful approach to poverty eradication emphasizes the *rights* of the poor. As Amartya Sen (1999) has said: 'it would be wrong, and have disastrous consequences, to consider that poverty is merely a question of *lack of material resources*. Ultimately, what the poor are denied is their human fulfilment. They are denied the *freedom* to fulfil themselves, as human beings and as citizens; they are blocked in their access to options and in their freedom of choice.' Freedom is meaningless so long as the necessary conditions for its effective

exercise have not been ensured. Freedom of choice, like any other form of freedom, is effective only when we are able to ensure the conditions necessary to exercise it. From the perspective of cultural diversity, human-rights-based strategies for poverty reduction can be strengthened when emphasis is placed on giving voice to marginalized groups (Mathews, 2007) and thereby empower them to contribute to defining their own way out of poverty and the paths for their own development. What is most often lacking is the means to initiate a virtuous circle.

Perceptions of poverty

Attempts to assess how poor populations perceive poverty have sought to nuance the one-size-fits-all grids such as those that inform the Human Development Index (HDI) and the Human Poverty Index (HIP-1) by capturing those populations' situations as they are rooted in traditional schemes and the collective imagination (Sall, 2002). UNESCO's work in this domain serves to illustrate the complexity of the channels through which poverty is perceived by way of surveys on popular perceptions of poverty and human rights, such as those recently conducted in Mali and in Burkina Faso (UNESCO, 2009).

Bamanan expressions used in Segou, Mali, generally link poverty to social rank, and the poor are referred to as 'powerless' or 'exhausted' (*fangantan, setan, dèsè, dèsèbagato, dogoto kolibagati*). In traditional Bamanan communities, wearing rags is not a sign of poverty but of modesty, especially for wealthy landlords. According to the traditionalist Nko in Mali, poverty (*fantanya*) and wealth/power (*setiguiya, fentigiya*) exist only in relation to one another: one is always poor in relation to someone else and not poor in relation to another. From this perspective, one has a responsibility to those who are poorer. While one cannot divest oneself of one's poverty, one has a particular responsibility to combat the incapacity to feed, to heal, to dress, or to have a home (*dogotoya*). In this way, poverty is understood as a relative phenomenon, and linked to notions of social responsibility and solidarity.

Among certain ethnic groups in Burkina Faso, wealth is related to physical health and the capacity to work (the individual ability to produce), and poverty is equated with sickness, incompetence and laziness — a person in good health simply cannot be poor. For the Mosse in Burkina

○ *In Roça Ribeira Peixe plantation in Sao Tome and Principe*

Faso, the best expression of human dignity is work. This is not related to the social recognition of wealth, however, for the wealthy are subject to particular scrutiny and are invited to put their wealth at the service of solving collective problems. Interestingly, the Mosse view poverty in terms of the smooth functioning of the community: on a community level, poverty is characterized as an absence of common understanding, and lack of solidarity and peace among individuals and groups; on an individual level, poverty is associated with an absence of sociability, an incapacity to integrate and a propensity for dissent.

Some of the groups surveyed discuss poverty as a loss of ability to stand up for one's rights and thus emphasize the need to help the poor to recover their self-esteem and dignity. The notion of the right to be protected against poverty appears in many different cultural contexts. The right to be protected against poverty through *zakat* is also a cornerstone of the Muslim tradition.

To ensure a complementarity between a universal approach to poverty eradication and recognition of the diversity of perceptions and values, holistic approaches that include all the relevant parameters (social, historical, economic and cultural) need to be identified, so as to take account of culture as the means by which *empowerment* becomes possible. People have to be empowered to become aware of their fundamental rights and make their own informed decisions. If they are not, they may be forced to adopt what they may perceive to be externally imposed solutions. A fruitful way to strike a balance between a human-rights-based approach to poverty eradication and the credit given to cultural parameters — that is, between a universal approach and the so-called 'relativistic' approach (see chapter 8) — is by ensuring self-determination.

The recognition of traditional communities' ability to address poverty through mutual assistance mechanisms or solidarity highlights the importance of focusing on cultural capacities for poverty alleviation. In Burkina Faso, despite obvious poverty-related problems, there exists an equilibrium between poverty, progress and culture (Tevoedjre, 1990); this makes it clear that well-being is related less to the abundance of material wealth than to mechanisms of solidarity, the enhancement of culture through knowledge and the will to progress.

Enabling cultural capacities

In the context of the UNDP's work on human development, Sen (1987, 1999) has proposed the 'capabilities approach', which emphasizes the substantial freedoms expressed in such categories as life, health, self-expression, relationships and control over one's environment. This approach moves away from the overly materialistic emphasis on income, employment and wealth towards an emphasis on amplifying people's choices, towards 'the expansion of the "capabilities" of persons to lead the kind of lives they value and have reason to value' (Sen, 1999). The capabilities approach advocates the promotion of opportunities for the poor, 'recognizing their vulnerability to risks, and the need for empowerment, including gender equality' (Ruggieri Laderchi et al., 2003). Two other approaches have been advanced in the context of poverty eradication strategies: the 'social exclusion approach', which stresses the integration of all, and the 'participatory approach', which focuses on the participation of stakeholders in decision-making about what constitutes poverty.

An approach that capitalizes on the synergies between cultural diversity and human rights resides in the dynamic idea that cultures are trajectories towards the future. Arjun Appadurai (2004) sums up the idea at the heart of this approach as follows: 'We need a sea change in the way we look at culture in order to create a more productive relationship between anthropology and economics, between culture and development, in the battle against poverty. This change requires us to place futurity, rather than pastness, at the heart of our thinking about culture.' The aim here is to unleash 'the capacity to aspire' and enable individuals and groups, once aware of their basic human rights and their value, to participate in the definition of their own development. To advance participatory initiatives, the World Bank utilizes participatory poverty assessments (PPAs) in poverty diagnostics and 'Voices of the Poor' exercises. The challenge, in line with the intercultural dialogue (see chapter 2), is to seek concrete means to enhance opportunities for the poor, the disadvantaged and the marginalized to 'exercise "voice," to debate, contest, and oppose vital directions for collective social life as they wish', especially when operating under 'adverse terms of recognition' (Appadurai, 2004). Culture in this sense is what enables individuals and groups to become the agents of their own development, even

Holistic approaches that include all the relevant parameters (social, historical, economic and cultural) need to be identified, so as to take account of culture as the means by which empowerment becomes possible ... The aim here is to unleash 'the capacity to aspire' and enable individuals and groups, once aware of their basic human rights and their value, to participate in the definition of their own development

| Box 7.2 | **The Fair trade movement** |

Fair trade began as an organized citizens' movement in the 1960s and 1970s, and the slogan 'Trade Not Aid' — in conjunction with poverty alleviation efforts through equitable trading relations with the South — began circulating in the international political arena about the time of the 1968 United Nations Conference on Trade and Development (UNCTAD). Since 1998, fair trade has been based on a chain extending from producers to sellers, under the aegis of four federations: the World Fair Trade Organization (WFTO), formerly the International Fair Trade Association, created in 1989; the European Fair Trade Association (EFTA), created in 1990; the Network of European Worldshops (NEWS), created in 1994; and the Fairtrade Labelling Organizations International (FLO), created in 1997. In 1998, these four created FINE (an acronym of the first letter of each body's name), an informal association to harmonize fair trade standards and guidelines and to streamline monitoring and awareness-raising systems. In 2007, the fair trade system benefited about 1.5 million workers/farmers in 58 developing countries in Africa, Asia and Latin America, estimated at 7.5 million people, including family and dependents.

Involving mainly local sectors (handicrafts and products such as coffee and cocoa), fair trade seeks to avoid the potentially harmful effects of production for foreign markets by paying close attention to workplace standards, balanced North-South trading relations and consumer guarantees regarding product origin. By focusing on the cultural dimension of products in the commodity sector and the related agricultural sector and its practices, fair trade helps to ensure that the human capital of individuals is turned to account for their own benefit. The symbolic value of certain products (such as the cocoa much appreciated by Andean cultures for their stimulating qualities) can help to stimulate a 'cultural' interest in the product on the part of foreign consumers, thereby generating a sense of pride among producers in the quality of their products.

While research into the impact of fair trade on poverty has so far been limited, the evidence available suggests that it has a positive development impact on livelihoods, not only by providing access to markets but also by empowering the poor to make choices that ensure non-exploitative market access. A key part of fair trade's success has been and continues to be its responsiveness and pragmatic approach to meeting the needs and aspirations of marginalized producers.

Although it has experienced rapid growth (40 percent annually on average over the past five years), with certified sales amounting to approximately €2.3 billion worldwide (a 47 percent year-to-year increase), the equitable trade market remains rather restricted; it accounts for only about 0.02 percent of global trade (and, most significantly, only 0.1 percent of the trade between Europe and the countries of the South).

The real interest of fair trade lies less in its economic potential than in its role as a consciousness-raising model for an equitable and sustainable global economy. South-South trade (currently representing only about 14 percent of the total exchange of goods in the countries of the South) is beginning to develop as part of an emerging consumer market, and fair trade practices could further benefit the poor through the development of other sectors, such as the service and tourism industries.

Source: WFTO and FLO websites.

Country	Estimated fair trade retail value (in million euros)			Licensees		
	2005	2006	% increase	2004	2005	% increase
Austria	25.6	41.7	63	31	37	19
Belgium	15.0	28.0	86	38	50	31
Canada	34.8	53.8	54	124	160	29
Denmark	14.0	21.5	54	10	21	110
Finland	13.0	22.5	73	16	20	25
France	109.1	160.0	47	72	106	47
Germany	70.9	110.0	55	66	87	32
Ireland	6.6	11.6	77	12	22	83
Italy	28.0	34.5	23	45	45	
Japan	3.4	4.1	23	13	24	84
Luxembourg	2.3	2.8	23	19	19	
Netherlands	36.5	41.0	12	36	41	14
Norway	6.7	8.6	28	19	24	26
Sweden	9.3	16.0	73	12	24	100
Switzerland	133.8	135.3	1	32	42	31
UK	276.8	409.5	48	157	193	23
USA	344.1	499.0	45	435	534	23
Australia/New Zealand	2.5	7.2	191	26	56	115
Spain	0.03	1.9	7.5	n.a.	n.a.	n.a.
TOTAL	**1,132.4**	**1,609.0**	**42**	**1,151**	**1,483**	**29**

Source: FLO.

when resources are limited, by providing the means for awareness-building based on their own assets and emphasizing the development of open-mindedness and cooperation.

Social policies that favour cultural diversity help to increase the level of self-determination among low-income or low-status minority groups by acknowledging or celebrating their distinctive cultural heritage. In addition to income redistribution and equal access to rights, institutions and other resources, poverty alleviation also requires measures to ensure that such groups can play an increased role in the public sphere. Public celebrations of cultural diversity can contribute to this end, along with the promotion of a positive collective identity among natives and immigrants. Research has shown that retaining cultural distinctiveness can provide important advantages, such as bilingualism (see chapter 3) and multiple cultural perspectives (see chapter 4). Breaking the spiral of poverty among low-income or low-status minority groups involves restoring their sense of pride, which entails valuing the intangible heritage of which they are depositories. 'Change in continuity' (UNESCO, 2000), as the key to effective development, involves the same competencies as successful intercultural dialogue, namely openness to difference without loss of identity (see chapter 2).

Public and private initiatives for poverty alleviation

Thus initiatives that are able to harness the cultural capacities of communities are the keys to unlocking the spiral or vicious circle of poverty: intangible heritage, alternative forms of education, community-based

media, community-based tourism and the equitable commerce in crafts and food products are means of contributing to improved socio-economic conditions while enhancing the creative link between cultures, traditions and modernity.

Fair trade — a trading partnership based on dialogue, transparency and mutual respect — has the potential to become an effective tool for poverty eradication insofar as it offers better trading conditions to, and secures the rights of, marginalized producers and workers, especially in the South. Fair trade is an excellent example of a productive partnership between social responsibility and economic interest as applied to the entire production and consumption cycle — from producers to distributors, down to the consumers themselves. By respecting the human and cultural dimensions of production and commerce, fair trade can make a significant contribution to economic justice and social understanding (see Box 7.2).

Community-based tourism, ecotourism and pro-poor tourism can likewise be effective means of escaping from poverty when they genuinely benefit local communities by improving their living conditions while revitalizing their local cultures and connecting them to the global marketplace (see chapter 6). New concepts are also emerging in the battle against poverty — concepts such as 'new museology' or 'ecomuseology' in countries such as Viet Nam — based on the recognition of the interdependencies between sustainable development and cultural diversity (Box 7.3). Crucial here is the insight that successful development

Box 7.3   **Ecomuseums and poverty alleviation in Viet Nam**

Viet Nam had already begun making new strides related to cultural heritage with the inauguration in 1997 of the Vietnam Museum of Ethnology in Hanoi. It has since intensified its commitment to harmonizing population needs and natural environmental protection by using ecomuseology as a critical holistic tool for promoting the concept of sustainable heritage development and local ownership. The concept of the ecomuseum arose when the Ha Long Bay began to face a number of challenges

related to rapid urbanization, heavy population pressure and the unplanned development of transport, tourism, seaport, coal mining and other industries. Viet Nam was the first country in Asia to apply a comprehensive management strategy to a World Heritage Site, the Ha Long Bay.

Initially funded by the UNDP and UNESCO in 2000, the Ha Long Ecomuseum has been an ongoing and open-ended project driven by the simple principle that the conflicts

between conservation and development can be adequately dealt with only by bringing people and their environment together through productive partnerships. The ecomuseum considers the entire Ha Long Bay area to be a living museum. It employs an 'interpretive' approach to its management, which views the components and processes of nature, culture and tangible heritage as continuously interacting with each other in a constantly changing equilibrium. Through intensive

A Fair Trade coffee farmer sorting through organic beans at a coffee plantation 🎧

Box 7.3	Ecomuseums and poverty alleviation in Viet Nam

research, managers and stakeholder-community groups monitor the bay's equilibrium and make carefully planned interventions to rebalance the components when necessary.

The ecomuseum concept encompasses the following actions:

- Supporting communities in securing their basic living needs (this may require advocacy with other agencies);

- Facilitating the community planning process within communities, including the identification of local resources;

- Supporting the protection of local resources, including cultural maintenance;

- Developing skills and providing other business support infrastructure, including funding and communications infrastructure;

- Launching businesses through contracting and outsourcing, as well as the provision of space for community markets;

- Promoting the growth of enterprises and employment by developing a plan for any business opportunity with good prospects for viability;

- Supporting communities in making wise investments and increasing their economic resources;

- Facilitating demonstration projects.

'New museology', or 'ecomuseology', has proven to be a valuable tool for mitigating development conflicts in several countries. Projects such as the Ha Long Ecomuseum could become models for promoting heritage economics without compromising conservation values, models in which community museological discourse is brought to bear on the economic dimension of conservation.

The Ha Long project has spurred the work of Vietnam's Poverty Task Force (PTF) — a government-donor forum for dialogue and consultation on poverty reduction. In a 2005 report, the PTF recommended that priority

be given to three targets as part of the main goal of eradicating poverty and preserving the culture and diversity of ethnic minorities:

1. Preserve and develop ethnic minority languages and promote bilingual literacy in areas where there are high concentrations of minority peoples.

2. Ensure that individual and collective land-use rights for all land-use types have been allocated to the majority of ethnic mountainous peoples.

3. Increase the proportion of government personnel of ethnic origin closer to the proportion in the national population.

These targets address the three pillars of sustainable development in concert with culture, emphasizing the importance of integrating cultural diversity in policy-making, planning, and project development and implementation at all levels.

Source: Galla, 2002.

Cultural approaches help to make poverty eradication strategies highly relevant at the local level, since they take the specificities of the concerned populations into account

planning is not just a function of addressing economics, social or political change, health advancement, human and cultural rights, the absence of physical violence, or sustainable physical environments in isolated fashion, but is achieved holistically, through the interplay of *all* these functions.

Cultural policies and culture-based projects have the potential to make significant contributions towards achieving the Millennium Development Goals (MDGs) and poverty eradication. As illustrated by the sub-Saharan countries of Africa, the identification, protection and appropriation of a culture and its integration in development strategies and in the fight against poverty is essential. Culturally based knowledge is a core resource for people in the desert and a lever for the daily activities (animal husbandry, agriculture, crafts, etc.),

enabling the survival of the people — and therefore their culture — over the short, middle and long term.

Moreover, cultural approaches help to make poverty eradication strategies highly relevant at the local level, since they take the specificities of the concerned populations (history, traditions, belief systems, social organization) into account. Developing multi-sectoral policies — with true collaboration and cooperation among different ministries — that are built on the linkages between culture, education, health, gender, decentralization and the environment (sustainable policies) are the most effective ways to successfully address the issue of poverty. It is essential that countries take ownership of Poverty Reduction Strategy Papers (PRSPs)[3] for these documents to become effective poverty reduction tools. To improve the local

3. The Poverty Reduction Strategy Papers (PRSPs) are policy documents prepared by low-income countries detailing development and poverty reduction priorities through policy matrices in order to avail of concessional lending from multinational donors. They were introduced by the World Bank and the International Monetary Fund (IMF) in 1999. They have become an important means for assessing priorities and resource allocation for poverty reduction.

appropriation of PRSPs and the conditions under which they are developed, it may be necessary to support multi-stakeholder approaches and partnerships, to strengthen government and institutional capacities in developing pro-poor growth policies, capacity-building in formulating, negotiating and implementing development policies, and to devise policies for the informal economy. In addition to economic growth strategies, targeted pro-poor policies, including job creation for vulnerable populations, must also be part of poverty reduction strategies. Development strategies must therefore recognize the poor as essential stakeholders in the development process. Poverty eradication strategies should tackle poverty in its multidimensional nature through multi-sectoral social intervention.

7.3 Cultural diversity and environmental sustainability

In issues ranging from the erosion of biodiversity to climate change, cultural diversity has an important — though often underestimated — role to play in addressing current ecological challenges and ensuring environmental sustainability. For while the international community has primarily sought technical and scientific responses to ecological challenges, there is increasing recognition that cultural practices are intimately linked to environmental integrity. The development of any culture arises from the constant interplay between the environment and human needs. Just as cultural identity and social stability can be strongly influenced by environmental conditions, cultural factors can influence consumer behaviours and values related to environmental stewardship. In this sense, culture and cultural diversity are fundamental drivers of environmental change (see Nelson, 2005).

Social anthropology has shown that there are numerous ways of perceiving and interacting with the natural environment, thereby challenging modes of thought that divorce culture and nature (Descola, 2005). One example is the Lakalaka system of dances and sung speeches of Tonga, which embodies the shared knowledge, beliefs and values that have supported culturally and environmentally appropriate fishing practices for generations. Thus, cultural expressions are not simply the product of human creativity independent of the environment in which they prosper; rather, they are the manifestations of our interactions with each other and our natural environment, as diversely reflected in different 'cosmovisions' of the world (see Descola, 2005; Ishizawa, 2004).

Much can be learned from the good practices of environmental management preserved by local, rural or indigenous peoples who view the human-environment relationship as a series of coevolving interactions. Most of these populations, including shifting and permanent cultivators, herders, hunters, gatherers and fishers, occupy ecosystems about which they have developed in-depth knowledge over time. Their unique experience with the use and management of such ecosystems encompasses multi-use strategies of appropriation, small-scale production with little surplus and low energy needs, and a custodial approach to land and natural resources that avoids waste and resource depletion.

The social and human sciences — particularly archaeology, history, social anthropology, ethnobiology and ethnoecology — have investigated whether and to what extent indigenous societies may offer solutions to contemporary environmental problems. While many books have highlighted cases in which societies failed

The Lakalaka, Tonga's national dance, a blend of choreography, oratory, and vocal and instrumental polyphony

⋒ *A toucan bird from Panama*

⋒ *A puma from Brazil*

⋒ *A chimpanzee in a National Park in Kenya*

to adapt to environmental change, episodes have been recorded of prolonged and successful shifts in livelihood and settlement patterns and innovative state policy in ancient times (Rosen, 2006; Butzer, 1971), the Middle Ages (Newman, 1990; Lamb, 1995; Rotberg and Rabb, 1983; Le Roy Ladurie, 1967), and the modern period (Orlove, 2005; Post, 1977)..In view of the considerable challenges our world currently faces, the time has come to draw on the riches of our cultures to find approaches to sustainable environmental management, as well as adaptation and mitigation in the face of natural hazards and climate change. The best way to proceed in this regard is to *empower* peoples whose local knowledge and experiences have long enabled them to conserve much of the earth's remaining biological diversity (Posey, 1999).

The links between biological and cultural diversity[4]

While biological and cultural diversity may have evolved differently, they have nonetheless constantly interacted to produce human and environmental diversity as we know it today (Toledo, 2007). The *Declaration of Belem* (ISE, 1998) points to the 'inextricable link between biological and cultural diversity' and recognizes the coevolving interdependence and reinforcement of these two components of the Earth's diversity. This is echoed in Article 1 of the 2001 *Universal Declaration on Cultural Diversity* in reference to the functional parallel between the two: 'As a source of exchange, innovation and creativity, cultural diversity is as necessary for humankind as biodiversity is for nature.'

UNESCO has long promoted the dynamic interdependence between human beings and nature, particularly since the launch in 1971 of the Man and the Biosphere (MAB) Programme and the adoption of the *World Heritage Convention* (UNESCO, 1972) the following year. These flagship programmes have contributed to the development of protected terrestrial and marine areas all over the world (see Map 7.2). The further inclusion of 'cultural landscapes' in the *World Heritage Convention* in 1992 (World Heritage Committee, 1992) has since enhanced the recognition of these linkages,

as has the adoption in 1995 of the Seville Strategy for Biosphere Reserves (UNESCO, 1996). The latter established the UNESCO Biosphere Reserves, under the MAB Programme, and stressed that they play a major role in achieving a new vision of the relationship between conservation and development, one that takes into account both cultural and natural dimensions (see UNESCO, 2008c). These linkages are reiterated within the 2003 UNESCO *Convention on the Safeguarding of the Intangible Cultural Heritage*, which focuses on the custodians of the various forms of intangible heritage, including 'knowledge and practices concerning nature and the universe' (CBD, 2008).

In the context of sustainable development, UNESCO has also played an important role in raising awareness of the links between biological and cultural diversity, notably with UNEP, through the High-Level Round Table on Cultural Diversity and Biodiversity for Sustainable Development at the 2002 Johannesburg Summit (UNESCO, 2002). As a follow-up, a more in-depth analysis has revealed seven 'areas of interdependence between biological and cultural diversity' (UNESCO, 2008b):

1. Language linguistic diversity (see chapter 3);

2. Material culture (e.g. objects created from and/or representing biodiversity);

3. Knowledge and technology (including traditional and local knowledge such as traditional medicine or early-warning systems);

4. Modes of subsistence (e.g. resource-based livelihoods, plant/animal domestication, selective breeding);

5. Economic relations (e.g. partnerships based on trading natural resources);

6. Social relations (including attachment to place);

7. Belief systems.

Efforts to further elucidate the links between cultural and biological diversity and their implications for sustainable

4. The Convention on Biological Diversity (CBD, 1993: art. 2) defines 'biological diversity' as 'the variability among living organisms from all sources including, inter alia, terrestrial, marine and other aquatic ecosystems and the ecological complexes of which they are part: this includes diversity within species, between species and of ecosystems.' In addition, it defines biological resources' as 'genetic resources, organisms or parts thereof, populations, or any other biotic component of ecosystems with actual or potential use or value for humanity.'

Map 7.2 Protected terrestrial and marine areas*, 2005

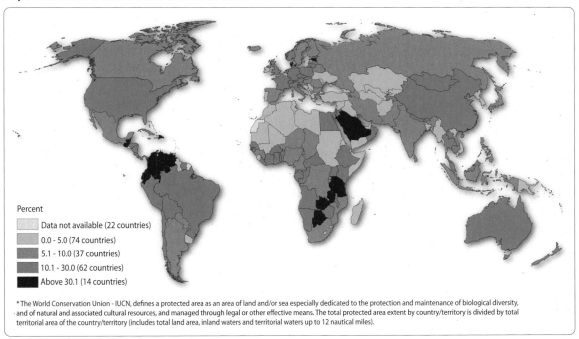

Percent

Data not available (22 countries)
0.0 - 5.0 (74 countries)
5.1 - 10.0 (37 countries)
10.1 - 30.0 (62 countries)
Above 30.1 (14 countries)

* The World Conservation Union - IUCN, defines a protected area as an area of land and/or sea especially dedicated to the protection and maintenance of biological diversity, and of natural and associated cultural resources, and managed through legal or other effective means. The total protected area extent by country/territory is divided by total territorial area of the country/territory (includes total land area, inland waters and territorial waters up to 12 nautical miles).

Source: United Nations, UNEP-WCMC, 2006.

development are currently underway in many contexts and across a wide array of disciplines — the academic world, UN agencies, programmes and forums (e.g. the UN Permanent Forum on Indigenous Issues [UNPFII], the International Indigenous Forum on Biodiversity [IIFB], the Inuit Circumpolar Council), and NGOs (e.g. International Union for Conservation of Nature [IUCN], Tebtebba, Terralingua, International Union of Forest Research [IUFRO], Resilience Alliance, Global Diversity Foundation), to name but a few (see UNESCO, 2008b).

Many new practices have been developed as a result of increased awareness of the interactions between landscapes, economics and cultures, both conceptually (Toledo 1992, 2002; Barrera-Bassols and Zinck, 2003) and on the ground, as illustrated by the renewed interest of decision-makers in the terroirs paradigm. The term 'terroirs', which in France designates culturally distinctive areas that have existed for several centuries (in Japan, the equivalent of the terroir is the *satoyama*), has been revitalized and updated, and consideration is currently being given to setting up an international network. The terroirs are focal points for the establishment of systems

for revitalizing biological, agricultural, cultural and other forms of diversity, including traditions, celebrations, family structures, language and knowledge. They also provide a way of reinforcing the cultural and economic dynamics between town and countryside by developing food-processing flows, promoting creative and participative tourism and highlighting new perspectives on preservation and economic and social development by turning to account the diverse facets of the rural world.

In many respects, local cultural practices, especially those corresponding to cosmologies that assume an intrinsic connection between human beings and nature, tend to favour a balanced relationship between human activities and environmental sustainability. A greater involvement of local and indigenous communities in the international community's decisions concerning the global environmental agenda may help to achieve some measure of harmony between the two perspectives when, for example, ancestral ways of living (e.g. whale hunting for the Makah Indians in the north-western US) are confronted with decisions taken by the international community to safeguard endangered species.

Chapter 7
Cultural diversity:
A key dimension of
sustainable development

Responding to climate change: A cultural challenge?

Climate change may become one of the greatest challenges facing humanity in the 21st century, especially for vulnerable communities already under stress, for whom the cumulative effects on water supply, disease patterns, farming systems and the habitability of coastal settlements will have devastating effects. Since cultural expressions and practices are very often developed in response to environmental conditions, the prospect of large-scale environmental upheavals represents a potentially major cultural challenge.

Box 7.4	Sustainable development assistance for displaced populations and refugees

By the end of 2007, the total population of concern to the UN High Commission for Refugees (UNHCR) was estimated at 31.7 million people, including some 11.4 million refugees, 740,000 asylum-seekers, 731,000 repatriated refugees (in 2007), 13.7 million internally displaced persons (IDPs), 2.1 million repatriated IDPs (in 2007), and about 3 million stateless persons or others, many of whom had been dislocated by environmentally related problems, from resource scarcity to desertification, deforestation, droughts and floods (UNHCR, 2008). While there is much debate on the concept of 'environmental refugees' (for natural factors alone cannot be said to be the sole cause of migration, which is also a by-product of economic, social and political factors), it is reasonable to assume that further environmental degradation linked to global warming will lead to major forced migration in the future, exacerbating current trends in rural depopulation, international wage migration and flight from conflict areas.

Beyond issues relating to basic security, health and human rights protection, not to mention the technical and administrative organization needed to deal adequately with refugees, a real understanding of the importance of culture and cultural disruption in humanitarian situations has yet to be fully developed and integrated on the ground. Refugee situations are often characterized by high degrees of cultural diversity and complexity (because different cultures are brought into contact with one another, both locally and internationally), which heightens the potential for intercultural miscommunication and necessarily affects group and organizational capacities and assistance outcomes (Ngai and Koehn, 2005).

In addition to genocide, warfare and/or exile, victims of dislocation often experience extreme cultural disruption, all of which leads to a fundamental re-examination of their cultural identity. Divorced from the material and symbolic representations of their past, new conditions of life alter the socio-cultural practices of a given community, weaken the transmission of traditional knowledge and lead to changes in established power relations, not only between men and women but also inter-generationally. This can be further exacerbated by the experience of entering into a worldwide globalization process — for example, through unaccustomed exposure to radio and television, and in contact with a wide range of development actors responding to displaced persons' needs.

The preservation of the languages of displaced persons in refugee camps and the maintenance of their traditional and religious beliefs, their history and their social norms and values are of fundamental importance to cementing their sense of common identity in the face of cultural disruption. These factors also help to foster solidarity and mutual aid and are a necessary prerequisite for reintegrating returnees in their homeland. In this sense, programmes that aim to facilitate the transmission of traditional knowledge, adapted to the new social and cultural realities, provide refugees with the tools they need to meet the new challenges they face.

The major objective of the UNESCO pilot project on the transmission of Burundian intangible cultural heritage in refugee camps in Tanzania relies on oral tradition (storytelling) as a means of facilitating sustainable adaptation and repatriation. Focusing on aspects of traditional knowledge that had undergone a number of changes — from agriculture and stockbreeding to social relations (notably gender relations, relations between elders and youth, family and community relations) and cultural and ritual performance — the storytelling activities provided a platform for transmitting and discussing Burundian culture (especially to younger generations), reviving social relations among Burundians, and awareness-raising for the humanitarian staff associated with the project. Furthermore, these storytelling activities were broadcast by radio to residents in Burundi, thereby connecting refugees to homeland populations and maintaining a sense of connectedness to help to ensure peaceful co-existence for returnees. The follow-up study (2007) demonstrated the effectiveness of this method not only for the transmission of intangible traditional heritage but also for social unity and awareness-raising among humanitarian workers about the value of cultural transmission and the importance of cultural diversity in refugee settings.

While international institutions, such as the UNHCR and the International Organization for Migration (IOM), and NGOs that address refugee and displacement issues, have begun to integrate cultural diversity factors into repatriation and reintegration planning, it will be increasingly necessary to cultivate upstream organizational and communication capacities related to social and cultural heritage loss, as well as to further study the cultural impacts of mass displacement in refugee settings so as to anticipate changes that may lie ahead.

Source: UNHCR, 2008.

Short-onset, acute hazards (earthquakes, tsunamis, floods, etc.) can have considerable impacts on cultural diversity; for example, the destruction of key cultural centres and monuments (temples, museums, schools) interrupts the transmission of traditions and beliefs and possibly even entire cultures. The earthquake in 2003 that ravaged the old city of Bam in Iran provides further testimony to the fragility of human heritage in the face of natural disasters.

In the medium and long term, livelihood security is placed at risk by the increasing occurrence of mega-disasters (hurricanes, cyclones, tropical storms, etc.), which produce cascades of secondary environmental hazards (such as landslides and flooding) that in turn have a domino effect on all aspects of life. In urban industrial landscapes, these can bring about further complications through damage to factories, storage facilities, and pipelines, resulting in 'natural-technological' (NATECH) hazards that are very expensive to clean up and can have long-term public health consequences (Cruz et al., 2004). The institutional systems for anticipating post-disaster 'surprises', including their effects on the diversity of cultural practices, have not been sufficiently developed, particularly in the case of slow-onset, pervasive hazards, such as water stress and climate change, which are recognized as potential sources of social conflict and instability (see IPCC, 2007; Hartmann, 2003, 2002, 1998).

The environmental consequences of climate change may create, among other things, massive population displacements that may seriously undermine cultural continuity and diversity. These include displacements due to large-scale projects undertaken by governments, conflicts over water and arable land, worsening rural livelihood conditions, deforestation and disease (see Box 7.4). For many rural and indigenous people, cultures remain very much place-based. Their homes and much of their material culture are made of locally available natural materials. Their stories, myths, songs and the imagery in their languages are also tied to place. As a result, forced displacement can be culturally devastating, as in the case of small islands.[5] Moreover, new intermixing of different population groups may create new challenges for our living together with our differences (see chapters 1 and 8). In these ways,

climate change can have serious effects on cultural transmission, especially in rural areas and among minority-language groups already under stress due to economic globalization, urban drift and years of neglect or even hostility from those in charge of government, language, education, and cultural policies.

Despite the growing awareness of good practices stemming from local knowledge of resource management and the efforts of the International Forum of Indigenous Peoples on Climate Change since 2000, most climate change research has focused on technical modelling and national policy formulation. It was not until November 2006, at the 12th session of the Conference of the Parties to the Climate Change Convention (COP 12) held in Nairobi, Kenya, that case studies could be presented as side contributions from indigenous peoples — collected by the International Alliance of the Indigenous and Tribal Peoples of the Tropical Forest (IAIPTF). The five-year Nairobi Work Programme on Impacts, Vulnerability, and Adaptation to Climate Change (UNFCC, 2007) was a significant outcome of COP 12, ensuring, for the first time, indigenous participation in the collection of information for mitigation and adaptation based on traditional knowledge, even though there is still no effective protection for traditional knowledge (see also chapter 6, Box 6.1). In December 2007, at the 13th session of the Conference of the Parties to the Climate Change Convention (COP 13) held in Bali, Indonesia, the implementation of the pilot phase for promoting the reduction of emissions by avoiding deforestation was approved, as were other initiatives involving greater participation of indigenous and local communities.

Towards holistic and participatory approaches to adaptation and mitigation

The emergence of a daunting nexus of environmental problems that threaten the stability, if not the very existence, of human societies has triggered widespread reflection on the limitations of purely technical and scientific responses to the ecological imperative and on the potential of a sustainable development perspective that would draw on a broad range of cultural experiences, institutions and practices, including those of local and indigenous knowledge systems.

⋂   *The streets of Konarak, India*

The environmental consequences of climate change may create, among other things, massive population displacements that may seriously undermine cultural continuity and diversity

Chapter 7
Cultural diversity:
A key dimension of
sustainable development

5. See UNESCO webpage on 'small island developing states'.

UNESCO has contributed to work and reflection on traditional knowledge, since the 1960s, when its Jakarta office published *An Ethnobotanical Guide for Anthropological Research in Malayo-Oceania* (Barrau, 1962), a study of the vast knowledge of plants possessed by the traditional societies of the area. In the 1980s, UNESCO actively supported investigations of customary marine resource management across the Asia-Pacific region through its Coastal Marine Programme (Ruddle and Johannes, 1985) and has continued to support policies and practices pertaining to traditional knowledge. The emergence in 2002 of the interdisciplinary programme on Local and Indigenous Knowledge Systems (LINKS) specifically addresses indigenous knowledge in the framework of biodiversity management, natural disaster response and climate change adaptation.

We have much to learn from the good practices of environmental management embedded within local, rural and traditional knowledge and know-how as it relates to the management of natural resources and local biodiversity. Indigenous peoples living in 'frontier lands' or 'refuge regions' — that is, remote areas where the structure of original ecosystems has been more or less safeguarded — make up most of the 15–21 million world fishers, some 25–30 million nomadic herders or pastoralists (in East Africa, the Sahel and Arabian Peninsula), most of the slash-and-burn agriculturalists and half the 1 million hunters and gatherers still in

---

| **Box 7.5** | **Local management of natural resources and biodiversity** |

Among the examples of local and indigenous management of natural resources and biodiversity, the following can be highlighted:

■ *Land management plans in the Amazon region*: These plans, involving the Shuar people of the south of Ecuador, the Sarayacu Association in the centre of the Amazon, and the Limoncocha Association, consist of mapping the land to better organize use and management of resources for the future by identifying community reserves; hunting, farming and extraction zones; and residential, riverside and sacred areas.

■ *Intercropping in West Africa*: In zones of intense, yet variable, rainfall and limited sunlight at the height of the growing season, intercropping has proven more effective than plough agriculture. Planting several (sometimes many) different species, and different varieties of the same species, on the same farm offers the benefits of minimized exposure of the soil to erosive rainfall, minimized spread of pests and diseases, minimized risk of crop failure, maximized use of available soil moisture and plant nutrients, as well as the suppression of weeds at later stages in the cropping sequence through competition by established crops approaching harvest (Richards, 1983).

■ *Community-based disaster risk reduction in the Indian State of Bihar*: Faced with increasing severity of flooding since the late 1970s and resultant loss of life, livestock and possessions, community-based programmes were implemented in India (in addition to government emergency assistance) which rely on a combination of physical interventions and social capacity-building. Village Development Committees (VDCs), which have specific responsibilities during floods (e.g. a village rescue and evacuation team and a women's self-help group), were created and trained. The programme has had positive outcomes for the community not only in terms of social relations and physical assets but also in terms of natural resources management.

■ *National Adaptation Programme of Action (NAPA) in the Samoa Islands*: Because the impacts of climate change on livelihoods are anticipated to be very severe (with food security challenges due to storms and landslides, fires, diseases linked to flooding and droughts, water quality and quantity challenges, as well as forced changes in land-use practices) in the Samoa Islands, adaptation programmes have been set up, including the introduction of new animal species suited to local climate, nurseries for cultivars and planting, logging quotas, Coastal Infrastructure Management Plans (CIMPs) and strategies, designation of marine protected areas (with respect to fisheries), leak detection (with respect to water) and family relocation.

Indigenous peoples have also transformed and managed wild biodiversities across a wide range of land- and seascapes. Perhaps one of the most powerful and dramatic of these cultural tools relates to the use of fire. While fire has traditionally been viewed by the Western scientific community as an agent of environmental destruction, indigenous peoples subsisting in a number of the world's ecosystems have used fire to modify entire landscapes for several millennia. In northern Australia, the Aboriginal peoples have used firestick farming to selectively burn specific habitats in specific seasons and thereby create a landscape mosaic of different habitats that are resource-rich and biologically diverse (Lewis, 1989). Biodiversity and landscape management through the astute application of fire was systematically practiced by indigenous peoples in numerous ecological settings around the world; other well-documented examples are the traditional burning practices of several indigenous peoples in the southwestern US (Anderson, 2006).
Source: Cerda, 2007 and UNESCO.

existence. They inhabit a substantial portion of the world's little-disturbed tropical and boreal forests, mountains, grasslands, tundra and desert, as well as large areas of the world's coasts and near-shore waters, including mangroves and coral reefs. As guardians of more than 1,000 species and thousands of varieties of domesticated plants and animals, indigenous communities are involved in on-farm conservation and breeding, selecting varieties and improving crops on a day-to-day basis (see Box 7.5). As the encounter between traditional knowledge and other techniques of managing natural resources begins to yield 'hybrid' local practices that combine traditional rural practices with technical external tools, deeper cultural changes — e.g. shifting gender divisions of labour — are also underway (Wisner, 2007).

Part of the difficulty in drawing on local and indigenous knowledge is that it tends to be tacit knowledge. Due to mistrust and language barriers, early European observers of shifting cultivation and polyculture in the Americas misunderstood these practices as chaotic, disorganized and wasteful. A more respectful and open-minded approach would have revealed the inherent rationale of these practices — soil fertility restoration and mobilization of nutrients in ash from burned forest on the one hand, and the benefits of shade and different rooting depths that hedge against drought on the other hand (Wisner, 1994, 2004; Wisner and Smucker, 2008). If tacit knowledge is to be made explicit and harnessed, justice must be done to the complexities of intercultural dialogue — for example, through inclusive and participatory methods such as those embedded in the Cultural Diversity Programming Lens (see 'In focus' below). A much more sophisticated and nuanced approach to local knowledge now understands that no single, homogeneous 'knowledge' exists in a given locality and that if we are to confront current environmental challenges, different knowledge systems need to be engaged together — cross-culturally, inter-generationally, and differentiated by gender, occupation and ethnicity.

Participatory approaches are conducive not only to co-learning in action but also to more rapid change. This is supported by recent and current projects in Africa, Latin America and Asia, which have fostered creative dialogue between indigenous understandings of natural processes and specialized external knowledge. Indeed, with active participation, people become more conscious of their own situation and their own knowledge and practices. Tacit knowledge embodied in conventional practice becomes explicit, can be articulated and then discussed critically. In turn, external research tools are more likely to be accepted in ways that complement local concepts and experience of change. Three-dimensional modelling, the use of geographical information systems (GIS),[6] and the adoption of on-farm crop trials and new livelihood elements (Wangui, 2003) have all successfully involved active participation by local stakeholders.

Conclusion

Sustainable, human-centred development presupposes the participation of empowered individuals and communities and reflects their cultural patterns and solidarities. In this way, it restores the pride of individuals and communities, particularly indigenous peoples and other vulnerable groups, on the basis of their cultural expressions, values and perspectives. This in turn contributes to capacity-building geared towards a consensual search for well-being and alternative development pathways. 'Identity' can then move from defensive positioning to a form of empowerment conducive to the achievement of self-defined and sustainable objectives. In this sense, 'development with identity' (Tauli-Corpuz, 2008) comes to mean 'development with dignity'.

Insofar as cultural diversity involves strategies that capitalize on traditional knowledge and its synergies with scientific knowledge, it is a powerful tool for the achievement of the MDGs:

Science exerts a powerful influence on our daily lives, our interactions with the environment, our value systems and worldview. However, it is just one knowledge system amongst many. Other knowledge systems, many of them embedded in a remarkable diversity of cultures and sustaining a broad spectrum of ways of life, constitute a rich and diverse intellectual heritage whose importance for attaining international development objectives,

⌒ A collection of stones in the Yuyuan garden, Shanghai, China

Chapter 7
Cultural diversity:
A key dimension of
sustainable development

6. See the websites of the Participatory GIS Network and the Integrated Approaches to Participatory Development (IAPAD).

Sustainable, human-centred development presupposes the participation of empowered individuals and communities and reflects their cultural patterns and solidarities

➲   *Rice fields in Indonesia, 1984*

including the Millennium Development Goals (MDGs), continues to be underestimated. (Matsuura, 2008)

Cultural diversity can help to reshape strategies for achieving MDG 1 (eradication of extreme poverty) and MDG 7 (environmental sustainability). Although not explicitly mentioned in the *Millennium Declaration* (UN, 2000), which commits the international community to the realization of the eight MDGs, cultural diversity was emphasized in the *2005 World Summit Outcome Document* by the High-Level Plenary Meeting of the 60th

Session of the General Assembly, which followed up on that Declaration.[7] Indeed, the integration of cultural diversity within the MDGs framework may reinforce the 'global partnership for development' foreseen in MDG 8. A major step towards the recognition of the positive contribution of local and traditional knowledge for development was the recent release of the *UN Development Group Guidelines on Indigenous Peoples' Issues* (2008), which was broadly distributed throughout the UN system, including to UN Country Teams. Other guidelines corresponding to other aspects of cultural diversity could follow.

Chapter 7 Recommendations

The principles of cultural diversity, as embodied in particular in the Cultural Diversity Lens, should be duly taken into account in the design, implementation and monitoring of all development policies.

To this end, action should be taken to:

a. Identify concrete measures to operationalize research on the cultural dimension of natural resources conservation and management, with particular reference to the knowledge and know-how of indigenous communities.

b. Establish a clearing-house for documenting participatory approaches to environmental problems, including indications as to their success.

c. Encourage the participation of members of all communities in defining resource allocation criteria on the basis of social justice, so as to foster a dynamic of social dialogue and promote intercultural solidarity.

7. 'Acknowledging the diversity of the world, we recognize that all cultures and civilizations contribute to the enrichment of humankind. We acknowledge the importance of respect and understanding for religious and cultural diversity throughout the world. In order to promote international peace and security, we commit ourselves to advancing human welfare, freedom and progress everywhere, as well as to encouraging tolerance, respect, dialogue and cooperation among different cultures, civilizations and peoples' (UN, 2005: para. 14).

The Cultural Diversity Programming Lens: A tool for monitoring development projects

Various indicators, models and tools, many of which have been discussed throughout this report, are already being used to help to capture the various facets of how cultural diversity is lived on the ground — from participatory methodologies to intercultural dialogue facilitation and cultural mapping (see chapters 1 and 2), multilingualism (chapter 3) to intercultural skills (chapter 4) and inventories of cultural practices and industries (see chapters 5 and 6). These can serve to stimulate reflection on the methodologies to be used in sustainable development projects.

Since the 1980s and the rise of a 'people-centred' approach to development — as opposed to a 'commodity-centred' approach (Throsby, 2008) — a paradigm shift has been underway which recognizes that sustainable economic growth cannot be the sole indicator of positive sustainable development. While the emergence of the concept of 'human development' marks clear progress towards greater recognition of the specificity of assets in a given society and a given cultural context, the Human Development Index (HDI) is methodologically limited in its categorizations (e.g. measuring a healthy life on the basis of life expectancy or measuring knowledge in terms of combined primary, secondary and tertiary gross enrolment ratios). That said, the aim to establish comparable standards for the assessment of each country's efforts to enhance human capabilities remains both useful and necessary, for varied efforts can ultimately yield indicators that do capture the cultural specificity of the values prevailing in each cultural context.

Because greater importance is given today to well-being and happiness in the assessment of development progress, different societies have begun to attempt to assess and measure their own quality of life, as determined by the specific values that give meaning to their existence and the criteria of a 'good life' (Agazzi, 2002). The Organization for Economic Co-operation and Development (OECD) also has recently become interested in the elaboration of indicators that take account of the diversity of cultural conceptions of progress and well-being through so-called 'happiness indicators' (Veenhoven, 2007). The goal thereby is to develop indicators that are comparable across societies, midway between local indicators of development (such as Bhutan's Gross Happiness Index) and the universal concept of human development. The reflection on the economic crisis may provide a new rationale for such initiatives, as recently indicated by an *ad hoc* committee of experts created by the French Government (Stiglitz, Sen and Fitoussi, 2009)

Still, the challenge remains to operationalize an approach to development that is both comprehensive and multidimensional, incorporating 'all the dimensions of life and the energies of a community' (UNESCO, 1982), and that integrates the fundamental purpose of development, namely:

- The realization of the potentialities of the human person in harmony with the community;

- The human person understood as a subject (and not the object) of development;

- The satisfaction of both material and non-material needs;

- Respect for human rights and the principles of equality and non-discrimination;

- The opportunity for full participation; and

- A degree of individual and collective self-reliance (as embodied in the 1986 United Nations *Declaration on the Right to Development*).

With the goal of monitoring and evaluating cultural and sustainable development projects and mainstreaming cultural diversity into programme design, development and implementation, the UNESCO Regional Office in Bangkok developed the *Cultural Diversity Programming Lens (CDPL)* to operationalize such principles and associated normative standards (see UNESCO, 2000). Designed for use by decision- and policy-makers, programme managers and community leaders, the CDPL works like a lens that augments vision. It is an interdisciplinary checklist of criteria and questions, supplemented by indicators, that provides a means for integrating cultural diversity issues while ensuring the participation of all stakeholders across all phases of a given project, including in upstream research and needs assessment. The CDPL facilitates reflection and analysis linking culture and development. Due to the increasing importance of intercultural dialogue as an entry point for policies that promote cultural diversity, UNESCO has started integrating such dialogue in the analytical framework of the Lens and intends to develop it further. The CDPL also makes a useful contribution to the implementation of the UN's human-rights-based approach to programming, focusing on cultural diversity and intercultural dialogue, including cultural rights.

The CDPL builds on ten main topics, each of which is further divided into a series of sub-topics that are adaptable to the development of appropriate lenses. The main topics include:

1. Understanding the social, economic, political and legal background
2. Access for and inclusion of all
3. Participation of all
4. Linguistic diversity, with a special focus on mother tongue
5. Safeguarding of cultural and natural heritage
6. Promotion of cultural industries, goods and services
7. Promotion of intercultural dialogue and cultural pluralism
8. Interactions between modern science and traditional knowledge
9. Exchange and cooperation
10. Other.

Each of these topics refers to key questions that each decision-maker should have in mind when elaborating a programming activity. The general matrix can then be articulated across thematic lenses according to needs.

Figure 7.1 Cultural Diversity Programming Lens (CDPL) general framework

	Themes	Key questions	Sub-themes

1	Social, economic, political and legal environment
	
	Ref.:
	UDCD: 4,5,6,7,8,9
	MLAP: 2, 4, 12, 13, 15, 16, 18
		Is a detailed socio-economic analysis in the target area available?
		
		How can the legal environment affect the implementation and outcomes of the programme?
			• Collecting disaggregated data (sex, age group, family situation, education, income, ethnicity, race, religion, sexual preferences, political affiliations)
			• Mapping and visualizing data using GIS
			• Identification of culturally-related international instruments which can influence the programme design or be promoted through the activities
			• Influence of the national legal system (laws on culture, cultural industries, intellectual property rights, socially-marginalized and minority groups, mobility, specifically for artists, etc.)
			• Advocacy for cultural rights
			  - Right not to be discriminated on the basis of race, colour, sex, language, religion, political or other opinion, ethnicity, national or social origin, birth, HIV and AIDS or other health conditions and disabilities
			  - Freedom of expression, thought, religion, media pluralism, and multilingualism
			  - Right to choose the kind of education for your children
			  - Right to participate freely in the cultural life of the community

2	Access and inclusion of all Ref.: UDCD: 2, 6, 8, 9 MLAP: 3, 10, 16, 17	Is the programme really accessible to all? Are the materials used and produced during the programme usable by all?	• Inclusion of persons or groups from diverse cultural backgrounds: ethnicity, religion, social group, sex, age, etc • Physical, economic, time-sensitive, legal and social accessibility to the programme • Content of materials linguistically and culturally-appropriate for all target groups • Formats and dissemination methods adapted to various levels of literacy and lifestyles
3	Participation of all Ref.: UDCD: 2 MLAP: 3, 19	Do stakeholders and interest groups from diverse backgrounds truly participate in the programme design and implementation? Does participation really contribute to empowerment and capacity-building among diverse cultural groups?	• Disaggregated data help identify cultural groups • Knowledge of local pressure groups and power structure
4	Linguistic diversity with special focus on the mother tongue Ref.: UDCD: 5, 6 MLAP: 5, 6, 10	How will the programme influence linguistic diversity? How will the programme increase (or decrease) access to resources and services in people's mother tongue?	• Expression in the greatest number of languages • Cultural creation in the greatest number of languages • Dissemination of programme documents, outputs and information in the greatest number of languages and understood by all stakeholders • Content and materials for both formal and informal education and relevant information are produced or translated in the reader's mother-tongue

	Themes	Key questions	Sub-themes
5	Safeguarding cultural and natural heritage Ref.: UDCD: 7 MLAP: 5, 13, 14	How can the programme encourage the safeguarding of cultural and natural heritage? How can the programme raise awareness and increase visibility of the heritage by utilizing its strengths?	• Assessment of cultural and natural heritage affected by the programme: identification, documentation, mapping, archiving, display of tangible and intangible assets • Revitalization of cultural and natural heritage: preservation, conservation, and protection, restoration and revitalization • Education of heritage professionals and civil society • Monitoring mechanisms on the use of cultural and natural resources through the programme • Use of heritage and cultural expressions as information platform and educational tools • Use of heritage and cultural expressions as a tool for development • Use of heritage and cultural expressions as a tool for peace and dialogue
6	Promotion of cultural industries and cultural goods and services Ref.: UDCD: 8, 9, 10 MLAP: 12, 15, 16, 17	How can the programme promote cultural industries and cultural goods? How can the programme raise awareness and increase visibility of the cultural industries by utilizing their strengths?	• Improvement of the production, dissemination, and exchange of diversified cultural products and services • Activities fostering creativity and diversity through recognition and protection of artists and authors' rights and cultural works • Improvement of the dissemination and exchange of diversified cultural products and services • Support in the emergence and consolidation of cultural industries and markets • Use of crafts, performing arts and other art forms as information platform and educational tools. • Use of crafts, performing arts and other art forms as therapeutic tools

7	Promotion of intercultural dialogue and cultural pluralism
	
	Ref.:
	UDCD: 1, 12
	MLAP: 2, 7, 18
		How does the programme integrate and reinforce intercultural dialogue?
		
		How does it recognize the positive value of a culturally diverse society and promote cultural pluralism?
			• The programme provides space for exchanging different perspectives on the issue and objectives of the intervention between people of different cultural groups (gender, ethnic, age/generation, religious, etc.)
			• The programme identify mediation/ conflict resolution mechanism within the implementation of the project and as its result
			• Programme includes activities to strengthen appreciation and respect of cultural diversity:
			  - Awareness-raising, advocacy, and research
			  - Educational and informational components
			  - Forum for dialogue

8	Interactions between modern science and traditional knowledge
	
	Ref.:
	UDCD: 8, 9, 10
	MLAP: 3, 8,
		Does the programme increase the opportunities to foster exchange and synergies between traditional and modern pedagogies, methods and knowledge?
		
		Does the programme protect traditional knowledge?
			• Exchanges and cooperation between traditional and modern experts and practitioners
			• Creating synergies between tradition and modernity
			  - Integration of traditional facets into the programme to build ownership
			  - Use of modern technologies as a transmission medium for indigenous knowledge
			• Legal protection of traditional knowledge
			• Maintaining a healthy balance between tradition and modernity

9	Exchange and cooperation Ref.: UDCD: 7, 10, 11, 12 MLAP: 2, 3, 9, 10, 11, 17, 19	How will the programme reinforce cooperation at local, national, and international level and increase opportunities for exchanges?	• Promotion of intergenerational and intercultural dialogue • Development of links between marginalized groups, technical experts, public sector, private sector, civil society, research institutions, etc. • Cooperation and exchanges in the development of necessary infrastructures and skills (e.g. technological/technical transfer) • Measures to counter the digital divide
10	Others	How will other cultural factors affect the programme?	

UDCD: Articles of the 2001 *Universal Declaration on Cultural Diversity*
MLAP: Main Lines of an Action Plan for the Implementation of the *Universal Declaration on Cultural Diversity*

The general framework of the CDPL is now being adapted
for use in the context of Joint UN Programming in 'Delivering
as One' pilot countries.

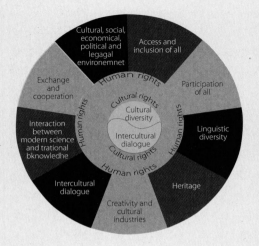

A beach in Mauritania

References and websites

Background documents and UNESCO Sources

Brosius, P. 2007. Cultural diversity and conservation. Background paper.

Cerda, J. 2007. Cultural diversity in a changing climate. Background paper.

Galla, A. 2007. Cultural diversity in human development. Background paper.

Guigané, J.-P. 2007. The human factor in development policies. Contribution to the second meeting of the Advisory Committee of Experts (UNESCO Venice Office, 2-3 April 2007)

Lamont, M. and Small, M. 2007. Cultural diversity and poverty eradication. Background paper.

Matsuura, K. 2008. Traditional knowledge in global policies and practice for education, science and culture. United Nations University.

Odora-Hoppers, C. 2007. Cultural diversity, traditions and modernities: complexities and opportunities in the 21st century. Background paper.

Regenvanu, R. 2007. Cultural pluralism and development policies. Contribution to the UNESCO International Meeting of Experts on 'Mainstreaming Principles of Intercultural Dialogue and Cultural Diversity' (UNESCO Headquarters, 21-23 May 2008)

Tillman, H. and Salas, M. A. 2007. Cultural diversity: A key component of sustainability. Background paper.

Toledo, V. M. 2007. Bio-cultural diversity and the search for a sustainable society. Background paper.

Tresilian, D. 2006. *Poverty Alleviation and Community-Based Tourism: Experiences from Central and South Asia*. Paris, UNESCO. http://unesdocdev.unesco.org/images/0017/001798/179864eo.pdf

UNESCO. 2009. *Statut de la Pauvreté dans l'agenda des droits de l'homme: cas de l'Afrique de l'Ouest* (forthcoming).

—. 2008a. *Building National Capacities for Research and Policy Analysis: Summary of the Findings and Recommendations of the Selected Research Projects*. Paris, UNESCO. http://unesdoc.unesco.org/images/0016/001609/160989E.pdf

—. 2008b. *Links between Biological and Cultural Diversity: Concepts, Methods and Experiences. Report of an International Workshop*. Paris, UNESCO. http://unesdoc.unesco.org/images/0015/001592/159255E.pdf

—. 2008c. *Madrid Action Plan for Biosphere Reserves (2008–2013)*. Paris, UNESCO. http://unesdoc.unesco.org/images/0016/001633/163301e.pdf

—. 2005. *Convention on the Protection and Promotion of the Diversity of Cultural Expressions*. Paris, UNESCO. http://unesdoc.unesco.org/images/0014/001429/142919e.pdf

—. 2003. *Convention on the Safeguarding of Intangible Cultural Heritage*. Paris, UNESCO. http://unesdoc.unesco.org/images/0013/001325/132540e.pdf

—. 2001. *Universal Declaration on Cultural Diversity*. Paris, UNESCO. http://unesdoc.unesco.org/images/0012/001271/127160m.pdf

—. 2000. *Change in Continuity: Concepts and Tools for a Cultural Approach to Development*. Paris, UNESCO.

—. 1996. *Biosphere Reserves: The Seville Strategy and the Statutory Framework of the World Network*. Paris, UNESCO. http://unesdoc.unesco.org/images/0010/001038/103849e.pdf

—. 1982. *Final Report*. World Conference on Cultural Policies (Mondiacult), Mexico City, 26 July–6 August. Paris, UNESCO. http://unesdoc.unesco.org/images/0005/000525/052505eo.pdf

—. 1972. *Convention Concerning the Protection of the World Cultural and Natural Heritage [= World Heritage Convention]*. http://whc.unesco.org/archive/convention-en.pdf

UNESCO and United Nations Environmental Programme (UNEP). 2002. High Level Round Table on Cultural Diversity and Biodiversity for Sustainable Development. World Summit on Sustainable Development (Johannesburg, 3 September 2002). http://portal.unesco.org/culture/en/ev.php-URL_ID=13658&URL_DO=DO_TOPIC&URL_SECTION=201.html

United Nations. 2008. *Development Group Guidelines on Indigenous Peoples' Issues*. New York, United Nations. http://www2.ohchr.org/english/issues/indigenous/docs/guidelines.pdf

—. 2005. *2005 World Summit Outcome*. http://daccessdds.un.org/doc/UNDOC/GEN/N05/487/60/PDF/N0548760.pdf?OpenElement

—. 2000. *United Nations Millennium Declaration*. http://www.un.org/millennium/declaration/ares552e.htm

—. 1986. *Declaration on the Right to Development*. http://www.un.org/documents/ga/res/41/a41r128.htm

Wisner, B. 2007. Climate change and cultural diversity: reflections from the bottom up and from the top down. Background paper.

World Heritage Committee. 1992. Report of the Sixteenth Session (Santa Fe, 7-14 December 1992)

Websites

Bhutan Gross Happiness Index: http://www.grossnationalhappiness.com

Convention on Biological Diversity (CBD): http://www.cbd.int *and* http://www.cbd.int/doc/legal/cbd-un-en.pdf

Cultural Diversity Programming Lens: http://www.unescobkk.org/culture/our-projects/empowerment-of-the-culture-profession/cultural-diversity-lens

European Fair Trade Association (EFTA): http://www.european-fair-trade-association.org

Fair Trade Labelling Organizations International (FLO): http://www.fairtrade.net

Food and Agriculture Organization of the United Nations (FAO): http://www.fao.org

Global Diversity Foundation: http://www.globaldiversity.org.uk

Ha Long Bay Ecomuseum: http://www.halongbay.net.vn/index.asp?lan=en *and* http://www.unesco.org/archives/multimedia/?s=films_details&id_page=33&id_film=146

Integrated Approaches to Participatory Development (IAPAD): http://www.iapad.org

International Alliance of the Indigenous and Tribal Peoples of the Tropical Forest (IAIPTF): http://www.international-alliance.org

International Conference on Population and Development (ICPD): http://www.un.org/popin/icpd2.htm

International Indigenous Forum on Biodiversity (IIFB): http://www.iifb.net

International Organization for Migration (IOM): http://www.iom.int

International Union for Conservation of Nature (IUCN): http://www.iucn.org

International Union of Forest Research (IUFRO): http://www.iufro.org

Inuit Circumpolar Council: http://www.inuit.org

LINKS Programme: http://portal.unesco.org/science/en/ev.php-URL_ID=1945&URL_DO=DO_TOPIC&URL_SECTION=201.html

Man and the Biosphere Programme (MAB): http://portal.unesco.org/science/en/ev.php-URL_ID=6393&URL_DO=DO_TOPIC&URL_SECTION=201.html

MDG Achievement Fund: http://www.undp.org/mdgf

Millennium Development Goals (MDGs): http://www.un.org/millenniumgoals

Millennium Ecosystem Assessment (MEA): http://www.millenniumassessment.org

National Adaptation Programme of Action (NAPAs): http://unfccc.int/national_reports/napa/items/2719.php

Network of European Worldshops (NEWS!): http://www.worldshops.org

Participatory GIS Network: http://www.iapad.org/participatory_gis.htm

Resilience Alliance: http://www.resalliance.org

Sarayacu Association: http://www.rainforestinfo.org.au/projects/rsdg/sarayacu.htm

Tebtebba: http://www.tebtebba.org

Terralingua: http://www.terralingua.org

UNESCO-MAB Biosphere Reserve Directory: http://www.unesco.org/mabdb/bios1-2.htm

UNESCO, Biosphere Reserves: http://portal.unesco.org/science/en/ev.php-URL_ID=4793&URL_DO=DO_TOPIC&URL_SECTION=201.html

UNESCO, Anti-poverty: http://portal.unesco.org/shs/en/ev.php-URL_ID=3905&URL_DO=DO_TOPIC&URL_SECTION=201.html

UNESCO, Biodiversity: http://portal.unesco.org/science/en/ev.php-URL_ID=4794&URL_DO=DO_TOPIC&URL_SECTION=201.html

UNESCO, Human Rights, HIV and AIDS: http://portal.unesco.org/en/ev.php-URL_ID=33525&URL_DO=DO_TOPIC&URL_SECTION=201.html

UNESCO, Small Island Developing States: http://www.unescobkk.org/education/esd/about-esd/esd-briefing/small-island-developing-states

United Nations Climate Change Conference — Nairobi 2006: http://unfccc.int/meetings/cop_12/items/3754.php

United Nations Conference on Trade and Development (UNCTAD): http://www.unctad.org

United Nations High Commissioner for Refugees (UNHCR): http://www.unhcr.org

United Nations Permanent Forum on Indigenous Issues (UNPFII): http://www.un.org/esa/socdev/unpfii

United Nations Population Fund (UNFPA): http://www.unfpa.org/public

United Nations, Delivering as One: http://www.undg.org/?P=7

Vietnam Museum of Ethnology: http://www.vme.org.vn

Voices of the Poor: http://web.worldbank.org/WBSITE/EXTERNAL/TOPICS/EXTPOVERTY/0,,contentMDK:20622514~menuPK:336998~pagePK:148956~piPK:216618~theSitePK:336992,00.html

World Fair Trade Organization (WFTO): http://www.wfto.com

World Health Organization (WHO): http://www.who.int

World Summit on Sustainable Development (Johannesburg, 2002): http://www.un.org/jsummit

References

Agazzi, E. 2002. La pauvreté au regard de la dignité humaine. *1ère Journée de la Philosophie à l'UNESCO.* http://portal.unesco.org/shs/en/files/5967/10918929981Agazzi.pdf/Agazzi.pdf

Anderson, K. M. 2006. *Tending the Wild: Native American Knowledge and the Management of California's Natural Resources.* Berkeley, Calif., University of California Press.

Appadurai, A. 2004. The capacity to aspire: Culture and the terms of recognition. V. Rao and M. Walton (eds.), *Culture and Public Action.* Stanford, Calif., Stanford University Press.

Arrow, K. 1962. The economic implications of learning-by-doing', *Review of Economic Studies,* Vol. 29, pp. 155–73.

Atkinson, A. B. 1987. On the measurement of poverty. *Econometrica,* Vol. 55, No. 4, pp. 749–64.

Barrau, J. 1962. *An Ethnobotanical Guide for Anthropological Research in Malayo-Oceania.* Paris, UNESCO.

Barrera-Bassols, N. and Zinck, J. A. 2003. Ethnopedology: a worldwide view on the soil knowledge of local people. *Geoderma,* Vol. 111, No. 3–4, pp. 171–95.

Bruto da Costa, A. 2008. Poverty and human rights. UNESCO (ed.), *Building National Capacities for Research and Policy Analysis: Summary of the Findings and Recommendations of the Selected Research Projects.* Paris, UNESCO, pp. 31–46. http://unesdoc.unesco.org/images/0016/001609/160989E.pdf

Butzer, K. W. 1971. *Environment and Archeology: An Ecological Approach to Prehistory.* London, Methuen.

Cardoso, F. H. and Faletto, E. 1979. *Dependency and Development in Latin America.* Translated by M. Mattingly Urquidi. Berkeley, Calif., University of California Press.

Convention on Biological Diversity (CBD). 2008. *Gincana 6: Towards the Nagoya Biodiversity Summit*. Montreal, CBD. http://www.cbd.int/doc/publications/cbd-gincana-06-en.pdf

Convention on Biological Diversity (CBD). 1993. *Convention on Biological Diversity*. Montreal, CBD. http://www.cbd.int/doc/legal/cbd-un-en.pdf

Cruz, A. M., Steinberg, L. J., Vetere Arellano, A. L., Nordvik, J.-P. and Pisano, F. 2004. State of the Art in Natech Risk Management. Brussels, DG Joint Research Centre, European Commission and United Nations International Strategy for Disaster Reduction. http://www.unisdr.org/preventionweb/files/2631_FinalNatechStateofthe20Artcorrected.pdf

Descola, P. 2005. *Par-delà Nature et Culture*. Paris, Gallimard.

Deutsch, K. W. 1961. Social mobilization and political development. *American Political Science Review*, Vol. 55, pp. 634–47.

Diamond, J. 2005. *Collapse: How Societies Choose to Fail or Succeed*. New York, Viking Press.

—. 1995. Easter Island's end. *Discover Magazine*, Vol. 16, No. 8 (August), pp. 62–69.

Domar, E. 1946. Capital expansion, rate of growth and employment. *Econometrica*, Vol. 14, pp. 137–47.

Esteva, G. 1991. Development. W. Sachs (ed.), *The Development Dictionary: A Guide to Knowledge as Power*. London, Zed Books, pp. 6–25.

Geertz, C. 1973. *The Interpretation of Cultures: Selected Essays*. New York, Basic Books.

Gould, H. 2007. What's culture got to do with HIV and AIDS? *Findings* No. 7 Healthlink Worldwide, February. http://www.healthlink.org.uk/PDFs/findings7_hiv_culture.pdf

Harragin, S. 2004. Relief and an understanding of local knowledge: the case of southern Sudan. V. Rao and M. Walton (eds.), *Culture and Public Action*. Stanford, Calif., Stanford University Press.

Harrison, L. E. 1985. *Underdevelopment is a State of Mind: The Latin American Case*. Lanham, Md., University Press of America.

Harrison, L. E. and Huntington, S. P. (eds.). 2000. *Culture Matters: How Values Shape Human Progress*. New York, Basic Books.

Harrod, R. F. 1939. An essay in dynamic theory. *Economic Journal*, Vol. 49, No. 193, pp. 14–33. http://www.usp.br/feaecon/media/fck/File/P2_Harrod_Essay_Dynamic_Theory.pdf

Hartmann, E. 2003. *Strategic Scarcity: The Origins and Impact of Environmental Conflict Ideas*. PhD Thesis, Development Studies, London School of Economics.

—. 2002. Degradation narratives: over-simplifying the link between population, poverty and the environment. *IHDP Update: Newsletter of the International Human Dimensions Program on Global Environmental Change*, No. 4, pp. 6–8. http://www.ihdp.uni-bonn.de/html/publications/update/update02_04/IHDPUpdate02_04_Hartmann.htm

—. 1998. Population, environment and security: a new trinity. *Environment and Urbanization*, Vol. 10, No. 2, pp. 113–27.

Hasan, Z. 2006. Sustainable development from an Islamic Perspective: meaning implications and policy concerns. MPRA Paper No. 2784. http://mpra.ub.uni-muenchen.de/2784/1/MPRA_paper_2784.pdf

Inkeles, A. and Smith, D. H. 1974. *Becoming Modern: Individual Change in Six Developing Countries*. Cambridge, Mass., Harvard University Press.

Intergovernmental Panel on Climate Change (IPCC). 2007. *Climate Change 2007: Impacts, Adaptation and Vulnerability*. Contribution of Working Group II to the Fourth Assessment Report (AR4) of the Intergovernmental Panel on Climate Change. Cambridge, Cambridge University Press. http://www.ipcc.ch/publications_and_data/publications_ipcc_fourth_assessment_report_wg2_report_impacts_adaptation_and_vulnerability.htm

International Society of Ethnobiology (ISE). 1988. *Declaration of Belem*. First International Congress of Ethnobiology. July. http://ise.arts.ubc.ca/_common/docs/DeclarationofBelem.pdf

Ishizawa, J. 2004. Cosmovisions and environmental governance: The case of in situ conservation of native cultivated plants and their wild relatives in Peru. Paper presented to the international conference 'Bridging Scales and Epistemologies: Linking Local Knowledge with Global Science in Multi-scale Assessments', Alexandria, Egypt, 17–20 March. http://ma.caudillweb.com/documents/bridging/papers/ishizawa.jorge.pdf

Jenkins, S. and Lambert, P. J. 1993. Poverty ordering, poverty gaps and poverty lines. Department of Economics Discussion Paper 93-07. Swansea, Wales, University College of Swansea.

Lamb, H. H. 1995. *Climate, History and the Modern World*. 2nd ed. London, Routledge.

Le Roy Ladurie, E. 1967. *Histoire du climat depuis l'an mil*. Paris, Flammarion. (English translation: *Times of Feast, Times of Famine: A History of Climate Since the Year 1000*. Translated by Barbara Bray. Garden City, N.Y., Doubleday, 1971.)

Lewis, H. T. 1989. Ecological and technological knowledge of fire: Aborigines versus park rangers in northern Australia. *American Anthropologist*, Vol. 91, pp. 940–61.

Lucas, R. E. 1988. On the mechanics of economic development. *Journal of Monetary Economics*, Vol. 22, No. 1, pp. 3–42.

Mathews, S. 2007. UNESCO concept paper for the experts meeting on Development of Minimum Norms for Poverty Reduction Strategy Papers (PRSPs) to Comply with the Human Rights Framework: A Decision-Making Tool for Funding Negotiations, 19–20 March.

Nelson, G. C. 2005. Drivers of ecosystem change: summary chapter. R. M. Hassan, R. Scholes and N. Ash (eds.), *Ecosystems and Human Well-Being: Current State and Trends; Findings of the Condition and Trends Working Group*. (Millennium Ecosystem Assessment Series, Vol. 1). Washington, DC, Island Press, pp. 73–76. http://www.millenniumassessment.org/documents/document.272.aspx.pdf

Newman, L. F. (ed.). 1990. *Hunger in History: Food Shortage, Poverty and Deprivation*. Oxford, Blackwell.

Ngai, P. and Koehn, P. 2005. Organizational communication and globally displaced perimeter populations: a neglected challenge for intercultural-communication training. G. Cheney and G. Barnett (eds.), *International and Multicultural Organizational Communication*. Cresskill, N.J., Hampton Press.

Nussbaum, M. 2003. *Beyond the Social Contract: Toward Global Justice*. The Tanner Lectures on Human Values. http://www.tannerlectures.utah.edu/lectures/documents/volume24/nussbaum_2003.pdf

Obuljen, N. 2002. Community cultural development, cultural policy networks and Culturelink. Don Adams and A. Goldbard (eds.), *Community, Culture and Globalization*. New York, The Rockefeller Foundation, pp. 211–23. http://arlenegoldbard.com/wp-content/uploads/2007/11/ccg_chapter_12.pdf

Office of the United Nations High Commissioner for Human Rights (OHCHR). 2004. *Human Rights and Poverty Reduction: A Conceptual Framework*. New York, United Nations. http://www2.ohchr.org/english/issues/poverty/docs/povertyE.pdf

Orlove, B. J. 2005. Human adaptation to climate change: A review of three historical cases and some general perspectives. *Environmental Science and Policy*, Vol. 8, No. 6, pp. 589–600.

Pogge, T. (ed.). 2007. *Freedom from Poverty as a Human Right: Who Owes What to the Very Poor?* New York, Oxford University Press.

Pogge, T. 2002. World Poverty and Human Rights: Cosmopolitan Responsibilities and Reforms. Cambridge, Polity.

Posey, D. A. (ed.). 1999. *Cultural and Spiritual Values of Biodiversity: A Complementary Contribution to the Global Biodiversity Assessment*. London, Intermediate Technology Publications for the United Nations Environment Programme (UNEP).

Rahnema, M. 1997. Development and people's immune system: The story of another variety of AIDS. M. Rahnema and V. Bawtree (eds.), *The Post-Development Reader*, London, Zed Books, pp. 377–404.

Post, J.D. 1977. *The Last Great Subsistence Crisis in the Western World*. Baltimore, Johns Hopkins University Press.

Richards, P. 1983. Ecological change and the politics of African land use. *African Studies Review*, Vol. 26, pp. 1–72.

Riddell, R. 2004. Approaches to poverty: a note from the 'development' perspective. Paper presented at 'Poverty: The Relevance of Human Rights to Poverty Reduction', International Council on Human Rights Policy, Geneva, 24–25 November. http://www.ichrp.org/files/papers/144/121_Riddell.pdf

Romer, P. 1990. Endogenous technological change. *Journal of Political Economy*, Vol. 98, No. 5, Pt. 2, pp. S71–S102. http://artsci.wustl.edu/~econ502/Romer.pdf

Rosen, S. A. 2006. The tyranny of texts: a rebellion against the primacy of written in defining archaeological agendas. A. M. Maeir and P. de Miroschedji (eds.), *"I Will Speak the Riddles of Ancient Times": Archaeological and Historical Studies in Honor of Amihai Mazar on the Occasion of His Sixtieth Birthday*, Vol. 2. Winona Lake, Ind., Eisenbrauns.

Rostow, W. W. 1960. *The Stages of Economic Growth: A Non-Communist Manifesto*. Cambridge, Cambridge University Press.

Rotberg, R. I. and Rabb, T. K. (eds.). 1983. *Hunger and History: The Impact of Changing Food Production and Consumption Patterns on Society*. Cambridge, Cambridge University Press.

Roué, M. and Nakashima, D. 2002. Indigenous knowledge, peoples and sustainable practice. P. Timmerman (ed.), *Social and Economic Dimensions of Global Environmental Change* (Vol. 5 of T. Munn [ed.], *Encyclopedia of Global Environmental Change*). Chichester, Wiley, pp. 314–24. http://portal.unesco.org/science/en/files/3519/10849731741IK_People/IK_People

Ruddle, K. and Johannes, R. E. (eds.). 1985. *The Traditional Knowledge and Management of Coastal Systems in Asia and the Pacific*. Jakarta, UNESCO.

Ruggieri Laderchi, C., Saith, R. and Stewart, F. 2003. Does it matter that we do not agree on the fefinition of poverty? A comparison of four approaches. *Oxford Development Studies*, Vol. 31, No. 3, pp. 243–74. http://www3.qeh.ox.ac.uk/pdf/qehwp/qehwps107.pdf

Sall, A. 2002. Pauvreté et sécurité humaine dans des environnements africains. Quelques reflexions et repères pour l'action. P. Sané (ed.), *La Pauvreté, une fatalité? Promouvoir l'autonomie et la sécurité humaine des groupes défavorisés. Bénin — Burkina Faso — Mali — Niger*. Paris, UNESCO.

Samoff, J. and Carrol, B. 2003. *From Manpower Planning to the Knowledge Era: World Bank Policies on Higher Education in Africa*. UNESCO Forum Occasional Paper No. 2. Paris, UNESCO. http://unesdoc.unesco.org/images/0013/001347/134782eo.pdf

Scott, J. C. 1999. *Seeing Like A State: How Certain Schemes to Improve the Human Condition Have Failed*. New Haven, Conn., Yale University Press.

Shiva, V. 2005. *Globalization's New Wars: Seed, Water and Life Forms*. New Delhi, Women Unlimited.

Sen, A. 2000. Culture and development. Keynote speech at the World Bank Tokyo Meeting, 13 December. http://info.worldbank.org/etools/docs/voddocs/354/688/sen_tokyo.pdf

—. 1999. *Development as Freedom*. New York, Random House.

—. 1987. *Commodities and Capabilities*. New Delhi, Oxford University Press.

—. 1976. Poverty: An ordinal approach to measurement. *Econometrica*, Vol. 44, pp. 219–31.

Solow, R. 1957. Technical change and the aggregate production function. *Review of Economics and Statistics*, Vol. 39, No. 3, pp. 312–20.

Spicker, P., Alvarez Leguizamon, S. and Gordon, D. 2007. *Poverty: An International Glossary*. 2nd ed. London, Zed Books.

Stiglitz, J., Sen, A. and Fitoussi, J.P. 2009. Report by the Commission on the Measurement of Economic Performance and Social Porgress. Paris, September 2009. http://www.stiglitz-sen-fitoussi.fr/documents/rapport_anglais.pdf

Swidler, A. 2007. Syncretism and subversion in AIDS governance: how locals cope with global demands. N. K. Poku, A. Whiteside and B. Sandkjaer (eds.), *AIDS and Governance*. Aldershot, Ashgate.

Tauli-Corpuz, V. 2008. *The Concept of Indigenous Peoples' Self-determined Development or Development with Identity and Culture: Challenges and Trajectories.* Baguio City, Philippines, Tebtebba Foundation. http://portal.unesco.org/culture/fr/files/37745/12197591975Concept_paper_Indigenous_Peoples__Development_with_Identity.pdf/Concept%2Bpaper%2BIndigenous%2BPeoples%2B%2BDevelopment%2Bwith%2BIdentity.pdf

Tevoedjre, A. 1990. Pauvreté, progrès et culture dans le contexte de l'Afrique et dans la perspective du développement endogène et centré sur l'homme. P.-M. Henry (ed.), *Pauvreté, progrès et développement.* Paris, l'Harmattan/UNESCO, pp. 245–53. http://unesdoc.unesco.org/images/0007/000733/073398fb.pdf

Throsby, D. 2008. Culture in sustainable development: Insights for the future implementation of art. 13 [of the *Convention on the Protection and Promotion of the Diversity of Cultural Expressions*]. http://unesdoc.unesco.org/images/0015/001572/157287E.pdf

Toledo, V. M. 2002. Ethnoecology: A conceptual framework for the study of indigenous knowledge of nature. J. R. Stepp, F. S. Wyndham, and R. K. Zarger (eds.), *Ethnobiology and Biocultural Diversity: Proceedings of the Seventh International Congress of Ethnobiology.* Bristol, Vt., International Society of Ethnobiology (ISE).

—. 1992. What is ethnoecology? origins, scope and implications of a rising discipline. *Etnoecologica*, Vol. 1, pp. 5–21.

UN Committee on Social, Economic and Cultural Rights (UNCSEC). 2001. Substantive Issues Arising in the Implementation of the International Covenant on Economic, Social and Cultural Rights: Poverty and the International Covenant on Economic, Social and Cultural Rights. Statement adopted by the CSEC on 4 May. http://www.unhchr.ch/tbs/doc.nsf/0/518e88bfb89822c9c1256a4e004df048?Opendocument

UN World Commission on Environment and Development (WCED). 1987. *Our Common Future* [= Bruntland Report]. New York, United Nations. http://www.un-documents.net/wced-ocf.htm *or* http://www.worldinbalance.net/agreements/1987-brundtland.html

United Nations Development Programme (UNDP). 2004. *Human Development Report 2004: Cultural Liberty in Today's World.* New York, UNDP. http://hdr.undp.org/en/media/hdr04_complete.pdf

United Nations Environment Programme (UNEP). 1972. *Report of the United Nations Conference on the Human Environment.* (Stockholm). Nairobi, UNEP. http://www.unep.org/Documents.Multilingual/Default.asp?DocumentID=97

United Nations Framework Convention on Climate Change (UNFCC). 2007. *Report of the Subsidiary Body for Scientific and Technological Advice on its twenty-fifth session, Nairobi, 6–14 November 2006.* FCCC/SBSTA/2006/11. http://unfccc.int/resource/docs/2006/sbsta/eng/11.pdf

United Nations High Commissioner for Refugees (UNHCR). 2008. *Statistical Yearbook 2007: Trends in Displacement, Protection and Solutions.* Geneva, UNHCR. http://www.unhcr.org/4981b19d2.html

United Nations Population Fund (UNFPA). 2004. *Culture Matters: Lessons from a Legacy of Engaging Faith-based Organizations.* New York, UNFPA. http://www.unfpa.org/webdav/site/global/shared/documents/publications/2008/Culture_Matter_II.pdf

Veenhoven, R. 2007. Measures of Gross National Happiness. Presentation at OECD Istanbul World Forum on Statistics, Knowledge and Policy, June. MPRA Paper No. 11280. http://mpra.ub.uni-muenchen.de/11280/1/MPRA_paper_11280.pdf

Wade, A. 2007. Excerpts from his address to the ILC. 96th International Labour Conference, Geneva, International Labour Organization (ILO), 12 June. http://www.ilo.org/global/About_the_ILO/Media_and_public_information/Broadcast_materials/B-rolls/lang--en/docName--WCMS_083037/index.htm

Wallerstein, I. 1974. *The Modern World-System I: Capitalist Agriculture and the Origins of the European World-Economy in the Sixteenth Century.* New York, Academic Press.

Wangui, E. E. 2003. *Links between Gendered Division of Labour and Land Use in Kajiado District, Kenya.* The Land Use Change, Impacts and Dynamics (LUCID) Project Working Paper No. 23. Nairobi, LUCID Project. http://www.lucideastafrica.org/publications/Wangui_LUCID_WP23.pdf

Weber, M. 2002. *The Protestant Ethic and the Spirit of Capitalism* (1905). M. Weber, *The Protestant Ethic and the Spirit of Capitalism, and Other Writings.* Edited and translated by P. Baehr and G. C. Wells. London, Penguin.

Wisner, B. 2004. Assessment of capability and vulnerability. G. Bankoff, G. Frerks and T. Hilhorst (eds.), *Vulnerability: Disasters, Development and People.* London, Earthscan, pp. 183–93.

Wisner, B. and Haghebaert, B. 2006. Fierce friends / friendly enemies: state / civil society relations in disaster risk reduction. Paper presented at the ProVention Consortium Forum 2006, Bangkok, 2–3 February. http://www.proventionconsortium.org/themes/default/pdfs/Forum06/Forum06_Session4_State-CommunityAction.pdf

Wisner, B. and Smucker, T. 2008. Changing household responses to drought in Tharaka, Kenya: persistence, change, and challenge. *Disasters*, Vol. 32, No. 2, pp. 190–215.

Wisner, B., Blaikie, P., Cannon, T. and Davis, I. 2004. *At Risk: Natural Hazards, People's Vulnerability, and Disasters.* 2nd ed. London: Routledge.

World Bank (Social Development Department, Environmentally and Socially Sustainable Development Network), 2006. Cultural Diversity and Delivery of Services: A Major Challenge for Social Inclusion. Report No 36414. Document of the World Bank

World Commission on Culture and Development. 1996. *Our Creative Diversity.* Paris, UNESCO. http://unesdoc.unesco.org/images/0010/001055/105586e.pdf

Young children playing, Alice Springs, Australia

Cultural diversity, human rights and democratic governance

It is argued throughout this report that respect for cultural diversity contributes to the dignity of each individual, group and community. Rights and freedoms are not exercised in a vacuum but are embedded within a social context. All rights and freedoms have a cultural dimension that contributes to their effective exercise. It is precisely this dimension that forms the link between the individual, the community and the group, which grounds universal values within a particular society.

Human rights are universal because they belong to all of humanity. This is the sense intended in the *Universal Declaration of Human Rights* (UN, 1948), which acknowledges that everyone, as a member of society, should exercise all rights 'indispensable for his dignity and the free development of his personality' (Art. 22).

Although sometimes portrayed as challenging to social cohesion, cultural diversity is, on the contrary, an enabler of dialogue and mutual enrichment and thus a source of economic, social, political and cultural creativity. Democratic governance presupposes forms of government and modes of decision-making that take account of the multicultural composition of contemporary societies and their wide variety of beliefs, projects and lifestyles. In promoting a more inclusive form of governance, the management of cultural diversity can turn a societal challenge into a democratic strength and thereby contribute to the establishment of that *culture of human rights and peace* to which UNESCO and the United Nations are committed.

Kutiyattam, a form of sacred theatre from Kerala, India

Cultural diversity, human rights and democratic governance

8.1 Cultural diversity and universally recognized human rights 223

Box 8.1 International case law highlighting cultural aspects of human rights 227

Box 8.2 Individual and collective dimensions of cultural rights 229

8.2 Cultural diversity: A parameter of social cohesion 231

Map 8.1 Government policies on immigration, 2005 231

Box 8.3 The challenges of social cohesion in Africa: from colonial empire to African nationhood 234

8.3 The challenge of cultural diversity for democratic governance 238

Map 8.2 Percentage of political positions in Parliaments held by women, 2007 239

Conclusion 242

Recommendations 242

In focus: Three examples of traditional mechanisms and intangible heritage in the service of democratic governance 243

References and websites 246

A billboard on Suva's main street, Fiji

8.1 Cultural diversity and universally recognized human rights

'No one may invoke cultural diversity to infringe upon human rights guaranteed by international law, nor to limit their scope'. This core provision of the 2001 *Universal Declaration on Cultural Diversity* (Art. 4) underlines the tension that is sometimes confusedly invoked between cultural diversity and the proclamation of universal human rights. This perception of cultural diversity as a possible impediment to universality stems from political and academic circles that tend to view cultural diversity as synonymous with relativism and thus as potentially in contradiction to universal principles. From this perspective, questions arise as to the relevance or legitimacy of accounting for cultural diversity in the implementation of international human rights standards, particularly when cultural diversity is used to sustain discriminatory or harmful practices. The present section argues that such criticisms are based on an assumption of the mutual exclusiveness between cultural diversity and universal human rights. Yet, since human rights emanate from the very fabric of cultures — as recognized by the countries that have become signatories to human rights instruments — universal human rights and cultural diversity cannot be philosophically, morally or legally opposed to one another. On the contrary, cultural diversity and intercultural dialogue can in fact become key levers for strengthening the universal grounding of human rights.

As stated by the 1993 *Vienna Declaration*, the challenge is to promote and protect all rights and fundamental freedoms 'regardless of [the States'] political, economic and cultural systems' (UN, 1993: Art. 5), while bearing in mind 'the significance of national and regional particularities and various historical, cultural and religious backgrounds.'

The cultural dimension of universal rights
The rights and freedoms universally recognized by the world community in the *Universal Declaration of Human Rights* (UN, 1948) are inherent in everyone, regardless of sex, ethnic or social origin, level of education, disabilities, or religious beliefs. In this sense, they are intangible. They are also inalienable since no one can renounce their rights and freedoms even if they should wish to do so, since this would compromise the rights and freedoms of all by virtue of being human. If someone voluntarily wished to accept slavery, this would be at odds with the right of everyone to be born free. Accordingly, no one can invoke slavery as a cultural practice in opposition to the right to freedom. In the same way, there can be no contradiction between the intangibility of human rights and fundamental freedoms and cultural diversity. The statement that cultural diversity constitutes an asset for humanity as a whole and consequently should be safeguarded is not the same as saying that any cultural value, tradition and practice must be preserved as intangible heritage. As shown in chapter 1, cultures have never been fixed and are in a state of perpetual change since they interact with the outside world and are expressed through human beings who themselves change.

The interdependency and indivisibility of human rights provide an interesting common ground for analysis of the relations among all human rights: the identification of one human right is connected to another because of the cultural dimension of all human rights.

Indeed, while civil and political rights and freedoms are sometimes regarded as covering the rights and freedoms that should be given prominence, some point out that the very indivisibility of human rights pleas for greater recognition of the linkages between all categories of rights. While international standards may seem far removed from the recognition of the importance of preserving cultural diversity insofar as it pertains to identities and values, the advancement of human rights in the last decades has begun to bridge this gap, particularly when due consideration has been given to the principles of non-discrimination, equality, gender parity and intercultural dialogue. This is illustrated below by the significant progress made both in the field of civil and political rights and in that of economic and social rights:

- Civil and political rights are essential for the freedom of thought, religion and association, as well as for taking part in decision-making processes that determine the development of one's community, among other things. If these rights, which have an obvious cultural component, are not guaranteed, there can be no political freedom. In addition, the right to vote is contingent on the right to education,

> 'No one may invoke cultural diversity to infringe upon human rights guaranteed by international law, nor to limit their scope'

Highlighting the cultural dimensions of all human rights should be understood as encouraging a sense of ownership of these rights by all, in their diversity

which is the condition upon which the language(s) written on ballot cards and used in political debates can be understood. The clarification of the cultural requisites of these rights and their implications across different cultural settings is crucial. This holds equally of the right to justice (see the European Court of Human Rights [ECHR], case Airey v. Ireland of 9 October 1979), the right to information (see ECHR case Conka v. Belgium of 5 February 2002), and the right to correspondence (see ECHR case Chishti v. Portugal of 2 October 2003). The cultural dimension of civil and political rights is also recognized in a series of other freedoms, such as the freedoms of expression, information and communication developed in Article 19 of the 1966 *International Covenant on Civil and Political Rights*. In this connection, language rights are particularly important since they provide access to a capacity essential to all other rights. This is made quite clear in the Covenant when it states that anyone charged with a criminal offence must be informed 'in a language which he understands of the nature and cause of the charge against him' (UN, 1966a: Art. 14.5) and 'have the free assistance of an interpreter if he cannot understand or speak the language used in court' (Art. 14.3.f).

◐ *African immigrants queue at the port of Lampedusa before being transferred to Sicily, Italy*

■ With respect to economic and social rights, Article 12 of the 1966 *International Covenant on Economic, Social and Cultural Rights* (UN, 1966b) emphasizes the right to enjoy the highest attainable standard of physical and mental health, which also has a cultural dimension. This was clarified when the UN Committee on Economic, Social and Cultural Rights (CESCR) affirmed that this right implies both freedoms and entitlements and that health services (in this case for indigenous people) should be 'culturally appropriate, taking into account traditional preventive care, healing practices and medicines' (CESCR, 2000). The CESCR also called on States to provide resources for indigenous peoples to design, deliver and control those services and offer protection of the vital medicinal plants, animals and minerals necessary to the full enjoyment of the right. Another example concerns the right to safe drinking water, which, in addition to being of sufficient quality, should include services and water facilities that are 'culturally appropriate'.

Highlighting the cultural dimensions of all human rights should in no way be understood as undermining universality but rather as encouraging a sense of ownership of these rights by all, in their diversity. What is needed, as the Fribourg Group underlined in the *Fribourg Declaration on Cultural Rights* (2007), is to take into account 'the cultural dimensions of all human rights in order to enhance universality through diversity and to encourage the appropriation of these rights by all persons, alone or in community with others' (Art. 9d).

Progress in the appropriation of universally recognized human rights is a multifaceted process: it builds on existing human rights treaties and institutions — to which States freely adhere — and takes account of developments in the human rights field, which are grounded in a diversity of experiences and priorities identified worldwide (An-Na'im, 1992, 2002, 2003; Forsythe and McMahon, 2003). Thus, as a common achievement of the international community representing hard-won consensus, the universal grounding of human rights in the social fabric of societies is reinforced by the promotion of cultural diversity and intercultural dialogue, which contribute to the flourishing debate in the international community on human rights. For example, the same principles of human dignity and self-determination that oppose external domination likewise oppose internal domination and advocate an open and evolving democratic governance. From this perspective, it is through dialogue and communication that standards protecting individual human rights and freedoms can be incorporated into a cultural context (An-Na'im, 1992). Thus, human rights do not appear as imposed at the expense of cultural integrity, but rather as being declared from within the cultures in order to fulfil a need (Laclau, 2000). In this sense, cultural diversity has the potential to become a useful instrument for facilitating consensus among different cultural traditions by engaging debate within and across cultures on human rights by virtue of our common humanity, despite possible divergences related to context.

Recognition of cultural diversity grounds the universality of human rights in the realities of our societies by drawing attention to their appropriation by *all* individuals who can identify these rights with a sense of ownership, regardless of language, tradition and location. In the same vein, the fact that these rights and freedoms are meant to be exercised in a wide variety of cultural environments by no means implies that universal norms can be relativized in terms of their application.

Cultural diversity and the effective exercise of human rights

All universal human-rights instruments allow for an application of rights and liberties according to given social and cultural realities, subject to the strict observance of the proclaimed norms and dispositions. As illustrated by some of the international human rights instruments related to gender, child protection, education and health — grounded in the core principles of non-discrimination, equality, justice, pluralism and tolerance — an increasing number of such international instruments make room for the integration of cultural diversity in the effective exercise of human rights:

- The *International Convention on the Elimination of All Forms of Racial Discrimination* (UN, 1965) proclaimed the exercise of human rights and fundamental freedoms in the political, economic, social, cultural or any other field

of public life to be guaranteed without any distinction, exclusion, restriction or preference based on race, colour, descent, or national or ethnic origin.

- The *Convention on the Elimination of All Forms of Discrimination Against Women* (CEDAW; UN, 1979) developed a similar approach regarding women, highlighting the principle of equal treatment of men and women, as well as the recognition, enjoyment or exercise by women, 'irrespective of their marital status, on a basis of equality of men and women, of human rights and fundamental freedoms in the political, economic, social, cultural, civil or any other field' (Art. 1). It became a cornerstone for the implementation of women's rights at school, at work and in healthcare, as well as for the support of women's organizations and their participation in cultural life. CEDAW is the only human-rights instrument that identifies culture and tradition as influential forces shaping gender roles and family relations.

- The *Convention on the Rights of the Child* (UN, 1989) — the most widely ratified of the Conventions — provides a number of recognitions and protections related to children under the guiding principle of the 'best interests of the child' (Art. 3) and State obligations to respect the right of the child to preserve his or her identity and to undertake actions in order to re-establish his or her identity speedily in case of deprivation (Art. 8). In cases of deprivation, the Convention stresses the State obligation to ensure alternative care that 'could include, inter alia, foster placement, *kafalah* of Islamic law, adoption or if necessary placement in suitable institutions for the care of children. When considering solutions, due regard shall be paid to the desirability of continuity in a child's upbringing and to the child's ethnic, religious, cultural and linguistic background' (Art. 20).

- The *Declaration on the Rights of Persons Belonging to National or Ethnic, Religious and Linguistic Minorities* (UN, 1992c),[1] although non-binding, provided a step forward in the debate on the importance of appropriate educational policies aimed at encouraging

An increasing number of international instruments make room for the integration of cultural diversity in the effective exercise of human rights

---

1. Recent emerging international norms relevant to indigenous peoples include: the *Convention Concerning Indigenous and Tribal Peoples in Independent Countries* (ILO, 1989); Art. 29 (c) and (d) and 30 of the *Convention on the Rights of the Child* (1989); Art. 8 (j) of the *Convention on Biological Diversity* (UN, 1992a); *Agenda 21* of UNCED (1992), esp. chap. 26; See also the preamble and Art. 3 of the *United Nations Framework Convention on Climate Change* (UN, 1992b); and Art. 10 (2) (e) of the *International Convention to Combat Desertification in Countries Experiencing Serious Drought and/or Desertification, Particularly in Africa* (UN, 1994).

knowledge of their traditions and customs, history, language and culture 'except where specific practices are in violation of national law and contrary to international standards' (Art. 4.2). With regard to indigenous populations, the 1993 *Vienna Declaration and Programme of Action* affirmed that 'States should, in accordance with international law, take concerted positive steps to ensure respect for all human rights and fundamental freedoms of indigenous people, on the basis of equality and non-discrimination' (UN, 1993: Art. 20). Thus civil and political, economic, cultural and social rights should be put on the same footing. The challenge, then, is to 'treat human rights globally in a fair and equal manner' (Art. 5).

All these universal human-rights instruments mark progressive developments in the concept of cultural diversity, while reaffirming its relation to *all* human rights. In the case of the principle, for example, of the 'best interests of the child' as enshrined in the *Convention on the Rights of the Child* (UN, 1989), while no exception can be tolerated, this principle will be interpreted according to the realities of kinship systems in a particular country, the relations within and between communities, etc.

From these examples it follows that the effective exercise of human rights is to be understood as a step towards equality and the recognition of particularities. By no means can it be said to support the domination, homogenization or 'Westernization' of cultures. Universal human-rights instruments are not a form of imperialism. They represent a dynamic base for respecting human dignity, even while States remain sovereign and have latitude to undertake measures related to cultural diversity.

However, in the implementation of human rights it can be extremely challenging to achieve a balance between States' unconditional commitment to implement and uphold human rights (notably through national and federal laws, judicial decisions or degrees of recognition in national legislation and policies) and the necessary recognition of cultural specificities. Indeed, problems arise when deeply rooted traditions and practices contravene the universal values inherent in human

> *The implementation of universal provisions of international law can be facilitated through appropriate reference to the meaningful cultural context in which rights and freedoms are rooted and appropriated*

rights (human dignity), as may arise in cases of slavery and punishments (e.g. physical mutilation), or in gender relations, religion and the rights of the child.

Where such conflicts arise, cross-cultural initiatives (An-Na'im, 1992), involving NGOs and the UN, have provided intermediary solutions through educational means and alternative arrangements aimed at preserving human dignity. For example, advances have been made regarding female genital mutilation (FGM) in Kenya, Nigeria and Uganda (More, 2005), which neither limit human rights to suit a given culture nor impose external values on a particular culture (see OHCHR et al., 2008). Another example of such conflict resolution concerns Egypt: an alliance of government agencies, civil court judges, women's groups, lawyers and progressive Muslim clerics won a major victory for women's rights in 2000 with the passage of a law that enables a woman to divorce without her husband's consent; this alliance succeeded mainly because it argued its case within the general framework of human rights, while also emphasizing historical aspects of Islam — examples from the Prophet Mohammed's life — that confer equal rights on women. The lesson here is that the implementation of universal provisions of international law can be facilitated through appropriate reference to the meaningful cultural context in which rights and freedoms are rooted and appropriated. The increasing relevance of cultural diversity in international law is confirmed by case law as detailed in Box 8.1.

Cultural rights

Both the *International Covenant on Civil and Political Rights* (UN, 1966a) and the *International Covenant on Economic, Social and Cultural Rights* (UN, 1966b) build on the fundamental proclamations in the *Universal Declaration of Human Rights* that 'All human beings are born free and equal in dignity and rights' (UN, 1948: Art. 1), that 'Everyone is entitled of universal dignity and to all the rights and freedoms, without distinction of any kind such as race, colour, sex, language, religion, political or other opinion, national or social origin, property, birth or other status' (Art. 2), and that 'Everyone has the right freely to participate in the cultural life of the community, to enjoy the arts and to share in scientific advancement and its benefits' (Art. 27).[2]

2. These proclamations are reinforced in the Preamble, which recognizes the importance of a human-rights-based legal framework to maintaining international peace and security, stating that the 'recognition of the inherent dignity and equal and inalienable rights of all members of the human family is the foundation of freedom, justice and peace in the world' (UN, 1948).

Box 8.1	International case law highlighting cultural aspects of human rights

Courts have played an important role in the development of integrated approaches to multiculturalism and have led to the defence of the principles of non-discrimination, inclusion, participation of minorities and promotion of their rights. Courts have the crucial task of integrating universal values with values of diversity and finding ways for individuals to enjoy these rights. Numerous cases have been heard by the different treaty bodies, as well as by national institutions and courts, notably those bearing on the enjoyment of culture in relation to traditional land-use.

Such a landmark case is that of *Lubicon Lake Band v. Canada* (Comm. N°. 167/1984). On behalf of the native Indian community, the Chief claimed a violation of the right of self-determination under Article 1 of the *International Covenant on Civil and Political Rights* (ICCPR; UN, 1966a). The United Nations Human Rights Committee (UNHRC), which is responsible for implementing the Covenant, found that, while it could not deal with cases concerning self-determination (since only *individuals* who are victims of violations of rights under the Covenant can submit claims, and an individual cannot be a victim of a violation of the right of self-determination), many of the claims presented by the applicants raised issues pertaining to the enjoyment of culture by individuals belonging to ethnic, religious or linguistic minorities (UN, 1966a:

Art. 27). The UNHRC has pursued its broad interpretation of 'enjoyment of culture' to include certain traditional use of land.

Other cases have arisen concerning the Sami community and its use of land to breed and herd reindeer in relation to the Swedish and Finnish governments' permitting companies to use the land for logging, mining or forestry, including: *Ivan Kitok v. Sweden*, where the UNHRC confirmed that the economic activity of reindeer husbandry is an essential component of the Sami culture and as such falls under Article 27 of the ICCPR (Comm. N°. 197/1985); the *Länsman* cases against Finland (Comm. N°. 511/1992 and 671/1995); the case of *Anni Äärelä and Jouni Näkkäläjärvi v. Finland*, where more attention was paid to the quality of the land (Comm. N°. 779/1997).

In the case of *Apirana Mahuika et al. v. New Zealand*, the petitioners were New Zealand Maoris who claimed that their rights under Article 27 of the Covenant had been violated in a dispute over fishing rights (UN Doc. CCPR/C/70/D/547/1993 and Comm. N°. 547/1993). In these cases, the UNHRC has employed a dynamic approach to the concept of culture, including economic activities linked to the culture of a community, without confining itself to the protection of traditional economic activities or means of livelihood. For example, the fact that technological innovations are used in such activities (e.g. reindeer herding) does not mean

that Article 27 no longer applies. Rather, as land claims fall under the enjoyment of culture, a close relationship between the two must be demonstrated. Thus, because in the case of *J. G. A. Diergaardt (the late Captain of the Rehoboth Baster Community) et al. v. Namibia* this relationship was not sufficiently demonstrated and the claimants did not prevail (UN Doc. CCPR/C/69/D/760/1997 and Comm. N°. 760/1997).

Other cases have concerned the enjoyment of culture in relation to linguistic rights, such as *Diergaardt v. Namibia*. The Namibian Constitution (1990: Art. 4) speficies that English is the country's sole official language. The claimants complained that the Constitution's prohibition on the use of their own language violated Article 26, which provides equality before the law and non-discrimination on any ground, and Article 27 of the ICCPR. The UNHRC's find that Namibia was indeed in violation of Article 26 confirmed the importance of non-discrimination in relation to cultural — in this case linguistic — diversity. However, the UNHRC's decision was not unanimous on the issues relating to language and cultural diversity: one committee member dissented on the finding of a violation of Article 26 because the use of minority languages had only been limited at the official level; he also stated that giving many tribal languages an official status would be an obstacle to nation-building.

Source: Donders, 2007.

These Covenants draw attention to the question of cultural identities and values: the *International Covenant on Civil and Political Rights*, by stating that no person (belonging to ethnic, religious or linguistic minorities) shall be denied the right to enjoy his or her own culture, to profess and practice his or her own religion or to use his or her own language (UN, 1966a: Art. 27); the *International Covenant on Economic, Social and Cultural Rights*, by proclaiming the right to take part in cultural life and the right to education, the latter of which 'shall be directed to the full development of the human personality and the sense of its dignity' (UN, 1966b: Art. 13), underlining the principle of non-discrimination.

Defining cultural rights is sometimes a complex issue since, as shown above, all human rights have a cultural dimension. Two sides of the debate emerge in legal discussions: whether cultural rights go beyond civil and political rights or whether the adoption of 'cultural rights', once recognized, imply a further need to *accommodate* the different identities and values of minorities (Kymlicka and Norman, 2000; Kukathas, 1992).

Five rights are generally understood as specifically referring to cultural issues, as they appear in the *Universal Declaration of Human Rights* (UN, 1948: Art. 26 and 27) and the two 1966 Covenants (especially

UN, 1966b: Art. 13, 14 and 15). These are: the right to education; the right to participate in cultural life; the right to enjoy the benefits of scientific progress and its implications; the right to benefit from the protection of the moral and material interests resulting from scientific, literary or artistic production of which the person is the author; and the freedom to pursue scientific research and creative activity.

Similar provisions exist in regional human-rights instruments, such as the *American Convention of Human Rights* (OAS, 1969: Art. 26), the *African [Banjul] Charter on Human and Peoples' Rights* (OAU, 1981: Art. 17 and 22), and the *Charter of Fundamental Rights of the European Union* (EU, 2000: Art. 14 and 22). Broader classifications of cultural rights include the right to freedom of expression, the right of parents to choose the kind of education given to their children, not to mention soft international laws adopted by the UN General Assembly (e.g. the 2007 *Declaration on the Rights of Indigenous Peoples*) or by UNESCO (e.g. the 1966 *Declaration of the Principles of International Cultural Cooperation* and the 2001 *Universal Declaration on Cultural Diversity*). Some other instruments, notably the 1976 *Algiers Declaration of the Rights of Peoples* (civil society, including labour unionists and NGOs) and the 1981 *African [Banjul] Charter on Human and Peoples' Rights* (OAU, 1981), recognize other cultural rights — such as the right to respect cultural identity, as well as traditions, languages and cultural heritage in the case of minority populations; the right of a people to its own artistic, historical and cultural wealth; the right of a people not to have an alien culture imposed on it; and the right to the equal enjoyment of the common heritage of humanity (see Levy, 1997).

Academic, judiciary and political circles throughout the world tend to point out that cultural rights are poorly developed in international human-rights law in comparison with civil, political, economic and social rights (see Türk, 1992; Symonides, 2000; Hansen, 2002). The situation is further complicated by the fact that provisions pertaining to cultural rights are scattered across a variety of international instruments, which does not make for consistency or understanding of them as a whole. This situation is somewhat paradoxical since many aspects of rights and obligations relating to tangible and intangible heritage have given rise to a wide range of legal instruments. These instruments

(often elaborated by UNESCO) refer to *all* human rights, seldom singling out cultural rights per se except that of heritage. In the same vein, the *Faro Framework Convention on the Value of Cultural Heritage for Society* (Council of Europe, 2005: Art. 1) recognizes that 'rights relating to cultural heritage are inherent in the right to participate in cultural life, as defined in the Universal Declaration of Human Rights.' The same article refers to 'the role of cultural heritage in the construction of a peaceful and democratic society, and in the processes of sustainable development and the promotion of cultural diversity'. Yet this central role accorded to cultural heritage is not reflected over the whole range of cultural rights as provided for in the *International Covenant on Economic, Social and Cultural Rights* (UN, 1966b).

There are a number of reasons why cultural rights are less developed than other human rights. First, the term 'culture' is elusive and difficult to translate into human rights standards. Where culture is interpreted narrowly, cultural rights include the protection of cultural creations such as works of art, literature and monuments, as well as access to museums, theatres, libraries, etc. If culture is understood as the process of artistic and scientific creation, then cultural rights include the right to freedom of expression, as well as the protection of the producers of cultural products, including copyright. If culture is considered in terms of a specific way of life, the sum of a community's material and spiritual activities and products (*Mexico City Declaration on Cultural Policies*, UNESCO, 1982), then cultural rights comprise the right of self-determination — particularly in the case of a community, including cultural development — and also the rights to maintain and develop one's own culture (Stavenhagen, 2001; Hansen, 2002; Marks, 2003). Regardless, violations of cultural rights are often dramatically lived by the individuals or groups concerned and can lead to social unrest.

The broad compass of cultural rights (as related to both arts and ways of life) poses numerous problems of definition and varying levels of opposability. The problems relating to the opposability, monitoring and verification of cultural rights take many forms, including the following: To whom are cultural rights opposable? Who can guarantee the exercise of such rights? The State? Public or private institutions? Are the guarantors accountable if these rights are violated? Can individuals take responsibility? For instance, once 'the right of everyone to take part in cultural life' is recognized (UN, 1966b: Art. 15.1.a), to whom is it opposable? In addition, if a State wishes to guarantee this right, how can its effectiveness be monitored? Is the State expected to create the conditions conducive to the exercise of such a right? This is implied by Article 15.2, since States Parties to that Covenant are expected to take the necessary steps 'for the conservation, the development and the diffusion of science and culture.' Thus, States have positive obligations in this regard, but they are also expected to refrain from undue interference 'to respect the freedom indispensable for scientific research and creative activity' (Art. 15.3).

Ongoing debate on whether the implementation of cultural rights might create tensions with other human rights, such as the right to equal treatment and non-discrimination, is also bound up with the concern that such rights might be assimilated to collective rights (see Box 8.2).

States often regard cultural rights — unlike civil and political rights — as constituting an objective to be attained progressively. This is patently the case of the *American Convention of Human Rights* (OAS, 1969), which declares that: 'The States Parties undertake to adopt measures […] with a view to achieving progressively […] the full realization of the rights implicit in the economic, social, educational, scientific, and cultural

---

Box 8.2	**Individual and collective dimensions of cultural rights**

Cultural rights can be divided into individual rights, group rights (rights of individuals as part of a community) and collective rights (rights of communities as a whole) (Prott, 1988). While cultural-rights provisions are mostly defined as individual rights, their enjoyment is firmly associated with other individuals and communities. For example, the individual right to participate in cultural life can be enjoyed only by members of a cultural community. Moreover, apart from individually defined cultural rights, such as the rights to freedom of religion, expression and association, communities have started claiming rights, such as the collective right to the protection of cultural identity, the right not to have an alien culture imposed on them, and the right of peoples to their own cultural heritage, as well as to participate in the cultural heritage of humankind.

States have approached cultural rights mainly as individual rights, because the provisions in international human-rights instruments have been defined primarily in individual terms — except the right of self-determination, which, as included in the *International Covenant on Economic, Social and Cultural Rights* and the *International Covenant on Civil and Political Rights* (both Art. 1), is a right of 'all peoples'. States have been anxious about endowing communities as a whole with cultural rights for fear that such

a collective approach might endanger the stability of their society. Despite this anxiety, however, the collective dimension of culture has not been entirely disregarded, as is illustrated by the development of rights of minorities and indigenous peoples. The *Declaration on the Rights of Persons Belonging to National or Ethnic, Religious and Linguistic Minorities* (UN, 1992) contains specific cultural rights for members of minorities, such as rights to enjoy their culture, to use their language and practice their religion (Art. 2), as well as linguistic and educational rights (Art. 4). The Declaration recognizes the collective dimension of these rights. The protection of the cultural, religious, ethnic and linguistic identity of minorities in Article 1, for example, is understood to be a duty of States. And Article 3 refers to the possibility of the collective enjoyment of the rights elaborated in the Declaration. The Declaration also refers to minorities as a whole, especially with regard to the protection of their identity and existence, thereby recognizing minorities as collectivities. However, the provisions referring to minorities as a whole are formulated not as rights for the communities involved but as duties on the part of States. This means that the communities are not the subjects but rather the beneficiaries of these provisions. On the other hand, the UN *Declaration on the Rights of Indigenous Peoples*, adopted by the

General Assembly in September 2007, goes much further in its collective approach. In its Preamble, it affirms that all *peoples* contribute to the diversity of cultures, which constitute the common heritage of humankind. The Declaration contains several collective rights for indigenous peoples, including rights related to non-discrimination, non-assimilation and not being forcibly removed from territory. It also contains several cultural rights, as discussed.

Even though there are collective dimensions to many human rights (e.g. the right of association), it is mainly the individual who is the 'holder' of a right. The collective dimensions of human rights are not to be confused with collective rights, which are 'essential for the integrity, survival and well-being of distinct nations and communities... inseparably linked to cultures, spirituality and worldviews… and also critical to the exercise and enjoyment of the rights of indigenous individuals' (Letter from 40 indigenous peoples' organizations to Tony Blair, September 2004; quoted in Survival International, 2005).

Few human-rights instruments recognize collective rights as such, and they remain at this point difficult to claim and to enforce.

Source: Donders, 2007.

New Jersey City skyline on the Hudson River, US

Houses in Celebes Islands, Toraja, Indonesia

Cultural diversity can serve as a reference point in the implementation of human rights, both for the enjoyment of cultural rights proper and for the observance of all human rights, given their cultural dimensions

without realizing that such a two-tiered approach misses the interrelatedness of all these aspects of human life. Indeed, the full enjoyment of the 'right to education' (UN, 1948: Art. 26) enhances access to hygiene and to work; the full enjoyment of the 'right to share in scientific advancement and its benefits' (Art. 27) enhances access to food and health; and the 'right to participate in the cultural life of the community' (Art. 27) enhances a sense of citizenship and belonging to the common human family. Cultural rights are all the more important as they contribute to self-realization. Hence, they should be seen not as 'supernumerary rights' but rather as *capacities of capacities*, as they have been called, insofar as they contribute to the effective exercise of other human rights, at the heart of which lies our sense of dignity (Meyer-Bisch, 2006).

Moreover, it is worth noting the adoption on 10 December 2008 of the *Optional Protocol to the International Covenant on Economic, Social and Cultural Rights* by the United Nations General Assembly, in the context of the 60th anniversary of the *Universal Declaration of Human Rights*. The entry into force of this Optional Protocol will undoubtedly add a new dimension to international doctrine and case law regarding the effective enjoyment of cultural rights.

standards set forth in the Charter of the Organization of American States as amended by the *Protocol of Buenos Aires'* (Art. 26). But this is equally true, albeit in a more nuanced way, of the *International Covenant on Economic, Social and Cultural Rights* (UN, 1966b): while stipulating that 'Primary education shall be compulsory and available free to all' (Art. 13, 2, a), it refers in the case of secondary and higher education to 'the progressive introduction of free education' (Art. 13, 2, b and c). This is particularly important since States do not always agree as to whether cultural rights are substantive human rights or policy-oriented rights, which do not entail direct and definite obligations.

While the UN and UNESCO have stressed on more than one occasion that all rights are indivisible and interdependent, there remains a tendency to consider the effective exercise of cultural rights to be subordinate to the achievement of other rights related to food, hygiene, health, shelter, labour and decent living,

The ongoing process of discussion and standard-setting concerning cultural diversity could lead to further elucidation or better implementation of human rights, as regional intergovernmental organizations (such as the Organization of African Unity, the European Union, the Council of Europe, the Organization of American States) are taking steps in this direction. Several NGOs (such as Amnesty International, Article 19 and Human Rights Watch) have gradually stressed the importance of the cultural dimension for the full enjoyment of civil and political rights, as well as for economic and social rights — for instance, for the right to decent living conditions and in the struggle against poverty. These developments, coupled with the work of the United Nations Committee on Economic, Social and Cultural Rights (CESCR), can help to make visible the important link between cultural diversity and the implementation of human rights. Indeed, cultural diversity can serve as a reference point in their implementation, both for the enjoyment of cultural rights proper and for the observance of all human rights, given their cultural dimensions.

8.2 Cultural diversity: A parameter of social cohesion

As highlighted throughout this report, cultural diversity represents a key challenge today in light of the increasingly multicultural composition of the social fabric of most countries. This multiculturalism is the result of long-standing, slow and pervasive processes of interaction, influence and syncretism, as well as of more recent increases in migration flows, where developed countries, for the most part, have become host countries to populations from all over the world. This phenomenon has resulted in a variety of immigration policies worldwide, as illustrated by Map 8.1.

Multiculturalism presents opportunities and risks, the latter most often discussed in terms of the looming potential for conflicts. However, it is not the context of cultural diversity that leads to conflict so much as how cultural diversity — including the social processes to which it gives rise — is understood and managed. The source of conflict lies neither in the recognition of multiculturalism nor in its negation; rather, it arises from conceptions that distinguish heterogeneous communities and from the interplay of economic, political or cultural factors with actual situations of domination.

The UNDP's 2004 Human Development Report, *Cultural Liberty in Today's Diverse World*, stresses the need to implement public policies that recognize difference, champion diversity and promote cultural freedoms. Yet this is only possible to the extent that we are fully cognizant of the conflicts that can arise in multicultural societies from the very recognition of diversity. Experience has shown that attempting to reinforce the national fabric by pretending that differences do not exist is not a genuine solution since it often leads to cultural backlashes and conflicts. Confronting the question of difference (with respect to all forms of exclusion, citizenship and values) is the only effective way of living together with our differences.

In the context of increased migration, what has tended to be regarded as an issue *between* different societies is increasingly becoming one *within* societies. It is therefore worth examining the issue of cultural diversity with respect to the challenges it creates for social cohesion. How can we implement culturally pluralistic policies that contribute to stronger dialogue and civic engagement as opposed to withdrawal into radicalized positions and

Map 8.1 Government policies on immigration, 2005

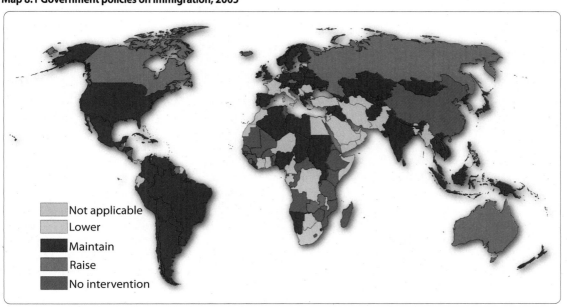

Not applicable
Lower
Maintain
Raise
No intervention

Source: United Nations, Department of Economic and Social Affairs, Population Division (2006), World Population Policies, 2005.

A key dimension of social cohesion policy would be to provide the means for minorities to express themselves, since this could lead to better understanding of their views within majority groups and help them to overcome intolerance, misconceptions and stereotyping

values? Seeking to answer this question would lead us towards new forms of conviviality and solidarity.

The challenges of diversity and multiculturalism

All societies consist — and have always consisted — of a web of diverse influences, interactions and exchanges, a situation that is becoming more complex as globalization takes hold (see chapters 1 and 2). There are no culturally homogenous societies, unless specific policies to this end — contradicting the right to cultural self-determination — have been implemented. Unfortunately, the history of humanity — with its genocides, ethnic cleansing and multiple forms of exclusion or 'ghettoization' — is full of such attempts. Cultural references are often mobilized to exacerbate the manifestation of conflict, as is attested by the inter-confessional riots in 2002 in the Indian State of Gujarat, which resulted in hundreds of fatalities, as well as by the inter-community clashes with Zimbabwean refugees in South Africa in 2007, which challenged the 'Rainbow Nation' model of successful integration.

In host countries, massive urbanization and immigration are also provoking questions related to accommodation and fuelling debates about cultural differences and sustainable social cohesion. Immigrant host countries such as France or Canada (Quebec) have been paying increasing attention to secularism or reasonable accommodation mechanisms and have created high-level commissions for investigating and debating these issues (e.g. the Stasi Commission in France in 2003–2004 and the Bouchard-Taylor Commission in Canada in 2007–2008).

It is worth reiterating that, in the majority of societies, diversity is perceived in terms of social constructs (see chapter 2 on stereotypes). Individuals tend to be categorized in ways that are at variance with how they perceive themselves. In reality, the very context of diversity is changing our concept of community and our sense of identities. Evidence of this is provided by ethnic endogamy (in-marriage) in the US: at the turn of the last century, in-marriage was caste-like for new immigrants from eastern and southern Europe, whereas by 1990 only one-fifth of so-called Caucasian Americans had spouses with identical migration origins (Paginini and Morgan, 1990; Alba, 1995; Putnam, 2007). Issues of perception are crucial here: most controversies surrounding accommodation issues involve significant misunderstandings and distortions between facts and perceptions.

While it may be true that diversity does not spontaneously cohere, particularly since the divisions and violence found in most contemporary societies render the social link even more problematic (Cornu, 2008), we nevertheless need to rethink the ways in which unity may be created, with reference to the idea that a society holds together through trust, particularly trust in a person's word or promise. The problem of *reciprocal trust* between culturally distinct communities has become even more complex due to the polarization of relations between a majority and minorities that feel themselves insufficiently recognized and integrated (as opposed to assimilated) in the social fabric.

The competition between majority and minority groups is a negative assumption that undermines most of social functioning. The scarcity of resources and the challenges of social justice are significant sources of negative attitudes towards others, particularly where the 'zero-sum competition belief' is prevalent. According to this belief, minorities, disadvantaged groups and indigenous populations absorb resources that would otherwise be accessible to majority groups (Vala and Costa-Lopes, 2007). One way of dealing with this negative assumption is to tailor persuasive messages that target these assumptions, including through public campaigns that demystify the perception of minorities and stigmatized people as consumers of scarce resources and as a threat to the economy and the welfare system. This was highlighted at the First EU Roma Summit (2008), a recent governmental and civil society summit on Roma migrants within the EU. Researchers in Canada are conducting studies that document the positive impacts of such persuasive messages on perceptions of immigrants and immigration; they are leading to new pathways, beyond affirmative action and preferential treatment initiatives, for advancing the cause of marginalized communities (Esses et al., 2001).

For example, a key dimension of social cohesion policy would be to provide the means for minorities to express themselves, since this could lead to better understanding of their views within majority groups and help them to overcome intolerance, misconceptions and stereotyping. Platforms and measures should be developed that ensure that minority voices and views can be heard and that debates with members of the communities involved can take place so as to shed light on fears, values and positions and to dispel misunderstandings. This could include the provision of cultural centres or media for minority groups, as well as the simplification of the procedures for setting up associations or for the receipt of subventions. Indeed, 'the challenge […] is to ensure that the values and principles guiding community interactions are geared towards positive outcomes, balancing the interests of the community as a whole, rather than serving alternative power structures which can appropriate the social wealth to the interests of a minority' (Gould, 2001).

Multiculturalism must begin to be seen as an opportunity to strengthen social cohesion, since contemporary societies must in any case manage the cultural differences that form them. This is nothing new, and

history is replete with examples of societies that have attempted to ensure social cohesion and peaceful coexistence. A case in point is the development of nation-states in the 19th century which sought essentially to maintain unity despite the existence of diversity:

At the height of the European nation-state, from around 1870 to 1945, it was widely assumed that all those who lived within a State boundary should assimilate to its predominant ethos, into which successive generations were socialised — via, inter alia, national, sometimes nationalistic, rituals. However, over the last centuries, Europe has also seen other more positive experiences, for instance during certain periods of the history of central and eastern Europe,

◔ *Outside the classes of the Majid Primary School Mahal, Bagh, Kashmir, Pakistan*

which helps us to understand how different cultures and religions could peacefully coexist in mutual tolerance and respect (Council of Europe, 2008).

On a broader scale, however, policies of assimilation during that period led to colonial imperialism, which has left an enduring mark on the societies of the countries of the South (see Box 8.3). Such policies of assimilation were however followed by multicultural policies oriented towards greater acceptance of culturally diverse populations.

Policies of multiculturalism

As a policy framework, multiculturalism has been advanced to ensure equality in diversity and the promotion of tolerance and respect for cultural diversity. In the early 1970s it was implemented primarily in immigration countries, notably Australia, Canada, the US, the UK, Sweden and the Netherlands, with specific objectives and programmatic components. In many countries, these policies have entailed different actions in the following fields:

- *Public 'recognition'*: Support for ethnic minority organizations, facilities and activities (see, for example, the Multicultural Centre Prague in the Czech Republic) and creation of public consultative bodies incorporating such organizations.

- *Education*: Often focused on dress, gender and other issues sensitive to the values of specific ethnic and religious minorities; creation of curricula reflecting the backgrounds of ethnic minority pupils; mother-tongue teaching and language support; the establishment of schools (publicly financed or not).

| Box 8.3 | The challenges of social cohesion in Africa: From colonial empire to African nationhood |

The question of cultural diversity in sub-Saharan Africa is a long-standing problem — one that greatly exercised the colonial administrations, as it did the African elites at the time of independence, the promoters of democracy and most recently the contemporary proponents of cosmopolitanism.

The British and French colonial administrations came face to face with the problem of cultural diversity. How was a colonial law to be applied to such different peoples within the same administrative constituency who had been brought together purely by chance as the result of a geographical boundary drawn on a colonial map? How could one legislate, discern the causes of revolt and set about recruiting collaborators in a population whose members did not speak the same language and were not governed by the same ontological system, the same legal principles and even less by the same founding myths? In other words, how was one to fathom this diversity of culture and then subordinate it to the new colonial norm? How could obedience to any one power ('the civilizer') encompass diversity? The response of French colonialism to this question was that diversity must be assimilated, that all concerned must practice self-denial and become more or less French. British colonization gave the opposite reply: all must be equal but in a state of servitude known as indirect rule. The colonized were allowed to keep their social structures, myths and hierarchies so long as they all served to magnify the British Crown.

African elites also faced the problem of diversity when they threw off the colonial yoke. How was unity achieved during the anti-colonial struggle to be maintained after independence? In other words, diversity came up here against the problem of nation-building. The legacy of colonialism took the form of States rather than nations. How was it possible to unite ethnic groups that often had nothing in common and have them construct a national founding narrative together? How was the problem of living together in harmony to be managed? What was to be the common bond? Some African elites invented political philosophies based, for example, on the notion of the family — such as the African socialism of Julius Nyerere, the former President of Tanzania. Others have replied to the question of diversity by promoting a very vague and rather essentialist notion of African authenticity, where diversity was accounted for by reference to some unchanging essence called 'Africanness'.

Marked by disillusion, economic failure and finally the loss of momentum of the States concerned, the 1990s ushered in — with the help of the new deal in international politics — the so-called democratization phase. The watchword at that time was to rethink the notion of citizenship and the relationship to politics, which were frequently restricted to the narrow confines of the State. Such democratization was a response to the notion of diversity. Multiparty democracy was to be the key to silencing ethnic rationales and creating a space for public discussion. Unfortunately, the response to the question of diversity fell far short of expectations. The multiparty approach, which was supposed to respond to the issue of diversity, simply produced more of the same, despite the fact that genuine diversity is not a mechanical duplication but the emergence of strangeness, otherness and the unexpected into the realm of sameness.

Source: Bidima, 2008.

- *Culturally sensitive practices*: Training and information established within social services, among healthcare providers, police and the courts.

- *Public material*: Such as health promotion campaigns provided in multiple languages.

- *Law*: Cultural exceptions to laws (such as allowing Sikh turbans instead of motorcycle helmets); oaths on sacred books other than the Bible; recognition of other marriage, divorce and inheritance traditions; protection from discrimination and incitement to hatred.

- *Religious accommodation*: Permission and support for the establishment of places of worship, cemeteries and funerary rites; allowance of time-off for worship. Practices of reasonable accommodation and concerted adjustment, while reflecting upon open and rigid secularism and the demand for fairness in harmonizing the practices of public institutions, and the acknowledgment of the importance of 'perception crisis' over identities, are crucial for the understanding of the issue of secularism and the peaceful coexistence of different religions (Bouchard and Taylor, 2008).

- *Food*: Allowance of ritual slaughter; provision of prescribed foods (halal, kosher, vegetarian) in public institutions.

- *Broadcasting and media*: Monitoring of group images to ensure non-discrimination or to avoid stereotypes; provision of media facilities for minority groups (see Australia's Special Broadcasting Service).

Despite progress, multicultural policies have more recently been marked by a number of shortcomings, such as the promotion of the 'feel good' celebration and consumption of ethno-cultural diversity (taught in multicultural school curricula, performed in multicultural festivals, displayed in multicultural media and museums), which mask a widespread failure to address the inequalities faced by immigrant populations (Alibhai-Brown, 2000). 'Multiculturalism' has in practice too often led to an 'ethnization of cultural values', a 'dependency on State largesse in political relations with minorities' and an 'overemphasis on cultural identity to the detriment of overcoming general inequality'

(Alliance of Civilizations, 2006). This in turn has fostered communitarianism or enclosure within the 'cultural tribe' and, by way of reaction, criticism of the multicultural policies alleged to be responsible for such trends.

In response to these issues, new approaches to multiculturalism emerged in the early 1990s, framing debates on cultural diversity within an opposition between 'liberalism' and 'communitarianism', highlighting issues relating to minority rights and their role in modern democracies, the nature of collective rights, the meaning of equality, the relation between equality and impartiality, equality and neutrality when speaking about cultural diversity, the principle of self-determination of minorities, and the appropriateness or universal standards when defining and shaping cultural diversity. The issue of cultural identities has given rise to substantial differences of opinion. Some political theorists defend the perspective of cultural identities as a question of total freedom, arguing, for example, in favour of a separation of State and religion (Taylor, 1994; Kymlicka, 1989, 1995 and 2007; Barry, 2003). In their opinion, the State is not to interfere with the expression of cultural identities, but must also refrain from promoting any specific cultural expression. The State is to observe a degree of neutrality by not supporting a specific model of culture but instead promoting neutral and abstract political principles that should lead to a conception of equality (Tomasi, 2001). Another approach, based on the concept of 'political multiculturalism', argues that the State should always, even implicitly, defend cultural identities and consider intervention in order to correct any imbalance between some identities and others. In this sense, multiculturalism would promote the integration and recognition of minorities into society, allowing for minority rights to be conceived as a compensation for prejudice.

Today governments in several countries face the challenge of finding *post-multiculturalist* models that fuse agendas for promoting national identity and agendas 'celebrating' diversity, fostering social capital and reducing socio-economic inequality. The challenge thereby is to adopt structures and programmes that are broad enough to permit strong group identities to endure within a legal framework that upholds the rights and obligations of citizenship — that is, to find solutions that can successfully combine national and multiple identities (King, 2005).

'Multiculturalism' has in practice too often led to an 'ethnization of cultural values'

In this respect, agendas promoting national identity and limiting immigration (most often perceived as an inherently divisive process) have been introduced in countries such as Germany, the UK, the Netherlands, Singapore and Australia, where governments have established policies and programmes to enable immigrants to acquire knowledge of the host country's cultural norms and values. Successful immigrants are rewarded with ceremonies celebrating the acquisition of national citizenship. In other countries, language requirements for immigrants are being augmented — again through compulsory courses and tests, sometimes even prior to entry — to ensure that newcomers demonstrate acceptable levels of competency in the official language. In these and other ways, the onus and obligation are being placed on immigrants and ethnic minorities to take up 'host' country values and cultural

An elderly woman in Surgut, Russia

practices and to actively demonstrate their desire to 'belong'. Such measures are seen by policy-makers as crucial steps to ensure immigrants' and ethnic minorities' own socio-economic mobility, to avoid unrest and to guarantee the security of all.

Despite a strong emphasis on conformity, cohesion and national identity in these practices, they are not intended to function as a return to 'assimilation' as understood and practiced in the first half of the 20th century. In almost all the contexts in which these new policies are being implemented, there remains an explicit and institutionally embedded attempt to include the significance and value of diversity by reducing socio-economic inequality among ethnic and cultural minorities. In the UK, plans and measures have been adopted to improve educational results and attainment among ethnic minority pupils and to recruit ethnic minority teachers to better represent the communities they serve, as well as to improve literacy and numeracy among ethnic-minority adults and implement housing policies to ensure decent accommodation of vulnerable tenants through home improvements initiatives (Joint Committee on Human Rights, 2005). Better support and training are also provided for prison officers 'to help address discrimination and serve all communities equally' (JCHR, 2005). Moreover, legislation is scheduled to be introduced that will require that providers of goods and services cannot discriminate against customers and refuse services on grounds of religion or belief.

The solution to the challenges of difference is clearly to be found neither in 'assimilationist' initiatives claiming to be 'blind to diversity' nor in communitarianism, understood as exclusive identification with a cultural, religious or linguistic community, which can lead to a potentially dangerous fragmentation of the public space. Post-multiculturalist policies require going beyond such extremes to embrace cultural diversity conceived in terms of multiple interactions and allegiances.

Towards new forms of solidarity

The search for solutions to the impasses of multiculturalism has much to gain from greater recognition of multiple identities (as described in chapter 2). This is not a matter of questioning the capacity of communities to provide their members with a shared outlook and services meeting their expectations so much as one of creating the conditions for renewed dialogue between communities in order to counter the temptation to withdraw into themselves or to become mistrustful of cultural differences. Since multiple cultural allegiances run counter to withdrawal into self and identity-based or culturalist reactions, the task is to mobilize such allegiances in the service of greater openness between communities, which represents one of the main challenges of intercultural dialogue.

At the policy level, the goal must be to determine how to account for the plurality of individual and group affiliations and identities and to translate them into effective policies. Indeed, it is the convergence of possible affiliations among members of different groups that makes it possible for them to meet on a common ground. And rather than creating new administrative categories, recognition of the multiple dimensions of individual and group identities can aid the rediscovery of common norms relevant to each kind of group. Too often, multicultural initiatives have focused on strengthening existing cultures' and communities' capacities in a competition for visibility and recognition. Yet for cultural diversity to contribute to pluralism, emphasis must be placed on providing *enabling environment* to facilitate access to other cultures.

Indeed, as numerous studies on the impacts of the new technologies and networking have shown, new forms of sociability and solidarity are emerging which can facilitate dialogue between communities and help to strengthen social cohesion. The development of civil society movements based on common ideas and goals has led to new kinds of project-based solidarity. *Campaign-oriented* forms of participation involve actions aimed at influencing the parliament and government of a representative democracy, primarily through political parties. *Cause-oriented* activities focused mainly on influencing specific issues and policies. These actions are exemplified by consumer politics (buying or boycotting certain products for political or ethical reasons), taking part in demonstrations and protests, and organizing or signing petitions. *Civic-oriented* activities, by contrast, involve membership and working together in voluntary associations, as well as collaboration with community groups to solve a local problem (Norris, 2003). Face-to-face deliberative activities and horizontal collaboration

within voluntary organizations far removed from the political sphere — such as trade unions, social clubs and philanthropic groups — promote interpersonal trust, social tolerance and cooperative behaviour. In turn, these norms are regarded as cementing the bonds of social life, laying the foundation for building local communities, civil society and democratic governance. Engagement in common causes illustrates people's 'capacity to aspire' and contributes to new forms of citizenship (civic engagement) based on shared overarching values.

The development of *networks* facilitates such new patterns of cohesion. Informal webs of solidarity further the exchange within and between minority groups and between majority and minority groups. These new forms of solidarity and networks play a crucial role in helping to respond to the demands for recognition of newcomers and minority groups that are not being fulfilled by established structures and often are not even registered by national or local administrations.

Social cohesion cannot be forged by glossing over differences since they remain present even when they go unrecognized in the public space, with the risk that they will reappear in expressions of violence due to frustration. Such policies serve only to exacerbate the clash of differences. If cultural diversity can contribute to the reinforcement of social cohesion, it does so by empowering individuals and groups through an enlargement of choice — thus, not by imprisoning them in the confines of a cultural 'tribe' but by fostering in them an openness to the cultures of others. It is crucial, therefore, to create new forms of governance designed to take greater account of differences in accordance with the principles mentioned above.

⌒ *Local architecture in the Dourrou village, Mali*

For cultural diversity to contribute to pluralism, emphasis must be placed on providing an enabling environment to facilitate access to other cultures ... new forms of sociability and solidarity are emerging which can facilitate dialogue between communities and help to strengthen social cohesion

8.3 The challenge of cultural diversity for democratic governance

Governance is understood as 'a system of values, policies and institutions by which a society manages its economic, political and social affairs through interaction within and among the State, civil society and the private sector' (Dwivedi, 2001). Over the past 20 years or so, the concept of *governance* has 'transcended the formal government apparatus' (Weiss, 2000) to include the processes of decision-making and those by which decisions are implemented. 'Good governance' has come to refer to open and enlightened policy-making, a bureaucracy imbued with a professional ethos acting in furtherance of the public good, the rule of law, transparent processes and a strong civil society participating in public affairs. 'Poor governance', by contrast, is characterized by arbitrary policy-making, unaccountable bureaucracies, un-enforced or unjust legal systems, the abuse of executive power, a civil society unengaged in public life, and widespread corruption (World Bank, 1994; Treisman, 2000).

🔊 *Moroccan pupils in a primary school class in Tifelte near Rabat*

Governance has thus come to include a range of activities involving all cultural communities and stakeholders in a given country, from governmental institutions to political parties, interest groups, NGOs, the private sector and the public at large, including the formal and informal actors involved in decision-making and implementation, and the formal and informal structures in which these all take place (Frederickson, 1997). Recognizing the interdependence of all these actors in the smooth functioning of society connects governance to a wider concern with social capital (see

section 8.2) and the underpinnings necessary for social cohesion which go beyond 'recourse to the authority and sanctions of government' and are related to the very interactions, power dependencies and networks for collective action (Stoker, 1998).

As governance theories evolve in order to better facilitate the implementation of multi-stakeholder initiatives, cultural diversity is increasingly pertinent to a proper understanding of the mechanisms through which a society regulates the relations between the individuals and groups within it and creates institutions to this end. With the acknowledgement of culture as a major factor influencing how governance is conceptualized and put into practice across administration, law enforcement, citizen participation and the promotion of equality, cultural diversity provides a key to new forms of governance, which are better attuned to the styles and practices of particular cultural contexts and the coexistence of specific cultural groups. This enables people and groups to express themselves and participate in their own way in the realization of the common objective of democratic ideals. This development has implications for both power-sharing mechanisms and the provision of rights.

It is worth recalling that the UN's commitment to the democratic ideal does not prejudge the particular arrangements that States may wish to implement and that, as the Preamble of UNESCO's Constitution (1945) says, 'dignity, equality and mutual respect' are not incompatible with a diversity of acceptable or respectable political regimes throughout the world. The UN system has evolved regarding its neutrality towards the political systems prevailing in its Member States. Only on rare occasions (as in the case of National-Socialist, fascist and racist regimes) has it condemned certain regimes. It was not until the 1980s, with the 'rediscovery' of Article 21, paragraph 3, of the *Universal Declaration of Human Rights* (UN, 1948), that the UN system made the transition from stressing the criterion of the effective exercise of power (or the equivalence of political regimes) to that of democratic legitimacy (or the preponderance of pluralistic democracy). This point was discussed at length at the 1991 International Forum on Culture and Democracy in Prague (Hermet, 1993). At the Forum,

Boutros Boutros-Ghali (1993), then the Secretary-General of the UN, stated that: 'democracy is the private domain of no one. It can and ought to be assimilated by all cultures. It can take many forms in order to accommodate local realities more effectively. Democracy is not a model to copy from certain States, but a goal to be achieved by all peoples. It is the political expression of our common heritage'. Nearly ten years later Boutros-Ghali (2002) made the point even more strongly when he reaffirmed that

> the recognition of universal values does not mean that a veil should be drawn over the specific historical, religious and cultural characteristics that make up the genius peculiar to each society and each nation State. For the general principles of democracy can be embodied in different ways, depending on the context. Thus, while democracy is the system in which 'sovereign power lies with the people', the methods with which it can be exercised can vary depending on the social system and economic development peculiar to each country. Those methods also tend to change depending on political, demographic, economic and social change.

It is essential to bear in mind that the enhancement of governance mechanisms in any society must be respectful of local contexts and perceptions, beyond the notion that there exists only one single 'good' organizational pattern possible for each and every society. Indeed, it is the way in which a given form of democratic governance is exercised within a particular cultural context that will determine its effectiveness.

Empowerment and participation

Insofar as multicultural societies continue to be perceived and experienced as divided societies (with a majority group and minorities striving for recognition), the major issue with respect to governance is that of access to political power by persons belonging to such minorities while remaining members of their communities. This is also the case for women (Map 8.2), who continue to be under-represented in high political positions. Building multicultural societies, without falling prey to the problems outlined in the previous section, requires the development and implementation of policies that ensure the political participation of diverse cultural groups. Indeed, many minorities and other historically marginalized groups are often excluded from real political power and so feel alienated from the State. In some cases, their exclusion is due to a lack of democracy or a denial of political rights. But very often it is because something more is required; for even when members of such groups have equal political rights in a democracy, they may be consistently under-represented

Cultural diversity provides a key to new forms of governance, which are better attuned to the styles and practices of particular cultural contexts and the coexistence of specific cultural groups

Map 8.2 Percentage of political positions in Parliaments held by women, 2007

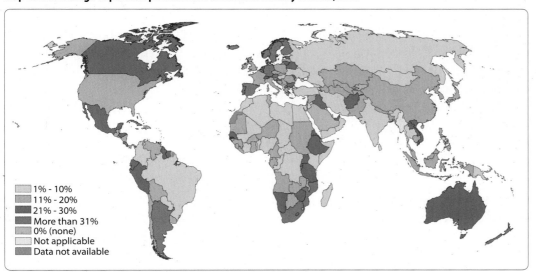

- 1% - 10%
- 11% - 20%
- 21% - 30%
- More than 31%
- 0% (none)
- Not applicable
- Data not available

Source: Inter-Parliamentary Union, 2007. Parline database.

or outvoted, or may be shackled by cultural obstacles because of there difference (UNDP, 2004).

In tandem with the international human rights standards and the international instruments allowing the autonomy and sovereignty of States, some scholars have made interesting proposals that could provide useful guidance in the formulation of policies concerning minorities (Stamatopoulou, 2008). The proposals include the following:

■ States are submitted to a general obligation related to freedom: this obligation entails respect for the freedom of minorities, as individuals and groups, to participate (or not) in cultural life and to express their values and practices in the ways they have chosen. In this sense and as a general principle, authorities should not intervene or interfere except under specific conditions.

■ States should prevent third parties from intervening.

■ States should develop laws and policies and all manner of measures for the fulfilment of cultural rights (provisions of resources, subsidies, international assistance, etc.).

■ Democratic and transparent processes should guarantee the participation and empowerment of minorities.

■ Education about cultural diversity is crucial. The media play an important role in promoting such knowledge.

Some human-rights-based initiatives for empowering and recognizing minorities have already been undertaken following some of these proposals. Indeed, at the national level, some States have recognized in their constitutions the 'autonomy' of minorities to develop their values and practices — such as in the Swiss Constitution (Art. 2, para. 2 and 3), the Colombian Constitution (Art. 7) and the Peruvian Constitution (Art. 7) — or have embraced multiculturalism, such as in Ecuador, whose Constitution refers to Ecuador as a 'pluricultural and multiethnic State' (Art. 1). Some have gone further and decreed an obligation of 'consultation' with indigenous communities and their participation in political decisions that could affect them (e.g. Colombian Constitution, Art. 11). Other initiatives include, for example, the creation of a special jurisdiction for indigenous peoples (see Colombian Constitution, Art. 246).

Other countries have developed specific models for the protection of cultural diversity — such as the National Cultural Autonomy Model (NCA), proposed by the former president of Austria, Karl Renner (2005), on the premise that ethnic and national communities should be allowed to organize themselves freely and autonomously within multinational States (Nimni, 2007). In the same way, the UK has developed a social policy linking arts and social inclusion with special emphasis on cultural diversity: the Arts Council England (2009) has focused its initiatives on community development and empowerment as means for preventing discrimination.

↻ *Fishermen children playing with a bicycle in Aral Sea region, Kazakhstan*

Power-sharing arrangements

In addition to institutional solutions, 'power-sharing arrangements' have enabled the political participation of diverse cultural groups through a process of consensus democracy designed to address the claims made by culturally diverse groups not territorially concentrated or not demanding autonomy or self-rule. Indeed, consensus democracy has proven to be an important advance in reflection on democracy in divided societies, particularly in response to 'authoritarian rulers trying to justify their non-democratic regimes by invoking the overriding need for national unity' (Bogaards, 2006).

More recently, such power-sharing arrangements have included the provision of limited territorial autonomy for indigenous groups, for example, in response to Inuit demand, in Alaska, the Canadian Arctic and Greenland, for political and territorial recognition accompanied by cultural and linguistic measures. So far, the Inuit community has secured the creation of a parliament in Greenland (1979) and a legislative assembly in Nunavut (1999), which will be followed in 2010 by the creation in Arctic Quebec of a legislative assembly to be called *uqarvimarik* ('the site of speech above all others'). Recent standard-setting initiatives for promoting cultural diversity, and particularly community-level empowerment initiatives encouraged by the *Convention on the Safeguarding of Intangible Heritage* (UNESCO, 2003), may also contribute to the revival of local modes of governance and initiation of new forms of public involvement which are more respectful of the worldviews and values of other cultural groups (Therrien, 2008; see also 'In focus' below).

Power-sharing arrangements must come to be seen as integral to the effective empowerment of marginalized populations insofar as they provide ethnic minorities or indigenous communities with the opportunity to engage actively in citizenship and democratic practices. Central in this regard are media policies that are respectful of cultural differences and that enable cultural minorities to exercise their citizenship fully (see chapter 5 above). Many countries have adopted radio, television and video, as well as traditional songs and theatre, as instruments for participatory governance, especially for illiterate citizens. In India, film and television — for which basic literacy is not required — are used to facilitate electoral consultations, and names on electoral ballots

are accompanied by parties' symbols, such as a flower or a sickle. In Cambodia, the Cambodian Institute of Human Rights (CIHR) uses television quiz shows to teach people about human rights. In the US, an artistic experiment aimed at reclaiming a conflict-ridden Chicago neighbourhood took the form of multiple video dialogues among neighbours displayed on monitors that lit the street and provided a neutral site for cultural and social exchange (Karim and Wayland, 2001).

Educational and cultural policies committed to both the empowerment of the disadvantaged and the building of communities of interest (see also chapters 3 and 4) are central to public policies committed to the same objective. For example, some cultural policies supportive of cultural diversity have incorporated in their agenda the need to devise means for extending governance participation to those who are on the society's margins (Council of Europe, 1997). This includes engaging groups in civic dialogue through literature, music, photography and other cultural goods and services from all parts of the world in order to promote democratic principles and human rights. From awareness-raising high-visibility rock concerts to awards shows, or photojournalism initiatives aimed at sensitizing the general public to such issues as living conditions, work situations, environmental challenges — there are multiple means for promoting active citizenship in service to more equitable and diversity-adapted governance mechanisms.

The overarching goal of these policies is to promote an *enabling environment* for realistic progress towards genuine democratic governance. Such a universalistic approach founded on mutual trust is the key to peaceful coexistence within societies; it is the point of departure for the forging of a wider international consensus in keeping with the goals of the United Nations. The more *human-centred governance* (going one step beyond the World Commission on Culture and Development's 'people-centred' development approach) advocated here would involve precisely the creation of networks and other forms of collaboration in which a bottom-up approach would permit the participation of all stakeholders and thus offer them the opportunity to articulate and promote their claims and views. The resultant empowerment would in turn increase the chances of successful collaborations and shield them against future disruptions; it would strengthen the

Measuring rice in the grain section of the Zumbahua market, Ecuador

Consensus democracy has proven to be an important advance in reflection on democracy in divided societies

self-esteem of cultural minorities and groups and the social fabric, and it would help to eliminate stereotyped perceptions related to 'passive welfare recipients' as opposed to individuals responsible for their own destiny. Empowerment can therefore be prioritized in the same way as information (one-way flow of information), consultation (two-way flow of information) and collaboration (shared control over decision-making).

Conclusion

Cultural diversity is central in two ways to nurturing a culture of human rights, which has been one of the international community's main goals for over 60 years. Firstly, it can favour the effective exercise of human rights by people everywhere, without discrimination or exclusion, by highlighting the diverse ways in which rights and freedoms can be exercised in a wide variety of cultural contexts and situations throughout the world. Secondly, it can help to ensure that universal human rights are also universally recognized by and embedded in all cultures.

Recognition of the value of each culture, in terms of its creative difference and originality, invests *all* individuals with a sense of pride essential to their empowerment. This recovered dignity is essential to social cohesion, in which differences unite rather than divide. Links of solidarity are in this way forged between individuals so as to transcend selfish competition over resources. Cultural diversity can thereby provide a means to renew the modes of democratic governance, so that groups — the young, the disenfranchised, the have-nots, minorities, indigenous populations and immigrants — can recover their trust in systems of democratic governance and see that their contribution is recognized and appreciated, and that it makes a difference.

By furthering human rights, social cohesion and democratic governance, cultural diversity creates a convergence of three factors that are essential for the establishment of peace and peaceful co-existence within and between nations. In this way, the triad of human rights, social cohesion and democratic governance is strengthened by the promotion and safeguarding of cultural diversity.

Chapter 8 Recommendations

As universally recognized human rights should be guaranteed to every individual, their effective exercise can be fostered through the recognition of cultural diversity, which can also reinforce social cohesion and encourage renewed modes of democratic governance. Policies that are conducive to the preservation and promotion of cultural diversity should be encouraged to this end.

Action should be taken in particular to:

a. Collect striking examples of cases in which the cultural context is a key factor in the effective exercise of universally recognized rights and freedoms, so as to highlight the cultural dimension of all rights and freedoms.

b. Map exchanges within and between minority groups and between majority and minority communities, especially in the context of 'global cities', in order to create informal networks of solidarity, and widely publicize such exchanges.

c. Study the diversity of intangible heritage as a source of examples of modes of democratic governance based on the empowerment and participation of all communities.

Three examples of traditional mechanisms and intangible heritage in the service of democratic governance

The Council of Wise Men and the Water Court (Murcia and Valencia, Spain)

The Council of Wise Men and the Water Court are the bodies responsible for administering justice within the traditional irrigator communities of the plains (*huertas* or *vegas*) of Murcia and Valencia. They are customary tribunals with jurisdiction in all matters pertaining to irrigation. Since the construction of the extensive and complex irrigation systems of Murcia and Valencia in the age of al-Andalus (9th to 13th centuries CE), these two bodies have contributed to the management and maintenance of irrigation canals and infrastructures (dams, flow separators, water mills, water wheels, sluices), as well as to the safeguarding and organization of the intangible water culture. They contribute to the maintenance of a society governed by shared community principles and a spirit of respect, survival and responsibility towards its living environment. Their proven effectiveness in the settlement of conflicts led the 13th-century Christian peoples to perpetuate the Islamic tradition by incorporating it in their cultural practices. They later exported this model to the Americas, where it is still in operation today.

This organization, which is a remarkable example of the intercultural transfer of techniques, skills and knowledge inherited from the medieval Islamic world (with traditions linked to Hindu, Iranian, Mesopotamian, Nabatean, Yemenite, Egyptian, Greek and Roman, and Berber cultures) and extended by the colonists of the most arid regions in the Americas, survived over the millennia due to its integration in the Spanish judicial system. It offers the same guarantees and has the same legal standing as any other civil court — immediacy, efficiency and due hearing of parties. Governed by the principles of cooperation, good government and the sustainable exploitation of a scarce common resource (water), the members of these two bodies are farmer-judges with no legal training who have been chosen independently and democratically by the users of the irrigation canals and who settle disputes with reference to the most basic human rights embodied in the *Universal Declaration of Human Rights* (UN, 1948): equality, the right to the presumption of innocence and the right to a fair trial. Their goal is to maintain social peace and mutual respect but also to ensure the optimal use of water resources, without compromising its enjoyment by other users and its transmission to future generations.

The participating farmers play numerous roles, such as the conservation and management of the irrigation system through their association in irrigator communities, the settlement of conflicts through their internal courts, the sharing of water through assemblies of landowners and trade unions, and the representation of their peers in the governing bodies of communities, enabling them to participate in the courts and other relevant institutions and public services. The two judicial bodies regulate conflicts between irrigators by means of orally based, rapid, and impartial procedures. The verdicts are usually respected because the two courts command authority and respect, their procedures are transparent and fair, and the farmer-judges are recognized by their peers as honest individuals familiar with usages and customs.

The council and court constitute the identity marker of the communities that create and compose them, the depositories and culmination of a millennial farming culture. They are the most visible expression of the customs of the living water culture heritage, its natural environment, its people and its language — in short, a comprehensive vision linked to soil and irrigation as it is practised in the fertile plains.

In addition to defending the collective interest, the two bodies are also involved in monitoring and sanction. For the immigrant community, the council and court therefore fulfil an extraordinary cultural function relating to the maintenance of the group's identity and cohesion, represented by the traditional black smock worn by the farmer-judges. The cultural identity function is also recognized by Murcian and Valencian society, while other local and international communities have recognized that the council and court contribute to intercultural dialogue and encourage sustainable development by promoting models of democratic self-governance, as well as respect for the wisdom of elders.

The council and the court represent a broad spectrum of intangible cultural heritage, which consists of non-material assets that are essentially economic in nature: trades and lifestyles that have survived from the pre-industrial world and that today are threatened by the global industrialization of production systems, despite the fact that such trades and lifestyles have been, as in the present case, decisive in forming the identities of communities and peoples. Such lifestyles are the product of centuries of wise adaptation by human groups to their surroundings through the creation of sustainable systems of resource exploitation. The council and court are the culmination of a complex system of sustainable, communal, autonomous and democratic water management by the irrigators, a system that has successfully adapted itself to its setting.

The council and court demonstrate human creativity through the rapidity and efficiency of their oral dispute-settlement procedures and the construction and maintenance of complex water-distribution systems. Moreover, the two bodies are open to change; they encourage any innovation that would help to ensure the continuity of the irrigator communities and the cultural landscapes upon which they depend without deforming them; and their members have always shown themselves ready to place their experience at the service of irrigators in other parts of the world. These are dynamic traits that are to be recognized.

The encouragement of mutual respect among water-users and the avoidance of conflicts pertaining to water — a resource that may one day lead to confrontations between communities at the global level — are the main reasons for the existence of the council and the court.

The Manden Charter (Mali)

The new Manden Charter was adopted in the early 13th century CE by the general assembly of the chiefs of the Manden in response to its proposal by Sundiata Keita, following his victory over Soumangourou Kanté, King of Sosso, at the historic battle of Kirina. Keita stated the principle of this document as follows: 'Now that we are masters of our destiny, we shall set our country on a firm and just footing. Let us therefore enact laws that the peoples must respect and apply.' At the conclusion of the general assembly, the Charter regulating the life of the Mandenka community was solemnly proclaimed to the world at large in Kurukan Fuga, a vast clearing extending from the village of Kenielen to the gates of the village of Kaaba (usually known as Kangaba) in the heart of the Manden, 90 km from Bamako.

Enacted in the form of an oath, the proclamation includes a preamble and seven chapters consisting of rules for the conduct of public and family life grouped under the following major headings: social understanding and peace in the context of ethnic and cultural diversity; the inviolability

of human life and the prohibition of physical or mental torture; education within the family out of respect for parents, support for family members and the supervision of children; the integrity of the homeland and the protection of the human person; food security; the abolition of slave raiding; and freedom of expression and enterprise.

The Manden Charter is one of the oldest of the Manden constitutions. Its effectiveness in the Manden and in all the territories conquered by Sundiata Keita had to do, firstly, with its character as an oath and founding document and, secondly, with the determination of the Ngwana (warlords and companions of Sundiata) to pacify the country. The repositories of the Manden Charter are therefore the Malinké, the founding clan of the empire of Sundiata, through their 'men of the word', namely the blacksmith and, above all, *griot* castes.

In Kurukan Fuga, Sundiata and his companions proclaimed human rights, the freedom of movement of people and goods, the freedom for all to enjoy the fruits of their labours; they laid the foundations for alliances, unity and integration between peoples. According to some, the African Union was born in Kurukan Fuga. Indeed, the Manden Charter laid the foundations for the politics, administration and functioning, as well as the rules of conduct of its men and women, of the great Mandingue community.

Over a span of eight centuries, the Manden Charter proclaims the importance of intercultural dialogue, peace and fraternity. It establishes a sense of belonging to a community, whose laws and prescriptions continue to govern everyday lives, even though the empire of Sundiata is no more.

For this reason, the highest authorities of Mali attach particular importance to the preservation and promotion of the Manden Charter, which remains a model and source of inspiration in the formulation of legal and administrative instruments governing our societies.

Traditional monarchs supporting the National Policy Agenda in Education, Science and Culture (Nigeria)

Traditional monarchs can play an important role in promoting cultural diversity for the development of their communities. As observed by Folarin Osotimehin, UNESCO's Senior Science Policy Advisor in Nigeria, 'the monarchs' exert a strong influence on their people. A few years ago, key traditional rulers in the North managed to convince their people, after government officials had failed to do so, to participate in a vaccination campaign against poliomyelitis in which they had initially refused to take part.

The three monarchs of the Yoruba, Ibo and Hausa ethnic groups in Nigeria visited UNESCO in March 2007. On this occasion, they announced plans to develop three initiatives: the teaching and communication of science and technology in the Yoruba, Ibo and Hausa languages; the integration of traditional knowledge in building local innovation systems; and the building of bridges between the language communities in the country and in the diasporas.

Indeed, although English is Nigeria's official language, about 85 percent of the country's 140 million inhabitants speak one of the three main mother tongues: Yoruba, Ibo and Hausa. In recent years, Nigerians from these ethnic groups have launched a number of initiatives to foster quality education and sustainable development by promoting the use of their mother tongue in their communities, as well as in diaspora communities all over the world. (Yoruba is spoken not only in much of Nigeria but also in parts of Benin and Togo, as well as in communities in Brazil, Cuba and the US — constituting about 150 million people with Yoruba affinities in different parts of the world.)

The commitment of traditional monarchs to the promotion of scientific development contributes to the cultural relevance of the national strategies implemented. As explained by the fiftieth *Ooni* (King) of Ife, Oba Okunade Sijuade, in a speech to UNESCO in March 2007 on behalf of the Council of Traditional Rulers of Nigeria:

> *Without doubt, science and technology are the basis for socio-economic development in any nation (…); however, technology must be culturally relevant and adapted to local situations and needs. Experience has shown that, in Nigeria, development strategies are designed and communicated in the English language, a language which is not accessible to a large percentage of the local people.*

The idea is to use an existing platform for dialogue and cooperation among African monarchs, the Group of Leading African Monarchs, to move initiatives forward. Their first meeting was held in Nigeria in 2006, and the second, in Kenya in 2007.

One of the projects for which the monarchs are mobilizing seed money is the setting-up of a conservation and analytical laboratory for the preservation of an 8,000-year-old canoe that Nigerian and German archaeologists recently excavated in the Nguru-Hadeija wetlands within the Lake Chad Basin of northern Nigeria. The canoe is the oldest in Africa and the third-oldest watercraft in the world. Another project concerns the establishment of the Yoruba Academy of Science to promote scientific cooperation among communities that use the Yoruba language. UNESCO is assisting with feasibility studies for the Academy, which will be launched at Ile-Ife in early 2010.

The monarchs' initiatives fall within the ongoing reform of science and technology undertaken by Nigeria with the support of UNESCO since 2004. They also accord with the African Union's decision in January 2007 to build constituencies to defend and champion science, technology and innovation in Africa.

◖ *Gelede ceremony, performed by the Yoruba-Nago community spread over Benin, Nigeria and Togo*

References and websites

Background documents and UNESCO Sources

An-Na'im, A. A. 2007. Human rights and cultural diversity. Background paper.

Boutros-Ghali, B. 2002. *The Interaction between Democracy and Development*. Paris, UNESCO. http://unesdoc.unesco.org/images/0012/001282/128283e.pdf

—. 1993. Address by the Secretary-General of the United Nations at the opening of the World Conference on Human Rights, Vienna, 14 June. http://www.unhchr.ch/huricane/huricane.nsf/view01/F4F957347797532 0C12570210077FC48?opendocument

Caluser, M. 2007. Good governance and consideration of the human dimension in different cultural contexts. Background paper.

Djabbarzade, M. 2007. Good governance and cultural diversity: An operational perspective. Background paper.

Donders, Y. 2007. Cultural diversity and human rights: A good match? Background paper.

Donders, Y. and Volodin, V. (eds.). 2007. *Human Rights in Education, Science and Culture: Legal Developments and Challenges*. Paris, UNESCO. http://www.unesco.org/library/Donders2007.pdf

Elmandjra, M. 2008. Cultural diversity: Key to the survival of humanity. Background paper.

Formisano, M. 2009. Cultural diversity and human rights beyond the dichotomy of universalism vs. particularism. Background paper.

Kymlicka, W. 2007. The rise and fall of multiculturalism? New debates on inclusion and accommodation in diverse societies. Background paper.

Meyer-Bisch, P. 2006. L'observation de la diversité et des droits culturels: propositions méthodologiques et stratégiques. Contribution pour la division des politiques culturelles et du dialogue interculturel.

Niec, H. (ed.). 1998. *Cultural Rights and Wrongs*. Paris, UNESCO.

Norris, P. 2003. Building knowledge societies: the renewal of democratic practices in knowledge societies. http://ksghome.harvard.edu/~pnorris/ACROBAT/UNESCO%20Report%20Knowledge%20Societies.pdf

Shayegan, D. 2008. La diversité culturelle et la civilisation planétaire. Background paper.

UNESCO. 2003. *Convention on the Safeguarding of Intangible Cultural Heritage*. Paris, UNESCO. http://unesdoc.unesco.org/images/0013/001325/132540e.pdf

—. 2001. *Universal Declaration on Cultural Diversity*. Paris, UNESCO. http://unesdoc.unesco.org/images/0012/001271/127160m.pdf

—. 1992. International Forum on Culture and Democracy (Prague, 4–6 September 1991), meeting papers CLT.91/CONF.015

—. 1982. *Mexico City Declaration on Cultural Policies*. World Conference on Cultural Policies, Mexico City, 26 July — 6 August. http://portal.unesco.org/culture/en/files/12762/11295421661mexico_en.pdf/mexico_en.pdf

—. 1945. *The Constitution of UNESCO*. http://unesdoc.unesco.org/images/0012/001255/125590e.pdf#constitution

United Nations. 2008. *Optional Protocol to the International Covenant on Economic, Social and Cultural Rights*. http://www2.ohchr.org/english/bodies/cescr/docs/A-RES-63-117.pdf

—. 2007. *Declaration on the Rights of Indigenous Peoples*. http://www.un.org/esa/socdev/unpfii/documents/DRIPS_en.pdf

—. 1994. *International Convention to Combat Desertification in Countries Experiencing Serious Drought and/or Desertification, Particularly in Africa*. http://www.un-documents.net/a49r234.htm

—. 1993. *Vienna Declaration and Programme of Action*. http://www.unhchr.ch/huridocda/huridoca.nsf/(Symbol)/A.CONF.157.23.En

—. 1992a. *Convention on Biological Diversity*. http://www.cbd.int/doc/legal/cbd-un-en.pdf

—. 1992b. *United Nations Framework Convention on Climate Change*. http://unfccc.int/resource/docs/convkp/conveng.pdf

—. 1992c. *Declaration on the Rights of Persons Belonging to National or Ethnic, Religious and Linguistic Minorities*. A/RES/47/135. 18 December. http://www.un.org/documents/ga/res/47/a47r135.htm

—. 1989. *Convention on the Rights of the Child*. http://www2.ohchr.org/english/law/crc.htm

—. 1979. *Convention on the Elimination of All Forms of Discrimination Against Women* (CEDAW). http://www.un.org/womenwatch/daw/cedaw/text/econvention.htm

—. 1966a. *International Covenant on Civil and Political Rights*. http://www2.ohchr.org/english/law/ccpr.htm

—. 1966b. *International Covenant on Economic, Social and Cultural Rights*. http://www2.ohchr.org/english/law/cescr.htm

—. 1965. *International Convention on the Elimination of All Forms of Racial Discrimination*. http://www2.ohchr.org/english/law/cerd.htm

—. 1948. *Universal Declaration of Human Rights*. 10 December. http://www.un.org/en/documents/udhr

Vala, J. and Costa-Lopes, R. 2007. Youth, intolerance and diversity. Background paper.

Vertovec, S. 2007. Towards post-multiculturalism? Changing communities, conditions and contexts of diversity. Background paper.

Web pages

African Union: http://www.africa-union.org

Amnesty International: http://www.amnesty.org

Article 19: http://www.article19.org

Citizenship and Immigration Canada, Multiculturalism: http://www.cic.gc.ca/multi/index-eng.asp

Convention on Biological Diversity (CBD): http://www.cbd.int and http://www.cbd.int/doc/legal/cbd-un-en.pdf

Council of Europe: http://www.coe.int

European Court of Human Rights (ECHR): http://www.echr.coe.int/echr

European Union (EU): http://europa.eu

First EU Roma Summit, 2008: http://ec.europa.eu/social/main.jsp?catId=88&langId=en&eventsId=105

Human Rights Watch: http://www.hrw.org

Multicultural Centre Prague: http://www.mkc.cz/en/home.html

Organization of African Unity (OAU): see African Union

Organization of American States (OAS): http://www.oas.org

Special Broadcasting Service (Australia): http://www.sbs.com.au

United Nations Framework Convention on Climate Change (UNFCCC): http://unfccc.int

United Nations Human Rights Council (UNHCR): http://www2.ohchr.org/english/bodies/hrcouncil

World Bank, What is Social Capital? http://go.worldbank.org/K4LUMW43B0

References

Alba, R. 1995. Assimilation's quiet tide. *Public Interest*, Vol. 119, pp. 3–18.

Alibhai-Brown, Y. 2000. *After Multiculturalism*. London, Foreign Policy Centre.

An-Na'im, A. A. 1992. Toward a cross-cultural approach to defining international standards of human rights: The meaning of cruel, inhuman, or degrading treatment or punishment. A. A. An-Na'im (ed.), *Human Rights in Cross-cultural Perspectives*. Philadelphia, Pa., University of Pennsylvania Press.

— (ed.). 2003. *Human Rights Under African Constitutions: Realizing the Promise for Ourselves*. Philadelphia, Pa., University of Pennsylvania Press.

— (ed.). 2002. *Cultural Transformation and Human Rights in Africa*. London, Zed Books.

— (ed.). 1992. *Human Rights in Cross-Cultural Perspective: A Quest for Consensus*. Philadelphia, Pa., University of Pennsylvania Press.

Algiers, 1976. *Algiers Declaration of the Rights of Peoples*. http://www.ciemen.org/pdf/ang.PDF

Arts Council England. 2009. *Annual Review 2009*. London, The Stationery Office. http://www.artscouncil.org.uk/downloads/annualreview2009.pdf

Barry, B. 2003. *Culture and Equality: An Egalitarian Critique of Multiculturalism*. Cambridge, Polity.

Berkes, F. and Folke, C. 1992. A systems perspective in the Interrelations between natural, human and cultural capital. *Ecological Economics*, Vol. 5, pp. 1–8. http://dlc.dlib.indiana.edu/archive/00002660/01/A_systems_perspective.pdf

Bidima, J.-G. 2008. African cultural diversity in the media. *Diogenes*, Vol. 55, No. 4, pp. 122–33.

Bogaards, M. 2006. Democracy and power-sharing in multinational states. *International Journal of Multicultural Societies*, Vol. 8, No. 2, pp. 119–26. http://unesdoc.unesco.org/images/0014/001499/149924E.pdf#page=3

Bouchard, G. and Taylor, C. 2008. *Building the Future: A Time for Reconciliation*. Montreal, Government of Quebec. http://www.accommodements.qc.ca/documentation/rapports/rapport-final-integral-en.pdf

Burger, J. H. 1990. The function of human rights as individual and collective rights. J. Berting et al. (eds.), *Human Rights in a Pluralist World: Individuals and Collectivities*. London, Meckler.

Cornu, L. 2008. Trust, strangeness and hospitality. *Diogenes*, Vol. 55, No. 4, pp. 15–26.

Council of Europe. 2008. *White Paper on Intercultural Dialogue: Living Together as Equals in Dignity*. Strasbourg, Council of Europe. http://www.coe.int/t/dg4/intercultural/Source/Pub_White_Paper/White%20Paper_final_revised_EN.pdf

—. 2005. *Faro Framework Convention on the Value of Cultural Heritage for Society*. http://conventions.coe.int/Treaty/Commun/QueVoulezVous.asp?NT=199&CM=8&CL=ENG

—. 1997. *In From the Margins: A Contribution to the Debate on Culture and Development in Europe*. Strasbourg: Council of Europe. http://www.coe.int/t/dg4/cultureheritage/Source/Resources/Publications/Culture/InFromTheMargins_Short_EN.pdf (Summary)

—. 1993. *Vienna Declaration*. 9 October. https://wcd.coe.int/ViewDoc.jsp?id=621771&BackColorInternet=9999CC&BackColorIntranet=FFBB55&BackColorLogged=FFAC75

Dwivedi, O. P. 2001. The challenge of cultural diversity for good governance. Paper presented at the United Nations Expert Group Meeting on Managing Diversity in the Civil Service, New York, 3–4 May. http://unpan1.un.org/intradoc/groups/public/documents/UN/UNPAN000573.pdf

Esses, V. M., Dovidio, J. F., Jackson, L. M. and Armstrong, T. L. 2001. The immigration dilemma: the role of perceived group competition, ethnic prejudice, and national identity. *Journal of Social Issues*, Vol. 57, pp. 389–412.

European Union (EU). 2000. *Charter of Fundamental Rights of the European Union*. http://www.europarl.europa.eu/charter/pdf/text_en.pdf

Federal Authorities of the Swiss Confederation. 1999. *Federal Constitution of the Swiss Confederation*. http://www.admin.ch/org/polit/00083/index.html?lang=en

Forsythe, D. P. and McMahon, P. C. (eds.). 2003. *Diversity and Human Rights: Area Studies Revisited*. Lincoln, Neb., University of Nebraska Press.

Frederickson, H. G. 1997. *The Spirit of Public Administration*. San Francisco, Calif., Jossey-Bass.

Fribourg Group. 2007. *Fribourg Declaration on Cultural Rights*. http://www.unifr.ch/iiedh/assets/files/declarations/eng-declaration.pdf

Gould, H. 2001. Culture and social capital. F. Matarasso (ed.), *Recognising Culture: A Series of Briefing Papers on Culture and Development*. Gloucester, Comedia, pp. 69–75. http://unesdoc.unesco.org/images/0015/001592/159227e.pdf

Chapter 8
Cultural diversity,
human rights
and democratic governance

Hansen, S. A. 2002. The Right to Take Part in Cultural Life: Toward Defining Minimum Core Obligations Related to Article 15(1)(a) of the International Covenant on Economic, Social and Cultural Rights. A. R. Chapman and S. Russell, *Core Obligations: Building a Framework for Economic, Social and Cultural Rights*. Antwerp, Intersentia.

Hermet, G. (ed.). 1993. *Culture et Démocratie*. Paris, UNESCO.

International Labour Organization (ILO). 1989. *Convention Concerning Indigenous and Tribal Peoples in Independent Countries*. Convention No. 169. Geneva, ILO. http://www.ilo.org/ilolex/cgi-lex/convde.pl?C169

Joint Committee on Human Rights (JCHR). 2005. *The Convention on the Elimination of all Forms of Racial Discrimination*. London, The Stationery Office. http://www.publications.parliament.uk/pa/jt200405/jtselect/jtrights/88/88.pdf

Karim, K. H. and Wayland, S. V. 2001. Culture, governance and human rights. F. Matarasso (ed.), *Recognising Culture: A Series of Briefing Papers on Culture and Development*. Gloucester, Comedia, pp. 45–50. http://unesdoc.unesco.org/images/0015/001592/159227e.pdf

King, D. 2005. Facing the future: America's post-multiculturalist trajectory. *Social Policy and Administration*, Vol. 39, No. 2, pp. 116–12.

Kukathas, C. 1992. Are There Any Cultural Rights? *Political Theory*, Vol. 20, No. 1, pp. 105–39.

Kymlicka, W. 2007. *Multicultural Odysseys: Navigating the New International Politics of Diversity*. Oxford, Oxford University Press.

—. 1995. *Multicultural Citizenship: A liberal Theory of Minority Rights*. Oxford, Clarendon Press.

—. 1989. *Liberalism, Community and Culture*. Oxford, Clarendon Press.

Kymlicka, W. and Norman, W. 2000. Citizenship in culturally diverse societies: issues, contexts and concepts. W. Kymlicka and (eds.), *Citizenship in Diverse Societies*. Oxford, Oxford University Press, pp. 1–44. http://fds.oup.com/www.oup.co.uk/pdf/0-19-829644-4.pdf

Laclau, E. 2000. Universalism, particularism and the question of identity. S. Schech and J. Haggis (eds.), *Development: A Cultural Studies Reader*. Oxford, Blackwell.

Levy, J. T. 1997. Classifying cultural rights. W. Kymlicka and I. Shapiro (eds.), *Ethnicity and Group Rights*. New York, New York University Press.

Lijphart, A. 1999. *Patterns of Democracy: Government Forms and Performance in Thirty-Six Countries*. New Haven, Conn., Yale University Press.

—. 1985. *Power-Sharing in South Africa*. Berkeley, Calif., University of California, Institute of International Studies.

—. 1977. *Democracy in Plural Societies*. New Haven, Conn., Yale University Press.

—. 1975. *The Politics of Accommodation: Pluralism and Democracy in the Netherlands*. 2nd rev. ed. Berkeley, Calif., University of California Press.

—. 1969. Consociational democracy. *World Politics*, Vol. 21, No. 1, pp. 207–25.

Lipset, S. M. 1959. Some social requisites of democracy: economic development and political legitimacy. *American Political Science Review*, Vol. 53, pp. 69–105.

Marks, S. 2003. Defining cultural rights. M. Bergsmo (ed.), *Human Rights and Criminal Justice for the Downtrodden: Essays in Honour of Asbjørn Eide*. Leiden, Brill.

Martin-Chenut, K. 2008. International law and democracy. *Diogenes*, Vol. 55, No. 4, pp. 33–43.

Meyer-Bisch, P. (ed.). 1993. *Les droits culturels. Une catégorie sous-développée de droits de l'homme*. Fribourg, Editions Universitaires.

More, E. 2005. The Universal Declaration of Human Rights in today's world. *Journal of International Communication*, Vol. 11, No. 2, pp. 26–46. http://www.internationalcommunicationsjournal.com/issues/volume-11-no-2/the-universal-declaration-of-human-rights-in-today's-world-.asp

Nimni, E. 2007. National cultural autonomy as an alternative to minority nationalism. *Ethnopolitics*, Vol. 3, No. 3, pp. 345–65.

OHCHR, UNAIDS, UNDP, UNECA, UNESCO, UNFPA, UNHCR, UNICEF, UNIFEM, WHO. 2008. *Eliminating Female Genital Mutilation: An Interagency Statement*. Geneva, World Health Organization (WHO). http://www.unfpa.org/upload/lib_pub_file/756_filename_fgm.pdf

Organization of African Unity (OAU). 1981. *African [Banjul] Charter on Human and Peoples' Rights*. http://www.achpr.org/english/_info/charter_en.html

Organization of American States (OAS). 1969. *American Convention of Human Rights*. http://www.cidh.oas.org/Basicos/English/Basic3.American%20Convention.htm

—. 1967. *Protocol of Buenos Aires*. http://www1.umn.edu/humanrts/oasinstr/buenosaires.html

—. 1967. *Charter of the Organization of American States*. Amended 1997. http://www.oas.org/juridico/english/charter.html

Paginini, D. L. and Morgan, S. P. 1990. Intermarriage and social distance among U.S. immigrants at the turn of the century. *American Journal of Sociology*, Vol. 96, pp. 405–32.

Prott, L. 1999. Understanding one another on cultural rights. H. Niec (ed.), *Cultural Rights and Wrongs*. Paris, UNESCO.

—. 1988. Cultural rights as peoples' rights in international law. J. Crawford (ed.), *The Rights of Peoples*. Oxford, Clarendon Press.

Putnam, R. D. 2007. *E Pluribus Unum*: diversity and community in the twenty-first century. *Scandinavian Political Studies*, Vol. 30, No. 2, pp. 137–74.

Renner, K. 2005. State and nation. E. Nimni (ed.), *National-Cultural Autonomy and its Contemporary Critics*. London, Routledge.

Republic of Columbia. 1991. *Constitución política de Colombia 1991*. http://pdba.georgetown.edu/Constitutions/Colombia/colombia91.pdf

Republic of Ecuador. 2008. *Constitución del Ecuador*. http://www.asambleaconstituyente.gov.ec/documentos/constitucion_de_bolsillo.pdf

Republic of Namibia. 1990. *The Constitution of the Republic of Namibia*. http://www.orusovo.com/namcon/constitution.pdf

Republic of Peru. 1993. *Constitución política del Perú 1993*. http://pdba.georgetown.edu/Constitutions/Peru/per93reforms05.html

Shweder, R. A. and Le Vine, R. (eds.). 1984. *Culture Theory: Essays on Mind, Self and Emotions*. Cambridge, Cambridge University Press.

Stamatopoulou, E. 2008. The right to take part in cultural life. Paper presented at the Committee on Economic, social and Cultural Rights, Day of General Discussion, 'Right to take part in cultural life (article 15 (1) (a) of the Covenant)', 9 May 2008. E/C.12/40/9. http://www.bayefsky.com/general/e_c12_40_9_2008.pdf

Stasi Commission. 2003. *Commission de réflexion sur l'application du principe de laïcité dans la République. Rapport au Président de la République.* 11 December. http://lesrapports.ladocumentationfrancaise.fr/BRP/034000725/0000.pdf. See video of debate in February 2004: http://www.assemblee-nationale.fr/histoire/50annees/20040203-chirac-raffarin-leg12.asp

Stavenhagen, R. 2001. Cultural rights: a social perspective. A. Eide, C. Krause and A. Rosas (eds.), *Economic, Social and Cultural Rights — A Textbook*, 2nd ed. Dordrecht: Martinus Nijhoff.

Stoker, G. 1998. Governance as a theory: five propositions. *International Social Science Journal*, Vol. 155, pp. 17–28. http://www.catedras.fsoc.uba.ar/rusailh/Unidad%201/Stoker%202002,%20Governance%20as%20theory,%20five%20propositions.pdf

Survival International. 2005. *Collective Rights*. London, Survival International. http://www.survival-international.org/files/related_material/71_72_172_collectiverights0502.pdf

Symonides, J. 2000. Cultural rights. J. Symonides (ed.), *Human Rights, Concept and Standards*. Paris: UNESCO.

Taylor, C. 1994. The politics of recognition. C. Taylor, *Multiculturalism*. Princeton, N.J., Princeton University Press.

Therrien, M. 2007. Democracy and recognition: building research partnerships. *Diogenes*, Vol. 55, No. 4, pp. 134–36.

Tierney, S. (ed.). 2008. *Multiculturalism and the Canadian Constitution*. Vancouver, B.C.: University of British Columbia Press.

Tomasi, J. 2001. *Liberalism beyond Justice: Citizens, Society, and the Boundaries of Political Theory*. Princeton, N.J., Princeton University Press.

Treisman, D. 2000. The causes of corruption: a cross-national study. *Journal of Public Economics*, Vol. 76, pp. 399-457. http://www.sscnet.ucla.edu/polisci/faculty/treisman/causes.pdf

Türk, D. 1992. *The Realization of Economic, Social and Cultural Rights*. E/CN.4/Sub.2/1992/16. 3 July. New York, United Nations. http://www.unhchr.ch/huridocda/huridoca.nsf/(Symbol)/E.CN.4.SUB.2.1992.16.En?Opendocument

UN Committee on Economic, Social and Cultural Rights (CESCR). 2002. *General Comment 14: The right to the highest attainable standard of health.* 18 November. E/C.12/2000/4. http://www.unhchr.ch/tbs/doc.nsf/(symbol)/E.C.12.2000.4.En.

United Nations Alliance of Civilizations (UNAOC). 2006. *Research Base for the High-Level Group Report — Education: Analysis and Existing Initiatives*. New York, Alliance of Civilizations. http://www.unaoc.org/repository/thematic_education.pdf

The obelisk of Buenos Aires

United Nations Conference on Environment & Development (UNCED). 1992. *Agenda 21*. http://www.unep.org/Documents.Multilingual/Default.asp?documentID=52

United Nations Development Programme (UNDP). *Human Development Report 2004: Cultural Liberty in Today's World*. New York, UNDP. http://hdr.undp.org/en/media/hdr04_complete.pdf

Weiss, T. G. 2000. Governance, good governance and global governance. *Third World Quarterly*, Vol. 21, No. 5, pp. 795–814.

World Bank (Social Development Department, Environmentally and Socially Sustainable Development Network), 2006. Cultural Diversity and Delivery of Services: A Major Challenge for Social Inclusion. Report No. 36414. Document of the World Bank.

World Bank. 1994. *Governance: The World Bank's Experience*. Washington, DC, World Bank.

General Conclusion

There is an urgent need to invest in cultural diversity and dialogue. Integrating cultural diversity into a wide range of public policies – including those somewhat remote from the cultural field proper – can help renew the international community's approaches to two key objectives: *development* and *peace building and conflict prevention*.

◑   *A man playing a trumpet in the old French Quarter of New Orleans, US*

Regarding *development*, culture is increasingly recognized as a cross-cutting dimension of the three economic, social and environmental pillars of sustainability; for there is a cultural dimension to development that should not be underestimated. In this respect, efforts by the international community to adopt new strategies for safeguarding and managing natural resources have been significantly enhanced by the approach offered by cultural diversity, which highlights some of the ways in which indigenous knowledge can direct us towards more sustainable modes of living. It also shows us that poverty – which is an intolerable violation of human rights in terms of both the hardships and the loss of dignity it causes – must be approached in terms of each specific social and cultural setting.

Regarding *peace* and *conflict prevention*, acknowledging cultural diversity places emphasis on 'unity in diversity', the shared humanity inherent in our differences. Far from representing a potential restriction on universally proclaimed human rights, cultural diversity furthers their effective exercise, strengthens social cohesion and provides sources of inspiration for renewing forms of democratic governance. For rights and freedoms are exercised in very varied cultural environments and all have a cultural dimension that needs to be acknowledged so as to ensure their effective integration in different cultural contexts. Similarly, ignoring the increasingly multicultural make-up of societies would amount to negating the existence of large sections of the population, which compartmentalizes society and damages the social fabric by creating competition between the different communities over access to resources (for education, health, social services) rather than promoting a sense

◔   *One of the 6ᵗʰ century Buddhas of Bamiyan destroyed in 2001 by the then Taliban government in Afghanistan*

of solidarity. Finally, forms of democratic governance can be renewed by deriving lessons from the different models adopted by diverse cultures.

Recognizing cultural diversity as a resource to be promoted requires that we refine our understanding of it and of intercultural dialogue so as to rid ourselves of a number of preconceptions.

Towards a new understanding of cultural diversity

The World Report sets out to promote such a renewed understanding by examining certain common preconceptions:

- *Globalization leads inevitably to cultural homogenization.* While globalization undoubtedly weakens cultural diversity in some respects by standardizing modes of life, production and consumption, it equally helps to reconfigure cultural diversity in many of the ways highlighted in the present report. The expansion of digital networks, for example, has sometimes helped to revitalize endangered or even extinct languages; and the development of new technologies has greatly increased the possibilities of communicating and exchanging cultural content in time and space. Moreover, in certain cultural contexts, global cities in particular, the varied cultural flows and sometimes unexpected encounters produced by globalization are reflected in a growing range of consumer habits and trends.

- *Cultural diversity is reducible to the diversity of national cultures.* Yet national identity is not a fixed quantity: it represents an historical construction; and identity that

◉ *Dancers and musicians of Cilipi, Croatia*

◑ *Group of tourists in front of the Giza sphinx in Egypt*

intellectual traditions), does not mean relinquishing our convictions but simply remaining open-minded. Intercultural dialogue must be seen as a complex and ongoing process that is never completed .

■ *Cultural diversity and the economy are mutually incompatible.* In practice, cultural diversity pervades all sectors of the economy, from marketing and advertising to finance and business management. Diversity is coming to be seen as a resource within the enterprise, since it stimulates creativity and innovation, particularly of a social kind. Recognition of the tools required for cultural diversity to flourish ('cultural intelligence') is one of the most tangible signs of this gradual shift in the economic sector.

■ *Scientific and technological progress and the diversity of cultural practices are mutually incompatible.* Cultural diversity is in no way incompatible with progress or development. Indeed, the emergence of genuine . 'knowledge societies' implies a diversity of forms of knowledge and of its sources of production, including of indigenous knowledge conducive to the preservation of the environment. By observing the balances between the different ecological niches more closely, indigenous peoples have often been able to preserve the biodiversity of their environment. Reason dictates that such knowledge should not be overlooked, while recognizing that it can be supplemented by other scientific inputs. Indeed, the new technologies have not rendered the older technologies obsolete. Both are mediums of cultural expressions that, while potentially very different, are nonetheless of equal value.

may appear seamless is in fact the product of multiple interactions, showing that all identities are multiple and that cultural diversity is present in all national contexts. As long been known, no culture has ever been totally isolated or immobile. Cultures interact and are continuously evolving, as underlined by the Mondiacult Conference some 30 years ago.

■ *Cultural diversity and intercultural dialogue are mutually exclusive.* Rather than viewing the world as a plurality of civilizations, whether in terms of conflict (the 'clash of civilizations') or dialogue (the 'alliance of civilizations'), we need to move towards the reconciliation of difference whereby the harmony of the whole is born of the resonance inherent in receptiveness to others. Cultural diversity is the precondition of intercultural dialogue, and vice versa. Without genuine dialogue, the dynamic of change (which is the very essence of cultural diversity) is not sustained, and diversity is lost or declines as a result of self-enclosure. Dialogue, including interreligious dialogue (conceived as dialogue between all spiritual and

■ *There is an irreconcilable contradiction between cultural diversity and universalism.* The assertion that cultural diversity leads inevitably to the relativization of rights and freedoms, seen as varying in time and space, rests on an unjustified conflation of standardization and universality. The rights and freedoms universally recognized by the world community are intrinsic to every human being and are in this sense intangible. They are also inalienable since no one can renounce his or her rights. On the other hand, these rights and freedoms are exercised in a wide variety of cultural environments, and all have a cultural dimension that needs to be underscored. This is not to say that universal norms are relative in terms of their application. It is rather that cultural diversity can further the exercise of rights and freedoms, since to ignore cultural realities would be tantamount to affirming formal rights and freedoms without ensuring that they can in practice be rooted and enjoyed in diverse cultural contexts.

It is all the more necessary to dispel these preconceptions since it is tempting to see cultural factors as the cause of conflicts, whereas they are only the pretext for conflict; the ultimate cause of conflict lies in political or socio-economic circumstances. To clarify the question, it is necessary – as the present report recommends – to establish new mechanisms for monitoring, data collection and the circulation of information.

In challenging such received notions, the World Report suggests a new approach that emphasizes the dynamic character of cultural diversity. It implies that policies to promote cultural diversity should not be confined to safeguarding the tangible and intangible heritage and creating the conditions in which creativity can flourish, but should also encompass measures aimed at assisting vulnerable individuals and groups ill-equipped to cope with cultural change.

The implications of cultural diversity for public policy

Although the cultural dimension of the challenges confronting the international community is not directly reflected in the Millennium Development Goals, an informed awareness of the implications of cultural diversity is essential to public policy-making in areas lying outside the cultural domain proper:

- *In the field of languages,* it is cultural impoverishment, as much as the political, social, administrative and cultural status of languages, which is at the root of language decline. Thus, in keeping with the demand for recognition of the dignity of every individual whatever his or her language, we see the emergence of claims for the promotion of endangered mother tongues or the revival of languages not spoken for over half a century. Multilingualism has in this way today become a necessity for knowing where we come from (mother tongue) and for knowing other people (a national or vernacular language) on a worldwide scale (an international language).

- *In education,* integration of the cultural dimension makes for greater relevance of educational methods and contents. The cultural dimension contributes to the full realization of the right to education and the diversification of forms of learning, including out-of-school learning, ensuring that no group in society (e.g. indigenous minorities, vulnerable groups) is overlooked. If cultural diversity is not taken into account, education cannot fulfil its role of learning to live together. Consequently, the development of intercultural competencies that are conducive to dialogue between cultures and civilizations should be an educational priority. A multi-pronged strategy is needed to meet the requirements of education through and for diversity. It should inform the education system as a whole, in all disciplines, at all levels and in its different branches (formal and non-formal). It should draw on the help of local communities, enjoy the backing of teachers and explain its objectives to parents in order to enlist their support. It calls for the training of teachers in the challenges of intercultural and inter-religious education, and presupposes the involvement of the larger community to help raise the profile of cultural diversity in educational practices, including in out-of-school activities.

- *In the area of communication and cultural content,* since the diversified communication of varied content contributes to the vitality of exchanges, and because globalization and the new technologies have expanded the scope of possible choices. When taken into account in this context, cultural diversity enables many communities to have a voice within the public sphere, even if continued efforts are necessary to curb the stereotypes and prejudices to which they may be subject. The contemporary media, in their many forms and formats, can help to give greater prominence to and ensure better awareness of cultural diversity. Thus it is important to ensure that they not only reach but that they reflect the widest possible audience.

- *In the private sector,* cultural diversity is impinging on all spheres of economic activity, since creativity and innovation are linked. It is moreover not sufficient for such diversity to be visually representative (in terms of gender or ethnic origin): other non-visible aspects are equally relevant, such as social background, educational profile, professional career, past experience, culturally distinct interpersonal relations, and so on.

Because cultural diversity cuts across a whole series of public-policy areas not obviously related to culture, UNESCO has a particular responsibility to assist Member States in the formulation of relevant policies in all its fields of competence (education, natural sciences, social sciences, culture, communication and information).

The main challenges to be addressed

The World Report highlights three challenges relating to cultural diversity that will confront the international community in the years ahead: combating cultural illiteracy; reconciling universalism and diversity; and supporting new forms of pluralism resulting from the assertion of multiple identities by individuals and groups.

- In a globalized world in which the contacts between cultures are expanding rapidly, *it is necessary to combat the spread of cultural illiteracy.* Indeed, the ability to accept cultural differences, to welcome

☉ *The Hudhud chanting of the Ifugao in the Philippines*

them without being unsettled by them, calls for intercultural competencies that some societies have learned to develop in particular contexts but which can sometimes appear sorely lacking at the individual level. Helping to equip individuals or groups with the tools they need to manage cultural diversity more effectively should be the new concern of public and private decision-makers. Intercultural dialogue should ensure equality between all stakeholders in society. Multilingualism and media and information literacy have an important role to play in this regard. *Multilingualism* (understood as the ability to master several languages) considerably strengthens the possibility of openness to others and is therefore one of the factors favouring intercultural competencies. Similarly, *information proficiency and media education* for all have today become a necessity in order to make critical choices based on quality amid the increasing flows of information and contents characterizing contemporary societies. For diversified communication can mask a 'false diversity', and the proliferation of channels can reflect the existence of closed audiences or groups that are not receptive to one another. Such a juxtaposition of cultural enclaves creates no more than the illusion of cultural diversity.

- *There is a need to strengthen the foundations of universalism* by showing how it can be embodied in a wide variety of practices without being compromised. Cultural diversity is central to human rights. These rights must be 'appropriated' at the local level, not as elements superimposed on cultural practices but as universal principles deriving from the practices themselves. For each cultural practice constitutes a pathway to the universal, testifying to our shared humanity.

- *There is a need to explore the new approach opened up by recognition of the multiple – multidimensional – identities of individuals and groups in order to further the development of cultural pluralism.* Increasingly, individuals decline to be limited to fixed categories (whether ethnic, linguistic, cultural, political or otherwise) and no longer identify with a unidimensional identity that some would assign to them. This is not to question the significance of collective identities – postmodern hyper-individualism being far from a planetwide phenomenon – but rather

places the stress on the increased circulation between groups characteristic of individual experiences today. This is an opportunity to be seized. The growing number of potential points of encounter between individuals can reduce the obstacles to intercultural dialogue, and the plasticity of identities can create a dynamic of change conducive to innovations of all kinds and at every level. Such an approach makes it possible to transcend the limits of the multiculturalist policies initiated in the 1970s, which tended to confine individuals within community categories rather than encouraging mutual exchanges from the standpoint of pluralism and openness.

It follows that States should invest increased financial and human resources in cultural diversity as a matter of priority. What are the main areas in which these investments should be made and what should be their goal? The recommendations that follow offer a number of pointers in this regard. The returns that can be expected on such investments are no less than progress towards the achievement of sustainable development and a peace based on 'unity in diversity'. The cost of such action may be high but the cost of inaction could be even greater. *If the international community is able in ten years time to measure the progress made along this long road, the approaches outlined in this World Report will have served their purpose.*

◑ *Children in a school in Bangkok, Thailand*

Recommendations

The following recommendations are addressed as appropriate to States, intergovernmental and non-governmental international and regional bodies, national institutions and private-sector entities.

Chapter 1 – CULTURAL DIVERSITY

1. Consideration should be given to establishing a World Observatory on Cultural Diversity to monitor the impacts of globalization and to serve as a source of information and data for comparative research with a forward-looking function.

To this end, action should be taken to:

a. Collect, compile and widely disseminate data and statistics on cultural diversity, building inter alia on the revised 2009 UNESCO Framework for Cultural Statistics.

b. Develop methodologies and tools for assessing, measuring and monitoring cultural diversity, adaptable to national or local conditions by governments and public and private institutions.

c. Establish national observatories to monitor policies and advise on appropriate measures for the promotion of cultural diversity.

Chapter 2 – INTERCULTURAL DIALOGUE

2. Support should continue to be given to networks and initiatives for intercultural and interfaith dialogue at all levels, while ensuring the full involvement of new partners, especially women and young people.
To this end, action should be taken to:

a. Develop measures to enable members of communities and groups subject to discrimination and stigmatization to participate in the framing of projects designed to counter cultural stereotyping.

b. Support initiatives aimed at developing real and virtual spaces and provide facilities for cultural interaction, especially in countries where inter-community conflict exists.

c. Showcase 'places of memory' that serve to symbolize and promote reconciliation between communities within an overall process of cultural rapprochement.

Chapter 3 – LANGUAGES

3. National language policies should be implemented with a view to both safeguarding linguistic diversity and promoting multilingual competencies.

To this end, action should be taken to:

a. Facilitate language use through appropriate measures, be they educational, editorial, administrative or other.

b. Make provision – as appropriate – for the learning, alongside mother tongues, of a national and an international language.

c. Encourage the translation by all possible means of written and audiovisual materials in order to promote the international circulation of ideas and artistic works, including through the use of new technologies.

d. Develop reliable and internationally comparable indicators for assessing the impact of language policies on linguistic diversity, and promote good practices in this regard.

Chapter 4 – EDUCATION

4. In order to further the process of learning to live together, there is a need to promote intercultural competencies, including those embedded in the everyday practices of communities, with a view to improving pedagogical approaches to intercultural relations.

To this end, action should be taken to:

a. Undertake a global comparative survey of educational contents and methods, including traditional modes of transmission, with particular reference to the recognition and accommodation of cultural diversity.

b. Support efforts to identify and/or create opportunities and facilities for culture-specific learning in each educational system, making use of existing instruments such as EFA National Assessment Reports.

c. Adapt teaching methods to the requirements of the everyday life of learners, with the necessary support of educational policy-makers, educational professionals at all levels and local communities, recognizing the cultural dimension as a central pillar of Education for Sustainable Development.

d. Develop international guidelines for the promotion of intercultural dialogue through the arts, based on the identification of good practices in arts education.

Chapter 5 – COMMUNICATION AND CULTURAL CONTENTS

5. There is a need to encourage cultural sensitivity in the production and consumption of communication and information contents, thereby facilitating access, empowerment and participation.

To this end, action should be taken to:

a. Support the production and distribution of innovative and diversified audiovisual materials, taking account of local needs, contents and actors, and having recourse as appropriate to public-private partnerships.

b. Assess the impact of ICT-driven changes on cultural diversity, with a view to highlighting good practices of multilingual access to written and audiovisual productions.

c. Promote media and information literacy for all age groups in order to increase the ability of media users to critically evaluate communication and cultural contents.

Chapter 6 – CREATIVITY AND THE MARKETPLACE

6. Creativity being a source of social and technological innovation, there is a need to invest in its development, both in the cultural sector and in the business sector, within which cultural diversity is to be understood as a source of profit and enhanced performance, conducive to corporate 'cultural intelligence'.

To this end, action should be taken to:

a. Facilitate the exchange of artistic productions and the circulation of artists, including through a system of cultural visas.

b. Develop appropriate systems for the protection of traditional know-how in the crafts sector, as well as ways and means of compensating the communities concerned for the commercial exploitation of such know-how.

c. Draw up and widely disseminate good practices in relation to tourism development with a view to maximizing its positive impacts on cultural diversity.

d. Develop 'cultural intelligence' in the business and marketing world through the establishment of real and virtual forums and the production of relevant research on the profitability of cultural diversity, not limited only to ethnic or gender difference.

Chapter 7 – CULTURAL DIVERSITY AND SUSTAINABLE DEVELOPMENT

7. The principles of cultural diversity, as embodied in particular in the Cultural Diversity Lens, should be duly taken into account in the design, implementation and monitoring of all development policies.

To this end, action should be taken to:

a. Identify concrete measures to operationalize research on the cultural dimension of natural resources conservation and management, with particular reference to the knowledge and know-how of indigenous communities.

b. Establish a clearing-house for documenting participatory approaches to environmental problems, including indications as to their success.

c. Encourage the participation of members of all communities in defining resource allocation criteria on the basis of social justice, so as to foster a dynamic of social dialogue and promote intercultural solidarity.

Chapter 8 – CULTURAL DIVERSITY, HUMAN RIGHTS AND DEMOCRATIC GOVERNANCE

8. As universally recognized human rights should be guaranteed to every individual, their effective exercise can be fostered through the recognition of cultural diversity, which can also reinforce social cohesion and encourage renewed modes of democratic governance. Policies conducive to the preservation and promotion of cultural diversity should be encouraged to this end.

Action should be taken in particular to:

a. Collect striking examples of cases in which the cultural context is a key factor in the effective exercise of universally recognized rights and freedoms, so as to highlight the cultural dimension of all rights and freedoms.

b. Map exchanges within and between minority groups and between majority and minority communities, especially in the context of 'global cities', in order to create informal networks of solidarities, and widely publicize such exchanges.

c. Study the diversity of the intangible heritage as a source of examples of modes of democratic governance based on the empowerment and participation of all communities.

GENERAL RECOMMENDATIONS:

9. There is a need to promote awareness among policy- and decision-makers about the benefits of intercultural and interfaith dialogue, while bearing in mind its potential instrumentalization.

10. Consideration should be given to establishing a national mechanism for monitoring public policies as they relate to cultural diversity, with a view to ensuring improved governance and the full implementation of universally recognized human rights.

Songs from the Garifuna, Belize, Guatemala, Honduras and Nicaragua

Annex

Introduction to the Statistical Annex.............. 260

Methodological explorations of the measurement of culture and cultural diversity 261

  Figure A.1 French labour force in cultural sector by type of activities in 2005.................... 264

  Figure A.2 The culture cycle.................... 267

  Figure A.3 Domains and activities.................... 268

  Figure A.4 Types of dichotomy useful to assess diversity.................... 270

  Figure A.5 Population of adults by ethnic group experiencing Taonga Tuku Iho activity during the last 12 months.................... 271

  Figure A.6 Share of foreign literature in French book publishing and in bestselling novels........ 272

  References and websites 273

Reader's guide 276

Table 1. Ratifications of the seven cultural conventions of UNESCO.......................... 277

Table 2. World Heritage sites and Intangible Cultural Heritage of Humanity 281

Table 3. Demographic context.......................... 286

Table 4. Telecommunication access 294

Table 5. Gender................................. 298

Table 6. Highlights of the World Values Survey 302

Table 7. Languages... 304

Table 8. Translations... 308

Table 9. Education and literacy 312

Table 10. Education and curricula 320

Table 11. International flows of mobile students at the tertiary level.................... 328

Table 12. Newspapers 332

Table 13. Broadcast content 340

Table 14. Movies 344

Table 15. Recorded music: Sales and repertoire 348

Table 16. International flows of selected cultural goods and services 352

Table 17. Tourism flows 360

Table 18. Environment, biodiversity and habitat 364

Table 19. Economic development and innovation 368

Glossary.. 372

Tamil workers planting tea in Sri Lanka

Introduction to the Statistical Annex

This Statistical Annex is divided into two parts. The first part discusses and explores the difficulties and methodological issues surrounding the measurement of cultural domains and activities, drawing attention to the limited coverage and scarcity of existing cultural data worldwide, especially regarding cultural participation and questions pertinent to heritage and indigenous issues. It also introduces the newly revised UNESCO Framework for Cultural Statistics (FCS), which updates the 1986 version and represents a methodological tool, which helps countries with varying capacities to organise their cultural statistics. The last section describes some initial approaches to measuring cultural diversity and the diversity of cultural expressions based on the conclusions of the first UNESCO Expert Meeting on Cultural Diversity (2007), which attempted to disentangle the complexities and sensitivities inherent to some of these issues.

The second part presents 19 statistical tables covering the areas described in the FCS and current coverage . across a wide range of topics and more than 200 countries and territories. Data were gathered from different sources but no specific surveys were carried out for the present report. UIS data covering culture, communication, education and science were collected from the standard UIS surveys. To complete the data set, data from international or regional agencies such as United Nations (UN) agencies or the World Bank were used as much as possible: regarding telecommunications access, data were gathered from the International Telecommunication Union (ITU); data for tourism flows were gathered from the UN World Tourism Organization (UNWTO), and for trade from the UN Statistical Division (UNSD); demographic data from the UN Department of Economics and Social affairs (UNDESA) and environmental data from the UN Environment Programme (UNEP), International Union for Conservation of Nature (IUCN) and Food and Agriculture Organization (FAO). Other data come the Organization for Economic Co-operation and Development (OECD) and the UN Development Programme (UNDP).

Still, most data originating from administrative sources lead but to a partial picture of the cultural domains as described in the FCS. For example, no harmonized data on cultural participation exist except from European countries. Alternative data from private sources (such as the International Federation of the Phonographic Industry (IFPI) for music or from household surveys) are also provided to complete the data set despite the fact that country coverage remains limited.

As cultural statistics are still under development in many countries, coverage varies immensely depending on the country and the domain in question. Generally speaking, economic data offer better coverage than social data (see methodology chapter). Most of the data on media are focused on content in radio, television or cinema. The low response rates for feature films or music reflect data scarcity, especially concerning Internet and interactive-media products such as e-newspapers, music downloads and e-books, all of which are difficult to capture using traditional statistical tools.

It is difficult to draw a global picture of cultural diversity and the diversity of cultural expressions from available data. Some information can be drawn from statistics on flows of students or goods (see methodology chapter). The statistics on media and culture provide a sense of the variety of cultural products and activities available, but cannot provide a full picture of the products actually 'consumed'. The scarcity of cultural data generally speaking highlights the urgent and overarching need to implement standards to improve cultural data collection worldwide.

⊃ *Old believers in the cultural space of the Semeiskie, east of Lake Baikal, Russian Federation*

Methodological explorations of the measurement of culture and cultural diversity

As illustrated throughout this report, the rise of cultural diversity on the international agenda is concomitant with the expansion of globalization, the speed of technological change and the emergence of the cultural and creative industries[1] – all of which are changing our very notions of culture and the ways in which we create, express and 'consume' it. As these industries become increasingly important components of contemporary post-industrial, knowledge-based economies, governments throughout the world have begun to recognize the potential value of the cultural and creative industries in growth, job creation and development (UIS and Global Alliance, 2002). As vectors of cultural identity, cultural activities play an important role in fostering cultural diversity, as well as in sustainable development and poverty alleviation.

While public policy has placed higher priority on culture and cultural diversity in recent decades, the sector of cultural activities is still poorly understood – largely because the accurate measurement of economic and social activity in the sector continues to pose considerable theoretical and political problems. While many developed countries (e.g. Australia, Canada, Finland, France and Spain) have finely tuned or dedicated systems for producing high-quality national cultural statistics, the intangible nature of culture (e.g. the valuation of heritage) and the differing definitions of it across the globe, compounded by cultural biases, tend to permeate many of the widely used statistical instruments and investigative approaches. This makes it difficult to accurately capture the extent of the field and the size of its workforce, much less to understand the social dynamics inherent in cultural activities.

International comparability remains highly problematic throughout the sector, and data scarcity is a major problem in all countries, but especially so in developing countries (with a few exceptions, such as Chile, Colombia and Singapore), which are for the most part unable to produce regular cultural statistics. The problem of data scarcity is particularly challenging on the African continent, despite the major role the cultural industries play in Africa's development, as has been acknowledged in the *Dakar Plan of Action* (UNESCO and OAU, 1992) and reiterated in the New Partnership for Africa's Development (NEPAD) plan for culture and development (UNESCO, 2003). Few cultural statistics are currently collected on a regular basis, despite the increasing importance of assessing the revenue generated from the music, crafts and films that thrive on the continent. The growth in the importance of such assessment is a general trend that can be observed all around the world. To meet the challenge posed therein would require, in many countries, better characterization of cultural industries in international classification systems in order to provide clear guidance to national statistics offices.

At international, regional and national levels, efforts to gather economic data in this sector have nevertheless intensified over the past decade (see the next section). However measurement strategies have tended to fall short of fully assessing the depth and breadth of cultural activities – from creation through dissemination and consumption of cultural expressions and products – and taking account of how globalization allows the transmission of cultural products throughout the world and is generating new communication tools (such as the Internet) which are engendering new forms of culture and new ways of accessing and practising culture. Digital technology has drastically changed the modes of producing and disseminating cultural products, and cultural industries that previously were kept separate by analogue systems of production (film, television, photography and printing) have now converged. As cultural consumption has grown with the rise of digital

---

1. The term 'cultural industries' refers to industries that combine the creation, production and commercialization of creative content that is intangible and cultural in nature. The content is typically protected by copyright and can take the form of goods or services. Cultural industries generally include printing, publishing and multimedia, audiovisual, phonographic and cinematographic productions, as well as crafts and design. The term 'creative industries' encompasses a broader range of activities, which include the cultural industries and all cultural or artistic production, whether live or produced as an individual unit. The creative industries are those in which the product or service contains a substantial element of artistic or creative endeavour and include activities such as architecture and advertising (see DCMS, 1998). The terms 'cultural industries' and 'creative industries' are often used interchangeably, but they are not synonymous. See also the Glossary following the statistical tables.

technology and the global exchange of goods, services, ideas, people and capital, so too has the range of products expanded, such that a 'product' now mediates most cultural experiences, which have themselves become multicultural in nature.

UNESCO sees culture as part of everyday life, reflected in many forms of human activity and expression, and involving beliefs, attitudes and practices including *all* forms of artistic and creative expression. Many of these can indeed be measured through cultural goods, services and practices, but so far a holistic methodological approach – based on a wider, more inclusive definition of cultural practices and consumption – has been lacking that would also take account of traditional forms of art that are expressed in non-commodified forms, such as intangible heritage, use of local languages and crafts. Since UNESCO's mandate goes far beyond a strictly economic evaluation of cultural activities, the UNESCO Institute for Statistics (UIS) has been tasked with redefining its 1986 *Framework for Cultural Statistics*, which represented the first comprehensive attempt to develop common methodologies to capture information about cultural activities on an international level while taking into account the needs and specificities of the developing world.[2]

The importance of the link between culture and development has received increased attention from aid agencies and specialists as culture has come to be recognized as a means for economic, social and individual development (UNESCO, 1995). In this sense, cultural activities (including tourism, crafts and artefacts) make an important contribution to poverty alleviation. Community cultural assets, such as intangible heritage, support sustainable local development and contribute to social and cultural revitalization. Many cultural industries are predominantly small or family businesses that offer opportunities to women, youth and socially disadvantaged groups to participate in productive activities that contribute in turn to gender equality, self-esteem and social awareness.[3]

UIS's statistical work in the field of culture was given new impetus with UNESCO's adoption in 2005 of the *Convention on the Protection and Promotion of the Diversity of Cultural Expressions*, which expressly obligates UNESCO to 'facilitate the collection, analysis and dissemination of all relevant information, statistics and best practices' regarding cultural diversity (Art. 19). At the same time, there has been a change of focus in UIS work, from data collection on infrastructure to new surveys and analyses that focus on content and reflect the digital era.[4] A UIS survey on print and electronic press was launched in 2005 with new questions related to languages and community newspapers; it was followed in 2006 by a survey on radio and television broadcasting which focused on the content and origin of programmes; and in 2007 a survey on cinema was conducted that includes questions on the digital production of feature films, languages used and the origin of co-productions. The results of these surveys are presented in the statistical tables.

This chapter surveys the field of cultural statistics, discussing some of the developments and challenges facing the assessment and measurement of cultural activities, and introduces the *2009 Framework for Cultural Statistics*. This revised Framework is a holistic organizational tool for capturing a wide range of cultural expressions based on consensual definitions of cultural practices, irrespective of the particular economic or social mode of its production. It is explicitly designed to provide a basis for producing comparable data on culture worldwide founded on this wider notion of culture, with the goal of enabling countries with varying capacities in statistics collection to work within their constraints, as may be posed by policy priorities, statistical expertise and human and financial resources.

2. UNESCO's 1986 *Framework for Cultural Statistics* was subsequently adopted by various national institutions, which then adapted and modified their methodology to reflect the specific cultural realities of their country. The Framework defined ten distinct categories: (0) cultural heritage; (1) printed matter and literature; (2/3) music and the performing arts; (4) visual arts; (5/6) audiovisual media (cinema and photography; radio and television); (7) socio-cultural activities; (8) sports and games; and (9) environment and nature. It also proposed cross-category matrices, such as creation/production, transmission/dissemination, consumption, registration/protection and participation (UIS, 1986).

3. The Jodhpur Initiatives, an interagency technical assistance programme launched in 2005 by UNESCO in cooperation with WIPO, UNIDO, UNDP, the World Bank and the Asian Development Bank, has developed a framework for strengthening national capacity-building projects related to the cultural industries sector as a strategy for poverty reduction and community regeneration. See UNESCO Bangkok, 2005; Askerud and Engelhardt, 2007.

4. UIS has also produced analytical reports on culture focusing on flows of cultural goods and services and on languages *Measuring Linguistic Diversity on the Internet*. It has also contributed analysis to the culture sector for reports such as *World Heritage: Challenges for the Millennium* (UNESCO, 2007).

In this way, it is hoped that the 2009 Framework will help to support appropriate policy implementation in the field of culture.

Overview of the challenges facing the field of cultural studies

At international, regional and national levels, efforts have intensified considerably in recent decades to measure the economic and social aspects of cultural activities through data on intellectual property rights, national accounts, cultural satellite accounts, trade and employment statistics, as well as household and time-use surveys. While these have enabled the production of a wide range of cultural data that can help to measure the contribution of culture to the national economy in terms of GDP and trends in cultural participation, consumption and employment (though often by means of a re-aggregation of classifications that are not directly cultural), data scarcity, differing definitions, and structural and operational challenges permeate the sector. One of the crucial tasks that we face today is to find a way to capture the social dimension of cultural activities beyond their economic value, in order to fully grasp their role in furthering sustainable development and promoting policy that supports cultural diversity.

The economic dimension

The identification of goods and services that generate *intellectual property rights* is a key component of the contribution of culture to the economy. The World Intellectual Property Organization (WIPO) has developed a framework that enables countries to estimate the size of their creative and information sector, with a breakdown into four categories of industries depending on their level of involvement in the creation, production and manufacturing of literary, scientific and artistic works: core copyright, interdependent copyright, partial copyright and non-dedicated support industries (WIPO, 2003).[5] In 2002, total copyright industries accounted for 12 percent of GDP and 8.4 percent of the workforce in the US, whereas in Hungary they accounted for 6.8 percent of GDP and 7.1 percent of the workforce; in

Singapore, 5.7 percent and 5.8 percent (in 2001); and in Canada, 5.3 percent and 7.0 percent, respectively (WIPO, 2006). Operationally, the notion of copyright is linked to a very clear policy goal, namely to ensure that countries protect their intellectual assets. However, it concerns only those economic activities that give rise to intellectual property rights, thus based on a definition of cultural industries that is more restrictive than that of UNESCO. Many areas of industry may be 'creative' or 'cultural', but it may be difficult to spell out a clear right to intellectual property in them (e.g. cultural practices such as the crafts sector or museum activities). Neither non-market cultural production nor the ownership of a cultural product are fully accounted for in the WIPO framework. Furthermore, when all copyright industries are factored into the economic model, the total value of their contribution to GDP nor to the workforce can vary considerably depending on how these are defined, and the results of the studies are not entirely comparable

National accounts, which oversee national economic activity, are another means for determining the extent of cultural industries' contribution to national economies, namely in the form of earnings and employment. In Canada, a recent study has shown that, on average from 1996 to 2003, the culture sector accounted for 3.8 percent of national output and 4 percent of national employment (Statistics Canada, 2007).

Yet because this approach focuses purely on financial factors, it is difficult to assess the value of non-commercial cultural products. Furthermore, precise assessment of a broad range of cultural products and services within national accounting systems requires very sophisticated data collection and technical skills, as well as dedicated resources, which are often lacking or incomplete. There is a widespread lack of resources and expertise to ensure high quality statistical work in this area, especially in the developing world, where data collection related to culture remains a low priority area for many countries. Differing definitions and categories further complicate comparability.

---

5. 'Core copyright industries' are usually those characterized as typical cultural industries that are wholly engaged in the creation, production and manufacturing, performance, broadcast, communication and exhibition, or distribution and sales of works and other protected subject matter. 'Interdependent copyright industries' are those engaged in the production, manufacture and sale of equipment whose function is wholly or primarily to facilitate the creation, production or use of works and other protected subject matter. 'Partial copyright industries' cover industries in which a portion of the activities is related to works and other protected subject matter and may involve creation, production and manufacturing, performance, broadcast, communication and exhibition or distribution and sales. 'Non-dedicated support industries' are those in which a portion of the activities is related to facilitating the broadcast, communication, distribution or sales of works and other protected subject matter.

The development of *cultural satellite accounts* is being promoted in Latin America to provide a macroeconomic view of the part that cultural goods play in the national economy. Initiatives in Brazil, Chile and Colombia are attempting to use national accounts data to measure the economic contribution of culture. The Convenio Andrés Bello (a group of Latin American countries and Spain) is developing a handbook on cultural satellite accounts, with the goal of providing a common methodology among countries, which aims to assess the cost of cultural products supply, the total expenditure on culture, and financial flows of cultural activities and uses. MERCOSUR countries have been very active in studying this area of potential economic growth. Initial results from a study for different Latin American countries show that the contribution of culture (here understood as publishing, leisure, cultural services and sports) to the GDP for the MERCOSUR countries was less than 2 percent in 2003 – except for Argentina and Uruguay, with 2.6 percent and 2.9 percent, respectively – in comparison to 2.6 percent in the EU (KEA, 2006). However, the studies were not strictly comparable as they use different methods. Statistical data and indicators are non-existent in other countries of the region, particularly in Central America.

The measurement of cultural employment is another significant means for obtaining data on cultural statistics, but it also presents problems. In France, the French labour force in the cultural sector was estimated to be 2 percent of total employment in 2005 (see Figure A.1).

To accurately assess cultural employment within a country, occupations within cultural industries would have to be supplemented with cultural occupations in non-cultural industries. These could include, for example, design activities in manufacturing and other sectors. However, cultural occupations in developing countries are often a secondary occupation for agricultural labourers or other workers and, as such, often are not declared or captured in censuses and labour force surveys.

The International Standard Classification by Occupations (ISCO) does not currently provide the level of detail required to identify cultural occupations in a truly comprehensive manner. In some cases, it is necessary to link employment data with industry data to calculate total cultural employment. These hidden or 'embedded' cultural occupations may not include a large enough number of practitioners to be accurately measured in sample surveys. Moreover, self-employed or informal work, and small companies employing less than ten people, are not captured in surveys. In this respect, even European statistics may well underestimate cultural employment. Nevertheless, national labour force surveys have a major role to play, especially in collecting data on secondary occupations, since cultural activities are often associated with part-time or amateur production but remain vital supplements to economic growth, especially in developing countries.

In many countries the cultural sector is more economically important than a number of older established industries (e.g. mining and car manufacturing) and contributes significantly to national export earnings. As a result, *trade statistics* may be more significant than employment data, especially in the developing world, with implications for the potential role of culture in development (Barrowclough and Kozul-Wright, 2006). The United Nations Conference on Trade and Development (UNCTAD) has for example developed models to measure trade flows within the creative industries, defined as 'the cycle of creation, production and distribution of goods and services that uses intellectual capital as primary input' (2008). UNCTAD estimates total trade of creative industries to have been US$445.2 billion in 2005. One major drawback of trade statistics, however, is that they fall short of assessing the value of ideas, creativity and innovation that may be transformed into productive capacity which may require intellectual property protection. Only the declared value of goods crossing a country's border is

Figure A.1 French labour force in cultural sector by type of activities in 2005

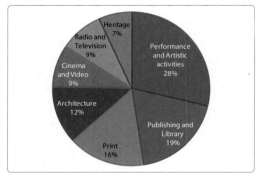

Source: Lacroix, 2003.

captured in customs data, not their actual market value, which is often considered far more important. Trade data on services are collected using balance of payments data, and only cover service transactions that relate to the cross-border supply of services (suppliers and consumers remain in their respective countries and the services cross the border). Thus, the results given in trade statistics provide only the tip of the iceberg of a far more global phenomenon (UIS and UNESCO, 2005).

The 2009 Framework seeks to incorporate these mechanisms while placing them within a holistic system that gives equal weight to the social dynamics within which they function.

The social dimension

The economic and social measurement of cultural participation is a particularly challenging but crucial dimension of cultural statistics. While participation in cultural activities and practices can be captured through attendance at formal and payable events, such as going to a movie or a concert, it often occurs in the informal sector where no economic transactions take place, such as participating in community activities and amateur artistic productions, or in everyday activities like reading a book.

A few commonly accepted statistical standards that focus on consumer expenditures on cultural goods and services and participation at paid cultural activities – namely, household and time-use surveys – are being used to capture facets of the economic dimension of cultural participation. However, such surveys are expensive and often designed for other purposes than strictly 'cultural' ones. Internationally comparable indicators on the social aspects of culture is an area requiring further development as regards both definitions and standard instruments. The term 'consumption' is normally used when referring to an activity for which the consumer has given a 'monetary' value, while the term 'participation' is used to designate taking part in amateur or unpaid activities. In practice this distinction can be difficult to make as consumers/participants may take part in informal activities 'paying' in kind or contributing to the 'cost' of the event in other ways. Moreover, cultural participation covers both active and passive behaviour. For example, it includes the person who is listening to a concert and the musician.

The purpose of cultural participation surveys should be to assess overall participation levels, even though it may be difficult to distinguish active from passive behaviour. For example, at some festivals, individuals may at one time be performers (active, creating, and inspiring others) and at other times be the audience (passive or seeking inspiration). Cultural participation does not concern activities carried out for employment purposes, however, which are defined by occupation (ILO, 1987); for example, cultural participation would include visitors to a museum but not the guide.

Pilot cultural participation surveys have been conducted mainly in the European Union. The European Leadership Group (LEG, 2000) attempted to produce a regional model, which was applied in the Eurobarometer. Three surveys have been carried out since then to collect harmonized data on European participation in cultural activities and to experiment with their applicability. The European conception of cultural participation includes the arts and everyday life activities that are related to enjoyment. It encompasses 'the ways in which ethnically marked differences in cultural tastes, values and behaviours inform not just artistic and media preferences but are embedded in the daily rhythms of different ways of life; and of the ways in which these connect with other relevant social characteristics – those of class and gender, for example' (Bennett, 2001).

In 2006 the UIS commissioned a study on cultural participation that looked at the European model of cultural participation surveys and its potential adaptability to cultural activities in developing countries (Morrone, 2006). The study reviewed the potential for cultural participation surveys in three developing countries, (Bhutan, Thailand and Uganda), as well as current data in New Zealand. It was found that surveys in these countries – when carried out – basically covered the same activities as those in the Eurobarometer, with additions adapted to the cultural practices and contexts of the countries themselves. Thailand carried out three rounds of cultural participation surveys, in 1985, 1995 and 2005, covering the Thai system of values and the protection of Thai culture. The Bhutan Living Standard Surveys, undertaken in 2003 and 2007, collected data on participation in community celebrations of cultural/historical events, community rites/events (non-religious), participation in community social, and household production of traditional crafts. While Uganda does not carry out participation surveys, the study suggested that such a survey would require items on food and nutrition, traditional dress, traditional medicine and oral tradition. One possible approach for obtaining data on cultural participation would be to add a module in the Ugandan National Household Survey, which collects information on the socio-economic characteristics at both the household and community levels. Finally, New Zealand cultural participation surveys included participation in rituals, ceremonies and practices of indigenous language by ethnic group, social group and gender, indicating the diversity of groups participating in different cultural activities (see the discussion of cultural diversity in the final section of this chapter).

The report of the study, *Guidelines for Measuring Cultural Participation* (Morrone, 2006), proposed a definition of cultural practices according to three categories: 1) *Home-based* refers to the amount of time spent watching television, listening to the radio, watching and listening to recorded sound and images, reading and using computers and the Internet; 2) *Going out* includes visits to cultural venues such as the cinema, the theatre, concerts, museums, monuments and heritage sites; and 3) *Identity-building* covers amateur cultural practices, membership in cultural associations, popular culture, ethnic culture, community practices and youth culture. Indeed, to reflect developing countries' views on cultural participation it would be necessary to extend the EU definition to include the language dimension (knowledge and transmission of particular languages, including story-telling, that contribute to community preservation) and the intangible cultural heritage (ICH)[6] or tradition dimension (everything from food to music, dress, traditional tools, indigenous knowledge, community social, cultural, historical events, religious and non-religious activities and festivals, etc.).

The 2009 Framework therefore seeks to establish some broad agreement on the overall conceptualization of the social model of culture and to provide some general guidance for developing additional statistical tools for defining the social element of culture and identifying appropriate indicators and definitions. It is acknowledged that carrying out frequent cultural participation surveys requires extensive human and financial resources, and that measuring the manifestations and expressions of ICH is extremely difficult and requires further methodological work in order to develop appropriate tools. At this stage, the Framework proposes that participation surveys concentrate on overall levels of participation and on recording the domain under which cultural activities take place. By using such surveys in a systematic way – for example, to survey participation in activities such as music, dance and reading – it will be possible to examine social issues, as well as to link amateur or informal cultural production to more formal activity. This link is vital for examining the economic relevance of the cultural sector and its impact on society as a whole.

Overview of the UNESCO 2009 Framework for Cultural Statistics

It is recognized that very few countries have sufficient resources for dedicated surveys of cultural activity, and that the 1986 UNESCO *Framework for Cultural Statistics* had been centred on OECD or EU perspectives rather than those of developing countries. As a result, UIS has concentrated on a pragmatic approach that builds on the most common international statistical classification systems[7] to maximize the potential of existing surveys to measure cultural activity, such as through labour force surveys and population censuses. Yet while the standards used for constructing the core definitions of the 2009 Framework are economic and social in nature in order to maximize international comparability, the updated Framework aims to be flexible enough to allow countries to select the domains that form part of their cultural statistics (a product that is highly cultural in one country, such as clothing and national dress, may have little cultural meaning in another). Furthermore, it allows for an interpretation of a resulting domain that is not limited to economic aspects of culture and extends to all aspects of that domain. So, for example, the definition for the

---

6. In the context of this statistical framework, 'intangible cultural heritage' (ICH) covers the 'practices, representations, expressions, knowledge, skills, as well as the associated instruments, objects, artefacts and cultural spaces'.

7. Principally, the International Standard Industrial Classification (ISIC) for cultural production activities, the International Standard Classification of Occupations (ISCO) for cultural employment, the Central Product Classification (CPC) for cultural goods and services, the Harmonised Commodity Description and Coding System Harmonised System (HS) for international flows of cultural goods, and the UN Trial International Classification of Activities for Time-Use Statistics (ICATUS).

measurement of 'performance' includes all performances, amateur and professional, whether they take place in formal concert halls or in open spaces in rural villages.

The Framework aims to assess cultural goods, services and activities arising within the cultural production cycle, conceived of in terms of its different cycles and the potential interactions between them: creation, production, dissemination, exhibition/reception and consumption and participation activities (see Figure A.2). While the concept of a culture cycle is not new, it seeks to highlight how a given 'cultural product' is embedded within both economic and social processes, regardless of funding or governance arrangements or whether activities take place in the formal or informal economy. The term 'culture cycle' is helpful since it suggests the interconnections across these activities, including the feedback processes by which activities (consumption) inspire the creation of new cultural products and artefacts. The model is an abstract analytical aid for thinking about cultural production and dissemination and functions as a lens for awareness-raising purposes. In practice, some of the phases of the cycle may overlap. For example, while musicians may compose (create) and perform (produce/disseminate), playwrights write (create) but rarely act (produce/disseminate). The individual craftsperson who may collect raw materials (informal resource input), use traditional skills (informal training) and sell the resulting product at the roadside (informal distribution and retail) personifies the whole cycle in an informal setting. Understanding which part of the process is being measured is an important element in designing the appropriate public policies for intervention in cultural production.

Central to this process is understanding and being able to track the totality of activities and necessary resources that are required to transform ideas into cultural goods and services, which then reach consumers, participants or users. In terms of cultural economy (which includes the informal economy), the artefact (whether painting, craft object, performance, etc.) is meaningless without a value system and a production system that gives it value or meaning. So, for example, having a particular site recognized as being of outstanding cultural heritage is of only limited economic use to a developing country, unless that country is also able to mobilize the assets of tourism, transport, preservation and hotels to capture

Figure A.2 The culture cycle

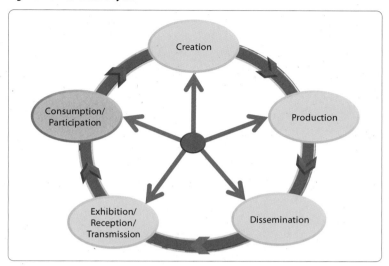

1. **Creation:** The origination and authoring of ideas and content (e.g. sculptors, writers, design companies) and the making of one-off products (e.g. crafts, fine arts).

2. **Production**: Reproducible cultural forms (e.g. television programmes), as well as the specialist tools, infrastructure and processes used in their realization (e.g. the production of musical instruments, the printing of newspapers).

3. **Dissemination:** Bringing generally mass reproduced cultural products to consumers and exhibitors (e.g. the wholesale, retail and rental of recorded music and computer games, film distribution). With digital distribution, goods and services can go directly from the creator to the consumer.

4. **Exhibition/Reception/Transmission:** Sites of exchange of rights to provide audiences with live and/or unmediated cultural experiences by granting or selling restricted access to consume/ participate in often time-based cultural activities (e.g. festival organization and production, opera houses, theatres, museums). Transmission relates to the transfer of knowledge that may not involve any commercial transaction and that often occurs in informal practices. It includes transmitting cultural identity from generation to generation, particularly in the form of intangible cultural heritage (ICH). It also includes festivals and events with open access.

5. **Consumption/Participation:** The activities of audiences and participants in consuming cultural products and taking part in cultural activities and experiences (e.g. book reading, dancing, participating in carnivals, listening to radio, visiting galleries).

Source: UIS, 2009.

the value of paying guests. At the same time, tangible and intangible heritage encompass artistic, aesthetic, symbolic and spiritual values. Thus, the characteristics of cultural goods and services differ from other products in that their value system is linked to their appreciation (Throsby, 2001).

Domains and activities
A review of selected cultural statistics frameworks from around the world (BOP, 2006) has shown that there is general agreement that culture is the result of a group of identifiable constituent activities. However, the review also suggested that this can be partly obscured by two

factors: a lack of agreement in identifying how these activities should be grouped together at a higher level as domains, and little shared understanding as to what functions should be included in the analysis of the cultural sector. In part, divergence related to the former is a genuine reflection of local differences in culture, but it is also related to the lack of a fully developed underlying model or logic for the analysis, which is the root cause of the latter.

Identifying sectoral breadth is necessary for measuring the cultural domain and defining which categories belong to it and which do not. For the purpose of the 2009 Framework, which follows a pragmatic approach, the operational definition of culture has been taken from the Preamble of the 2001 *Universal Declaration on Cultural Diversity*: 'culture should be regarded as the set of distinctive spiritual, material, intellectual and emotional features of society or a social group, and that it encompasses, in addition to art and literature, lifestyles, ways of living together, value systems, traditions and beliefs'. The pragmatic definition of culture used in the Framework is based on the representation of culture in terms of *domains* in order to measure the cultural activities, goods and services generated by industrial and non-industrial processes. It is understood that these cultural activities embody

or convey cultural expressions, irrespective of their commercial value, and may give rise to the production of cultural goods and services (UNESCO, 2005).

Unlike in the 1986 Framework, this definition of cultural domains is based on a hierarchical model that comprises core cultural domains and related cultural domains. The cultural domains include cultural activities, goods and services that are involved in all the different phases of the cultural production cycle. The related domains are linked to the broader definition of culture, which encompasses social and recreational activities. In contrast to the 1986 Framework, intangible cultural heritage (ICH) has been added as a core transversal dimension (previously covered only partially by the category 'community's services'). In addition, equipment/material and education/archives are presented as transversal domains because they can be applied to all the different core and related domains (see Figure A.3). To avoid double counting, each activity can be classified only once within the Framework, even though there are instances where activities logically span more than one domain. For instance, music would fall under both 'Performance and Celebration' and 'Audiovisual', as it consists of live music (Performance) and recorded music (Audiovisual). But the 2009 Framework prioritizes the subject rather than the form in which the cultural content can appear.

Figure A.3 Domains and activities

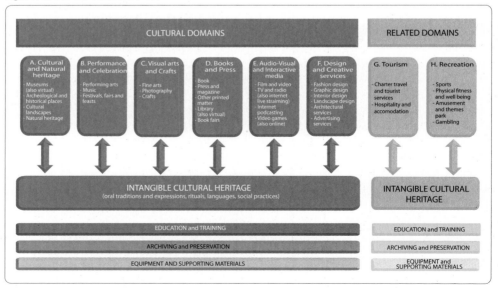

Souce: UIS, 2009.

At this stage, the purpose of the Framework is to show how statistics derived from economic data, household and visitor surveys, and valuation of cultural assets can be combined to present a holistic view of the culture sector that will allow for international comparability. Only after the revised Framework has been adopted and has entered into its implementation stage can the development of guidelines, indicators, pilot exercises, and training and capacity-building begin.

As has been pointed out, on reviewing the existing cultural statistics frameworks in several countries and regions of the world, it was found that very little cultural data is actually collected even in developed countries. The new Framework should be therefore understood as the starting point of a process of building cultural statistics from an international perspective, with the aim of highlighting the importance of culture and increase its visibility. Its primary purpose at this stage is to assist countries in developing their own locally sensitive frameworks and to relate them and make possible adaptations to existing frameworks. The Framework may also serve as a basis for negotiations between cultural policy and practitioners and national statistics offices, whose participation is critical for developing cultural statistics. In this sense, the Framework can act as a tool for stimulating demand and as a means for providing the culture sector with guidelines for requesting data collection.

Measuring cultural diversity and the diversity of cultural expressions
As we have seen, many comparability issues arise when discussing cultural statistics, and even more so when assessing diversity, particularly when trying to make international comparisons or accounting for differences between countries (e.g. in attitudes towards social participation). This section describes approaches to measuring diversity of cultural expressions and presents some initial thoughts for discussion, based on conclusions of the first UNESCO Expert Meeting on Cultural Diversity, which attempted to disentangle the complexities and sensitivities inherent to some of these issues (UIS, 2007).

Diversity is an aspect of different elements of culture, from personal identity to preferences, quality of life, indigenous/ethnic affiliation, or even culture as an individual emancipatory experience. Diversity requires an enabling environment in order to flourish, where 'environment' is understood as the set of conditions that allow for freedom of expression, ethnic diversity and the availability of social and cultural capital, technology, infrastructure, education, social networks and representation of social groups within institutions. Cultural expressions generate cultural goods, services and activities, which in turn can be (or become) commercial in nature, though not necessarily. While commodified goods can usually be measured through economic statistics, non-commodified goods, services and activities have to be identified through household surveys and qualitative studies, which can serve to evaluate amateur practices and non-formal cultural activities.

Cultural diversity is a multifaceted policy area with a number of different roots and with different emphasis and articulation at different territorial levels: intra-state, inter-state or transnational. In the latter context, the drive towards active policy on cultural diversity has a number of interconnected aspects:

- In general terms, there has been a growing demand for cultural products originating in the developing world or, in some cases, a hybridization of these products with those from the developed world. But developing countries are often poorly positioned to negotiate returns on their cultural exports that are comparable with returns received by developed nations. This is partly due to a lack of local institutional capacity but also to the absolute power of an oligopolistic industrial sector.

- The blurring of boundaries between (largely Western) notions of high and low culture, and between the West and 'the rest'.

- The commercialization of crafts production and its role in strategies of economic development in the developing world.

A range of issues is emerging as a result of these changes, perhaps the most debated of which concerns intellectual property rights (IPR). Since culture is seen increasingly as a commodity, a system of rights (and determination of which rights may be accorded to individual producers) dictates the degree of protection that should be given to individuals and communities for the exploitation of their ideas. As has been well publicized, there are particular problems – mainly argued on behalf of large corporations seeking to protect their assets – associated with copying or theft. At the same time, areas of culture that are untraded may not develop a robust identification of rights, leaving them vulnerable to theft. This problem exists in developing countries and often goes unreported, posing a threat to the diversity of cultural expressions. Furthermore, while the connections between copyright protection and diversity are still unclear and ill-defined, intellectual property rights may have a paradoxical effect on diversity, namely by either enhancing it (fostering the creation of products and their distribution) or depleting it (developing new entry barriers for users). It could also accelerate phenomena such as homogenization, where common cultural patterns can be identified around the world (consumption of the same movies) or hybridization of culture (new forms of culture).

Diversity between nations
The diversity of cultural expressions can be studied by looking at the types of dichotomy in the supply and demand of cultural goods and services, as shown in Table 1 below. Not all dichotomies in the diversity of

cultural expressions can be easily measured, however, and depending on the market or section, assessing the demand for diversity may be extremely complex. Household surveys would be required to assess the demand, which is a costly instrument.

Studying cultural flows between nations is a common tool for looking at diversity between nations. Imports and exports of films can be used to represent production and exchange diversity by indicating the origin of films entering a country, but measurement is severely limited by the technical constraints of customs and balance of payments data. Typically, films are exported to the destination market and then copied and distributed locally. As a result, the level of exports may bear little relation to the volume distributed in the recipient country. While an exported film has an almost negligible value at customs, the bulk of international exchanges relating to its export are compiled in data from balance of payments, in the form of receipts for royalties and licences through copies, exhibition rights and reproduction licence fees. Customs statistics provide information about the country of origin and the country of destination of each good. Unfortunately, the 'cultural origin' of a cultural good is not easily identifiable. Only limited information is available on the origin of the cultural content of traded products. The rules applied to origin and destination of imported and exported products relate to the location of processing, but do not specify the origin of its cultural content. It is possible for the original work and its copies to be produced in different locations. For example, many films created and projected in country A may have been imported in the form of release prints from country B, which benefits from competitive laboratories that process at lower prices. In trade records, the products are declared as originating from country B. However, from a cultural point of view, country B is not considered to be the country of origin of this product (UIS and UNESCO, 2005).

Diversity within nations: Internal diversity
The diversity within a nation is expressed not just by diversity of products but also by diversity of creators, consumers and actors of cultural activities and products. The study of different social/ethnic groups, as well as the use of languages, could be undertaken to assess domestic diversity (gender, various social groups, including people belonging to minorities or indigenous

Figure A.4 Types of dichotomy useful to assess diversity

Types of dichotomy		What to assess?
Variety of offers (goods and services produced)	Demand for cultural goods and services	*Variety of offers for a given good, sector, activity, etc.* *Diversity of supply does not imply that all types of products are consumed.*
Supply of diversity	Diversity in means of distribution	*For a given good, sector, activity, etc. Existence of a monopoly, oligopoly, barriers of access.*
Stocks	Flows	*What is produced / what is exchanged.*
Foreign	Domestic	*Origin of goods, services, activities. Important for exports.*
Rural	Urban	*Where cultural activities occur and goods and services are produced and by whom.*
Commodified	Non-commodified	*For good/object, activity, expression, etc. Also includes dimensions of paying vs. non-paying or profit vs. non-profit or traditional knowledge vs. commercial knowledge.*
Tangible heritage	Intangible heritage	*Built heritage vs. vernacular traditions and knowledge.*
Physical/analogue	Digital	*New forms of cultural expression: Internet, eBooks, etc.*

Source: UIS, 2007.

peoples).[8] Some countries are quite advanced in this domain, such as Canada, the Netherlands and New Zealand, where detailed social statistics are available with data broken down by social/ethnic groups or types of languages. This diversity can be studied by analyzing differences or commonalities in cultural practices of different ethnic groups or by gender.

In New Zealand many analyses look at the representation of minorities in different cultural practices. Statistics New Zealand has developed cultural indicators to monitor trends in the cultural sector, broken down into five themes: engagement, cultural identity, diversity, social cohesion, and economic development. The indicators aim to measure whether New Zealand's growing cultural diversity is freely expressed, respected and valued (MacKenzie, 2007). The list of potential indicators is as follows:

- Percentage of grants New Zealand's national lottery has distributed to arts and cultural activities for ethnic organizations

- Percentage of the population involved in ethnic cultural activities

- Level of minority cultural activities presented to wider audiences

- Proportion of local content on New Zealand television

- Speakers of te Reo Māori

- Involvement in community arts, culture and heritage groups by members of ethnic groups that are not Maori or New Zealand European.

Maori cultural heritage is an integral part of the New Zealand *Framework for Cultural Statistics*. The first category of the Framework contains the category *Taonga tuku iho*,[9] which is exclusive to Maori culture and comprises four sub-categories: learning about traditional Maori customs, practices, history or beliefs; visiting the ceremonial centre of a community, the fore-court of a meeting house (*marae*); visiting sites of historic importance to Maori; and viewing exhibitions of Maori ancestral treasures. Statistics New Zealand initiated the Cultural Experience Survey (CES) in 2002 as a supplement to its Household Labour Force Survey (HLFS). The survey results provided the percentage of the population involved in ethnic cultural activities. Figure 4 below shows that more than two-thirds of Maori adults experienced one or more Maori activities during the 12 months before the survey. This level was more than twice that for Europeans. A socio-economic portrait of the adults experiencing at least one Maori activity indicated that four out of ten of these adults had a tertiary qualification and more than 40 percent of adults under 45 years of age experienced at least one Maori experience, which was double the rate among the population over 65 years of age.

Figure A.5 Population of adults by ethnic group experiencing Taonga Tuku Iho activity during the last 12 months

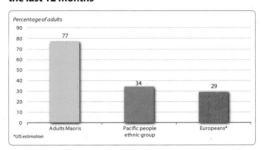

Source: Statistics New Zealand, 2003.

Assessing the diversity of cultural expressions
As discussed throughout this chapter, severe limitations in current data render the measurement of cultural activities problematic, and this holds even more for the evaluation and assessment of changes in the diversity

---

8. The United Nations Permanent Forum on Indigenous Issues (UNPFII) identified the need to develop indicators relevant to indigenous peoples and the Millennium Development Goals (MDGs). The work undertaken by the Working Group on Indicators of the International Indigenous Forum on Biodiversity (IIFB) was set up by the Secretariat of the Convention on Biological Diversity and is supported by the UNPFII. The IIFB has developed indicators pertinent to indigenous peoples for assessing progress towards the 2010 biodiversity target, which covers the status of traditional knowledge, innovations and practices (CBD, 2008). The indicators relate to indigenous rights, 'enabling environments', cultural practices and the use of traditional languages.

9. Refers to valued items relative to Maori passed down from earlier generations.

of cultural expressions (loss of diversity, endangered languages, impact of globalization, etc.).

A basic theoretical model of diversity was developed by Andrew Stirling (1998) and can be used to analyze diversity, while drawing on developments in other fields and tested in cultural domains such as publishing and music. The model is based on three components:

- *Variety*: Number of categories, cultural types (e.g. in book publishing, it refers to different genres of books, such as literature, academic books, comics, art books, etc.)

- *Balance*: Market share, frequency or any measure of the proportion revealing the pattern in the distribution of that quantity across the relevant categories (e.g. percentage of academic books in a shop as compared to the percentage of children's books)

- *Disparity*: Degree to which each category differs from the others (e.g. is the distinction between adult and children's literature greater than that between university and school textbooks?)

Disparity is more difficult to measure and can often be subjective. Disparity of cultural expressions can be captured as a distance defined between types within a hierarchy. The application of this model would concentrate on the first two aspects of variety and balance.

Figure A.6 Share of foreign literature in French book publishing and in bestselling novels

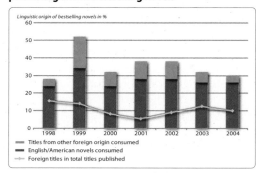

Source: Benhamou and Peltier, 2007.

Françoise Benhamou and Stéphanie Peltier (2007) applied Stirling's model to the book publishing industry in France, based on the definition of cultural diversity as 'the quantitative and qualitative diversity of the production and consumption of cultural goods and services in a given country'. They evaluated the supplied and consumed diversity of that industry in terms of three categories: title, genre and original language. The differentiation in supplied and consumed diversity highlighted the fact that while the choice of products can be quite large, the products consumed can involve a smaller range, as reflected, for example, in the superstar phenomenon[10] (Ranaivoson, 2007), which leads to less diversity.

The analysis of the linguistic origin of the books has led to the observation that the share of books of foreign origin in French publishing fell between 1997 and 2004. But in the meantime, the pattern of distribution of books of foreign origin has changed, with a decline of books in English in favour of books from different origins. Nevertheless, the share of bestselling novels consumed is still dominated by English/American literature. As illustrated in Figure A.5, the variety of books supplied is greater than the variety of books consumed.

There is still no clear common understanding or definition of the diversity of cultural expressions, and additional in-depth research projects need to be carried out in other cultural sectors before any conclusions can be drawn about the pertinence of this model. Cultural expressions should be examined and measured at all stages in the value chain, from production to distribution to consumption, and include both commodified cultural goods and services and un-commodified activities (e.g. amateur practices or Internet use). The diversity of cultural expressions should be measured at both the national and the international levels. Relevant definitions for the examination of social diversity need to be explicitly debated. The enabling environment – that is, the conditions that allow diversity to flourish – should also be taken into account. Developments of these measures should bear in mind policy relevance and the specific needs of the countries concerned.

10. 'Superstars' are products and producers that stimulate a great deal of consumption and attract even more attention.

References

Askerud, P. and Engelhardt, R. (eds.). 2007. *Statistics on Cultural Industries: Framework for the Elaboration of National Data Capacity Building Projects*. Bangkok, UNESCO Bangkok. http://unesdoc.unesco.org/images/0015/001549/154956e.pdf

Barrowclough, D. and Kozul-Wright, Z. (eds.). 2006. *Creative Industries and Developing Countries: Voice, Choice and Economic Growth*. London, Routledge.

Benhamou, F. and Peltier, S. 2007. How should cultural diversity be measured? An application using the French publishing industry. *Journal of Cultural Economics*, Vol. 31, No. 2, pp. 85–107.

Bennett, T. 2001. *Cultural Policy and Cultural Diversity: Mapping the Policy Domain*. Policy Note 7. Strasbourg, Council of Europe.

Burns Owens Partnership (BOP), Pratt, A. and Taylor, C. 2006. *Creating Global Statistics for Culture: Expert Scoping Study*. Report to UIS.

Convention on Biological Diversity (CBD). 2008. Indigenous languages in the Context of the Convention on Biological Diversity. Paper presented at the UNPFII International Expert Group Meeting on Indigenous Languages, New York, 8–10 January. http://www.un.org/esa/socdev/unpfii/documents/EGM_IL_SCBD.doc

Culture Statistics Program, Statistics Canada. 2007. *Economic Contribution of the Culture Sector to Canada's Provinces*. Ottawa, Statistics Canada. http://www.statcan.gc.ca/pub/81-595-m/81-595-m2006037-eng.pdf

Departamento Administrativo Nacional de Estadística (DANE). 2008. *Colombia: Cuenta Satélite de Cultura*. Bogata, DANE, Government of Colombia. http://www.dane.gov.co/index.php?option=com_content&task=category&sectionid=33&id=416&Itemid=915

Department for Culture Media and Sport, United Kingdom (DCMS). (1998). *Creative Industries Mapping Document 1998*. London, DCMS. http://www.culture.gov.uk/reference_library/publications/4740.aspx

European Leadership Group (LEG). 2000. *Cultural Statistics in the EU*. Eurostat Working Papers. Population and Social Conditions Series, 3/2000/E/No1. Final report of the LEG. Luxembourg, Eurostat.

Hui, D. (ed.). 2003. *Baseline Study of Hong Kong's Creative Industries*. For the Central Policy Unit, Hong Kong, Special Administrative Region Government. Hong Kong, Centre for Cultural Policy Research, University of Hong Kong. http://www.cpu.gov.hk/english/documents/new/press/baseline%20study(eng).pdf

International Labour Organisation (ILO). 2007. *International Standard Classification of Occupations 2008 (ISCO 08)*. Draft. Geneva, ILO. http://www.ilo.org/public/english/bureau/stat/isco/docs/draft08.pdf

—. 1987. *International Standard Classification of Occupations 1988 (ISCO 88)*. Geneva, ILO. http://www.ilo.org/public/english/bureau/stat/isco/isco88/index.htm

Kahneman, D. and Knetsch, J. 1992. Valuing public goods: the purchase of moral satisfaction. *Journal of Environmental Economics and Management*, Vol. 22, pp. 57–70.

KEA. 2006. *The Economy of Culture in Europe*. Study prepared for the European Commission. Brussels, KEA European Affairs. http://www.keanet.eu/Ecoculture/Study%20new.pdf

Lacroix, C. 2009. *Statistiques de la culture. Chiffre clés. Edition 2009*. Paris, Ministère de la culture et de la communication, Département des Etudes de la Prospective et des Statistiques (DEPS).

MacKenzie, J. 2007. *Best practices, methodologies and approaches to measure the diversity of cultural expressions*. http://www.uis.unesco.org/template/pdf/cscl/Cultdiv/McKenzie.pdf

Observer Delegation of Canada. 2008. Statement by the Observer Delegation of Canada to the United Nations Permanent Forum on Indigenous Issues' International Expert Group Meeting on Indigenous Languages. 9 January, New York. http://www.un.org/esa/socdev/unpfii/documents/EGM_IL_Canada_en.doc

Organisation for Economic Co-operation and Development (OECD). 2007a. *International Measurement of the Economic and Social Importance of Culture*. Paris, OECD. http://www.oecd.org/dataoecd/56/54/38348526.pdf

—. 2007b. *PISA 2006: Science Competencies for Tomorrow's World*. 2 vols. Paris, OECD. Vol. 1 (http://www.oei.es/evaluacioneducativa/InformePISA2006-FINALingles.pdf) and Vol. 2 (http://www.oecd.org/dataoecd/30/18/39703566.pdf).

Ranaivoson, H. 2007. Measuring cultural diversity: A definition based on an overview of existing literature. Paper presented at the First Expert Group Meeting on the Statistical Measurement of the Diversity of Cultural Expressions in Montreal, September. http://www.uis.unesco.org/template/pdf/cscl/cultdiv/Ranaivoson.pdf

Traditional Japanese puppet theatre, Ningyo Johruri Bunraku

Statistics New Zealand. 2003. *A Measure of Culture: Cultural Experiences and Cultural Spending in New Zealand*. Wellington, Statistics New Zealand. http://www.stats.govt.nz/~/media/Statistics/Publications/Analytical-reports/Measure%20of%20Culture/measure-of-culture.ashx

Stirling, A. 1998. *On the Economics and Analysis of Diversity*. Electronic Working Papers Series Paper No. 28. Brighton, Science Policy Research Unit, University of Sussex. http://www.uis.unesco.org/template/pdf/cscl/cultdiv/Stirling.pdf

Throsby, D. 2001. *Economics and Culture*. Cambridge, Cambridge University Press.

Tran, H. T. and Navrud, S. 2007. Valuing cultural heritage in developing countries: comparing and pooling contingent valuation and choice modelling estimates. *Environmental and Resource Economics,* Vol. 38, No. 1, pp. 51–69.

UNESCO. 2007. *World Heritage: Challenges for the Millennium*. Paris, UNESCO World Heritage Centre. http://whc.unesco.org/uploads/activities/documents/activity-558-1.pdf

—. 2005. *Convention on the Protection and Promotion of the Diversity of Cultural Expressions*. Paris, UNESCO. http://unesdoc.unesco.org/images/0014/001429/142919e.pdf

—. 2003. *Atelier sur la culture et le développement dans le programme d'action du NEPAD*. Paris, UNESCO. http://ocpa.irmo.hr/resources/docs/NEPAD_Draft_Final_Report-fr.pdf

—. 2002. *Universal Declaration on Cultural Diversity*. Paris, UNESCO. http://unesdoc.unesco.org/images/0012/001271/127160m.pdf

—. 1986. *The UNESCO Framework for Cultural Statistics*. http://www.uis.unesco.org/template/pdf/cscl/framework/1986original.pdf

UNESCO and Organization of African Unity (OAU). 1992. *Culture Industries for Development in Africa: Dakar Plan of Action*. http://unesdoc.unesco.org/images/0011/001131/113126eo.pdf

UNESCO Bangkok. 2005. *The Jodhpur Initiatives*. Bangkok, UNESCO Bangkok. http://cms.unescobkk.org/fileadmin/user_upload/culture/Cultural_Industries/Jodhpur_Initiatives.pdf

UNESCO Institute for Statistics (UIS). *The 2009 UNESCO Framework for Cultural Statistics: August 2009*. Montreal.

—. 2009. UNESCO Framework for Cultural Statistics: Task Force Meeting Summary. May 2009. Montreal. http://www.uis.unesco.org/template/pdf/cscl/framework/TFM_Summary_EN.pdf

—. 2006a. *Guidelines for Measuring Cultural Participation*. Montreal. Paper submitted by A. Morrone. http://www.uis.unesco.org/template/pdf/cscl/framework/CUL_particip.pdf

—. 2006b. *Evaluating Language Statistics: The Ethnologue and Beyond*. Paper submitted to the UIS by John C. Paolillo. Montreal: UNESCO Institute of Statistics.

UNESCO. 2007. *Expert Group Meeting (EGM) on the Statistical Measurement of the Diversity of Cultural Expressions. Final Report*. Montreal, UIS. http://www.uis.unesco.org/template/pdf/cscl/cultdiv/mtgreport.pdf

UNESCO Institute for Statistics (UIS) and Global Alliance for Cultural Diversity. 2002. *Understanding Creative Industries: Cultural Statistics for Public Policy-making*. http://portal.unesco.org/culture/en/files/30297/11942616973cultural_stat_EN.pdf/cultural_stat_EN.pdf

UNESCO Institute for Statistics (UIS) and UNESCO. 2005. *International Flows of Selected Cultural Goods and Services, 1994–2002*. Montreal, UIS. http://www.uis.unesco.org/template/pdf/cscl/IntlFlows_EN.pdf

United Nations. 1948. *Universal Declaration of Human Rights*. http://www.un.org/en/documents/udhr

United Nations Conference on Trade and Development (UNCTAD). 2008. Background paper. Secretary-General's high-level panel on the creative economy and industries for development. UNCTAD pre-conference event, 14–15 January. http://www.unctad.org/en/docs/tdxiibpd4_en.pdf

United Nations Permanent Forum on Indigenous Issues (UNPFII). 2007. *Handbook for Participants*. New York, United Nations. http://www.un.org/esa/socdev/unpfii/documents/handbook_participants_en.pdf

Van der Pol, H. 2008. Key role of cultural and creative industries in the economy. *Statistics Knowledge and Policy 2007: Measuring and Fostering the Progress of Societies*. Paris, OECD. http://www.oecd.org/dataoecd/11/47/38703999.pdf?contentId=38704000

World Intellectual Property Organisation (WIPO). 2006. *National studies on Assessing the Economic Contribution of the Copyright-Based Industries*. Geneva, WIPO.

—. 2003. *Guide on Surveying the Economic Contribution of the Copyright-based Industries*. Geneva, WIPO. http://www.wipo.int/copyright/en/publications/pdf/copyright_pub_893.pdf

Websites

Central Product Classification (CPC): http://unstats.un.org/unsd/statcom/doc02/cpc.pdf

Convenio Andrés Bello (CAB): http://www.convenioandresbello.info

Eurobarometer Surveys: http://ec.europa.eu/public_opinion/index_en.htm

Harmonised Commodity Description and Coding System Harmonised System (HS): http://www.wcoomd.org/home_wco_topics_hsoverviewboxes_hsoverview_hsharmonizedsystem.htm

International Standard Classification of Occupations (ISCO): http://www.ilo.org/public/english/bureau/stat/isco/index.htm

International Standard Industrial Classification (ISIC): http://www.ilo.org/public/english/bureau/stat/class/isic.htm

New Zealand Cultural Experience Survey (CES): http://www2.stats.govt.nz/domino/external/omni/omni.nsf/outputs/12860FC8DE9BF3D1CC256D3B00704A8D

New Zealand Framework for Cultural Statistics: http://www.stats.govt.nz/methods_and_services/surveys-and-methods/classifications-and-standards/classifications-and-related-statistical-standards/framework-for-cultural-statistics.aspx

New Zealand Household Labour Force Survey (HLFS): http://www.stats.govt.nz/browse_for_stats/work_income_and_spending/Employment/HouseholdLabourForceSurvey_HOTPJun09qtr/Technical%20Notes.aspx

UIS, New Tools and Frameworks to Monitor Information Societies and Critical Issues in the Field of Culture: http://www.uis.unesco.org/ev.php?URL_ID=3754&URL_DO=DO_TOPIC&URL_SECTION=201

UN Trial International Classification of Activities for Time-Use Statistics (ICATUS): http://unstats.un.org/unsd/methods/timeuse/icatus/icatus_1.htm

United Nations Permanent Forum on Indigenous Issues (UNPFII): http://www.un.org/esa/socdev/unpfii/index.html

Storytellers and street performers in Jemaa el-Fna Square in Marrakesh, Morocco.

Reader's guide

The following symbols and groupings are used in the Statistical Tables:

…	No data available
*	National estimation
**	UIS estimation
0	Magnitude negligible (less than half the last decimal shown)
.	Not applicable
±	Partial data
+n	Data refer to the year n years after the reference year
-n	Data refer to the year n years before the reference year
(.)	= Numbers in parenthesis indicate a different beginning year for Average annual % change calculation.

Population

Unless specified, all of the indicators in the statistical tables were calculated using the population estimates produced by the United Nations Population Division in its 2006 revision.

Trade data

Data for cultural trade in goods were extracted in June 2008 from the UN Comtrade database using the Harmonized System (HS) classification, version 1996.

Data on audiovisual and related services were extracted from the IMF Balance of Payments Statistics in current US$. The source of other services data is from the publication *OECD Statistics on International Trade in Services*.

Regional averages

Calculations for regional aggregates and the world were done where data coverage was sufficient to do so. Regional figures for literacy rates, gross enrolment ratios, school life expectancy are weighted averages, taking into account the relative size of the population of each country in each region. The averages are derived from both published data and broad estimates for countries for which no reliable publishable data are available.

The Glossary following the statistical tables defines the concepts used in the tables.

Regional groupings

The regional country groupings follow the UNESCO system detailed by country groupings by geographical regions (continents) and by geographical sub-regions. Some changes have been made in order to fulfil the purpose of this report.

Arab States
Algeria, Bahrain, Djibouti, Egypt, Iraq, Jordan, Kuwait, Lebanon, Libyan Arab Jamahiriya, Mauritania, Morocco, Oman, Palestinian Autonomous Territories, Qatar, Saudi Arabia, Sudan, Syrian Arab Republic, Tunisia, United Arab Emirates, Yemen.

Sub-Saharan Africa
Angola, Benin, Botswana, Burkina Faso, Burundi, Cameroon, Cape Verde, Central African Republic, Chad, Comoros, Congo, Democratic Republic of the Congo, Côte d'Ivoire, Equatorial Guinea, Eritrea, Ethiopia, Gabon, Gambia, Ghana, Guinea, Guinea-Bissau, Kenya, Lesotho, Liberia, Madagascar, Malawi, Mali, Mauritius, Mozambique, Namibia, Niger, Nigeria, Rwanda, Saint Helena, Sao Tome and Principe, Senegal, Seychelles, Sierra Leone, Somalia, South Africa, Swaziland, United Republic of Tanzania, Togo, Uganda, Zambia, Zimbabwe.

Central and South Asia
Afghanistan, Armenia, Azerbaijan, Bangladesh, Bhutan, Georgia, India, Islamic Republic of Iran, Kazakhstan, Kyrgyzstan, Maldives, Nepal, Pakistan, Sri Lanka, Tajikistan, Turkmenistan, Uzbekistan.

East Asia
Brunei Darussalam, Cambodia, China (Hong Kong Special Administrative Region of China and Macao Special Administrative Region of China), Indonesia, Japan, Democratic People's Republic of Korea, Republic of Korea, Lao People's Democratic Republic, Malaysia, Mongolia, Myanmar, Philippines, Singapore, Thailand, Timor-Leste, Viet Nam.

Europe
Albania, Andorra, Austria, Belarus, Belgium, Bosnia and Herzegovina, Bulgaria, Croatia, Cyprus, Czech Republic, Denmark, Estonia, Finland, France, Germany, Gibraltar, Greece, Holy See, Hungary, Iceland, Ireland, Israel, Italy, Latvia, Liechtenstein, Lithuania, Luxembourg, the Former Yugoslav Republic of Macedonia, Malta, Republic of Moldova, Monaco, Montenegro, the Netherlands, Norway, Poland, Portugal, Romania, the Russian Federation, San Marino, Serbia, Slovakia, Slovenia, Spain, Sweden, Switzerland, Turkey, Ukraine, the United Kingdom of Great Britain and Northern Ireland.

North America
Canada, United States of America

Latin America and the Caribbean
Anguilla, Antigua and Barbuda, Argentina, Aruba, Bahamas, Barbados, Belize, Bermuda, Bolivia, Brazil, British Virgin Islands, Cayman Islands, Chile, Colombia, Costa Rica, Cuba, Dominica, Dominican Republic, Ecuador, El Salvador, Grenada, Guatemala, Guyana, Haiti, Honduras, Jamaica, Mexico, Montserrat, Netherlands Antilles, Nicaragua, Panama, Paraguay, Peru, Saint Kitts and Nevis, Saint Lucia, Saint Vincent and the Grenadines, Suriname, Trinidad and Tobago, Turks and Caicos Islands, Uruguay, Venezuela.

Pacific
Australia, Cook Islands, Fiji, Kiribati, Marshall Islands, Federated States of Micronesia, Nauru, New Zealand, Niue, Palau, Papua New Guinea, Samoa, Solomon Islands, Tokelau, Tonga, Tuvalu, Vanuatu.

Table 1. Ratifications of the seven cultural conventions of UNESCO[1]

Country or Territory	Universal Copyright Convention (1952,1971)		Convention for the Protection of Cultural Property in the Event of Armed Conflict (1954)	Convention on the Means of Prohibiting and Preventing the Illicit Import, Export and Transfer of Ownership of Cultural Property (1970)	Convention Concerning the Protection of the World Cultural and Natural Heritage (1972)	Second Protocol to the Hague Convention of 1954 for the Protection of Cultural Property in the Event of Armed Conflict (1999)	Convention on the Protection of the Underwater Cultural Heritage (2001)	Convention for the Safeguarding of the Intangible Cultural Heritage (2003)	Convention on the Protection and Promotion of the Diversity of Cultural Expressions (2005)
Arab States									
Algeria	1973	1973	...	1974	1974	...	...	2004	...
Bahrain	...	...	2008	...	1991	2008	...	...	...
Djibouti	...	...	...	...	2007	...	...	2007	2006
Egypt	...	...	1955	1973	1974	2005	...	2005	2007
Iraq	...	...	1967	1973	1974	...	...	...	...
Jordan	...	...	1957	1974	1975	2009	...	2006	2007
Kuwait	...	...	1969	1972	2002	...	...	...	2007
Lebanon	1959	...	1960	1992	1983	...	2007	2007	...
Libyan Arab Jamahiriya	...	...	1957	1973	1978	2001	2005	...	...
Mauritania	...	...	...	1977	1981	...	...	2006	...
Morocco	1972	1975	1968	2003	1975	...	...	2006	...
Oman	...	...	1977	1978	1981	...	...	2005	2007
Palestinian A.T.	...	...	...	...	...	...	...	...	...
Qatar	...	...	1973	1977	1984	2000	...	2008	2009
Saudi Arabia	1994	1994	1971	1976	1978	2007	...	2008	
Sudan	...	...	1970	...	1974	...	...	2008	2008
Syrian Arab Republic	...	...	1958	1975	1975	...	...	2005	2008
Tunisia	1969	1975	1981	1975	1975	...	2009	2006	2007
United Arab Emirates	...	...	...	...	2001	...	...	2005	...
Yemen	...	...	1970	...	1980	...	...	2007	...
Sub-Saharan Africa									
Angola	...	...	...	1991	1991	...	...	...	...
Benin	...	...	...	...	1982	...	...	...	2007
Botswana	...	...	2002	...	1998	...	...	...	...
Burkina Faso	...	...	1969	1987	1987	...	...	2006	2006
Burundi	...	...	...	...	1982	...	...	2006	2008
Cameroon	1973	1973	1961	1972	1982	...	...	...	2006
Cape Verde	...	...	...	...	1988	...	...	...	...
Central African Republic	...	...	...	1972	1980	...	...	2004	...
Chad	...	...	2008	2008	1999	...	...	2008	2008
Comoros	...	...	...	...	2000	...	...	...	...
Congo	...	...	...	...	1987	...	...	...	2008
Congo (Dem. Rep.)	...	...	1961	1974	1974	...	...	...	...
Côte d'Ivoire	...	...	1980	1990	1981	...	...	2006	2007
Equatorial Guinea	...	...	2003	...	...	2003	...	...	...
Eritrea	...	...	2004	...	2001	...	...	...	...
Ethiopia	...	...	...	...	1977	...	...	2006	2008
Gabon	...	...	1961	2003	1986	2003	...	2004	2007
Gambia	...	...	...	...	1987	...	...	...	...
Ghana	1962	...	1960	...	1975	...	...	...	...
Guinea	1981	1981	1960	1979	1979	...	...	2008	2008
Guinea-Bissau	...	...	...	...	2006	...	...	...	...
Kenya	1966	1974	...	...	1991	...	...	2007	2007
Lesotho	...	...	...	...	2003	...	...	2008	...
Liberia	1956	...	...	...	2002	...	...	...	...
Madagascar	...	...	1961	1989	1983	...	...	2006	2006
Malawi	1965	...	...	...	1982	...	...	...	...
Mali	...	...	1961	1987	1977	...	...	2005	2006
Mauritius	1970	...	2006	1978	1995	...	...	2004	2006
Mozambique	...	...	...	...	1982	...	...	2007	2007
Namibia	...	...	...	...	2000	...	...	2007	2006
Niger	1989	1989	1976	1972	1974	2006	...	2007	2007
Nigeria	1961	...	1961	1972	1974	2005	2005	2005	2008
Rwanda	1989	1989	2000	2001	2000	...	...	...	...
Saint Helena[c]	...	...	...	...	...	...	...	...	...
Sao Tome and Principe	...	...	...	...	2006	...	...	2006	...
Senegal	1974	1974	1987	1984	1976	...	...	2006	2006
Seychelles	...	...	2003	2004	1980	...	...	2005	2008
Sierra Leone	...	...	...	...	2005	...	...	...	...
Somalia	...	...	...	...	...	...	...	...	...
South Africa	...	...	2003	2003	1997	...	...	...	2006

Ratification[a] Year of Convention per Member State

Table 1. Ratifications of the seven cultural conventions of UNESCO[1]

Country or Territory	Universal Copyright Convention (1952,1971)		Convention for the Protection of Cultural Property in the Event of Armed Conflict (1954)	Convention on the Means of Prohibiting and Preventing the Illicit Import, Export and Transfer of Ownership of Cultural Property (1970)	Convention Concerning the Protection of the World Cultural and Natural Heritage (1972)	Second Protocol to the Hague Convention of 1954 for the Protection of Cultural Property in the Event of Armed Conflict (1999)	Convention on the Protection of the Underwater Cultural Heritage (2001)	Convention for the Safeguarding of the Intangible Cultural Heritage (2003)	Convention on the Protection and Promotion of the Diversity of Cultural Expressions (2005)
Swaziland	...	...	...	...	2005	...	...	...	...
Tanzania (United Rep.)	...	...	1971	1977	1977	...	...	...	...
Togo	2003	2003	...	...	1998	...	...	2009	2006
Uganda	...	...	...	...	1987	...	...	2009	...
Zambia	1965	...	...	1985	1984	...	...	2006	...
Zimbabwe	...	...	1998	2006	1982	...	...	2006	2008
Central and South Asia									
Afghanistan	...	...	...	2005	1979	...	...	2009	2009
Armenia	...	...	1993	1993	1993	2006	...	2006	2007
Azerbaijan	1997	...	1993	1999	1993	2001	...	2007	...
Bangladesh	1975	1975	2006	1987	1983	...	...	2009	2007
Bhutan	...	...	...	2002	2001	...	...	2005	...
Georgia	...	...	1992	1992	1992	...	...	2008	2008
India	1957	1988	1958	1977	1977	...	...	2005	2006
Iran (Islamic Rep.)	...	...	1959	1975	1975	2005	2009	2006	...
Kazakhstan	1992	...	1997	...	1994	...	...	...	...
Kyrgyzstan	...	...	1995	1995	1995	...	...	2006	...
Maldives	...	...	...	...	1986	...	...	...	...
Nepal	...	...	...	1976	1978	...	...	...	...
Pakistan	1954	...	1959	1981	1976	...	...	2005	...
Sri Lanka	1983	1983	2004	1981	1980	...	...	2008	...
Tajikistan	1992	...	1992	1992	1992	2006	...	...	2007
Turkmenistan	...	...	...	...	1994	...	...	...	...
Uzbekistan	...	...	1996	1996	1993	...	...	2008	...
East Asia									
Brunei Darussalam	...	...	...	...	...	...	...	...	...
Cambodia	1953	...	1962	1972	1991	...	2007	2006	2007
China	1992	1992	2000	1989	1985	...	...	2004	2007
Indonesia	...	...	1967	...	1989	...	...	2007	...
Japan	1956	1977	2007	2002	1992	2007	...	2004	...
Korea (Dem. People's Rep.)	...	...	...	1983	1998	...	...	2009	...
Korea (Rep.)	1987	1987	...	1983	1988	...	...	2005	...
Lao (People's Dem. Rep.)	1954	...	...	...	1987	...	...	...	2007
Malaysia	...	...	1960	...	1988	...	...	...	...
Mongolia	...	...	1964	1991	1990	...	...	2005	2007
Myanmar	...	...	1956	...	1994	...	...	...	...
Philippines	...	...	...	...	1985	...	...	2006	...
Singapore	...	...	...	...	...	...	...	...	...
Thailand	...	...	1958	...	1987	...	...	...	...
Timor-Leste	...	...	...	...	...	...	...	...	...
Viet Nam	...	...	...	2005	1987	...	...	2005	2007
Europe									
Albania	2003	2003	1960	2002	1989	...	2009	2006	2006
Andorra	1952	...	...	...	1997	...	...	...	2007
Austria	1957	1982	1964	...	1992	2002	...	2009	2006
Belarus	1994	...	1957	1988	1988	2000	...	2005	2006
Belgium	1960	...	1960	2009	1996	...	...	2006	...
Bosnia and Herzegovina	1993	1993	1993	1993	1993	2009	2009	2009	2009
Bulgaria	1975	1975	1956	1971	1974	2000	2003	2006	2006
Croatia	1992	1992	1992	1992	1992	2006	2004	2005	2006
Cyprus	1990	1990	1964	1979	1975	2001	...	2006	2006
Czech Republic	1993	1993	1993	1993	1993	2007	...	2009	...
Denmark	1961	1979	2003	2003	1979	...	...	...	2006
Estonia	...	...	1995	1995	1995	2005	...	2006	2006
Finland	1963	1986	1994	1999	1987	2004	...	...	2006
France	1955	1972	1957	1997	1975	...	...	2006	2006
Germany	1955	1973	1967	2007	1976	...	...	...	2007
Gibraltar	...	...	...	...	...	...	...	...	...
Greece	1963	...	1981	1981	1981	2005	...	2007	2007
Holy See[c]	1955	1980	1958	...	1982	...	...	...	...

Table 1. Ratifications of the seven cultural conventions of UNESCO[1]

Country or Territory	Universal Copyright Convention (1952,1971)		Convention for the Protection of Cultural Property in the Event of Armed Conflict (1954)	Convention on the Means of Prohibiting and Preventing the Illicit Import, Export and Transfer of Ownership of Cultural Property (1970)	Convention Concerning the Protection of the World Cultural and Natural Heritage (1972)	Second Protocol to the Hague Convention of 1954 for the Protection of Cultural Property in the Event of Armed Conflict (1999)	Convention on the Protection of the Underwater Cultural Heritage (2001)	Convention for the Safeguarding of the Intangible Cultural Heritage (2003)	Convention on the Protection and Promotion of the Diversity of Cultural Expressions (2005)
Country or Territory									
Hungary	1970	1972	1956	1978	1985	2005	...	2006	2008
Iceland	1956	...	...	2004	1995	...	...	2005	2007
Ireland	1958	...	...	...	1991	...	...	...	2006
Israel	1955	...	1957	...	1999	...	...	...	...
Italy	1956	1979	1958	1978	1978	2009	...	2007	2007
Latvia	...	...	2003	...	1995	...	...	2005	2007
Liechtenstein	1958	1999	1960	...	...	...	...	...	...
Lithuania	...	...	1998	1998	1992	2002	2006	2005	2006
Luxembourg	1955	...	1961	...	1983	2005	...	2006	2006
Macedonia (TFYR)	1997	1997	1997	1997	1997	2002	...	2006	2007
Malta	1968	...	...	...	1978	...	...	...	2006
Moldova (Rep.)	1997	...	1999	2007	2002	...	...	2006	2006
Monaco	1955	1974	1957	...	1978	...	...	2007	2006
Montenegro	2007	2007	2007	2007	2006	2007	2008	...	2008
Netherlands	1967	1985	1958	2009	1992	2007	...	...	...
Norway	1962	1974	1961	2007	1977	...	...	2007	2007
Poland	1976	1976	1956	1974	1976	...	...	...	2007
Portugal	1956	1981	2000	1985	1980	...	2006	2008	2007
Romania	...	...	1958	1993	1990	2006	2007	2006	2006
Russian Federation	1973	1994	1957	1988	1988	...	...	...	...
San Marino	...	...	1956	...	1991	...	...	...	...
Serbia	2001	2001	2001	2001	2001	2002	...	...	2009
Slovakia	1993	1993	1993	1993	1993	2004	2009	2006	2006
Slovenia	1992	1992	1992	1992	1992	2004	2008	2008	2006
Spain	1954	1974	1960	1986	1982	2001	2005	2006	2006
Sweden	1961	1973	1985	2003	1985	...	...	...	2006
Switzerland	1955	1993	1962	2003	1975	2004	...	2008	2008
Turkey	...	...	1965	1981	1983	...	...	2006	...
Ukraine	1994	...	1957	1988	1988	...	2006	2008	...
United Kingdom	1957	1972	...	2002	1984	...	...	...	2007
North America									
Canada	1962	...	1998	1978	1976	2005	...	...	2005
United States of America	1954	1972	2009	1983	1973	...	...	...	...
Latin America and the Caribbean									
Anguilla^c	...	...	...	...	...	...	...	...	...
Antigua and Barbuda	...	...	...	...	1983	...	...	...	...
Argentina	1957	...	1989	1973	1978	2002	...	2006	2008
Aruba	...	...	...	...	...	...	...	...	...
Bahamas	1976	1976	...	1997	...	...	...	...	...
Barbados	1983	1983	2002	2002	2002	2008	2008	2008	2008
Belize	1982	...	...	1990	1990	...	...	2007	...
Bermuda^c	...	...	...	...	...	...	...	...	...
Bolivia	1989	1989	2004	1976	1976	...	...	2006	2006
Brazil	1959	1975	1958	1973	1977	2005	...	2006	2007
British Virgin Islands	...	...	...	...	...	...	...	...	...
Cayman Islands	...	...	...	...	...	...	...	...	...
Chile	...	...	2008	...	1980	2008	...	2008	2007
Colombia	1976	1976	1998	1988	1983	...	...	2008	...
Costa Rica	1954	1979	1998	1996	1977	2003	...	2007	...
Cuba	1957	...	1957	1980	1981	...	2008	2007	2007
Dominica	...	...	...	...	1995	...	...	2005	...
Dominican Republic	1983	1983	1960	1973	1985	2009	...	2006	...
Ecuador	1957	1991	1956	1971	1975	2004	2006	2008	2006
El Salvador	1978	1978	2001	1978	1991	2002	...	...	...
Grenada	...	...	...	1992	1998	...	2009	2009	2009
Guatemala	1964	...	1985	1985	1979	2005	...	2006	2006
Guyana	...	...	...	...	1977	...	...	...	...
Haiti	1954	...	...	...	1980	...	...	...	...
Honduras	...	...	2002	1979	1979	2003	...	2006	...
Jamaica	...	...	...	...	1983	...	...	...	2007
Mexico	1957	1975	1956	1972	1984	2003	2006	2005	2006

Table 1. Ratifications of the seven cultural conventions of UNESCO[1]

	Ratification[a] Year of Convention per Member State								
Country or Territory	Universal Copyright Convention (1952,1971)		Convention for the Protection of Cultural Property in the Event of Armed Conflict (1954)	Convention on the Means of Prohibiting and Preventing the Illicit Import, Export and Transfer of Ownership of Cultural Property (1970)	Convention Concerning the Protection of the World Cultural and Natural Heritage (1972)	Second Protocol to the Hague Convention of 1954 for the Protection of Cultural Property in the Event of Armed Conflict (1999)	Convention on the Protection of the Underwater Cultural Heritage (2001)	Convention for the Safeguarding of the Intangible Cultural Heritage (2003)	Convention on the Protection and Promotion of the Diversity of Cultural Expressions (2005)
Montserrat[c]	...	...	...	...	...	...	...	...	...
Netherlands Antilles	...	...	...	...	...	...	...	...	...
Nicaragua	1961	...	1959	1977	1979	2001	...	2006	2009
Panama	1962	1980	1962	1973	1978	2001	2003	2004	2007
Paraguay	1961	...	2004	2004	1988	2004	2006	2006	2007
Peru	1963	1985	1989	1979	1982	2005	...	2005	2006
Saint Kitts and Nevis	...	...	...	...	1986	...	...	...	...
Saint Lucia	...	...	...	...	1991	...	2007	2007	2007
Saint Vincent and the Grenadines	1985	1985	...	...	2003	...	...	...	...
Suriname	...	...	...	...	1997	...	...	...	...
Trinidad and Tobago	1988	1988	...	...	2005	...	...	...	...
Turks and Caicos Islands[c]	...	...	...	...	...	...	...	...	...
Uruguay	1993	1993	1999	1977	1989	2007	...	2007	2007
Venezuela	1966	1996	2005	2005	1990	...	...	2007	...
Pacific									
Australia	1969	1977	1984	1989	1974	...	...	...	...
Cook Islands	...	...	...	...	2009	...	...	...	...
Fiji	1971	...	...	...	1990	...	...	...	...
Kiribati	...	...	...	...	2000	...	...	...	...
Marshall Islands	...	...	...	...	2002	...	...	...	...
Micronesia (Fed. States)	...	...	...	...	2002	...	...	...	...
Nauru	...	...	...	...	...	...	...	...	...
New Zealand	1964	...	2008	2007	1984	...	...	...	2007
Niue	...	...	...	...	2001	...	...	...	...
Palau	...	...	...	...	2002	...	...	...	...
Papua New Guinea	...	...	...	...	1997	...	...	2008	...
Samoa	...	...	...	...	2001	...	...	...	...
Solomon Islands	...	...	...	...	1992	...	...	...	...
Tokelau	...	...	...	...	...	...	...	...	...
Tonga	...	...	...	...	2004	...	...	...	...
Tuvalu	...	...	...	...	...	...	...	...	...
Vanuatu	...	...	...	...	2002	...	...	...	...
Total number of State Parties	99	65	123	117	186	53	26	114	98

% per region[b]	% of members or associate members having ratified the designated convention								
WORLD	50	33	62	59	93	26	13	56	49
Arab States	26	21	79	74	100	26	16	79	47
Sub-Saharan Africa	29	16	49	47	96	9	2	51	51
Central and South Asia	41	18	71	82	100	24	...	65	35
East Asia	31	19	50	44	81	6	6	56	31
Europe	89	56	91	76	100	46	26	65	78
North America	100	50	100	100	100	50	...	...	50
Latin America and the Caribbean	62	43	54	59	86	43	22	62	46
Pacific	18	6	12	12	82	...	...	6	6

Source:

1. Data extracted from UNESCO, Standard-Setting Instruments, as of 3 August 2009. For details, see http://portal.unesco.org/en/ev.php-URL_ID=12024&URL_DO=DO_TOPIC&URL_SECTION=201.html

Notes:

a. Year of deposit of either ratification, acceptance, accession or notification of succession.

b. Calculated using the sum of UNESCO Member States per region.

c. Not a Member State of UNESCO.

... Data not available

. Not applicable

Table 2. World Heritage sites and Intangible Cultural Heritage of Humanity[1]

Country or Territory	World Heritage — Properties included in the World Heritage List[a]							Tentative List (Properties submitted for consideration)	List of Intangible Cultural Heritage in Need of Urgent Safeguarding	Intangible Cultural Heritage — Representative List of the Intangible Cultural Heritage of Humanity[g]
	Cultural	Natural	Mixed	Total	Endangered site	Before 1995	1995 and after			
Arab States										
Algeria	6	.	1	7	.	7	.	6		The Ahellil of Gouara
Bahrain	1	.	.	1	.	.	1	6		.
Djibouti	.	.	.	.	.	.	.	.		.
Egypt	6	1	.	7	1	5	2	31		The Al-Sirah Al-Hilaliyyah Epic
Iraq	3	.	.	3	2	1	2	7		The Iraqi Maqam
Jordan	3	.	.	3	.	2	1	16		The Cultural Space of the Bedu in Petra and Wadi Rum
Kuwait	.	.	.	.	.	.	.	.		.
Lebanon	5	.	.	5	.	4	1	9		.
Libyan Arab Jamahiriya	5	.	.	5	.	5	.	.		.
Mauritania	1	1	.	2	.	1	1	3		.
Morocco	8	.	.	8	.	3	5	14		The Cultural Space of Jemaa el Fna Square / The Moussem of Tan-Tan
Oman	4	1[b]	.	4	.	2	2	2		.
Palestinian A. T.	1	.	.	1	1	.	1	.		The Palestinian Hikaye
Qatar	.	.	.	.	.	.	.	2		.
Saudi Arabia	1	.	.	1	.	.	1	2		.
Sudan	1	.	.	1	.	.	1	7		.
Syrian Arab Republic	5	.	.	5	.	4	1	15		.
Tunisia	7	1	.	8	.	7	1	4		.
United Arab Emirates	.	.	.	.	.	.	.	1		.
Yemen	3	1	.	4	1	3	1	10		The Song of Sana'a
Sub-Saharan Africa										
Angola	.	.	.	.	.	.	.	11		.
Benin	1	.	.	1	.	1	.	6		The Oral Heritage of Gelede[f] (w/ Nigeria, Togo)
Botswana	1	.	.	1	.	.	1	4		.
Burkina Faso	1	.	.	1	.	.	1	5		.
Burundi	.	.	.	.	.	.	.	10		.
Cameroon	.	1	.	1	.	1	.	13		.
Cape Verde	1	.	.	1	.	.	1	5		.
Central African Republic	.	1	.	1	1	1	.	10		The Polyphonic Singing of the Aka Pygmies of Central Africa
Chad	.	.	.	.	.	.	.	9		.
Comoros	.	.	.	.	.	.	.	4		.
Congo	.	.	.	.	.	.	.	5		.
Congo (Dem. Rep.)	.	5	.	5	5	4	1	3		.
Côte d'Ivoire	.	3	.	3	2	3	.	4		The Gbofe of Afounkaha — the Music of the Transverse Trumps of the Tagbana Community
Equatorial Guinea	.	.	.	.	.	.	.	.		.
Eritrea	.	.	.	.	.	.	.	1		.
Ethiopia	7	1	.	8	1	7	1	2		.
Gabon	.	.	1	1	.	.	1	7		.
Gambia	2	.	.	2	.	.	2	2		The Kankurang, Manding Initiatory Rite[f] (w/ Senegal)
Ghana	2	.	.	2	.	2	.	6		.
Guinea	.	1	.	1	1	1	.	3		The Cultural Space of Sosso-Bala
Guinea-Bissau	.	.	.	.	.	.	.	1		.
Kenya	2	2	.	4	.	.	4	6		.
Lesotho	.	.	.	.	.	.	.	2		.
Liberia	.	.	.	.	.	.	.	.		.
Madagascar	1	2	.	3	.	1	2	7		The Woodcrafting Knowledge of the Zafimaniry
Malawi	1	1	.	2	.	1	1	3		The Vimbuza Healing Dance / The Gule Wamkulu[f] (w/ Mozambique, Zambia)
Mali	3	.	1	4	.	3	1	9		The Cultural Space of the Yaaral and Degal
Mauritius	2	.	.	2	.	.	2	1		.
Mozambique	1	.	.	1	.	1	.	4		The Chopi Timbila / The Gule Wamkulu[f] (w/ Malawi, Zambia)
Namibia	1	.	.	1	.	.	1	4		.
Niger	.	2	.	2	1	1	1	19		.
Nigeria	2	.	.	2	.	.	2	12		The Oral Heritage of Gelede[f] (w/ Benin, Togo) / The Ifa Divination System
Rwanda	.	.	.	.	.	.	.	.		.
Saint Helena	.	.	.	.	.	.	.	.		.
Sao Tome and Principe	.	.	.	.	.	.	.	.		.
Senegal	3	2	.	5	1	3	2	10		The Kankurang, Manding Initiatory Rite[f] (w/ Gambia)
Seychelles	.	2	.	2	.	2	.	.		.

Note (List of Intangible Cultural Heritage in Need of Urgent Safeguarding): The first elements included in the List of Intangible Cultural Heritage in Need of Urgent Safeguarding will only be known following the Fourth Session of the Intergovernmental Committee for the Safeguarding of the Intangible Cultural Heritage, to be held in Abu Dhabi from 28 September to 2 October 2009, i.e. immediately after the completion of this report. For updated information, please refer to http://www.unesco.org/culture/ich/index.php?pg=home

Table 2. World Heritage sites and Oral and Intangible Heritage of Humanity[1]

Country or Territory	World Heritage — Properties included in the World Heritage List[a]							Tentative List (Properties submitted for consideration)	Intangible Cultural Heritage — Representative List of the Intangible Cultural Heritage of Humanity[g]
	Cultural	Natural	Mixed	Total	Endangered site	Before 1995	1995 and after		
Sierra Leone	.	.	.	.	.	.	.	.	
Somalia	.	.	.	.	.	.	.	.	
South Africa	4	3	1	8	.	.	8	10	
Swaziland	.	.	.	.	.	.	.	1	
Tanzania (United Rep.)	3	4	.	7	1	5	2	7	
Togo	1	.	.	1	.	.	1	7	The Oral Heritage of Gelede[f] (w/ Benin, Nigeria)
Uganda	1	2	.	3	.	2	1	5	Barkcloth Making in Uganda
Zambia	.	1	.	1	.	1	.	7	The Makishi Masquerade / The Gule Wamkulu[f] (w/ Malawi, Mozambique)
Zimbabwe	3	2	.	5	.	4	1	1	The Mbende Jerusarema Dance
Central and South Asia									
Afghanistan	2	.	.	2	2	.	2	3	
Armenia	3	.	.	3	.	.	3	4	The Dukuk and its Music
Azerbaijan	2	.	.	2	.	.	2	10	The Azerbaijani Mugham
Bangladesh	2	1	.	3	.	2	1	5	Baul Songs
Bhutan	.	.	.	.	.	.	.	.	The Mask Dance of the Drums from Drametse
Georgia	3	.	.	3	1	2	1	15	Georgian Polyphonic Singing
India	22	5	.	27	1	21	6	27	Kutiyattam, Sanskrit Theatre / The Tradition of Vedic Chanting / Ramlila — the Traditional Performance of the Ramayana
Iran (Islamic Rep.)	10	.	.	10	1	3	7	59	
Kazakhstan	2	1	.	3	.	.	3	11	
Kyrgyzstan	1	.	.	1	.	.	1	6	The Art of Akyns, Kyrgyz Epic Tellers
Maldives	.	.	.	.	.	.	.	1	
Nepal	2	2	.	4	.	3	1	15	
Pakistan	6	.	.	6	1	5	1	18	
Sri Lanka	6	1	.	7	.	7	.	2	
Tajikistan	.	.	.	.	.	.	.	17	Shashmaqom Music[f] (w/ Uzbekistan)
Turkmenistan	3	.	.	3	.	.	3	7	
Uzbekistan	4	.	.	4	.	2	2	30	The Cultural Space of the Boysun District / Shashmaqom Music[f] (w/ Tajikistan)
East Asia									
Brunei Darussalam	.	.	.	.	.	.	.	.	
Cambodia	2	.	.	2	.	1	1	9	The Royal Ballet of Cambodia / Sbek Thom, Khmer Shadow Theatre
China	27	7	4	38	.	14	24	51	Kun Qu Opera / The Guqin and its Music / The Uyghur Muqam of Xinjiang / Urtiin Duu — Traditional Folk Long Song[f] (w/ Mongolia)
Indonesia	3	4	.	7	.	4	3	24	The Wayang Puppet Theatre / The Indonesian Kris
Japan	11	3	.	14	.	5	9	12	Nôgaku Theatre / Ningyo Johruri Bunraku Puppet Theatre / Kabuki Theatre
Korea (Dem. People's Rep.)	1	.	.	1	.	.	1	6	
Korea (Rep.)	8	1	.	9	.	.	9	7	The Royal Ancestral Ritual in the Jongmyo Shrine and its Music / The Pansori Epic Chant / The Gangneung Danoje Festival
Lao (People's Dem. Rep.)	2	.	.	2	.	.	2	2	
Malaysia	1	2	.	3	.	.	3	2	Mak Yong Theatre
Mongolia	1	1	.	2	.	.	2	7	The Traditional Music of the Morin Khuur / Urtiin Duu — Traditional Folk Long Song[f] (w/ China)
Myanmar	.	.	.	.	.	.	.	8	
Philippines	3	2	.	5	1	2	3	28	The Hudhud Chants of the Ifugao / The Darangen Epic of the Maranao People of Lake Lanao
Singapore	.	.	.	.	.	.	.	.	
Thailand	3	2	.	5	.	4	1	2	
Timor-Leste	.	.	.	.	.	.	.	.	
Viet Nam	3	2	.	5	.	2	3	7	Nha Nhac, Vietnamese Court Music / The Space of Gong Culture
Europe									
Albania	2	.	.	2	.	1	1	2	Albanian Folk Iso-polyphony

List of Intangible Cultural Heritage in Need of Urgent Safeguarding: The first elements included in the List of Intangible Cultural Heritage in Need of Urgent Safeguarding will only be known following the Fourth Session of the Intergovernmental Committee for the Safeguarding of the Intangible Cultural Heritage, to be held in Abu Dhabi from 28 September to 2 October 2009, i.e. immediately after the completion of this report. For updated information, please refer to http://www.unesco.org/culture/ich/index.php?pg=home

Table 2. World Heritage sites and Oral and Intangible Heritage of Humanity[1]

Country or Territory	World Heritage — Properties included in the World Heritage List[a]							Tentative List (Properties submitted for consideration)	List of Intangible Cultural Heritage in Need of Urgent Safeguarding	Intangible Cultural Heritage — Representative List of the Intangible Cultural Heritage of Humanity[g]
	Cultural	Natural	Mixed	Total	Endangered site	Before 1995	1995 and after			
Andorra	1	.	.	1	.	.	1	2		.
Austria	8	.	.	8	.	.	8	11		.
Belarus	3	1	.	4	.	1	3	10		.
Belgium	10	.	.	10	.	.	10	16		The Carnival of Binche / Processional Giants and Dragons in Belgium and France[f] (w/ France)
Bosnia and Herzegovina	2	.	.	2	.	.	2	8		.
Bulgaria	7	2	.	9	.	9	.	14		The Bistritsa Babi — Archaic Polyphony, Dances and Rituals from the Shoplouk Region
Croatia	6	1	.	7	.	3	4	15	The first elements included in the List of Intangible Cultural Heritage in Need of Urgent Safeguarding will only be known following the Fourth Session of the Intergovernmental Committee for the Safeguarding of the Intangible Cultural Heritage, to be held in Abu Dhabi from 28 September to 2 October 2009, i.e. immediately after the completion of this report. For updated information, please refer to http://www.unesco.org/culture/ich/index.php?pg=home	.
Cyprus	3	.	.	3	.	2	1	12		.
Czech Republic	12	.	.	12	.	4	8	15		Slovácko Verbůnk, Recruit Dances
Denmark	3	1	.	4	.	1	3	5		.
Estonia	2	.	.	2	.	.	2	4		The Kihnu Cultural Space / The Baltic Song and Dance Celebrations[f] (w/ Latvia, Lithuania)
Finland	6	1	.	7	.	3	4	6		.
France	30	2	1	33	.	19	14	35		Processional Giants and Dragons in Belgium and France[f] (w/ Belgium)
Germany	32[c]	2	.	33	.	16	18	13		.
Gibraltar	.	.	.	.	.	.	.	.		.
Greece	15	.	2	17	.	13	4	8		.
Holy See	2	.	.	2	.	2	.	.		.
Hungary	7	1	.	8	.	2	6	11		.
Iceland	1	1	.	2	.	.	2	9		.
Ireland	2	.	.	2	.	1	1	8		.
Israel[d]	6	.	.	6	1	1	5	19		.
Italy	42	2	.	43	.	9	35	40		Opera dei Pupi, Sicilian Puppet Theatre / Canto tenore, Sardinian Pastoral Songs
Latvia	2	.	.	2	.	.	2	5		The Baltic Song and Dance Celebrations[f] (w/ Estonia, Lithuania)
Liechtenstein	.	.	.	.	.	.	.	.		.
Lithuania	4	.	.	4	.	1	3	1		Cross-crafting and its Symbolism / The Baltic Song and Dance Celebrations[f] (w/ Estonia, Latvia)
Luxembourg	1	.	.	1	.	1	.	2		.
Macedonia (TFYR)	.	.	1	1	.	1	.	3		.
Malta	3	.	.	3	.	3	.	7		.
Moldova (Rep.)	1	.	.	1	.	.	1	1		.
Monaco	.	.	.	.	.	.	.	.		.
Montenegro	1	1	.	2	.	2	.	.		.
Netherlands	7	1	.	8	.	.	8	12		.
Norway	6	1	.	7	.	4	3	5		.
Poland	12	1	.	13	.	6	7	4		.
Portugal	12	1	.	13	.	6	7	13		.
Romania	6	1	.	7	.	4	3	14		Căluş Ritual
Russian Federation	15	8	.	23	.	8	15	25		The Cultural Space and Oral Culture of the Semeiskie / The Olonkho, Yakut Heroic Epos
San Marino	1	.	.	1	.	.	1	.		.
Serbia	4	.	.	4	1	2	2	5		.
Slovakia	5	2	.	7	.	3	4	14		The Fujara and its Music
Slovenia	.	1	.	1	.	1	.	4		.
Spain	36	3	2	41	.	21	20	25		The Mystery Play of Elche / The Patum of Berga
Sweden	12	1	1	14	.	5	9	2		.
Switzerland	7	3	.	10	.	3	7	2		.
Turkey	7	.	2	9	.	8	1	23		The Arts of the Meddah, Public Storytellers / The Mevlevi Sema Ceremony
Ukraine	3	1	.	4	.	1	3	14		.
United Kingdom	23	4	1	28	.	14	14	16		.
North America										.
Canada	6	9	.	15	.	10	5	9		.
United States of America	8	12	.	20	.	18	2	14		.
Latin America and the Caribbean										.
Anguilla	.	.	.	.	.	.	.	.		.
Antigua and Barbuda	.	.	.	.	.	.	.	.		.
Argentina	4	4	.	8	.	3	5	7		.
Aruba	.	.	.	.	.	.	.	.		.

Table 2. World Heritage sites and Oral and Intangible Heritage of Humanity[1]

| | World Heritage | | | | | | | | Intangible Cultural Heritage |
| | Properties included in the World Heritage List[a] | | | | | Before 1995 | 1995 and after | Tentative List (Properties submitted for consideration) | Representative List of the Intangible Cultural Heritage of Humanity[g] |
Country or Territory	Cultural	Natural	Mixed	Total	Endangered site				
Bahamas	.	.	.	.	.	.	.	.	.
Barbados	.	.	.	.	.	.	.	3	
Belize	.	1	.	1	1	.	1	.	Language, Dance and Music of the Garifuna[f] (w/ Guatemala, Honduras, Nicaragua)
Bermuda	.	.	.	.	.	.	.	.	
Bolivia	5	1	.	6	.	3	3	6	The Carnival of Oruro / The Andean Cosmovision of the Kallawaya
Brazil	10	7	.	17	.	8	9	17	Oral and Graphic Expressions of the Wajápi / The Samba de Roda of Recôncavo of Bahia
British Virgin Islands	.	.	.	.	.	.	.	.	
Cayman Islands	.	.	.	.	.	.	.	.	
Chile	5	.	.	5	1	.	5	18	
Colombia	4	2	.	6	1	2	4	6	The Carnival of Barranquilla / The Cultural Space of Palenque de San Basilio
Costa Rica	.	3	.	3	.	1	2	2	Oxherding and Oxcart Traditions in Costa Rica
Cuba	7	2	.	9	.	2	7	3	La Tumba Francesa
Dominica	.	1	.	1	.	.	1	.	
Dominican Republic	1	.	.	1	.	.	1	14	The Cultural Space of the Brotherhood of the Holy Spirit of the Congos of Villa Mella The Cocolo Dance Drama Tradition
Ecuador	2	2	.	4	1	3	1	6	The Oral Heritage and Cultural Manifestations of the Zápara People[f] (w/ Peru)
El Salvador	1	.	.	1	.	.	.	6	
Grenada	.	.	.	.	.	.	.	3	
Guatemala	2	.	1	3	.	3	.	18	Language, Dance and Music of the Garifuna[f] (w/ Belize, Honduras, Nicaragua) The Rabinal Achí Dance Drama Tradition
Guyana	.	.	.	.	.	.	.	5	
Haiti	1	.	.	1	.	1	.	1	
Honduras	1	1	.	2	.	2	.	.	Language, Dance and Music of the Garifuna[f] (w/ Belize, Guatemala, Nicaragua)
Jamaica	.	.	.	.	.	.	.	3	The Maroon Heritage of Moore Town
Mexico	25	4	.	29	.	14	15	39	The Indigenous Festivity dedicated to the Dead
Montserrat	.	.	.	.	.	.	.	.	
Netherlands Antilles	.	.	.	.	.	.	.	.	
Nicaragua	1	.	.	1	.	.	1	6	Language, Dance and Music of the Garifuna[f] (w/ Belize, Guatemala, Honduras) El Güegüense
Panama	2	3	.	5	.	3	2	.	
Paraguay	1	.	.	1	.	.	1	4	
Peru	7	2	2	11	1	9	2	5	The Oral Heritage and Cultural Manifestations of the Zápara People[f] (w/ Ecuador) Taquile and its Textile Art
Saint Kitts and Nevis	1	.	.	1	.	.	1	2	
Saint Lucia	.	1	.	1	.	.	1	.	
Saint Vincent and the Grenadines	.	.	.	.	.	.	.	.	
Suriname	1	1	.	2	.	.	2	1	
Trinidad and Tobago	.	.	.	.	.	.	.	.	
Turks and Caicos Islands	.	.	.	.	.	.	.	.	
Uruguay	1	.	.	1	.	.	1	3	
Venezuela	2	1	.	3	1	2	1	3	
Pacific									
Australia	2	11	4	17	.	11	6	2	
Cook Islands	.	.	.	.	.	.	.	.	
Fiji	.	.	.	.	.	.	.	4	
Kiribati	.	.	.	.	.	.	.	1	
Marshall Islands	.	.	.	.	.	.	.	4	
Micronesia (Fed. States)	.	.	.	.	.	.	.	1	
Nauru	.	.	.	.	.	.	.	.	
New Zealand	.	2	1	3	.	2	1	8	
Niue	.	.	.	.	.	.	.	.	
Palau	.	.	.	.	.	.	.	5	
Papua New Guinea	1	.	.	1	.	.	1	7	
Samoa	.	.	.	.	.	.	.	2	
Solomon Islands	.	1	.	1	.	.	1	2	
Tokelau	.	.	.	.	.	.	.	.	
Tonga	.	.	.	.	.	.	.	2	The Lakalaka, Dances and Sung Speeches of Tonga

List of Intangible Cultural Heritage in Need of Urgent Safeguarding: The first elements included in the List of Intangible Cultural Heritage in Need of Urgent Safeguarding will only be known following the Fourth Session of the Intergovernmental Committee for the Safeguarding of the Intangible Cultural Heritage, to be held in Abu Dhabi from 28 September to 2 October 2009, i.e. immediately after the completion of this report. For updated information, please refer to http://www.unesco.org/culture/ich/index.php?pg=home

Table 2. World Heritage sites and Oral and Intangible Heritage of Humanity[1]

	World Heritage							Tentative List (Properties submitted for consideration)	Intangible Cultural Heritage	
	Properties included in the World Heritage List[a]								List of Intangible Cultural Heritage in Need of Urgent Safeguarding	Representative List of the Intangible Cultural Heritage of Humanity[g]
	Cultural	Natural	Mixed	Total	Endangered site	Before 1995	1995 and after			
Country or Territory										
Tuvalu	.	.	.	.	.	.	.	.		
Vanuatu	1	.	.	1	.	.	1	5		Vanuatu Sand Drawings
Regions										
WORLD[e]	689	176	25	890	31	438	453	1,463		
Arab States	60	4	1	65	5	45	20	135		
Sub-Saharan Africa	43	35	3	81	12	44	37	226		
Central and South Asia	68	10	0	78	6	45	33	230		
East Asia	65	24	4	93	1	32	61	165		
Europe	370	43	10	422	2	181	241	460		
North America	14	21	0	35	0	28	7	23		
Latin America and the Caribbean	84	36	3	123	6	59	64	181		
Pacific	4	14	5	23	0	13	10	43		

Source:

1. UNESCO, World Heritage Center, Intangible Cultural Heritage section, 2009. The table was generated following the 33rd Session of the World Heritage Committee meeting of 22–30 June 2009 in Seville, Spain.

Notes:

a: The complete list of properties with description is available online at the UNESCO World Heritage Center, http://whc.unesco.org.

b. Arabian Oryx Sanctuary in Oman was delisted in 2007.

c. Dresden Elbe Valley in Germany was delisted in 2009.

d. Old City of Jerusalem and its Walls (listed in 1981) is included in both Israel and Palestinian Autonomous Territories, but only within the Arab States region.

e. Transboundary properties counting for only one site.

f. Multinational masterpiece.

g. New elements will be incorporated in the Representative List on the occasion of the Fourth Session of the Intergovernmental Committee for the Safeguarding of the Intangible Cultural Heritage, to be held in Abu Dhabi from 28 September to 2 October 2009 i.e. immediately after the completion of this report. For updated information, please refer to http://www.unesco.org/culture/ich/index.php?pg=home.

... Data not available

. Not applicable

Table 3. Demographic context

Country or Territory	Total Population[1] ('000)	Net migration (average annual) Rate per 1,000 pop.	Net migration (average annual) Rate per 1,000 pop.	Population growth[1] Natural increase (average annual) Crude birth rate	Population growth[1] Natural increase (average annual) Crude death rate	Population growth[1] Natural increase (average annual) Rate of natural increase	Total annual growth rate Rate per 1,000 pop.	Age structure[1] Less than 15	Age structure[1] Over 65	Migrant stock[2] % of population	Migrant stock[2] Definition Code[a]
	2005	1995/2000	2000/2005	2000/2005	2000/2005	2000/2005	2000/2005	2005	2005	2005	2005
Arab States											
Algeria	32,854	-1.0	-0.9	20.7	5.0	15.7	14.8	29.6	4.5	0.7	C
Bahrain	725	5.4	5.5	19.3	3.1	16.2	21.8	26.3	3.1	40.7	C
Djibouti	804	8.9	0.0	31.4	12.0	19.4	19.4	38.5	3.0	2.6	I
Egypt	72,850	-1.7	-1.5	25.5	5.9	19.6	18.2	33.3	4.8	0.2	B
Iraq	27,996	1.0	-2.8	35.6	10.6	25.0	22.2	41.5	2.8	0.1	C
Jordan	5,544	-6.2	5.0	27.9	4.1	23.8	28.9	37.2	3.2	39.0	C
Kuwait	2,700	32.1	21.5	18.6	1.7	16.8	38.4	23.8	1.8	62.1	C
Lebanon	4,011	...	...	19.3	7.0	12.3	12.3	28.6	7.2	18.4	B
Libyan Arab Jamahiriya	5,918	0.4	0.4	24.0	4.1	20.0	20.4	30.3	3.8	10.5	C
Mauritania	2,963	0.8	2.2	35.3	8.7	26.5	28.8	40.3	3.6	2.1	C
Morocco	30,495	-3.6	-3.7	20.9	6.0	15.0	11.3	30.3	5.2	0.4	C
Oman	2,507	-6.1	-12.2	23.5	2.8	20.8	8.6	33.8	2.6	24.4	C
Palestinian A. T.	3,762	0.0	0.6	39.1	4.2	34.8	35.6	45.9	3.1	45.4	B
Qatar	796	15.1	35.6	17.8	2.6	15.2	51.1	21.7	1.3	78.3	C
Saudi Arabia	23,612	0.7	2.6	26.5	3.8	22.7	25.3	34.5	2.8	25.9	C
Sudan	36,900	-1.4	-3.0	34.4	11.2	23.2	20.2	40.7	3.5	1.8	B
Syrian Arab Republic	18,894	-1.7	2.3	28.2	3.6	24.7	27.0	36.6	3.2	5.2	C
Tunisia	10,105	-0.4	-0.6	17.1	5.5	11.6	11.0	26.0	6.3	0.4	C
United Arab Emirates	4,104	40.3	31.4	16.7	1.4	15.2	46.9	19.8	1.1	71.4	C
Yemen	21,096	-1.2	-1.0	39.3	8.6	30.7	29.7	45.9	2.3	1.3	C
Sub-Saharan Africa											
Angola	16,095	-1.8	2.3	48.6	22.1	26.5	28.9	46.4	2.4	0.4	B
Benin	8,490	-0.9	2.5	42.2	12.6	29.6	32.2	44.2	2.7	2.1	C
Botswana	1,836	2.8	2.2	26.0	16.3	9.8	12.0	35.6	3.4	4.5	C
Burkina Faso	13,933	-2.2	1.5	45.9	15.7	30.2	31.9	46.2	3.1	5.8	B
Burundi	7,859	-12.4	5.3	44.2	16.7	27.5	32.9	45.1	2.6	1.3	B
Cameroon	17,795	0.0	0.1	37.9	15.0	22.9	23.0	41.8	3.5	0.8	B
Cape Verde	507	-2.3	-2.1	30.9	5.3	25.6	23.5	39.5	4.3	2.2	B
Central African Republic	4,191	0.6	-2.2	37.9	19.4	18.5	16.3	42.7	3.9	1.9	C
Chad	10,146	1.8	4.7	47.4	16.0	31.4	36.2	46.2	3.0	4.5	B
Comoros[d]	798	-1.8	-2.7	36.5	7.4	29.1	26.5	42.0	2.7	8.4	B
Congo	3,610	2.8	-0.6	37.2	12.7	24.5	23.9	41.9	3.2	7.2	B
Congo (Dem. Rep.)	58,741	-5.7	-0.9	49.6	19.3	30.3	29.5	47.2	2.6	0.9	BC
Côte d'Ivoire	18,585	2.2	-3.8	37.5	16.5	21.0	17.3	41.7	3.2	13.1	CB
Equatorial Guinea	484	0.0	0.0	39.8	16.4	23.4	23.4	42.4	4.1	1.2	C
Eritrea	4,527	-0.5	11.2	40.5	10.6	29.9	41.2	43.0	2.3	0.3	I
Ethiopia	78,986	-0.2	-0.4	40.7	14.4	26.3	25.9	44.5	2.9	0.7	B
Gabon	1,291	2.6	1.5	27.7	11.7	16.0	17.6	35.9	4.7	17.7	C
Gambia	1,617	7.1	4.1	38.1	11.2	26.9	31.1	41.2	3.7	15.3	B
Ghana	22,535	-0.5	0.1	32.2	10.0	22.3	22.4	39.0	3.6	7.5	B
Guinea	9,003	-5.8	-9.9	42.0	13.5	28.5	18.6	43.4	3.1	4.3	C
Guinea-Bissau	1,597	-1.7	0.2	49.9	19.5	30.4	30.6	47.4	3.0	1.2	B
Kenya	35,599	-0.1	0.2	39.1	13.2	25.9	26.1	42.6	2.7	1.0	B
Lesotho	1,981	-4.0	-3.7	31.3	17.7	13.6	9.9	40.4	4.7	0.3	C
Liberia	3,442	42.6	-7.3	49.9	19.8	30.1	22.8	46.9	2.2	1.5	B
Madagascar	18,643	-0.1	-0.1	39.3	11.0	28.3	28.3	43.8	3.1	0.3	C
Malawi	13,226	-1.6	-0.5	43.8	17.5	26.3	25.8	47.1	3.0	2.2	B
Mali	11,611	-6.1	-2.5	48.6	16.4	32.2	29.8	47.7	3.6	0.3	C
Mauritius[e]	1,241	-0.3	0.0	15.9	6.8	9.1	9.1	24.4	6.6	1.7	B
Mozambique	20,533	0.9	-0.2	43.5	19.2	24.4	24.2	44.2	3.2	2.1	B
Namibia	2,020	1.8	-0.1	27.4	12.9	14.5	14.4	39.1	3.5	7.1	B
Niger	13,264	0.5	-0.5	51.2	15.6	35.6	35.2	48.0	3.1	0.9	B
Nigeria	141,356	-0.2	-0.3	42.7	17.5	25.2	25.0	44.3	2.9	0.7	C
Rwanda	9,234	57.2	1.0	41.7	18.4	23.3	24.3	43.5	2.5	1.3	B
Saint Helena[f]	6	...	...	...	...	...	14.6	...	...	24.8	B
Sao Tome and Principe	153	-9.0	-9.6	34.9	8.2	26.6	17.1	41.6	4.4	4.8	C
Senegal	11,770	-2.1	-1.8	37.6	9.8	27.8	26.0	42.2	4.2	2.8	B
Seychelles	86	...	...	...	...	...	10.6	...	...	6.1	B
Sierra Leone	5,586	-5.1	18.7	46.9	23.5	23.5	42.3	42.8	3.3	2.2	C
Somalia	8,196	-3.0	2.6	45.8	18.5	27.3	30.0	44.1	2.6	3.4	I
South Africa	47,939	1.8	0.3	24.1	13.5	10.6	10.9	32.1	4.2	2.3	B
Swaziland	1,125	-2.4	-1.1	30.4	17.2	13.3	12.2	39.8	3.2	4.4	B

Number of refugees[3, b] ('000)		Diaspora remittances[4]		Government policies[6]							
				Immigration			Emigration		Fertility		
By destination	By origin	Total[c] (Millions of US dollars)	% of Gross Domestic Product[5]	Overall policy	Highly skilled workers	Integration of non-citizens	Overall policy	Encouraging the return of citizens	View on fertility level	Policy to modify fertility	
2006	2006	2004		2005			2005		2005		Country or Territory
											Arab States
94	8	2,460	3.05	↔	...	...	<>	Yes	Too high	↓↓	Algeria
0	0	...	...	↔	...	...	<>	...	Too high	↓↓	Bahrain
9	0	...	...	↓↓	...	No	<>	No	Too high	<>	Djibouti
88	8	3,341	3.76	↓↓	↔	Yes	↔	Yes	Too high	↓↓	Egypt
44	1,451	...	...	↔	↔	Yes	↓↓	...	Satisf.	<>	Iraq
2,359	2	2,287	21.15	↓↓	↓↓	No	↑↑	No	Too high	↓↓	Jordan
0	1	...	...	↓↓	↔	Yes	<>	No	Too low	↑↑	Kuwait
429	12	2,700	13.54	↓↓	<>	No	↓↓	Yes	Too high	↓↓	Lebanon
3	2	8	0.04	↔	...	...	↔	No	Satisf.	<>	Libyan Arab Jamahiriya
1	33	2	0.16	<>	...	...	<>	...	Too high	↓↓	Mauritania
1	95[k]	4,218	8.47	↓↓	↔	Yes	↔	Yes	Satisf.	↓↓	Morocco
0	0	40	0.16	↓↓	↔	No	<>	No	Too high	↓↓	Oman
1,739	4,783	692	20.19	.	.	.	.	.	...	...	Palestinian A. T.
0	0	...	...	↓↓	↔	...	<>	...	Satisf.	↔	Qatar
241	1	...	...	↓↓	↓↓	Yes	↓↓	Yes	Satisf.	↑↑	Saudi Arabia
196	686	1,403	7.03	↔	...	...	↓↓	...	Too high	↓↓	Sudan
1,145	12	803	3.43	↓↓	...	...	↓↓	...	Satisf.	<>	Syrian Arab Republic
0	3	1,432	5.09	<>	<>	No	↑↑	No	Satisf.	↓↓	Tunisia
0	0	...	...	↓↓	↓↓	...	<>	Yes	Satisf.	↔	United Arab Emirates
96	1	1,283	9.81	↓↓	↔	...	↑↑	...	Too high	↓↓	Yemen
											Sub-Saharan Africa
13	207	...	...	<>	...	...	<>	No	Too high	↔	Angola
11	0	84	2.06	<>	<>	No	↓↓	No	Too high	↓↓	Benin
3	0	27	0.32	↓↓	↓↓	Yes	<>	No	Too high	↓↓	Botswana
1	0	50	1.12	<>	<>	No	<>	Yes	Too high	↓↓	Burkina Faso
13	397	...	...	<>	...	...	<>	...	Too high	↓↓	Burundi
35	10	11	0.07	↓↓	...	...	<>	...	Too high	↓↓	Cameroon
...	0	92	9.54	<>	<>	No	↔	Yes	Too high	↓↓	Cape Verde
12	72	...	...	<>	...	...	<>	...	Satisf.	<>	Central African Republic
287	36	...	...	↔	...	...	<>	...	Satisf.	<>	Chad
0	0	12	3.61	<>	...	...	<>	...	Too high	↓↓	Comoros[d]
56	21	1	0.02	<>	...	...	<>	...	Too high	↓↓	Congo
208	402	...	...	↓↓	...	...	<>	...	Satisf.	<>	Congo (Dem. Rep.)
27	26	148	0.91	↓↓	↔	No	<>	No	Too high	↓↓	Côte d'Ivoire
...	0	...	...	<>	...	...	↓↓	...	Satisf.	↔	Equatorial Guinea
5	194	...	...	<>	...	...	<>	Yes	Too high	↓↓	Eritrea
97	74	46	0.57	<>	<>	No	<>	Yes	Too high	↓↓	Ethiopia
8	0	6	0.09	↓↓	...	...	↓↓	No	Too low	↑↑	Gabon
14	1	8	1.93	↓↓	<>	...	<>	No	Too high	↓↓	Gambia
45	10	82	0.94	↓↓	<>	No	↓↓	Yes	Too high	↓↓	Ghana
31	7	42	1.08	<>	<>	No	<>	No	Too high	↓↓	Guinea
8	1	23	8.49	<>	...	...	↓↓	...	Too high	<>	Guinea-Bissau
273	5	494	3.33	<>	<>	No	<>	No	Too high	↓↓	Kenya
...	0	355	25.86	<>	...	...	<>	Yes	Too high	↓↓	Lesotho
16	161	...	...	↔	...	Yes	<>	Yes	Too high	↓↓	Liberia
...	0	16	0.40	<>	...	...	<>	No	Too high	↓↓	Madagascar
4	0	1	0.05	↓↓	...	Yes	<>	Yes	Too high	↓↓	Malawi
11	1	154	3.11	<>	...	No	↓↓	Yes	Too high	↓↓	Mali
...	0	215	3.40	<>	<>	Yes	<>	No	Satisf.	↔	Mauritius[e]
3	0	58	0.91	<>	...	...	<>	...	Too high	↓↓	Mozambique
5	1	13	0.24	↔	...	Yes	<>	No	Satisf.	↓↓	Namibia
0	1	25	0.93	↓↓	...	No	<>	...	Too high	↓↓	Niger
9	13	2,751	3.60	↔	...	...	<>	Yes	Too high	↓↓	Nigeria
49	93	7	0.38	↔	<>	Yes	↔	Yes	Too high	↓↓	Rwanda
...	...	...	...	.	.	.	.	.	...	...	Saint Helena[f]
...	0	1	1.47	<>	...	...	<>	...	Too high	<>	Sao Tome and Principe
21	15	511	6.68	<>	...	...	<>	Yes	Too high	↓↓	Senegal
...	0	2	0.28	↔	...	...	↔	...	Satisf.	<>	Seychelles
27	43	26	2.49	<>	...	...	<>	...	Too high	↓↓	Sierra Leone
1	464	...	...	.	.	.	...	...	Satisf.	<>	Somalia
35	1	521	0.24	↓↓	↔	Yes	↓↓	Yes	Satisf.	↔	South Africa
1	0	62	2.69	↔	...	...	<>	...	Too high	↓↓	Swaziland

Table 3. Demographic context

	Total Population[1] ('000)	Net migration (average annual)		Population growth[1] — Natural increase (average annual)			Total annual growth rate	Age structure[1]		Migrant stock[2]	
		Rate per 1,000 pop.	Rate per 1,000 pop.	Crude birth rate	Crude death rate	Rate of natural increase	Rate per 1,000 pop.	Less than 15	Over 65	% of population	Definition Code[a]
Country or Territory	2005	1995/2000	2000/2005	2000/2005				2005		2005	
Tanzania (United Rep.)	38,478	-1.3	-1.9	42.1	14.6	27.5	25.6	44.4	3.0	2.1	B
Togo	6,239	5.2	-0.1	39.6	10.8	28.8	28.8	43.3	3.1	3.0	B
Uganda	28,947	-0.4	0.0	47.3	15.5	31.8	31.8	49.4	2.5	1.8	B
Zambia	11,478	1.7	-1.5	41.9	21.7	20.2	18.8	45.7	2.9	2.4	B
Zimbabwe	13,120	-2.5	-1.2	28.9	20.5	8.4	7.2	39.5	3.5	3.9	B
Central and South Asia											
Afghanistan	25,067	-4.1	9.7	49.7	21.6	28.1	37.9	47.0	2.2	0.1	I
Armenia	3,018	-14.3	-6.6	11.2	8.9	2.3	-4.2	20.8	12.1	7.8	B
Azerbaijan	8,352	-3.2	-2.4	14.3	6.9	7.5	5.1	25.3	7.2	2.2	B
Bangladesh	153,281	-0.5	-0.7	27.8	8.2	19.6	18.9	35.2	3.5	0.7	B
Bhutan	637	0.1	11.7	22.4	7.8	14.5	26.3	33.0	4.6	0.5	I
Georgia	4,473	-14.4	-10.8	11.1	11.1	0.1	-10.7	18.9	14.3	4.3	B
India	1,134,403	-0.3	-0.2	25.1	8.7	16.4	16.2	33.0	5.0	0.5	B
Iran (Islamic Rep.)	69,421	-1.7	-3.7	19.0	5.5	13.4	9.7	28.8	4.5	2.8	B
Kazakhstan	15,211	-17.1	-2.7	16.7	10.6	6.1	3.4	24.2	8.0	16.9	B
Kyrgyzstan	5,204	-1.1	-3.0	21.0	7.9	13.1	10.1	31.0	5.9	5.5	B
Maldives	295	0.0	0.0	22.2	6.5	15.7	15.7	34.0	3.8	1.0	I
Nepal	27,094	-0-9	-0.8	30.2	8.7	21.5	20.8	39.0	3.7	3.0	B
Pakistan	158,081	-0.1	-1.6	27.5	7.7	19.8	18.2	37.2	3.9	2.1	B
Sri Lanka	19,121	-4.3	-4.7	16.3	7.3	9.0	4.3	24.2	6.5	1.8	C
Tajikistan	6,550	-11.6	-10.8	29.4	6.6	22.7	11.9	39.4	3.9	4.7	B
Turkmenistan	4,833	-2.3	-0.4	22.9	8.3	14.6	14.2	31.8	4.7	4.6	B
Uzbekistan	26,593	-3.4	-2.3	23.7	6.8	16.9	14.6	33.2	4.7	4.8	B
East Asia											
Brunei Darussalam	374	2.2	2.0	23.6	2.8	20.8	22.9	29.6	3.2	33.2	B
Cambodia	13,956	1.3	0.2	27.5	10.0	17.4	17.6	37.6	3.1	2.2	C
China[g]	1,312,979	-0.2	-0.3	13.6	6.6	7.0	6.7	21.6	7.7	0.0	I
Hong Kong (SAR China)	7,057	9.3	8.7	8.1	5.3	2.8	11.5	15.1	12.0	42.6	B
Macao (SAR China)	473	7.1	10.9	7.4	4.3	3.1	14.0	16.1	7.5	55.9	B
Indonesia	226,063	-0.9	-0.9	20.7	6.6	14.0	13.1	28.4	5.5	0.1	C
Japan	127,897	0.4	0.4	9.0	8.0	0.9	1.4	13.9	19.7	1.6	C
Korea (Dem. People's Rep.)	23,616	0.0	0.0	15.1	9.3	5.8	5.8	24.2	8.5	0.2	I
Korea (Rep.)	47,870	-0.3	-0.3	10.4	5.4	4.9	4.6	18.6	9.4	1.2	B
Lao (People's Dem. Rep.)	5,664	-3.5	-4.2	28.4	8.0	20.4	16.2	39.8	3.5	0.4	C
Malaysia	25,653	4.5	1.2	22.7	4.5	18.2	19.5	31.4	4.4	6.5	B
Mongolia	2,581	-7.4	-4.0	19.7	6.9	12.8	8.8	28.9	3.9	0.3	C
Myanmar	47,967	0.0	-0.4	19.5	10.2	9.3	8.9	27.3	5.6	0.2	C
Philippines	84,566	-2.5	-2.2	28.1	5.1	23.0	20.8	36.2	3.8	0.5	C
Singapore	4,327	19.6	9.6	10.1	4.9	5.3	14.9	19.5	8.5	42.6	B
Thailand	63,003	1.7	0.7	15.4	8.6	6.8	7.6	21.7	7.8	1.6	C
Timor-Leste	1,067	-40.8	21.2	41.7	10.2	31.6	53.1	45.0	2.7	0.6	I
Viet Nam	85,029	-0.5	-0.5	20.2	5.2	15.0	14.5	29.6	5.6	0.0	C
Europe											
Albania	3,154	-17.9	-7.0	17.2	5.5	11.8	4.7	26.3	8.4	2.6	C
Andorra	73	…	…	…	…	…	20.1	…	…	77.9	C
Austria	8,292	1.2	4.4	9.5	9.5	0.0	4.4	15.8	16.2	15.1	B
Belarus	9,795	0.0	0.0	9.3	14.5	-5.2	-5.2	15.7	14.4	12.2	B
Belgium	10,398	1.2	3.5	10.8	10.3	0.5	4.0	17.0	17.3	6.9	C
Bosnia and Herzegovina	3,915	16.3	6.0	9.4	8.7	0.7	6.7	17.6	13.7	1.0	I
Bulgaria	7,745	-2.5	-1.1	8.7	14.2	-5.5	-6.6	13.8	17.2	1.3	B
Croatia	4,551	-6.5	4.4	9.1	11.5	-2.4	2.0	15.5	17.2	14.5	B
Cyprus	836	7.6	7.1	12.1	7.0	5.2	12.3	19.9	12.1	13.9	B
Czech Republic	10,192	0.2	1.3	9.0	10.8	-1.9	-0.6	14.8	14.2	4.4	B
Denmark	5,417	2.8	1.7	12.0	10.7	1.3	3.0	18.8	15.1	7.2	B
Estonia	1,344	-5.2	0.1	9.8	13.7	-3.9	-3.8	15.2	16.6	15.2	B
Finland	5,246	0.8	1.3	11.0	9.5	1.4	2.7	17.4	15.9	3.0	B
France[h]	60,991	0.3	2.4	12.8	9.2	3.6	6.0	18.4	16.3	10.7	B
Germany	82,652	2.8	2.4	8.7	10.3	-1.6	0.8	14.4	18.8	12.3	C
Gibraltar	29	…	…	…	…	…	12.2	…	…	26.4	B
Greece	11,100	5.6	2.8	9.4	9.9	-0.5	2.3	14.3	18.3	8.8	C
Holy See	0.78	…	…	…	…	…	-1.0	…	…	100.0	I

Number of refugees[3, b] ('000)		Diaspora remittances[4]		Government policies[6]							
					Immigration			Emigration		Fertility	
By destination	By origin	Total[c] (Millions of US dollars)	% of Gross Domestic Product[5]	Overall policy	Highly skilled workers	Integration of non-citizens	Overall policy	Encouraging the return of citizens	View on fertility level	Policy to modify fertility	Country or Territory
2006	2006	2004			2005		2005		2005		
485	2	7	0.06	<>	...	No	<>	No	Too high	↓↓	Tanzania (United Rep.)
6	27	149	7.16	<>	<>	Yes	<>	...	Too high	↓↓	Togo
272	22	291	3.74	↔	...	No	<>	...	Too high	↓↓	Uganda
120	0	...	...	↑↑	↔	Yes	↓↓	Yes	Too high	↓↓	Zambia
4	13	...	...	<>	↑↑	...	↓↓	...	Too high	↓↓	Zimbabwe
											Central and South Asia
0	2,108	...	...	↔	...	...	↓↓	Yes	Too high	<>	Afghanistan
114	15	336	9.29	↑↑	↔	Yes	↓↓	Yes	Too low	↑↑	Armenia
3	126	228	2.75	↔	↔	Yes	↓↓	Yes	Satisf.	<>	Azerbaijan
26	8	3,372	5.47	↓↓	...	No	↑↑	No	Too high	↓↓	Bangladesh
...	108	...	...	↓↓	↓↓	...	↓↓	...	Too high	↓↓	Bhutan
1	6	303	5.93	↔	↔	...	↓↓	...	Too low	↑↑	Georgia
158	18	21,727	3.19	↔	↔	...	↑↑	...	Too high	↓↓	India
968	102	1,032	0.62	↓↓	↔	...	↓↓	Yes	Too high	↓↓	Iran (Islamic Rep.)
4	7	167	0.41	↔	↑↑	Yes	↓↓	Yes	Too low	↑↑	Kazakhstan
0	2	189	8.74	↔	↔	Yes	↔	Yes	Satisf.	↔	Kyrgyzstan
...	0	3	0.40	↓↓	...	...	<>	...	Too high	↓↓	Maldives
128	3	785	12.07	↔	↔	No	↑↑	Yes	Too high	↓↓	Nepal
1,044	26	3,945	4.21	↓↓	↔	No	↑↑	Yes	Too high	↓↓	Pakistan
0	117	1,564	8.13	↔	↔	...	↔	...	Satisf.	↔	Sri Lanka
1	1	252	13.19	↔	...	...	<>	Yes	Too high	↓↓	Tajikistan
1	1	...	...	↓↓	...	No	↓↓	...	Satisf.	↔	Turkmenistan
1	9	...	...	↔	↔	...	↔	...	Satisf.	↔	Uzbekistan
											East Asia
...	0	...	...	↔	↑↑	No	<>	No	Satisf.	<>	Brunei Darussalam
0	18	138	3.17	↔	↔	No	<>	No	Too high	↓↓	Cambodia
301	161	21,283	1.29	<>	↔	No	↔	No	Satisf.	↔	China[g]
2	0	240	0.15	.		.	.	.	...	...	Hong Kong (SAR China)
...	0	...	...	.	.		.	.	...	...	Macao (SAR China)
0	35	1,700	0.76	↔	↔	No	↑↑	No	Too high	↓↓	Indonesia
2	0	931	0.02	↔	↑↑	No	<>	No	Too low	↑↑	Japan
...	0	...	...	↔	↑↑	No	↔	...	Too low	<>	Korea (Dem. People's Rep.)
0	1	832	0.12	↑↑	↑↑	Yes	<>	No	Too low	↑↑	Korea (Rep.)
...	26	1	0.04	↔	↑↑	...	<>	Yes	Too high	↓↓	Lao (People's Dem. Rep.)
37	1	987	0.84	↔	↔	Yes	<>	Yes	Satisf.	<>	Malaysia
0	1	56	4.41	↔	↑↑	No	↔	Yes	Too low	↑↑	Mongolia
...	203	78	0.71	↓↓	↔	No	↔	Yes	Satisf.	↔	Myanmar
0	1	11,634	13.46	↔	↔	Yes	↔	Yes	Too high	↓↓	Philippines
0	0	...	...	↑↑	↑↑	Yes	↓↓	Yes	Too low	↑↑	Singapore
133	3	1,622	1.01	↔	↔	...	↑↑	No	Satisf.	↔	Thailand
0	0	...	...	↔	↔	...	<>	...	Too high	<>	Timor-Leste
2	374	3,200	6.98	↔	↔	Yes	↑↑	Yes	Satisf.	↔	Viet Nam
											Europe
0	14	889	11.19	↔	↔	No	↔	Yes	Satisf.	↔	Albania
...	0	...	...	↔	<>	Yes	↔	No	Satisf.	↔	Andorra
25	0	2,475	0.85	↔	↔	Yes	<>	Yes	Too low	↑↑	Austria
1	9	244	1.07	↔	↔	Yes	↓↓	Yes	Too low	↑↑	Belarus
17	0	6,840	1.94	↔	↔	Yes	<>	No	Satisf.	<>	Belgium
10	200	1,824	23.14	↔	...	...	↓↓	Yes	Too low	<>	Bosnia and Herzegovina
5	3	103	0.42	↔	↔	Integration	↔	...	Too low	↑↑	Bulgaria
2	94	1,222	3.56	↔	↑↑	Yes	↓↓	Yes	Too low	↑↑	Croatia
1	0	242	1.58	↓↓	↔	Yes	↔	Yes	Too low	↑↑	Cyprus
2	2	454	0.42	↑↑	↑↑	Yes	<>	No	Too low	↑↑	Czech Republic
37	0	941	0.39	↓↓	↑↑	Yes	<>	No	Satisf.	<>	Denmark
0	1	164	1.49	↓↓	↔	Yes	↔	Yes	Too low	↑↑	Estonia
12	0	672	0.36	↔	↔	Yes	<>	No	Too low	↑↑	Finland
146	0	12,650	0.62	↓↓	↑↑	Yes	<>	No	Too low	↑↑	France[h]
605	0	6,497	0.24	↔	↑↑	Yes	<>	No	Too low	<>	Germany
...	...	...	...	.	.	.	.	.	...	...	Gibraltar
2	0	1,242	0.61	↔	↔	Yes	<>	Yes	Too low	↑↑	Greece
...	...	...	...	↔	...	...	↔	...	Satisf.	<>	Holy See

Table 3. Demographic context

Country or Territory	Total Population[1] ('000)	Net migration (average annual) Rate per 1,000 pop.	Net migration (average annual) Rate per 1,000 pop.	Population growth[1] Natural increase (average annual) Crude birth rate	Population growth[1] Natural increase (average annual) Crude death rate	Population growth[1] Natural increase (average annual) Rate of natural increase	Total annual growth rate Rate per 1,000 pop.	Age structure[1] Less than 15	Age structure[1] Over 65	Migrant stock[2] % of population	Migrant stock[2] Definition Code[a]
	2005	1995/2000	2000/2005	2000/2005	2000/2005	2000/2005		2005	2005	2005	2005
Hungary	10,086	1.7	1.3	9.5	13.3	-3.8	-2.5	15.8	15.2	3.1	B
Iceland	296	1.1	1.8	14.4	6.1	8.3	10.2	22.1	11.7	7.8	B
Ireland	4,143	4.9	9.5	15.2	7.6	7.6	17.1	20.7	11.1	14.1	B
Israel	6,692	9.6	3.6	21.1	5.6	15.4	19.1	27.9	10.1	39.6	B
Italy	58,646	2.1	3.9	9.4	9.9	-0.6	3.3	14.0	19.7	4.3	B
Latvia	2,302	-3.3	-1.7	8.7	13.6	-4.9	-6.6	14.4	16.6	19.5	B
Liechtenstein	35	...	...	...	...	...	10.3	...	...	33.9	C
Lithuania	3,425	-6.2	-1.7	9.0	11.8	-2.8	-4.5	16.8	15.3	4.8	B
Luxembourg	457	9.7	5.7	12.0	8.9	3.2	8.9	18.5	14.2	37.4	C
Macedonia (TFYR)	2,034	-0.5	-1.0	12.0	8.6	3.4	2.4	19.7	11.1	6.0	B
Malta	403	1.3	4.5	10.0	7.7	2.4	6.9	17.4	13.2	2.7	C
Moldova (Rep.)	3,877	-11.7	-12.5	11.4	12.4	-0.9	-13.4	20.0	11.1	10.5	B
Monaco	33	...	...	...	...	...	3.0	...	...	69.9	B
Montenegro	608	7.7	-24.4	13.2	8.2	5.0	-19.5	19.6	13.8	...	...
Netherlands	16,328	2.3	1.4	12.4	8.7	3.6	5.0	18.4	14.2	10.1	B
Norway	4,639	2.4	3.7	12.3	9.5	2.9	6.6	19.6	14.7	7.4	B
Poland	38,196	-1.6	-1.0	9.4	9.6	-0.2	-1.2	16.3	13.3	1.8	B
Portugal	10,528	3.5	5.3	10.9	10.4	0.5	5.8	15.7	16.9	7.3	B
Romania	21,628	-3.1	-2.5	10.0	12.2	-2.2	-4.7	15.7	14.8	0.6	B
Russian Federation	143,953	3.0	1.3	9.9	15.9	-6.0	-4.8	15.1	13.8	8.4	B
San Marino	30	...	...	...	...	...	22.9	...	...	33.5	B
Serbia	9,863	-2.9	-6.8	12.5	11.0	1.4	-5.4	18.5	14.7	...	...
Slovakia	5,387	0.0	0.1	9.7	9.8	-0.1	0.0	16.8	11.7	2.3	B
Slovenia	1,999	2.5	2.2	8.9	9.4	-0.6	1.6	14.1	15.6	8.5	B
Spain	43,397	4.0	13.6	10.2	8.7	1.5	15.2	14.4	16.8	11.1	B
Sweden	9,038	1.1	3.4	10.9	10.5	0.4	3.8	17.4	17.2	12.4	B
Switzerland	7,424	0.8	2.7	9.8	8.1	1.7	4.4	16.7	15.4	22.9	B
Turkey	72,970	0.3	-0.1	19.5	5.8	13.7	13.6	28.3	5.6	1.8	B
Ukraine	46,918	-2.2	-0.7	8.4	15.8	-7.4	-8.1	14.7	16.1	14.7	B
United Kingdom	60,245	1.7	3.2	11.6	10.2	1.4	4.6	18.0	16.1	9.1	B
North America											
Canada	32,271	4.9	6.6	10.7	7.2	3.4	10.1	17.6	13.1	18.9	B
United States of America	299,846	4.5	4.4	14.1	8.3	5.8	10.3	20.8	12.3	12.9	B
Latin America and the Caribbean											
Anguilla	12	...	...	...	...	...	17.4	...	...	41.8	B
Antigua and Barbuda	83	...	...	...	...	...	15.7	...	...	22.4	B
Argentina	38,747	-0.6	-0.5	18.0	7.7	10.3	9.8	26.4	10.2	3.9	B
Aruba	103	6.0	16.7	16.2	6.9	9.3	26.1	22.0	7.8	24.6	B
Bahamas	323	1.4	1.3	18.1	6.5	11.6	12.9	27.6	6.2	9.8	B
Barbados	292	-0.9	-0.9	11.9	7.3	4.7	3.8	18.9	9.2	9.7	B
Belize	276	-0.9	-0.8	28.3	3.8	24.5	23.8	37.6	4.2	15.0	B
Bermuda	64	...	...	...	...	...	4.1	...	...	29.3	B
Bolivia	9,182	-2.5	-2.3	30.2	8.2	22.1	19.8	38.1	4.5	1.3	B
Brazil	186,831	-0.3	-0.3	20.6	6.3	14.3	14.1	27.8	6.1	0.3	B
British Virgin Islands	22	...	...	...	...	...	14.1	...	...	38.3	B
Cayman Islands	46	...	...	...	...	...	25.0	...	...	35.8	B
Chile	16,295	0.8	0.4	15.7	5.0	10.8	11.2	24.9	8.1	1.4	B
Colombia	44,946	-0.8	-0.6	21.2	5.6	15.6	15.1	30.3	5.1	0.3	B
Costa Rica	4,327	6.9	4.1	19.1	3.9	15.2	19.3	28.4	5.8	10.2	B
Cuba	11,260	-2.2	-2.3	12.0	7.6	4.4	2.1	19.2	11.2	0.7	B
Dominica	68	...	...	...	...	...	-1.8	...	...	5.7	B
Dominican Republic	9,470	-3.3	-3.2	25.2	6.0	19.2	15.9	33.5	5.6	1.8	B
Ecuador	13,061	-5.1	-6.3	23.2	5.0	18.2	11.9	32.6	5.9	0.9	B
El Salvador	6,668	-2.6	-4.4	25.1	5.9	19.2	14.7	34.1	5.5	0.3	B
Grenada	105	-7.8	-0.3	18.4	8.8	9.6	9.4	34.2	6.8	10.5	B
Guatemala	12,710	-7.3	-5.0	35.8	6.0	29.7	24.8	43.1	4.3	0.4	B
Guyana	739	-16.3	-10.9	21.3	9.1	12.2	1.4	31.1	5.7	0.1	B
Haiti	9,296	-3.3	-3.1	29.8	10.5	19.3	16.2	38.0	4.1	0.4	B
Honduras	6,834	-6.1	-4.6	30.2	6.0	24.2	19.6	40.0	4.1	0.4	B
Jamaica	2,682	-7.9	-7.6	21.8	7.1	14.7	7.1	31.7	7.5	0.7	B
Mexico	104,266	-2.5	-7.8	21.4	4.7	16.7	8.9	30.8	5.8	0.6	B
Montserrat	6	...	...	...	...	...	25.4	...	...	2.5	B

Number of refugees[3,b] ('000)		Diaspora remittances[4]		Government policies[6]							
				Immigration			Emigration		Fertility		
By destination	By origin	Total[c] (Millions of US dollars)	% of Gross Domestic Product[5]	Overall policy	Highly skilled workers	Integration of non-citizens	Overall policy	Encouraging the return of citizens	View on fertility level	Policy to modify fertility	Country or Territory
2006	2006	2004		2005			2005		2005		
8	3	307	0.31	↔	...	Yes	<>	No	Too low	↑↑	Hungary
0	0	112	0.92	<>	<>	No	<>	No	Satisf.	↔	Iceland
8	0	358	0.20	↔	↑↑	Yes	<>	Yes	Satisf.	↔	Ireland
1	1	398	0.32	↑↑	↔	Yes	↓↓	Yes	Too low	↑↑	Israel
27	0	2,172	0.13	↓↓	<>	Yes	<>	No	Too low	↑↑	Italy
0	1	229	1.68	↔	↔	Yes	<>	Yes	Too low	↑↑	Latvia
0	...	...	...	↔	↔	Yes	<>	No	Too low	<>	Liechtenstein
1	1	308	1.40	↔	↑↑	Yes	<>	No	Too low	↑↑	Lithuania
2	0	951	2.98	↔	...	Yes	<>	...	Satisf.	↔	Luxembourg
1	8	171	3.25	↔	...	No	↓↓	No	Satisf.	<>	Macedonia (TFYR)
2	0	16	0.28	↔	...	No	<>	No	Too low	<>	Malta
0	12	703	27.09	↔		...	<>	...	Too low	↑↑	Moldova (Rep.)
...	...	...	...	↔	...	...	↔	...	Satisf.	↔	Monaco
7	0	...	...								Montenegro
101	0	1,522	0.26	↓↓	↑↑	Yes	<>	No	Satisf.	<>	Netherlands
43	0	392	0.16	↔	↑↑	Yes	<>	No	Satisf.	↔	Norway
7	14	2,709	1.12	↔	↔	Yes	<>	No	Too low	<>	Poland
0	0	3,212	1.92	↔	↔	Yes	↔	No	Too low	↑↑	Portugal
2	7	132	0.18	↓↓	<>	Yes	↓↓	No	Too low	↑↑	Romania
1	159	2,668	0.46	↑↑	↑↑	Yes	<>	...	Too low	↑↑	Russian Federation
...	0	...	...	<>	<>	No	<>	No	Satisf.	<>	San Marino
99	174	...	...	...	...	...	...	...	...	...	Serbia
0	1	425	1.03	↔	↔	Yes	<>	No	Too low	↑↑	Slovakia
0	2	267	0.83	↔	↔	Yes	<>	Yes	Too low	↑↑	Slovenia
5	2	6,859	0.66	↔	↔	Yes	↓↓	Yes	Too low	↑↑	Spain
80	0	578	0.17	↔	↔	Yes	<>	No	Satisf.	<>	Sweden
49	0	1,760	0.49	↔	↑↑	Yes	<>	No	Too low	<>	Switzerland
3	227	804	0.27	↓↓	↑↑	No	↔	No	Satisf.	↔	Turkey
2	64	411	0.63	↔	↔	No	↓↓	No	Too low	↑↑	Ukraine
302	0	6,350	0.30	↔	↑↑	Yes	<>	No	Satisf.	<>	United Kingdom
											North America
152	0	...	...	↑↑	↑↑	Yes	<>	No	Too low	<>	Canada
843	1	3,038	0.03	↔	↔	Yes	<>	No	Satisf.	<>	United States of America
											Latin America and the Caribbean
...	...	...	...	.	.	.	.		...	...	Anguilla
...	0	11	1.59	↔	↔	...	<>	Yes	Satisf.	<>	Antigua and Barbuda
3	1	288	0.19	↔	↔	Yes	↓↓	Yes	Satisf.	<>	Argentina
...	...	16	0.77	.	.	.	.	.	...	...	Aruba
...	0	...	...	↓↓	↔	...	<>	...	Satisf.	<>	Bahamas
...	0	113	3.99	↔	↑↑	No	<>	Yes	Too low	↑↑	Barbados
0	0	21	2.21	↓↓	↔	No	<>	No	Too high	↔	Belize
...	...	...	...	.	.	.	.	.	...	...	Bermuda
1	0	158	1.88	↔	↔	No	<>	...	Satisf.	<>	Bolivia
3	1	3,575	0.60	↔	↔	Yes	<>	No	Satisf.	<>	Brazil
...	...	...	...	.	.	.	.	.	...	...	British Virgin Islands
...	...	...	...	.	.	.	.	.	...	...	Cayman Islands
1	1	13	0.01	↔	↔	Yes	↔	No	Satisf.	<>	Chile
0	73	3,190	3.33	↔	↑↑	Yes	↓↓	Yes	Too high	↓↓	Colombia
12	0	320	1.74	↔	...	Yes	<>	No	Satisf.	↓↓	Costa Rica
1	34	...	...	↔	↔	No	↔	No	Satisf.	<>	Cuba
...	0	4	1.47	↔	↔	Yes	<>	Yes	Satisf.	<>	Dominica
...	0	2,471	10.41	↔	...	No	<>	No	Too high	↓↓	Dominican Republic
12	1	1,604	5.34	↓↓	↔	No	↓↓	Yes	Satisf.	↔	Ecuador
0	6	2,564	16.48	<>	↔	No	↓↓	Yes	Satisf.	<>	El Salvador
...	0	23	5.81	↔	↔	...	↓↓	Yes	Too high	↓↓	Grenada
0	6	2,591	9.77	<>	↔	Yes	<>	No	Too high	↓↓	Guatemala
...	1	64	8.23	↔	↔	...	<>	...	Satisf.	<>	Guyana
...	21	876	22.12	↔	...	...	↓↓	Yes	Too high	↓↓	Haiti
0	1	1,142	15.49	↔	↔	...	<>	...	Too high	↓↓	Honduras
...	1	1,398	16.42	↔	↔	No	<>	Yes	Too high	↓↓	Jamaica
3	3	18,143	2.68	↔	↑↑	Yes	↓↓	Yes	Satisf.	↓↓	Mexico
...	...	...	...	.	.	.	.	.	...	...	Montserrat

Table 3. Demographic context

Country or Territory	Total Population[1] ('000)	Net migration (average annual)		Population growth[1]			Total annual growth rate	Age structure[1]		Migrant stock[2]	
		Rate per 1,000 pop.	Rate per 1,000 pop.	Crude birth rate	Crude death rate	Rate of natural increase	Rate per 1,000 pop.	Less than 15	Over 65	% of population	Definition Code[a]
	2005	1995/2000	2000/2005	2000/2005				2005		2005	
Netherlands Antilles	186	-20.2	-0.8	14.5	7.5	7.0	6.2	22.5	9.8	26.5	B
Nicaragua	5,463	-6.5	-7.9	26.3	5.0	21.4	13.4	37.9	4.0	0.5	B
Panama	3,232	0.8	0.5	22.7	5.0	17.7	18.2	30.4	6.0	3.2	B
Paraguay	5,904	-1.7	-1.6	26.9	5.6	21.3	19.7	35.8	4.8	2.7	B
Peru	27,274	-4.4	-3.9	22.2	6.2	16.0	12.2	31.8	5.6	0.1	B
Saint Kitts and Nevis	49	...	...	...	...	...	13.0	...	...	10.4	B
Saint Lucia	161	-3.6	-1.3	19.1	7.0	12.2	10.9	27.9	7.2	5.4	B
Saint Vincent and the Grenadines	119	-8.7	-8.5	20.8	6.9	13.9	5.4	29.3	6.5	8.7	B
Suriname	452	-7.5	-7.2	21.2	6.8	14.4	7.2	29.8	6.3	1.2	C
Trinidad and Tobago	1,324	-3.1	-3.0	14.5	7.9	6.6	3.5	22.2	6.5	2.9	B
Turks and Caicos Islands	24	...	...	...	...	...	51.9	...	...	11.9	B
Uruguay	3,326	-1.6	-6.3	16.0	9.3	6.7	0.5	23.8	13.5	2.4	B
Venezuela	26,726	0.3	0.3	22.9	5.0	17.9	18.2	31.3	5.0	3.8	B
Pacific											
Australia[i]	20,310	5.0	6.0	12.7	6.8	5.9	11.9	19.5	13.1	20.3	B
Cook Islands	14	...	...	...	...	...	-26.7	...	...	17.0	B
Fiji	828	-10.7	-10.3	23.1	6.4	16.8	6.5	32.9	4.2	2.0	B
Kiribati	92	...	...	...	...	...	18.2	...	...	2.6	B
Marshall Islands	57	...	...	...	...	...	16.8	...	...	2.7	B
Micronesia (Fed. States)	110	-25.4	-17.9	29.7	6.3	23.4	5.5	38.6	3.8	3.2	B
Nauru	10	...	...	...	...	...	1.5	...	...	36.1	C
New Zealand	4,097	2.1	5.1	14.2	7.1	7.1	12.2	21.5	12.2	15.9	B
Niue	1.63	...	...	...	...	...	-28.0	...	...	7.6	B
Palau	20	...	...	...	...	...	8.6	...	...	15.2	B
Papua New Guinea	6,070	0.0	0.0	34.0	9.9	24.1	24.1	40.6	2.4	0.4	C
Samoa	184	-16.2	-16.6	29.4	5.7	23.7	7.1	40.8	4.6	5.0	B
Solomon Islands	472	0.0	0.0	33.6	7.9	25.7	25.7	40.5	2.9	0.7	B
Tokelau	1.40	...	...	...	...	...	-15.9	...	...	12.5	B
Tonga	.99	-19.5	-16.1	24.3	5.7	18.7	2.6	37.5	6.4	1.1	B
Tuvalu	10	...	...	...	...	...	5.0	...	...	3.1	C
Vanuatu	215	-7.9	0.0	31.0	5.7	25.3	25.4	39.8	3.3	0.5	B
World[j]	**6,514,751**	**0.0**	**0.0**	**21.1**	**8.8**	**12.4**	**12.4**	**28.3**	**7.3**	**2.9**	.
Arab States	308,638	-0.5	-0.5	27.4	6.6	20.8	20.3	35.0	4.0	6.5	.
Sub-Saharan Africa	727,896	0.0	-0.2	41.0	15.9	25.1	24.9	43.6	3.1	2.1	.
Central and South Asia	1,661,633	-0.8	-0.6	25.4	8.6	16.9	16.2	33.5	4.7	1.1	.
East Asia	2,080,141	-0.2	-0.3	15.3	6.7	8.5	8.2	23.2	7.9	0.6	.
Europe	811,310	1.2	2.0	11.1	11.1	0.0	2.0	15.9	15.9	8.4	.
North America	332,117	4.5	4.7	13.8	8.2	5.6	10.2	20.5	12.3	13.5	.
Latin America and the Caribbean	552,955	-1.5	-2.5	21.5	6.0	15.5	13.0	29.8	6.3	1.1	.
Pacific	32,593	2.9	4.0	17.7	7.4	10.2	14.2	24.9	10.3	14.9	.

Sources:

1. United Nations, Department of Economic and Social Affairs, Population Division, 2007. World Population Prospects: The 2006 Revision.

2. United Nations, Department of Economic and Social Affairs, Population Division, 2006. Trends in Total Migrant Stock: The 2005 Revision.

3. United Nations High Commissioner for Refugees, 2007. 2006 Global Trends: Refugees, Asylum-seekers, Returnees, Internally Displaced and Stateless Persons; United Nations Relief and Welfare Agency, 2007. UNRWA figures as of 31 December 2006. Published in June 2007, revised 16 July 2007.

4. United Nations, Department of Economic and Social Affairs, Population Division, 2006. International Migration 2006 Wall Chart.

5. World Bank, Global Economic Prospects 2006: Economic Implications of Remittances and Migration; United Nations, Department of Economic and Social Affairs, Statistics Division.

6. United Nations, Department of Economic and Social Affairs, Population Division, 2006. World Population Policies 2005.

Notes:

a. Migrant Stock: The letter code indicates the type of data underlying the estimates: B (birthplace): indicates the data referring to the foreign born; C (citizenship): indicates the data referring to non-citizens; I (imputed): indicates that no data were available and were estimated by a model.

b. Data refer to the end of year; zero indicates that there are less than 500 refugees. Also included are Palestinian refugees registered with the United Nations Relief and Welfare Agency (UNRWA).

c. Credits only; Remittances include workers' remittances, compensation of employees, and migrants' transfers; Regional aggregations were prepared by the United Nations Population Division.

d. Including Mayotte.

By destination	By origin	Total[c] (Millions of US dollars)	% of Gross Domestic Product[5]	Overall policy	Highly skilled workers	Integration of non-citizens	Overall policy	Encouraging the return of citizens	View on fertility level	Policy to modify fertility	Country or Territory
2006	2006	2004			2005		2005		2005		
...	...	5	0.16	.	.	.	.	.	...	...	Netherlands Antilles
0	2	519	11.77	<>	<>	No	<>	No	Too high	↓↓	Nicaragua
2	0	127	0.94	↓↓	...	...	<>	Yes	Satisf.	↔	Panama
0	0	260	3.70	↔	↔	No	<>	Yes	Too high	<>	Paraguay
1	7	1,123	1.67	↔	↔	No	↔	Yes	Too high	↓↓	Peru
...	0	4	1.02	↔	↔	...	<>	Yes	Satisf.	<>	Saint Kitts and Nevis
...	0	4	0.56	↔	↔	...	<>	-	Too high	↓↓	Saint Lucia
...	0	3	0.75	↔	↔	...	<>	...	Satisf.	↔	Saint Vincent and the Grenadines
...	0	9	0.81	↑↑	↑↑	Yes	↓↓	No	Satisf.	↔	Suriname
...	0	79	0.69	↔	↔	Yes	<>	No	Satisf.	↔	Trinidad and Tobago
...	0	...	...	.	.	.	.	.	...	...	Turks and Caicos Islands
0	0	32	0.24	↔	↔	No	<>	No	Too low	<>	Uruguay
1	4	20	0.02	↔	↔	...	<>	No	Satisf.	↓↓	Venezuela
											Pacific
69	0	2,744	0.44	↑↑	↑↑	Yes	<>	No	Too low	↑↑	Australia[i]
...	...	...	...	↓↓	<>	Yes	↓↓	Yes	Too low	↑↑	Cook Islands
...	2	24	0.88	↓↓	...	Yes	↓↓	No	Satisf.	↓↓	Fiji
...	0	7	8.86	↔	...	...	↔	...	Too high	↓↓	Kiribati
...	...	...	...	↔	...	...	↔	No	Too high	↓↓	Marshall Islands
0	...	...	...	↓↓	↔	...	<>	...	Too high	↓↓	Micronesia (Fed. States)
...	0	...	...	↔	...	...	↔	...	Satisf.	↔	Nauru
5	0	1,132	1.16	↔	↑↑	Yes	<>	Yes	Satisf.	↔	New Zealand
...	...	...	...	↑↑	...	...	↓↓	Yes	Too low	↑↑	Niue
...	...	...	...	<>	...	...	↓↓	Yes	Satisf.	<>	Palau
10	0	6	0.13	↔	↑↑	Yes	<>	Yes	Too high	↓↓	Papua New Guinea
...	0	45	12.43	↔	↔	...	↔	...	Too high	↓↓	Samoa
...	0	2	0.74	↔	↔	...	↔	...	Too high	↓↓	Solomon Islands
...	...	...	...	.	.	.	.	.	...	...	Tokelau
...	0	66	33.50	↔	↔	...	↔	...	Satisf.	↔	Tonga
...	0	...	...	↔	...	...	↑↑	...	Too high	↓↓	Tuvalu
...	...	9	3.09	<>	...	...	<>	...	Too high	↓↓	Vanuatu
14,326	14,326[l]	225,810	0.55	.	.	.	.	.	.	.	**World**[j]
6,444	7,099	20,669	...	.	.	.	.	.	.	.	Arab States
2,216	2,320	6,291	...	.	.	.	.	.	.	.	Sub-Saharan Africa
2,451	2,657	33,903	...	.	.	.	.	.	.	.	Central and South Asia
478	825	42,702	...	.	.	.	.	.	.	.	East Asia
1,617	1,000	70,273	...	.	.	.	.	.	.	.	Europe
995	1	3,038	...	.	.	.	.	.	.	.	North America
41	164	40,770	1.92	.	.	.	.	.	.	.	Latin America and the Caribbean
84	2	4,035	0.54	.	.	.	.	.	.	.	Pacific

e. Including Agalega, Rodrigues and Saint Brandon.

f. Including Ascension and Tristan da Cunha.

g. For statistical purposes, the data for China do not include Hong Kong and Macao Special Administrative Regions (SAR) of China.

h. Not including DOM-TOM.

i. Including Christmas Island, Cocos (Keeling) Islands and Norfolk Island.

j. Including American Samoa, Faeroe Islands, Falkland Islands (Malvinas), French Guiana, French Polynesia, Greenland, Guadeloupe, Guam, Martinique, New Caledonia, Northern Mariana Islands, Pitcairn, Puerto Rico, Réunion, Saint-Pierre-et-Miquelon, Western Sahara, Channel Islands, Isle of Man, United States Virgin Islands, Wallis and Futuna Islands (not included elsewhere).

k. Including 90,614 refugees from Western Sahara, as defined by the UNHCR.

l. Including 11,259 refugees defined as 'stateless': 246,736 coming from 'various' origins and 4,448,429 Palestinians compiled separately by the UNRWA.

... Data not available

. Not applicable

↓↓ = Lower

↔ = Maintain

↑↑ = Raise

<> = No Intervention

Satisf. = Satisfactory

Table 4. Telecommunication access[1]

Country or Territory	Radio % of households with radio	Television % of households with TV set	Television % of households with cable or satellite	Personal computer per 1,000 inhabitants	Personal computer Average annual % change	Internet[a] Users per 1,000 inhabitants	Internet[a] Broad-band (% of subscribers)	Internet[a] % of montly GNI per capita for 20 hours usage (cheapest)	Telephone Fixed lines Subscribers per 1,000 inhabitants	Telephone Fixed lines Average annual % change	Telephone Fixed lines Cost of 3-min local call (peak—US$)	Telephone Mobile cellular[b] Sub-scribers per 1,000 in-habitants	Telephone Mobile cellular[b] Average annual % change	Telephone Mobile cellular[b] Cost of 3-min local call (peak—US$)	Ratio Mobile/ Fixed subscribers	International traffic Incoming minutes per person	International traffic Outgoing minutes per person
	2002	2005	2005	2005	2000/ 2005	2006	2006	2006	2006	2001–2006	2005	2006	2001–2006	2005	2006	2005	2005
Arab States																	
Algeria	71	90	70.0[s,-4]	11	10.2	74	0.0[-5]	5.0	85	7.0	0.08[+1]	630	187	0.22[+1]	7.39	11.5	5.4
Bahrain	…	95	62.2[s,-3]	177	3.9	213	64.9	2.5	262	0.0	0.06[+1]	1,216	22	0.32	4.65	252.7[-2]	407.5
Djibouti	57	43	5.3[s,-4]	24	21.5	13	1.2[-1]	51.9	13[-1]	0.2	0.08	55[-1]	92	0.51[+1]	4.09	18.9[-2]	24.5
Egypt	88	88	32.6	37	25.2	81	10.3	4.8	146	8.1	0.01	243	43	0.16	1.67	23.9	6.2
Iraq	…	…	…	8[-3]	…	…	1[-2]	0.0[-4]	…	38[-2]	12.8	…	21[-2]	.	…	0.55	…
Jordan	80	96	37.5[s,-3]	64	15.4	139	23.6	6.1	107	-4.4	0.06	758	34	0.21	7.07	69.8	65.6
Kuwait	95	95	100.0[s,-1]	222	14.6	294	8.8[-1]	1.2	189[-1]	-1.6	0.00	881[-1]	24	3.07	4.66	…	202.8
Lebanon	98[-1]	96	87.5[c]	102	17.1	234	54.8	2.0	168	0.5	0.10[+1]	272	6	0.13[+1]	1.62	234.2	44.9
Libyan Arab Jamahiriya	…	50	71.0[s,-3]	22	-2.0[(+1)]	39[-1]	…	6.0	80	-7.9	0.00[+1]	650	135	0.34[+1]	8.13	26.0[+1]	31.4
Mauritania	50	25	…	26	22.1	33	20.6	122.8	11	4.0	0.11	348	53	0.51	30.40	15.0[-2]	9.1
Morocco	79[+3]	78	30.3[s,-1]	24	15.0	198	97.8	20.5	41	0.1	0.15	519	26	1.14[+1]	12.64	58.8	5.5
Oman	67	79	…	52	9.3	125	23.7	1.9	109	2.8	0.06	714	40	0.31	6.53	76.2[-1]	122.8
Palestinian A. T.	83	93	66.5[s,-3]	52	12.2[(+1)]	68	29.1	16.7	88	-0.4	0.01	211	18	0.46[-2]	2.41	52.6[-1]	11.7
Qatar	…	90	14.0[c]	182	4.5	353	66.7	…	278	1.5	0.00	1,120	33	0.45	4.03	339.5	503.4
Saudi Arabia	…	99	0.2[c,-3]	133	16.4	194	12.1	2.5	163	1.5	0.04	813	47	0.32	4.98	69.4	141.8
Sudan	39[+3]	16	1.6[-3]	88	96.6	93	0.2	148.3	17	5.1	0.01[-3]	124	110	0.26	7.35	9.5	2.7
Syrian Arab Republic	…	95	36.9[-3]	42	22.8	77	1.8	13.6	167	9.3	0.02[+1]	241	83	0.22	1.44	31.5[-1]	14.4
Tunisia	77	92	46.8[s,-1]	56	20.9	127	11.7[-1]	5.6	124	2.6	0.02[+1]	718	78	0.34	5.79	58.7	24.4
United Arab Emirates	…	86	44.6[c,-1]	256	15.7	402	35.2	0.7	308	0.1	0.24	1,299	18	0.07	4.21	…	780.4
Yemen	…	43	…	19	58.0	12	0.0[-4]	23.8	46[-1]	19.4	0.02[-1]	95[-1]	85	0.08[-1]	2.07	9.7[-3]	2.2
Sub-Saharan Africa																	
Angola	18	9	3.1	6	40.1	5[-1]	0.0[-1]	44.2	6	2.0	0.09[-3]	137	92	0.74	23.07	4.3[-3]	2.4
Benin	91	20	…	4	22.2	80	2.2	55.3	9	2.1	0.16	121	48	0.96[+1]	13.65	3.2	3.2
Botswana	92	10	3.2[s,-4]	47	6.2	33[-1]	0.0[-6]	5.9	74	-2.7	0.13[+1]	527	23	1.06	7.15	37.3[-1]	40.7
Burkina Faso	65	8	0.4[-1]	2	12.3	6	18.6	310.5	7	6.9	0.19	71	63	0.77	10.73	4.3	3.1
Burundi	63	14	0.0[-3]	7	63.5	7	…	693.3	4[-1]	7.1	0.07	19[-1]	41	0.58[+1]	4.92	1.0[-4]	0.4
Cameroon	62[+3]	26	…	11	28.9	20	1.3[-1]	66.0	6[-1]	-3.7	0.11	127[-1]	49	1.32[+1]	22.45	5.9	2.9
Cape Verde	66	61	…	109	14.4	57[-1]	24.3	28.1	138	-0.1	0.05	210	25	1.18	1.52	121.4	18.1
Central African Republic	51	5	0.3[s]	3	13.0	3	0.0[-1]	572.1	2[-1]	1.3	0.57	24[-1]	71	0.57	10.00	1.1[-5]	1.9
Chad	44	4	0.1[s,-3]	2	3.9	6	0.0[-2]	414.5	1	0.4	0.14	45	78	1.05[+1]	35.85	1.5[-2]	0.5
Comoros	59	13	…	7	9.5	26	0.4[-1]	81.3	21[-1]	14.5	0.19	20[-1]	.	0.70[+1]	20.1[-3]	4.9	
Congo	32	7	…	5	8.9	19	0.0[-2]	133.4	4[-1]	-9.9	0.15	136[-1]	31	…	30.80	…	2.2
Congo (Dem. Rep.)	15	4	…	0	11.0[(+1)]	3	4.4	1,017.2	0	-3.6	0.15	73	91	…	455.44	3.5	1.8
Côte d'Ivoire	79	35	…	17	26.9	16	6.9[-1]	105.9	14	-4.0	0.29[+1]	215	39	2.26[+1]	15.58	13.6[-1]	3.2
Equatorial Guinea	…	26	…	19	32.0	16	15.0[-1]	180.8	8	-0.4	0.04	13	-1	0.33	1.65	7.4	1.2
Eritrea	79[+1]	16	0.7	6	27.0	21	0.0	150.3	9	17.6	0.02[+1]	11	94	0.25	1.20	2.5	0.3
Ethiopia	21	4	…	4	34.4	2[-1]	1.0[-1]	254.5	9	-2.1	0.28	11	36	0.56	20.97	38.7	35.3
Gabon	77	56	10.8	35	28.0	62	11.4	11.8	28	5.4	0.03[-3]	583	45	0.67[-4]	7.65	…	20.2
Gambia	73	12	…	15	7.4	36[-1]	3.4[-1]	76.2	32	5.5	0.17	243	80	0.20	14.61	17.2	2.9
Ghana	71[+1]	26	0.2[c,-4]	6	13.8	27	58.4	74.4	15	-1.1	0.07[-1]	226	33	0.54[-1]	7.19	5.8[-3]	0.7
Guinea	56	11	0.9[s,-3]	5	7.2	5	0.0[-3]	72.3	3[-1]	-2.3	…	21[-1]	.	0.00[-2]	9.32	6.7[-5]	1.2
Guinea-Bissau	28	31	0.3[s,-4]	2	0.5[(+1)]	22	0.0[-4]	562.1	6[-1]	-3.6	0.11	59[-1]	57	0.64	22.10	4.4	1.2
Kenya	87	18	0.2[c,-4]	14	23.6	76	0.0[-1]	189.8	8	21.3	0.26	177	43	0.46	5.21	7.7	10.3
Lesotho	29	2	…	1	5.0[(+1)]	26[-1]	1.8[-1]	63.4	24[-1]	.	…	126[-1]	193	0.00[-5]	21.88	…	1.9[-4]
Liberia	…	…	…	…	…	0[-5]	…	…	2[-4]	.	…	46[-1]	.	0.45[-1]	8.06	1.0[-1]	0.3
Madagascar	41	10	…	5	20.4	6	0.0[-1]	190.1	7	14.1	0.20[-1]	55	44	0.60[+1]	4.18	2.0[-3]	2.8[-3]
Malawi	55	3	0.4[-4]	2	12.9	4	2.7[-1]	314.4	8[-1]	14.2	0.10	32[-1]	62	0.85[+1]	18.33	5.9[-4]	4.8
Mali	71	17	0.1[s,-3]	4	24.4	6	3.4	103.4	7	6.8	0.07	126	96	0.11[+1]	2.16	96.5	53.6
Mauritius	90	93	4.2[s,-3]	169	10.8	145	15.9	4.5	286	2.2	0.15	617	22	0.38	34.93	11.9	0.8
Mozambique	46	6	…	14	33.1	9[-1]	…	146.1	3	-7.8	0.06[-1]	112	69	1.18	3.56	26.8[-3]	31.2
Namibia	89	39	14.0[-3]	123	25.3	40[-1]	0.0[-1]	24.6	69[-1]	2.9	0.14[+1]	245[-1]	45	0.92[+1]	13.52	1.9[-2]	0.2
Niger	33	7	…	1	10.9	3	5.9[-1]	581.8	2[-1]	-1.0	0.14	24[-1]	239	0.89	19.15	1.9[-4]	2.3
Nigeria	62	32	0.2[c,-4]	8	7.1	55	0.0[-1]	140.7	12	20.0	0.08[+1]	223	135	0.79	19.02	…	0.2
Rwanda	41	2	…	2	15.6[(+1)]	7	40.0	172.2	2	-7.1	0.14	33	34	…	…	…	…
Saint Helena	…	…	…	…	…	0[-5]	…	…	…	…	…	…	.	0.00[-5]	2.43	37.0	14.3
Sao Tome and Principe	54	35	0.2[s,-3]	39	41.5[(+1)]	187	0.0	163.7	49	5.1	0.22	119	54	0.57[+1]	10.56	26.0	13.4
Senegal	73	31	0.8[s,-2]	21	6.5	54	95.3	48.7	23	0.9	0.13	247	12	1.63	2.75	…	1,097.1
Seychelles	92[+3]	89	5.8	193	7.3	253[-1]	26.6	4.6	258[-1]	-0.3	…	710[-1]	…	0.90	4.50	…	1.6[-4]
Sierra Leone	53	7[-3]	0.2[s,-4]	…	…	2[-2]	…	60.4	5[-4]	.	0.03[-3]	22[-3]	…	…	…	…	

Table 4. Telecommunication access[1]

Country or Territory	Radio — % of households with radio	Television — % of households with TV set	Television — % of households with cable or satellite	Personal computer — per 1,000 inhabitants	Personal computer — Average annual % change	Internet[a] — Users per 1,000 inhabitants	Internet[a] — Broad-band (% of subscribers)	Internet[a] — % of montly GNI per capita for 20 hours usage (cheapest)	Telephone / Fixed lines — Subscribers per 1,000 inhabitants	Telephone / Fixed lines — Average annual % change	Telephone / Fixed lines — Cost of 3-min local call (peak — US$)	Telephone / Mobile cellular[b] — Sub-scribers per 1,000 in-habitants	Telephone / Mobile cellular[b] — Average annual % change	Telephone / Mobile cellular[b] — Cost of 3-min local call (peak — US$)	Ratio Mobile/ Fixed subscribers	International traffic — Incoming minutes per person	International traffic — Outgoing minutes per person
	2002	2005	2005	2005	2000/2005	2006	2006	2006	2006	2001–2006	2005	2006	2001–2006	2005	2006	2005	2005
Somalia	17	8	0.0[s,-2]	9	91.0[(+1)]	11	0.0[-2]	...	12[-1]	26.2	0.10	61[-1]	51	0.04	5.00	...	...
South Africa	81[+2]	59	4.4[-3]	83	5.3	106[-1]	3.9[-1]	20.9	99[-1]	-2.0	0.19	708[-1]	32	1.27	7.18	17.4[-3]	10.7
Swaziland	58	18	3.0[s,-3]	37	26.9	37[-1]	0.0[-3]	37.4	39	4.3	0.09	221	34	1.23	5.69	22.4[-2]	22.5
Tanzania (United Rep.)	52	14	0.1[c,-4]	9	25.6	10[-1]	0.0[-3]	351.0	4	-4.9	0.16	146	79	0.69	36.66	1.1[-3]	0.5
Togo	86	16	0.2[s,-3]	30	9.9	50	0.0[-3]	173.0	13	8.1	0.22	110	45	0.72[+1]	8.63	17.9	3.6
Uganda	65[+4]	10[+1]	0.2[c,-3]	10	33.7	25	0.0[-2]	478.0	4	10.4	0.28[+1]	67	43	0.67	18.58	1.7[-2]	1.3
Zambia	61	26[-3]	0.6[c,-4]	11	11.2	43	25.8	205.3	8	-0.1	0.13	142	66	0.62[-1]	17.80	5.7[-2]	0.9
Zimbabwe	64	34	0.8[s]	65	33.3	92	10.5	47.6	25	4.8	0.00[+1]	63	21	7.62	2.51	17.7	6.5
Central and South Asia																	
Afghanistan	58[-1]	6	3.0	3	.	21	0.8	...	6	36.1	0.00[+1]	97	.	0.00	15.27	0.2	0.1
Armenia	42	91	0.5[c,-4]	98	64.7	57	1.1[-2]	59.4	197[-1]	3.2	0.03	105[-1]	89	0.26	0.54	112.0	15.9
Azerbaijan	103	99	17.2[-2]	23	34.9[(+1)]	99	3.0[-1]	12.8	141	6.0	0.11	395	35	0.30	2.80	26.2[-1]	8.1
Bangladesh	30[+2]	23[-1]	20.3[c,-1]	15	59.2	3	0.0[-1]	65.5	7	12.8	0.02[+1]	123	102	0.28	16.87	3.7	1.4
Bhutan	77[+1]	53	4.4[c,-1]	20	17.9	46	0.0	23.5	49	9.7	0.03[+1]	127	.	0.34	2.60	13.1[+1]	8.8
Georgia	82	89	5.0[-3]	47	14.7	75	16.7	11.2	125	0.5	0.25	384	43	0.48	3.08	39.0[-2]	14.1
India	35	32	30.1[c]	15	27.8	53[-1]	18.2	13.1	35	-0.5	0.07	144	88	0.07	4.07	2.3[-3]	0.9
Iran (Islamic Rep.)	83	77[-3]	...	125	15.7	256	4.2	1.2	313	13.9	0.01	194	44	0.18	0.62	2.9	5.8
Kazakhstan	41	...	2.7[c,-3]	...	...	81	8.5	8.4	191	8.0	0.00[-3]	511	67	0.79	2.67	17.4[-3]	14.2
Kyrgyzstan	...	...	1.7[c]	19	30.0	57	17.6[-1]	36.0	85[-1]	2.2	0.07	104[-1]	110	0.24	1.23	13.9	15.3
Maldives	...	92	8.2[s,-4]	152	33.0	68[-1]	77.4	25.5	108	2.0	0.06	875	67	0.40	8.08	64.1[-1]	30.2
Nepal	43[-1]	13	...	5	11.2	9	0.0[-1]	38.9	22	12.5	0.03	38	122	0.12[+1]	1.75	4.3	1.3
Pakistan	38[+1]	46	...	5	4.5	75	2.4	19.0	33	8.1	0.03[+1]	214	112	0.26	6.59	9.2	1.2
Sri Lanka	63	32	0.2[c,-2]	38	39.7	22	22.4	5.4	98	17.4	0.09	282	51	0.33	2.87	23.1	5.6
Tajikistan	...	79	0.0[c,-3]	13	.	3[-1]	2.2[-3]	52.8	43[-1]	4.2	0.01[-2]	40[-1]	253	0.20	0.95	8.6[-2]	2.5
Turkmenistan	...	93[-5]	...	72	47.2[(+1)]	13	0.0[-5]	114.2	82[-1]	-0.8	...	22[-1]	87	...	0.26	2.5[-5]	8.2
Uzbekistan	...	...	2.0[c,-3]	28	33.6[(+3)]	63	7.4[-3]	15.1	67[-1]	0.4	0.01[+1]	27[-1]	52	0.30	0.40	9.3	2.9
East Asia																	
Brunei Darussalam	...	98	40.0[c,-4]	88	5.1	433	54.8	...	210	-4.1	0.05[-1]	665	10	0.72	3.17	69.9[-5]	74.8
Cambodia	...	43	...	3	21.9	3[-1]	11.7[-1]	113.4	2	-2.1	0.03	80	36	0.19	34.78	8.6	0.9
China	...	89	26.9[c,-3]	42	21.1	104	65.8	7.8	278	14.6	0.03	349	25	0.22	1.25	5.5	1.7
Hong Kong (SAR China)	99[+2]	99	61.0	591	8.0	529	65.5	0.2	540	-1.4	0.00	1,312	9	0.05	2.43	300.7	837.3
Macao (SAR China)	...	94	15.0	338	16.3	419	87.6	1.0	370	-1.3	0.00	1,333	25	0.45[+1]	3.60	293.8	203.4
Indonesia	74	65	7.6[-4]	15	7.9	71[-1]	7.2[-1]	18.2	65	14.0	0.04	279	56	0.11[-1]	4.30	4.0[-1]	1.0
Japan	...	99	25.7[s,-1]	675	16.5	684	44.0[-3]	0.4	431	-2.2	0.08	795	6	0.56[-3]	1.84	16.6[-1]	29.0
Korea (Dem. People's Rep.)	...	...	...	...	...	0[-5]	0.0[-5]	...	42[-3]	.	...	0[-4]	...	0.00[-4]	0.00	...	...
Korea (Rep.)	...	...	85.8	537	6.2	710	100.0	2.8	559	0.4	0.04	837	6	0.32	1.50	30.0	62.5
Lao (People's Dem. Rep.)	...	30	0.6[-4]	18	45.8	4[-1]	2.2[-1]	84.9	13[-1]	7.6	0.06	113[-1]	112	0.20	8.48	4.2	2.4
Malaysia	...	95	34.8[s]	218	18.2	432	19.1	2.0	166	-3.4	0.03	745	19	0.43	4.48	43.3[-3]	68.5
Mongolia	...	63	12.4	132	59.0	104[-1]	3.1[-1]	21.4	60[-1]	4.9	0.01	216[-1]	29	0.47	3.57	2.7	2.1
Myanmar	2[+1]	3	0.7[s]	8	30.8	2	10.6	...	11[-1]	13.3	0.04	4	55	0.01[-3]	0.42	2.6[-1]	0.2
Philippines	71[+1]	63	18.4[c,-3]	53	22.5	55[-1]	8.5[-1]	1.9	42	-0.2	0.00	497	26	0.44	11.80	26.5[-1]	1.7
Singapore	...	98	42.7	684	7.2	392	34.5	1.0	423	-2.3	0.01[+1]	1,093	8	0.42[+1]	2.58	357.0	691.9
Thailand	...	92	7.1[-3]	70	19.9	133	1.9[-3]	3.3	111	2.4	0.07	643	39	0.37	5.77	5.3	8.8
Timor-Leste	...	...	...	...	...	...	...	...	...	...	...	...	...	...	...	...	...
Viet Nam	...	83	...	14	12.7	170	12.7	23.7	186[-1]	48.8	0.02[+1]	180	63	0.43[+1]	0.97	7.4[-3]	1.2
Europe																	
Albania	82	90	67.2[c]	17	16.1	149	0.0[-3]	9.2	112[-1]	15.0	0.03	485[-1]	40	0.75	4.33	140.8	19.2
Andorra	...	99[+1]	...	...	...	286	60.7[-1]	...	451[-1]	-3.8	0.15	822[-1]	16	1.07[+1]	1.82	...	944.8
Austria	87	98[+1]	85.6	603	11.0	504	74.6	0.6	428	-2.7	0.18	1,111	7	1.21	2.60	114.7[-2]	148.3
Belarus	48	97	38.5[c]	8	.	562	2.8	5.9	346	3.9	0.01[+1]	612	113	0.11	1.77	33.4[-1]	32.0
Belgium	71[-1]	98	90.2[c]	380	11.0	462[-1]	91.9[-1]	1.4	452	-2.0	0.25	926	4	1.34	2.05	166.8[-5]	170.8
Bosnia and Herzegovina	...	87	58.2	54	9.9[(+1)]	242	16.7	4.6	252	2.7	0.05	481	33	0.65	1.91	144.4	63.2
Bulgaria	...	97	36.4[c]	63	7.0	243	85.8	3.2	312	-3.0	0.10	1,073	41	0.86	3.44	51.8	19.9
Croatia	...	98	5.7[c]	194	11.9	346	19.6	2.8	402	0.3	0.04	981	20	0.61	2.44	142.9	82.8
Cyprus	99	99	...	364	11.1	458	57.2	1.5	524	-3.2	0.07[+1]	999	18	0.26	1.90	215.3[-2]	609.9
Czech Republic	80	127	38.6[c]	275	17.6	348	30.1[-1]	2.5	316[-1]	-4.4	0.20	1,192	12	0.45	3.78	53.8	41.4
Denmark	...	97	57.3[c]	696	6.6	584	91.8	0.7	571	-4.6	0.13	1,076	8	0.38	1.89	200.3	117.6
Estonia	88[+2]	93[-2]	40.6[c]	484	24.7	567	94.9	1.8	404	1.7	0.12	1,238	21	0.36	3.06	52.4[-1]	54.6

Table 4. Telecommunication access[1]

Country or Territory	Radio % of households with radio	Television % of households with TV set	Television % of households with cable or satellite	Personal computer per 1,000 inhabitants	Personal computer Average annual % change	Internet[a] Users per 1,000 inhabitants	Internet[a] Broad-band (% of subscribers)	Internet[a] % of montly GNI per capita for 20 hours usage (cheapest)	Fixed lines Subscribers per 1,000 inhabitants	Fixed lines Average annual % change	Fixed lines Cost of 3-min local call (peak — US$)	Mobile cellular[b] Sub-scribers per 1,000 in-habitants	Mobile cellular[b] Average annual % change	Mobile cellular[b] Cost of 3-min local call (peak — US$)	Telephone Ratio Mobile/Fixed subscribers	International traffic Incoming minutes per person	International traffic Outgoing minutes per person
	2002	2005	2005	2005	2000/2005	2006	2006	2006	2006	2001-2006	2005	2006	2001-2006	2005	2006	2005	2005
Finland	96	94	63.2[-2]	500	4.8	556	57.1[-2]	0.8	365	-7.6	0.19	1,078	6	0.30	2.95	87.9[-5]	35.6
France	...	97	40.0[-1]	574	13.6	491	83.3	0.5	553	-0.7	0.20	842	6	1.68	1.52	115.0	67.5
Germany	76[+1]	98	89.4	605	12.5	467	53.5[-1]	0.3	656	0.6	0.13	1020	8	1.46	1.56	78.5[-5]	121.0
Gibraltar	...	74[-5]	...	...	...	218[-2]	...	...	880[-2]	...	0.22	638[-2]	...	0.83	0.73	954.9[-5]	643.0[-5]
Greece	...	100	11.6[-3]	92	6.1	184	53.2	1.2	556	1.8	0.10	998	7	1.24	1.79	94.7	87.2
Holy See	...	...	...	...	...	...	...	...	...	...	...	...	...	...	...	...	44.5
Hungary	...	96	51.3[c]	149	11.9	348	75.6	1.6	333	-1.9	0.17	991	15	0.53	2.97	60.6	44.5
Iceland	97[-1]	98	6.1[c-2]	480	4.2	650	89.3	1.9	649	-1.3	0.15	1,101	5	0.52	1.70	134.3	106.5
Ireland	95	98	80.7	530	8.2	340	49.9	1.1	497	0.6	0.18	1,111	8	1.20	2.24	381.2[-5]	277.4
Israel	...	92	94.1[-2]	251[-2]	...	279	73.3[-1]	1.5	441	-2.0	0.07	1,234	7	0.59	2.80	167.4	209.4
Italy	...	96	21.9	366	15.5	491	38.5[-1]	1.1	427[-1]	-2.5	0.08	1,219[-1]	8	0.04	2.85	130.5[-2]	61.3
Latvia	80[+1]	98	54.7	246	11.5	468	94.5	2.7	287	-1.2	0.14	954	28	0.05	3.32	49.3	17.3
Liechtenstein	99[-1]	98[-3]	95.8[c-3]	...	...	583[-3]	63.1	...	580[-3]	...	0.16[+1]	729[-3]	...	0.70	1.26	...	1,269.8[-3]
Lithuania	...	98	21.6[c]	180	21.3	318	88.3	1.5	232	-6.8	0.18	1,384	36	0.36	5.95	33.0	15.9
Luxembourg	99[-1]	99	100.0	635	6.8	735	71.4	0.6	535	-1.7	0.11	1,547	11	0.40[+1]	2.89	464.3	935.1
Macedonia (TFYR)	39[+2]	98	...	222	57.8[+1]	132	28.0	12.6	241	-2.0	0.06[+1]	696	44	1.47[+1]	2.89	55.5	7.8
Malta	...	93	74.8[c-2]	165	-4.3	316[-1]	58.5	0.9	500	-1.2	0.16	857	7	1.73	1.71	167.9[-2]	59.3
Moldova (Rep.)	...	82	13.7	97	40.9	190	23.3	40.2	266	8.6	0.05	354	42	1.59	1.33	93.8	24.6
Monaco	...	...	...	...	...	...	...	...	...	...	...	...	...	...	...	...	...
Montenegro	...	...	...	...	...	...	...	...	465[-1]	-2.2	0.11[-1]	970[-1]	6	1.31	2.08	150.7[-5]	96.1
Netherlands	99	99	11.2[s-1]	854	16.6	888	45.8[-2]	0.5	440	-3.2	0.19	1,080	6	0.43	2.45	71.0	121.2
Norway	99[-1]	100	42.6[c-2]	592	3.8	873	84.1	0.7	301	0.3	0.09[-2]	963	30	0.71	3.20	37.9[-2]	11.8
Poland	95[-2]	91	32.4[c]	242	28.4	288	81.6	2.2	304	0.3	0.12	961	8	0.45	3.16	122.3	56.2
Portugal	88[-2]	99	39.2[c]	134	5.4	304	90.3	3.2	400	-1.3	0.12	1,156	8	0.58	2.89	39.2[-3]	11.5
Romania	...	94	49.7[c]	129	32.1	325	53.7	6.9	195	0.9	0.09	808	36	0.45	4.14	6.9[-3]	8.1
Russian Federation	...	98	15.4[-3]	121	13.9	179	0.6[-4]	4.5	279[-1]	5.3	0.02	834[-1]	99	0.45	2.99	...	...
San Marino	...	...	32.8[s]	...	...	...	25.7	...	...	...	0.07	...	...	...	...	...	...
Serbia	...	...	...	...	...	...	...	...	...	...	...	...	...	...	...	...	...
Slovakia	69[+3]	98	29.1[c]	358	21.1	419	80.2	3.5	217	-5.6	0.22	908	18	0.87	4.19	58.8	31.2
Slovenia	92	96	82.3[-2]	404	7.9	625	70.7	1.5	419	0.7	0.08[-1]	909	4	0.23	2.17	...	52.9
Spain	88[+3]	99	8.3[c]	277	9.7	423	92.6	1.8	419	-0.5	0.13[+1]	1,052	8	0.79	2.51	64.8	108.4
Sweden	93	94	57.0[c-2]	835	10.5	769	67.6	0.6	595	-1.4	0.15	1,058	6	0.24	1.78	...	131.6
Switzerland	...	99	93.2[c]	866	6.0	585	74.1	0.2	676	-1.7	0.24	995	7	0.96[+1]	1.47	296.3[-5]	335.2
Turkey	...	92	7.7[c]	56	8.8	166	87.2	3.7	255	-1.4	0.16	712	20	0.65[-2]	2.80	16.9	9.9
Ukraine	...	97	11.8[-3]	39	16.2	119	0.0[-4]	7.2	265	3.8	0.03[+1]	1,054	87	0.59	3.98	33.3	11.7
United Kingdom	79[-1]	98	44.5[-1]	758	17.2	554	78.4	1.0	555	-1.0	0.22[+1]	1,151	8	0.55	2.07	129.7[-4]	95.4
North America																	
Canada	...	99	80.9	877	15.8	682[-1]	80.4[-1]	0.4	644[-1]	-1.4	0.00	527[-1]	11	0.62	0.82	235.4[-5]	292.8
United States of America	99[-1]	99	80.1	754[-1]	7.5	687	44.7[-3]	0.4	568	-3.1	0.00	769	12	1.35	1.35	62.4[-1]	233.7
Latin America and the Caribbean																	
Anguilla	...	...	...	...	...	379	63.9[-1]	2.8	474	-0.4	0.06	1,210	30	1.00	2.55	389.8[-2]	214.3[-2]
Antigua and Barbuda	90[-1]	98	...	146	8.9[+1]	...	...	...	242	2.1	0.03[+1]	805	35	0.39[+1]	3.33	22.9	9.6
Argentina	...	97	58.4[c-4]	90	5.4	209	57.5	4.8	368[-1]	-2.1	0.09[+1]	1,040[-1]	16	1.17	2.83	...	442.2
Aruba	...	76	...	76	...	231[-1]	0.0[-5]	...	412[-1]	0.6	...	705[-1]	38	0.99	1.71	346.7[-2]	250.2
Bahamas	113[-1]	93	...	124	11.2[+2]	319[-1]	49.2[-1]	2.0	462[-1]	0.8	0.00	706[-1]	40	0.45	1.53	388.5[-2]	425.2
Barbados	...	93	0.5[s-1]	137	12.3	548[-1]	...	...	420	-3.0	0.15	...	22	1.27	3.49	137.0[-1]	49.8
Belize	...	93	...	149	3.9	121	67.6	13.9	120	-3.0	0.15	420	22	1.27	3.49	1.00	...
Bermuda	...	...	73.9[c-1]	225[-1]	-17.4	661[-1]	62.4	...	825[-1]	-2.1	0.20	829[-1]	40	0.90	1.00	...	1,909.8
Bolivia	...	50	3.5[c-2]	24	7.3	62	15.0[-1]	15.3	71	2.9	0.06[+1]	288	26	0.62	4.05	41.8[-1]	6.9
Brazil	88[+2]	91	7.7	161	26.9	225	26.5[-1]	10.4	205	-0.7	0.11	528	27	1.35	2.58	7.4[-4]	3.5
British Virgin Islands	...	...	...	...	...	...	...	...	907[-5]	.	0.16	764[-2]	23	1.10	0.84	842.6[-2]	745.2[-2]
Cayman Islands	...	...	...	...	...	404	...	...	202	-2.0	0.02	756	18	1.77	3.74	34.4	13.8
Chile	99	90	23.9[-3]	141	8.9	252	89.4	5.9	173	-0.2	0.14	653	53	0.37	3.78	60.4	7.8
Colombia	124	90	...	42	3.2	147	70.7	4.6	168	-0.2	0.02	653	53	0.37	3.78	91.9	34.9
Costa Rica	100	89	24.5[c]	231	8.6	276	34.6	7.5	307	5.5	0.09[+1]	328	32	0.19	1.07	27.9	2.7
Cuba	...	70	...	33	22.5	21	0.0[-3]	...	86	10.9	0.09[+1]	14	78	1.39	0.16	2.00	139.2[-4]
Dominica	87[-1]	76[-4]	...	184[-1]	24.4	367[-1]	54.0[-2]	6.8	297[-2]	-3.4	0.08	593[-2]	76	0.78	2.00	192.9[-4]	37.0
Dominican Republic	62[+3]	76	...	22	3.3[+1]	208	36.2	10.7	93	-2.8	0.09[+1]	479	27	0.57	5.13	...	...
Ecuador	85[-1]	80	4.3	66	24.3	117	19.5[-1]	20.1	133	4.4	0.03	643	56	1.50	4.84	206.7	8.9

Table 4. Telecommunication access[1]

Country or Territory	Radio — % of households with radio	Television — % of households with TV set	Television — % of households with cable or satellite	Personal computer — per 1,000 inhabitants	Personal computer — Average annual % change	Internet[a] — Users per 1,000 inhabitants	Internet[a] — Broad-band (% of subscribers)	Internet[a] — % of montly GNI per capita for 20 hours usage (cheapest)	Fixed lines — Subscribers per 1,000 inhabitants	Fixed lines — Average annual % change	Fixed lines — Cost of 3-min local call (peak — US$)	Mobile cellular[b] — Sub-scribers per 1,000 in-habitants	Mobile cellular[b] — Average annual % change	Mobile cellular[b] — Cost of 3-min local call (peak — US$)	Ratio Mobile/ Fixed subscribers	International traffic — Incoming minutes per person	International traffic — Outgoing minutes per person
	2002	2005	2005	2005	2000/2005	2006	2006	2006	2006	2001–2006	2005	2006	2001–2006	2005	2006	2005	2005
El Salvador	...	83	12.5[c-1]	52	22.1	96[-1]	33.2[-1]	11.7	153	8.2	0.01	570	33	0.03	3.71	348.5	61.4
Grenada	...	94[-5]	...	152[-1]	6.7	182[-3]	76.1	7.1	259	-4.0	0.08	432	47	0.78	1.67	539.9	87.4
Guatemala	...	50	...	21	12.2	101	...	29.8	104	9.6	0.08[+1]	551	41	0.40[+1]	5.30	147.7	27.0
Guyana	...	92	...	39	5.5	216[-1]	4.2[-1]	14.7	149[-1]	8.2	0.00	380[-1]	39	0.56	2.55	93.6[-1]	26.7
Haiti	5[+1]	27	3.7[-2]	2	3.6[(+1)]	69	0.0[-2]	213.0	16[-1]	14.2	0.13[-1]	54[-1]	50	0.39	3.44	...	2.7
Honduras	74[-1]	58	9.7[c]	18	9.2	48	0.0[-1]	38.5	102	15.7	0.06	322	54	0.78	3.16	88.1	8.3
Jamaica	...	70	...	67	7.6	459[-1]	9.5[-4]	12.5	119[-1]	-11.7	0.03	1,045[-1]	46	0.48	8.79	182.6[-2]	59.3
Mexico	89[+3]	93	17.7	134	18.6	174[-1]	77.6	3.5	189	6.7	0.14[+1]	541	20	0.41	2.87	150.7	21.3
Montserrat	...	...	...	...	...	...	...	...	...	...	...	...	...	...	...	...	...
Netherlands Antilles	...	...	...	...	...	...	...	...	449[-5]	.	0.16	1,086[-2]	...	1.42	2.42	...	...
Nicaragua	...	60	11.3[c-1]	40	11.4	28	80.6	40.6	45	8.0	0.05	331	60	1.21	7.38	55.4[-1]	6.5
Panama	83	79	...	46	5.1	67	21.3[-1]	11.0	132	0.7	0.09[+1]	524[-1]	35	0.54[+1]	3.98	39.9[-4]	15.4[-2]
Paraguay	...	79	8.8[c-4]	78	42.9	43	24.6	12.3	55	0.8	0.04	537	21	0.35	9.77	23.8	7.5
Peru	72[+1]	71	7.2[c]	103	20.2	221	47.1	12.0	85	6.9	0.05[+1]	308	35	1.20[+1]	3.64	88.9	10.1
Saint Kitts and Nevis	90[-1]	71[-4]	...	257[-1]	10.4	241[-4]	10.9[-4]	3.8	585[-2]	2.1	...	234[-2]	66	1.50[-2]	0.40	348.8[-2]	284.8[-2]
Saint Lucia	93[-1]	79[-4]	...	163[-1]	3.1	345[-2]	...	6.4	328[-4]	.	0.08	655[-1]	147	0.78	2.00	120.5[-2]	101.5[-2]
Saint Vincent and the Grenadines	...	79	38.0[c]	138	6.0	84[-1]	86.1	7.8	189	-3.3	0.10	732	63	0.78	3.87	203.7[-2]	75.5
Suriname	...	66	4.2	44	-0.7[(+1)]	71[-1]	32.2	16.3	179	0.4	0.05	703	29	0.69	3.93	183.2	93.5
Trinidad and Tobago	98[-1]	88	24.9[c-3]	97	9.6	123[-1]	25.4	1.8	245	0.5	0.04	1,246	45	0.76	5.08	287.4[-1]	111.3
Turks and Caicos Islands	...	...	...	...	...	...	...	...	...	...	...	...	...	...	...	...	...
Uruguay	95[-1]	92	...	135	5.1	227	51.0	7.3	296	0.7	0.14	699	35	0.37[-5]	2.36	79.7	34.2
Venezuela	...	90	18.4[c]	93	15.5	152	70.7	12.7	155	7.4	0.02	691	22	1.38	4.46	15.0[-5]	26.3
Pacific																	
Australia	99[+3]	99	21.5[c]	760	10.1	745	58.6	1.0	484	-1.4	0.23	962	11	2.35	1.99	98.1[-4]	181.7
Cook Islands	...	...	...	...	...	...	...	...	...	...	...	...	...	...	...	...	...
Fiji	94[+1]	60	0.1[s-3]	60	6.1	96	52.6[-1]	10.0	136[-1]	4.4	0.07[+1]	248[-1]	25	1.07	1.82	83.6[-3]	27.8
Kiribati	58[+1]	26[-2]	0.0[-3]	11[-1]	3.8	21	0.0[-4]	...	51[-4]	.	0.12[-2]	7[-2]	14	1.32[-1]	0.13	18.5[-4]	7.5[-4]
Marshall Islands	...	...	...	90[-1]	23.6	39	0.0[-3]	...	82[-3]	.	0.00	12[-2]	8	0.30[-2]	0.14	67.5[-2]	15.4[-2]
Micronesia (Fed. States)	50[+1]	16	2.5[c-2]	55	43.0[(+1)]	145	2.0[-1]	...	113[-1]	4.8	0.00	128[-1]	.	0.30[+1]	1.13	58.9[-2]	30.1
Nauru	...	.	...	...	...	30[-5]	...	...	184[-5]	.	...	149[-5]	...	...	0.81	...	...
New Zealand	99[+1]	98	30.6[s-2]	507	7.2	773	27.6[-1]	0.7	422[-1]	-2.5	0.00	862[-1]	10	2.56[-1]	2.04	223.4[-1]	130.0
Niue	...	...	...	...	...	...	...	...	...	...	...	...	...	...	...	...	...
Palau	...	...	...	...	...	261[-2]	0.0[-4]	...	365	1.2[(+1)]	...	416	36[(+1)]	...	1.14	...	361.2
Papua New Guinea	26[+1]	10	2.0[c-4]	64	4.4	18	...	53.5	10[-1]	-1.5	0.08[-2]	12[-1]	59	0.63[-2]	1.18	3.6[-5]	0.0
Samoa	99[+1]	88	...	19	27.6	43	0.0[-4]	7.4	106[-1]	18.4	0.04[+1]	131[-1]	75	0.86[-1]	1.23	108.7[-2]	40.4
Solomon Islands	72[+1]	5	...	47	3.9	17	23.7[-1]	217.8	16[-1]	-2.5	0.09	13[-1]	54	1.22[+1]	0.81	16.0[-5]	12.5
Tokelau	...	...	...	...	...	...	...	...	...	...	...	...	...	...	...	...	...
Tonga	...	26	...	60	35.4	31	37.0[-1]	193.5	138[-1]	5.9	0.10[+1]	301[-1]	234	0.10[+1]	2.17	...	25.2
Tuvalu	...	60	0.1[s-4]	87	72.8[(+1)]	176[-1]	0.0[-3]	...	92[-1]	12.4	...	135[-1]	.	0.00[-5]	1.46	...	15.6
Vanuatu	...	6	...	14	1.9	35[-1]	3.7[-1]	50.3	32[-1]	-1.8	0.36[+1]	59[-1]	139	0.72[+1]	1.82	...	14.6[-3]

Source:

1. International Telecommunication Union (ITU), 2007. World Telecommunication/ICT Indicators database 2007. Data source for population figures (excepted households): UNPD (2007); World Population Prospects (2006 Revision).

Notes:

a. 'Internet Users' is based on nationally reported data. In some cases, surveys have been carried out that give a more precise figure for the number of Internet users. However surveys differ across countries regarding the age and frequency of use covered. The reported figure for Internet users may refer only to users above a certain age. Countries that do not have surveys generally base their estimates on derivations from reported Internet Service Provider subscriber counts, calculated by multiplying the number of subscribers by a multiplier.

b. Some countries go beyond the 100% rate because either: a) People may subscribe to more than one mobile cellular service (for example, one for work and one for private use); b) Inactive prepaid subscribers may be counted by operators; c) People may subscribe in the country they work but not reside, thus not adding up to the population figure, especially for small countries (i.e. Luxembourg).

c = Cable only, satellite subscribers (if any) not included

s = Satellite only, cable subscribers (if any) not included

... Data not available

. Not applicable

+n Data refer to the year n years after the reference year

-n Data refer to the year n years before the reference year

(..) = Numbers in parenthesis indicate a different beginning year for Average annual % change calculation.

Table 5. Gender

Country or Territory	Female activity rate[1] % of men rate	Female activity rate[1] Economic activity index (1990=100)	Gender Parity Index Enrolment in tertiary level education[2] F/M	Political positions held by women Seats in parliament[a,3] % of total	Political positions held by women At ministerial level[b,4] % of total	Female legislators, senior officials and managers[c,5] % of total	Female professional and technical workers[c,5] % of total	Female in Research & Development[6] % of total	Income disparity ratio[d,7] F/M
	2006	2006	2007	2007	2005	1994–2005	1994–2005	2007	1996–2005
Arab States									
Algeria	46	164	1.40	7***	11	…	32	35[-2, ±]	0.34
Bahrain	35	106	2.46[-1]	14***	9	…	…	…	0.35
Djibouti	65	95	0.69	11	5	…	…	…	0.48
Egypt	28	78	…	4***	6	9	30	36[±]	0.23
Iraq	27	129	0.59[**, -2]	25	…	…	…	…	…
Jordan	37	159	1.10	8***	11	…	…	21[-4]	0.31
Kuwait	60	144	2.32[-1]	2[i]	…	…	…	35[±, t]	0.35
Lebanon	44	107	1.20	5	7	…	…	…	0.31
Libyan Arab Jamahiriya	43	184	…	8	…	…	…	…	0.30
Mauritania	66	98	0.36[-1]	18***	9	…	…	…	0.50
Morocco	34	112	0.89	6***	6	12	35	28[-1, **]	0.25
Oman	30	157	1.18	9***	10	9	33	…	0.19
Palestinian A. T.	16	115	1.22	…	…	11	35	…	…
Qatar	42	123	2.87	…	8	8	24	…	0.24
Saudi Arabia	23	122	1.46[-1]	…	…	31	6	17[-5, ±]	0.16
Sudan	34	87	…	17***	3	…	…	30[-3, *]	0.25
Syrian Arab Republic	45	136	…	12	6	…	40[e]	…	0.34
Tunisia	41	144	1.51	20***	7	…	…	45[-2]	0.29
United Arab Emirates	44	159	2.32[+1]	23	6	8	25	…	0.25
Yemen	40	110	0.37[**, -1]	1***	3	4	15	…	0.30
Sub-Saharan Africa									
Angola	82	99	…	15	6	…	…	…	0.62
Benin	63	92	…	8	19	…	…	…	0.47
Botswana	67	80	1.00[-2]	11	27	33	51	31[-2, ±]	0.31
Burkina Faso	88	101	0.46	15	15	…	…	13[±, t]	0.66
Burundi	99	101	0.46	32***	11	…	…	…	0.77
Cameroon	67	93	0.79	14	11	…	…	19[-2, ±]	0.49
Cape Verde	47	82	1.21	15	19	…	…	52[-5, ±]	0.35
Central African Republic	79	99	0.28[-1]	10	10	…	…	42[±]	0.61
Chad	86	102	0.14[**, -2]	6	12	…	…	…	0.65
Comoros	68	92	…	3	…	…	…	…	0.51
Congo	65	98	…	9***	15	…	…	13[-7, ±, n]	0.50
Congo (Dem. Rep.)	69	101	0.35*	8***	13	…	…	…	0.52
Côte d'Ivoire	45	90	0.50	9	17	…	…	17[-2, ±]	0.32
Equatorial Guinea	56	106	…	18	5	…	…	…	0.43
Eritrea	66	95	…	22	18	…	…	…	0.45
Ethiopia	81	99	0.34	21***	6	20	30	7[±]	0.60
Gabon	76	98	…	14***	12	…	…	25[-1, ±]	0.57
Gambia	69	95	…	9	20	…	…	9[-2, ±]	0.53
Ghana	94	93	0.54	11	12	…	…	…	0.71
Guinea	94	100	0.28[-1]	19	15	…	…	6[-7]	0.69
Guinea-Bissau	68	104	…	14	38	…	…	…	0.51
Kenya	80	94	0.57	7	10	…	…	…	0.83
Lesotho	65	82	1.19[-1]	25***	28	…	…	56[-3, ±, o]	0.52
Liberia	66	100	…	14***	…	…	…	…	…
Madagascar	92	101	0.89	9***	6	…	…	35[±]	0.70
Malawi	96	100	0.51	14	14	…	…	…	0.73
Mali	89	100	0.52[**, -2]	10	19	…	…	12[-1, ±]	0.68
Mauritius	56	104	1.17[+1]	17	8	25	43	…	0.41
Mozambique	103	96	0.49[-2]	35	13	…	…	34[-1, ±, t]	0.81
Namibia	75	95	0.88[-1]	27***	19	30	55	…	0.57
Niger	76	101	0.33	12	23	…	…	…	0.57
Nigeria	54	96	0.69[-2]	7***	10	…	…	17[-2]	0.41
Rwanda	97	93	0.62[**, -2]	45***	36	…	…	…	0.74
Saint Helena	…	…	…	…	…	…	…	25[-8, ±, n]	…
Sao Tome and Principe	41	79	.	2[j]	14	…	…	…	0.30
Senegal	70	92	0.51**	29***	21	…	…	10[±, *]	0.54
Seychelles	…	…	.	24	13	…	…	36[-2, ±]	…
Sierra Leone	62	105	…	13	13	…	…	…	0.45
Somalia	64	97	…	8	…	…	…	…	…
South Africa	60	86	1.24[-1]	33[***, f]	41	…	…	40[-2]	0.45
Swaziland	44	85	0.98[-1]	17***	13	…	…	…	0.29
Tanzania (United Rep.)	97	98	0.48	30	15	49	32	…	0.73
Togo	57	93	…	9	20	…	…	12[±, **]	0.43

Table 5. Gender

Country or Territory	Female activity rate[1] % of men rate	Female activity rate[1] Economic activity index (1990=100)	Gender Parity Index Enrolment in tertiary level education[2] F/M	Political positions held by women Seats in parliament[a,3] % of total	Political positions held by women At ministerial level[b,4] % of total	Female legislators, senior officials and managers[c,5] % of total	Female professional and technical workers[c,5] % of total	Female in Research & Development[6] % of total	Income disparity ratio[d,7] F/M
	2006	2006	2007	2007	2005	1994–2005	1994–2005	2007	1996–2005
Uganda	94	99	...	30	23	...	...	41	0.70
Zambia	74	101	...	15	25	...	...	27[-2, ±, **]	0.55
Zimbabwe	75	92	...	22***	15	...	...	...	0.58
Central and South Asia									
Afghanistan	45	105	...	26***	...	...	...	...	...
Armenia	84	72	1.20	9	-	...	...	45[±]	0.63
Azerbaijan	86	98	0.88*	11	15	...	...	52	0.65
Bangladesh	63	85	0.57	15[g]	8	23	12	...	0.46
Bhutan	62	142	0.51	3	-	...	...	...	...
Georgia	68	65	1.12	9	22	26	62	53	0.33
India	43	94	0.72[-1]	9***	3	...	...	12[-7, n]	0.31
Iran (Islamic Rep.)	55	186	1.15	4	7	16	34	23[-1]	0.39
Kazakhstan	93	109	1.44	12***	18	38	67	52	0.63
Kyrgyzstan	77	92	1.30	-	13	25	57	44	0.58
Maldives	69	248	...	12	12	15	40	...	0.50
Nepal	66	105	...	17	7	8	19	15[-5, *]	0.50
Pakistan	40	119	0.85*	20***	6	2	26	27	0.29
Sri Lanka	47	79	...	5	10	21	46	35[-3, t]	0.41
Tajikistan	75	88	0.38	20***	3	...	...	39[-1]	0.57
Turkmenistan	85	94	...	16	10	...	...	...	0.64
Uzbekistan	80	95	0.71	16***	4	...	...	...	0.60
East Asia									
Brunei Darussalam	56	98	1.88	.[k]	9	26	44	41[-1, ±, t]	0.42
Cambodia	96	96	0.56	11***	7	14	33	21[-5, ±, *]	0.74
China	86	95	1.01	20	6	17	52	...	0.64
Hong Kong (SAR China)	78	118	1.03	...	...	27	40	...	0.56
Macao (SAR China)	84	138	0.92	...	...	...	...	22[-2, ±, *]	...
Indonesia	61	102	1.00	11	11	...	...	...	0.46
Japan	72	106	0.88	12***	13	10[e]	46[e]	12[-1]	0.45
Korea (Dem. People's Rep.)	62	90	...	20	6	8	39	...	0.40
Korea (Rep.)	70	109	0.67	13	...	...	...	13[-1, ±]	...
Lao (People's Dem. Rep.)	69	101	0.72	25	-	...	...	...	0.51
Malaysia	58	107	1.22[-1]	13***	9	23	40	38[-1]	0.36
Mongolia	68	95	1.56	7	6	50	54	48[±]	0.50
Myanmar	80	99	...	[m]	...	...	...	86[-5, ±, s]	...
Philippines	68	118	1.24[-1]	20***	25	58	61	52	0.61
Singapore	69	105	...	24	-	26	44	27[-1]	0.51
Thailand	85	91	1.23	9	8	29	54	50[-2]	0.62
Timor-Leste	68	117	...	28	22	...	...	...	...
Viet Nam	94	97	...	26	12	22	51	43[-5]	0.70
Europe									
Albania	72	86	...	7	5	...	...	...	0.54
Andorra	...	...	1.25[*, -1]	29	...	...	...	...	...
Austria	83	117	1.20	31***	35	27	49	25[-1]	0.46
Belarus	92	91	1.41	30***	10	...	...	43	0.63
Belgium	80	125	1.26	36***	21	32	49	30[-2]	0.55
Bosnia and Herzegovina	91	109	...	14***	11	...	...	...	...
Bulgaria	83	71	1.22	22	24	34	60	45[-1]	0.65
Croatia	82	105	1.23	22	33	24	50	44[-1]	0.67
Cyprus	81	116	0.99*	14	-	15	45	32[-1]	0.60
Czech Republic	84	87	1.26	15***	11	30	52	28	0.51
Denmark	90	95	1.41	38	33	25	53	30[-2]	0.73
Estonia	88	85	1.63	22	15	37	70	43[g]	0.62
Finland	95	101	1.23	42	47	30	55	32[-1]	0.71
France	85	109	1.27	18***	18	37	47	28[-1]	0.64
Germany	86	120	...	31***	46	37	50	21[-2]	0.58
Gibraltar	...	...	.	...	...	...	...	...	...
Greece	72	132	1.10	16	6	26	49	36[-2]	0.55
Holy See	...	...	...	...	...	...	...	...	...
Hungary	81	94	1.46	10	12	35	62	34[-1]	0.64
Iceland	92	108	1.86	32	27	27	56	39	0.72
Ireland	79	150	1.27	14***	21	31	52	30[-2]	0.53
Israel	91	126	1.32	14	17	26	54	...	0.65

Table 5. Gender

Country or Territory	Female activity rate[1] % of men rate 2006	Female activity rate Economic activity index (1990=100) 2006	Gender Parity Index Enrolment in tertiary level education[2] F/M 2007	Political positions held by women Seats in parliament[a,3] % of total 2007	Political positions held by women At ministerial level[b,4] % of total 2005	Female legislators, senior officials and managers[c,5] % of total 1994-2005	Female professional and technical workers[c,5] % of total 1994-2005	Female in Research & Development[6] % of total 2007	Income disparity ratio[d,7] F/M 1996-2005
Italy	69	114	1.40	16***	8	32	46	33[-1]	0.47
Latvia	88	84	1.85	19	24	42	65	48[-1]	0.65
Liechtenstein	...	...	0.49*	24	...	...	...	...	...
Lithuania	92	94	1.57	25	15	43	67	49[-1]	0.69
Luxembourg	75	128	1.12[-1]	23	14	...	...	18[-2]	0.51
Macedonia (TFYR)	66	91	1.27	28	17	29	52	50[-1]	0.48
Malta	55	176	1.35[-2]	9	15	20	38	26[-1]	0.50
Moldova (Rep.)	85	90	1.39*	22	11	39	66	45[±]	0.63
Monaco	...	...	...	21	...	...	...	50[-2, ±]	...
Montenegro	...	...	...	9	...	...	...	41	...
Netherlands	83	132	1.09	36***	36	26	50	18[-2, p]	0.64
Norway	93	111	1.57	38	44	30	50	32[-2]	0.77
Poland	84	88	1.40	18***	6	33	61	40[-1]	0.60
Portugal	86	116	1.22	21	17	34	50	44[-2]	0.59
Romania	81	89	1.33	11***	13	29	57	43[-1]	0.69
Russian Federation	89	94	1.35	8***	-	39	65	42[o]	0.62
San Marino	...	...	...	12	...	...	...	...	...
Serbia	74	103	...	20	...	...	...	45[-1, ±]	...
Slovakia	82	88	1.49	19	-	31	58	42	0.58
Slovenia	89	106	1.45	11***	6	33	57	35[-1]	0.61
Spain	72	138	1.24	31***	50	32	48	37[-1]	0.50
Sweden	95	91	1.57	47	52	30	51	36[-2, r, t]	0.81
Switzerland	87	121	0.93	27***	14	8	22	27[-3]	0.63
Turkey	36	80	0.76	9	4	7	32	36[-1]	0.35
Ukraine	86	89	1.24	8	6	38	64	44	0.55
United Kingdom	85	103	1.40	19***	29	34	47	...	0.66

North America

Country or Territory	% of men rate 2006	Economic activity index 2006	F/M 2007	Seats % 2007	Ministerial % 2005	% 1994-2005	% 1994-2005	% 2007	F/M 1996-2005
Canada	89	107	...	24***	23	36	56	...	0.64
United States of America	86	104	1.41	16***	14	42	56	...	0.63

Latin America and the Caribbean

Country or Territory	% of men rate 2006	Economic activity index 2006	F/M 2007	Seats % 2007	Ministerial % 2005	% 1994-2005	% 1994-2005	% 2007	F/M 1996-2005
Anguilla	...	...	4.86[**, -1]	...	...	...	...	...	...
Antigua and Barbuda	...	...	...	14***	15	45	55	...	...
Argentina	75	143	1.52[-1]	37***	8	33	53	51[-1]	0.54
Aruba	...	...	1.45	...	...	...	...	...	0.70
Bahamas	94	107	...	23***	27	46	60	...	0.63
Barbados	87	104	2.18	18***	29	43	52	...	0.40
Belize	54	137	...	12***	6	41	50	...	...
Bermuda	...	...	1.80[*, -2]	...	...	...	...	...	...
Bolivia	77	130	...	15***	7	36	40	40[-6, t]	0.57
Brazil	74	129	1.29	9***	11	34	52	50[-1]	0.58
British Virgin Islands	...	...	2.28[**, -2]	...	...	...	...	...	...
Cayman Islands	...	...	...	...	...	...	...	...	...
Chile	55	117	1.01	13***	17	25[e]	52[e]	30[-3]	0.40
Colombia	78	138	1.09	10***	36	38[e]	50[e]	36[-1]	0.63
Costa Rica	59	142	1.26[**, -2]	39	25	25	40	39[-2]	0.53
Cuba	62	117	1.85	36	16	34[e]	62[e]	46[o]	0.45
Dominica	...	...	...	13	...	48	55	...	...
Dominican Republic	59	132	...	17***	14	32	51	...	0.43
Ecuador	76	194	1.22	25	14	35	48	45	0.56
El Salvador	66	96	1.22	17	35	33	45	31	0.40
Grenada	...	...	...	29***	40	...	...	25[-1]	0.32
Guatemala	42	117	1.00	12	25	...	...	...	0.41
Guyana	54	123	2.09	29	22	...	...	...	0.52
Haiti	69	99	...	6***	25	...	...	27[-4]	0.46
Honduras	64	168	...	23	14	41[e]	52[e]	...	0.56
Jamaica	76	83	...	14***	18	...	...	32[-4]	0.39
Mexico	52	119	0.93	21***	9	29	42	...	...
Montserrat	...	...	...	...	...	...	...	...	...
Netherlands Antilles	76	102	...	...	...	...	...	43[-5, **]	0.32
Nicaragua	43	101	...	18	14	43	51	41[-3, t]	0.57
Panama	68	135	1.61[-1]	17	14	23	54[e]	47[-2]	0.34
Paraguay	80	127	1.13[**, -2]	10***	31	34	46	...	0.55
Peru	75	128	1.06[**, -1]	29	12	...	...	...	...
Saint Kitts and Nevis	...	...	...	7	...	...	...	...	...

Table 5. Gender

Country or Territory	Female activity rate[1]		Gender Parity Index Enrolment in tertiary level education[2]	Political positions held by women		Female legislators, senior officials and managers[c,5]	Female professional and technical workers[c,5]	Female in Research & Development[6]	Income disparity ratio[d,7]
	% of men rate	Economic activity index (1990=100)	F/M	Seats in parliament[a,3] % of total	At ministerial level[b,4] % of total	% of total	% of total	% of total	F/M
	2006	2006	2007	2007	2005	1994–2005	1994–2005	2007	1996–2005
Saint Lucia	71	115	2.41	14***, h	8	55	53	33-8, **	0.51
Saint Vincent and the Grenadines	72	124	.	18	20	...	...	...	0.51
Suriname	52	94	...	25	12	...	...	...	0.40
Trinidad and Tobago	63	113	1.28**, -2	29***	18	43	53	39-1	0.46
Turks and Caicos Islands	...	...	.	...	...	...	...	...	...
Uruguay	78	123	1.75	11***	...	40	54	42-1	0.56
Venezuela	74	160	...	19	14	27e	61e	52±	0.53
Pacific									
Australia	84	110	1.29	28***	20	37	56	...	0.70
Cook Islands	...	...	...	...	...	...	...	...	...
Fiji	67	108	1.20**, -2	.l	9	...	...	...	0.48
Kiribati	...	...	.	4	...	...	...	...	...
Marshall Islands	...	...	...	3	...	...	...	...	...
Micronesia (Fed. States)	...	...	...	...	...	...	...	...	...
Nauru	...	...	.	...	...	...	...	...	...
New Zealand	86	114	1.49	32	23	36	53	39-6	0.70
Niue	...	...	.	...	...	...	...	...	...
Palau	...	...	...	...	...	...	...	...	...
Papua New Guinea	96	101	...	1	...	...	...	...	0.72
Samoa	53	102	...	6	8	...	...	...	0.38
Solomon Islands	67	97	.	...	...	...	...	...	0.50
Tokelau	...	...	...	...	...	...	...	...	...
Tonga	63	123	...	3	...	...	...	...	0.48
Tuvalu	...	...	.	...	...	...	...	...	...
Vanuatu	90	100	...	4	8	...	...	...	0.68

Sources:

1. Calculated on the basis of data from the International Labour Organization (ILO), 2008. Key Indicators of the Labour Market. 5th Edition. Geneva. http://www.ilo.org/kilm
2. UNESCO Institute for Statistics, 2009. Education Database.
3. IPU (Inter-Parliamentary Union), 2007a. Parline Database. Geneva. http://www.ipu.org
4. IPU (Inter-Parliamentary Union), 2007b. Correspondence on women in government at the ministerial level. June 2007. Geneva. Data from the Human Development Report 2007/2008, Table 33.
5. ILO (International Labour Organization), 2007. LABORSTA Database. Geneva. http://laborsta.ilo.org. Data from the Human Development Report 2007/2008, Table 29.
6. UNESCO Institute for Statistics, Science & Technology Database, 2009.
7. UNDP (United Nations Development Programme), 2007. Human Development Report 2007/2008, Table 29. Human Development Report Office, New York.

Notes:

a. Data as of 30 November 2007 from the latest election results.
b. Data as of 1 January 2005. The total includes deputy prime ministers and ministers. Prime ministers who hold ministerial portfolios and vice-presidents and heads of ministerial level departments or agencies who exercise a ministerial function in the government structure are also included.
c. Data refer to the most recent year available between 1994 and 2005. Estimates for countries that have implemented the International Standard Classification of Occupations (ISCO-88) are not strictly comparable with those for countries using the previous classification (ISCO-68).
d. Calculated on the basis of incomes estimates based on data for the most recent year available between 1996 and 2005. For more details, see Technical note 1 from the Human Development Report 2007/2008, p. 358.
e. Data follow the ISCO-68 classification.
f. South Africa: The figures on the distribution of seats do not include the 36 special rotating delegates appointed on an ad hoc basis, and all percentages given are therefore calculated on the basis of the 54 permanent seats.
g. Bangladesh: In 2004, the number of seats in parliament was raised from 300 to 345, with the addition of 45 reserved seats for women. These reserved seats were filled in September and October 2005, being allocated to political parties in proportion to their share of the national vote received in the 2001 election.

h. Saint Lucia: Although no woman was elected in the 2006 elections, Ms. Flood-Beaubrun became a member of the House by virtue of her election as Speaker. However, in November 2007, a by-election was won by Ms. Jeannine Rambally, making her the first woman to be elected in Saint Lucia. There are therefore two women members of parliament.
i. Kuwait: No woman candidate was elected in the 2006 elections. One woman was appointed to the 16-member cabinet sworn in in July 2006. A new cabinet sworn in in March 2007 included two women. As cabinet ministers also sit in parliament, there are two women out of a total of 65 members. One female minister resigned in August 2007, bringing the number of women down to one.
j. Sao Tome and Principe: Four women were elected on 26 March 2006. However, after the formation of the new government on 21 April 2006, the total number of women parliamentarians decreased to one (1.82 percent).
k. Brunei Darussalam: Does not currently have a parliament.
l. Fiji: Parliament has been dissolved or suspended for an indefinite period.
m. Myanmar: The parliament elected in 1990 has never been convened nor authorized to sit, and many of its members were detained or forced into exile.
n. Based on full-time equivalent instead of headcount.
o. Underestimated or based on underestimated data.
p. Provisional.
q. Eurostat estimation.
r. University graduates instead of researchers.
s. Overestimated or based on overestimated data.
t. Break in series.

...   Data not available
*   National estimation
**   UIS estimation
***   Including both upper and lower houses
.   Not applicable
±   Partial data
+n   Data refer to the year n years after the reference year
-n   Data refer to the year n years before the reference year

Table 6. Highlights of the World Values Survey[1]

Country or Territory	Survey year[a]	How proud of nationality[b] ('Very proud' + 'Quite proud') %	Geographical groups belonging to first[c] — Locality %	Geographical groups belonging to first[c] — Country %	Geographical groups belonging to first[c] — The world %	Important child qualities[d] — Tolerance and respect for other people % mentioning	Important child qualities[d] — Imagination % mentioning	Education, arts, music or cultural activities[e] — Belong to %	Education, arts, music or cultural activities[e] — Unpaid work for %	Most people can be trusted[f] %	Confidence in...[g] ('A great deal' + 'Quite a lot') — The Press %	Confidence in...[g] — Television %	Confidence in...[g] — The United Nations %	Immigrants should maintain distinct customs and traditions[h] %	Respect for human rights in country[i] ('There is not much' + 'Not at all') %	Freedom of choice and control[j] Mean score out of 10
OECD Countries																
Australia	1995	97	32	44	10	81	26	...	...	40	17	26	50	...	...	7.6
Austria	1999	91	35	24	3	71	24	13	7	34	32	...	42	18	24	7.5
Belgium	1999	75	35	27	9	83	23	20	9	31	37	...	45	25	37	6.6
Canada	2000	95	33	39	13	81	33	21	11	39	35	38	65	...	16	7.6
Czech Republic	1999	81	43	35	5	63	7	10	6	24	38	50-1	48	31	36	6.9
Denmark	1999	93	56	19	2	87	37	17	5	67	33	...	64	23	12	7.3
Finland	2000	94	49	31	4	83	28	14	5	58	36	50-4	44	32	12	7.4
France	1999	89	44	28	11	85	18	8	5	22	36	...	54	27	40	6.4
Germany	1999	68	55	10	2	73	29	8	3	35	36	22-2	52	24	21	7.4
Greece	1999	88	38	35	13	53	22	21	14	24	31	...	19	77	37	7.0
Hungary	1999	89	67	20	4	66	11	3	3	22	31	41-1	59	33	43	6.2
Iceland	1999	98	38	51	4	84	18	15	6	41	39	...	72	27	14	7.6
Ireland	1999	98	59	22	1	75	25	10	4	36	34	...	62	57	24	7.3
Italy	1999	88	53	23	9	75	12	10	6	33	35	...	68	60	38	6.3
Japan	2000	59	57	24	1	71	35	11	4	43	73	68	61	...	38	6.0
Korea (Rep.)	2001	78	45	31	3	65	33	19	9	27	66	63	62	...	53	7.1
Luxembourg	1999	89	43	24	8	78	25	17	8	26	46	...	65	57	9	7.0
Mexico	2000	95	35	35	16	71	24	8	5	21	42	47	45	...	52	8.2
Netherlands	1999	80	39	41	8	91	32	45	16	60	56	...	55	30	21	6.7
New Zealand	1998	96	29	53	8	78	28	...	...	49	34	38	56	...	...	7.8
Norway	1996	89	56	20	3	66	37	...	...	65	33	49	73	...	...	7.2
Poland	1999	97	63	19	1	80	13	2	2	19	47	47-2	58	48	43	6.2
Portugal	1999	97	36	42	4	65	15	3	2	10	66	...	71	49	38	6.8
Slovakia	1999	77	54	27	4	57	3	7	6	16	49	50-1	52	40	41	6.3
Spain	2000	92	41	29	7	77	25	6	3	34	41	39	55	52-1	37	6.7
Sweden	1999	87	59	22	5	93	40	26	11	66	46	49-3	74	36	25	7.4
Switzerland	1996	75	27	30	15	79	23	...	...	41	22	31	43	...	...	7.3
Turkey	2001	87	34	41	9	63	22	1	1	16	34	37	46	...	74	5.3
United Kingdom	1999	90	49	28	7	84	38	10	3	30	16	...	60	45	34	7.2
United States of America	1999	96	32	35	20	80	30	37	20	36	27	25	57	...	26	8.0
Others																
Albania	2002	94	51	37	2	80	29	14	10	24	35	54	86	...	63	6.0
Algeria	2002	96	28	56	4	54	12	12	12	11	48	45	15	...	64	6.7
Argentina	1999	92	31	42	9	70	24	9	4	15	38	33	42	...	78	7.4
Armenia	1997	82	33	45	10	48	16	...	...	25	34	45	70	...	77	5.7
Azerbaijan	1997	95	21	45	18	59	14	...	...	21	32	42	33	...	39	5.6
Bangladesh	2002	97	47	37	2	71	36	29	28	24	93	84	93	...	27	5.7
Belarus	2000	72	66	25	7	72	10	2	2	42	41	48-4	53	48	64	5.6
Bosnia and Herzegovina	2001	69	57	23	7	72	27	4	3	16	25	35	39	...	65	6.3
Brazil	1997	84	31	29	27	59	8	...	...	3	61	57	70	...	...	7.4
Bulgaria	1999	69	47	41	4	59	19	4	2	27	26	69-2	40	60	66	6.2
Chile	2000	93	32	40	8	76	36	9	7	23	48	53	58	...	43	7.2
China	2001	82	24	55	3	73	35	2	16	55	69	74	69	...	12	7.1
Colombia	1998	97	53	28	10	69	20	...	...	11	42	45	...	...	...	7.9
Croatia	1999	88	62	22	7	64-3	17-3	6	3	18	18	22-3	47	56	42	6.9
Dominican Republic	1996	93	42	9	20	68	12	...	...	26	33	38	44	...	...	7.4
Egypt	2000	99	35	45	1	65	15	...	...	38	69	68	32	...	28	5.5
El Salvador	1999	96	...	...	...	59	10	...	...	15	46	49	51	...	...	7.5
Estonia	1999	67	61	21	4	71	11	8	5	23	42	68-3	43	52	46	6.0
Georgia	1996	94	28	49	11	54	10	...	...	19	60	61	61	...	75	6.2
India	2001	93	31	53	4	63	28	15	12	41	70	72	53	...	25	5.7
Indonesia	2001	93	75	13	2	63	29	...	...	52	55	61	48	...	38	7.2
Iran (Islamic Rep.)	2000	95	34	52	6	59	11	...	...	65	36	49	36	...	27	6.6
Iraq	2004	95	22	60	1	78	...	...	...	48	...	56	16	...	58	5.9
Israel	2001	84	...	...	...	82	23	...	...	23	...	...	...	...	...	...
Jordan	2001	99	10	4	46	67	5	...	...	28	59	58	36	...	26	7.3
Kyrgyzstan	2003	82	29	47	11	65	38	11	3	17	44	52	59	...	68	7.1
Latvia	1999	81	41	39	5	69	7	4	4	17	45	58-3	48	47	48	5.8
Lithuania	1999	61	51	37	4	58	5	2	2	25	77	76-2	47	36	77	6.3
Macedonia (TFYR)	2001	82	45	39	6	75	13	12	7	14	20	22	37	...	68	5.8

Table 6. Highlights of the World Values Survey[1]

Country or Territory	Survey year[a]	How proud of nationality[b] ('Very proud' + 'Quite proud') %	Geographical groups belonging to first[c] Locality %	Country %	The world %	Important child qualities[d] Tolerance and respect for other people % mentioning	Imagination % mentioning	Education, arts, music or cultural activities[e] Belong to %	Unpaid work for %	Most people can be trusted[f] %	Confidence in...[g] ('A great deal' + 'Quite a lot') The Press %	Television %	The United Nations %	Immigrants should maintain distinct customs and traditions[h] %	Respect for human rights in country[i] ('There is not much' + 'Not at all') %	Freedom of choice and control[j] Mean score out of 10
Malta	1999	97	...	...	...	61	7	5	4	21	36	...	63	56	25	7.4
Moldova (Rep.)	2002	65	37	35	16	78	26	12	9	15	44	49	74	...	79	6.0
Morocco	2001	97	18	62	4	65	9	3	...	24	37	30	13	...	58	6.3
Nigeria	2000	91	42	31	2	59	11	...	...	26	64	72	70	...	37	7.1
Pakistan	2001	97	4	90	0	53	7	...	...	31	52	57	22	...	46	4.7
Peru	2001	94	35	38	0	73	23	13	10	11	23	25	44	...	55	7.2
Philippines	2001	98	53	11	3	60	14	5	4	8	67	71	76	...	21	6.8
Romania	1999	86	45	30	3	58	14	3	2	10	38	49-1	44	62	76	6.7
Russian Federation	1999	70	51	25	16	67	7	1	0	24	30	47-4	27	43	84	5.6
Saudi Arabia	2003	95	22	49	5	56	31	...	...	53	63	67	33	...	28	6.6
Serbia	2001	74	52	20	6	64	10	3	1	20	29	30	19	...	52	6.0
Singapore	2002	93	...	...	...	70	13	14	6	17	...	...	...	...	...	7.1
Slovenia	1999	91	53	32	4	70	12	9	7	22	61	53-4	49	31	59	7.2
South Africa	2001	95	30	42	8	74	20	17	7	12	65	77	67	...	44	6.8
Tanzania (United Rep.)	2001	95	55	25	3	84	61	28	26	8	76	79	82	...	31	5.8
Uganda	2001	89	24	43	6	57	11	21	16	8	67	67	87	...	30	6.8
Ukraine	1999	61	49	26	15	65	11	3	2	27	47	48-3	55	46	77	5.4
Uruguay	1996	95	24	52	11	70	31	...	...	22	61	57	56	...	...	7.0
Venezuela	2000	99	29	40	12	80	24	18	...	16	65	64	52	...	52	8.3
Viet Nam	2001	98	30	54	1	68	20	17	16	41	84	93	61	...	5	7.5
Zimbabwe	2001	91	28	43	6	78	11	7	4	12	54	59	70	...	68	5.9
World (Total of sample)		88	40	35	8	68	19	12	7	27	45	51	54	42	47	6.6

Source:

1. World Values Survey database, 2008. Data can be downloaded at http://www.worldvaluessurvey.org

Notes:

a. Year the survey was taken, unless otherwise specified.

b. *Question:* How proud are you to be [Nationality]? (Very proud, Quite proud, Not very proud, Not at all proud). Percentages of people answering 'Very proud' or 'Quite proud' are presented in the table.

c. Question: To which of these geographical groups would you say you belong to first of all? [Locality, Region (not listed here), Country, Continent (not listed here), The world].

d. Question: Here is a list of qualities that children can be encouraged to learn at home. Which, if any, do you consider to be especially important? Please choose up to five. (Choices: good manners, independence, hard work, feeling of responsibility, imagination, tolerance and respect for other people, thrift saving money and things, determination and perseverance, religious faith, unselfishness, obedience).

e. Question: Please look carefully at the following list of voluntary organizations and activities and say... which, if any, do you belong to? And for which, if any, are you currently doing unpaid voluntary work? [Education, arts, music or cultural activities].

f. Question: Generally speaking, would you say that most people can be trusted or that you need to be very careful in dealing with people? (Two choices: 'Most people can be trusted' and 'Can't be too careful').

g. Question: I am going to name a number of organizations. For each one, could you tell me how much confidence you have in them: is it a great deal of confidence, quite a lot of confidence, not very much confidence or none at all? (Percentage answering 'A great deal' or 'Quite a lot' for: The Press, Television, The United Nations).

h. Question: Which of these statements is the nearest to your opinion? For the greater good of society it is better if immigrants... A) maintain their distinct customs and traditions; B) do not maintain their distinct customs and traditions but take over the customs of the country. (Percentage answering 'A' is shown here).

i. Question: How much respect is there for individual human rights nowadays in our country? Do you feel there is: [a lot of respect, some respect, not much respect, no respect at all]. Percentage answering 'There is not much' or 'Not at all' is presented in the tables.

j. Question: Some people feel they have completely free choice and control over their lives, while other people feel that what they do has no real effect on what happens to them. Please use this scale where 1 means 'none at all' and 10 means 'a great deal' to indicate how much freedom of choice and control you feel you have over the way your life turns out.

... Data not available

+n Data refer to the year n years after the reference year

-n Data refer to the year n years before the reference year

Table 7. Languages[a]

Country or Territory	Living languages according to Ethnologue 2005 edition[1] Number of living languages Indigenous	Immigrant	% of world languages?	Linguistic Diversity Index[b]	Total yearly instructional hours devoted to languages (average) grades 1–6	grades 7–8	Official or National Language(s) %[h] grades 1–6	Local or Regional Language(s) %[i] grades 1–6	International Language(s) %[j] grades 1–6	Official or National Language(s) %[h] grades 7–8	Local or Regional Language(s) %[i] grades 7–8	International Language(s) %[j] grades 7–8
Arab States												
Algeria[d]	18	4	0.32	0.313	...	...	...	...	...	...	...	...
Bahrain	3	8	0.16	0.663	310	321	74.9	0.0	25.1	54.5	0.0	45.5
Djibouti	5	1	0.09	0.592	443	...	100.0	0.0	0.0	...	...	...
Egypt[e]	11	10	0.30	0.509	383	359	89.7	0.0	10.3	61.5	0.0	38.5
Iraq[d]	21	4	0.36	0.666	263	272	87.6	0.0	12.4	52.2	0.0	47.8
Jordan[d]	9	6	0.22	0.484	288	378	84.0	0.0	16.0	56.1	0.0	43.9
Kuwait[d]	3	4	0.10	0.556	309	265	71.2	0.0	28.8	50.0	0.0	50.0
Lebanon[e]	6	3	0.13	0.161	351	394	50.0	0.0	50.0	50.0	0.0	50.0
Libyan Arab Jamahiriya[d]	9	5	0.20	0.362	177	233	100.0	0.0	0.0	60.0	0.0	40.0
Mauritania[e]	6	3	0.13	0.172	...	...	100.0	0.0	0.0	100.0	0.0	0.0
Morocco[d]	9	1	0.14	0.466	434	352	59.5	0.0	40.5	50.0	0.0	50.0
Oman[d]	13	8	0.30	0.693	227	192	64.7	0.0	35.3	58.3	0.0	41.7
Palestinian A. T.	4	2	0.09	0.208	284	360	84.4	0.0	15.6	54.9	0.0	45.1
Qatar	3	3	0.09	0.608	309	260	62.7	0.0	37.3	53.8	0.0	46.2
Saudi Arabia[f]	5	15	0.29	0.609	230	283	100.0	0.0	0.0	60.0	0.0	40.0
Sudan[e]	134	...	1.94	0.587	284	515	100.0	0.0	0.0	100.0	0.0	0.0
Syrian Arab Republic[d]	15	3	0.26	0.503	262	284	90.8	0.0	9.2	54.5	0.0	45.5
Tunisia[d]	6	4	0.14	0.012	484	321	61.2	0.0	38.8	50.0	0.0	50.0
United Arab Emirates[d]	7	29	0.52	0.777	304	285	53.9	0.0	46.1	53.8	0.0	46.2
Yemen[d]	8	6	0.20	0.579	226	297	100.0	0.0	0.0	54.5	0.0	45.5
Sub-Saharan Africa												
Angola	41	...	0.59	0.785	199	227	100.0	0.0	0.0	50.0	0.0	50.0
Benin[d]	54	1	0.80	0.901	364	361	100.0	0.0	0.0	60.0	0.0	40.0
Botswana	28	9	0.54	0.444	...	...	...	...	...	...	...	...
Burkina Faso	68	1	1.00	0.773	...	...	...	...	...	...	...	...
Burundi[d]	3	1	0.06	0.004	401	386	100.0	0.0	0.0	84.0	0.0	16.0
Cameroon[e]	279	1	4.05	0.942	...	...	98.0	0.0	2.0	...	...	...
Cape Verde	2	...	0.03	0.070	179	232	100.0	0.0	0.0	50.0	0.0	50.0
Central African Republic	69	10	1.14	0.960	...	...	...	...	...	63.6	0.0	36.4
Chad[d]	132	1	1.92	0.950	...	...	71.2	0.0	28.8	61.5	0.0	38.5
Comoros	7	1	0.12	0.551	...	...	100.0	0.0	0.0	...	...	...
Congo[d]	62	4	0.95	0.820	...	...	100.0	0.0	0.0	56.1	0.0	43.9
Congo (Dem. Rep.)[e]	214	2	3.12	0.948	...	...	100.0	0.0	0.0	...	...	...
Côte d'Ivoire	78	14	1.33	0.917	...	...	...	...	...	...	...	...
Equatorial Guinea	14	...	0.20	0.453	...	...	...	...	...	...	...	...
Eritrea	12	6	0.26	0.749	...	...	...	...	...	...	...	...
Ethiopia[f]	84	2	1.24	0.843	331	378	25.9	33.2	41.0	35.7	21.4	42.9
Gabon	41	...	0.59	0.919	...	...	...	...	...	...	...	...
Gambia	9	13	0.32	0.748	...	...	...	...	...	...	...	...
Ghana[d]	79	4	1.20	0.805	340	225	100.0	0.0	0.0	100.0	0.0	0.0
Guinea[d]	34	4	0.55	0.748	...	...	...	...	...	80.0	0.0	20.0
Guinea-Bissau	21	4	0.36	0.853	...	...	...	...	...	...	...	...
Kenya[d]	61	3	0.93	0.901	280	281	79.7	20.3	0.0	100.0	0.0	0.0
Lesotho[d]	5	1	0.09	0.260	279	...	100.0	0.0	0.0	0.0	0.0	0.0
Liberia	30	1	0.45	0.912	...	...	...	...	...	...	...	...
Madagascar[d]	13	2	0.22	0.656	...	...	100.0	0.0	0.0	76.9	0.0	23.1
Malawi[d]	14	8	0.32	0.519	...	...	100.0	0.0	0.0	100.0	0.0	0.0
Mali	50	4	0.78	0.876	...	...	...	...	...	...	...	...
Mauritius[d]	6	7	0.19	0.641	305	...	100.0	0.0	0.0	...	...	...
Mozambique[d]	43	...	0.62	0.929	266	177	100.0	0.0	0.0	77.9	0.0	22.1
Namibia[d]	28	8	0.52	0.808	340	310	46.3	0.0	53.7	50.0	0.0	50.0
Niger[d]	21	...	0.30	0.646	329	368	100.0	0.0	0.0	60.0	0.0	40.0
Nigeria	510	6	7.47	0.870	...	...	...	...	...	...	...	...
Rwanda[d]	3	2	0.07	0.004	293	420	67.1	0.0	32.9	57.1	0.0	42.9
Saint Helena	...	...	...	...	...	...	...	...	...	...	...	...
Sao Tome and Principe	4	1	0.07	0.389	...	...	...	...	...	...	...	...
Senegal[d]	36	5	0.59	0.772	401	330	100.0	0.0	0.0	50.1	0.0	49.9
Seychelles	3	...	0.04	0.067	...	...	...	...	...	...	...	...
Sierra Leone	24	1	0.36	0.817	...	...	...	...	...	...	...	...
Somalia	13	...	0.19	0.179	...	...	...	...	...	...	...	...
South Africa[f]	24	11	0.51	0.869	273	222	100.0	0.0	0.0	100.0	0.0	0.0

Table 7. Languages[a]

Country or Territory	Living languages — Number of living languages Indigenous	Immigrant	% of world languages?	Linguistic Diversity Index[b]	Total yearly instructional hours (average) grades 1–6	grades 7–8	Official or National Language(s) %[h] grades 1–6	Local or Regional Language(s) %[i] grades 1–6	International Language(s) %[j] grades 1–6	Official or National Language(s) %[h] grades 7–8	Local or Regional Language(s) %[i] grades 7–8	International Language(s) %[j] grades 7–8
Swaziland	4	…	0.06	0.228	…	…	…	…	…	…	…	…
Tanzania (United Rep.)[d]	127	1	1.85	0.965	287	…	100.0	0.0	0.0	…	…	…
Togo[f]	39	3	0.61	0.897	…	…	100.0	0.0	0.0	63.6	0.0	36.4
Uganda	43	3	0.67	0.928	…	…	…	…	…	…	…	…
Zambia[e]	41	3	0.64	0.855	…	…	100.0	0.0	0.0	0.0	0.0	0.0
Zimbabwe[e]	19	2	0.30	0.526	…	…	50.0	0.0	50.0	45.4	0.0	54.6
Central and South Asia												
Afghanistan[d]	47	4	0.74	0.732	265	336	87.8	0.0	12.2	71.4	0.0	28.6
Armenia	6	5	0.16	0.174	…	…	…	…	…	…	…	…
Azerbaijan[f]	14	21	0.51	0.373	216	176	100.0	0.0	0.0	100.0	0.0	0.0
Bangladesh	39	7	0.67	0.332	…	…	…	…	…	…	…	…
Bhutan	24	7	0.45	0.846	…	…	…	…	…	…	…	…
Georgia[d]	12	12	0.35	0.576	295	312	89.8	0.0	10.2	77.4	0.0	22.6
India[f,g]	415	12	6.18	0.930	227	288	100.0	0.0	0.0	100.0	0.0	0.0
Iran (Islamic Rep.)[d]	75	4	1.14	0.797	231	226	96.4	0.0	3.6	71.4	0.0	28.6
Kazakhstan[e]	7	36	0.62	0.701	304	277	100.0	0.0	0.0	100.0	0.0	0.0
Kyrgyzstan[e]	3	29	0.46	0.670	348	320	83.1	0.0	16.9	79.1	0.0	20.9
Maldives	1	1	0.03	0.010	…	…	…	…	…	…	…	…
Nepal[d]	123	2	1.81	0.742	292	316	76.4	0.0	23.6	57.1	0.0	42.9
Pakistan[f]	72	5	1.11	0.762	…	328	…	…	…	37.5	25.0	37.5
Sri Lanka[f]	7	…	0.10	0.313	270	253	79.4	0.0	20.6	50.0	0.0	50.0
Tajikistan	9	24	0.48	0.482	…	…	…	…	…	…	…	…
Turkmenistan[e]	3	24	0.39	0.386	328	278	83.2	16.8	0.0	84.5	15.5	0.0
Uzbekistan[d]	7	33	0.58	0.428	296	289	93.0	0.0	7.0	72.7	0.0	27.3
East Asia												
Brunei Darussalam	17	2	0.27	0.456	400	257	50.0	0.0	50.0	36.4	0.0	63.6
Cambodia[d]	21	3	0.35	0.157	250	299	91.6	0.0	8.4	52.4	0.0	47.6
China[e]	235	6	3.49	0.491	309	271	81.9	18.1	0.0	57.9	0.0	42.1
Hong Kong (SAR China)	…	…	…	…	…	…	…	…	…	…	…	…
Macao (SAR China)	…	…	…	…	…	…	…	…	…	…	…	…
Indonesia[e]	737	5	10.73	0.846	220	285	100.0	0.0	0.0	60.0	0.0	40.0
Japan[d]	15	1	0.23	0.028	186	198	100.0	0.0	0.0	53.9	0.0	46.1
Korea (Dem. People's Rep.)	…	…	…	…	…	…	…	…	…	…	…	…
Korea (Rep.)[d]	2	2	0.06	0.003	217	203	89.8	0.0	10.2	60.0	0.0	40.0
Lao (People's Dem. Rep.)[d]	82	4	1.24	0.678	204	212	94.8	0.0	5.2	60.0	0.0	40.0
Malaysia[e]	140	7	2.13	0.758	373	226	78.5	0.0	21.5	54.5	0.0	45.5
Mongolia[d]	13	2	0.22	0.331	194	176	85.0	0.0	15.0	54.0	0.0	46.0
Myanmar[d]	108	5	1.63	0.521	276	…	59.5	0.0	40.5	…	…	…
Philippines[d]	171	9	2.60	0.849	416	242	50.0	0.0	50.0	50.0	0.0	50.0
Singapore[d]	21	9	0.43	0.748	363	322	100.0	0.0	0.0	100.0	0.0	0.0
Thailand[f]	74	9	1.20	0.753	176	133	100.0	0.0	0.0	100.0	0.0	0.0
Timor-Leste	19	…	0.27	0.897	…	…	…	…	…	…	…	…
Viet Nam	102	2	1.50	0.234	…	…	…	…	…	…	…	…
Europe												
Albania[d]	7	…	0.10	0.257	224	160	100.0	0.0	0.0	100.0	0.0	0.0
Andorra	3	2	0.07	0.574	…	…	…	…	…	…	…	…
Austria[d]	9	10	0.27	0.540	282	210	65.7	0.0	34.3	57.1	0.0	42.9
Belarus[e]	1	8	0.13	0.397	324	290	72.1	17.1	10.8	62.5	20.8	16.6
Belgium[e]	9	19	0.41	0.734	255	…	90.2	0.0	9.8	…	…	…
Bosnia and Herzegovina	4	4	0.12	0.416	…	…	…	…	…	…	…	…
Bulgaria	11	5	0.23	0.224	172	209	85.8	0.0	14.2	55.6	0.0	44.4
Croatia[d]	6	2	0.12	0.087	211	209	83.1	0.0	16.9	57.1	0.0	42.9
Cyprus	4	2	0.09	0.366	322	345	92.9	0.0	7.2	64.5	0.0	35.5
Czech Republic[d]	8	1	0.13	0.069	299	244	83.1	0.0	16.9	57.1	0.0	42.9
Denmark[d]	8	6	0.20	0.051	258	303	85.7	0.0	14.3	66.7	0.0	33.3
Estonia[f]	2	14	0.23	0.476	242	206	72.6	0.0	27.4	58.7	0.0	41.3
Finland	12	11	0.33	0.140	…	…	…	…	…	…	…	…
France[d]	29	37	0.95	0.272	326	255	78.8	7.0	14.2	51.1	6.5	42.3
Germany	27	42	1.00	0.189	…	…	…	…	…	…	…	…
Gibraltar	2	1	0.04	0.498	…	…	…	…	…	…	…	…

Table 7. Languages[a]

Country or Territory	Living languages according to Ethnologue 2005 edition[1] Number of living languages Indigenous	Immigrant	% of world languages?	Linguistic Diversity Index[b]	Total yearly instructional hours devoted to languages (average) grades 1–6	grades 7–8	Type of language taught in school as % of Total Yearly Instructional Hours devoted to languages according to IBE[2] Official or National Language(s) %[h] grades 1–6	Local or Regional Language(s) %[i] grades 1–6	International Language(s) %[j] grades 1–6	Official or National Language(s) %[h] grades 7–8	Local or Regional Language(s) %[i] grades 7–8	International Language(s) %[j] grades 7–8
					2000s		2000s					
Greece[d]	14	10	0.35	0.175	263	287	86.1	0.0	13.9	47.4	0.0	52.6
Holy See	...	...	...	...	...	...	...	...	...	...	...	...
Hungary[d]	12	9	0.30	0.158	228	204	82.4	0.0	17.6	57.1	0.0	42.9
Iceland	3	...	0.04	0.019	211	241	63.3	0.0	36.7	63.3	0.0	36.7
Ireland[d]	5	...	0.07	0.223	275	285	100.0	0.0	0.0	66.7	0.0	33.3
Israel[e]	33	15	0.69	0.665	...	...	...	...	...	50.9	0.0	49.1
Italy[d]	33	9	0.61	0.593	...	308	...	...	...	70.0	0.0	30.0
Latvia[d]	5	7	0.17	0.595	225	199	77.8	0.0	22.2	68.5	0.0	31.5
Liechtenstein	3	1	0.06	0.128	...	...	...	...	...	...	...	...
Lithuania[d]	4	7	0.16	0.339	209	246	84.0	0.0	16.0	60.1	0.0	39.9
Luxembourg	3	3	0.09	0.498	336	...	100.0	0.0	0.0	...	...	...
Macedonia (TFYR)	9	1	0.14	0.566	151	213	84.0	0.0	16.0	66.7	0.0	33.3
Malta	3	...	0.04	0.016	311	303	100.0	0.0	0.0	100.0	0.0	0.0
Moldova (Rep.)[e]	5	8	0.19	0.589	224	180	80.2	0.0	19.8	66.7	0.0	33.3
Monaco	3	...	0.04	0.521	...	...	...	...	...	...	...	...
Montenegro	...	...	...	...	...	...	...	...	...	...	...	...
Netherlands	15	23	0.55	0.389	...	...	...	...	...	...	...	...
Norway[d]	11	10	0.30	0.657	241	241	58.9	0.0	41.1	54.3	0.0	45.7
Poland	11	6	0.25	0.060	257	210	71.4	0.0	28.6	58.9	0.0	41.1
Portugal[d]	7	1	0.12	0.022	...	281	...	...	...	42.1	0.0	57.9
Romania[d]	15	8	0.33	0.168	208	222	74.3	0.0	25.7	47.1	0.0	52.9
Russian Federation[d]	101	28	1.87	0.283	250	245	66.5	33.5	0.0	66.6	33.4	0.0
San Marino[d]	2	...	0.03	0.494	...	...	...	...	...	58.3	0.0	41.7
Serbia[c]	11	3	0.20	0.359	165	168	82.0	0.0	18.0	66.7	0.0	33.3
Slovakia[d]	10	2	0.17	0.307	247	195	88.0	0.0	12.0	57.1	0.0	42.9
Slovenia[d]	4	6	0.14	0.174	175	189	83.2	0.0	16.8	61.5	0.0	38.5
Spain	13	7	0.29	0.438	...	...	...	...	...	...	...	...
Sweden	15	17	0.46	0.167	...	...	...	...	...	...	...	...
Switzerland	12	14	0.38	0.547	...	...	...	...	...	...	...	...
Turkey[d]	34	11	0.65	0.289	244	223	86.9	0.0	13.1	55.6	0.0	44.4
Ukraine[d]	10	29	0.56	0.492	211	253	87.6	0.0	12.4	66.7	0.0	33.3
United Kingdom	12	43	0.80	0.139	...	...	...	...	...	...	...	...
North America												
Canada[d]	85	60	2.10	0.549	...	...	100.0	0.0	0.0	100.0	0.0	0.0
United States of America	162	149	4.50	0.353	...	...	...	...	...	...	...	...
Latin America and the Caribbean												
Anguilla	2	...	0.03	0.140	...	...	...	...	...	...	...	...
Antigua and Barbuda	2	2	0.06	0.057	...	...	...	...	...	...	...	...
Argentina[d]	25	14	0.56	0.213	187	192	96.4	0.0	3.6	62.5	0.0	37.5
Aruba	3	2	0.07	0.387	...	...	...	...	...	...	...	...
Bahamas	2	2	0.06	0.386	...	...	...	...	...	...	...	...
Barbados	2	...	0.03	0.091	...	...	...	...	...	...	...	...
Belize	8	4	0.17	0.693	...	...	...	...	...	...	...	...
Bermuda	...	...	...	...	...	...	...	...	...	...	...	...
Bolivia	36	3	0.56	0.680	...	...	...	...	...	...	...	...
Brazil[d]	188	12	2.89	0.032	242	226	90.8	0.0	9.2	69.2	0.0	30.8
British Virgin Islands	2	...	0.03	0.167	...	...	...	...	...	...	...	...
Cayman Islands	1	2	0.04	0.547	...	...	...	...	...	...	...	...
Chile[d]	9	3	0.17	0.034	176	218	88.9	0.0	11.1	66.7	0.0	33.3
Colombia	80	3	1.20	0.030	...	...	...	...	...	...	...	...
Costa Rica[d]	9	4	0.19	0.050	...	...	...	...	...	45.5	0.0	54.5
Cuba[d]	2	2	0.06	0.001	299	203	96.0	0.0	4.0	54.7	0.0	45.3
Dominica	3	...	0.04	0.313	399	...	100.0	0.0	0.0	...	...	...
Dominican Republic	4	4	0.12	0.053	242	318	82.6	0.0	17.4	55.6	0.0	44.4
Ecuador[d]	23	2	0.36	0.264	186	222	100.0	0.0	0.0	62.5	0.0	37.5
El Salvador	5	2	0.10	0.004	...	...	...	...	...	...	...	...
Grenada	3	...	0.04	0.064	216	...	100.0	0.0	0.0	...	...	...
Guatemala[d]	54	...	0.78	0.691	...	198	...	...	...	62.5	0.0	37.5
Guyana	16	3	0.27	0.078	411	...	100.0	0.0	0.0	...	...	...
Haiti	2	...	0.03	0.000	...	...	...	...	...	...	...	...
Honduras[d]	10	3	0.19	0.056	107	203	100.0	0.0	0.0	62.5	0.0	37.5

Table 7. Languages[a]

Country or Territory	Number of living languages — Indigenous	Number of living languages — Immigrant	% of world languages?	Linguistic Diversity Index[b]	Total yearly instructional hours (average) grades 1–6	Total yearly instructional hours (average) grades 7–8	Official or National Language(s) %[h] grades 1–6	Local or Regional Language(s) %[i] grades 1–6	International Language(s) %[j] grades 1–6	Official or National Language(s) %[h] grades 7–8	Local or Regional Language(s) %[i] grades 7–8	International Language(s) %[j] grades 7–8
					2000s					2000s		
Jamaica	3	3	0.09	0.011	…	…	…	…	…	…	…	…
Mexico[d]	291	6	4.30	0.135	280	267	100.0	0.0	0.0	62.5	0.0	37.5
Montserrat	2	…	0.03	0.026	…	…	…	…	…	…	…	…
Netherlands Antilles	4	2	0.09	0.266	…	…	…	…	…	…	…	…
Nicaragua[d]	7	…	0.10	0.081	256	258	100.0	0.0	0.0	62.5	0.0	37.5
Panama[d]	14	4	0.26	0.324	210	216	69.8	0.0	30.2	55.6	0.0	44.4
Paraguay[d]	20	6	0.38	0.347	235	134	75.5	24.5	0.0	75.0	25.0	0.0
Peru[f]	93	1	1.36	0.376	…	156	…	…	…	61.5	0.0	38.5
Saint Kitts and Nevis	2	…	0.03	0.010	…	…	100.0	0.0	0.0	66.7	0.0	33.3
Saint Lucia[f]	2	…	0.03	0.020	307	225	100.0	0.0	0.0	100.0	0.0	0.0
Saint Vincent and the Grenadines	2	1	0.04	0.009	…	…	…	…	…	…	…	…
Suriname	16	4	0.29	0.788	388	…	100.0	0.0	0.0	…	…	…
Trinidad and Tobago	6	1	0.10	0.696	…	186	…	…	…	75.0	0.0	25.0
Turks and Caicos Islands	2	…	0.03	0.145	…	…	…	…	…	…	…	…
Uruguay[d]	2	9	0.16	0.092	206	190	100.0	0.0	0.0	50.0	0.0	50.0
Venezuela[d]	40	6	0.67	0.026	218	216	100.0	0.0	0.0	100.0	0.0	0.0
Pacific												
Australia[d]	231	44	3.98	0.126	…	…	87.0	0.0	13.0	66.7	0.0	33.3
Cook Islands	5	1	0.09	0.379	…	…	…	…	…	…	…	…
Fiji	10	10	0.29	0.607	…	…	…	…	…	…	…	…
Kiribati	2	1	0.04	0.033	…	…	…	…	…	…	…	…
Marshall Islands	2	…	0.03	0.027	…	…	…	…	…	…	…	…
Micronesia (Fed. States)	18	1	0.27	0.792	…	…	…	…	…	…	…	…
Nauru	3	6	0.13	0.596	…	…	…	…	…	…	…	…
New Zealand	3	18	0.30	0.102	…	…	…	…	…	…	…	…
Niue	2	1	0.04	0.071	…	…	…	…	…	…	…	…
Palau	4	1	0.07	0.077	…	…	…	…	…	…	…	…
Papua New Guinea[d]	820	…	11.86	0.990	…	…	…	…	…	100	0	0
Samoa	2	…	0.03	0.002	…	…	…	…	…	…	…	…
Solomon Islands	70	…	1.01	0.965	…	…	…	…	…	…	…	…
Tokelau	2	…	0.03	0.054	…	…	…	…	…	…	…	…
Tonga	3	…	0.04	0.014	…	…	…	…	…	…	…	…
Tuvalu	2	…	0.03	0.139	…	…	…	…	…	…	…	…
Vanuatu	109	6	1.66	0.972	…	…	…	…	…	…	…	…
World	**6,912**											

Sources:

1. Gordon, 2005. Ethnologue: Languages of the World, Fifteenth edition. Dallas, Tex.: SIL International. http://www.ethnologue.com. The year of publication does not necessarily reflect the year of assessment.
   Ethnologue data tend to be higher than other sets of data (e.g. data collected in a National Census) because Ethnologue's definition of 'languages' tends to include 'dialects' or other sub-categories of a given 'language'. The distinction between a language and a dialect is fluid and often political. A great number of languages are considered to be dialects of another language by some experts and separate languages by others. The Ethnologue data are routinely cited by a very large number of linguists, although there is widespread agreement that they are not always accurate, and quite often problematic.

2. International Bureau of Education, 2009. The IBE contributes to the identification of educational trends worldwide by commissioning and conducting studies and research on a variety of educational and curricular topics.
   Yearly instructional time is defined as the number of hours devoted for curricula during the working school year. http://www.ibe.unesco.org/en.html

Notes:

a. Data in this table relates to Ethnologue data. Other data sets may be equally relevant, although not directly comparable, such as data from the UNESCO Interactive Atlas of the World's Languages in Danger (2009), available at http://www.unesco.org/culture/ich/index.php?pg=00206

b. Linguistic Diversity Index: The highest possible value, 1, indicates total diversity (that is, no two people have the same mother tongue) while the lowest possible value, 0, indicates no diversity at all (that is, everyone has the same mother tongue). The computation of the diversity index is based on the population of each language as a proportion of the total population.

c. Includes Montenegro for number of living languages, linguistic diversity index and type of language taught in school.

d. Country for which IBE's designation of either 'national' or 'official' language(s) overlaps completely with Ethnologue's designation of 'official' language(s).

e. Country for which a comparison between Ethnologue's official language designation and IBE's coded timetable information was possible, the result of which highlighted certain inconsistencies

f. Country for which IBE's collected national timetables do not stipulate the exact name(s) of the language(s) taught in the curriculum, which cannot be compared with Ethnologue's designation of 'official' language(s).

g. There are two offical languages for the federal state and 16 official languages for Indian states in India.

h. Combining previous estimates of instructional time for national/official languages.

i. Referring to time devoted to non-official indigenous languages.

j. Referring to time allocated to non-official exogenous languages.

… Data not available

Table 8. Translations[1]

Country or Territory	1995	1996	1997	1998	1999	2000	2001	2002	2003	2004	2005	Published translations[b] — Major languages into which translated (Target languages) 2005 — First language	Second language	Third language	for first target language 2005 — First language	Second language	Third language
Albania	94	110	41	41	149	177	231	258	303	347	384	Albanian	English	Serbian	English	French	Italian
Australia	.	.	.	.	.	.	.	.	.	.	.	English	Chinese	Greek, Italian	Chinese, French	Greek, Italian	German, Japanese
Austria	292	269	316	559	433	250	290	279	193	195	236	German	English	Slovenian	English	Italian	French
Belarus	267	308	287	213	219	215	221	240	140	257	331	Russian	Belarusian	English	English	German	Belorusian
Belgium	909	1066	1,099	1,130	1,349	1,207	1,066	1,243	1,522	1,624	1,177	Dutch	French	English	English	French	German
Brazil	1,253	2033	2,577	1,658	3,145	2,983	3,201	2,857	.	.	662	Portuguese	English	French	English	French	German
Bulgaria	1,502	1225	894	1,344	1,077	715	.	742	1,138	1,134	1,251	Bulgarian	English	Russian	English	Russian	French
Canada	1,029	994	1,094	1,201	1,525	1,292	1,166	1,161	1,507	1,325	1,614	French	English	Spanish	English	Spanish	Italian
Croatia	534	648	833	808	706	934	1,334	1,398	1,582	1,962	1,873	Croatian	English	German	English	German	French
Cyprus	.	.	.	.	.	.	.	.	.	.	.	English	Greek	Turkish	Greek	Turkish	…
Czech Republic	2,643	2775	3,113	3,181	3,303	3,477	3,702	3,655	4,082	4,159	4,324	Czech	English	German	English	German	French
Denmark	2,121	2546	2,574	2,859	3,261	3,291	3,120	3,104	3,167	3,116	2,776	Danish	English	German	English	Swedish	Norwegian
Egypt	.	.	.	393	358	464	425	313	.	.	325	Arabic	…	…	English	French	Spanish
Estonia	725	774	903	982	962	1,291	1,364	1,373	1,454	1,524	1,332	Estonian	Russian	English	English	Russian	German, French
Finland	1,901	1,857	1,977	2,003	2,265	2,173	2,025	2,060	2,005	2,106	2,340	Finnish	Swedish	English	English	Swedish	French
France	6,609	7292	7,879	8,565	8,718	8,989	9,504	9,501	9,857	11,533	10,306	French	English	German	English	Japanese	German
Germany	9,143	10,354	9,827	10,263	10,756	10,831	11,130	10,372	.	.	10,093	German	English	French	English	French	Italian
Greece	1,664	.	.	.	1,633	2,044	2,270	2,515	2,443	2,619	2,193	Greek	English	French	English	French	German
Hungary	2,036	1,425	2,403	2,430	2,672	2,770	2,706	2,323	2,699	2,756	2,580	Hungarian	English	French	English	German	French
India	283	289	331	459	611	699	590	372	488	551	312	English	Tamil	Malayalam	Bengali	Hindi	Sanskrit
Israel	25	54	170	256	438	776	966	449	468	530	590	Hebrew	English	French	English	French	German
Kuwait	.	.	.	.	.	.	.	.	.	.	.	Arabic[d]	English[d]	French[d]	English[d]	French[d]	German[d]
Italy	2,585	2,196	2,615	2,825	3,083	2,414	2,799	2,462	2,586	2,534	.	Italian[d]	…	…	English[d]	French[d]	German[d]
Japan	5,445	5,431	5,754	5,743	5,561	5,444	5,782	6,333	6,470	6,742	6,860	Japanese	English	Italian	English	French	German
Latvia	250	234	317	370	293	324	406	349	449	512	544	Latvian	…	…	English	German	Russian
Lithuania	563	720	806	898	851	720	654	736	707	881	759	Lithuanian	English	Polish	English	German	French
Macedonia (TFYR)	158	200	139	268	189	103	.	302	246	317	313	Macedonian	Albanian	English	English	French	Russian
Moldova (Rep.)	84	92	119	133	135	142	192	294	311	.	273	Russian	Moldavian	English	Moldavian	English	German, Greek, Italian, Yiddish
Netherlands	4,960	4,620	4,480	4,024	.	.	5,768	5,939	6,119	5,921	5,782	Dutch	English	Danish	English	German	French
New Zealand	.	.	.	.	.	.	.	.	.	.	.	Maori	English	Chinese	English	…	…

for second target language			Overall			Most frequently translated authors[c]						Country or Territory
First language	Second language	Third language	First language	Second language	Third language	Name	Worldwide number of translations	Worldwide number of countries translating	Name	Worldwide number of translations	Worldwide number of countries translating	
2005			2005			1979-1989			1995-2005			
Albanian	...	...	English	French	Italian	Hoxha, Enver	947	30	Dostoevsky, Fedor / Freud, Sigmund	715 / 384	46 / 42	Albania
English	...	...	English	Chinese	French	Wilson, Lorraine			Baum, Lyman Frank	174	38	Australia
German	Farsi	French	English	German	French, Italian	Christie, Agatha	72	18	Mankell, Henning	480	31	Austria
Russian	Polish	French	English	Russian	German	...			Christie, Agatha	2,388	46	Belarus
English	Dutch	German	English	French	German	Vandersteen, Willy	328	5	Horowitz, Anthony	186	22	Belgium
Portugese	French	...	English	French	Portugese	Christie, Agatha	2,615	39	Steel, Danielle	1,911	41	Brazil
Bulgarian	Russian	German	English	Russian	French	Živkov, Todor			Roberts, Nora	1,518	36	Bulgaria
French	German	Italian	English	French	Spanish	Joannes Paulus II, papa	2,615	39	Stine, Robert L.	1,648	32	Canada
Croatian	Italian	Polish	English	German	Croatian	...	1,550	24	Stine, Robert L.	1,648	32	Croatia
English	Turkish	Russian	Greek	English	Turkish	Frankl, Viktor Emil	1,721	26	Nikita, Eleni S.	12	1	Cyprus
Czech	German	Slovak	English	German	Czech	...	2,121	41	Vandenberg, Patricia	684	5	Czech Republic
Danish	French	German, Kalaallisut, Russian, Swedish	English	Danish	Swedish	Grover, Marshall	3,269	33	Milne, Alan Alexander	593	31	Denmark
...	...	...	English	French	Spanish	Christie, Agatha	98	6	Stine, Robert L.	1,648	32	Egypt
Estonian	English	German	English	Estonian	German	...	1,216		Cartland, Barbara	988	24	Estonia
Finnish	English, Russian	Danish, Latin, Norwegian	English	Swedish	French	Christie, Agatha	78	48	Milne, Alan Alexander	593	31	Finland
French	German	Italian	English	Japanese	German	Cartland, Barbara	13	24	Christie, Agatha	2,388	46	France
German	French	Russian	English	German	French	Blyton, Enid	1,550	24	Blyton, Enid	1,250	33	Germany
Greek	English	Ancient Greek	English	French	German	Verne, Jules	159	26	Hargreaves, Roger	295	9	Greece
Italian	...	...	English	German	French	Lenin, Vladimir	364	16	Courths-Mahler, Hedwig	607	6	Hungary
English	Russian	Malayalam	English	Bengali	Hindi	Vivekananda, Swami			Tagore, Rabindranath	240	38	India
Hebrew	Russian	...	English	French	German	Shakespeare, William / Aleichem, Shalom			Stine, Robert L.	1,648	32	Israel
English[d]	...	...	English[d]	Arabic[d]	German[d]	Euripides			Brown, Simon	72	23	Kuwait
...	...	...	English[d]	French[d]	German[d]	Cartland, Barbara			Shakespeare, William	1,608	53	Italy
Japanese	German	...	English	French	German	Mather, Anne	2,615	39	Roberts, Nora	1,518	36	Japan
...	...	...	English	German	Russian	...	13	6	Steel, Danielle	1,911	41	Latvia
Lithuanian	Russian	...	English	German	French	...	1,550	24	Christie, Agatha	2,388	46	Lithuania
Macedonian	Arabic	Turkish	English	French	Macedonian	...	1,216	48	Acovski, Duško	56	1	Macedonia (TFYR)
English	Russian	French	Moldavian	English	Russian	...	414	6	Singer, Mihaela	27	1	Moldova (Rep.)
Dutch	French	Bulgarian, German, Spanish	English	German	French	Christie, Agatha			Steel, Danielle	1,911	41	Netherlands
Maori	German	Chinese, Swedish	English	Maori	German	Cowley, Joy			Randell, Beverley	97	3	New Zealand

Table 8. Translations[1]

Country or Territory	Published translationsb											Major languages into which translated (Target languages)			for first target language		
												First language	Second language	Third language	First language	Second language	Third language
	1995	1996	1997	1998	1999	2000	2001	2002	2003	2004	2005	2005			2005		
Norway	1,181	1,316	1,759	1,902	1,791	1,340	1,936	2,032	2,092	2,080	2,055	Norwegian, Bokmål	Norwegian, Nynorsk	English	English	Swedish	Danish
Poland	2,876	3,623	3,760	3,917	3,792	4,300	5,784	4,041	4,367	4,192	3,644	Polish	English	German	English	German	French
Romania	769	910	802	1,054	948	886	1,146	.	.	1,162	1,472	Romanian	English	French	English	French	German
Russian Federationa	3,534	3,214	2,942	3,132	3,133	3,954	4,381	4,603	4,871	6,239	9,101	Russian	English	Bashkir	English	French	German
Slovak Republic	976	472	605	912	961	.	958	776	737	1,024	1,083	Slovak	Czech	Hungarian	English	German	French
Slovenia	733	877	932	978	957	866	750	778	838	989	1,009	Slovenian	English	German, French	English	German	French
Spain	6,728	6,399	6,850	7,802	9,403	9,647	10,161	9,313	11,507	9,507	10,640	Spanish	Catalan	English	English	French	German
Switzerland	1,076	1,041	1,041	1,226	1,062	.	762	1,135	997	930	1,046	German	French	English	English	French	Italian
Tunisia	.	.	.	.	.	.	.	.	.	.	.	Arabic	French	English, Italian	French	German	English

Source:

1. Index Translationum, based on available data reported regularly by countries as of 20 August 2009. Language denominations are based on ISO/DIS 639-3.5 and SIL.

Notes:

a. Update ongoing based on the new data received in 2008 and 2009.

b. UIS estimates are provided in cases in which the reported data do not seem to be coherent with the overall trend of translations.

c. In some cases, where the name sorted out by the Index seems to result from bias in data collection, the second best result has been retained as the accurate one.

d. 2004 figures.

... Data not available

. Not applicable

Major languages translated (Original languages)						Most frequently translated authors[c]						
for second target language			Overall									
First language	Second language	Third language	First language	Second language	Third language	Name	Worldwide number of translations	Worldwide number of countries translating	Name	Worldwide number of translations	Worldwide number of countries translating	
2005			2005			1979-1989			1995-2005			**Country or Territory**
French	Danish, English	Swedish	English	Swedish	Danish	Cartland, Barbara			Lindgren, Astrid	829	40	Norway
Polish	English, German	French, Serbian	English	German	French	Shakespeare, William	2,121	41	Christie, Agatha	2,388	46	Poland
Romanian	German	French	English	French	German	Ceaușescu, Nicolae	2,615	39	Villiers, Gérard de	203	11	Romania
Russian	Bashkir	…	English	French	German	…	12	3	Chase, James Hadley	578	22	Russian Federation[a]
English	Slovak	German	English	German	Slovak	…			Dailey, Janet	180	18	Slovak Republic
Slovenian	…	…	English	German	French	…			Cartland, Barbara	988	24	Slovenia
Spanish	English	French	English	French	Spanish	Verne, Jules			Verne, Jules	1,352	50	Spain
German	English	Italian	English	German	French	Christie, Agatha	2,121	41	Simenon, Georges	567	34	Switzerland
Arabic	…	…	French	Arabic	German	Marchal, Guy	2,615	39	Rousseau, Jean-Jacques	174	35	Tunisia

Table 9. Education and literacy[1]

Country or Territory	Compulsory education (age group) 2007	Legal guarantee of free education[2]	School life expectancy (expected years of schooling from primary to tertiary education) 1991	School life expectancy 2007	Pre-primary and other ECCE %	Primary %	Primary GPI (F/M)	Secondary %	Secondary GPI (F/M)	Tertiary %	Tertiary GPI (F/M)	Private: Pre-primary and other ECCE	Private: Primary	Private: Secondary	Private: Tertiary
Arab States															
Algeria	6–14	Yes	9.99	12.77**, -2	...	109.65	0.94	83.22**, -2	1.08**, -2	24.02	1.40	34.09	...	...	...
Bahrain	6–14	Yes	13.62	15.14**, -1	54.87-1	119.50-1	1.00-1	102.09-1	1.04-1	32.05-1	2.46-1	100.00-1	24.74-1	16.52-1	...
Djibouti	6–15	No	...	4.72**	3.16+1	46.51	0.86	25.35	0.69	2.63	0.69	89.01+1	13.64+1	12.20+1	...
Egypt	6–14	Yes	9.64	...	17.24	104.65	0.95	...	...	34.75**, -2	...	29.76	7.79	...	...
Iraq	6–11	Yes	9.81	9.69**, -2	5.76**, -2	99.45**, -2	0.83**, -2	45.33**, -2	0.66**, -2	15.79**, -2	0.59**, -2	...	...	...	...
Jordan	6–15	Yes	12.46	13.07**	31.61	95.72	1.02	89.34	1.03	39.91	1.10	91.89	32.57	17.01	30.57
Kuwait	6–14	Yes	...	12.51**, -1	76.59	98.49	0.98	90.79	1.02	17.56-1	2.32-1	39.57-1	34.46-1	29.27-1	25.63-1
Lebanon	6–14	Yes	11.90	13.20**	67.50+1	95.38	0.97	81.06	1.12	51.55	1.20	80.33+1	69.76+1	56.24+1	54.32+1
Libyan Arab Jamahiriya	6–14	Yes	12.93	...	8.88-1	110.37-1	0.95-1	93.53-1	1.17-1	...	...	16.92-1	4.65-1	2.16-1	...
Mauritania	6–14	Yes	4.13	8.20**	...	103.24	1.06	25.16**	0.89**	3.97	0.36-1	77.80**, -2	9.24	16.78*, -1	...
Morocco	6–14	Yes	6.49	10.49**	59.70	107.24	0.90	55.85	0.86**	11.31	0.89	96.32	8.37	5.20-1	10.40
Oman	...	Yes	8.17	11.51**	31.16	80.33	1.01	89.77	0.96	25.49	1.18	31.00	6.16	1.34	24.71-1
Palestinian A. T.	6–15	...	...	13.19	29.90	80.39	1.00	92.44	1.06	46.16	1.22	99.75	10.44	4.61	55.25
Qatar	6–17	Yes	12.39	13.60	...	109.42	0.99	103.47	0.98	15.93	2.87	88.29	49.05	34.16	30.84
Saudi Arabia	6–11	Yes	7.84	13.18**, -2	...	98.14	0.96*	93.92	0.91*, -2	30.24-1	1.46-1	48.89	8.21	11.39	...
Sudan[c]	6–13	Yes	4.12	...	23.06	66.37	0.86	33.35	0.93	...	...	37.88	3.71	9.85	...
Syrian Arab Republic	6–14	Yes	9.82	...	10.04	126.25	0.96	72.08	0.97	...	...	71.96	4.15	3.84	...
Tunisia	6–16	Yes	10.45	13.98**	...	104.65	0.97	88.04	1.10**, -1	30.81	1.51	...	1.44	4.66	1.07-1
United Arab Emirates	6–14	Yes	11.37	...	84.68	106.53	0.99	92.41**	1.03**	22.85+1	2.32+1	77.55	66.78	48.78**	58.24+1
Yemen	6–14	Yes	5.14	8.65**, -2	...	87.33-2	0.74-2	45.63-2	0.49-2	9.39**, -1	0.37**, -1	48.96-2	2.33-2	2.18-2	14.85-2
Sub-Saharan Africa															
Angola	6–11	No	4.04	...	...	...	...	...	...	2.87-1	...	...	...	...	33.93-1
Benin	6–11	No	3.76	8.37**, -2	...	95.91-1	0.83-1	32.48**, -2	0.57**, -2	5.11-1	...	37.48-2	13.14-1	25.15**, -2	...
Botswana	6–15	No	9.62	11.93**, -2	15.37-2	106.73-2	0.99-2	76.46-2	1.05-2	5.12-2	1.00-2	95.73-2	...	...	100.00-2
Burkina Faso	6–16	No	2.73	5.20	2.95	65.31	0.84	15.51	0.73	2.50	0.46	...	13.10+1	42.84+1	17.22+1
Burundi	7–12	No	4.89	8.19**	2.18	114.46	0.93	15.24	0.72	1.90	0.46	46.46	1.14	6.96	31.72**, -2
Cameroon	6–11	No	8.27	8.98**	21.00	109.64	0.86	25.15*	0.79*	7.15	0.79	62.29	22.12	28.10*	12.40
Cape Verde	6–11	No	...	11.38**	52.60	101.45	0.94	79.35	1.18	8.94	1.21	...	0.35	12.04	54.91
Central African Republic	6–15	No	4.76	...	3.22	70.67	0.70	...	...	1.10-1	0.28-1	35.25-2	12.96+1	...	...
Chad	6–11	Yes	3.44	5.87**, -2	...	73.98	0.70	18.83	0.45	1.16**, -2	0.14**, -2	33.59-1	23.06-1	...	...
Comoros	6–13	No	5.83	...	...	85.42**, -2	0.88**, -2	35.14**, -2	0.76**, -2	...	...	62.25**, -2	10.01**, -2	41.07**, -2	...
Congo	6–15	Yes	11.01	...	9.58	105.86	0.93	...	...	...	...	80.06	35.00	...	...
Congo (Dem. Rep.)	6–13	No	5.75	7.77**	2.72	85.13	0.81	33.35	0.53	4.07	0.35-1	68.71	11.16	...	...
Côte d'Ivoire	6–15	No	5.82	...	3.22	72.13	0.79	...	...	7.89	0.50	46.37	11.71	...	36.30
Equatorial Guinea	7–11	Yes	10.83	...	...	124.24	0.95	...	...	...	...	49.19-2	29.91-2	...	...
Eritrea	7–14	No	...	...	13.64	54.95	0.83	29.24	0.70	...	...	44.80	8.76	5.19	...
Ethiopia	7–12	No	2.70	7.61**	2.94	90.75	0.88	30.47	0.67	2.75	0.34	95.33	...	...	16.32
Gabon	6–16	Yes	10.76	...	...	...	...	...	...	...	...	...	...	...	...
Gambia	7–12	Yes	...	...	...	86.42	1.05	48.77	0.90	...	...	100.00	17.52+1	25.36+1	...
Ghana	6–14	Yes	6.65	9.29**	77.65+1	97.67	0.99	49.25**	0.88**	5.84	0.54	19.22+1	17.29+1	15.95+1	...
Guinea	7–12	No	2.95	8.22-1	10.34	90.83	0.85	37.62**	0.57**	5.29-1	0.28-1	85.95	26.57	15.86-1	5.62-1
Guinea-Bissau	7–12	Yes	3.49	...	...	...	...	...	...	...	...	...	...	...	...
Kenya	6–13	No	9.27	10.46**	48.00	112.64	0.99	52.79	0.88	3.47	0.57	35.28	9.63	11.35	15.15
Lesotho	6–12	No	9.51	10.26-1	...	114.36-1	1.00-1	37.04-1	1.27-1	3.63-1	1.19-1	100.00-1	0.41-1	2.63-1	...
Liberia	6–11	No	3.23	...	124.74-1	83.37-1	0.89+1	...	...	...	...	23.69+1	29.74+1	...	...
Madagascar	6–10	Yes	6.22	9.42**	8.47	141.38	0.97	26.35**	0.95**	3.18	0.89	94.27	19.10	40.99**	14.04
Malawi	6–13	No	5.96	9.11**	...	116.50	1.04	28.27	0.83	0.49	0.51	...	1.08-1	10.36-1	...
Mali	7–15	Yes	2.02	7.24**	3.35	83.13	0.80	31.63	0.64	4.42	0.52**, -2	...	38.48	28.25	...
Mauritius	5–16	Yes	10.45	13.53**, -2	99.25	101.39	1.00	88.42**, -2	0.99**, -2	13.96+1	1.17+1	82.20	26.12	...	...
Mozambique	6–12	No	3.66	8.26**, -2	...	111.02	0.87	18.34	0.73	1.46-2	0.49-2	...	1.85	12.75	33.34-2
Namibia	7–16	Yes	11.65	10.77**, -1	...	109.21	0.99	58.99	1.17	6.37-1	0.88-1	...	4.25	4.92	82.48-1
Niger	7–12	Yes	2.02	4.02**	2.03	53.34	0.75	10.61	0.61	1.04	0.33	28.56	3.85	15.02	29.06
Nigeria	6–14	Yes	6.68	...	15.21-1	96.75-1	0.85-1	31.86-1	0.81-1	10.15-2	0.69-2	...	5.00-1	11.85-1	...
Rwanda	7–12	Yes	6.07	8.58**, -2	...	147.36	1.02	18.08	0.89	2.56**, -2	0.62**, -2	...	1.68	41.07	...
Saint Helena	...	...	...	...	...	...	...	...	...	...	...	...	...	...	...
Sao Tome and Principe	7–12	Yes	...	10.44	...	127.36	1.00	49.77	1.08	...	...	0.52+1	...	...	...
Senegal	7–12	Yes	4.46	7.18**	...	83.54	1.00	26.28**	0.76**	6.71**	0.51**	51.05	12.38	23.48-2	...
Seychelles[d]	6–15	Yes	...	14.71*	108.66*	125.34*	0.99*	111.80*	1.13*	...	...	6.03	6.18	5.77	...
Sierra Leone	6–11	No	5.07	...	...	147.08	0.90	31.63	0.69	...	...	50.25	3.13	6.93	...
Somalia	6–13	No	1.22	...	...	...	...	...	...	...	...	...	...	...	...
South Africa	7–15	No	11.92	13.08**, -1	...	102.50	0.97	97.08**	1.05**	15.41-1	1.24-1	5.65	2.47	2.84-2	...

Pupil/teacher ratio	Female teachers as % of total teachers	Pupil/teacher ratio	Female teachers as % of total teachers	Pupil/teacher ratio	Female teachers as % of total teachers	Pupil/teacher ratio	Female teachers as % of total teachers	Youth % (15–24)		Adults % (15 and over)		Country or Territory
Pre-primary and other ECCE		**Primary**		**Secondary**		**Tertiary**		1985–1994[b]	2000–2007[b]	1985–1994[b]	2000–2007[b]	
2007												
												Arab States
24.80	67.40	23.96	52.86	...	...	28.46	35.15**	74.33	92.45**	49.63	75.39**	Algeria
15.95⁻¹	99.92⁻¹	...	...	...	...	24.92**,⁻²	40.74**,⁻²	96.94	99.77**	84.01	88.76**	Bahrain
16.68**,⁺¹	87.18**,⁺¹	34.03⁺¹	25.77⁺¹	34.27⁺¹	23.31⁺¹	18.12	16.53	...	...	...	...	Djibouti
24.81	98.93	27.08**	55.80**	...	41.74**	...	...	63.33	84.88	44.42	66.37	Egypt
15.51**,⁻²	100.00**,⁻²	20.53**,⁻²	72.16**,⁻²	18.79**,⁻²	58.28**,⁻²	22.09**,⁻²	35.10**,⁻²	...	84.80	...	74.05	Iraq
19.29	99.98	...	...	...	...	25.47	23.03	...	98.98	...	91.13	Jordan
11.90	99.80	9.61	88.43	9.49	53.46**	18.89**,⁻¹	27.34**,⁻¹	87.46	98.45	74.49	94.46	Kuwait
15.83⁺¹	99.39⁺¹	13.87⁺¹	85.67⁺¹	8.94⁺¹	54.50⁺¹	8.43⁺¹	38.87⁺¹	...	98.71	...	89.61	Lebanon
8.95⁻¹	96.38⁻¹	...	...	...	...	...	...	94.88**	98.88**	76.28**	86.78**	Libyan Arab Jamahiriya
19.35**,⁻²	100.00**,⁻²	42.51	34.62	26.58**	10.38**	28.77⁻¹	4.25⁻¹	...	66.36**	...	55.80**	Mauritania
17.48	61.07	27.38	47.23	...	...	19.99	19.35	58.43	75.14**	41.59	55.58**	Morocco
18.81	99.79	13.02**	62.70**	14.89**	55.63**	23.32	29.20	...	98.37**	...	84.37**	Oman
24.03	99.69	30.08	66.63	25.10	48.68	30.63	16.67	...	99.04	...	93.81	Palestinian A. T.
17.89⁻¹	99.32⁻¹	10.68⁻¹	85.49⁻¹	9.48⁻¹	56.15⁻¹	7.70	37.38	89.54	99.06	75.64	93.08	Qatar
10.94*	100.00*	11.23*	52.48*	11.13**,⁻²	52.63**,⁻²	22.76⁻¹	33.04⁻¹	87.86	96.99**	70.82	84.95**	Saudi Arabia
17.41	100.00	36.68	63.70	18.49	51.65	...	...	...	77.18	...	60.93	Sudan[c]
23.60	97.80	...	...	...	...	...	...	...	93.69**	...	83.12**	Syrian Arab Republic
...	...	18.15	53.14	15.91	44.99⁻²	18.00	41.39	...	95.68**	...	77.70**	Tunisia
20.79	99.71	17.19	84.50	12.88**	55.36**	16.44⁺¹	30.68⁺¹	82.47	95.01	71.24	90.03	United Arab Emirates
15.26⁻²	96.78⁻²	...	...	...	...	33.16**,⁻²	15.92**,⁻²	60.22	80.38**	37.09	58.86**	Yemen
												Sub-Saharan Africa
...	...	...	...	...	...	37.86⁻¹	...	...	72.18	...	67.41	Angola
49.13⁻¹	78.27⁻¹	43.62⁻¹	17.36⁻¹	...	...	...	...	39.88	52.42**	27.25	40.54**	Benin
22.32⁻²	54.75⁻²	24.24⁻²	77.63⁻²	13.64**,⁻²	53.88**,⁻²	20.70⁻²	36.67⁻²	89.26	94.12**	68.58	82.85**	Botswana
23.60	70.63**	48.92⁺¹	32.93⁺¹	30.33⁺¹	16.86⁺¹	18.61⁺¹	8.15⁺¹	20.18	39.26	13.57	28.73	Burkina Faso
36.77*	86.79*	52.00	52.75	27.99	24.41	15.51	14.46**,⁻²	53.56	73.33	37.38	59.30	Burundi
17.60	96.79	44.43	42.51	16.17**,⁻¹	26.41**,⁻¹	43.47	...	...	...	...	67.90	Cameroon
21.71	100.00	24.86	66.69	19.02	39.44	8.96	38.81	88.17	97.27**	62.80	83.78**	Cape Verde
34.37	91.92	89.62⁺¹	12.70⁺¹	...	...	...	...	48.20	58.52	33.62	48.57	Central African Republic
37.75**,⁻²	...	60.38	13.37	32.91**	...	9.52**,⁻²	3.18**,⁻²	16.96	44.44**	12.22	31.76**	Chad
...	...	34.98**,⁻²	32.85**,⁻²	13.81**,⁻²	12.97**,⁻²	...	...	77.28**	89.45**	62.70**	75.06**	Comoros
20.49	94.43	58.48	44.32	...	14.37**,⁻²	...	...	...	...	...	...	Congo
25.55	95.37	38.30	25.91	15.67	10.11	14.06	...	...	70.42	...	67.17	Congo (Dem. Rep.)
17.04	97.46	41.00	24.50	...	...	...	...	48.51	60.72	34.14	48.73	Côte d'Ivoire
23.90	87.43	27.62	34.37	...	...	...	...	...	94.86	...	86.99	Equatorial Guinea
35.09	96.89	47.87	47.94	49.35	11.77	...	...	...	86.34**	...	64.15**	Eritrea
27.33	61.56	...	...	...	...	25.19	9.24	33.59	49.90**	27.01	35.90**	Ethiopia
...	...	...	...	...	...	...	...	93.21	96.97**	72.23	86.17**	Gabon
...	...	40.88	33.14	22.72	15.87	...	...	...	...	...	...	Gambia
35.22⁺¹	83.61⁺¹	32.16⁺¹	33.03⁺¹	17.47⁺¹	22.08⁺¹	34.91	11.14	...	77.78**	...	65.03**	Ghana
33.32	50.12	45.36	26.09	38.15**	6.34**	29.68⁻¹	3.06⁻¹	...	46.55	...	29.48	Guinea
...	...	...	...	...	...	...	...	...	...	...	...	Guinea-Bissau
22.16	87.31	45.56**	44.15**	26.64**	39.64**	...	...	...	80.32	...	73.61	Kenya
18.70⁻¹	99.13⁻¹	40.41⁻¹	77.53⁻¹	25.23⁻¹	54.74⁻¹	13.32⁻¹	47.49⁻¹	...	...	...	82.22	Lesotho
142.24⁺¹	51.52⁺¹	23.83⁺¹	12.07⁺¹	...	...	...	...	51.41**	71.78**	40.84**	55.55**	Liberia
30.83	97.47	48.73	60.60	24.35**	47.13**,⁻¹	19.23	30.05	...	70.24	...	70.68	Madagascar
...	...	66.82	37.72	...	...	7.50	33.57**	59.02	82.99**	48.54	71.79**	Malawi
36.15	93.38	51.67	26.59	35.56	...	52.04	...	...	38.82	...	26.18	Mali
14.51	100.00	21.51	64.71	17.21**,⁻²	56.45	...	...	61.34**	96.25**	51.21**	87.41**	Mauritius
...	...	64.83	33.51	36.88	16.45	9.40⁻²	21.17⁻²	...	52.94**	...	44.38**	Mozambique
...	...	29.95	64.67**	24.62	49.79**	17.28⁻¹	42.20⁻¹	88.11	92.66**	75.82	87.96**	Namibia
23.40	87.66	39.67	42.93	27.25	16.94	10.24⁻¹	6.21**,⁻¹	...	36.55	...	28.67	Niger
...	...	40.42⁻¹	50.47⁻¹	31.85⁻¹	38.24⁻¹	...	...	71.19	86.68**	55.45	72.01**	Nigeria
...	...	69.29	53.45	22.02	53.36	14.52**,⁻²	12.11**,⁻²	74.90	77.63	57.85	64.90	Rwanda
...	...	...	...	...	...	...	...	...	...	...	...	Saint Helena
22.81**,⁻¹	...	30.79**,⁻¹	55.40**,⁻¹	21.71**,⁻¹	12.53**,⁻¹	.	.	93.85	95.23**	73.24	87.93**	Sao Tome and Principe
17.47	67.92	34.21	27.97	25.25**	15.43**	.	.	37.87	50.85	26.87	41.89	Senegal
14.84	100.00	12.47	85.37	13.29	55.27	.	.	98.81	99.06	87.81	91.84	Seychelles[d]
20.27	79.17	43.73	25.68	23.90	16.04	...	...	...	54.12**	...	38.10**	Sierra Leone
...	...	...	...	...	...	...	...	...	...	...	...	Somalia
...	...	30.98	76.52	29.02**	53.20**	16.78⁻¹	50.77⁻¹	...	95.43**	...	88.00**	South Africa

Statistical Annex

Table 9. Education and literacy[1]

Country or Territory	Compulsory education (age group)	Legal guarantee of free education[2]	School life expectancy 1991	School life expectancy 2007	Pre-primary and other ECCE %	Primary %	Primary GPI (F/M)	Secondary %	Secondary GPI (F/M)	Tertiary %	Tertiary GPI (F/M)	Private Pre-primary and other ECCE	Private Primary	Private Secondary	Private Tertiary
	2007		1991	2007				2007					2007		
Swaziland	6–12	Yes	9.27	10.55**,-1	16.76**,-2	113.43	0.93	54.42	0.89	4.16-1	0.98-1	.	.	...	...
Tanzania (United Rep.)	7–13	No	5.44	...	34.53+1	111.85	0.98	...	...	1.48	0.48	9.61+1	0.98	...	...
Togo	6–15	No	7.58	9.00**	3.81	97.10	0.86	39.35	0.53**	5.20	...	55.14	42.24	31.33-1	...
Uganda	6–12	No	5.60	...	3.54	116.17	1.01	22.53**	0.83**	...	...	100.00	10.09	...	...
Zambia	7–13	No	7.67	...	...	118.96	0.97	43.14	0.89	...	...	...	3.13	...	...
Zimbabwe	6–12	No	10.59	...	...	101.16-1	0.99-1	39.97-1	0.93-1	...	...	...	...	...	...
Central and South Asia															
Afghanistan	7–15	Yes	2.46	...	...	102.56	0.63	27.60	0.38	...	...	...	...	...	...
Armenia	7–14	Yes	10.44	11.96	...	109.54	1.03	89.05	1.05	34.20	1.20	1.47	1.55	1.44	22.76
Azerbaijan	6–16	Yes	10.60	12.76**	29.92*	115.83*	0.99*	88.81*	0.96*	15.24*	0.88*	0.15	0.26	0.46	16.47
Bangladesh	6–10	Yes	6.10	7.96	...	91.43	1.08	43.34	1.06	7.25	0.57	...	42.45	95.63	49.23
Bhutan	...	Yes	1.52	10.33**,-1	1.21+1	111.03+1	1.00+1	56.39+1	0.93+1	5.28	0.51	100.00+1	2.51+1	9.17+1	...
Georgia	6–14	Yes	12.37	12.67	...	99.03	0.97	90.17	1.00**	37.26	1.12	...	6.45	4.83	21.20
India[c]	6–14	Yes	8.09	10.01**,-1	...	111.91-1	0.96-1	54.63-1	0.83-1	11.85-1	0.72-1	...	...	...	...
Iran (Islamic Rep.)	6–13	Yes	9.65	12.83**,-2	54.16	120.87	1.29	80.95-2	0.94-2	31.39	1.15	8.25	5.24	7.98**,-2	51.96
Kazakhstan	7–17	Yes	12.56	15.05	...	105.29	1.00	92.80	0.99	51.18	1.44	4.66+1	0.84+1	0.76+1	48.91
Kyrgyzstan	7–15	Yes	10.42	12.51	15.62	95.33	0.99	86.41	1.01	42.80	1.30	1.13	1.16	1.36	8.69
Maldives	6–12	No	...	12.26**,-1	85.01	110.61	0.97	83.10**,-1	1.07**,-1	...	...	90.20	1.24	12.23**,-1	...
Nepal	5–9	Yes	7.47	9.83**	57.11+1	126.32	0.99	42.64**	0.91**	11.33	...	62.57+1	10.25+1	14.36+1	41.97
Pakistan	5–9	No	4.52	7.13**	...	92.04	0.82	32.54	0.76	5.12*	0.85*	...	33.71-1	31.41	8.00-2
Sri Lanka[c]	5–13	No	11.22	...	...	109.24	1.00	...	...	...	...	...	...	...	...
Tajikistan	7–15	Yes	11.70	11.03**	...	99.76	0.96	83.57	0.84	19.75	0.38	.	.	.	...
Turkmenistan	7–15	Yes	12.13	...	...	...	...	...	...	...	...	...	...	...	...
Uzbekistan	7–17	Yes	11.58	11.56	...	95.48	0.97	102.41	0.98	9.80	0.71	0.54	.	.	...
East Asia															
Brunei Darussalam	6–15	No	12.55	13.90**	55.20	105.51	0.99	97.38	1.04	15.37	1.88	66.18	36.50	12.82	0.26
Cambodia	...	Yes	7.19	9.82**	11.44	119.20	0.93	40.37	0.82	5.35	0.56	29.72	0.75	1.97	58.44
China[g]	6–14	Yes	9.30	11.41**	41.61	112.33	0.99	77.33	1.01	22.89	1.01	34.26	3.84	8.32	...
Hong Kong (SAR China)	6–14	Yes	...	13.68-2	82.38	97.94-2	0.95-2	86.22	1.00	33.84	1.03	100.00	12.80	12.97	6.26
Macao (SAR China)	5–14	...	11.52	15.01	85.01	107.83	0.92	99.31	1.00	56.98	0.92	96.19	95.90	95.15	61.01
Indonesia	7–15	No	10.05	12.32	43.65	117.25	0.96	73.48	1.01	17.46	1.00	99.03	18.20	48.77	73.82
Japan	6–15	Yes	13.31	14.97**	101.79	100.16	1.00	100.88	1.00	58.06	0.88	67.36	1.01	19.12	79.65
Korea (Dem. People's Rep.)	6–15	Yes	...	...	...	...	...	...	...	...	...	...	...	...	...
Korea (Rep.)	6–14	Yes	13.63	16.87	106.24	106.54	0.98	98.30	0.93	94.67	0.67	78.11	1.29	32.13	80.15
Lao (People's Dem. Rep.)	6–10	No	7.02	9.36**	12.82	117.73	0.90	43.82	0.79	11.56	0.72	28.44	2.78	1.55	23.52
Malaysia	6–11	No	10.13	12.73-2	56.92-1	97.90-1	0.99-1	69.07-2	1.10-2	30.24-1	1.22-1	45.48-1	0.83-2	3.21-2	33.10-1
Mongolia	7–15	Yes	9.37	13.05	69.77	99.86	1.02	91.69	1.11	47.69	1.56	2.99	5.03	5.55	34.36
Myanmar	5–9	Yes	6.81	...	...	...	...	...	...	...	...	55.75	...	...	...
Philippines	6–12	Yes	10.81	11.78**,-1	46.28	109.39	0.98	83.26	1.10	28.47-1	1.24-1	41.63	7.98	20.28	65.78-1
Singapore	6–11	No	11.92	...	...	...	...	...	...	...	...	...	5.33	5.89	60.60
Thailand	6–14	Yes	8.72	13.93**	94.95+1	106.00	1.00	83.50	1.10	49.51	1.23	20.73+1	18.01+1	17.98	17.40**,-1
Timor-Leste	6–11	Yes	...	...	10.16-2	90.92	0.94	53.44-2	1.00-2	...	...	...	...	10.10	...
Viet Nam	6–14	Yes	7.52	...	...	...	...	...	...	...	...	56.81	0.53	11.39	11.77
Europe															
Albania	6–13	Yes	11.51	...	...	...	...	...	...	...	...	...	...	...	...
Andorra[d]	6–16	...	...	11.13**,-1	100.67*	88.19*	0.98*	82.45*	1.08*	9.89*,-1	1.25*,-1	1.99	1.63	3.12	...
Austria	6–14	Yes	13.91	15.20	91.59	100.98	0.99	101.62	0.96	51.07	1.20	27.37	5.21	9.68	14.09
Belarus	6–14	Yes	13.06	14.63	121.02	97.11	0.99	95.40	1.02	68.54	1.41	4.40	0.05	0.05	13.28
Belgium	6–18	Yes	13.95	16.01	121.98	102.68	1.00	110.06	0.97	62.48	1.26	52.50	54.26	68.35	55.82
Bosnia and Herzegovina	...	Yes	8.75	12.49**	...	97.83	0.93	85.50	1.03	36.85	...	...	...	...	...
Bulgaria	7–14	Yes	12.34	13.68	81.49	101.05	0.99	105.65	0.96	49.52	1.22	0.49	0.55	0.95	19.59
Croatia	7–14	Yes	11.05	13.65	51.80	98.89	1.00	91.68	1.03	45.78	1.23	11.14	0.21	1.30	5.06
Cyprus[d]	6–14	Yes	10.32	13.79*	79.63*	102.47*	0.99*	97.78*	1.02*	36.17*	0.99*	49.68	6.29	14.38	67.82
Czech Republic	6–15	Yes	11.88	15.17	114.68	100.56	0.99	95.71	1.01	54.82	1.26	1.42	1.26	7.79	12.12
Denmark	7–16	Yes	14.16	16.86	...	99.00	1.00	119.22	1.03	80.30	1.41	...	12.15	13.36	2.20
Estonia	7–15	Yes	12.76	15.83	...	98.97	0.99	99.77	1.02	65.04	1.63	2.77	2.76	2.34	83.76
Finland	7–16	Yes	15.17	17.13	63.86	97.59	1.00	111.32	1.05	93.81	1.23	8.63	1.33	6.82	10.63
France	6–16	Yes	14.30	16.23	113.08	110.28	0.99	113.43	1.01	55.57	1.27	12.83	14.88	25.59	17.08
Germany	6–18	Yes	14.61	...	107.04	104.24	1.00	99.72	0.98	...	...	63.45	3.34	8.37	...
Gibraltar	5–14	Yes	...	...	...	...	...	...	...	...	...	.	...	...	...

		Teaching Staff						Literacy rate[a]				
Pre-primary and other ECCE		Primary		Secondary		Tertiary		Youth % (15–24)		Adults % (15 and over)		
Pupil/teacher ratio	Female teachers as % of total teachers	Pupil/teacher ratio	Female teachers as % of total teachers	Pupil/teacher ratio	Female teachers as % of total teachers	Pupil/teacher ratio	Female teachers as % of total teachers	1985-1994[b]	2000-2007[b]	1985-1994[b]	2000-2007[b]	Country or Territory
				2007								
32.27**,-2	74.94**,-2	32.44	70.46	19.06	47.64	12.32-1	40.26-1	83.75	94.01**	67.24	83.82**	Swaziland
43.06	56.23	52.62+1	49.01**,+1	...	...	18.36	18.05	81.75	77.55**	59.11	72.31**	Tanzania (United Rep.)
25.46	91.65	39.14	12.09	35.51**	6.75**	69.15	10.85**	...	74.37	...	53.16	Togo
41.67-1	70.49-1	56.97	39.20	18.44**	21.80**	...	...	69.80	86.29**	56.11	73.60**	Uganda
...	...	49.34	48.04	42.63	39.00	...	...	66.38	75.09**	65.00	70.64**	Zambia
...	...	38.21-1	...	...	...	...	...	95.41	91.17**	83.51	91.17**	Zimbabwe
												Central and South Asia
...	...	42.77	27.69	31.56	27.59	...	...	...	34.26	...	28.00	Afghanistan
9.49	99.70	19.31	99.68	7.77	84.03	8.58	47.34	99.91	99.77**	98.75	99.48**	Armenia
8.73	99.99	11.63	86.61	7.82	66.12	8.23	40.43	...	100.00	...	99.50	Azerbaijan
...	89.42-2	44.75	40.44	25.24	19.77	17.91	17.56	44.68	72.13**	35.32	53.48**	Bangladesh
22.50**,-1	...	29.88+1	49.81-1	23.75+1	33.14+1	11.04-1	...	...	74.41	...	52.81	Bhutan
10.73	100.00	...	...	...	...	8.85	52.49	...	...	...	...	Georgia
40.31-1	100.00-1	...	...	...	...	...	...	61.90	82.09**	48.22	66.02**	India[c]
26.91-2	89.44-2	19.18	57.54	18.75-2	48.05-2	21.19	23.51	86.97	96.64	65.53	82.33	Iran (Islamic Rep.)
10.41+1	98.77+1	16.63+1	98.35+1	10.01+1	85.64+1	17.47+1	63.14+1	99.73	99.82**	97.53	99.62**	Kazakhstan
25.36	98.90	24.23	97.38	13.56	74.45	17.77	56.08	...	99.60**	...	99.30**	Kyrgyzstan
24.31	96.56	14.52	71.09	...	...	...	...	98.20	98.07**	96.02	97.05**	Maldives
41.29+1	92.63+1	37.82+1	35.50+1	40.95+1	14.85+1	32.30	...	49.60	79.31**	32.98	56.50**	Nepal
...	...	39.95	45.90	...	...	18.27*	37.21*	...	69.17	...	54.15	Pakistan
...	...	23.81	84.60	...	...	...	...	...	97.48	...	90.81	Sri Lanka[c]
12.63	100.00	21.61	64.15	16.54	49.06	18.98	31.88	99.70	99.86**	97.69	99.64**	Tajikistan
...	...	...	...	...	...	...	...	...	99.82**	...	99.51**	Turkmenistan
9.27	95.02	18.24	84.93	13.06	63.29	12.36	36.14	...	99.34	...	96.90	Uzbekistan
												East Asia
21.15	96.76	12.67	73.84	10.80	59.99	8.14	42.68	98.10	99.59**	87.80	94.85**	Brunei Darussalam
25.16	96.51	50.88	42.89	28.92	31.71	23.30-1	11.41-1	...	86.20**	...	76.32**	Cambodia
22.43	97.62	17.68	55.54	16.37	45.08**	19.11	43.17	94.28	99.26**	77.79	93.31**	China[g]
13.56	99.17	16.94	77.84	17.48**,-1	56.08**,-1	...	...	...	...	...	...	Hong Kong (SAR China)
19.50	99.58	20.35	88.13	20.55	59.46	13.84	31.25	...	99.64	...	93.50	Macao (SAR China)
13.32	96.49	18.82	57.58	13.04	48.89	14.14	40.89	96.21	96.65	81.52	91.98	Indonesia
28.30	97.80**,-1	18.49	64.88**,-1	12.22	...	7.82	17.90*,-1	...	...	...	...	Japan
...	...	...	...	...	...	...	...	...	...	...	...	Korea (Dem. People's Rep.)
18.67	99.36	25.59	76.55	18.06	52.51	15.90	31.51	...	...	...	...	Korea (Rep.)
16.74	99.18	30.12	47.20	23.60	42.78	24.75	33.30	...	83.93	...	72.70	Lao (People's Dem. Rep.)
22.63-2	95.90-2	16.08-1	67.78-1	16.99-2	63.23-2	18.82-1	48.16-1	95.56	98.30**	82.92	91.90**	Malaysia
29.03	99.79	31.60	94.86	19.75	73.72	16.27	56.05	...	95.44**	...	97.28**	Mongolia
18.67	99.45	29.11	82.63	32.78	83.07	47.58	82.21	...	94.52	...	89.89	Myanmar
32.87-1	96.99-1	33.67	87.27	35.13	76.23	21.27**,-2	55.70**,-2	96.58	94.41**	93.57	93.40**	Philippines
...	...	20.42	80.71	16.96	65.62	12.92	34.53	98.97	99.72**	89.10	94.43**	Singapore
24.34+1	78.45+1	15.99+1	59.98+1	21.22+1	55.25+1	32.13**,+1	68.07**,+1	...	98.18**	...	94.15**	Thailand
29.48-2	97.05-2	30.85	31.99	23.68-2	22.87	...	...	...	...	87.60	...	Timor-Leste
19.01	99.13	20.44	77.66	21.82	63.73	29.66	44.43	93.73	...	87.60	...	Viet Nam
												Europe
...	...	...	...	...	...	...	...	...	99.38**	...	99.04**	Albania
12.79	95.00	10.25	76.85	7.75-2	59.34-2	4.95-1	39.51-1	...	...	...	...	Andorra[d]
13.53	98.77	11.86	89.33	10.85	61.94	8.89	32.06	...	...	...	...	Austria
6.17	99.10	15.97	99.29	8.10	80.34	13.21	55.91	99.77	99.78**	97.88	99.71**	Belarus
13.94	98.02	11.20	79.75	10.04**,-1	57.42**,-1	14.97	42.14	...	...	...	...	Belgium
13.17	94.49	...	...	...	...	...	...	...	99.79	...	96.66	Bosnia and Herzegovina
11.45	99.68	15.94	93.30	11.55	77.85	12.06	45.44	...	97.48**	...	98.28**	Bulgaria
14.17	99.30	16.69	91.11	9.30	67.93	10.71	41.22	99.64	99.65**	96.70	98.72**	Croatia
17.42	99.20	15.63	82.07	10.68	62.01	12.19	39.86	99.62	99.85**	94.36	97.72**	Cyprus[d]
13.59	99.84	18.73	94.21	10.55-1	64.84-1	14.99-1	37.55-1	...	...	...	...	Czech Republic
...	...	...	...	...	...	...	...	...	...	...	...	Denmark
7.52-1	99.64-1	12.83	93.62	9.93	77.35	10.74**,-1	48.47**,-1	99.87	99.79**	99.73	99.79**	Estonia
11.43	96.87	15.03	76.96	12.40**,-2	66.82**,-2	16.45**,-1	46.35**,-1	...	...	...	...	Finland
18.34	81.90	18.95	82.09	12.10	58.81	...	...	...	...	...	...	France
11.67	98.04	13.63	84.03	13.46	57.18	...	35.57	...	...	...	...	Germany
...	...	...	...	...	...	...	...	...	...	...	...	Gibraltar

Table 9. Education and literacy[1]

Country or Territory	Compulsory education (age group)	Legal guarantee of free education[2]	School life expectancy (expected years of schooling from primary to tertiary education) 1991	School life expectancy 2007	Gross Enrolment Ratio (GER) Pre-primary and other ECCE %	Primary %	Primary GPI (F/M)	Secondary %	Secondary GPI (F/M)	Tertiary %	Tertiary GPI (F/M)	Private Enrolment as % of Total Enrolment Pre-primary and other ECCE	Private Primary	Private Secondary	Private Tertiary
	2007		1991	2007				2007						2007	
Greece	6–14	Yes	13.38	16.48	68.93	101.31	1.00	101.82	0.95	90.81	1.10	3.09	7.17	5.19	...
Holy See	...	...	.	.	.	.	.	.	.	.	.	.	.	.	.
Hungary	7–16	Yes	11.39	15.14	87.94	95.74	0.98	95.53	1.00	69.10	1.46	5.34	7.34	10.77	15.46
Iceland	6–16	Yes	15.31	18.32	96.64	97.46	1.00	110.56	1.06	73.43	1.86	8.82	1.57	6.80	20.60
Ireland	6–15	Yes	12.72	17.83	...	104.44	1.00	113.47	1.07	61.06	1.27	...	0.91	0.67	8.54
Israel	5–15	Yes	13.10	15.56	97.54	110.81	1.01	91.51	1.00	60.41	1.32	5.38	.	.	86.07
Italy	6–14	Yes	13.46	16.47	103.28	104.64	0.99	101.14	0.99	68.12	1.40	32.15	6.98	5.01	7.71
Latvia	7–15	Yes	12.39	14.55**	88.90⁻¹	95.38	0.97	97.92**	1.01**	71.31	1.85	3.16	1.23⁻¹	1.08**	95.79
Liechtenstein	6–14	Yes	...	14.58*	102.21*	109.62*	0.99*	106.09*	0.87*	31.19*	0.49*	3.56	4.23	4.20	100.00
Lithuania	7–15	Yes	12.71	15.75	69.46	95.30	0.99	97.81	0.99	75.56	1.57	0.28	0.56	0.65	9.26
Luxembourg	6–15	Yes	11.06	13.53⁻¹	87.10	102.36	1.00	97.21	1.04	10.21⁻¹	1.12⁻¹	6.67	7.66	18.11	...
Macedonia (TFYR)	7–14	Yes	11.00	12.41	39.51	95.10	1.00	84.28	0.97	35.51	1.27	...	...	0.63	17.06
Malta	5–15	Yes	12.91	14.84⁻²	97.25⁻²	100.12⁻²	0.98⁻²	99.46⁻²	1.00⁻²	31.60⁻²	1.35⁻²	38.57⁻²	37.71⁻²	27.86⁻²	...
Moldova (Rep.)[d, e]	7–15	Yes	11.88	12.14*	70.14*	94.42*	0.98*	88.55*	1.03*	41.20*	1.39*	0.14	0.83	1.11	15.41*
Monaco[f]	6–16	No	...	...	...	...	...	...	...	.	.	19.53⁺¹	24.84⁺¹	22.32⁺¹	...
Montenegro	...	...	...	...	...	...	...	...	...	...	...	...	...	...	...
Netherlands	5–17	Yes	14.86	16.63	101.63	106.76	0.98	119.58	0.98	60.32	1.09	...	...	...	...
Norway	6–16	Yes	14.27	17.54	92.46	98.72	1.00	112.81	0.99	76.24	1.57	44.27	2.20	6.62⁻²	13.73
Poland	7–15	Yes	12.23	15.25	60.33	97.05	1.00	99.85	0.99	66.95	1.40	9.35	2.05	3.10	32.20
Portugal	6–14	Yes	12.16	15.43	79.44	115.11	0.95	101.03	1.07	55.96	1.22	47.64	11.08	15.67	24.93
Romania	7–14	Yes	11.46	14.34	72.35	104.63	0.99	87.46	0.99	58.26	1.33	1.63	0.33	1.00	30.97
Russian Federation	6–15	Yes	12.40	13.72**	88.41	95.76	1.00	84.31	0.98	74.72	1.35	1.95	0.59	0.64	...
San Marino[f]	6–16	No	...	...	...	...	...	...	...	...	...	...	...	...	...
Serbia[c, d]	...	Yes	8.84	...	...	...	...	...	...	...	...	0.15	...	0.20	...
Slovakia	6–15	Yes	11.99	14.85	94.04	101.87	0.99	93.72	1.01	50.85	1.49	2.53	5.30	8.48	7.31
Slovenia	6–14	Yes	12.32	16.82**	80.57	103.65	0.99	93.80	0.99	85.53	1.45	1.67	0.15	1.27	10.47
Spain	6–16	Yes	14.54	16.23	122.39	105.69	0.99	119.84	1.06	68.91	1.24	35.86	33.02	28.22	13.79
Sweden	7–16	Yes	13.00	15.64	95.23⁻¹	94.46	1.00	103.63	0.99	75.18	1.57	12.00⁻¹	7.71	12.07	7.98
Switzerland	7–15	Yes	13.58	14.88	99.10	97.35	0.99	92.66	0.96	47.00	0.93	9.39	4.07	7.28	18.53
Turkey	6–14	Yes	8.48	11.62**	...	96.03**	0.95**	80.16**	0.82**	36.30	0.76	9.44	1.82**, ⁻¹	2.25**, ⁻¹	5.07
Ukraine	6–17	Yes	12.20	14.56	94.47	99.82	1.00*	94.22	1.00*	76.38	1.24	2.14	0.53	0.42	...
United Kingdom	5–16	Yes	14.15	15.95**	73.04	103.90	1.01	97.46	1.02	59.10	1.40	28.97	5.33	25.72	100.00

North America

Country or Territory	Compulsory education	Legal guarantee	1991	2007	Pre-primary %	Primary %	GPI	Secondary %	GPI	Tertiary %	GPI	Private Pre-primary	Private Primary	Private Secondary	Private Tertiary
Canada	6–16	Yes	16.91	...	...	98.98⁻¹	0.99⁻¹	101.55⁻¹	0.98⁻¹	...	...	5.82⁻¹	5.82⁻¹	5.82⁻¹	...
United States of America	6–17	No	15.30	15.82**	62.22	99.04	1.00	94.22	1.01	81.68	1.41	35.36	10.00	8.76	25.78

Latin America and the Caribbean

Country or Territory	Compulsory education	Legal guarantee	1991	2007	Pre-primary %	Primary %	GPI	Secondary %	GPI	Tertiary %	GPI	Private Pre-primary	Private Primary	Private Secondary	Private Tertiary
Anguilla	5–17	Yes	...	11.17**, ⁻¹	...	92.93**, ⁻¹	0.99**, ⁻¹	82.75**, ⁻¹	1.02**, ⁻¹	4.56**, ⁻¹	4.86**, ⁻¹	100.00⁺¹	9.32⁺¹	.	81.48⁺¹
Antigua and Barbuda	5–16	Yes	...	...	112.32*	102.48*	0.94*	105.17*	0.96*	...	...	94.65	49.70	18.98	...
Argentina	5–14	Yes	13.07	15.38⁻¹	66.55⁻¹	113.77⁻¹	0.98⁻¹	84.12⁻¹	1.12⁻¹	67.13⁻¹	1.52⁻¹	30.63⁻¹	22.17⁻¹	27.94⁻¹	25.22⁻¹
Aruba[d]	6–16	...	...	13.79	96.39	113.65	0.97	105.07	1.06	33.05	1.45	74.26	77.85	92.28	17.29
Bahamas	5–16	No	12.23	...	...	102.77	1.00	94.02	1.03	...	...	...	29.20	31.69	...
Barbados	5–16	Yes	7.84	14.97**	91.12	105.10	1.00	103.22	1.03	53.13	2.18	14.86	10.45	5.13	...
Belize	5–14	Yes	10.92	...	34.62	123.11	0.99	78.73	1.07	...	...	81.76⁺¹	95.19⁺¹	70.11⁺¹	...
Bermuda[d]	5–16	...	...	13.13*, ⁻²	...	100.26*, ⁻¹	0.85*, ⁻¹	84.50*, ⁻¹	1.06*, ⁻¹	18.80*, ⁻²	1.80*, ⁻²	...	35.42⁻¹	42.32⁻¹	...
Bolivia	6–13	Yes	10.37	...	49.31	108.26	1.00	81.85	0.97	...	...	10.43	8.07	13.49	...
Brazil	7–14	Yes	10.32	13.78	...	129.61	0.93	100.12	1.11	29.99	1.29	24.45	10.67	11.44	72.91
British Virgin Islands[d]	5–16	...	...	17.26**, ⁻²	166.38*, ⁻¹	107.60**	0.96**	100.79**	1.11**	75.47**, ⁻²	2.28**, ⁻²	100.00⁻¹	27.79	12.44	...
Cayman Islands	5–16	...	...	...	...	89.70**, ⁻²	0.89**, ⁻²	101.66**, ⁻²	0.92**, ⁻²	...	...	91.87⁻¹	35.48	28.87	...
Chile	6–13	Yes	12.17	14.53	55.76	105.65	0.95	90.60	1.03	52.06	1.01	55.56	54.86	54.60	76.59
Colombia	5–14	No	9.03	12.61**	40.54	116.34	0.99	85.12	1.11	31.80	1.09	41.40	19.11	23.46	44.90
Costa Rica	5–14	Yes	9.98	11.73**, ⁻²	64.60	110.17	0.99	87.39	1.05	25.34**, ⁻²	1.26**, ⁻²	13.41	7.51	10.03	...
Cuba	6–14	Yes	12.26	17.15**	...	101.52	0.98	92.67	1.00	109.03	1.85	.	.	.	.
Dominica[d]	5–16	No	...	13.02**, ⁻²	...	85.70*, ⁻¹	1.02*, ⁻¹	105.98*, ⁻¹	0.98*, ⁻¹	.	.	100.00	31.92	25.56	...
Dominican Republic	5–13	Yes	8.06	...	31.96	106.83	0.94	79.12	1.20	...	...	51.40⁺¹	20.80⁺¹	22.09⁺¹	...
Ecuador	5–14	Yes	11.37	13.34	215.62	118.50	1.00	69.63	1.01	35.32	1.22	38.92	28.17	32.01	25.53
El Salvador	7–15	Yes	8.85	12.22	49.41	117.82	1.00	64.40	1.04	21.69	1.22	19.03	10.29	18.54	66.23
Grenada[d]	5–16	Yes	...	12.09**, ⁻²	80.24	81.14	0.96	98.60	0.99	...	...	55.95	77.48	59.68	...
Guatemala	7–15	Yes	6.66	10.64**	28.63	113.43	0.94	55.62	0.92	17.71	1.00	20.00	11.37	74.04	...
Guyana	6–15	Yes	9.87	12.67**	86.70	112.15	0.98	106.59	0.93	12.32	2.09	2.11	1.78	2.07	...
Haiti	6–11	No	4.59	...	...	...	...	...	...	...	...	...	...	...	...
Honduras	6–11	Yes	8.68	...	45.74	119.39	1.00	64.02	1.25	...	...	13.66⁻¹	7.28⁻¹	...	...

	Teaching Staff							Literacy rate[a]				
Pre-primary and other ECCE		Primary		Secondary		Tertiary						
Pupil/teacher ratio	Female teachers as % of total teachers	Pupil/teacher ratio	Female teachers as % of total teachers	Pupil/teacher ratio	Female teachers as % of total teachers	Pupil/teacher ratio	Female teachers as % of total teachers	Youth % (15–24) 1985–1994[b]	Youth % (15–24) 2000–2007[b]	Adults % (15 and over) 1985–1994[b]	Adults % (15 and over) 2000–2007[b]	Country or Territory
2007												
11.92	99.21	10.29	65.33	7.88	57.54	20.79	35.19	98.98	99.32**	92.61	97.08**	Greece
10.69	99.80	10.06	96.01	10.53**,-1	71.52**,-1	18.40	37.08	...	...	...	...	Holy See
6.31	96.71	10.48**,-1	79.61**,-1	10.78**,-1	65.17**,-1	8.07	44.67	98.94**	...	98.89**	98.89**	Hungary
...	...	15.94	84.04	10.54-1	62.14-1	15.36	39.21	...	...	...	...	Iceland
...	...	13.41	86.20	11.88	71.14			...	...	...	...	Ireland
11.62	99.07	10.33	95.25	10.10	67.39	19.48	34.97	...	99.89**	...	98.87**	Israel
10.37	99.68	11.41	97.18	9.74**	82.89	18.86	56.68	...	99.72**	...	99.78**	Italy
8.36	98.94	7.12	77.14	8.59	49.86			99.78	99.72**	99.45	99.78**	Latvia
7.15	99.55	13.26	97.21	9.45	81.13	12.65	54.52	99.67	99.77**	98.44	99.68**	Liechtenstein
11.94	98.37	11.08	71.88	10.18	47.08			...	...	...	...	Lithuania
11.32	97.80	18.28	72.22	13.72	53.76	20.98	44.95	...	...	...	...	Luxembourg
9.78-2	98.63-2	11.52-2	85.60-2	9.77-2	57.27-2	13.26**,-2	22.61**,-2	98.86	98.72	94.06	...	Macedonia (TFYR)
9.87	100.00	16.25	97.49	12.10	75.66	17.32*	57.85*	98.21	98.27	87.98	92.36	Malta
...	...	...	...	5.81+1	68.40+1	.	.	99.73	99.69**	96.38	96.99**	Moldova (Rep.)[d, e]
...	...	...	...					...	...	...	...	Monaco[f]
...	...	...	...	13.32	46.38	13.22	36.90	...	...	...	...	Montenegro
...	...	...	...	...	...	11.22	41.11	...	...	...	...	Netherlands
17.56	97.98	10.64	84.30	12.71**,-1	69.14**,-1	21.68	42.01	99.65**	...**	99.06**	99.31**	Norway
15.90	97.11	11.73	81.78	7.32	68.67	10.17	43.16	99.20	99.66**	87.95	94.88**	Poland
17.75	99.75	16.54	86.70	12.70	66.84	30.35	43.93	99.11	97.42**	96.71	97.60**	Portugal
7.38	100.00*	17.12	98.67	8.63	81.00	13.80	56.61	99.72	99.70**	97.99	99.52**	Romania
7.50+1	97.08+1	6.34+1	91.13+1	...	...	...	...	...	...	...	...	Russian Federation
16.90	97.94	13.25**	...	11.86**	...			...	...	...	...	San Marino[f]
13.38	99.94	15.35	84.60	12.81	74.09	16.02	43.28	98.56	99.36	92.29	99.36	Serbia[c, d]
18.22**,-1	99.66**,-1	15.57	97.58	10.23	71.88	20.67	35.35	...	...	...	...	Slovakia
12.96	87.98	12.83	71.99	10.81	56.77	12.34	39.14	99.76	99.85**	99.52	99.68**	Slovenia
9.67-1	96.26-1	9.80	81.20	9.62	58.76	11.34	43.42	99.55	99.57	96.49	97.94	Spain
...	...	...	...	...	...	6.30-1	31.39-1	...	...	...	...	Sweden
25.87	95.23	...	...	...	...	27.47	39.28	...	...	...	...	Switzerland
8.50	98.74	16.34	98.87*	10.57	79.45*	14.32	...	92.54	96.36	79.23	88.66	Turkey
22.47-1	97.09-1	18.08-1	81.34-1	14.54*,-1	60.91*,-1	18.60-1	40.79-1	...	99.79**	...	99.69**	Ukraine
								...	...	...	...	United Kingdom
												North America
...	...	...	...	...	...	...	...	...	...	...	...	Canada
16.04	91.32	13.80	88.62	14.56	62.44	13.55	44.63	...	...	...	...	United States of America
												Latin America and the Caribbean
10.47+1	100.00+1	14.12+1	90.35+1	10.43	68.75	3.86+1	42.86+1	...	...	...	...	Anguilla
12.88	100.00	21.50	92.38					...	...	...	98.95	Antigua and Barbuda
18.52-1	96.24-1	16.34-1	88.29-1	12.76-1	69.10-1	15.48-1	53.15-1	98.30	99.11**	96.13	97.64**	Argentina
20.67	99.29	17.42	82.83	14.46	56.54	10.05	50.00	...	99.29**	...	98.14**	Aruba[d]
...	...	13.83	84.58	12.27	69.58			...	...	...	...	Bahamas
18.94	96.91	14.54	77.98	14.58-1	58.81-1	14.51	48.73	...	...	...	...	Barbados
16.67+1	99.14+1	22.62+1	71.90+1	16.96+1	59.24+1	...	49.48**,-2	76.42	...	70.30	...	Belize
...	...	8.25-1	89.42-1	6.05-1	67.47-1	10.07	54.55	...	...	...	...	Bermuda[d]
40.90**,-2	92.18**,-2	...	...	...	...	...	...	93.90	99.44	79.99	90.74	Bolivia
19.93	96.74	23.86	91.03	18.55	69.10	14.34	43.73	...	97.80	...	90.01	Brazil
14.51-1	100.00-1	14.16	90.23	8.61	73.99	10.91**,-2	54.55**,-2	...	...	...	...	British Virgin Islands[d]
12.77-1	100.00-1	11.06	89.55	9.17-1	58.23-1	11.57-1	24.49-1	...	98.91	...	98.87	Cayman Islands
18.64	98.17	25.11	78.40	23.71	62.86	13.79	38.69	98.43	99.06**	94.29	96.54**	Chile
21.83	95.71	28.21	76.49	28.31	51.60	15.54**	35.27**	90.52	97.97	81.38	92.65	Colombia
13.44	93.81	19.49	79.85	17.91*	57.68*	...	...	...	98.01**	...	95.95**	Costa Rica
15.98+1	100.00+1	9.61+1	76.56+1	9.67+1	54.54+1	6.72+1	58.69+1	...	99.98**	...	99.79**	Cuba
13.84	100.00	17.32	84.37	15.95	65.25	.	.	...	...	...	...	Dominica[d]
24.20+1	94.49+1	19.62+1	69.22+1	24.47+1	59.29+1			...	95.99**	...	89.14**	Dominican Republic
16.84	87.04	22.57	70.04	14.66	49.76	19.53	27.58	96.19	95.43	88.30	84.19	Ecuador
31.33	91.26	39.67	68.22	26.90	47.77	15.80	33.37	84.95	93.56	74.14	82.03	El Salvador
13.96	100.00	15.77	77.04	15.43*,-2	59.14-2			...	...	...	...	Grenada[d]
24.21	91.29	30.45	64.85	16.11	43.56	29.20*,-1	31.20-1	75.99	85.48**	64.21	73.20**	Guatemala
14.72	99.43	26.18	87.54	14.08	57.27	12.92	49.91	...	...	...	...	Guyana
...	...	...	...	...	...	...	...	...	...	...	...	Haiti
25.75-1	...	27.93-1	...	...	...	...	...	...	93.92	...	83.59	Honduras

Table 9. Education and literacy[1]

Country or Territory	Compulsory education (age group) 2007	Legal guarantee of free education[2]	School life expectancy 1991	School life expectancy 2007	Pre-primary and other ECCE %	Primary GER %	Primary GPI (F/M)	Secondary GER %	Secondary GPI (F/M)	Tertiary GER %	Tertiary GPI (F/M)	Private Pre-primary and other ECCE	Private Primary	Private Secondary	Private Tertiary
Jamaica	6–11	No	10.96	...	86.86	91.33	1.01	89.79	1.05	...	...	90.56	7.83	5.79⁻²	
Mexico	6–15	Yes	10.56	13.63	114.14	113.89	0.97	88.75	1.03	26.93	0.93	15.23	8.11	15.16	32.97
Montserrat[d]	5–16	...	...	15.08**	90.63*	106.65*	1.12*	102.06*	1.02*	.	.	...	30.58		
Netherlands Antilles	6–15	...	...	...	...	...	...	...	...	...	...	...	...	...	...
Nicaragua	6–11	Yes	8.38	...		115.77	0.98	68.86	1.13	...	...	15.61	14.92	23.74	...
Panama	6–14	Yes	11.15	13.39**,⁻¹	70.43	112.58	0.97	70.23	1.08	44.93⁻¹	1.61⁻¹	15.87	11.10	15.75	25.52*
Paraguay	6–14	Yes	8.70	12.03**,⁻²	34.30⁻²	111.34⁻²	0.97⁻²	66.48⁻²	1.03⁻²	25.50**,⁻²	1.13**,⁻²	27.68⁻²	16.61⁻²	21.09⁻²	56.90*
Peru	6–16	Yes	12.03	14.03**,⁻¹	72.49	117.10	1.01	98.01	1.04	35.06**,⁻¹	1.06**,⁻¹	23.64	18.96	25.81	54.37*
Saint Kitts and Nevis[d]	5–16	No	13.74	12.30**,⁻²	160.77**	93.73**	1.01**	104.65**	0.91**	.	.	74.24	21.55	3.78	...
Saint Lucia	5–15	No	12.86	13.44**	...	109.11	0.97	93.47	1.13	8.59	2.41	100.00	3.17	3.75	6.82
Saint Vincent and the Grenadines	5–15	No	12.27	12.03**,⁻²	87.54**,⁻²	102.45	0.94	74.87⁻²	1.24⁻²	.	.	100.00**,⁻²	3.80	24.61⁻²	
Suriname	7–12	Yes	11.06	...	85.08	118.71	0.98	79.62	1.39	...	...	44.41	45.62	18.34	
Trinidad and Tobago	5–11	Yes	11.15	11.25**,⁻²	80.88*	99.96	0.97	85.98**	1.07**	11.39**,⁻²	1.28**,⁻²	100.00**,⁻²	72.77	23.53*,⁻²	
Turks and Caicos Islands	4–16	...	...	11.36**,⁻²	118.36**,⁻²	89.81**,⁻²	1.04**,⁻²	85.98**,⁻²	0.94**,⁻²	.	.	65.47⁻²	29.86⁻²	16.37**,⁻²	...
Uruguay	6–15	Yes	12.95	15.69	80.34	114.17	0.97	92.03	0.99	64.27	1.75	33.38	14.34	12.51	11.50
Venezuela	5–14	Yes	10.76	12.72*,⁻¹	83.78	106.04	0.97	79.37	1.12	51.96*,⁻¹	...	20.08	16.03⁺¹	27.11⁺¹	44.72*
Pacific															
Australia	5–15	Yes	13.42	20.67	104.21⁻¹	107.27	1.00	148.59	0.96	75.06	1.29	66.63⁻¹	29.85	27.55	4.29
Cook Islands[d]	5–15	...	...	9.43**	94.11**	72.51**	0.97**	73.13**	1.08**	.	.	28.60	21.27	15.07	
Fiji	6–15	No	8.61	13.01**,⁻²	15.81⁻¹	94.49	0.97	82.36	1.12	15.41**,⁻²	1.20**,⁻²	100.00⁻¹	98.90**,⁻²	91.99**,⁻²	...
Kiribati[d]	6–15	No	...	12.31*,⁻²	...	112.76*,⁻²	1.01*,⁻²	87.93*,⁻¹	1.14*,⁻¹	.	.	...	...	...	...
Marshall Islands	6–14	No	...	...	44.97*	93.05*	0.97*	66.40*	1.02*	.	.	...	...	...	...
Micronesia (Fed. States)	6–13	No	...	...	...	109.90	1.01	90.61**	1.07⁻²	...	...	...	8.09**	...	...
Nauru[d]	6–16	No	...	8.49*,⁻¹	88.61**	78.81**	1.03**	46.06**	1.19**	.	.	.	.	.	.
New Zealand	5–16	Yes	14.66	19.85	93.27	101.57	1.01	121.07	1.03	79.84	1.49	97.55	12.34	20.33	11.05
Niue[d]	5–16	...	...	12.29*,⁻²	119.23*,⁻²	104.71**,⁻²	0.95**,⁻²	98.56**,⁻²	1.07**,⁻²	.	.	20.15**,⁻²	23.06	28.23	...
Palau[d]	6–14	Yes	...	...	63.59**,⁻²	98.78*	1.02**	96.91**	0.97**	...	...	...	...	...	...
Papua New Guinea	6–14	No	4.81	...	...	55.16⁻¹	0.84⁻¹	...	...	...	...	...	...	...	...
Samoa	5–12	No	11.26	...	48.13	95.43	1.00	80.56**,⁻²	1.13**,⁻²	...	...	100.00	16.97**,⁻²	32.16**,⁻²	...
Solomon Islands	...	No	...	8.49⁻²	...	100.52⁻²	0.96⁻²	30.05⁻²	0.84⁻²	...	...	...	...	...	...
Tokelau[d]	...	...	...	...	...	...	...	...	...	...	...	...	...	...	...
Tonga	6–14	No	14.01	...	22.80**,⁻²	113.09⁻¹	0.95⁻¹	93.68⁻¹	1.04⁻¹	...	...	...	...	...	...
Tuvalu[d]	7–14	No	...	...	...	105.57*,⁻¹	0.99*,⁻¹	...	...	...	...	...	...	...	...
Vanuatu	6–12	No	...	...	7.30⁻¹	108.42	0.97	...	...	...	...	94.07⁻¹	27.26	...	...
World	...	.	9.78	12.65	...	102.32	0.96	77.47	0.97	33.88	1.18	43.80	16.17	18.21	33.92
Arab States	...	.	9.43	11.59	...	97.48	0.95	73.83	0.95	24.38	1.37	64.44	19.86	16.24	30.59
Sub-Saharan Africa	...	.	6.32	9.24	...	101.13	0.91	41.29	0.83	4.85	0.64	54.18	13.50	18.89	34.46
Central and South Asia	...	.	8.93	11.28	...	106.02	0.98	70.29	0.92	21.73	0.90	29.88	9.61	16.33	29.91
East Asia	...	.	9.99	12.99	...	106.32	0.97	78.43	1.00	36.31	1.07	54.85	13.81	19.81	43.29
Europe	...	.	12.57	15.07	...	100.67	0.99	99.39	1.00	58.03	1.30	15.01	7.35	9.49	29.45
North America	...	.	16.11	15.82	...	99.01	1.00	97.88	0.99	81.68	1.41	20.59	7.91	7.29	25.78
Latin America and the Caribbean	...	.	10.43	13.32	...	107.19	0.98	87.23	1.05	37.22	1.65	50.30	26.24	26.12	42.86
Pacific	...	.	11.13	13.07	...	97.00	0.98	85.84	1.05	56.77	1.33	72.43	29.72	35.89	7.67

Sources:

1. UNESCO Institute for Statistics, 2009. Education Database.
2. Tomasevski, 2006. The State of the Right to Education Worldwide. Free or Fee: 2006 Global Report.

Notes:

a. Literacy data should be used and interpreted with literacy metadata that can be found at UIS website: http://stats.uis.unesco.org/unesco/ReportFolders/ReportFolders.aspx. For countries indicated with (*), national observed literacy data are used. For all others, UIS literacy estimates are used. The estimates were generated using the UIS Global Age-specific Literacy Projections model. They are based on the latest available national data.

b. Data are for the most recent year available during the period specified. See the introduction to the statistical tables of the EFA Global Monitoring Report 2009 for a broader explanation of national literacy definitions, assessment methods, and sources and years of data: http://www.unesco.org/en/efareport. National literacy definitions may differ.

c. Literacy data for the most recent year do not include some geographic regions.

d. National population data were used to calculate enrolment ratios.

e. Enrolment and population data exclude Transnistria.

f. Enrolment ratios were not calculated due to lack of United Nations population data by age.

g. Children can enter primary school at age 6 or 7.

Pre-primary and other ECCE		Primary		Secondary		Tertiary		Literacy rate[a]				
								Youth % (15–24)		Adults % (15 and over)		
Pupil/teacher ratio	Female teachers as % of total teachers	Pupil/teacher ratio	Female teachers as % of total teachers	Pupil/teacher ratio	Female teachers as % of total teachers	Pupil/teacher ratio	Female teachers as % of total teachers	1985–1994[b]	2000–2007[b]	1985–1994[b]	2000–2007[b]	Country or Territory
			2007									
23.82	97.83	27.68**,-2	88.98**,-2	19.77	68.68	...	...	...	94.34**	...	85.98**	Jamaica
28.39	95.96	27.99	66.53	17.92	47.31	9.21	...	95.42	98.16	87.56	92.80	Mexico
10.55	100.00	16.03	100.00	11.97	65.52	.	.	...	...	...	...	Montserrat[d]
...	...	...	...	...	...	...	...	96.98	98.22**	95.10	96.35**	Netherlands Antilles
22.17	94.27	30.56	75.68	31.11	58.59	...	...	...	87.01	...	78.00	Nicaragua
18.38	94.04	24.54	75.97	15.47	58.45	11.35-1	46.02-1	95.09	96.32**	88.78	93.39**	Panama
20.70	95.58	22.22	64.60	18.01	45.33-1	...	...	95.61	98.79	90.27	94.56	Paraguay
6.61	100.00	16.59	86.83	10.12	63.98	...	...	95.37	97.36	87.15	89.59	Peru
10.83	100.00	22.73	87.41	16.70	66.37	4.87	54.24	...	...	...	...	Saint Kitts and Nevis[d]
11.45**,-2	100.00**,-2	17.07	77.06	17.88**,-2	57.77**,-2	.	.	...	...	...	...	Saint Lucia
20.04	99.88	13.23	91.92	14.00	59.74	.	.	...	...	...	...	Saint Vincent and the Grenadines
13.53*	100.00*,-2	15.94	76.69	13.99**,-2	62.04**,-2	...	...	...	95.17**	...	90.38**	Suriname
12.45**,-2	95.40**,-2	15.00**,-2	89.19**,-2	9.06**,-2	61.83**,-2	9.40**,-2	33.33**,-2	99.30	99.51**	96.94	98.69**	Trinidad and Tobago
23.39	...	15.51	...	13.80	...	10.06	...	...	...	...	...	Turks and Caicos Islands
15.37-2	94.36-2	16.19+1	81.27+1	10.23+1	63.95+1	12.72*,-1	...	98.63	98.76	95.38	97.86	Uruguay
								95.44	98.40	89.83	95.15	Venezuela
												Pacific
14.97	100.00	16.25	76.80	14.67	78.20	...	...	...	...	...	...	Australia
19.21-1	99.02**,-2	28.16**,-2	56.91**,-2	22.90	50.01	.	.	...	...	...	...	Cook Islands[d]
...	...	24.67-2	75.23-2	17.04-2	47.37-2	...	...	...	...	...	...	Fiji
...	...	...	...	...	...	...	...	...	...	...	...	Kiribati[d]
...	...	16.63**	...	...	...	...	...	...	...	...	...	Marshall Islands
17.15	97.44	19.92	90.32	20.88	78.79	.	.	...	...	...	...	Micronesia (Fed. States)
13.53	98.83	15.68	83.28	14.63	61.60	17.23	49.92	...	...	...	...	Nauru[d]
...	...	11.87**,-2	100.00**,-2	8.24-2	68.00-2	.	.	...	...	...	...	New Zealand
...	...	12.50**,-2	...	...	...	...	...	...	...	...	...	Niue[d]
...	...	35.82**,-1	42.66**,-1	...	...	...	...	...	...	...	...	Palau[d]
...	...	23.80	78.25	...	...	...	...	...	64.06**	...	57.77**	Papua New Guinea
...	...	...	...	...	...	...	...	99.04	99.42**	97.94	98.70**	Samoa
...	...	...	...	...	...	.	.	...	...	...	...	Solomon Islands
...	...	22.29-1	...	...	...	...	...	...	...	...	...	Tokelau[d]
.	.	...	...	...	...	...	...	...	99.58**	...	99.22**	Tonga
11.86-1	90.99-1	...	...	...	...	...	...	...	...	...	...	Tuvalu[d]
								80.77**	91.73**	65.53**	78.09**	Vanuatu
19.89	**94.15**	**25.06**	**68.85**	**17.41**	**53.31**	**17.63**	**37.23**	**83.90**	**88.46**	**74.10**	**81.27**	**World**
17.86	94.90	22.40	62.08	17.16	46.67	21.70	27.79	79.55	91.25	62.52	79.20	Arab States
31.19	82.86	42.96	42.98	25.73	29.83	22.55	23.02	65.69	73.96	52.00	64.08	Sub-Saharan Africa
20.16	96.70	26.02	67.41	19.00	51.45	16.08	40.58	80.09	87.61	71.51	79.69	Central and South Asia
22.18	96.83	24.10	68.67	20.55	56.26	20.38	42.75	96.20	95.49	85.76	90.31	East Asia
12.66	97.63	13.51	86.28	10.60	65.86	15.05	42.01	99.01	99.22	95.04	97.84	Europe
16.04	91.32	13.80	88.62	14.56	62.44	13.55	44.63	...	...	...	...	North America
18.30	97.03	20.02	81.24	15.75	59.97	12.47	43.68	92.91	96.64	86.23	91.70	Latin America and the Caribbean
15.34	97.26	20.69	75.43	16.39	63.99	17.23	49.92	89.91	88.70	81.74	83.45	Pacific

... Data not available

* National estimation

** UIS estimation

. Not applicable

+n Data refer to the year n years after the reference year

-n Data refer to the year n years before the reference year

Table 10. Education and curricula

Columns: **Intended Annual Hours of Instruction** (Average grades 1–6; Average grades 7–8) and **Emphasis on Curriculum Categories as % of Median Yearly Instructional Hours** (Average grades 1–6; and grades 7–8 for the last three categories). Each category reports 1980s and 2000s.

Country or Territory	AnnHrs 1–6 1980s	2000s	AnnHrs 7–8 1980s	2000s	Language Ed. 1980s	2000s	Mathematics 1980s	2000s	Science, Comp. & Tech. 1980s	2000s	Social Sciences 1980s	2000s	Religion 1980s	2000s	Moral Ed. 1980s	2000s	Arts 1980s	2000s	Sports 1980s	2000s	Skills & Comp. 1980s	2000s	Optional & others 1980s	2000s	Lang. Ed. (7–8) 1980s	2000s	Math. (7–8) 1980s	2000s	Sci. Comp.Tech. (7–8) 1980s	2000s
Arab States																														
Algeria	702	810	858	955	51.1	…	20.4	…	7.1	…	2.9	…	0.0	…	6.5	…	7.4	…	4.6	…	0.0	…	0.0	…	42.9	36.7	14.3	16.7	9.5	13
Bahrain	734	812	972	875	40.2	38.2	18.1	18.1	3.7	8.9	5.2	5.9	7.7	9.2	0.0	…	13.7	10.9	7.7	7.2	3.7	1.7	0.0	0.0	…	…	…	…	…	…
Djibouti	…	805	…	837	…	55.1	…	21.1	…	2.2	…	2.1	…	0.0	…	0.0	…	13.2	…	5.4	…	0.0	…	0.8	18.2	…	15.2	…	3.0	
Egypt	685	944	755	995	31.7	40.5	19.6	17.4	5.1	5.7	6.2	2.8	9.8	8.7	0.0	0.0	10.4	5.6	8.3	4.2	8.9	15.2	0.0	0.0	46.7	36.1	16.7	8.3	10.0	8
Iraq	846	792	829	792	36.9	33.2	20.3	17.1	2.0	9.0	7.3	8.6	8.0	12.1	0.0	2.0	6.9	8.0	5.1	7.6	6.8	2.5	6.7	0.0	25.0	34.3	15.1	14.9	26.0	14
Jordan	693	841	746	998	36.2	34.3	15.0	17.1	12.5	12.5	7.5	7.8	11.3	10.3	0.0	0.0	6.3	6.8	3.8	6.8	7.5	4.4	0.0	0.0	38.9	37.9	13.9	13.9	11.1	13
Kuwait	695	777	780	705	35.2	39.8	13.1	13.6	7.9	8.4	2.7	3.7	18.7	9.4	0.0	0.0	8.4	11.0	6.9	7.9	2.5	3.1	4.5	3.1	…	37.5	…	12.5	…	9
Lebanon	756	810	800	1,050	…	43.3	…	16.7	…	11.1	…	10.0	…	0.0	…	0.0	…	6.1	…	6.7	…	6.1	…	0.0	43.6	37.5	12.9	15.6	14.5	21
Libyan Arab Jamahiriya	805	651	893	837	21.5	27.2	17.5	21.6	6.4	9.2	5.3	6.1	18.4	14.4	0.0	0.0	9.2	10.8	18.4	10.8	3.3	0.0	0.0	0.0	41.9	27.8	9.9	16.7	7.4	19
Mauritania	…	…	…	…	…	53.5	…	19.5	…	0.0	…	6.9	…	7.0	…	0.0	…	5.2	…	5.5	…	2.4	…	0.0	…	36.7	…	20.0	…	6
Morocco	878	924	880	1,056	47.9	47.0	15.9	17.9	4.0	5.4	8.1	1.8	5.0	11.9	3.9	0.0	3.6	8.9	3.3	7.1	1.4	0.0		7.0	16.7	33.3	11.9	16.7	11.9	16
Oman	…	640	…	640	…	35.5	…	17.6	…	12.2	…	5.0	…	13.8	…	0.0	…	6.7	…	5.0	…	2.5	…	1.7	37.8	30.0	18.9	20.0	12.2	19
Palestinian A.T.	…	832	…	945	…	34.2	…	18.5	…	11.5	…	8.8	…	10.1	…	0.0	…	6.7	…	6.7	…	3.5	…	0.0	29.3	38.1	12.0	14.9	6.0	12
Qatar	856	693	944	720	34.7	44.6	16.8	15.6	6.0	4.5	5.2	3.4	19.9	15.2	0.0	0.0	8.3	6.1	7.6	6.1	0.0	4.5	1.4	0.0	33.9	36.1	15.4	13.9	15.4	4
Saudi Arabia	740	664	842	765	26.9	34.7	16.2	16.6	4.2	4.2	3.5	5.7	32.4	21.4	0.0	0.0	5.4	5.4	7.2	4.0	4.2	4.0	0.0	4.0	…	37.0	…	14.8	…	7
Sudan	669	677	933	965	32.8	42.0	20.8	18.8	3.9	1.3	7.8	0.0	14.5	16.1	0.0	0.0	6.8	18.3	6.8	3.6	6.8	0.0	0.0		…	53.4	…	0.0	…	13
Syrian Arab Republic	811	768	842	925	31.3	34.1	16.2	16.0	4.8	4.2	7.9	6.8	8.6	8.5	0.0	0.0	12.4	11.2	8.7	8.5	4.8	4.2	5.4	6.4	32.4	30.7	14.7	11.2	5.9	9
Tunisia	870	825	756	900	53.4	58.7	15.1	14.8	5.9	5.6	2.6	3.9	7.4	6.0	0.0	0.0	2.6	4.8	0.0	3.7	6.7	2.5	6.4	0.0	36.1	35.7	13.9	14.3	5.6	9
United Arab Emirates	…	766	…	788	…	39.7	…	16.7	…	10.6	…	2.8	…	9.2	…	0.0	…	12.2	…	6.1	…	2.8	…	0.0	37.7	36.1	18.9	16.7	18.9	11
Yemen	…	653	…	864	…	34.6	…	19.5	…	0.0	…	5.4	…	16.2	…	1.1	…	0.0	…	7.1	…	8.8	…	7.1	…	34.4	…	18.8	…	0
Sub-Saharan Africa																														
Angola	655	689	918	851	28.3	28.9	23.9	24.5	14.2	14.6	8.0	10.2	0.0	0.0	0.0	1.2	7.6	12.4	8.0	8.2	10.2	0.0	0.0	0.0	…	26.7	…	16.7	…	20
Benin	1,026	939	1,055	1,116	29.7	38.8	16.2	19.3	0.0	10.4	18.2	8.8	0.0	0.0	0.0	0.0	13.5	5.2	5.8	6.2	15.3	3.0	1.2	8.3	36.1	32.4	20.8	16.2	13.9	16
Botswana	…	…	…	…	…	…	…	…	…	…	…	…	…	…	…	…	…	…	…	…	…	…	…	…	…	…	…	…	…	…
Burkina Faso	…	574	…	624	…	…	…	…	…	…	…	…	…	…	…	…	…	…	…	…	…	…	…	…	…	…	…	…	…	…
Burundi	888	823	888	1,080	…	48.8	…	25.6	…	0.0	…	11.5	…	2.6	…	0.0	…	0.0	…	5.3	…	3.6	…	2.6	29.4	35.7	14.7	18.6	20.6	14
Cameroon	875	…	…	…	63.6	53.9	16.0	12.4	3.4	2.7	3.6	2.6	0.0	0.0	1.3	0.0	0.0	3.8	3.1	8.0	9.1	5.3	0.0	10.5	…	…	…	…	…	…
Cape Verde	…	646	…	869	…	27.7	…	27.7	…	19.3	…	0.0	…	0.0	…	0.0	…	16.6	…	8.7	…	0.0	…	0.0	…	26.7	…	13.4	…	20
Central African Republic	…	…	…	…	…	…	…	…	…	…	…	…	…	…	…	…	…	…	…	…	…	…	…	…	19.2	42.3	14.9	19.2	16.1	7
Chad	…	…	…	…	…	67.4	…	14.6	…	2.4	…	4.4	…	0.0	…	1.7	…	5.4	…	1.8	…	2.4	…	0.0	40.0	43.3	15.0	16.7	15.0	16
Comoros	…	…	…	…	…	42.3	…	20.0	…	4.9	…	8.4	…	4.0	…	2.0	…	7.3	…	7.7	…	3.3	…	0.0	…	…	…	…	…	…
Congo	…	…	…	36.8	52.8	27.4	15.3	0.0	0.0	0.0	0.9	0.0	0.0	4.1	0.9	6.1	6.3	2.7	3.0	10.9	1.2	12.0	19.7	41.4	43.9	17.2	16.5	17.2	13
Congo (Dem. Rep.)	…	…	…	29.9	37.8	21.8	20.7	5.2	4.9	15.5	14.7	0.0	0.0	3.7	3.5	1.8	6.9	7.3	3.5	3.7	6.9	5.5	6.9	0.0	…	…	…	…	…
Côte d'Ivoire	…	…	…	…	…	…	…	…	…	…	…	…	…	…	…	…	…	…	…	…	…	…	…	…	…	…	…	…	…	…
Equatorial Guinea	…	…	…	…	…	…	…	…	…	…	…	…	…	…	…	…	…	…	…	…	…	…	…	…	…	…	…	…	…	…
Eritrea	…	…	…	…	…	…	…	…	…	…	…	…	…	…	…	…	…	…	…	…	…	…	…	…	22.2	…	16.7	…	19.4	
Ethiopia	819	900	1,063	945	31.3	36.8	19.1	15.1	8.0	15.1	5.4	12.1	0.0	0.0	0.0	0.0	11.1	14.0	7.3	7.0	11.4	0.0	6.4	0.0	…	40.0	…	14.3	…	25
Gabon	…	…	…	…	…	…	…	…	…	…	…	…	…	…	…	…	…	…	…	…	…	…	…	…	…	…	…	…	…	…
Gambia	…	616	…	770	…	…	…	…	…	…	…	…	…	…	…	…	…	…	…	…	…	…	…	…	…	…	…	…	…	…
Ghana	…	900	600	1,013	…	37.8	…	22.2	…	5.6	…	12.2	…	3.9	…	3.9	…	6.7	…	7.8	…	0.0	…	0.0	…	22.2	…	13.3	…	15
Guinea	…	…	…	…	…	…	…	…	…	…	…	…	…	…	…	…	…	…	…	…	…	…	…	…	26.0	33.3	15.5	20.0	19.6	23
Guinea-Bissau	…	…	…	…	…	…	…	…	…	…	…	…	…	…	…	…	…	…	…	…	…	…	…	…	…	…	…	…	…	…
Kenya	902	797	1,024	997	36.0	35.2	16.4	15.9	5.6	9.3	8.8	6.4	8.8	6.6	0.0	0.0	7.1	8.0	9.6	9.1	7.9	6.9	0.0	2.7	28.6	28.2	20.7	18.0	12.7	10
Lesotho	…	760	…	893	…	36.7	…	23.3	…	20.0	…	0.0	…	0.0	…	0.0	…	0.0	…	0.0	…	20.0	…		…	16.5			19.0	
Liberia	…	…	…	…	…	…	…	…	…	…	…	…	…	…	…	…	…	…	…	…	…	…	…	…	23.7	…	16.5	…	19.0	
Madagascar	784	…	…	…	…	46.0	…	18.3	…	3.6	…	15.6	…	0.0	…	0.0	…	3.8	…	4.4	…	0.0	…	8.3	…	41.3	…	12.7	…	20
Malawi	…	…	…	39.6	38.6	13.0	18.0	5.8	1.6	11.7	3.2	7.6	5.5	0.0	0.0	6.8	10.1	5.0	4.4	10.5	10.2	0.0	8.4	35.0	24.5	12.5	13.2	15.0	4
Mali	…	…	…	…	…	…	…	…	…	…	…	…	…	…	…	…	…	…	…	…	…	…	…	…	29.5	…	16.4	…	21.3	
Mauritius	925	966	…	962	…	31.6	…	15.0	…	11.4	…	12.8	…	0.0	…	0.0	…	6.3	…	3.2	…	3.2	…	16.5	…	…	…	…	…	…
Mozambique	675	653	847	783	32.6	40.7	22.6	24.4	7.3	6.6	10.0	7.7	0.0	0.0	0.0	0.0	1.5	6.2	8.3	8.3	5.6	6.2	12.1	0.0	…	22.6	…	17.6	…	22
Namibia	…	936	…	979	…	36.3	…	22.3	…	5.1	…	11.5	…	5.8	…	0.0	…	7.8	…	2.9	…	3.6	…	4.6	25.2	31.7	12.0	17.5	15.6	21
Niger	…	743	…	810	…	44.3	…	18.2	…	4.2	…	7.9	…	0.0	…	0.0	…	6.7	…	7.3	…	11.4	…	0.0	32.9	45.5	12.1	18.2	6.6	5
Nigeria	…	…	…	…	…	…	…	…	…	…	…	…	…	…	…	…	…	…	…	…	…	…	…	…	…	…	…	…	…	…
Rwanda	648	662	1,110	1,110	32.3	44.3	27.8	17.2	4.6	10.9	13.8	7.8	6.2	3.1	0.0	3.1	4.6	4.7	7.7	4.2	3.1	3.1	0.0	1.6	43.0	37.9	16.1	16.2	7.2	16
Saint Helena	…	…	…	…	…	…	…	…	…	…	…	…	…	…	…	…	…	…	…	…	…	…	…	…	…	…	…	…	…	…
Sao Tome and Principe	…	…	…	…	…	…	…	…	…	…	…	…	…	…	…	…	…	…	…	…	…	…	…	…	…	…	…	…	…	…
Senegal	…	775	…	853	…	51.8	…	18.7	…	3.6	…	5.4	…	0.0	…	1.2	…	9.7	…	7.1	…	2.6	…	0.0	…	38.7	…	16.2		
Seychelles[a]	998	…	997	…	37.3	…	18.6	…	7.5	…	8.7	…	5.0	…	0.0	…	10.6	…	6.1	…	0.0	…	6.2	…	…	…	…	…	…	…
Sierra Leone	…	…	…	…	…	…	…	…	…	…	…	…	…	…	…	…	…	…	…	…	…	…	…	…	…	…	…	…	…	…
Somalia	…	…	…	…	…	…	…	…	…	…	…	…	…	…	…	…	…	…	…	…	…	…	…	…	…	…	…	…	…	…
South Africa	…	780	…	865	…	35.0	…	26.4	…	10.0	…	7.1	…	0.0	…	0.0	…	3.9	…	0.0	…	17.5	…		…	25.7	…	17.9	…	20
Swaziland	…	…	…	…	…	…	…	…	…	…	…	…	…	…	…	…	…	…	…	…	…	…	…	…	…	…	…	…	…	…

Average grades 7–8 | **Total % of tertiary students[2]**

Right-hand group figures refer to **2007**.

Social Sciences: History, Geography, Civics, Social Studies 1980s	2000s	Religion 1980s	2000s	Moral Education 1980s	2000s	Arts 1980s	2000s	Sports 1980s	2000s	Skills and Competencies 1980s	2000s	Optional and Others 1980s	2000s	Agriculture	Education	Education, Manufacturing and Construction	Humanities and Arts	Health and Welfare	Science	Social Sciences, Business and Law	Services	Non-specified programmes	Country or Territory
																							Arab States
4.3	10.0	9.5	6.7	0.0	0.0	4.8	3.3	0.0	0.0	6.7	4.8	6.7	0.0	2.0	1.7	9.2	18.6	6.1	7.7	38.7	0.9	15.2	Algeria
...	...	...	...	...	...	...	...	...	...	...	...	...	...	.	2.1[-1]	8.6[-1]	8.8[-1]	7.0[-1]	9.2[-1]	51.8[-1]	3.0[-1]	9.6[-1]	Bahrain
...	...	4.6	...	...	...	10.6	...	3.0	...	37.9	...	0.0	...			5.9[-1]	23.3[-1]	.	22.6[-1]	43.9[-1]	4.3[-1]	...	Djibouti
8.3	11.1	3.3	5.6	0.0	0.0	8.3	5.0	5.6	5.0	2.8	0.0	...	13.9	...	...	...	...	...	...	...	...	...	Egypt
5.1	14.9	0.0	9.0	0.0	0.0	3.3	4.5	4.4	6.0	0.0	1.5	0.0	0.0	...	...	...	...	...	...	...	...	...	Iraq
3.3	9.1	5.6	9.1	0.0	0.0	5.6	6.1	5.6	4.5	0.0	6.1	11.1	0.0	1.6	13.7	13.2	15.4	14.2	14.9	25.2	0.4	1.4	Jordan
...	6.3	...	6.3	...	...	...	6.3	...	6.3	...	9.4	...	6.3	...	...	...	...	...	...	...	...	...	Kuwait
8.1	12.5	8.1	0.0	0.0	0.0	3.2	6.3	3.2	6.3	6.5	0.0	0.0	0.0	0.4[+1]	3.6[+1]	11.2[+1]	16.2[+1]	9.3[+1]	12.4[+1]	45.4[+1]	0.9[+1]	0.5[+1]	Lebanon
8.6	13.9	14.8	8.3	0.0	0.0	5.1	8.3	3.7	5.6	4.9	0.0	3.7	0.0	...	...	...	...	...	...	...	...	...	Libyan Arab Jamahiriya
...	13.3	...	3.3	3.3	...	...	10.0	...	6.7	...	0.0	...	0.0		3.6[-2]		13.0[-2]		6.2[-2]	19.8[-2]		57.4[-2]	Mauritania
...	8.3	14.3	5.6	...	...	7.1	2.8	11.9	5.6	14.3	0.0	0.0	11.1	0.7	1.3	6.7	14.5	5.0	22.2	48.2	1.4	...	Morocco
2.3	10.0	6.3	10.0	0.0	0.0	3.2	5.0	9.4	2.5	0.0	2.5	0.0	5.0	2.0	25.4	7.4	6.3	7.0	13.6	21.9	...	16.3	Oman
2.0	10.5	24.1	7.5	0.0	0.0	6.0	6.0	1.5	5.2	9.0	5.2	0.0	0.0	0.6	34.5	6.6	10.7	6.1	9.6	31.7	0.2	0.0	Palestinian A.T.
5.4	11.1	6.2	13.9	0.0	0.0	3.1	6.9	6.2	5.6	4.6	7.6	0.0	0.0	.	5.3	17.6	24.0	7.3	12.2	32.2	0.9	0.6	Qatar
...	3.7	...	0.0	...	7.4	...	1.9	...	7.4	...	1.9	...	...	0.9[-1]	4.3[-1]	5.3[-1]	39.5[-1]	6.7[-1]	20.6[-1]	16.6[-1]		6.1[-1]	Saudi Arabia
...	13.4	...	...	...	0.0	...	6.7	...	10.0	...	...	...	...	...	...	...	...	...	...	...	...	...	Sudan
8.8	10.9	5.9	5.6	0.0	0.0	5.9	6.9	5.9	5.6	20.6	13.9	0.0	5.6	...	...	...	...	...	...	...	...	...	Syrian Arab Republic
11.1	16.1	13.9	5.4	0.0	0.0	6.9	7.1	5.6	10.7	6.9	5.4	0.0	0.0	2.7[-1]	1.0[-1]	10.7[-1]	20.0[-1]	7.7[-1]	14.8[-1]	17.5[-1]	12.9[-1]	12.6[-1]	Tunisia
2.0	11.1	0.0	8.3	0.0	0.0	6.3	11.1	6.3	5.6	0.0	0.0	0.0	0.0	0.1[+1]	4.5[+1]	10.6[+1]	9.1[+1]	5.8[+1]	10.4[+1]	38.8[+1]	0.9[+1]	19.9[+1]	United Arab Emirates
...	14.1	...	9.4	...	1.6	...	0.0	...	3.1	...	15.6	...	3.1	...	...	...	...	...	...	...	...	...	Yemen
																							Sub-Saharan Africa
...	15.0	...	0.0	...	1.7	...	6.7	...	6.7	...	6.7	...	0.0	...	...	...	...	...	...	...	...	...	Angola
3.9	15.8	1.4	0.0	1.4	0.0	0.0	0.0	2.8	9.7	8.3	9.7	1.4	0.0	...	...	...	...	...	...	...	...	...	Benin
...	...	...	...	...	...	...	...	...	...	...	...	...	...	...	...	...	...	...	...	...	...	...	Botswana
...	...	...	...	...	...	...	...	...	...	...	...	...	...	0.6[+1]	5.1[+1]	1.2[+1]	15.2[+1]	6.5[+1]	16.1[+1]	54.7[+1]	0.5[+1]	...	Burkina Faso
7.7	14.3	0.0	0.0	0.0	0.0	2.9	2.9	2.9	5.7	11.8	8.6	0.0	0.0	...	...	...	...	...	...	...	...	...	Burundi
...	...	...	...	...	...	...	...	...	...	...	...	...	...	0.5	6.9	2.7	6.9	1.8	18.7	61.3	0.6	0.6	Cameroon
...	18.4	...	0.0	...	0.0	...	10.0	...	6.7	...	0.0	...	4.8	...	...	...	...	...	...	...	...	...	Cape Verde
2.6	11.5	7.0	0.0	0.0	0.0	8.1	0.0	4.8	11.5	17.4	7.7	0.0	0.0	...	...	...	...	...	...	...	...	...	Central African Republic
0.0	16.7	5.0	0.0	0.0	0.0	5.0	0.0	5.0	6.7	0.0	0.0	5.0	0.0	...	...	...	...	...	...	...	...	...	Chad
...	...	...	...	...	...	...	...	...	...	...	...	...	...	...	...	...	...	...	...	...	...	...	Comoros
3.8	13.2	0.0	0.0	0.0	0.0	3.5	6.6	6.9	6.6	0.0	0.0	0.0	0.0	...	...	...	...	...	...	...	...	...	Congo
...	...	...	...	...	...	...	...	...	...	...	...	...	...	...	...	...	...	...	...	...	...	...	Congo (Dem. Rep.)
...	...	...	...	...	...	...	...	...	...	...	...	...	...	0.4	1.5	9.2	13.1	6.3	14.7	48.1	4.3	2.4	Côte d'Ivoire
...	...	...	...	...	...	...	...	...	...	...	...	...	...	...	...	...	...	...	...	...	...	...	Equatorial Guinea
6.7	...	0.0	...	0.0	...	8.3	...	5.6	...	11.1	...	0.0	...	...	...	...	...	...	...	...	...	...	Eritrea
...	11.4	...	0.0	...	0.0	...	0.0	...	8.6	...	0.0	...	0.0	8.5	26.8	8.0	2.9	9.1	7.0	36.9	...	0.8	Ethiopia
...	...	...	...	...	...	...	...	...	...	...	...	...	...	...	...	...	...	...	...	...	...	...	Gabon
...	...	...	...	...	...	...	...	...	...	...	...	...	...	...	...	...	...	...	...	...	...	...	Gambia
...	6.7	...	3.3	3.3	...	...	4.4	...	4.4	...	13.3	...	13.3	...	...	...	...	...	...	...	...	...	Ghana
3.8	16.7	0.0	0.0	0.0	0.0	0.0	0.0	13.8	6.7	11.2	0.0	0.0	0.0	10.9[-1]	4.3[-1]	3.9[-1]	11.1[-1]	7.8[-1]	19.4[-1]	32.0[-1]	1.1[-1]	9.5[-1]	Guinea
...	...	...	...	...	...	...	...	...	...	...	...	...	...	...	...	...	...	...	...	...	...	...	Guinea-Bissau
9.0	10.3	3.2	7.7	3.2	0.0	6.4	7.7	6.4	7.7	0.0	7.7	0.0	2.6	...	...	...	...	...	...	...	...	...	Kenya
...	...	...	...	...	...	...	...	...	...	...	...	...	...	1.1[-2]	32.4[-2]	0.7[-2]	8.2[-2]	1.1[-2]	23.2[-2]	33.3[-2]			Lesotho
5.1	...	4.7	...	0.0	...	3.8	...	2.5	...	11.5	...	3.3	...	...	...	...	...	...	...	...	...	...	Liberia
...	19.1	...	0.0	...	0.0	...	6.4	...	0.0	...	0.0	...	0.0	2.3	2.4	7.2	10.8	7.0	11.5	57.9	0.3	0.7	Madagascar
6.0	9.4	0.0	3.8	0.0	0.0	7.5	11.3	5.0	3.8	10.0	29.3	0.0	0.0	...	...	...	...	...	...	...	...	...	Malawi
9.7	...	0.0	...	0.0	...	6.6	...	6.6	...	0.0	...	...	...	2.8[+1]	14.6[+1]	19.9[+1]	5.7[+1]	0.0[+1]	11.4[+1]	45.4[+1]	0.2[+1]	...	Mauritius
...	17.8	...	0.0	...	0.0	...	7.0	...	8.9	...	3.7	...	0.0	5.2[-2]	7.6[-2]	9.9[-2]	11.1[-2]	5.2[-2]	13.9[-2]	43.9[-2]	2.7[-2]	0.5[-2]	Mozambique
9.5	13.9	4.0	4.1	1.4	1.2	7.8	4.1	1.4	17.6	4.7	2.7	0.0	0.0	...	...	...	...	...	...	...	...	...	Namibia
1.0	7.3	6.6	10.9	0.0	0.0	4.4	0.0	4.4	7.3	22.0	3.6	0.0	0.0	3.0	2.0	...	27.5	19.5	6.2	34.9	-	6.9	Niger
...	...	...	...	...	...	...	...	...	...	...	...	...	...	...	...	...	...	...	...	...	...	...	Nigeria
2.2	16.2	0.0	1.4	0.0	1.4	7.2	2.7	7.2	2.7	7.2	5.4	0.0	0.0	...	...	...	...	...	...	...	...	...	Rwanda
...	...	...	...	...	...	...	...	...	...	...	...	...	...	...	...	...	...	...	...	...	...	...	Saint Helena
...	...	...	...	...	...	...	...	...	...	...	...	...	...	.	.	.	.	.	.	.	.	.	Sao Tome and Principe
...	16.2	...	0.0	...	0.0	...	6.5	...	6.5	...	9.7	...	0.0	.	.	.	.	.	.	.	.	.	Senegal
...	...	...	...	...	...	...	...	...	...	...	...	...	...	.	.	.	.	.	.	.	.	.	Seychelles[a]
...	...	...	...	...	...	...	...	...	...	...	...	...	...	.	.	.	.	.	.	.	.	.	Sierra Leone
...	...	...	...	...	...	...	...	...	...	...	...	...	...	...	...	...	...	...	...	...	...	...	Somalia
...	12.0	...	0.0	...	0.0	...	7.9	...	0.0	...	7.9	...	7.9	1.8[-1]	13.3[-1]	9.5[-1]	4.9[-1]	5.9[-1]	10.4[-1]	52.9[-1]	1.2[-1]	0.0[-1]	South Africa
...	...	...	...	...	...	...	...	...	...	...	...	...	...	6.1[-1]	10.7[-1]	3.1[-1]	21.1[-1]	7.0[-1]	5.7[-1]	45.5[-1]	0.8[-1]	...	Swaziland

Table 10. Education and curricula

	Intended Annual Hours of Instruction				Emphasis on Curriculum Categories as % of Median Yearly Instructional Hours																									
					Average grades 1–6																									
	Average grades 1–6		Average grades 7–8		Language Education		Mathematics		Science, Computer and Technology		Social Sciences: History, Geography, Civics, Social Studies		Religion		Moral Education		Arts		Sports		Skills and Competencies		Optional and others		Language Education		Mathematics		Science, Computer ar[d] Technology	
Country or Territory	1980s	2000s	1980s	2000s	1980s	2000s	1980s	2000s	1980s	2000s	1980s	2000s	1980s	2000s	1980s	2000s	1980s	2000s	1980s	2000s	1980s	2000s	1980s	2000s	1980s	2000s	1980s	2000s	1980s	200
Tanzania (United Rep.)	849	802	...	987	38.3	35.8	22.9	21.2	4.5	9.7	6.0	8.2	5.9	5.7	0.0	0.0	10.0	11.1	5.9	0.0	6.5	8.5	0.0	0.0	...	...	...	...	...	..
Togo	...	...	...	...	...	52.9	...	18.8	...	0.0	...	6.4	...	0.0	...	1.3	...	5.4	...	5.0	...	8.9	...	1.4	...	40.7	...	14.8	...	14.
Uganda	...	...	...	...	32.5	...	13.4	...	13.9	...	9.3	...	10.8	...	0.0	...	8.5	...	10.4	...	1.1	...	0.0	...	...	...	...	...	...	.
Zambia	688	...	908	...	...	44.5	...	18.2	...	4.4	...	18.2	...	...	...	0.0	...	2.2	...	10.4	...	2.2	...	0.0	...	...	...	...	...	.
Zimbabwe	...	...	910	...	...	35.6	...	9.3	...	0.0	...	14.4	...	...	...	3.1	...	10.4	...	5.2	...	6.1	...	13.0	...	31.0	...	12.7	...	0.
Central and South Asia																														
Afghanistan	...	648	...	864	...	40.8	...	18.8	...	1.7	...	3.3	...	15.0	...	0.0	...	15.0	...	3.8	...	1.7	...	0.0	...	38.9	...	13.9	...	16.
Armenia	...	...	...	...	...	...	...	...	...	...	...	...	...	...	...	...	...	...	...	...	...	...	...	...	...	...	...	...	...	..
Azerbaijan	...	550	...	736	...	39.2	...	8.5	...	18.4	...	2.1	...	0.0	...	0.0	...	7.9	...	7.9	...	4.0	...	12.0	...	24.0	...	7.0	...	28
Bangladesh	716	...	...	...	32.9	...	18.0	...	1.9	...	16.7	...	4.7	...	3.9	...	10.5	...	8.6	...	2.1	...	0.8	...	...	...	...	...	...	.
Bhutan	...	...	...	...	...	...	...	...	...	...	...	...	...	...	...	...	...	...	...	...	...	...	...	...	...	...	...	...	...	.
Georgia	...	676	...	825	...	43.6	...	19.4	...	3.0	...	4.0	...	0.0	...	0.0	...	9.9	...	7.8	...	0.0	...	12.3	...	37.9	...	17.3	...	22.
India	892	750	932	900	29.9	30.3	15.2	14.5	10.2	2.0	7.3	14.5	0.0	0.0	0.0	0.0	8.3	10.0	5.3	5.0	23.9	23.7	0.0	0.0	...	32.0	...	12.0	...	12.
Iran (Islamic Rep.)	756	648	972	792	...	35.7	...	19.3	...	9.6	...	3.2	...	5.6	...	0.0	...	10.3	...	7.3	...	9.0	0.0	0.0	...	28.6	...	16.3	...	16.
Kazakhstan	...	676	...	731	...	45.0	...	11.8	...	5.2	...	3.5	...	0.0	...	0.0	...	7.5	...	7.5	...	0.0	...	19.6	...	37.9	...	0.0	...	14.
Kyrgyzstan	...	699	...	893	...	49.8	...	18.2	...	1.1	...	3.3	...	0.0	...	2.6	...	10.1	...	7.5	...	2.2	...	5.2	...	35.9	...	17.9	...	16.
Maldives	...	...	...	...	...	...	...	...	...	...	...	...	...	...	...	...	...	...	...	...	...	...	...	...	25.0	...	15.0	...	11.3	.
Nepal	...	803	...	858	...	36.3	...	21.5	...	2.6	...	8.5	...	0.0	...	0.0	...	8.6	...	10.1	...	4.3	...	8.0	29.6	36.8	15.9	15.8	15.9	15.
Pakistan	919	780	...	820	32.1	...	14.2	...	12.1	...	9.2	...	14.2	...	0.0	...	8.4	...	2.2	...	7.7	...	0.0	...	...	40.0	...	10.0	...	7.
Sri Lanka	850	834	1,120	1,013	...	32.4	...	24.7	...	4.2	...	7.4	...	5.9	...	0.0	...	...	...	2.5	...	6.2	...	0.4	...	25.0	...	17.5	...	15.
Tajikistan	...	...	...	...	...	...	...	...	...	...	...	...	...	...	...	...	...	...	...	...	...	...	...	...	...	...	...	...	...	.
Turkmenistan	...	713	...	980	...	46.1	...	21.9	...	5.2	...	5.9	...	0.0	...	0.0	...	6.7	...	7.1	...	7.1	...	0.0	...	28.3	...	19.3	...	26.
Uzbekistan	...	644	...	867	...	46.0	...	20.3	...	4.7	...	4.7	...	0.0	...	3.0	...	8.1	...	8.1	...	5.1	...	0.0	...	33.3	...	15.2	...	22.
East Asia																														
Brunei Darussalam	...	910	...	933	...	44.0	...	24.2	...	7.7	...	8.7	...	6.6	...	0.0	...	4.4	...	4.4	...	0.0	...	0.0	...	27.5	...	15.0	...	15.
Cambodia	...	634	...	941	...	39.4	...	16.7	...	14.4	...	9.7	...	0.0	...	3.1	...	6.7	...	6.7	...	3.3	...	0.0	...	31.8	...	13.6	...	19.
China[d]	633	816	814	927	...	37.9	...	18.8	...	0.0	...	8.4	...	0.0	...	4.0	...	14.9	...	9.6	...	2.8	...	3.6	36.1	29.2	18.0	13.9	9.8	13.
Hong Kong (SAR China)	...	...	...	...	...	...	...	...	...	...	...	...	...	...	...	...	...	...	...	...	...	...	...	...	...	...	...	...	...	.
Macao (SAR China)	...	...	...	...	...	...	...	...	...	...	...	...	...	...	...	...	...	...	...	...	...	...	...	...	...	...	...	...	...	..
Indonesia	804	874	992	1,197	25.4	25.2	19.1	25.2	9.6	8.6	3.8	12.9	7.7	5.5	6.4	0.0	9.6	5.5	4.1	2.8	4.1	2.8	10.1	11.6	28.2	23.8	12.8	14.3	10.3	14.
Japan	723	671	875	817	26.7	27.6	17.5	17.3	9.6	6.8	9.6	10.9	0.0	0.0	3.6	3.9	14.5	14.3	10.9	10.8	2.3	2.3	5.4	6.2	15.0	24.2	11.7	11.2	10.0	11.
Korea (Dem. People's Rep.)	...	...	...	...	...	...	...	...	...	...	...	...	...	...	...	...	...	...	...	...	...	...	...	...	...	...	...	...	...	..
Korea (Rep.)	638	648	854	867	...	33.5	...	18.2	...	7.0	...	7.0	...	0.0	...	2.3	...	9.3	...	7.0	...	2.2	...	13.5	28.2	23.4	11.0	12.5	11.0	13.
Lao (People's Dem. Rep.)	635	615	848	874	36.8	33.2	29.4	17.4	3.2	2.9	3.4	8.7	0.0	0.0	5.2	0.0	11.1	7.0	5.2	7.0	5.8	5.2	0.0	18.6	26.4	24.2	22.7	19.4	22.6	25.
Malaysia	943	836	...	988	...	44.6	...	15.0	...	5.2	...	4.2	...	5.9	...	5.9	...	8.6	...	2.7	...	4.8	...	3.2	33.7	22.9	11.2	10.4	11.2	10.
Mongolia	...	556	...	699	...	34.9	...	17.4	...	5.6	...	9.2	...	0.0	...	4.0	...	12.8	...	8.0	...	2.7	...	5.3	...	25.1	...	17.4	...	23.
Myanmar	...	798	...	945	...	34.6	...	18.3	...	7.1	...	12.4	...	0.0	...	1.0	...	6.0	...	7.7	...	1.0	...	11.9	...	...	...	...	...	.
Philippines	905	972	1,180	1,089	41.4	42.8	13.8	14.3	3.9	4.2	9.2	12.2	0.0	0.0	12.3	7.9	3.9	2.1	3.9	2.1	11.5	8.4	0.0	6.1	21.1	22.2	10.5	11.1	23.7	22.
Singapore	...	873	...	960	...	41.6	...	20.4	...	5.3	...	10.0	...	0.0	...	6.9	...	7.6	...	5.5	...	0.7	...	2.1	...	33.5	...	16.4	...	17.
Thailand	889	1,000	1,000	1,000	18.0	17.6	18.0	17.6	0.0	0.0	6.4	18.6	0.0	0.0	7.6	22.2	7.6	0.0	7.6	0.0	28.9	18.3	6.1	5.6	...	13.3	...	10.0	...	10.
Timor-Leste	...	...	...	...	...	...	...	...	...	...	...	...	...	...	...	...	...	...	...	...	...	...	...	...	...	...	...	...	...	..
Viet Nam	671	487	851	592	...	...	...	...	...	...	...	...	...	0.0	...	...	...	...	...	...	...	...	...	...	...	...	...	...	...	..
Europe																														
Albania	683	586	810	707	40.2	38.3	23.2	20.5	4.8	6.9	5.2	9.8	0.0	0.0	3.9	0.0	8.9	10.1	6.6	8.7	7.2	5.7	0.0	0.0	23.9	22.7	11.9	15.1	11.9	17.
Andorra[a]	...	...	...	...	...	...	...	...	...	...	...	...	...	...	...	...	...	...	...	...	...	...	...	...	37.2	...	14.3	...	6.7	..
Austria	805	765	...	990	...	36.8	...	15.4	...	4.9	...	9.8	...	7.7	...	0.0	...	11.2	...	11.2	...	2.2	...	0.8	29.3	21.2	10.9	15.9	11.8	12.
Belarus	744	694	873	855	44.3	46.7	22.1	15.0	5.8	0.0	5.9	9.5	0.0	0.0	0.0	0.0	7.4	8.5	7.4	10.5	7.4	2.3	0.0	7.5	24.0	33.9	13.6	12.7	20.4	15.
Belgium	840	869	1,048	910	29.7	29.4	20.0	18.8	3.9	3.8	16.1	14.4	0.0	3.5	7.3	3.5	9.3	9.3	7.3	7.1	0.0	3.5	6.3	6.6	...	...	...	...	...	..
Bosnia and Herzegovina	...	573	...	739	...	...	...	...	...	...	...	...	...	...	...	...	...	...	...	...	...	...	...	...	...	...	...	...	...	..
Bulgaria	623	593	692	789	30.2	29.0	13.8	14.5	4.0	5.1	6.7	7.6	0.0	0.0	0.0	0.0	6.2	14.0	7.3	10.8	8.5	5.7	23.3	13.3	28.4	26.5	15.8	11.8	18.9	17.
Croatia	...	648	...	805	...	32.6	...	22.9	...	2.3	...	13.6	...	0.0	...	0.0	...	10.9	...	0.0	...	1.9	...	15.8	...	25.9	...	14.8	...	22.
Cyprus[a]	711	804	932	972	39.8	40.0	17.8	17.1	3.9	5.9	11.4	10.5	6.3	5.2	0.0	0.0	12.6	12.2	6.3	6.1	1.9	2.1	0.0	1.0	...	35.5	0.0	12.6	0.0	15.
Czech Republic	740	670	900	836	...	44.6	...	22.2	...	6.8	...	6.2	...	0.0	...	0.0	...	4.6	...	7.9	...	2.3	...	5.4	...	29.2	...	18.8	...	31.
Denmark	683	720	897	910	35.2	35.9	17.6	17.3	3.2	7.6	6.5	3.3	5.7	5.8	0.0	0.0	17.1	12.4	9.2	9.1	1.2	4.3	4.4	4.3	...	33.3	...	14.8	...	14.
Estonia	...	665	...	805	...	36.4	...	19.5	...	1.2	...	5.1	...	0.0	...	0.0	...	16.6	...	12.8	...	7.1	...	1.2	...	25.6	...	16.7	...	13.
Finland	912	627	827	855	31.0	...	14.7	...	0.0	...	17.0	...	7.1	...	0.0	...	14.2	...	7.9	...	1.3	...	6.8	...	...	...	...	...	...	..
France	928	923	858	858	31.2	35.4	20.4	18.8	11.1	7.0	10.8	13.0	0.0	0.0	0.0	0.6	7.4	10.5	17.3	11.8	0.0	0.0	1.9	2.9	28.6	29.7	12.7	12.1	25.4	15.
Germany	...	...	...	...	45.0	...	21.3	...	3.6	...	3.6	...	0.0	...	0.0	...	8.6	...	9.0	...	7.9	...	1.1	...	...	...	0.0	...	0.0	..
Gibraltar	...	...	...	...	...	...	...	...	...	...	...	...	...	...	...	...	...	...	...	...	...	...	...	...	...	...	...	...	...	..
Greece	...	713	...	919	33.1	36.9	12.3	16.0	3.9	3.5	17.5	13.1	6.1	7.3	0.0	0.0	14.9	12.3	8.6	7.3	1.9	0.0	1.7	3.7	...	31.2	...	13.1	...	14.
Holy See	...	...	...	...	...	...	...	...	...	...	...	...	...	...	...	...	...	...	...	...	...	...	...	...	...	...	...	...	...	..

Average grades 7–8 | **Total % of tertiary students[2]** (2007)

Social Sciences: History, Geography, Civics, Social Studies		Religion		Moral Education		Arts		Sports		Skills and Competencies		Optional and Others		Agriculture	Education	Education, Manufacturing and Construction	Humanities and Arts	Health and Welfare	Science	Social Sciences, Business and Law	Services	Non-specified programmes	Country or Territory
1980s	2000s	1980s	2000s	1980s	2000s	1980s	2000s	1980s	2000s	1980s	2000s	1980s	2000s										
...	...	...	...	...	...	...	...	...	...	...	...	...	...	4.7**,-2	12.9**,-2	9.0**,-2	7.1**,-2	6.6**,-2	15.2**,-2	20.2**,-2	1.7**,-2	22.4**,-2	Tanzania (United Rep.)
...	11.1	...	0.0	...	0.0	...	7.4	...	7.4	...	3.7	...	0.0	...	...	...	...	...	...	...	...	...	Togo
...	...	...	...	...	...	...	...	...	...	...	...	...	...	...	...	...	...	...	...	...	...	...	Uganda
...	...	...	...	...	...	...	...	...	...	...	...	...	...	...	...	...	...	...	...	...	...	...	Zambia
...	12.7	...	1.7	...	1.7	...	5.6	...	2.8	...	24.9	...	6.9	...	...	...	...	...	...	...	...	...	Zimbabwe
																							Central and South Asia
...	13.9	...	11.1	...	2.8	...	0.0	...	2.8	...	0.0	...	0.0	...	...	...	...	...	...	...	...	...	Afghanistan
...	8.4	...	0.0	...	0.0	...	4.3	...	5.6	...	2.8	...	19.7	4.7	14.7	6.5	4.4	15.6	0.2	28.4	2.9	22.5	Armenia
...	...	...	...	...	...	...	...	...	...	...	...	...	...	1.1	2.3	3.3	25.0	2.2	10.5	44.6	0.2	10.8	Azerbaijan
...	...	...	...	...	...	...	...	...	...	...	...	...	...	2.8	36.1	8.5	12.2	0.5	2.3	11.7	...	26.0	Bangladesh
...	8.5	...	0.0	...	0.0	...	1.8	...	6.9	...	0.0	...	5.2	2.8	3.4	8.9	38.2	9.1	5.1	30.0	2.5	0.0	Bhutan
...	12.0	...	0.0	...	0.0	...	10.0	...	5.0	...	17.0	...	0.0	...	1.3-2	5.9-2	36.0-2	2.2-2	14.3-2	13.5-2	...	26.8-2	Georgia
...	12.3	...	8.2	...	0.0	...	4.1	...	0.0	...	12.3	...	2.0	4.5	5.4	28.5	12.1	4.8	12.0	30.2	2.4	...	India
...	11.9	...	0.0	...	0.0	...	5.1	...	6.9	...	0.0	...	24.2	...	...	...	...	...	...	...	...	...	Iran (Islamic Rep.)
...	13.5	...	0.0	...	0.0	...	4.5	...	6.0	...	6.0	...	0.0	1.3	25.4	11.3	10.4	3.1	5.7	36.1	6.7	...	Kazakhstan
13.7	...	5.0	...	0.0	...	7.5	...	5.0	...	12.5	...	5.0	...	...	...	...	...	...	...	...	...	...	Kyrgyzstan
13.6	15.8	0.0	0.0	0.0	0.0	4.0	6.8	4.0	18.2	7.9	0.0	0.0	...	...	...	...	...	...	...	...	...	...	Maldives
...	7.5	...	5.0	...	5.0	...	0.0	...	3.8	...	6.3	...	15.0	1.5*	4.6*	5.6*	11.5*	7.5*	4.6*	18.3*	.	46.3*	Nepal
...	12.5	...	5.0	...	0.0	...	7.5	...	2.5	...	12.5	...	2.5	...	...	...	...	...	...	...	...	...	Pakistan
...	...	...	...	...	...	...	...	...	...	...	...	...	...	2.1	7.9	8.5	27.8	3.4	14.6	33.6	1.7	0.3	Sri Lanka
...	16.6	...	0.0	...	0.0	...	1.1	...	6.6	...	2.2	...	0.0	...	...	...	...	...	...	...	...	...	Tajikistan
...	...	...	...	...	...	...	...	...	...	...	...	...	...	...	...	...	...	...	...	...	...	...	Turkmenistan
...	13.6	...	0.0	...	0.0	...	3.0	...	6.1	...	4.6	...	1.5	4.0	34.3	14.5	11.6	6.7	6.2	20.3	2.3	...	Uzbekistan
																							East Asia
...	22.5	...	7.5	...	0.0	...	0.0	...	5.0	...	0.0	...	7.5	...	51.7	7.3	9.4	7.2	7.5	12.5	...	4.3	Brunei Darussalam
...	12.1	...	0.0	...	3.0	...	6.1	...	6.1	...	7.6	...	0.0	3.2	19.8	3.5	0.7	6.4	11.0	51.4	...	4.0	Cambodia
23.0	20.1	0.0	0.0	0.0	0.0	6.6	6.2	6.6	8.5	0.0	6.2	0.0	3.1	...	...	...	...	...	...	...	...	...	China[d]
...	...	...	...	...	...	...	...	...	...	...	...	...	...	...	5.4*	16.4*	10.6*	6.2*	13.1*	36.4*	3.9*	8.0*	Hong Kong (SAR China)
...	...	...	...	...	...	...	...	...	...	...	...	...	...	...	4.1	2.0	7.2	5.3	3.7	66.3	11.5	...	Macao (SAR China)
0.3	19.1	5.1	4.8	5.1	0.0	5.1	4.8	3.9	2.4	11.5	2.4	7.7	14.3	4.9	15.0	16.4	0.5	3.9	8.1	50.7	...	0.4	Indonesia
3.3	11.2	0.0	0.0	3.3	3.7	13.3	8.5	5.0	5.6	11.7	13.0	16.7	11.4	2.2	7.3	15.8	15.7	12.5	2.9	29.1	5.7	8.8	Japan
...	...	...	...	...	...	...	...	...	...	...	...	...	...	...	...	...	...	...	...	...	...	...	Korea (Dem. People's Rep.)
0.8	9.4	0.0	0.0	5.8	6.3	11.6	7.8	8.7	9.4	11.5	5.5	1.5	12.5	1.2	6.3	27.8	18.2	9.3	8.8	21.9	6.4	...	Korea (Rep.)
1.3	16.1	0.0	0.0	1.9	0.0	3.9	1.6	3.8	6.5	7.6	0.0	0.0	6.5	5.7	21.9	6.3	20.1	1.9	2.8	38.8	2.5	...	Lao (People's Dem. Rep.)
9.0	12.5	4.5	8.3	0.0	0.0	4.5	4.2	4.5	2.1	2.3	10.4	19.1	18.8	2.8-1	9.4-1	22.9-1	9.2-1	6.4-1	19.3-1	26.9-1	3.0-1	0.1-1	Malaysia
...	11.4	...	0.0	...	3.9	...	0.0	...	7.7	...	0.0	...	11.4	2.9	10.6	15.9	9.6	8.1	6.7	39.7	5.6	0.8	Mongolia
0.5	11.1	0.0	0.0	10.5	11.1	3.5	3.7	3.5	3.7	16.7	14.8	0.0	0.0	...	1.5	...	48.2	...	21.7	28.5	...	...	Myanmar
...	13.5	...	0.0	...	0.0	...	6.8	...	5.2	...	4.2	...	3.4	...	...	...	...	...	...	...	...	...	Philippines
...	6.7	...	0.0	...	0.0	...	3.3	...	1.7	...	1.7	...	53.3	...	3.2	30.7	9.0	5.6	16.9	34.1	0.6	...	Singapore
...	...	...	...	...	...	...	...	...	...	...	...	...	...	...	...	...	...	...	...	...	...	...	Thailand
...	...	...	...	...	...	...	...	...	...	...	...	...	...	...	...	...	...	...	...	...	...	...	Timor-Leste
...	...	...	0.0	...	...	...	0.0	...	...	...	0.0	...	...	6.5	25.6	23.5	3.6	3.0	...	34.1	...	3.7	Viet Nam
																							Europe
4.9	18.9	3.0	0.0	3.0	0.0	4.5	11.3	4.5	7.6	1.5	7.6	20.9	0.0	...	...	...	...	...	...	...	...	...	Albania
6.7	...	6.7	...	0.0	...	13.3	...	8.6	...	6.7	...	0.0	...	...	...	...	6.7-1	13.5-1	24.7-1	55.1-1	...	...	Andorra[a]
1.3	15.2	5.5	6.1	0.0	0.0	10.9	10.7	8.2	9.1	12.3	9.8	0.0	0.0	1.1	12.4	12.7	15.4	7.9	12.0	36.5	1.8	0.2	Austria
3.6	9.8	0.0	0.0	3.2	0.0	6.8	2.8	6.8	8.5	8.4	8.5	3.2	8.5	8.0	12.2	25.7	6.5	4.1	2.3	38.4	3.6	...	Belarus
...	...	...	...	...	...	...	...	...	...	...	...	...	...	2.5	12.3	9.5	10.9	19.4	6.5	29.5	1.9	7.5	Belgium
2.6	11.8	0.0	0.0	3.2	0.0	7.9	11.8	0.0	5.9	13.4	2.9	0.0	11.8	...	...	...	...	...	...	...	...	...	Bosnia and Herzegovina
...	14.8	...	0.0	...	0.0	...	7.4	...	0.0	...	3.7	...	11.1	2.5	6.4	19.7	7.9	6.2	5.1	44.0	8.0	0.2	Bulgaria
0.0	3.2	0.0	6.3	0.0	0.0	0.0	12.6	0.0	9.5	0.0	4.7	...	0.0	3.8	4.1	15.7	9.7	7.0	7.7	41.7	10.2	...	Croatia
...	20.8	...	0.0	...	0.0	...	0.0	...	0.0	...	0.0	...	0.0	0.1	9.7	6.8	9.5	6.1	11.9	49.9	6.1	...	Cyprus[a]
...	14.8	...	1.9	...	0.0	...	1.9	...	7.4	...	3.7	...	7.4	3.7	12.7	14.2	8.7	11.9	8.7	28.6	4.1	7.4	Czech Republic
...	14.1	...	0.0	...	1.9	...	7.0	...	7.0	...	7.0	...	7.0	1.5	11.3	10.1	15.3	22.0	8.7	29.0	2.2	...	Denmark
...	...	...	...	...	...	...	...	...	...	...	...	...	...	2.4	6.9	13.1	11.4	8.3	9.9	39.8	8.1	...	Estonia
7.4	10.6	0.0	0.0	0.0	0.0	6.4	7.6	6.4	9.1	0.0	0.0	3.2	15.1	2.2	5.2	25.4	14.6	13.7	11.2	22.7	4.9	...	Finland
0.0	...	0.0	...	...	...	0.0	...	0.0	...	0.0	...	0.0	...	1.1	2.8	12.8	16.0	15.1	12.4	35.6	3.4	0.8	France
...	...	...	...	...	...	...	...	...	...	...	...	...	...	...	...	...	...	...	...	...	...	...	Germany
...	...	...	...	...	...	...	...	...	...	...	...	...	...	...	...	...	...	...	...	...	...	...	Gibraltar
...	13.1	...	6.6	...	0.0	...	6.6	...	9.8	...	4.9	...	0.0	5.8	5.7	17.0	13.5	9.6	13.6	31.8	3.1	...	Greece
...	...	...	...	...	...	...	...	...	...	...	...	...	...	...	...	...	...	...	...	...	...	...	Holy See

Table 10. Education and curricula

The table below reports *Intended Annual Hours of Instruction* and *Emphasis on Curriculum Categories as % of Median Yearly Instructional Hours* (Average grades 1–6), followed by three additional curriculum categories. Each category is reported for the 1980s and the 2000s.

Country or Territory	Hrs 1–6 1980s	Hrs 1–6 2000s	Hrs 7–8 1980s	Hrs 7–8 2000s	Language 1980s	Language 2000s	Math 1980s	Math 2000s	Science/Comp/Tech 1980s	Science/Comp/Tech 2000s	Social Sciences 1980s	Social Sciences 2000s	Religion 1980s	Religion 2000s	Moral Educ. 1980s	Moral Educ. 2000s	Arts 1980s	Arts 2000s	Sports 1980s	Sports 2000s	Skills & Comp. 1980s	Skills & Comp. 2000s	Optional & others 1980s	Optional & others 2000s	Language 1980s	Language 2000s	Math 1980s	Math 2000s	Sci/Comp/Tech 1980s	Sci/Comp/Tech 2000s
Hungary	652	624	768	786	35.2	36.5	19.8	16.8	7.4	7.4	10.5	7.4	0.0	0.0	0.0	0.0	13.8	12.9	10.9	11.3	0.0	0.4	2.3	7.4	...	26.0	...	11.1	...	24
Iceland	697	695	887	794	21.0	30.3	15.0	17.2	6.1	15.2	15.0	5.1	15.0	5.1	0.0	0.0	19.4	11.1	8.5	10.1	0.0	4.0	0.0	2.0	...	30.3	...	17.2	...	15
Ireland	859	824	859	950	...	33.3	...	13.3	...	4.4	...	10.0	...	11.1	...	0.0	...	8.9	...	4.4	...	1.1	...	13.3	31.8	30.0	6.7	10.0	13.4	12
Israel	866	...	932	...																					...	20.8	...	13.0	...	15
Italy	...	911	...	922																					20.6	33.4	11.8	5.0	8.8	15
Latvia	...	572	...	793	...	39.3	...	18.7	...	3.7	...	3.2	...	0.0	...	0.0	...	14.3	...	9.6	...	3.0	...	8.2	21.9	25.1	12.5	16.5	23.4	13.
Liechtenstein																									39.6		14.2		9.0	
Lithuania	...	621	...	884	...	33.6	...	17.8	...	4.1	...	8.1	...	2.1	...	2.1	...	13.8	...	10.3	...	0.0	...	8.1	30.1	27.9	11.3	14.8	20.8	14
Luxembourg	972	840	1,080	900	46.9	40.0	18.3	17.8	0.0	6.7	5.5	2.2	11.0	10.0	0.0	0.0	3.7	7.2	3.7	10.0	5.5	2.8	5.5	3.3						
Macedonia (TFYR)	...	500	...	639	...	30.3	...	18.9	...	5.5	...	5.5	...	0.0	...	0.0	...	13.5	...	5.5	...	5.5	...	15.4	...	33.3	...	14.8	...	22
Malta	988	808	...	840	46.2	38.5	20.1	19.7	1.6	19.7	6.4	4.9	10.0	8.2	0.0	0.0	5.6	2.5	10.0	3.3	0.0	0.0	0.0	3.3	...	36.1	...	13.9	...	13
Moldova (Rep.)[a,b]	...	621	...	808	...	36.1	...	17.6	...	8.6	...	4.8	...	0.0	...	0.0	...	8.8	...	8.8	...	0.0	...	15.3	...	22.3	...	14.8	...	27
Monaco[c]																									45.0		11.7		5.0	
Montenegro																														
Netherlands	960	883	1,000	989																					...	20.3	...	12.7	...	16.4
Norway	585	637	855	827	29.0	37.8	16.8	13.9	0.0	2.6	0.0	8.7	10.1	3.7	0.0	3.7	18.7	12.7	7.9	6.7	1.9	1.8	15.7	8.4	...	29.1	...	12.1	...	4.
Poland	680	741	833	865	33.6	34.7	20.7	19.8	3.0	3.4	11.2	9.9	0.0	4.0	0.0	4.0	9.8	7.1	9.8	14.9	10.1	1.0	1.9	1.3	...	24.3	...	13.3	...	15.
Portugal	749	866	992	972																					...	28.9	...	12.2	...	17
Romania	595	657	803	850	37.7	31.7	20.3	13.7	3.4	6.1	9.4	6.1	0.0	3.8	1.2	0.0	11.8	11.5	8.1	8.5	5.2	4.1	3.0	14.6	23.3	26.2	15.0	12.3	17.5	18
Russian Federation	687	678	786	884	...	36.8	13.0	8.7	2.2	13.2	0.0	7.6	0.0	0.0	0.0	0.0	2.2	8.1	4.4	4.1	4.4	8.9	0.0	12.7	...	27.7	...	7.7	...	24
San Marino[c]																									37.5	37.5	12.5	4.7	10.0	14.
Serbia[c]	...	563	...	715	37.5	29.3	20.6	23.4	4.7	10.3	10.8	7.1	0.0	0.0	0.0	0.0	13.2	16.6	4.4	13.4	4.4	0.0	4.4	0.0	21.5	23.5	18.3	15.7	20.6	29
Slovakia	...	722	...	848	...	34.3	...	18.6	...	7.9	...	10.7	...	0.6	...	0.6	...	11.1	...	10.5	...	0.0	...	5.8	...	23.0	...	14.8	...	19
Slovenia	...	741	...	931	...	23.6	...	19.0	...	7.3	...	8.8	...	0.0	...	0.0	...	12.0	...	12.1	...	0.0	...	17.3	...	20.3	...	12.5	...	22
Spain	875	788	...	1,073																					...	23.0	...	11.5	...	9.8
Sweden	704	741	893	741	38.2	...	16.2	...	0.0	...	0.0	...	0.0	...	0.0	...	13.9	...	8.5	...	23.1	...	0.0	...	...	28.3	...	10.0	...	6.7
Switzerland					...	35.0	...	23.4	...	5.0	...	9.9	...	0.0	...	0.0	...	13.4	...	0.0	...	13.4	...	0.0	...	35.9	...	13.6	...	19.3
Turkey	856	720	1,073	744	32.0	33.9	17.4	13.3	7.4	5.0	6.0	13.3	1.8	1.7	1.8	1.7	6.4	10.0	4.3	6.1	2.6	3.6	20.2	11.4	40.0	30.0	8.9	13.3	6.7	10
Ukraine	757	635	880	899	...	33.2	...	18.4	...	1.2	...	6.1	...	0.0	...	0.0	...	8.0	...	8.0	...	7.2	...	18.0	...	28.2	...	14.1	...	15
United Kingdom	867	...	...	...																					...	19.1	...	12.0	...	0.0
North America																														
Canada	...	...	...	...	43.7	28.7	14.3	12.4	8.2	13.8	9.5	14.1	0.0	3.3	0.0	0.0	12.1	10.6	10.0	5.3	0.0	5.3	2.2	6.6	...	25.3	...	13.7	...	9
United States of America																														
Latin America and the Caribbean																														
Anguilla																														
Antigua and Barbuda																														
Argentina	731	720	774	900	28.0	26.0	26.0	26.3	10.0	14.5	16.0	16.0	0.0	0.0	0.0	1.0	8.0	10.3	8.0	6.0	4.0	0.0	0.0	0.0	36.0	21.3	16.1	13.3	8.7	16
Aruba[a]																														
Bahamas																														
Barbados	...	796																												
Belize																														
Bermuda[a]																														
Bolivia	...	855	...	893	26.0	...	21.0	...	11.5	...	11.2	...	1.3	...	0.7	...	3.5	...	3.5	...	17.8	...	3.5	...	20.0	...	16.7	...	10.0	
Brazil	780	800	936	833	...	30.2	...	21.4	...	10.2	...	20.5	...	2.2	...	0.0	...	6.6	...	8.8	...	0.0	...	0.0	46.4	27.1	10.7	18.8	10.7	12
British Virgin Islands[a]																														
Cayman Islands																														
Chile	833	878	833	965	...	20.0	...	15.6	...	17.1	...	13.8	...	6.7	...	0.0	...	5.8	...	0.0	...	0.0	...	21.1	...	22.6	...	15.1	...	15.
Colombia	832	900	...	...	22.5	...	16.0	...	12.5	...	16.1	...	4.5	...	4.5	...	11.1	...	8.5	...	0.0	...	4.3	...	20.0	...	14.3	...	8.6	
Costa Rica	...	660																							25.6	29.0	10.3	13.2	12.8	13.
Cuba	715	710	...	748	42.2	...	20.3	...	2.9	...	7.5	...	0.0	...	0.0	...	8.1	...	...	8.1	...	0.0			26.2	27.2	17.9	14.4	19.1	15
Dominica[a]	...	798	...	798	50.0	...	50.0	...	0.0	...	0.0	...	0.0	...	0.0	...	0.0	...	0.0	...	0.0	...	0.0	...						
Dominican Republic	...	788	...	884	30.7	...	22.7	...	12.0	...	12.0	...	0.7	...	0.7	...	10.7	...	10.7	...	0.0	...	0.0	...	31.3	36.0	31.3	20.0	0.0	12.
Ecuador	790	842	922	971	22.2	22.0	22.0	20.0	19.8	10.0	9.9	13.3	13.2	0.0	0.0	0.0	10.0	11.0	7.8	7.7	10.0	9.9	6.7	6.6	22.9	22.9	14.3	14.3	14.3	14.
El Salvador	729	750	...	750	20.0	...	20.0	...	20.0	...	16.0	...	0.0	...			16.0	...	8.0	...	0.0	...	0.0	...	24.0	...	16.0	...	20.0	
Grenada[a]	...	756	...	945	...	28.6	...	28.6	...	4.8	...	7.1	...	2.4	...	0.0	...	11.9	...	4.8	...	11.9	...	0.0						
Guatemala	999	828	999	864	24.3	...	13.5	...	13.5	...	13.5	...	0.0	...	0.0	...	16.2	...	5.4	...	13.5	...	0.0	...	24.3	22.9	13.5	14.3	13.5	14.
Guyana	661	780	...	...	31.0	52.6	14.3	26.3	6.6	10.5	6.6	10.5	0.0	0.0	0.0	0.0	8.8	6.0	6.0	0.0	0.0	15.6	6.0	0.0	17.3	...	13.7	...	6.5	
Haiti																														
Honduras	773	800	918	864	16.5	13.4	13.2	13.4	13.2	13.4	9.9	10.1	0.0	0.0	3.3	3.4	9.9	8.8	8.0	5.0	4.0	29.1	33.5	0.9	22.2	23.5	13.9	14.7	13.9	14.
Jamaica	891	855	...	...	...	34.0	...	30.0	...	12.7	...	5.6	...	3.1	...	0.0	...	5.6	...	3.1	...	6.1	...	0.0						
Mexico	716	800	1,079	1,167	27.0	35.0	20.3	26.7	20.2	11.3	12.1	17.1	0.0	0.0	0.0	0.0	9.2	5.0	5.4	5.0	5.8	0.0	0.0	0.0	20.0	22.9	11.4	14.3	37.1	28
Montserrat[a]																														

Average grades 7–8 | **Total % of tertiary students[2]**

2007

Social Sciences, History, Geography, Civics, Social Studies 1980s	Social Sciences ... 2000s	Religion 1980s	Religion 2000s	Moral Education 1980s	Moral Education 2000s	Arts 1980s	Arts 2000s	Sports 1980s	Sports 2000s	Skills and Competencies 1980s	Skills and Competencies 2000s	Optional and Others 1980s	Optional and Others 2000s	Agriculture	Education	Education, Manufacturing and Construction	Humanities and Arts	Health and Welfare	Science	Social Sciences, Business and Law	Services	Non-specified programmes	Country or Territory
...	13.9	...	0.0	...	0.9	...	7.4	...	7.4	...	0.9	...	7.4	2.7	11.8	11.5	8.6	8.8	6.9	40.6	9.1	...	Hungary
...	5.1	...	5.1	...	0.0	...	11.1	...	10.1	...	4.0	...	2.0	0.6	16.5	7.7	14.6	12.7	7.9	38.5	1.5	...	Iceland
.6	10.0	3.4	2.5	0.0	2.5	13.4	7.5	6.7	5.0	10.1	0.0	0.0	20.0	1.2	5.6	10.3	14.7	13.1	11.0	22.0	4.9	17.2	Ireland
...	19.5	...	18.1	...	0.0	...	3.2	...	4.6	...	0.0	...	5.6	0.5	14.9	17.8	10.6	7.5	9.1	38.5	.	1.2	Israel
.2	13.0	11.8	0.0	0.0	0.0	8.8	13.4	5.9	6.7	4.4	10.0	14.7	3.3	2.3	7.3	15.6	15.3	12.9	7.9	35.6	2.7	0.4	Italy
.1	11.5	0.0	0.0	0.0	1.5	9.4	8.6	9.4	7.2	0.0	5.7	9.4	10.6	1.1	10.5	10.4	7.2	6.3	5.1	53.7	5.6	0.1	Latvia
.7	...	7.6	...	0.0	...	3.8	...	7.6	...	1.9	...	3.8	...	...	...	22.9	0.7	2.1	...	74.3	...	...	Liechtenstein
.1	14.8	0.0	1.9	0.0	1.9	7.6	7.4	3.8	7.4	7.6	0.0	3.8	9.2	2.2	12.2	18.2	7.1	8.4	5.9	42.8	3.1	...	Lithuania
...	...	...	...	...	...	...	...	...	...	...	...	...	...	...	22.7[-1]	15.0[-1]	8.2[-1]	0.4[-1]	8.4[-1]	45.2[-1]	...	...	Luxembourg
...	14.8	...	0.0	...	0.0	...	7.4	...	3.7	...	3.7	...	0.0	4.0[-2]	13.3[-2]	18.1[-2]	10.9[-2]	9.0[-2]	7.4[-2]	32.8[-2]	4.5[-2]	...	Macedonia (TFYR)
...	16.7	...	5.6	...	0.0	...	2.8	...	5.6	...	0.0	...	5.6	0.8[-2]	15.7[-2]	7.8[-2]	13.5[-2]	14.5[-2]	5.9[-2]	41.6[-2]	0.2[-2]	...	Malta
...	11.1	...	0.0	...	0.0	...	5.6	...	7.4	...	0.0	...	11.0	...	...	...	...	...	...	...	...	...	Moldova (Rep.)[a,b]
.7	0.0	...	6.7	10.0	...	8.3	...	1.7	...	0.0	...	...	...	...	...	...	...	...	...	...	...	...	Monaco[c]
...	...	...	...	...	...	...	...	...	...	...	...	...	...	...	...	...	...	...	...	...	...	...	Montenegro
.7	...	0.0	...	0.0	...	5.1	...	5.1	...	17.7	...	10.1	...	1.1	14.5	8.0	8.4	16.6	6.4	37.0	6.1	1.8	Netherlands
...	13.5	...	3.6	...	3.6	...	13.4	...	8.0	...	3.2	...	9.3	0.8	14.1	7.0	11.6	19.8	8.8	32.3	4.0	1.7	Norway
...	14.3	...	3.3	...	3.3	...	3.3	...	10.0	...	0.0	...	13.3	2.2	13.6	12.6	10.2	6.1	9.5	40.3	5.6	...	Poland
...	18.7	...	0.0	...	0.0	...	6.1	...	9.1	...	0.0	...	8.1	1.9	5.8	22.3	8.5	16.5	7.3	32.0	5.7	...	Portugal
.7	14.6	0.0	3.1	0.0	0.0	6.7	6.9	6.7	4.6	9.2	0.0	5.0	13.9	2.7	2.5	17.2	9.9	5.6	6.2	51.0	4.3	0.6	Romania
...	13.3	...	0.0	...	0.0	...	6.1	...	3.1	...	6.8	...	10.7	...	...	...	...	...	...	...	...	...	Russian Federation
.5	12.5	5.0	0.0	0.0	2.5	12.5	5.0	6.3	20.0	9.4	0.0	...	3.1	...	...	...	...	...	...	...	...	...	San Marino[c]
.2	15.7	0.0	0.0	0.0	0.0	1.6	7.8	6.1	7.8	9.2	0.0	7.6	0.0	...	...	...	...	...	...	...	...	...	Serbia[c]
...	16.4	...	1.6	...	1.6	...	6.6	...	6.6	...	0.0	...	9.8	2.6	15.5	15.7	6.2	16.2	8.9	29.4	5.5	...	Slovakia
...	14.8	...	0.0	...	0.0	...	6.3	...	6.3	...	1.6	...	15.6	3.2	8.4	16.7	7.8	7.2	5.6	41.7	9.5	...	Slovenia
.8	...	6.6	...	0.0	...	13.1	...	8.2	...	4.8	...	13.3	...	2.0	9.2	17.6	10.3	11.7	10.5	31.6	5.6	1.4	Spain
.7	...	3.3	...	0.0	...	8.3	...	6.7	...	8.3	...	11.7	...	0.9	15.0	16.1	12.5	17.7	9.4	26.3	2.0	0.2	Sweden
.5	...	0.0	...	0.0	...	7.7	...	5.6	...	0.0	...	5.6	...	1.1	10.3	13.2	12.7	11.0	10.5	37.0	3.5	0.6	Switzerland
.7	11.7	8.9	3.3	0.0	3.3	2.2	6.7	3.3	3.3	23.3	7.5	0.0	10.8	3.7	11.5	13.1	6.2	5.6	7.5	48.7	3.8	...	Turkey
...	7.8	...	0.0	...	0.0	...	4.7	...	6.3	...	7.8	0.0	15.6	4.5	9.0	22.0	5.1	5.1	4.1	42.5	6.1	1.7	Ukraine
.0	...	0.0	...	0.0	...	12.2	...	9.0	...	36.6	...	11.0	...	0.9	9.2	8.4	17.1	16.0	13.4	26.9	3.1	5.0	United Kingdom

North America

...	8.4	...	1.5	...	1.5	...	12.2	...	7.0	...	9.8	...	10.7	...	...	...	...	...	...	...	...	...	Canada
...	...	...	...	...	...	...	...	...	...	...	...	...	...	0.6	9.4	6.7	10.6	13.9	8.9	27.3	5.1	17.6	United States of America

Latin America and the Caribbean

														29.6[+1]	.	.	.	.	.	70.4[+1]	.	.	Anguilla
...	...	...	...	...	...	...	...	...	...	...	...	...	...	...	...	...	...	...	...	...	...	...	Antigua and Barbuda
.6	13.3	0.0	0.0	0.0	2.7	8.4	8.0	7.1	8.0	4.2	0.0	0.0	17.3	3.5[-1]	10.2[-1]	8.1[-1]	12.4[-1]	12.8[-1]	9.5[-1]	39.6[-1]	3.0[-1]	0.9[-1]	Argentina
...	...	...	...	...	...	...	...	...	...	...	...	...	...	...	14.5	18.7	...	17.6	...	49.2	...	...	Aruba[a]
...	...	...	...	...	...	...	...	...	...	...	...	...	...	...	...	...	...	...	...	...	...	...	Bahamas
...	...	...	...	...	...	...	...	...	...	...	...	...	...	...	...	...	...	...	...	...	...	...	Barbados
...	...	...	...	...	...	...	...	...	...	...	...	...	...	...	...	...	...	...	...	...	...	...	Belize
...	...	...	...	...	...	...	...	...	...	...	...	...	...	...	4.1	6.0	9.3	7.7	12.5	33.0	3.3	24.3	Bermuda[a]
.0	...	3.3	...	0.0	...	6.7	...	3.3	...	26.7	...	3.3	...	...	...	...	...	...	...	...	...	...	Bolivia
.9	25.0	0.0	2.1	0.0	0.0	8.9	6.3	5.4	8.3	0.0	0.0	0.0	0.0	2.1	19.4	7.8	3.2	14.5	7.7	40.5	1.9	2.9	Brazil
...	...	...	...	...	...	...	...	...	...	...	...	...	...	...	...	...	...	...	...	...	...	...	British Virgin Islands[a]
														...	...	...	...	...	16.4[-1]	81.0[-1]	.	2.6[-1]	Cayman Islands
...	7.6	...	7.6	...	0.0	...	0.0	...	0.0	...	0.0	...	32.1	3.4	13.8	17.8	6.4	15.6	7.2	27.0	8.3	0.5	Chile
.4	...	4.3	...	4.3	...	5.7	...	5.7	...	0.0	...	25.7	...	2.1	10.4	28.0	4.3	9.2	2.2	43.8	...	...	Colombia
.8	13.2	2.6	2.6	0.0	0.0	10.3	10.5	5.1	5.3	7.7	7.9	12.8	5.3	...	...	...	...	...	...	...	...	...	Costa Rica
.7	20.9	0.0	0.0	0.0	0.0	6.0	3.8	7.1	7.2	7.1	10.9	0.0	0.0	1.6[+1]	24.7[+1]	1.6[+1]	1.9[+1]	24.4[+1]	2.3[+1]	34.3[+1]	8.0[+1]	1.4[+1]	Cuba
...	...	...	...	...	...	...	...	...	...	...	...	...	...	...	...	...	...	...	...	...	...	...	Dominica[a]
.0	12.0	0.0	2.0	0.0	0.0	25.0	8.0	12.5	8.0	0.0	0.0	0.0	0.0	...	...	...	...	...	...	...	...	...	Dominican Republic
.3	14.3	0.0	0.0	0.0	0.0	5.7	5.7	5.7	5.7	17.1	17.1	5.7	5.7	3.1	14.2	11.7	0.7	10.6	6.6	49.1	0.6	3.4	Ecuador
.0	...	0.0	...	0.0	...	16.0	...	8.0	...	0.0	...	0.0	...	1.2	9.2	11.9	4.7	16.4	11.2	45.4	0.0	...	El Salvador
...	...	...	...	...	...	...	...	...	...	...	...	...	...	...	...	...	...	...	...	...	...	...	Grenada[a]
.5	14.3	0.0	0.0	0.0	0.0	16.2	17.1	5.4	8.6	13.5	8.6	0.0	0.0	2.9*[-1]	13.1*[-1]	18.6*[-1]	0.7*[-1]	7.0*[-1]	2.3*[-1]	46.0*[-1]	...	9.4*[-1]	Guatemala
.4	...	0.0	...	0.0	...	8.6	...	6.6	...	34.9	...	5.1	...	3.7	30.3	4.9	3.1	9.5	8.2	38.2	0.7	1.4	Guyana
...	...	...	...	...	...	...	...	...	...	...	...	...	...	...	...	...	...	...	...	...	...	...	Haiti
.4	20.6	0.0	0.0	0.0	0.0	11.1	11.8	5.6	0.0	13.9	14.7	0.0	0.0	...	...	...	...	...	...	...	...	...	Honduras
...	...	...	...	...	...	...	...	...	...	...	...	...	...	...	...	...	...	...	...	...	...	...	Jamaica
.0	22.9	0.0	0.0	0.0	0.0	5.7	5.7	5.7	5.7	0.0	0.0	0.0	0.0	2.4	10.2	18.8	4.6	8.9	12.2	39.8	3.0	0.2	Mexico
...	...	...	...	...	...	...	...	...	...	...	...	...	...	...	...	...	...	...	...	...	...	...	Montserrat[a]

Statistical Annex

Table 10. Education and curricula

Country or Territory	Avg 1–6 1980s	Avg 1–6 2000s	Avg 7–8 1980s	Avg 7–8 2000s	Lang. Ed. 1980s	Lang. Ed. 2000s	Math 1980s	Math 2000s	Sci/Comp/Tech 1980s	Sci/Comp/Tech 2000s	Social Sci. 1980s	Social Sci. 2000s	Religion 1980s	Religion 2000s	Moral Ed. 1980s	Moral Ed. 2000s	Arts 1980s	Arts 2000s	Sports 1980s	Sports 2000s	Skills 1980s	Skills 2000s	Optional 1980s	Optional 2000s	Lang. Ed. (7–8) 1980s	Lang. Ed. (7–8) 2000s	Math (7–8) 1980s	Math (7–8) 2000s	Sci (7–8) 1980s	Sci (7–8) 2000s
Netherlands Antilles	.	...	...	...	...	...	...	...	...	...	...	...	...	...	...	...	...	...	...	...	...	...	...	...	...	...	...	...	...	...
Nicaragua	560	695	708	840	...	36.9	...	23.4	...	9.9	...	7.3	0.0	0.0	0.0	3.8	...	0.0	...	9.4	...	9.4	0.0	0.0	...	30.8	...	19.2	...	21
Panama	768	816	840	960	...	25.7	...	18.0	...	17.0	...	9.6	...	3.0	...	3.0	...	8.9	...	5.9	...	0.0	...	8.9	...	22.5	...	12.5	...	27
Paraguay	642	720	...	720	31.8	32.7	18.1	20.1	5.0	9.0	10.1	19.6	0.0	0.0	0.0	0.0	0.0	4.6	0.0	0.0	23.2	9.1	11.9	5.0	...	18.6	...	11.6	...	12
Peru	722	810	941	945	25.6	...	21.4	...	12.4	...	16.5	...	0.0	0.0	0.0	0.0	3.8	0.0	0.0	0.0	12.4	0.0	7.9	0.0	22.6	16.5	16.1	11.4	12.9	7
Saint Kitts and Nevis[a]	...	...	...	...	...	30.0	...	30.0	...	20.0	...	20.0	...	0.0	...	0.0	...	0.0	...	0.0	...	0.0	...	0.0	...	36.4	...	15.2	...	12.
Saint Lucia	...	927	...	975	...	33.1	...	18.4	...	3.8	...	10.6	...	11.6	...	0.0	...	9.4	...	4.6	...	8.5	...	0.0	...	23.1	...	17.6	...	5
Saint Vincent and the Grenadines	...	...	...	...	...	...	...	...	...	...	...	...	...	...	...	...	...	...	...	...	...	...	...	...	...	...	...	...	...	...
Suriname	...	833	...	...	...	46.6	...	18.3	...	5.4	...	6.7	...	0.0	...	0.0	...	9.3	...	6.9	...	0.0	...	6.9	...	...	...	...	...	...
Trinidad and Tobago	...	767	...	800	28.3	...	21.7	...	10.9	...	10.9	...	6.5	...	0.0	...	13.0	...	4.4	...	4.4	...	0.0	...	25.9	23.3	18.2	17.4	11.3	23.
Turks and Caicos Islands	...	...	...	...	...	...	...	...	...	...	...	...	...	...	...	...	...	...	...	...	...	...	...	...	...	...	...	...	...	...
Uruguay	768	630	1,224	720	21.7	32.7	18.2	28.9	8.5	11.5	12.4	14.4	3.2	0.0	3.2	0.0	5.5	9.6	4.2	2.9	23.1	0.0	0.0	0.0	23.5	26.3	11.8	13.2	11.8	13.
Venezuela	785	756	999	999	20.6	28.8	7.4	20.3	22.2	5.3	14.1	17.0	0.0	0.0	0.0	0.0	9.4	10.5	4.7	6.7	15.0	11.5	6.7	0.0	18.0	21.6	7.6	9.9	22.7	10.
Pacific																														
Australia	...	...	...	...	...	28.9	...	21.6	...	14.5	...	8.4	...	0.0	...	0.0	...	12.1	...	3.6	...	3.6	...	7.3	...	24.3	...	16.2	...	8
Cook Islands[a]	...	800	...	800	...	...	...	...	...	...	...	...	...	...	...	...	...	...	...	...	...	...	...	...	...	...	...	...	...	...
Fiji	...	...	...	...	...	...	...	...	...	...	...	...	...	...	...	...	...	...	...	...	...	...	...	...	...	...	...	...	...	...
Kiribati[a]	...	...	...	...	...	...	...	...	...	...	...	...	...	...	...	...	...	...	...	...	...	...	...	...	...	...	...	...	...	...
Marshall Islands	...	...	...	...	...	...	...	...	...	...	...	...	...	...	...	...	...	...	...	...	...	...	...	...	...	...	...	...	...	...
Micronesia (Fed. States)	...	...	...	...	...	...	...	...	...	...	...	...	...	...	...	...	...	...	...	...	...	...	...	...	...	...	...	...	...	...
Nauru[a]	...	...	...	...	...	...	...	...	...	...	...	...	...	...	...	...	...	...	...	...	...	...	...	...	...	...	...	...	...	...
New Zealand	950	985	945	...	...	...	...	...	...	...	...	...	...	...	...	...	...	...	...	...	...	...	...	...	...	...	...	...	...	...
Niue[a]	...	...	...	...	...	...	...	...	...	...	...	...	...	...	...	...	...	...	...	...	...	...	...	...	...	...	...	...	...	...
Palau[a]	...	...	...	...	...	...	...	...	...	...	...	...	...	...	...	...	...	...	...	...	...	...	...	...	...	...	...	...	...	...
Papua New Guinea	...	...	...	...	...	...	...	...	...	...	...	...	...	...	...	...	...	...	...	...	...	...	...	...	...	10.9	...	10.9	...	10
Samoa	...	...	...	...	...	...	...	...	...	...	...	...	...	...	...	...	...	...	...	...	...	...	...	...	...	...	...	...	...	...
Solomon Islands	...	...	...	...	...	...	...	...	...	...	...	...	...	...	...	...	...	...	...	...	...	...	...	...	...	...	...	...	...	...
Tokelau[a]	...	...	...	...	...	...	...	...	...	...	...	...	...	...	...	...	...	...	...	...	...	...	...	...	...	...	...	...	...	...
Tonga	...	...	...	...	42.6	...	14.2	...	0.0	...	16.0	...	4.3	...	0.0	...	10.6	...	0.0	...	7.3	...	5.0	...	...	...	...	...	...	...
Tuvalu[a]	...	...	...	...	...	...	...	...	...	...	...	...	...	...	...	...	...	...	...	...	...	...	...	...	...	...	...	...	...	...
Vanuatu	...	...	...	...	...	...	...	...	...	...	...	...	...	...	...	...	...	...	...	...	...	...	...	...	...	...	...	...	...	...
MEDIAN																														
World	768	765	893	868	32.6	36.4	18.1	18.4	5.6	5.6	8.8	7.9	0.0	0.0	0.0	0.0	8.8	8.5	6.8	6.8	5.8	2.8	1.1	2.6	28.3	29.1	13.9	14.7	12.2	15
Arab States	748	792	842	875	35.2	39.7	16.8	17.4	5.1	5.7	5.3	5.4	9.8	10.1	0.0	0.0	7.4	6.8	6.9	6.7	4.2	2.8	0.0	0.0	36.9	36.1	14.5	14.9	10.6	11
Sub-Saharan Africa	849	778	918	919	32.6	38.7	19.1	18.7	5.6	5.0	8.8	8.1	0.0	0.0	0.0	0.0	7.1	6.5	6.1	5.2	7.9	3.1	0.0	1.5	29.5	33.3	15.8	16.5	15.9	16.
Central and South Asia	850	688	972	861	32.1	40.8	15.2	19.3	10.2	4.2	9.2	4.0	4.7	0.0	0.0	0.0	8.4	9.3	5.3	7.5	7.7	4.3	0.0	0.4	27.3	34.6	15.5	15.5	13.0	16.
East Asia	723	807	865	937	26.7	34.9	18.0	17.6	3.9	5.6	6.4	9.7	0.0	0.0	6.4	3.9	9.6	7.0	5.2	6.7	5.8	2.8	5.4	5.6	28.2	24.2	11.7	13.7	11.0	14
Europe	749	695	880	855	35.2	35.6	19.1	17.8	3.9	5.7	8.1	7.9	0.0	0.3	0.0	0.0	10.8	11.1	7.9	9.0	3.5	2.2	1.9	7.0	28.4	28.0	12.0	13.3	11.8	15
North America	...	...	...	...	43.7	28.7	14.3	12.4	8.2	13.8	9.5	14.1	0.0	3.3	0.0	0.0	12.1	10.6	10.0	5.3	0.0	5.3	2.2	6.6	...	25.3	...	13.7	...	9
Latin America and the Caribbean	768	798	929	884	25.6	30.7	20.0	21.4	12.4	10.1	12.4	11.3	0.0	0.0	0.0	0.0	9.2	8.1	5.0	4.8	11.6	0.0	0.0	0.0	23.5	23.1	14.3	14.3	12.8	14
Pacific	950	893	945	800	42.6	28.9	14.2	21.6	0.0	14.5	16.0	8.4	4.3	0.0	0.0	0.0	10.6	12.1	0.0	3.6	7.3	3.6	5.0	7.3	...	17.6	...	13.6	...	9

Sources:

1. International Bureau of Education and Benavot, 2008.
2. UNESCO Institute for Statistics, 2009. Education Database.

Notes:

a. National population data were used to calculate enrolment ratios for % of tertiary students in each domain.

b. Enrolment and population data exclude Transnistria. For % of tertiary students in each domain.

c. Enrolment ratios were not calculated due to lack of United Nations population data by age. For % of tertiary students in each domain.

d. Children can enter primary school at age 6 or 7.

... Data not available
* National estimation
** UIS estimation

0 Magnitude negligible (less than half the last decimal shown)
. Not applicable
± Partial data
+n Data refer to the year n years after the reference year
-n Data refer to the year n years before the reference year

	Average grades 7–8													Total % of tertiary students[2]									
	Social Sciences: History, Geography, Civics, Social Studies		Religion		Moral Education		Arts		Sports		Skills and Competencies		Optional and Others		Agriculture	Education	Education, Manufacturing and Construction	Humanities and Arts	Health and Welfare	Science	Social Sciences, Business and Law	Services	Non-specified programmes	Country or Territory
	1980s	2000s	1980s	2000s	1980s	2000s	1980s	2000s	1980s	2000s	1980s	2000s	1980s	2000s	2007									
Netherlands Antilles	…	13.5	0.0	0.0	0.0	0.0	0.0	0.0	…	7.7	…	7.7	0.0	0.0	…	…	…	…	…	…	…	…	…	
Nicaragua	…	12.5	…	2.5	…	2.5	…	10.0	…	5.0	…	0.0	…	5.0	1.1[-1]	14.9[-1]	11.2[-1]	9.8[-1]	8.0[-1]	8.0[-1]	39.6[-1]	6.9[-1]	0.5[-1]	
Panama	…	16.9	…	0.0	…	3.5	…	9.3	…	4.7	…	11.6	…	11.6	…	…	…	…	…	…	…	.	…	
Paraguay	19.4	10.1	3.2	5.1	0.0	0.0	6.5	6.3	6.5	6.3	9.7	6.3	3.2	30.4	…	…	…	…	…	…	…	…	…	
Peru	24.2	…	…	0.0	…	0.0	…	0.0	…	0.0	…	12.1	…	0.0	…	…	…	…	…	…	…	…	…	
Saint Kitts and Nevis[a]	…	12.5	…	11.0	…	0.0	…	10.7	…	5.1	…	14.9	…	0.0	…	…	…	…	…	…	…	…	…	
Saint Lucia	…	…	…	…	…	…	…	…	…	…	…	…	…	…	.	5.1	0.2	0.2	.	7.0	15.9	.	71.6	
Saint Vincent and the Grenadines	…	…	…	…	…	…	…	…	…	…	…	…	…	…	…	…	…	…	…	…	…	…	…	
Suriname	11.3	5.8	4.7	0.0	0.0	0.0	12.4	11.6	3.6	5.8	9.5	0.0	2.9	12.8	…	…	…	…	…	…	…	…	…	
Trinidad and Tobago	…	…	…	…	…	…	…	…	…	…	…	…	…	…	…	…	…	…	…	…	…	…	…	
Turks and Caicos Islands	11.8	13.2	5.9	0.0	0.0	0.0	5.9	10.5	4.4	5.3	25.0	0.0	0.0	18.4	…	…	…	…	…	…	…	…	…	
Uruguay	16.0	18.0	0.0	0.0	0.0	0.0	6.7	4.5	3.8	5.4	18.1	30.2	7.2	0.0	3.2	16.0	9.6	4.7	13.3	11.7	40.2	1.2	-	
Venezuela	…	…	…	…	…	…	…	…	…	…	…	…	…	…	…	…	…	…	…	…	…	…	…	
Pacific																								
Australia	…	8.1	…	0.0	…	0.0	…	10.8	…	4.1	…	4.1	…	24.3	1.3	8.8	10.3	11.6	16.1	9.7	38.5	3.5	0.1	
Cook Islands[a]	…	…	…	…	…	…	…	…	…	…	…	…	…	…	…	…	…	…	…	…	…	…	…	
Fiji	…	…	…	…	…	…	…	…	…	…	…	…	…	…	…	…	…	…	…	…	…	…	…	
Kiribati[a]	…	…	…	…	…	…	…	…	…	…	…	…	…	…	…	…	…	…	…	…	…	…	…	
Marshall Islands	…	…	…	…	…	…	…	…	…	…	…	…	…	…	…	…	…	…	…	…	…	…	…	
Micronesia (Fed. States)	…	…	…	…	…	…	…	…	…	…	…	…	…	…	…	…	…	…	…	…	…	…	…	
Nauru[a]	…	…	…	…	…	…	…	…	…	…	…	…	…	…	…	…	…	…	…	…	…	…	…	
New Zealand	…	…	…	…	…	…	…	…	…	…	…	…	…	…	1.0	10.2	6.8	17.0	12.8	13.6	33.7	2.3	2.6	
Niue[a]	…	…	…	…	…	…	…	…	…	…	…	…	…	…	…	…	…	…	…	…	…	…	…	
Palau[a]	…	…	…	…	…	…	…	…	…	…	…	…	…	…	…	…	…	…	…	…	…	…	…	
Papua New Guinea	…	10.9	…	3.6	…	0.0	…	10.9	…	14.6	…	0.0	…	27.3	…	…	…	…	…	…	…	…	…	
Samoa	…	…	…	…	…	…	…	…	…	…	…	…	…	…	…	…	…	…	…	…	…	…	…	
Solomon Islands	…	…	…	…	…	…	…	…	…	…	…	…	…	…	…	…	…	…	…	…	…	…	…	
Tokelau[a]	…	…	…	…	…	…	…	…	…	…	…	…	…	…	…	…	…	…	…	…	…	…	…	
Tonga	…	…	…	…	…	…	…	…	…	…	…	…	…	…	…	…	…	…	…	…	…	…	…	
Tuvalu[a]	…	…	…	…	…	…	…	…	…	…	…	…	…	…	…	…	…	…	…	…	…	…	…	
Vanuatu	…	…	…	…	…	…	…	…	…	…	…	…	…	…	…	…	…	…	…	…	…	…	…	
MEDIAN																								
World	2.7	13.2	0.0	0.0	0.0	0.0	6.4	6.3	5.6	6.1	8.3	4.4	0.0	3.1	2.2	10.2	10.6	10.4	7.7	9.2	37.6	3.0	1.8	
Arab States	1.9	11.1	6.2	7.1	0.0	0.0	5.3	6.3	5.3	5.6	5.0	5.3	0.0	0.0	0.9	4.0	8.9	15.4	7.0	12.4	32.2	0.9	9.6	
Sub-Saharan Africa	3.9	13.9	0.7	0.0	0.0	0.0	5.7	4.4	5.0	6.7	10.6	5.4	0.0	0.0	2.8	7.6	7.6	10.8	6.5	13.9	45.4	1.0	0.8	
Central and South Asia	3.7	12.4	2.5	0.0	0.0	0.0	3.8	4.0	5.9	5.3	15.3	5.3	2.5	1.8	2.8	6.7	8.5	12.1	4.1	5.9	29.2	2.4	22.5	
East Asia	0.8	12.3	0.0	0.0	3.3	0.0	5.1	4.5	4.5	5.4	11.5	4.2	1.5	9.4	3.1	9.4	16.1	9.4	6.3	8.5	34.1	4.8	3.9	
Europe	2.7	14.0	0.0	0.0	0.0	0.0	7.6	7.2	6.4	7.1	7.6	3.5	3.8	8.3	2.2	11.3	14.6	10.2	9.6	8.5	38.4	4.3	1.2	
North America	…	8.4	…	1.5	…	1.5	…	12.2	…	7.0	…	9.8	…	10.7	0.6	9.4	6.7	10.6	13.9	8.9	27.3	5.1	17.6	
Latin America and the Caribbean	4.3	13.5	0.0	0.0	0.0	0.0	7.5	8.0	5.7	5.7	9.5	7.7	0.0	0.0	2.7	14.0	11.2	4.4	11.7	8.0	40.2	3.0	2.0	
Pacific	…	9.5	…	1.8	…	0.0	…	10.9	…	9.3	…	2.0	…	25.8	1.2	9.5	8.5	14.3	14.5	11.7	36.1	2.9	1.3	

Table 11. International flows of mobile students at the tertiary level[1]

| | Total enrolment in tertiary level ('000) | Outbound mobile students | | | | Inbound mobile students | | |
		Number of out-bound students	Outbound mobility ratio (%)	Gross outbound enrolment ratio (%)	Main destination (% of total)	Number of students from abroad	Inbound mobility rate (%)	Main country of origin (% of total)
Country or Territory					2007			
Arab States								
Algeria	902	23,213	2.7	0.6	France (86%)	5,709	0.6	...
Bahrain	18[-1]	2,576**	14.1[-1]	4.4**	United Kingdom (30%)	672[-1]	3.7[-1]	Saudi Arabia (34%)[-1]
Djibouti	2	1,440	73.6	1.7	France (73%)	...	...	...
Egypt	2,594**,[-2]	7,802	0.3**,[-2]	0.1	United Kingdom (17%)	...	...	...
Iraq	425**,[-2]	5,112**	0.9**,[-2]	0.2**	Jordan (39%)[-1]	...	...	...
Jordan	232	9,042	4.5	1.6	Ukraine (19%)	21,509[-1]	9.8[-1]	Palestinian A. T. (25%)[-1]
Kuwait	38[-1]	5,573**	17.1[-1]	2.6**	Jordan (30%)[-1]	...	...	...
Lebanon	197[+1]	12,702	7.0	3.5	France (47%)	22,674	12.1	...
Libyan Arab Jamahiriya	...	3,548	...	0.5	United Kingdom (33%)	...	...	...
Mauritania	12	2,880	27.0	1.0	France (45%)	...	...	...
Morocco	369	41,502	11.7	1.3	France (69%)	7,029	1.9	Mauritania (12%)
Oman	69	5,090**	7.7**	1.9**	Jordan (26%)[-1]	165	0.2	Bahrain (15%)
Palestinian A. T.	169	8,119[-1]	6.2[-1]	2.3[-1]	Jordan (69%)[-1]	...	...	...
Qatar	9	1,492	20.2	2.7	United Kingdom (34%)	2,487	28.0	Palestinian A. T. (14%)
Saudi Arabia	636[-1]	17,067	1.9[-1]	0.8	United Kingdom (27%)	13,687[-1]	2.2[-1]	Yemen (25%)[-1]
Sudan	...	2,793**	...	0.1**	Malaysia (17%)[-1]	...	...	...
Syrian Arab Republic	...	13,278	...	0.6	France (20%)	...	...	...
Tunisia	326	17,420	5.6	1.6	France (62%)	...	...	...
United Arab Emirates	77[+1]	5,742	...	1.7	United Kingdom (31%)	...	...	...
Yemen	209**,[-1]	7,364[-1]	4.0**,[-1]	0.3[-1]	Saudi Arabia (47%)[-1]	...	...	...
Sub-Saharan Africa								
Angola	49[-1]	7,327	15.0[-1]	0.4	Portugal (68%)	...	...	...
Benin	43[-1]	3,625	10.2[-1]	0.4	France (73%)	...	...	...
Botswana	11[-2]	6,882	88.8[-2]	3.1	South Africa (68%)	654[-2]	6.0[-2]	...
Burkina Faso	42[+1]	2,379	8.0	0.2	France (59%)	880[-2]	3.1[-2]	...
Burundi	16	973**	8.2**	0.1**	France (32%)	...	...	...
Cameroon	132	16,952	14.5	0.9	France (36%)	1,417	1.1	Chad (87%)
Cape Verde	5	4,847	102.7	8.2	Portugal (92%)	...	...	...
Central African Republic	4[-1]	885	20.6[-1]	0.2	France (75%)	485[-1]	10.9[-1]	Chad (82%)[-1]
Chad	10**,[-2]	2,697	...	0.3	Cameroon (48%)	...	...	...
Comoros	...	2,673	...	3.2	France (49%)	...	...	...
Congo	...	4,504	...	1.3	France (68%)	...	...	...
Congo (Dem. Rep.)	238	3,377	1.6	0.1	South Africa (38%)	...	...	...
Côte d'Ivoire	157	5,792	4.2	0.3	France (71%)	...	...	...
Equatorial Guinea	...	793	...	1.8	Spain (62%)	...	...	...
Eritrea	...	863**	...	0.2**	Jordan (16%)[-1]	...	...	...
Ethiopia	210	3,822	2.1	...	...	...	...	...
Gabon	...	4,418	...	3.4	France (81%)	...	...	...
Gambia	...	962	...	0.7	United Kingdom (38%)	...	...	...
Ghana	140	7,552	6.0	0.3	United Kingdom (37%)	1,899	1.4	Nigeria (71%)
Guinea	43[-1]	4,059	9.4[-1]	0.5	France (66%)	899[-1]	2.1[-1]	...
Guinea-Bissau	...	653	...	0.4	Portugal (67%)	...	...	...
Kenya	140	13,313	10.6	0.3	United Kingdom (29%)	...	...	...
Lesotho	9[-1]	3,901	47.5[-1]	1.6	South Africa (95%)	53[-1]	0.6[-1]	...
Liberia	...	554	...	0.2	Ghana (19%)	...	...	...
Madagascar	58	4,155	8.0	0.2	France (89%)	1,080	1.9	Comoros (88%)
Malawi	6	1,837	30.7	0.1	South Africa (31%)	...	...	...
Mali	51	3,075	6.9	0.3	France (66%)	...	...	...
Mauritius	14[+1]	7,448	41.0[-1]	7.7	France (21%)	...	...	...
Mozambique	28[-2]	2,409	10.6[-2]	0.1	Portugal (42%)	...	...	...
Namibia	13[-1]	10,663	60.8[-1]	4.9	South Africa (95%)	189[-1]	1.4[-1]	Angola (37%)[-1]
Niger	11	2,083	21.8	0.2	France (54%)	205	1.9	Cameroon (24%)
Nigeria	1,392[-2]	22,712	1.6[-2]	0.2	United Kingdom (40%)	...	...	...
Rwanda	26**,[-2]	1,726**	6.6**,[-2]	0.2**	France (39%)	...	...	...
Saint Helena	...	...	...	...	...	...	...	...
Sao Tome and Principe	.	792	.	4.6	Portugal (84%)	...	...	...
Senegal	91[+1]	11,709	17.4**	1.0	France (84%)	...	...	...
Seychelles	.	510	.	6.7	Australia (25%)	...	...	...
Sierra Leone	...	854	...	0.2	United Kingdom (33%)	...	...	...
Somalia	...	1,202[-1]	...	0.2[-1]	Malaysia (25%)[-1]	...	...	...
South Africa	741[-1]	5,746	0.8[-1]	0.1	United Kingdom (30%)	60,552**	7.2[-1]	Zimbabwe (24%)
Swaziland	6[-1]	3,059	57.9[-1]	2.2	South Africa (94%)	122[-1]	2.1[-1]	Burkina Faso (64%)[-1]
Tanzania (United Rep.)	55	4,138	8.3	0.1	United Kingdom (27%)	...	...	...

Table 11. International flows of mobile students at the tertiary level[1]

	Total enrolment in tertiary level ('000)	Outbound mobile students				Inbound mobile students		
		Number of outbound students	Outbound mobility ratio (%)	Gross outbound enrolment ratio (%)	Main destination (% of total)	Number of students from abroad	Inbound mobility rate (%)	Main country of origin (% of total)
Country or Territory					2007			
Togo	33	3,073	10.7	0.5	France (61%)	459	1.4	...
Uganda	...	2,622	...	0.1	United Kingdom (33%)	...	...	...
Zambia	...	3,817	...	0.3	South Africa (40%)	...	...	...
Zimbabwe	...	20,584	...	1.2	South Africa (68%)	...	...	...
Central and South Asia								
Afghanistan	...	3,023	...	0.1	Iran, Islamic Republic of (31%)	...	...	...
Armenia	107	3,910	3.9	1.2	Russian Federation (61%)	4,239	3.9	Iran, Islamic Republic of (28%)
Azerbaijan	135	4,743	3.9	0.5	Turkey (37%)	4,286	3.2	Turkey (71%)
Bangladesh	1,145	14,758	1.4	0.1	Australia (19%)	669	0.1	...
Bhutan	4	709**,[-1]	19.3**,[-1]	0.9**,[-1]	Australia (27%)	...	...	...
Georgia	141	8,233	6.0	2.2	Germany (36%)	428	0.3	Turkey (58%)
India	12,853[-1]	153,312	1.1[-1]	0.1	Australia (27%)	...	...	...
Iran (Islamic Rep.)	2,829	22,523	0.9	0.2	United Kingdom (11%)	2,092	0.1	Afghanistan (43%)
Kazakhstan	720[+1]	30,052	4.3	2.0	Russian Federation (66%)	10,928[+1]	1.5[+1]	Uzbekistan (33%)[+1]
Kyrgyzstan	239	3,969	1.8	0.7	Russian Federation (24%)	27,205	11.4	Uzbekistan (70%)
Maldives	...	1,153[-1]	...	3.1[-1]	Malaysia (44%)[-1]	...	...	...
Nepal	321	14,575	5.1	0.5	Australia (32%)	...	...	...
Pakistan	955*	24,617	3.0	0.1	United Kingdom (32%)	...	...	...
Sri Lanka	...	12,697	...	0.7	Australia (27%)	...	...	...
Tajikistan	147	2,909	2.3	0.4	Russian Federation (46%)	2,829	1.9	Uzbekistan (71%)
Turkmenistan	...	5,075	28.2	0.9	Turkey (29%)	...	...	...
Uzbekistan	289	31,889	12.6	1.1	Kyrgyzstan (59%)	248	0.1	Turkmenistan (17%)
East Asia								
Brunei Darussalam	5	2,384	47.4	6.9	United Kingdom (34%)	80	1.5	Malaysia (34%)
Cambodia	92	2,863	3.9	0.2	France (24%)	68[-1]	0.1[-1]	Viet Nam (75%)[-1]
China	25,346	421,148	1.9	0.4	Japan (21%)	42,138	0.2	...
Hong Kong (SAR China)	158	32,726	20.2	7.0	Australia (39%)	6,274	4.0	China (93%)
Macao (SAR China)	24	1,210	6.2	2.9	Australia (44%)	11,930	50.0	China (95%)
Indonesia	3,755	29,580	0.8	0.1	Australia (46%)	3,023	0.1	Timor-Leste (47%)
Japan	4,033	54,506	1.2	0.8	United Kingdom (24%)	125,877	3.1	China (64%)
Korea (Dem. People's Rep.)	...	6,029**	...	0.3**	Canada (31%)[-1]	...	...	...
Korea (Rep.)	3,209	105,327	3.1	3.1	Japan (49%)	31,943	1.0	China (72%)
Lao (People's Dem. Rep.)	75	3,544	5.5	0.5	Viet Nam (62%)	254	0.3	Viet Nam (75%)
Malaysia	749[-1]	46,473	6.1[-1]	1.9	Australia (33%)	24,404[-1]	3.3[-1]	China (23%)[-1]
Mongolia	142	6,427	5.0	2.2	Germany (20%)	1,111	0.8	Russian Federation (56%)
Myanmar	508	3,372**	...	...	Thailand (24%)[+1]	57	...	Republic of Korea (46%)
Philippines	2,484[-1]	7,843	0.3[-1]	0.1	Australia (19%)	5,136[-1]	0.2[-1]	Democratic People's Republic of Korea (22%)[-1]
Singapore	184	18,207	11.3	6.2	Australia (53%)	...	...	...
Thailand	2,422**,[+1]	24,485	0.9	0.5	Australia (24%)	10,915[+1]	0.5**,[+1]	China (39%)[+1]
Timor-Leste	...	2,127	...	1.9	Indonesia (61%)	...	...	...
Viet Nam	1,588	27,865	1.9	0.3	France (22%)	3,230	0.2	Lao People's Democratic Republic (70%)
Europe								
Albania	...	19,930	...	6.7	Italy (62%)	...	...	...
Andorra	0.40[-1]	997	91.1[-1]	24.2	Spain (81%)	...	...	...
Austria	261	10,458	4.3	2.0	Germany (46%)	43,572	16.7	Germany (28%)
Belarus	557	14,802	2.7	1.8	Russian Federation (58%)	4,423	0.8	China (24%)
Belgium	394	10,596	2.8	1.7	France (21%)	25,202	6.4	France (36%)
Bosnia and Herzegovina	99	8,634	8.7	3.2	Croatia (36%)	...	...	...
Bulgaria	259	24,680	8.8	4.7	Germany (53%)	9,100	3.5	Macedonia, FYR (40%)
Croatia	140	5,544	3.9	1.8	Italy (27%)	3,488	2.5	Bosnia and Herzegovina (85%)
Cyprus	22	22,898	110.7	37.3	Greece (37%)	5,590	25.1	Bangladesh (21%)
Czech Republic	363	7,359	1.7	1.1	Germany (25%)	24,483	6.7	Slovakia (67%)
Denmark	232	5,035	2.1	1.7	United Kingdom (28%)	12,695	5.5	Norway (15%)
Estonia	69	3,245	5.0	3.1	Finland (19%)	966	1.4	Finland (46%)
Finland	309	5,964	1.9	1.8	United Kingdom (24%)	10,066	3.3	China (17%)
France	2,180	54,021	2.5	1.4	United Kingdom (22%)	246,612	11.3	Morocco (11%)
Germany	...	77,534	...	1.6	United Kingdom (17%)	206,875	...	China (12%)
Gibraltar	.	642	...	...	United Kingdom (50%)	...	...	...
Greece	603	32,588	4.6	4.9	United Kingdom (34%)	21,160	3.5	Cyprus (54%)
Holy See	...	15	...	...	Spain (42%)	...	...	...
Hungary	432	7,214	1.4	1.2	Germany (28%)	15,110	3.5	Romania (22%)
Iceland	16	2,480	15.7	11.5	Denmark (40%)	783	4.9	Germany (14%)

Table 11. International flows of mobile students at the tertiary level[1]

		Outbound mobile students				Inbound mobile students		
	Total enrolment in tertiary level	Number of out-bound students	Outbound mobility ratio	Gross outbound enrolment ratio	Main destination (% of total)	Number of students from abroad	Inbound mobility rate (%)	Main country of origin (% of total)
	('000)		(%)	(%)				
Country or Territory					2007			
Ireland	190	19,357	9.7	6.2	United Kingdom (47%)	16,758	8.8	United States (15%)
Israel	327	11,882	3.7	2.2	Jordan (20%)[-1]	...	...	...
Italy	2,034	35,133	1.6	1.2	Austria (18%)	57,271	2.8	Albania (21%)
Latvia	129	3,858	3.2	2.1	United Kingdom (21%)	1,433	1.1	Lithuania (29%)
Liechtenstein	0.67	884	132.6	41.0	Switzerland (75%)	582	86.5	Austria (51%)
Lithuania	200	6,762	3.7	2.6	United Kingdom (19%)	1,901	1.0	Belarus (27%)
Luxembourg	2.69[-1]	7,201	269.2[-1]	26.7	Germany (32%)	1,137[-1]	42.2[-1]	France (34%)[-1]
Macedonia (TFYR)	58	6,424	10.9	3.9	Bulgaria (58%)	884	1.5	Serbia and Montenegro (69%)
Malta	9[-2]	1,033	8.6[-2]	3.5	United Kingdom (45%)	605[-2]	6.4[-2]	China (30%)[-2]
Moldova (Rep.)	148*	10,073	7.1	2.8	Romania (41%)	1,882	1.3*	Ukraine (23%)
Monaco		376	...	...	France (71%)	...	...	...
Montenegro[a]	...	10 195	...	1.7**, [-2]	Austria (14%)	...	...	...
Netherlands	590	10,447	1.9	1.1	United Kingdom (24%)	27,449	4.7	Germany (37%)
Norway	215	11,873	5.8	4.2	United Kingdom (22%)	15,618	7.3	Sweden (8%)
Poland	2,147	32,888	1.5	1.0	Germany (35%)	13,021	0.6	Ukraine (21%)
Portugal	367	11,200	2.8	1.7	United Kingdom (23%)	17,950	4.9	Angola (27%)
Romania	928	22,852	2.2	1.4	France (23%)	9,383	1.0	Moldova (43%)
Russian Federation	9,370	42,881	0.5	0.3	Germany (30%)	60,288	0.6	Kazakhstan (33%)
San Marino	1[+1]	899	...	...	Italy (82%)	...	...	...
Serbia[a]	...	10 195	...	1.7**, [-2]	Austria (14%)	...	...	Czech Republic (25%)
Slovakia	218	24,206	10.3	5.6	Czech Republic (68%)	1,901	0.9	Croatia (50%)
Slovenia	116	2,244	1.8	1.7	Austria (24%)	1,195	1.0	Portugal (11%)
Spain	1,777	23,914	1.2	0.9	United Kingdom (24%)	21,315	1.2	Germany (10%)
Sweden	414	13,723	3.6	2.5	United Kingdom (24%)	22,135	5.4	Germany (22%)
Switzerland	213	10,485	5.3	2.3	Germany (19%)	38,317	18.0	Azerbaijan (9%)
Turkey	2,454	36,840	1.5	0.5	Germany (26%)	19,257	0.8	China (15%)
Ukraine	2,819	26,720	0.9	0.7	Russian Federation (28%)	29,614	1.1	China (14%)
United Kingdom	2,363	24,115	1.1	0.6	France (17%)	351,470	14.9	China (14%)
North America								
Canada	...	43,918	...	2.0	United Kingdom (25%)	68,520[-1]	...	China (18%)[-1]
United States of America	17,759	50,265	0.3	0.2	United Kingdom (24%)	595,874	3.4	China (14%)
Latin America and the Caribbean								
Anguilla	0.05[+1]	96[-2]	305.8**, [-2]	9.6**, [-2]	...	...	...	...
Antigua and Barbuda	...	564	147.0	8.4	Cuba (40%)[+1]	...	...	...
Argentina	2,202[-1]	8,032	0.4[-1]	0.2	Spain (17%)	169[-1]	8.1[-1]	Netherlands Antilles (44%)[-1]
Aruba	2.23	131	6.7	1.9	United Kingdom (38%)	...	...	...
Bahamas	...	2,500	...	8.8	Canada (27%)[-1]	...	...	...
Barbados	11	1,454**	12.7**	6.8**	United Kingdom (29%)	890	7.8	Trinidad and Tobago (22%)
Belize	...	719	...	2.5	Cuba (51%)[+1]	...	...	...
Bermuda	1	1,101**	200.3[-2]	32.0[-1]	Canada (39%)[-1]	...	...	...
Bolivia	...	8,776**, [+1]	...	0.9**, [+1]	Cuba (70%)	...	...	...
Brazil	5,273	21,556	0.4	0.1	France (17%)	...	...	...
British Virgin Islands	1.20**, [-2]	365	32.6**, [-2]	20.5**	United Kingdom (34%)	...	...	...
Cayman Islands	1[-1]	368	...	13.8**, [-2]	United Kingdom (45%)	200[-1]	35.3[-1]	Jamaica (34%)[-1]
Chile	753	5,815	0.9	0.4	Germany (16%)	7,946	1.1	Peru (19%)
Colombia	1,373	17,531	1.3	0.4	France (21%)	...	...	...
Costa Rica	111**, [-2]	1,859	1.5**, [-2]	0.4	Cuba (26%)[+1]	...	...	...
Cuba	987[+1]	1,265	0.2	0.2	Spain (35%)	29,697[+1]	3.0[+1]	Bolivia (18%)[+1]
Dominica	.	637		12.9[-1]	Cuba (22%)[+1]	...	...	...
Dominican Republic	...	2,045	...	0.2	Cuba (35%)[+1]	...	...	...
Ecuador	444	7,098	1.6	0.6	Cuba (38%)[+1]	...	...	...
El Salvador	132	2,552	1.9	0.4	Cuba (49%)[+1]	768	0.6	Guatemala (25%)
Grenada	.	552	.	4.8	Cuba (23%)[+1]	...	...	...
Guatemala	234	2,620	1.2	0.2	Cuba (40%)[+1]	...	...	...
Guyana	7.53	1,385**, [+1]	7.4	2.4**, [+1]	Cuba (61%)[+1]	34	0.5	...
Haiti	...	4,405	...	0.4	France (45%)	...	...	...
Honduras	...	2,500	...	0.3	Cuba (64%)[+1]	...	...	...
Jamaica	...	6,101	...	2.3	United Kingdom (31%)	...	...	...
Mexico	2,529	24,950	1.0	0.3	Spain (17%)	...	...	...
Montserrat	.	57	.	19.6	United Kingdom (32%)	.	...	...
Netherlands Antilles	.	307**	...	2.7**	Aruba (65%)[-1]	...	...	...
Nicaragua	...	1,897	...	0.3	Cuba (53%)[+1]	...	...	...
Panama	131[-1]	1,985	1.6[-1]	0.7	Cuba (48%)[+1]	...	...	...

Table 11. International flows of mobile students at the tertiary level[1]

Country or Territory	Total enrolment in tertiary level ('000)	Number of out-bound students	Outbound mobility ratio (%)	Gross outbound enrolment ratio (%)	Main destination (% of total)	Number of students from abroad	Inbound mobility rate (%)	Main country of origin (% of total)
			Outbound mobile students				**Inbound mobile students**	
				2007				
Paraguay	156**, -2	2,105	1.2**, -2	0.3	Cuba (48%)+1	...	...	...
Peru	952**, -1	13,130	1.2**, -1	0.5	Chile (16%)	...	...	...
Saint Kitts and Nevis	.	515	.	11.8**	Cuba (18%)+1	...	...	...
Saint Lucia	1.44	1,209	88.4	7.2	Cuba (30%)+1	94	6.5	Canada (56%)
Saint Vincent and the Grenadines	.	688	37.6	5.3	Barbados (25%)	...	...	...
Suriname	...	555	...	1.2	Netherlands (67%)	...	...	...
Trinidad and Tobago	17**, -2	5,011	29.6**, -2	3.5	United Kingdom (30%)	...	...	...
Turks and Caicos Islands	.	273	.	13.6**, -2	United Kingdom (40%)	...	...	...
Uruguay	159	2,510**	1.6**	1.0**	...	...	...	...
Venezuela	1,381*, -1	11,844	0.7-1	0.4	Cuba (51%)+1	...	...	...
Pacific								
Australia	1,084	9,968	1.0	0.7	New Zealand (31%)	211,526	19.5	China (24%)
Cook Islands	.	46**, -1	.	2.7**, -1	Australia (100%)	.	.	...
Fiji	13**, -2	1,675	13.6**, -2	2.1	Australia (55%)	...	...	...
Kiribati	.	144	.	1.2**, -1	New Zealand (29%)	...	...	...
Marshall Islands	...	70	...	1.0	New Zealand (25%)	...	...	...
Micronesia (Fed. States)	...	248	...	1.9	Australia (36%)	...	...	...
Nauru	.	20**	.	2.1**	Thailand (36%)+1	...	...	...
New Zealand	243	4,104	1.9	1.4	Australia (53%)	33,047	13.6	China (41%)
Niue	.	7	.	3.7-1	Australia (100%)	.	.	...
Palau	...	29	...	2.2	Japan (28%)	...	...	...
Papua New Guinea	...	754	...	0.1	Australia (75%)	...	...	...
Samoa	...	253	...	1.5	New Zealand (49%)	...	...	...
Solomon Islands	.	320**	.	0.7**	Australia (59%)	...	...	...
Tokelau	.	3	.	0.6-1	Australia (100%)	.	.	...
Tonga	...	508	...	4.6	New Zealand (76%)	...	...	...
Tuvalu	.	98	.	6.8**, -2	Australia (22%)	.	.	...
Vanuatu	...	175**	...	0.8**	Australia (46%)	...	...	...

Source:
1. UNESCO Institute for Statistics, 2009. Education Database.

Notes:
a. Data for Serbia and Montenegro are combined.

... Data not available

* National estimation

** UIS estimation

. Not applicable

+n Data refer to the year n years after the reference year

-n Data refer to the year n years before the reference year

Table 12. Newspapers[1]

Country or Territory	Daily newspapers						Non-daily newspapers					
	Titles (per million inhabitants)		Circulation Total ('000)		Circulation per thousand inhabitants		Titles (per million inhabitants)		Circulation Total ('000)		Circulation per thousand inhabitants	
	2000	2004	2000	2004	2000	2004	2000	2004	2000	2004	2000	2004
Arab States												
Algeria	...	0.5^c	...	...	...	...	...	...	...	...	...	...
Bahrain	...	8.5^c	...	...	...	...	...	...	...	...	...	...
Djibouti	...	...	...	...	...	...	...	...	...	...	...	...
Egypt	...	...	...	...	...	...	...	...	...	...	...	...
Iraq	...	...	...	...	...	...	...	...	...	...	...	...
Jordan	1.0	0.7^c	...	...	...	...	4.2	...	...	...	...	...
Kuwait	3.6	3.1	...	...	...	...	16.6	34.8	...	...	...	...
Lebanon	3.5^c	3.8^c	215^c	215^c	57.0^c	54.2^c	1.9	1.0$^{-1,\,c}$	...	400$^{-1,\,c}$	...	102.1$^{-1,\,c}$
Libyan Arab Jamahiriya	...	0.7^c	...	...	...	...	...	...	...	...	...	...
Mauritania	...	1.0^c	...	...	...	...	...	...	...	...	...	...
Morocco	0.8	0.8	846	350**$^{,\,-1,\,c}$	29.3	11.7**$^{,\,-1,\,c}$	17.6^o	19.7	4,108	...	142.5^o	...
Oman	2.1	2.4	...	...	...	...	...	1.6^{+2}	...	...	...	...
Palestinian A. T.	1.0	0.8	...	35**$^{,\,c}$	...	9.6**$^{,\,c}$	4.1	2.8	51	22	16.2	5.9
Qatar	8.1	6.5	...	...	...	...	...	...	...	...	...	...
Saudi Arabia	...	0.5^c	...	...	...	...	...	...	...	...	...	...
Sudan	0.4	0.6	...	...	...	...	...	0.1	...	615	...	17.0
Syrian Arab Republic	...	0.2^c	...	...	...	...	...	...	...	...	...	...
Tunisia	0.7	1.0^c	180	219$^{-3,\,c}$	18.8	22.7$^{-3,\,c}$	3.0	4.0^{-3}	940	964^{-3}	98.3	99.7^{-3}
United Arab Emirates	2.5^c	2.3^c	...	...	...	...	...	...	...	...	...	...
Yemen	0.2	0.3	50	83	2.8	4.1	2.4	3.3	291	205	16.0	10.0
Sub-Saharan Africa												
Angola	0.1	0.1	35*	35*	2.5*	2.2*	...	...	...	...	...	...
Benin	2.5*	4.1	2*	3	0.2*	0.4	2.2*	2.9$^{\pm,\,e}$	2	2$^{\pm,\,e}$	0.2*	0.2$^{\pm,\,e}$
Botswana	0.6	1.1	51	75	29.4	41.5	4.6	5.0	...	...	...	...
Burkina Faso	...	0.4^c	...	...	...	...	...	...	...	...	...	...
Burundi	...	0.1^c	...	...	...	...	...	...	...	...	...	...
Cameroon	0.6*$^{,\,i}$	0.6*$^{,\,i}$	...	...	...	...	9.5*$^{,\,i}$	14.4*$^{,\,i}$	...	...	...	...
Cape Verde	...	...	...	...	...	...	11.1	10.1	...	...	...	...
Central African Republic	...	...	...	...	...	...	...	...	...	...	...	...
Chad	...	...	...	...	...	...	...	...	...	...	...	...
Comoros	...	1.3^c	...	...	...	...	...	...	...	...	...	...
Congo	...	...	...	...	...	...	...	...	...	...	...	...
Congo (Dem. Rep.)	0.2	0.2	...	...	...	...	3.2	2.9	...	...	...	...
Côte d'Ivoire	...	1.2^c	...	...	...	...	...	...	...	...	...	...
Equatorial Guinea	...	...	...	...	...	...	...	2.1^c	...	...	...	...
Eritrea	...	...	...	...	...	...	...	0.7^c	...	...	...	...
Ethiopia	0.1	0.0	338	358	4.9	4.6	1.8	1.8	...	...	...	...
Gabon	...	0.8^c	...	...	...	...	...	...	...	...	...	...
Gambia	...	1.3^c	...	...	...	...	...	...	...	...	...	...
Ghana	...	...	...	...	...	...	...	...	...	...	...	...
Guinea	...	0.2^c	...	...	...	...	...	...	...	...	...	...
Guinea-Bissau	...	...	...	...	...	...	...	...	...	...	...	...
Kenya	0.1	0.1	...	...	...	...	0.1	0.1	...	...	...	...
Lesotho	...	...	...	...	...	...	9.6*	9.2*	1	5*	0.7*	2.5*
Liberia	0.7^c	0.9^c	...	...	...	...	...	...	...	...	...	...
Madagascar	...	0.5^c	...	...	...	...	...	...	...	...	...	...
Malawi	...	0.2	...	...	...	...	...	...	...	...	...	...
Mali	...	0.8^c	...	...	...	...	...	...	...	...	...	...
Mauritius	4.2	8.1	138	95	116.4	77.2	27.8	27.6	150	370	126.5	300.7
Mozambique	0.6	1.0	51	55	2.8	2.7	1.4	2.5	146	210	8.0	10.5
Namibia	1.6	2.0	36	56	18.9	28.0	2.1$^{\pm,\,i}$	1.5$^{\pm,\,i}$	33	24$^{\pm,\,i}$	17.6$^{\pm,\,i}$	12.0$^{\pm,\,i}$
Niger	0.1	0.1	3	3	0.2	0.2	2.0	2.2	28	34	2.5	2.7
Nigeria	0.6	0.3^c	...	...	...	...	0.4	0.7	...	...	...	...
Rwanda	...	...	...	...	...	...	1.2	2.8	...	...	...	...
Saint Helena	...	...	...	...	...	...	...	...	...	...	...	...
Sao Tome and Principe	...	6.7^c	...	...	...	...	...	...	...	...	...	...
Senegal	0.8	1.1	...	100	...	8.7	...	...	...	...	...	...
Seychelles	...	12.1^c	...	...	...	...	...	...	...	...	...	...
Sierra Leone	...	...	...	...	...	...	...	...	...	...	...	...
Somalia	...	...	...	...	...	...	...	...	...	...	...	...
South Africa	0.4	0.4	1,118	1,408	24.6	29.6	5.9$^{\pm,\,h}$	6.6$^{\pm,\,h}$	5,504	7,630$^{\pm,\,h}$	121.2$^{\pm,\,h}$	160.5$^{\pm,\,h}$
Swaziland	1.0	1.8	20	27	18.9	24.2	3.8	5.4	18	35	17.0	31.4

	Community newspapers			On-line newspapers				Press Freedom Indexes		Journalists killed			
								RSF[a,2]	Freedom House[3]	according to IPI[4]	according to CPJ[5]		
Availability	Number of titles	per million inhabitants	Availability	Number of titles	per million inhabitants	% of on-line papers not printed					confirmed	unconfirmed	
2004	2004	2004	2004	2004	2004	2004		2008	2008	1999–2008	1999–2008	1999–2008	Country or Territory
													Arab States
...	...	...	...	...	...	...		31.3	62	.	2	.	Algeria
...	...	...	...	...	...	...		21.2	71	.	.	.	Bahrain
...	...	...	...	...	...	...		41.5	72	.	.	.	Djibouti
...	...	...	...	...	...	...		50.3	59	.	.	.	Egypt
...	...	...	...	...	...	...		59.4	69	235	136	21	Iraq
...	...	...	...	...	...	...		36.0	63	.	.	.	Jordan
Y[+2]	515[+2]	185.34[+2]	...	...	...	...		12.6	54	2	.	1	Kuwait
Y	...	...	Y	14	3.53	57		14.0	55	5	4	.	Lebanon
...	...	...	...	...	...	...		61.5	94	1	1	.	Libyan Arab Jamahiriya
...	...	...	...	...	...	...		23.9	56	.	.	.	Mauritania
N	...	...	Y[+1]	10[+1]	0.33[+1]	100[+1]		32.3	64	1	.	.	Morocco
N	...	...	N	...	...	.		32.7	71	.	.	.	Oman
N	...	...	Y	15	4.13	7		66.9	84	99	5	1	Palestinian A. T.
N[+1]	...	...	Y[+1]	3[+1]	3.77[+1]	...		15.5	64	.	.	.	Qatar
...	...	...	...	...	...	...		61.8	81	1	1	.	Saudi Arabia
Y	...	...	Y	8	0.22	75		42.0	78	1	1	.	Sudan
...	...	...	...	...	...	...		59.6	83	.	.	.	Syrian Arab Republic
...	...	...	...	...	...	...		48.1	81	.	.	.	Tunisia
...	...	...	...	...	...	...		14.5	68	.	.	.	United Arab Emirates
Y	7	0.34	Y	10	0.49	40		59.0	78	1	.	.	Yemen
													Sub-Saharan Africa
Y	...	...	Y[+1]	2[+1]	0.12[+1]	...		29.5	63	4	.	1	Angola
Y	4	0.49	Y[+1]	1[+1]	0.12[+1]	100[+1]		15.0	31	.	.	.	Benin
Y	1	0.55	N	...	...	.		14.0	36	.	.	.	Botswana
...	...	...	...	...	...	...		13.0	41	.	.	.	Burkina Faso
...	...	...	...	...	...	...		21.0	74	.	.	.	Burundi
...	...	...	Y	30	1.72	67		36.9	65	.	.	.	Cameroon
N	-	-	Y[+1]	6[+1]	11.84[+1]	33[+1]		8.0	28	.	.	.	Cape Verde
...	...	...	...	...	...	...		18.5	61	.	.	.	Central African Republic
...	...	...	...	...	...	...		41.3	74	.	.	.	Chad
...	...	...	...	...	...	...		20.0	54	.	.	.	Comoros
Y[+1]	5[+1]	1.39[+1]	Y[+1]	1[+1]	0.28[+1]	100[+1]		20.8	51	.	.	.	Congo
Y	20[l]	0.35[l]	Y	9	0.16	...		51.3	81	87	.	4	Congo (Dem. Rep.)
...	...	...	...	...	...	...		26.5	66	3	2	2	Côte d'Ivoire
...	...	...	...	...	...	...		59.3	89	.	.	.	Equatorial Guinea
...	...	...	...	...	...	...		97.5	94	1	2	.	Eritrea
...	...	...	...	...	...	...		47.8	76	.	.	.	Ethiopia
...	...	...	...	...	...	...		26.8	69	.	.	1	Gabon
...	...	...	...	...	...	...		42.8	79	2	1	.	Gambia
...	...	...	...	...	...	...		7.5	27	.	.	.	Ghana
...	...	...	...	...	...	...		21.5	66	.	.	.	Guinea
...	...	...	...	...	...	...		16.3	53	.	.	.	Guinea-Bissau
Y	2[m]	0.06[m]	N	.	.	.		21.3	60	1	.	2	Kenya
Y[+1]	1[+1]	0.50[+1]	Y	5	2.54	20[+1]		29.5	46	.	.	.	Lesotho
...	...	...	...	...	...	...		9.8	65	.	.	.	Liberia
...	...	...	...	...	...	...		21.0	48	.	.	.	Madagascar
N	...	...	Y[+1]	2[+1]	0.15[+1]	...		15.0	55	.	.	.	Malawi
Y	4	0.36	Y	...	...	...		7.5	27	.	.	.	Mali
N	...	...	Y[+1]	11[+1]	8.86[+1]	...		9.0	26	.	.	.	Mauritius
Y	5[n]	0.25[n]	Y	4	0.20	...		20.5	40	1	1	.	Mozambique
Y	6	3.01	Y	5	2.51	...		5.5	30	.	.	.	Namibia
...	...	...	...	...	...	...		37.0	63	.	.	.	Niger
Y	180	1.30	N	...	...	...		37.8	53	8	3	2	Nigeria
...	...	...	Y	1	0.11	100		50.0	84	.	.	.	Rwanda
...	...	...	...	...	...	...		...	...	.	.	.	Saint Helena
...	...	...	...	...	...	...		...	28	.	.	.	Sao Tome and Principe
N[+1]	...	...	Y[+1]	16[+1]	1.36[+1]	25[+1]		19.0	49	.	.	.	Senegal
...	...	...	...	...	...	...		15.5	59	.	.	.	Seychelles
...	...	...	...	...	...	...		27.8	59	14	14	.	Sierra Leone
...	...	...	...	...	...	...		58.0	84	97	14	1	Somalia
Y	...	...	Y	...	...	...		8.0	28	1	.	.	South Africa
N	...	...	Y[+1]	2[+1]	1.78[+1]	...		50.5	76	1	.	.	Swaziland

Table 12. Newspapers[1]

	Daily newspapers						Non-daily newspapers					
	Titles		Circulation				Titles		Circulation			
	per million inhabitants		Total ('000)		per thousand inhabitants		per million inhabitants		Total ('000)		per thousand inhabitants	
Country or Territory	2000	2004	2000	2004	2000	2004	2000	2004	2000	2004	2000	2004
Tanzania (United Rep.)	0.3	0.4	20	60	0.6	1.6	5.0	17.0	...	...	...	...
Togo	0.2	0.2[c]	10	...	1.9	...	...	...	...	...	...	...
Uganda	0.2	0.3	...	...	...	...	0.2	0.4	...	...	...	...
Zambia	0.3	0.3	...	55[**, c]	...	4.9[**, c]	...	...	...	...	...	...
Zimbabwe	0.2	0.2	...	...	...	...	0.6	1.2	...	...	...	...
Central and South Asia												
Afghanistan	...	0.8[+1]	...	...	...	...	...	...	...	...	...	...
Armenia	2.0	1.7	16	23	5.2	7.6	27.6	54.5	286	577	92.8	190.6
Azerbaijan	...	2.9[-1, c]	...	132[-3, c]	...	16.1[-3, c]	...	...	...	...	...	...
Bangladesh	...	0.1[c]	...	...	...	...	...	...	...	...	...	...
Bhutan	...	...	...	...	...	...	1.8[c]	1.6[c]	...	15[c]	...	24.1[c]
Georgia	...	2.0[±, i]	...	18[±, i]	...	3.9[±, i]	25.6[±, i]	25.0[±, i]	13	18[±, i]	2.8[±, i]	3.9[±, i]
India	1.5[±, i]	1.7[±, i]	59,913[±, i]	79,243[±, i]	57.3[±, i]	70.9[±, i]	4.2[±, i]	4.8[±, i]	67,050	77,476[±, i]	64.1[±, i]	69.4[±, i]
Iran (Islamic Rep.)	1.7	2.5[c]	...	...	...	...	13.7	...	...	...	...	...
Kazakhstan	...	...	...	...	...	...	...	...	...	...	...	...
Kyrgyzstan	0.6	0.4	14	5	2.7	1.0	36.6	41.2	33	34	6.7	6.6
Maldives	...	10.3[c]	...	...	...	...	...	...	...	...	...	...
Nepal	...	...	...	...	...	...	103.0	130.5	...	...	...	...
Pakistan	1.1	1.9	5,700	7,818	39.5	50.3	4.6	6.4	1,759	2,166	12.2	13.9
Sri Lanka	0.7	0.6	...	493[**, -2, c]	...	26.1[**, -2, c]	2.4	2.8	...	...	...	...
Tajikistan	...	...	...	...	...	...	...	...	...	...	...	...
Turkmenistan	0.4	0.4[c]	32	45[c]	7.0	9.4[c]	4.9	4.6[c]	338	307[c]	75.2	64.4[c]
Uzbekistan	...	0.2[c]	...	...	...	...	...	...	...	...	...	...
East Asia												
Brunei Darussalam	...	5.5[c]	...	25[c]	...	68.4[c]	...	...	...	...	...	...
Cambodia	...	...	...	...	...	...	...	...	...	...	...	...
China	0.7[c]	0.7[c]	75,603[c]	96,704[c]	59.5[c]	74.1[c]	0.9[c]	0.7[c]	103,284	98,662[c]	81.3[c]	75.6[c]
Hong Kong (SAR China)	8.9	6.6	1,481	...	223.1	...	...	3.3[c]	...	...	...	...
Macao (SAR China)	22.7	25.7	167	...	379.3	...	15.9	12.8	20	...	44.7	...
Indonesia	5.0	3.8[+1]	...	...	...	...	3.5[c]	1.6[c]	...	5,617[c]	...	25.2[c]
Japan	0.9[±, 2, h]	0.9[c]	71,896[**, c]	70,446[c]	566.0[**, c]	551.2[c]	...	...	...	...	...	...
Korea (Dem. People's Rep.)	...	0.6[c]	...	...	...	...	...	0.3[c]	...	...	...	...
Korea (Rep.)	2.5	2.9	...	...	...	...	46.3	48.4	...	...	...	...
Lao (People's Dem. Rep.)	1.0	1.1	12	15	2.3[c]	2.6	3.1	3.2	21	35	4.1	6.2
Malaysia	1.3[c·]	1.4[c]	2,191[c]	2,753[c]	94.1[c]	109.3[c]	...	...	...	...	...	...
Mongolia	2.0[c]	2.4[c]	44[c]	50[c]	17.8[c]	19.6[c]	...	...	...	...	...	...
Myanmar	...	...	...	...	...	...	...	...	...	...	...	...
Philippines	1.0	1.0	5,511	6,514	72.3	78.6	5.2	6.0	756	971	9.9	11.7
Singapore	2.7[c]	2.6[c]	1,334[c]	1,542[c]	332.1[c]	360.8[c]	2.5[c]	2.1[c]	1,203	1,134[c]	299.4[c]	265.3[c]
Thailand	...	...	...	...	...	...	...	...	...	...	...	...
Timor-Leste	1.2[c]	2.0[c]	...	...	...	...	1.2[c]	3.0[c]	...	...	...	...
Viet Nam	...	...	...	...	...	...	...	1.0	...	...	...	...
Europe												
Albania	5.2[c]	6.7[c]	...	76[-1, c]	...	24.4[-1, c]	25.7[c]	25.2[c]	...	...	...	...
Andorra	...	...	...	...	...	...	...	...	...	...	...	...
Austria	2.0	2.1	2,503	2,570	308.6	311.4	14.8[±, 2]	12.6[±, b]	...	...	...	...
Belarus	1.0	1.3	1,101	800	109.5	81.3	59.7	72.0	10,339	10,121	1,028.5	1,027.7
Belgium	2.9[c]	2.8[c]	1,768[c]	1,706[c]	173.5[c]	164.7[c]	...	...	...	...	...	...
Bosnia and Herzegovina	...	1.8[c]	...	...	...	...	...	...	...	...	...	...
Bulgaria	7.3	7.4	1,100	616	137.4	79.0	60.9	47.0	2,557	3,342	319.5	428.7
Croatia	3.1	2.9	...	...	...	...	50.8	63.2	...	...	...	...
Cyprus	11.5[±, f]	10.7[±, f]	...	...	...	...	20.1[±, f]	29.4[±, f]	...	...	...	...
Czech Republic	7.4	8.0	1,900	1,861	185.9	182.5	15.1	19.4[b]	4,694	1,039[b]	459.3	101.9[b]
Denmark	6.2	6.5[c]	1,507	1,906[c]	282.5	352.8[c]	1.9	...	1,415	...	265.2	...
Estonia	11.7	9.6	262	257	191.3	190.6	67.9	89.0	333	229	243.1	169.8
Finland	10.6[-2]	10.1[b]	2,304[-2]	2,255[b]	445.1[-2]	431.1[b]	41.2[-2]	39.0[b]	951	973[b]	183.7[-2]	186.0[b]
France	1.5[*, k]	1.7[*, +1, k]	9,741[**, k]	9,973[**, +1, k]	164.6[**, k]	163.5[**, +1, k]	...	...	...	...	...	...
Germany	4.3	4.2	23,900	22,100	290.4	267.5	0.4	0.4	6,500	6,100	79.0	73.8
Gibraltar	...	...	6[*]	6[*]	...	...	...	...	6[*]	6[*]	...	...
Greece	...	...	...	...	...	...	...	...	...	...	...	...
Holy See	...	...	...	...	...	...	...	...	...	...	...	...

| Community newspapers | | | On-line newspapers | | | | Press Freedom Indexes | | Journalists killed | | | |
Availability	Number of titles	per million inhabitants	Availability	Number of titles	per million inhabitants	% of on-line papers not printed	RSF[a,2]	Freedom House[3]	according to IPI[4]	according to CPJ[5] confirmed	unconfirmed	Country or Territory
2004	2004	2004	2004	2004	2004	2004	2008	2008	1999–2008	1999–2008	1999–2008	
Y	...	...	N	...	...	...	15.0	48	.	.	.	Tanzania (United Rep.)
...	...	...	...	...	...	...	10.0	74	.	.	.	Togo
Y	...	...	Y	6	0.21	...	26.0	53	1	1	.	Uganda
Y	24	2.13	N	...	...	...	15.5	64	1	.	.	Zambia
Y	10	0.77	N	...	...	.	54.0	89	1	1	.	Zimbabwe
Central and South Asia												
N	...	...	N	...	...	.	59.3	71	87	16	.	Afghanistan
Y+1	...	...	Y+2	45+2	14.95+2	7*,+2	22.8	66	1	.	1	Armenia
...	...	...	...	...	...	...	53.6	77	2	1	.	Azerbaijan
...	...	...	...	...	...	...	42.7	68	83	10	3	Bangladesh
...	...	...	...	...	...	...	15.5	61	.	.	.	Bhutan
Y	16	3.54	Y	40	8.86	...	31.3	60	6	4	1	Georgia
Y	...	...	...	...	...	...	30.0	35	61	11	13	India
...	...	...	...	...	...	...	80.3	85	1	1	.	Iran (Islamic Rep.)
Y	2	0.39	Y+2	19+2	3.61+2	32+2	35.3	78	1	.	1	Kazakhstan
...	...	...	...	...	...	...	27.0	70	2	1	1	Kyrgyzstan
N	...	...	N	...	...	...	23.3	66	.	.	.	Maldives
...	...	...	...	...	...	.	43.3	57	71	6	5	Nepal
Y+1	5+1	0.26+1	Y+1	12+1	0.63+1	...	54.9	66	90	19	4	Pakistan
...	...	...	...	...	...	...	78.0	67	86	16	6	Sri Lanka
...	...	...	...	...	...	...	25.5	77	1	.	1	Tajikistan
...	...	...	...	...	...	...	95.5	96	1	1	.	Turkmenistan
...	...	...	...	...	...	...	62.7	92	.	.	.	Uzbekistan
East Asia												
...	...	...	...	...	...	...	...	75	.	.	.	Brunei Darussalam
...	...	...	...	...	...	...	35.5	60	2	2	.	Cambodia
...	...	...	...	...	...	...	85.5	84	4	2	1	China
N+1	...	...	N+1	...	...	.	9.8	30	.	.	.	Hong Kong (SAR China)
Y	...	...	...	...	...	...	...	...	.	.	.	Macao (SAR China)
Y	...	...	Y	...	...	...	27.0	54	4	2	1	Indonesia
Y	...	...	Y	...	...	...	6.5	21	1	1	.	Japan
Y	341	7.15	Y	510	10.70	15	96.5	98	.	.	.	Korea (Dem. People's Rep.)
N	...	...	Y	4	0.72	...	9.0	30	.	.	.	Korea (Rep.)
N	...	...	Y	7	0.28	14	70.0	83	.	.	.	Lao (People's Dem. Rep.)
...	...	...	...	...	...	...	39.5	65	.	.	.	Malaysia
...	...	...	...	...	...	...	20.8	38	.	.	.	Mongolia
Y	580	7.00	Y	18	0.22	...	94.4	97	3	3	.	Myanmar
...	...	...	...	...	...	...	45.0	45	100	28	20	Philippines
...	...	...	...	...	...	...	49.0	69	.	.	.	Singapore
...	...	...	...	...	...	...	34.5	56	6	5	6	Thailand
...	...	...	...	...	...	...	13.8	38	2	2	.	Timor-Leste
Y	19	0.23	Y	50	0.60	4	86.2	82	.	.	.	Viet Nam
Europe												
...	...	...	...	...	...	...	16.0	50	.	.	.	Albania
N	...	...	Y	...	...	...	...	13	.	.	.	Andorra
Y	228	27.63	Y	...	...	...	3.5	21	.	.	.	Austria
Y	280	28.43	Y	...	...	...	58.3	91	3	1	3	Belarus
Y	...	...	Y+2	8+2	0.77+2	...	3.0	11	.	.	.	Belgium
...	...	...	...	...	...	...	8.0	45	.	.	.	Bosnia and Herzegovina
Y	154	19.76	Y	...	...	...	12.5	33	.	.	1	Bulgaria
...	...	...	...	...	...	...	8.5	36	2	1	.	Croatia
Y	30[9]	40.04[9]	Y	9	12.01	11	10.0	22	1	.	.	Cyprus
Y	...	...	Y+1	12+1	1.18+1	8+1	4.0	18	.	.	.	Czech Republic
...	...	...	...	...	...	...	3.5	10	.	.	.	Denmark
Y	163	120.89	Y	...	...	...	2.0	16	1	.	.	Estonia
N	...	...	Y	120	22.94	...	2.0	9	.	.	.	Finland
...	...	...	...	...	...	...	7.7	22	1	.	1	France
Y	...	..°	Y	...	...	...	4.5	16	.	.	.	Germany
...	...	...	...	...	...	...	...	...	.	.	.	Gibraltar
Y	...	...	Y	...	...	...	7.5	27	.	.	.	Greece
...	...	...	...	...	...	...	...	...	.	.	.	Holy See

Table 12. Newspapers[1]

Country or Territory	Daily newspapers — Titles per million inhabitants 2000	2004	Circulation Total ('000) 2000	2004	per thousand inhabitants 2000	2004	Non-daily newspapers — Titles per million inhabitants 2000	2004	Circulation Total ('000) 2000	2004	per thousand inhabitants 2000	2004
Hungary	3.4	3.4	1,782	2,195	174.5	217.0	7.9	9.6	1,470	1,368	143.9	135.3
Iceland	10.7	10.2	91	162	323.6	551.6	67.6	81.9	57	76	203.8	258.6
Ireland	1.6^c	1.7^c	574^c	742^c	150.9^c	182.4^c	17.4^c	15.5^c	2,180	2,117^c	573.1^c	520.4^c
Israel	...	...	...	...	...	...	...	...	...	...	...	...
Italy	1.6^c	1.6^c	7,123^c	8,017^c	123.5^c	137.1^c	...	1.2$^{±, j}$	...	...	...	...
Latvia	10.9	9.9	327	357	137.5	154.1	84.5	98.9	1,754	2,062	737.3	890.6
Liechtenstein	...	58.3^{-1}	17	18	...	513.6^{-1}	...	29.2^{-1}	16	33	...	924.4^{-1}
Lithuania	3.7	4.1	287	371	81.9	107.8	99.4	94.8	1,984	1,832	566.4	532.5
Luxembourg	11.5^c	13.3^c	120^c	115^c	275.4^c	254.5^c	50.4^c	42.0^c	...	374^c	...	826.4^c
Macedonia (TFYR)	3.0	4.9	...	180	...	88.8	16.4	13.8	47	115	23.5	56.6
Malta	10.3	10.0	...	...	...	...	30.9	30.0	...	...	...	...
Moldova (Rep.)	1.7	...	...	...	...	...	46.7	...	...	...	...	...
Monaco	...	...	...	8	...	...	...	...	...	6	...	...
Montenegro	...	...	...	...	...	...	...	...	...	...	...	...
Netherlands	2.4^c	2.3^c	4,992^c	5,001^c	313.5^c	307.5^c	41.0^c	34.3^c	20,317	18,205^c	1,275.9^c	1,119.4^c
Norway	18.1	16.1	2,545	2,378	567.0	516.0	30.7	32.8	567	641	126.3	139.1
Poland	1.1	1.1	3,928	4,345	102.2	113.6	0.6	0.9	584	613^{-1}	15.2	16.0^{-1}
Portugal	2.6	2.6	...	...	...	...	61.9	56.9	...	...	...	...
Romania	6.6	7.5	...	1,528	...	70.3	14.5*	11.4	...	672	...	30.9
Russian Federation	1.9	1.7	14,334	13,280	97.2	91.8	37.1	50.2	94,439	164,070	640.6	1,133.9
San Marino	...	...	...	...	...	...	...	...	...	...	...	...
Serbia	...	...	...	...	...	...	...	...	...	...	...	...
Slovakia	3.0	2.4	705	677	130.9	125.7	80.7	82.1	2,651	2,853	492.1	529.7
Slovenia	2.5	2.5	335	344$^{**, -2, c}$	168.9	172.8$^{**, -2, c}$	100.8	125.2	...	...	...	...
Spain	3.5^c	3.5^c	4,401^c	6,183^c	109.4^c	144.5^c	...	...	...	...	...	...
Sweden	10.2	10.3^c	3,627	4,324^c	409.0	480.6^c	...	...	...	...	...	...
Switzerland	14.9^c	13.0^c	3,311^c	3,105^c	455.9^c	420.0^c	17.6^c	15.8^c	1,548	1,351^c	213.1^c	182.8^c
Turkey	8.0	8.2	...	...	...	...	10.1	24.6	...	...	...	...
Ukraine	1.3	1.2	8,683	6,192	177.7	131.0	53.3	62.6	38,985	81,462	798.0	1,722.9
United Kingdom	1.8^c	1.8^c	19,259^c	17,375^c	327.2^c	289.8^c	17.9^c	16.8^c	50,075	44,906^c	850.6^c	748.9^c
North America												
Canada	3.5^c	3.2^c	5,500^c	5,578^c	179.2^c	174.6^c	...	...	...	...	...	...
United States of America	5.2^c	5.0^c	56,141^c	57,347^c	197.1^c	193.2^c	26.3^c	25.6^c	107,592	107,568^c	377.7^c	362.4^c
Latin America and the Caribbean												
Anguilla	...	...	...	...	...	...	177.7	159.7	...	...	...	...
Antigua and Barbuda	...	24.6^c	...	...	...	...	...	...	...	...	...	...
Argentina	3.0^c	4.8^c	2,300^c	1,363^c	62.3^c	35.5^c	...	...	...	...	...	...
Aruba	87.9	90.8	...	...	...	...	-	-	...	...	...	...
Bahamas	13.2^c	12.5^c	...	...	...	...	...	...	...	...	...	...
Barbados	7.0^c	6.9^c	...	...	...	...	...	...	...	...	...	...
Belize	...	...	...	...	...	...	...	37.1^c	...	...	...	...
Bermuda	16.1	15.8	15	17	241.4	263.9	48.3	31.6	29	23	466.8	357.7
Bolivia	2.0^c	2.1^c	...	...	...	...	2.9^c	4.4^c	...	...	...	...
Brazil	2.7	2.9	7,883	6,552	45.3	35.5	11.6	13.4	...	...	...	...
British Virgin Islands	...	46.1^c	...	...	...	...	...	368.7^c	...	...	...	...
Cayman Islands	49.0	45.2	15	15	362.7	348.1	...	22.6	...	3	...	67.8
Chile	3.4$^{±, d}$	3.7^c	1,303$^{**, d}$	816^c	84.6$^{**, d}$	50.6^c	0.6$^{±, d}$	2.0$^{±, d}$	...	...	...	...
Colombia	0.6$^{±, h}$	0.5$^{±, h}$	...	1,004$^{±, h}$	...	22.7$^{±, h}$	0.1$^{±, h}$	0.1$^{±, h}$	...	289$^{±, h}$	...	6.5$^{±, h}$
Costa Rica	1.5^c	1.7^c	275^c	275^c	70.0^c	64.7^c	6.9	9.9^c	...	168$^{-2, c}$	...	41.0$^{-2, c}$
Cuba	0.2	0.2	600	728	53.8	64.7	3.1	3.7	935	1,207	83.9	107.3
Dominica	...	...	...	...	...	...	...	42.6^c	...	...	...	...
Dominican Republic	1.0	1.2^c	230	365^c	26.3	39.1^c	0.9	0.8^c	215	...	24.6	...
Ecuador	2.9	...	1,220	...	99.1	...	3.3	...	...	...	...	...
El Salvador	...	0.8^c	...	250^c	...	38.0^c	...	...	...	...	...	...
Grenada	...	...	...	...	...	...	...	38.0^c	...	...	...	...
Guatemala	...	...	...	...	...	...	...	...	...	...	...	...
Guyana	2.7	4.1^c	57	...	77.3	...	5.5	...	48	...	65.0	...
Haiti	...	0.2^c	...	...	...	...	...	...	...	...	...	...
Honduras	...	...	...	...	...	...	...	...	...	...	...	...
Jamaica	...	1.1^c	...	...	...	...	...	...	...	...	...	...
Mexico	3.1	3.0$^{-2, c}$	9,251	...	92.8	...	0.3	0.1$^{-2, c}$	614	...	6.2	...
Montserrat	...	...	...	...	...	...	...	427.3^c	...	...	...	...

	Other information sources						Press Freedom Indexes		Journalists killed			
	Community newspapers			On-line newspapers			RSF[a,2]	Freedom House[3]	according to IPI[4]	according to CPJ[5]		
Availability	Number of titles	per million inhabitants	Availability	Number of titles	per million inhabitants	% of on-line papers not printed				confirmed	unconfirmed	
2004	2004	2004	2004	2004	2004	2004	2008	2008	1999–2008	1999–2008	1999–2008	**Country or Territory**
Y	...	...	Y+1	19+1	1.88+1	68+1	5.5	21	.	.	.	Hungary
Y	22	75.11	Y	21	71.70	...	1.5	9	.	.	.	Iceland
...	...	...	...	...	...	...	2.0	15	.	.	.	Ireland
...	...	...	...	...	...	...	8.8	28	.	4	.	Israel
Y	...	...	Y+2	145+2	2.49+2	37-1	8.4	29	.	.	.	Italy
Y	118	50.97	N	...	...	.	3.0	22	.	1	.	Latvia
...	...	...	...	...	...	...	...	14	.	.	.	Liechtenstein
Y	100	29.07	Y	...	...	...	4.0	18	.	.	.	Lithuania
...	...	...	...	...	...	...	1.5	12	.	.	.	Luxembourg
N	...	...	Y	10	4.93	...	8.3	47	.	.	.	Macedonia (TFYR)
N	...	...	Y	14	34.99	43	...	20	.	.	.	Malta
...	...	...	...	...	...	...	21.4	66	.	.	.	Moldova (Rep.)
Y	1	...	Y	1	...	100	10.0	16	.	.	.	Monaco
...	...	...	...	...	...	...	10.0	38	1	.	.	Montenegro
...	...	...	...	...	...	...	4.0	13	1	.	.	Netherlands
Y	193	41.88	Y	...	...	...	1.5	10	.	.	.	Norway
Y	14	0.37	Y	45	1.18	18	9.0	24	.	.	.	Poland
N	...	...	Y-1	98-1	9.41-1	3*,-1	4.0	16	.	.	.	Portugal
N	...	...	N	...	...	.	9.0	44	.	.	.	Romania
Y	1,667	11.52	Y	...	...	...	47.5	78	120	22	13	Russian Federation
...	...	...	...	...	...	...	...	17	.	.	.	San Marino
...	...	...	...	...	...	...	13.5	39	29	10	3	Serbia
Y	260	48.27	Y	31	5.75	...	3.0	22	.	.	.	Slovakia
Y	67	33.55	Y	97	48.57	63	7.3	23	.	.	.	Slovenia
...	...	...	...	...	...	...	8.0	23	2	1	.	Spain
...	...	...	...	...	...	...	3.0	11	.	.	.	Sweden
Y	...	...	Y	...	...	...	3.0	13	.	.	.	Switzerland
Y	2,322	32.24	Y+2	87+2	1.18+2	66+2	22.8	51	4	2	.	Turkey
Y	68	1.44	Y	...	...	...	19.3	53	6	2	3	Ukraine
...	...	...	...	...	...	...	5.5	18	2	1	1	United Kingdom
												North America
Y+1	1,522+1	47.16+1	Y+1	...	...	...	3.3	18	.	.	.	Canada
Y+1	7,000+1	23.35+1	Y+1	8,183+1	27.29+1	...	8.0	17	8	3	1	United States of America
												Latin America and the Caribbean
N	...	...	Y	1	79.86	...	...	...	.	.	.	Anguilla
...	...	...	...	...	...	...	...	39	.	.	.	Antigua and Barbuda
Y	...	...	Y	...	...	...	14.1	47	1	1	.	Argentina
N	...	...	Y	6	60.54	...	...	...	.	.	.	Aruba
...	...	...	...	...	...	...	...	20	.	.	.	Bahamas
...	...	...	...	...	...	...	...	19	.	.	.	Barbados
...	...	...	...	...	...	...	...	22	.	.	.	Belize
N	...	...	Y	3	47.38	...	...	...	.	.	.	Bermuda
...	...	...	...	...	...	...	28.2	39	3	2	.	Bolivia
Y	...	...	Y	...	...	...	18.0	42	57	8	2	Brazil
...	...	...	...	...	...	...	...	...	.	.	.	British Virgin Islands
N	...	...	Y	3	67.81	...	...	...	.	.	.	Cayman Islands
Y	...	...	Y	46	2.85	2	11.5	30	.	.	.	Chile
...	...	...	Y	24	0.54	...	35.5	59	117	23	21	Colombia
...	...	...	...	...	...	...	5.1	19	2	1	.	Costa Rica
Y	10	0.89	Y	25	2.22	...	88.3	94	.	.	.	Cuba
...	...	...	...	...	...	...	...	22	.	.	.	Dominica
...	...	...	...	...	...	...	18.0	39	43	1	1	Dominican Republic
Y+1	...	...	Y+1	2+1	0.15+1	50+1	15.5	41	2	1	1	Ecuador
...	...	...	...	...	...	...	12.8	42	1	.	1	El Salvador
...	...	...	...	...	...	...	...	24	.	.	.	Grenada
...	...	...	...	...	...	...	22.6	58	64	3	5	Guatemala
...	...	...	...	...	...	...	19.8	31	1	.	.	Guyana
...	...	...	...	...	...	...	15.1	56	65	5	3	Haiti
...	...	...	...	...	...	...	21.5	51	2	1	1	Honduras
...	...	...	...	...	...	...	4.9	15	.	.	.	Jamaica
...	...	...	...	...	...	...	46.1	51	78	9	15	Mexico
...	...	...	...	...	...	...	...	...	.	.	.	Montserrat

Table 12. Newspapers[1]

	Daily newspapers						Non-daily newspapers					
	Titles		Circulation				Titles		Circulation			
	per million inhabitants		Total ('000)		per thousand inhabitants		per million inhabitants		Total ('000)		per thousand inhabitants	
Country or Territory	2000	2004	2000	2004	2000	2004	2000	2004	2000	2004	2000	2004
Netherlands Antilles	...	27.1[c]	...	...	...	...	...	...	...	...	...	...
Nicaragua	...	1.1[c]	...	...	...	...	...	...	...	...	...	...
Panama	...	2.5	...	207	...	65.1	...	1.6	...	127	...	40.0
Paraguay	...	...	...	...	...	...	...	...	...	...	...	...
Peru	...	2.7[c]	...	...	...	...	...	...	...	...	...	...
Saint Kitts and Nevis	...	23.4[c]	...	...	...	...	...	93.6[c]	...	...	...	...
Saint Lucia	...	...	...	...	...	...	32.7	31.4	...	...	...	...
Saint Vincent and the Grenadines	.	25.2[+1]	...	...	...	...	.	.	...	...	...	...
Suriname	4.6	8.8[+1]	40	36[+1]	91.1	80.1[+1]	13.8	8.8[+1]	66	43[+1]	150.2	95.0[+1]
Trinidad and Tobago	2.3	2.3	166	196[-1, c]	127.6	149.1[-1, c]	5.4	5.3	141	170[-1]	108.4	129.3[-1]
Turks and Caicos Islands	...	...	...	...	...	...	...	72.7[c]	...	...	...	...
Uruguay	...	...	...	...	...	...	...	...	...	...	...	...
Venezuela	...	3.5[c]	...	2,450[c]	...	93.3[c]	...	...	...	...	...	...
Pacific												
Australia	2.6[c]	2.4[c]	3,173[c]	3,114[c]	165.8[c]	155.1[c]	18.5[c]	21.7[c]	381	433[c, g]	19.9[c, g]	21.6[c, g]
Cook Islands	...	50.3[c]	...	...	...	...	...	...	...	...	...	...
Fiji	3.7	3.7	53	44	66.1	53.5	3.7	3.7	...	...	...	...
Kiribati	...	...	...	...	...	...	...	33.0[c]	...	...	...	...
Marshall Islands	...	...	...	...	...	...	19.3	18.1	3	3	58.0	54.2
Micronesia (Fed. States)	...	...	...	...	...	...	...	27.4[c]	...	...	...	...
Nauru	...	...	...	...	...	...	...	495.1[c]	...	...	...	...
New Zealand	7.3	5.7[±, h]	765	739[**, c]	198.5	182.5[**, c]	32.7[±, h]	31.9[±, h]	...	...	...	...
Niue	496.5	627.8	...	...	...	...	...	...	...	...	...	...
Palau	...	...	...	...	...	...	104.6	96.6	5	5	235.2	217.4
Papua New Guinea	...	0.3[c]	...	51[c]	...	8.6[c]	...	...	...	...	...	...
Samoa	...	11.0[c]	...	...	...	...	...	...	...	...	...	...
Solomon Islands	...	2.2[c]	...	5[c]	...	10.8[c]	...	...	...	...	...	...
Tokelau	...	...	...	...	...	...	...	...	...	...	...	...
Tonga	...	...	...	...	...	...	...	30.3[c]	...	...	...	...
Tuvalu	...	...	...	...	...	...	89.0[c]	103.8[c]	...	...	...	...
Vanuatu	...	4.8[c]	...	3[c]	...	14.3[c]	...	...	...	...	...	...

Sources:

1. UNESCO Institute for Statistics, Communication database, 2008 and World Association of Newspapers, 2007. Both institutions share similar methodologies and definitions.
2. Press Freedom Index: Reporters sans frontières 2007. http://www.rsf.org
3. Freedom of the Press Index: Freedom House 2008. http://www.freedomhouse.org
4. Death watch: International Press Institute 2008. http://www.freemedia.at
5. Death watch: Committee for the Protection of Journalists, 2008. http://www.cpj.org.

Notes:

a. Compiled from questionnaires with 52 criteria for assessing the state of press freedom in each country. It includes every kind of violation directly affecting journalists (murders, imprisonment, physical attacks and threats) and news media (censorship, confiscation of issues, searches and harassment). The index should in no way be taken as an indication of the quality of the press in the countries concerned.

b. Does not include free newspapers.

c. Source: World Association of Newspapers.

d. Does not include newspapers from remote areas.

e. Does not include newspapers on literacy in local languages.

f. Does not include newspapers published in the Turkish occupied area of Cyprus.

g. Does not include Sunday editions.

h. Includes only newspapers affiliated to a national association.

i. Includes only newspapers that report to a governmental or national institution.

j. Includes only weekly titles.

k. Includes specialized daily newspapers for the general public and specialized technical and professional daily newspapers.

l. Does not include newspapers published in the provinces of Maniema, Equateur, Bandundu, Kasaï-Oriental and Kasaï-Occidental.

m. Does not include newspapers from the Kikuyu and Luo communities.

n. Does not include newspapers published in the north of the country.

Community newspapers			Other information sources On-line newspapers				Press Freedom Indexes		Journalists killed		
Availability	Number of titles	per million inhabitants	Availability	Number of titles	per million inhabitants	% of on-line papers not printed	RSF[a,2]	Freedom House[3]	according to IPI[4]	according to CPJ[5] confirmed	unconfirmed
2004	2004	2004	2004	2004	2004	2004	2008	2008	1999-2008	1999-2008	1999-2008	Country or Territory
...	...	...	...	...	...	...	...	...	.	.	.	Netherlands Antilles
N	...	...	Y	2	0.37	...	12.5	43	3	2	.	Nicaragua
Y+1	2+1	0.62+1	Y+1	11+1	3.40+1	18+1	11.8	44	.	.	.	Panama
...	...	...	...	...	...	...	20.5	60	2	2	.	Paraguay
...	...	...	...	...	...	...	37.4	44	5	2	1	Peru
...	...	...	...	...	...	...	...	19	.	.	.	Saint Kitts and Nevis
N	...	...	Y	3	18.82	...	...	16	.	.	.	Saint Lucia
N+1	...	...	Y+1	2+1	16.79+1	.	...	17	.	.	.	Saint Vincent and the Grenadines
N+1	...	...	N+1	...	...	.	6.0	23	.	.	.	Suriname
Y	...	...	Y+2	5+2	3.76+2	...	6.1	23	.	.	.	Trinidad and Tobago
...	...	...	...	...	...	...	...	...	.	.	.	Turks and Caicos Islands
...	...	...	...	...	...	...	8.3	30	1	1	.	Uruguay
...	...	...	...	...	...	...	27.3	74	79	2	3	Venezuela
												Pacific
...	...	...	...	...	...	...	6.3	21	.	.	.	Australia
...	...	...	...	...	...	...	...	...	.	.	.	Cook Islands
Y	...	...	Y	4	4.86	...	16.0	37	.	.	.	Fiji
...	...	...	...	...	...	...	...	26	.	.	.	Kiribati
N	...	...	Y	1	18.06	...	...	17	.	.	.	Marshall Islands
...	...	...	...	...	...	...	...	21	.	.	.	Micronesia (Fed. States)
...	...	...	...	...	...	...	...	28	.	.	.	Nauru
...	107	26.42	Y	...	...	...	3.0	13	.	.	.	New Zealand
N	...	...	Y+2	1+2	628.54	100+2	...	...	.	.	.	Niue
N	...	...	N	...	...	.	...	14	.	.	.	Palau
...	...	...	...	...	...	...	...	28	.	.	.	Papua New Guinea
...	...	...	...	...	...	...	...	29	.	.	.	Samoa
...	...	...	...	...	...	...	...	30	.	.	.	Solomon Islands
...	...	...	...	...	...	...	...	...	.	.	.	Tokelau
...	...	...	...	...	...	...	18.0	31	.	.	.	Tonga
...	...	...	...	...	...	...	...	26	.	.	.	Tuvalu
...	...	...	...	...	...	...	...	23	.	.	.	Vanuatu

o. Data does not include non-dailies issued 2 or 3 times a week

... Data not available

* National estimation

** UIS estimation

. Not applicable

± Partial data

+n Data refer to the year n years after the reference year

-n Data refer to the year n years before the reference year

Table 13. Broadcast content[1]

Country or Territory	National regulation on media	Televison Institutions[a] Total number	Televison Institutions[a] % public	Televison % of annual broadcasting time programmed National production content	Televison % of annual broadcasting time programmed Cultural & arts content	Televison % of annual broadcasting time programmed Film and series content	Radio Institutions[a] Total number	Radio Institutions[a] % public	Radio % of annual broadcasting time programmed National production content	Radio % of annual broadcasting time programmed Cultural & arts content	Radio % of annual broadcasting time programmed Music content	Broadcast journalists Total per million hab.	Broadcast journalists Sex ratio F/M
							2005						
Arab States													
Algeria	Y	...	...	...	...	13.4	...	...	100.0	...	45.9	...	...
Bahrain	...	...	...	...	...	...	...	...	...	...	...	...	...
Djibouti	Y[-1]	2[-1]	50.0[-1]	71.5[-1]	3.7[-1]	27.1[-1]	2[-1]	50.0[-1]	94.7[-1]	...	...	34[-1]	0.3[-1]
Egypt	Y	8	12.5	...	...	...	2	50.0	...	...	...	...	...
Iraq	...	...	...	...	...	...	...	...	...	...	...	...	...
Jordan	Y	5	100.0	...	...	...	15	46.7	...	...	...	...	...
Kuwait	...	...	...	...	...	...	...	...	...	...	...	...	...
Lebanon	Y	10	10.0	...	...	...	11	9.1	...	...	...	...	...
Libyan Arab Jamahiriya	...	...	...	...	...	...	...	...	...	...	...	...	...
Mauritania	Y[+1]	1[+1]	100.0[+1]	89.3[+1]	8.8[+1]	18.5[+1]	1[+1]	100.0[+1]	...	...	...	176[+1]	0.3[+1]
Morocco	...	...	...	...	...	...	...	...	...	...	...	...	...
Oman	N	...	...	...	...	...	...	...	...	...	...	346	0.3
Palestinian A. T.	N	31	3.2	...	...	...	33	3.0	...	...	...	299	0.3
Qatar	Y	...	...	31.7	10.8	30.1	...	...	76.4	15.1	24.7	183	0.5
Saudi Arabia	...	...	...	...	...	...	...	...	...	...	...	...	...
Sudan	Y[+1]	56	100.0	...	...	...	66	83.3	...	...	...	15[+1]	1.4[+1]
Syrian Arab Republic	Y	...	...	75.0	3.4	11.4	...	...	100.0	12.5	25.0	19	0.8
Tunisia	N	...	...	...	...	...	...	...	...	...	...	28[+1]	1.0[+1]
United Arab Emirates	N	...	...	...	...	...	...	...	...	...	...	...	...
Yemen	...	...	...	...	...	...	...	...	...	...	...	...	...
Sub-Saharan Africa													
Angola	...	...	...	...	...	...	...	...	...	...	...	...	...
Benin	...	...	...	...	...	...	...	...	...	...	...	...	...
Botswana	...	...	...	...	...	...	...	...	...	...	...	...	...
Burkina Faso	...	...	...	...	...	...	...	...	...	...	...	...	...
Burundi	...	...	...	...	...	...	...	...	...	...	...	...	...
Cameroon	Y	81	1.2	78.8	...	...	35	2.9	96.3	...	...	...	...
Cape Verde	N	1	100.0	...	...	...	10	10.0	...	...	...	195	0.8
Central African Republic	...	...	...	...	...	...	...	...	...	...	...	...	...
Chad	...	...	...	...	...	...	...	...	...	...	...	...	...
Comoros	...	...	...	...	...	...	...	...	...	...	...	...	...
Congo	...	2	100.0	...	...	...	8	37.5	...	...	...	24	0.6
Congo (Dem. Rep.)	Y	86	2.3	73.0	11.8	22.2	206	1.0	99.2	...	...	127	0.7
Côte d'Ivoire	Y	4	75.0	...	...	...	...	...	...	...	...	16	0.2
Equatorial Guinea	...	...	...	...	...	...	...	...	...	...	...	...	...
Eritrea	...	...	...	...	...	...	...	...	...	...	...	...	...
Ethiopia	Y	1	100.0	98.0	8.4	40.1	8	62.5	96.0	8.2	29.4	10	0.3
Gabon	...	...	...	...	...	...	...	...	...	...	...	...	...
Gambia	N	2	100.0	40.0	...	...	...	...	96.4	5.7	8.0	57	0.3
Ghana	...	28	7.1	...	...	...	85	14.1	...	...	...	...	...
Guinea	...	...	...	...	...	...	...	...	...	...	...	...	...
Guinea-Bissau	...	...	...	...	...	...	...	...	...	...	...	...	...
Kenya	...	...	...	...	...	...	...	...	...	...	...	...	...
Lesotho	...	...	...	...	...	...	...	...	...	...	...	...	...
Liberia	...	...	...	...	...	...	...	...	...	...	...	...	...
Madagascar	...	...	...	...	...	...	...	...	...	...	...	...	...
Malawi	...	...	...	...	...	...	...	...	...	...	...	...	...
Mali	...	...	...	...	...	...	...	...	...	...	...	...	...
Mauritius	Y	3	33.3	...	...	...	4	25.0	...	...	...	...	...
Mozambique	...	...	...	...	...	...	...	...	...	...	...	...	...
Namibia	...	...	...	...	...	...	...	...	...	...	...	...	...
Niger	Y	5	60.0	26.6	...	...	14	14.3	96.5	3.5	16.5	5[+1]	0.3[+1]
Nigeria	...	128	86.7	...	...	...	98	76.5	...	...	...	...	...
Rwanda	N	2[+1]	50.0[+1]	...	...	...	...	...	...	...	...	...	...
Saint Helena	...	...	...	...	...	...	...	...	...	...	...	...	...
Sao Tome and Principe	...	...	...	...	...	...	...	...	...	...	...	...	...
Senegal	...	...	...	...	...	...	...	...	...	...	...	...	...
Seychelles	...	...	...	...	...	...	...	...	...	...	...	...	...
Sierra Leone	...	...	...	...	...	...	...	...	...	...	...	...	...
Somalia	...	...	...	...	...	...	...	...	...	...	...	...	...
South Africa	Y	3	33.3	...	...	...	6	16.7	...	...	...	...	...

Table 13. Broadcast content[1]

Country or Territory	National regulation on media	Television Institutions[a] Total number	% public	% of annual broadcasting time programmed National production content	Cultural & arts content	Film and series content	Radio Institutions[a] Total number	% public	% of annual broadcasting time programmed National production content	Cultural & arts content	Music content	Broadcast journalists Total per million hab.	Sex ratio F/M
							2005						
Swaziland	...	...	...	...	...	...	...	...	...	...	...	...	...
Tanzania (United Rep.)	Y[+1]	22	4.5	75.7[+1]	...	...	39	5.1	...	...	...	5	1.5
Togo	Y	6	16.7	48.4	1.0[b]	41.5	81	2.5	90.3	...	...	45	0.5
Uganda	Y	13	15.4	...	...	...	101	2.0	...	...	...	...	...
Zambia	...	...	...	...	...	...	...	...	82.4	4.6	35.6	...	...
Zimbabwe	...	...	...	...	...	...	...	...	...	...	...	...	...
Central and South Asia													
Afghanistan	...	...	...	...	...	...	...	...	...	...	...	...	...
Armenia	...	...	...	...	...	...	...	...	...	...	...	...	...
Azerbaijan	Y	17	11.8	...	...	...	6	33.3	...	...	...	...	...
Bangladesh	N	...	...	95.5	1.9	18.1	...	...	...	...	...	...	...
Bhutan	N	...	...	97.1	2.9	3.7	...	...	98.7	2.6	14.3	151	0.4
Georgia	N	...	...	54.0	...	...	...	...	94.9	...	...	...	...
India	Y	83	1.2	...	...	...	23	4.3	...	...	...	...	...
Iran (Islamic Rep.)	...	...	...	...	...	...	...	...	...	...	...	...	...
Kazakhstan	...	...	...	...	...	...	...	...	...	...	...	...	...
Kyrgyzstan	...	...	...	...	...	...	...	...	...	...	...	...	...
Maldives	...	...	...	...	...	...	...	...	...	...	...	...	...
Nepal	N	6	16.7	...	...	...	57	1.8	100.0	2.6	31.6	42*	0.3*
Pakistan	Y	52	17.3	95.8	8.3	20.8	66	57.6	100.0	16.7	8.3	39	0.7
Sri Lanka	...	...	...	...	...	...	...	...	...	...	...	...	...
Tajikistan	...	...	...	...	...	...	...	...	...	...	...	...	...
Turkmenistan	...	...	...	...	...	...	...	...	...	...	...	...	...
Uzbekistan	...	...	...	...	...	...	...	...	...	...	...	...	...
East Asia													
Brunei Darussalam	...	...	...	...	...	...	...	...	...	...	...	...	...
Cambodia	...	...	...	80.7	5.6	10.1	...	...	...	...	...	...	...
China	Y	2,234	100.0	...	...	...	2,205	100.0	...	...	...	...	...
Hong Kong (SAR China)	Y	7	28.6	99.7	2.8	1.4	4	50.0	82.4	6.2	36.7	21	1.2
Macao (SAR China)	...	...	...	...	...	...	...	...	...	...	...	...	...
Indonesia	...	...	...	...	...	...	...	...	...	...	...	...	...
Japan	...	...	...	...	...	...	...	...	...	...	...	...	...
Korea (Dem. People's Rep.)	...	...	...	...	...	...	...	...	...	...	...	...	...
Korea (Rep.)	Y	499	5.6	...	...	...	...	...	...	...	...	49	0.2
Lao (People's Dem. Rep.)	...	...	...	...	...	...	...	...	...	...	...	...	...
Malaysia	...	...	...	...	...	...	...	...	...	...	...	...	...
Mongolia	Y	37	48.6	77.5	6.4	23.0	43	14.0	96.9	...	...	98	0.9
Myanmar	Y	3	100.0	88.9	6.5	22.2	3	100.0	85.4	0.7	33.3	1	3.3
Philippines	...	...	...	...	...	...	...	...	...	...	...	...	...
Singapore	...	...	...	...	...	...	...	...	...	...	...	...	...
Thailand	...	...	...	...	...	...	...	...	...	...	...	...	...
Timor-Leste	...	...	...	...	...	...	...	...	...	...	...	...	...
Viet Nam	...	...	...	...	...	...	...	...	...	...	...	...	...
Europe													
Albania	N	74	1.4	50.0	15.2	21.3	50	2.0	60.0	11.4	50.2	...	...
Andorra													
Austria	Y	74	1.4	...	...	...	64	1.6	100.0	...	...	...	...
Belarus	...	...	...	...	...	...	...	...	...	...	...	...	...
Belgium	Y	...	...	...	...	...	...	...	...	...	...	...	...
Bosnia and Herzegovina	Y	93	23.7	...	...	...	148	45.3	...	...	...	...	...
Bulgaria	Y[-2]	...	...	...	...	...	...	...	...	...	...	...	...
Croatia	...	16	6.3	...	-	...	135	14.8	100.0	2.4	54.8	358	1.4
Cyprus	Y	13	7.7	...	...	...	50	2.0	...	...	...	...	...
Czech Republic	Y	106	0.9	...	...	...	73	1.4	...	...	...	...	...
Denmark	Y[-1]	...	...	...	...	...	...	...	...	...	...	...	...
Estonia	Y	...	...	56.7	9.3[b]	33.1	17	5.9	77.1	9.5	43.1	...	...
Finland	Y	...	...	...	...	...	78	1.3	...	...	...	900	1.0
France	Y[-1]	140	7.1	78.2[-1]	5.5[-1]	25.3[-1]	1,028	5.4	...	...	...	136[-1]	...
Germany	Y[-1]	292	5.1	...	...	...	233	4.7	...	...	...	...	...
Gibraltar	...	...	...	...	...	...	...	...	...	...	...	...	...

Table 13. Broadcast content[1]

Country or Territory	National regulation on media	Television					Radio					Broadcast journalists	
		Institutions[a]		% of annual broadcasting time programmed			Institutions[a]		% of annual broadcasting time programmed				
		Total number	% public	National production content	Cultural & arts content	Film and series content	Total number	% public	National production content	Cultural & arts content	Music content	Total per million hab.	Sex ratio F/M
							2005						
Greece	Y	...	...	...	...	...	...	...	...	...	...	...	...
Holy See	N	...	...	...	...	...	...	...	...	...	...	...	...
Hungary	Y	571	25.7	...	...	...	135	6.7	94.2*	4.9*	60.7*	...	...
Iceland	N[-1]	10	10.0	55.1[-1]	10.4[-1]	28.1[-1]	10	10.0	...	...	...	...	...
Ireland	...	...	...	...	...	...	...	...	...	...	...	...	...
Israel	...	...	...	...	...	...	...	...	...	...	...	28[-1]	0.4[-1]
Italy	Y[-1]	...	...	...	...	...	...	...	...	...	...	...	...
Latvia	Y	22	4.5	23.4	5.5	26.6	28	3.6	22.7	6.3	53.6	101	2.1
Liechtenstein	...	...	...	...	...	...	...	...	...	...	...	...	...
Lithuania	Y	36	5.6	84.1	15.8	32.8	53	3.8	95.0	20.7	39.7	...	...
Luxembourg	Y	2	50.0	...	...	...	21	4.8	...	...	...	...	...
Macedonia (TFYR)	Y	64	17.2	...	...	...	95	31.6	...	...	...	1343	0.6
Malta	Y	9	33.3	...	...	...	16	18.8	...	...	...	...	...
Moldova (Rep.)	Y	40	10.0	...	...	...	45	8.9	...	...	...	...	...
Monaco	N	2	50.0	100.0	26.8	...	4	...	...	...	...	...	...
Montenegro	...	...	...	...	...	...	...	...	...	...	...	...	...
Netherlands	Y	...	...	...	...	...	...	...	...	...	...	...	...
Norway	Y	41	4.9	...	...	...	249	0.8	...	...	...	...	...
Poland	Y	25	4.0	88.2	0.7	15.8	191	9.4	96.2	1.5	59.1	48	1.1
Portugal	Y	8[+1]	12.5[+1]	73.8	0.9	8.8	336[+1]	0.3[+1]	93.9	2.7	72.6	195*	0.7*
Romania	Y	221	0.5	54.7	13.6	31.0	151	0.7	...	...	...	131	1.2
Russian Federation	...	...	...	...	...	...	...	...	...	...	...	...	...
San Marino	Y	...	...	...	...	...	...	...	100.0	...	...	...	...
Serbia	...	...	...	...	...	...	...	...	...	...	...	...	...
Slovakia	Y	93	1.1	54.4	0.4	30.0	27	3.7	...	...	...	301	1.0
Slovenia	...	...	...	...	...	...	...	...	...	...	...	...	...
Spain	...	...	...	...	...	...	...	...	...	...	...	...	...
Sweden	Y	165	1.2	...	...	...	92	2.2	...	...	...	...	...
Switzerland	Y	...	...	...	...	...	...	...	...	...	...	...	...
Turkey	...	529	0.2	...	...	...	1,266	0.1	...	...	...	...	...
Ukraine	Y	1,640	4.3	86.5	...	...	1,517	4.4	97.4	22.8	11.3	47	2.1
United Kingdom	...	...	...	...	...	...	...	...	...	...	...	...	...
North America													
Canada	...	...	...	...	...	...	...	...	...	...	...	...	...
United States of America	...	...	...	...	...	...	...	...	...	...	...	...	...
Latin America and the Caribbean													
Anguilla	...	1	...	89.3	16.1	7.1	...	...	71.1	0.2	19.3	2,494**	0.3
Antigua and Barbuda	...	...	...	...	...	...	...	...	...	...	...	...	...
Argentina	...	...	...	...	...	...	...	...	...	...	...	...	...
Aruba	N	3	33.3	14.0	0.9	5.7	18	-	...	...	...	480	0.6
Bahamas	...	...	...	...	...	...	...	...	...	...	...	...	...
Barbados	...	...	...	...	...	...	...	...	...	...	...	...	...
Belize	...	...	...	...	...	...	...	...	...	...	...	...	...
Bermuda	...	...	...	...	...	...	...	...	...	...	...	...	...
Bolivia	...	...	...	...	...	...	...	...	...	...	...	...	...
Brazil	Y	747	10.0	75.0	...	...	4,220	15.0	100.0	...	...	32	0.6
British Virgin Islands	...	...	...	...	...	...	...	...	...	...	...	...	...
Cayman Islands	N	1	...	...	...	...	11	18.2	...	...	...	...	...
Chile	Y	125[-1]	0.8[-1]	...	...	...	893[-1]	...	...	...	...	...	...
Colombia	Y[+1]	53[+1]	26.4[+1]	...	...	...	836[+1]	21.8[+1]	...	...	...	...	...
Costa Rica	...	...	...	...	...	...	...	...	...	...	...	...	...
Cuba	Y	2	100.0	71.0	6.4	17.4	2	100.0	100.0	4.5	36.2	193	1.1
Dominica	...	...	...	...	...	...	...	...	...	...	...	...	...
Dominican Republic	Y	46	2.2	...	...	...	354	5.1	...	...	...	104	0.7
Ecuador	...	203	2.0	...	...	...	831	7.5	...	...	...	...	...
El Salvador	...	...	...	...	...	...	...	...	...	...	...	...	...
Grenada	...	...	...	...	...	...	...	...	...	...	...	...	...
Guatemala	...	33	6.1	...	...	...	268	1.5	...	...	...	...	...
Guyana	...	...	...	...	...	...	...	...	...	...	...	...	...
Haiti	Y	32[+1]	3.1[+1]	...	...	...	156[+1]	0.6[+1]	...	...	...	7[+1]	0.3[+1]
Honduras	...	...	...	...	...	...	...	...	...	...	...	...	...

Table 13. Broadcast content[1]

| Country or Territory | National regulation on media | Television Institutions[a] | | Television % of annual broadcasting time programmed | | | Radio Institutions[a] | | Radio % of annual broadcasting time programmed | | | Broadcast journalists | |
		Total number	% public	National production content	Cultural & arts content	Film and series content	Total number	% public	National production content	Cultural & arts content	Music content	Total per million hab.	Sex ratio F/M
							2005						
Jamaica	Y	4	25.0	...	...	...	20	...	...	...	...	...	...
Mexico	Y	...	...	...	...	...	...	...	...	...	...	...	...
Montserrat	...	...	...	...	...	...	...	...	...	...	...	...	...
Netherlands Antilles	...	...	...	...	...	...	...	...	...	...	...	...	...
Nicaragua	N	15	6.7	...	...	...	258	1.2	...	...	...	...	...
Panama	Y	17	5.9	...	...	...	138	2.2	...	...	...	...	...
Paraguay	...	8	...	...	...	...	236	0.4	...	.	.	46	0.4
Peru	N	459	0.2	94.4	39.3	...	1,145	0.1	98.4	...	36.8[c]	...	...
Saint Kitts and Nevis	...	...	...	...	...	...	...	...	...	...	...	...	...
Saint Lucia	N	8	25.0	...	...	...	11	18.2	...	...	...	...	...
Saint Vincent and the Grenadines	N[+1]	3[+1]	...	25.0[+1]	...	...	10[+1]	10.0[+1]	...	...	...	334[+1]	0.7[+1]
Suriname	N	27	7.4	...	...	...	41	4.9	...	...	...	...	...
Trinidad and Tobago	...	...	...	...	...	...	...	...	...	...	...	...	...
Turks and Caicos Islands	...	...	...	...	...	...	...	...	...	...	...	...	...
Uruguay	Y	313	10.5	...	...	...	284	8.8	...	...	...	...	...
Venezuela	Y	...	...	...	...	...	...	...	...	...	...	...	...
Pacific													
Australia	Y	...	...	...	...	...	263	0.8	...	...	...	...	...
Cook Islands	...	...	...	...	...	...	...	...	...	...	...	...	...
Fiji	...	...	...	...	...	...	...	...	...	...	...	...	...
Kiribati	...	...	...	...	...	...	...	...	...	...	...	...	...
Marshall Islands	...	...	...	...	...	...	...	...	...	...	...	...	...
Micronesia (Fed. States)	...	...	...	...	...	...	...	...	...	...	...	...	...
Nauru	...	...	...	...	...	...	...	...	...	...	...	...	...
New Zealand	Y	...	...	36.2	...	...	...	...	...	...	...	...	...
Niue	...	...	...	...	...	...	...	...	...	...	...	...	...
Palau	...	...	...	...	...	...	...	...	...	...	...	...	...
Papua New Guinea	Y	2	...	...	...	...	43	2.3	95.3	1.2	30.5	9	0.9
Samoa	...	...	...	...	...	...	...	...	...	...	...	...	...
Solomon Islands	...	...	...	...	...	...	...	...	...	...	...	...	...
Tokelau	N	...	...	...	...	...	3	100.0	100.0	...	...	6,392*	3.5
Tonga	...	...	...	...	...	...	...	...	...	...	...	...	...
Tuvalu	...	...	...	...	...	...	...	...	...	...	...	...	...
Vanuatu	...	...	...	...	...	...	...	...	...	...	...	...	...

Source:

1. UNESCO Institute for Statistics, 2008. Communication database. http://www.uis.unesco.org

Notes:

a. Includes institutions providing both radio and television services.

b. Includes education and sciences.

c. Includes other entertainment.

... Data not available

* National estimation

** UIS estimation

Table 14. Movies

Country or Territory	Production			Distribution		Infrastructure	
	Number of national feature films produced	% of feature films 100% nationally produced	% of feature films co-produced	Number of distribution companies	% of nationally controlled distrib. company	Number of cinemas	% of multiplexes[i]
				2006			
Arab States							
Algeria[3]	...	...	...	...	...	69[j]	...
Bahrain	...	...	...	...	...	26[l,a,-1]	...
Djibouti	...	...	...	...	...	...	...
Egypt	23[1,±,g]	...	...	11	...	218	...
Iraq	...	...	...	...	...	...	...
Jordan	...	...	...	...	...	...	...
Kuwait	...	...	...	...	...	...	...
Lebanon	8	25	75	14	57	150	3
Libyan Arab Jamahiriya	...	...	...	...	...	...	...
Mauritania	...	...	...	...	...	...	...
Morocco	12	83	17	7	100	96	2
Oman	1	100	...	9	56	18	...
Palestinian A. T.	...	...	...	...	...	...	...
Qatar	...	...	...	...	...	...	...
Saudi Arabia	...	...	...	...	...	...	...
Sudan	...	...	...	...	...	...	...
Syrian Arab Republic	...	...	...	...	...	...	...
Tunisia[3]	...	...	...	...	...	29[j]	...
United Arab Emirates	...	...	...	...	...	202[b,j]	...
Yemen	...	...	...	...	...	...	...
Sub-Saharan Africa							
Angola	...	...	...	...	...	...	...
Benin	...	...	...	...	...	7[a,l,-4]	...
Botswana	...	...	...	...	...	...	...
Burkina Faso	5	40	60	...	...	19[a,l,-2]	...
Burundi	...	...	...	...	...	...	...
Cameroon	7	86	14	...	...	13	...
Cape Verde	...	...	...	...	...	...	...
Central African Republic	...	...	...	...	...	...	...
Chad	...	...	...	...	...	...	...
Comoros	...	...	...	...	...	...	...
Congo	...	...	...	...	...	...	...
Congo (Dem. Rep.)	...	...	...	...	...	...	...
Côte d'Ivoire	...	...	...	...	...	...	...
Equatorial Guinea	...	...	...	...	...	...	...
Eritrea	...	...	...	...	...	...	...
Ethiopia	...	...	...	...	...	...	...
Gabon	...	...	...	...	...	...	...
Gambia	...	...	...	...	...	...	...
Ghana	...	...	...	...	...	...	...
Guinea	...	...	...	...	...	...	...
Guinea-Bissau	...	...	...	...	...	...	...
Kenya	...	...	...	...	...	...	...
Lesotho	...	...	...	...	...	...	...
Liberia	...	...	...	...	...	...	...
Madagascar	40[±,g]	...	...	...	...	...	...
Malawi	...	...	...	...	...	...	...
Mali	...	...	...	...	...	11[a,l,-5]	...
Mauritius	...	...	...	6	100	17	...
Mozambique	1	100	...	...	...	12[±]	...
Namibia	1[-1]	100[-1]	...	1[-1]	...	3	...
Niger	...	...	...	...	...	5	...
Nigeria	...[-1,j]	...	...	139	97	4,871	...
Rwanda	...	...	...	...	...	...	...
Saint Helena	...	...	...	...	...	...	...
Sao Tome and Principe	...	...	...	...	...	...	...
Senegal	...	...	...	...	...	22[a,l,-4]	...
Seychelles	...	...	...	...	...	...	...
Sierra Leone	...	...	...	...	...	...	...
Somalia	...	...	...	...	...	...	...
South Africa[4]	10	...	...	...	...	815[b,j]	...
Swaziland	...	...	...	...	...	...	...
Tanzania (United Rep.)	...	...	...	...	...	...	...
Togo	...	...	...	...	...	...	...
Uganda	...	...	...	...	...	...	...

Table 14. Movies

Country or Territory	Production			Distribution		Infrastructure	
	Number of national feature films produced	% of feature films 100% nationally produced	% of feature films co-produced	Number of distribution companies	% of nationally controlled distrib. company	Number of cinemas	% of multiplexes[i]
				2006			
Zambia	...	...	...	...	...	...	...
Zimbabwe	...	...	...	...	...	...	...
Central and South Asia							
Afghanistan	...	...	...	...	...	...	...
Armenia	8	75	25	...	...	...	...
Azerbaijan	3	100	...	...	...	19	...
Bangladesh	102[-1,p]	...	...	...	...	...	...
Bhutan	...	...	...	...	...	...	...
Georgia	...	...	...	...	...	...	...
India	1,091[b]	...	...	...	...	11,183[b,l,-1]	3[b,m]
Iran (Islamic Rep.)	26[-1,p]	...	...	...	...	244[b,l,-1]	...
Kazakhstan	...	...	...	...	...	...	...
Kyrgyzstan	1	...	100	...	...	53	...
Maldives	...	...	...	...	...	...	...
Nepal	...	...	...	...	...	...	...
Pakistan	18[-1,p]	...	...	...	...	...	...
Sri Lanka	...	...	...	...	...	...	...
Tajikistan	...	...	...	...	...	...	...
Turkmenistan	...	...	...	...	...	...	...
Uzbekistan	...	...	...	...	...	...	...
East Asia							
Brunei Darussalam	...	...	...	...	...	...	...
Cambodia	62	98	2	...	...	14	0
China	330[p]	...	...	...	...	37,753[b,l]	...
Hong Kong (SAR China)	51[b]	...	...	...	...	212[b,l]	...
Macao (SAR China)	1	100	...	...	...	4	...
Indonesia	60[b]	...	...	...	...	929[b,l]	...
Japan	417[b]	...	...	...	...	3,062[b,l]	...
Korea (Dem. People's Rep.)	...	...	...	...	...	...	...
Korea (Rep.)	110[b]	...	...	...	...	1,880[b,l]	...
Lao (People's Dem. Rep.)	...	...	...	1	100	5	...
Malaysia	28	100	...	529[±]	100	68	15
Mongolia	1[±,g]	...	...	...	...	...	...
Myanmar	...	...	...	...	...	...	...
Philippines	65	100	...	239	21	211	9
Singapore	10	70	30	7	100	27	26
Thailand	42[b]	...	...	...	...	671[b,l]	...
Timor-Leste	...	...	...	...	...	...	...
Viet Nam	12[-1,p]	...	...	...	...	...	...
Europe							
Albania	...	...	...	...	...	...	...
Andorra	...	...	...	...	...	6	...
Austria	34[c]	68[c]	32[c]	24[d,-1]	38	582[c,l]	37[c,m]
Belarus	2	100	...	7	100	139	...
Belgium	67[c]	16[c]	84[c]	28[±,d,-1]	...	507[c,l]	...
Bosnia and Herzegovina	...	...	...	...	...	...	...
Bulgaria	10	40	60	56	98	68	7
Croatia	2	...	100	7	100	87[±]	1
Cyprus	4	25	75	5	...	10	...
Czech Republic	35[c]	80[c]	20[c]	17[±,d,-1]	...	701[c,l]	...[c,m]
Denmark	34[±,g]	100	...	18[±,d,-1]	...	385[±]	...
Estonia	7	43	57	5	80	55	2
Finland	19	84	16	11	55	205	2
France	203[e]	63[e]	37[e]	238[e]	...	2,070[e]	7[e]
Germany	174	67	33	89	94	1,823	7
Gibraltar	...	...	...	...	...	...	...
Greece	22[c]	82[c]	18[c]	14[±,d,-1]	...	...	...
Holy See	...	...	...	...	...	...	...
Hungary	46[c]	80[c]	20[c]	13	...	216	6
Iceland	6	50	50	4	100	22	...
Ireland	19	37	63	7	43	64	39
Israel	22	100	...	12	100	58	17
Italy	116	78	22	36	...	1,910[c,l]	5[c,m]
Latvia	2	100	...	4	...	42	2

Table 14. Movies

Country or Territory	Production			Distribution		Infrastructure	
	Number of national feature films produced	% of feature films 100% nationally produced	% of feature films co-produced	Number of distribution companies	% of nationally controlled distrib. company	Number of cinemas	% of multiplexes[i]
	2006						
Liechtenstein	...	...	...	...	...	...	...
Lithuania	1	...	100	6	67	48	4
Luxembourg	12[c]	17[c]	83[c]	...	...'	24[c,l]	42[c,m]
Macedonia (TFYR)	...	...	...	1[±,d,-1]	...	...	...
Malta	...	...	...	...	...	43[c,l]	...
Moldova (Rep.)	3	100	...	7	100	8[±]	...
Monaco	...	...	...	...	...	...	...
Montenegro	...	...	...	...	...	...	...
Netherlands	21	71	29	14[d,-1]	64	163	9
Norway	21	95	5	16[±,d,-1]	...	235[±]	3
Poland	37	95	5	28	75	514	7
Portugal	32	41	59	15	87	141	11
Romania	18	78	22	17	...	73	3
Russian Federation	67[a,o]	...	...	47[±,d,1]	...	1,294[±,c,l]	...
San Marino	...	...	...	...	...	...	...
Serbia	...	...	...	...	...	...	...
Slovakia	3	...	100	11	73	217	1
Slovenia	3	67	33	20	85	57	7
Spain	150	73	27	176[±]	97	990	18
Sweden	46[c]	70[c]	30[c]	25[±,d,-1]	...	1,171[c,l]	...
Switzerland	38	37	63	46*	91*	414*	2*
Turkey	35	89	11	16[±,d,-1]	...	302	8
Ukraine	7	100	...	13	100	2,740	...
United Kingdom	107[f]	47[f]	53[f]	67[f]	...	697[f]	...
North America							
Canada	74	72	28	...	...	...	...
United States of America	485[±,a]	...	...	...	...	38,415[c,l]	...
Latin America and the Caribbean							
Anguilla	...	...	...	...	...	...	...
Antigua and Barbuda	...	...	...	...	...	...	...
Argentina[2]	63	...	...	...	...	978[c,l]	...
Aruba	...	...	...	...	...	...	...
Bahamas	...	...	...	...	...	...	...
Barbados	...	...	...	...	...	...	...
Belize	...	...	...	...	...	...	...
Bermuda	...	...	...	...	...	...	...
Bolivia[2]	7	...	...	...	...	56[b,l]	...
Brazil	27[±,n]	...	...	29	79	880	7
British Virgin Islands	...	...	...	...	...	1	...
Cayman Islands	...	...	...	...	...	...	...
Chile	11	82	18	20	20	63	22
Colombia[2]	8	...	...	...	...	447[l,-1]	...
Costa Rica	...	...	...	2	100	20	20
Cuba	6	33	67	1	100	437	...
Dominica	...	...	...	...	...	...	...
Dominican Republic	9	89	11	1[h]	100	21	38
Ecuador	...	...	...	...	...	...	...
El Salvador	...	...	...	...	...	...	...
Grenada	...	...	...	...	...	...	...
Guatemala[2]	1[-1]	...	...	...	...	...	...
Guyana	...	...	...	...	...	...	...
Haiti	...	...	...	...	...	...	...
Honduras	...	...	...	...	...	...	...
Jamaica	...	...	...	...	...	...	...
Mexico	64	88	13	17	71	802*	32*
Montserrat	...	...	...	...	...	...	...
Netherlands Antilles	...	...	...	...	...	...	...
Nicaragua	...	...	...	...	...	...	...
Panama[2]	1[-1]	...	...	...	...	...	...
Paraguay	4	...	...	...	...	...	...
Peru[2]	6	...	...	...	...	262[l]	...
Saint Kitts and Nevis	...	...	...	...	...	...	...
Saint Lucia	...	...	...	...	...	...	...
Saint Vincent and the Grenadines	...	...	...	...	...	2	...

Table 14. Movies

Country or Territory	Production			Distribution		Infrastructure	
	Number of national feature films produced	% of feature films 100% nationally produced	% of feature films co-produced	Number of distribution companies	% of nationally controlled distrib. company	Number of cinemas	% of multiplexes[i]
				2006			
Suriname	...	...	...	...	...	...	...
Trinidad and Tobago	...	...	...	...	...	...	...
Turks and Caicos Islands	...	...	...	...	...	...	...
Uruguay[2]	2	...	...	...	...	110[b,l]	...
Venezuela[2]	14	...	...	...	...	402[b,l]	...
Pacific							
Australia	28	89	11	29	...	494	21[k]
Cook Islands	...	...	...	...	...	...	...
Fiji	...	...	...	...	...	...	...
Kiribati	...	...	...	...	...	...	...
Marshall Islands	...	...	...	...	...	...	...
Micronesia (Fed. States)	...	...	...	...	...	...	...
Nauru	...	...	...	...	...	...	...
New Zealand	6	67	33	...	...	...	...
Niue	...	...	...	...	...	...	...
Palau	...	...	...	...	...	...	...
Papua New Guinea	...	...	...	...	...	...	...
Samoa	...	...	...	...	...	...	...
Solomon Islands	...	...	...	...	...	...	...
Tokelau	...	...	...	...	...	...	...
Tonga	...	...	...	...	...	...	...
Tuvalu	...	...	...	...	...	...	...
Vanuatu	...	...	...	...	...	...	...

Source:

1. UNESCO Institute for Statistics, Culture statistics database, 2009.
2. Fundación del Nuevo Cine Latinoamericano. http://www.cinelatinoamericano.org/cifras.aspx
3. European Audiovisual Observatory, 2008. Focus: World Film Market Trends 2008.
4. European Audiovisual Observatory, 2009. Focus: World Film Market Trends 2009.

Notes:

a. Source: European Audiovisual Observatory, 2007. Focus: World Film Market Trends 2007.
b. Source: European Audiovisual Observatory, 2008. Focus: World Film Market Trends 2008.
c. Source: European Audiovisual Observatory, 2007, 2006. Yearbook 2008: Film and Video, Vol. 3.
d. Source: European Audiovisual Observatory, 2007. Film Distribution Companies in Europe.
e. Source: Centre national de la cinématographie.
f. Source: UK Film Council.
g. Only includes films that were 100% nationally produced.
h. Only includes companies with majority nationally-controlled
i. Multiplex = Cinema with 8 screens or more.

j. Films produced in Nigeria are shot on digital video. This country produced 872 feature films in 2005.
k. In Australia, multiplexes are defined as cinemas comprising at least 7 screens.
l. Number of screens.
m. Percentage (%) of screens in multiplexes.
n. Includes only co-productions with majority national financing.
o. Only films produced and exhibited nationally
p. Data extracted from http://www.screendigest.com

... Data not available
* National estimation
± Partial data
-n Data refer to the year n years before the reference year

Table 15. Recorded music: Sales and repertoire

Country or Territory	Retail sales[a] US$ per capita		Repertoire[b] % Domestic		% International		% Classical		Piracy level in %
	1998[3]	2004[2]	1998[3]	2006[1]	1998[3]	2006[1]	1998[3]	2006[1]	2006[1]
Arab States									
Algeria	...	...	...	...	...	...	...	...	...
Bahrain	...	4.9	...	...	...	...	...	...	10–24
Djibouti	...	...	...	...	...	...	...	...	...
Egypt	0.8	0.2	81[f]	...	19	...	0	...	Above 50
Iraq	...	...	...	...	...	...	...	...	...
Jordan	...	...	...	...	...	...	...	...	Above 50
Kuwait	4.5	3.3	57	...	43[f]	...	0	...	Above 50
Lebanon	4.0	1.7	60[f]	...	40	...	0	...	Above 50
Libyan Arab Jamahiriya	...	...	...	...	...	...	...	...	...
Mauritania	...	...	...	...	...	...	...	...	...
Morocco	...	...	...	...	...	...	...	...	Above 50
Oman	0.7	1.3	60[f]	...	40	...	0	...	25–50
Palestinian A. T.	...	...	...	...	...	...	...	...	...
Qatar	...	4.8	...	...	...	...	...	...	10–24
Saudi Arabia	2.7	1.2	63[f]	...	37	...	0	...	Above 50
Sudan	...	...	...	...	...	...	...	...	...
Syrian Arab Republic	...	...	...	...	...	...	...	...	...
Tunisia	...	...	...	...	...	...	...	...	...
United Arab Emirates	15.3	7.2	46[f]	...	54	...	0	...	10–24
Yemen	...	...	...	...	...	...	...	...	...
Sub-Saharan Africa									
Angola	...	...	...	...	...	...	...	...	...
Benin	...	...	...	...	...	...	...	...	...
Botswana	...	...	...	...	...	...	...	...	...
Burkina Faso	...	...	...	...	...	...	...	...	...
Burundi	...	...	...	...	...	...	...	...	...
Cameroon	...	...	...	...	...	...	...	...	...
Cape Verde	...	...	...	...	...	...	...	...	...
Central African Republic	...	...	...	...	...	...	...	...	...
Chad	...	...	...	...	...	...	...	...	...
Comoros	...	...	...	...	...	...	...	...	...
Congo	...	...	...	...	...	...	...	...	...
Congo (Dem. Rep.)	...	...	...	...	...	...	...	...	...
Côte d'Ivoire	...	...	...	...	...	...	...	...	...
Equatorial Guinea	...	...	...	...	...	...	...	...	...
Eritrea	...	...	...	...	...	...	...	...	...
Ethiopia	...	...	...	...	...	...	...	...	...
Gabon	...	...	...	...	...	...	...	...	...
Gambia	1.3	...	71	...	29	...	0	...	...
Ghana	...	...	...	...	...	...	...	...	...
Guinea	...	...	...	...	...	...	...	...	...
Guinea-Bissau	...	...	...	...	...	...	...	...	...
Kenya	0.1	...	34	...	66	...	0	...	...
Lesotho	...	...	...	...	...	...	...	...	...
Liberia	...	...	...	...	...	...	...	...	...
Madagascar	...	...	...	...	...	...	...	...	...
Malawi	...	...	...	...	...	...	...	...	...
Mali	...	...	...	...	...	...	...	...	...
Mauritius	...	...	...	...	...	...	...	...	...
Mozambique	...	...	...	...	...	...	...	...	...
Namibia	...	...	...	...	...	...	...	...	...
Niger	...	...	...	...	...	...	...	...	...
Nigeria	0.0	...	66	...	34	...	0	...	Above 50
Rwanda	...	...	...	...	...	...	...	...	...
Saint Helena	...	...	...	...	...	...	...	...	...
Sao Tome and Principe	...	...	...	...	...	...	...	...	...
Senegal	...	...	...	...	...	...	...	...	...
Seychelles	...	...	...	...	...	...	...	...	...
Sierra Leone	...	...	...	...	...	...	...	...	...
Somalia	...	...	...	...	...	...	...	...	...
South Africa	4.4	5.0	24	45	70	55	6	0	25–50
Swaziland	...	...	...	...	...	...	...	...	...
Tanzania (United Rep.)	...	...	...	...	...	...	...	...	...
Togo	...	...	...	...	...	...	...	...	...
Uganda	...	...	...	...	...	...	...	...	...

Table 15. Recorded music: Sales and repertoire

Country or Territory	Retail sales[a] US$ per capita		Repertoire[b] % Domestic		% International		% Classical		Piracy level in %
	1998[3]	2004[2]	1998[3]	2006[1]	1998[3]	2006[1]	1998[3]	2006[1]	2006[1]
Zambia	...	...	...	...	...	...	...	...	...
Zimbabwe	0.8	1.3	65	...	35	...	0	...	...
Central and South Asia									
Afghanistan	...	...	...	...	...	...	...	...	...
Armenia	...	...	...	...	...	...	...	...	...
Azerbaijan	...	...	...	...	...	...	...	...	...
Bangladesh	...	...	...	...	...	...	...	...	Above 50
Bhutan	...	...	...	...	...	...	...	...	...
Georgia	...	...	...	...	...	...	...	...	...
India	0.3	0.1	96	91	3	9[f]	1	0	Above 50
Iran (Islamic Rep.)	...	...	...	...	...	...	...	...	...
Kazakhstan	...	...	...	...	...	...	...	...	...
Kyrgyzstan	...	...	...	...	...	...	...	...	...
Maldives	...	...	...	...	...	...	...	...	...
Nepal	...	...	...	...	...	...	...	...	...
Pakistan	0.0	0.2	90	...	10	...	0	...	Above 50
Sri Lanka	...	...	...	...	...	...	...	...	...
Tajikistan	...	...	...	...	...	...	...	...	...
Turkmenistan	...	...	...	...	...	...	...	...	...
Uzbekistan	...	...	...	...	...	...	...	...	...
East Asia									
Brunei Darussalam	...	...	...	...	...	...	...	...	...
Cambodia	...	...	...	...	...	...	...	...	...
China	0.1	0.2	66	13[c]	33[f]	78[c,f]	1	9[c]	Above 50
Hong Kong (SAR China)	18.8	11.6	42	36	46[f]	53[f]	12	11	10–24
Macao (SAR China)	...	...	...	...	...	...	...	...	...
Indonesia	0.3	0.4	81	65	18	35[f]	1	0	Above 50
Japan	51.8	40.4	78	72	22	24	...	4	Under 10
Korea (Dem. People's Rep.)	...	...	...	...	...	...	...	...	...
Korea (Rep.)	3.3	2.8	39	56	43	27[f]	18	17	Under 10
Lao (People's Dem. Rep.)	...	...	...	...	...	...	...	...	...
Malaysia	2.4	1.3	24	21	71[f]	77[f]	5	2	25–50
Mongolia	...	...	...	...	...	...	...	...	...
Myanmar	...	...	...	...	...	...	...	...	...
Philippines	0.6	0.3	30	38	67	61[f]	3	1	Above 50
Singapore	15.4	10.7	27[f]	24[f]	64	71	9	5	Under 10
Thailand	1.9	2.2	82	70	18	30[f]	0	0	25–50
Timor-Leste	...	...	...	...	...	...	...	...	...
Viet Nam	...	...	...	...	...	...	...	...	...
Europe									
Albania	...	...	...	...	...	...	...	...	...
Andorra	...	...	...	...	...	...	...	...	...
Austria	42.3	35.0	15	9	73	79	12	12	Under 10
Belarus	...	...	...	...	...	...	...	...	...
Belgium	36.1	26.6	20	21	71	74	19	5	Under 10
Bosnia and Herzegovina	...	...	...	...	...	...	...	...	...
Bulgaria	0.4	0.7	62	...	38	...	0	...	25–50
Croatia	3.9	3.9	62	...	38	...	0	...	...
Cyprus	...	...	...	...	...	...	...	...	...
Czech Republic	7.6	3.9	42	56	48	37	10	7	25–50
Denmark	49.5	34.7	35	48	57	49	8	3	Under 10
Estonia	...	8.5	...	...	...	...	...	...	...
Finland	26.9	25.5	42	52	48	40	10	8	Under 10
France	36.4	32.6	44	63[d]	46	31[d]	10	6	Under 10
Germany	36.6	26.0	43	47	47	46	10	7	Under 10
Gibraltar	...	...	...	...	...	...	...	...	...
Greece	10.9	8.1	59	57	37	41	4	2	Above 50
Holy See	...	...	...	...	...	...	...	...	...
Hungary	5.6	5.8	32	42	59	51	9	7	10–24
Iceland	56.9	59.0[-1]	45	...	55	...	...	...	10–24
Ireland	31.6	35.8	16	21	79	79	5	0	10–24
Israel	8.3	6.8	33	...	60	...	7	...	...
Italy	10.5	11.2	44	53	51	43	5	4[e]	10–24
Latvia	3.9	1.9	47	...	53	...	0	...	Above 50

Table 15. Recorded music: Sales and repertoire

Country or Territory	Retail sales[a] US$ per capita		Repertoire[b] % Domestic		% International		% Classical		Piracy level in %
	1998[3]	2004[2]	1998[3]	2006[1]	1998[3]	2006[1]	1998[3]	2006[1]	2006[1]
Liechtenstein	...	...	...	...	...	...	...	...	...
Lithuania	1.7	...	...	...	...	...	...	...	...
Luxembourg	...	...	...	...	...	...	...	...	...
Macedonia (TFYR)	...	...	...	...	...	...	...	...	...
Malta	...	...	...	...	...	...	...	...	...
Moldova (Rep.)	...	...	...	...	...	...	...	...	...
Monaco	...	...	...	...	...	...	...	...	...
Montenegro	...	...	...	...	...	...	...	...	...
Netherlands	35.7	31.2	27	25	64	74	9	1	10–24
Norway	62.8	59.4	19	47	77	49	4	4	Under 10
Poland	3.9	2.4	22	38	67	51	11	11	25–50
Portugal	18.7	12.2	31	39	65	57	4	4	10–24
Romania	0.3	1.2[-1]	41	...	52	...	7	...	Above 50
Russian Federation	0.6	3.4	68	70	26	28	6	2	Above 50
San Marino	...	...	...	...	...	...	...	...	...
Serbia	...	...	...	...	...	...	...	...	...
Slovakia	4.0	1.9[-1]	19	...	74	...	7	...	25–50
Slovenia	4.8	6.8[-1]	23	...	77	...	0	...	...
Spain	17.1	13.4	42	46	51	48	7	6	10–24
Sweden	44.2	29.8	25	40	71	57	4	3	Under 10
Switzerland	45.0	35.0	8	9	82	83	10	8	Under 10
Turkey	2.0	2.3	79	92	21	8	0	0	Above 50
Ukraine	0.4	0.9	6	...	92	...	2	...	Above 50
United Kingdom	49.0	58.5	48	50	45	45	7	5	Under 10
North America									
Canada	32.1	21.7	11	25	83	71	6	4	Under 10
United States of America	48.2	40.9	91	93	5	5	4	2	Under 10
Latin America and the Caribbean									
Anguilla	...	...	...	...	...	...	...	...	...
Antigua and Barbuda	...	...	...	...	...	...	...	...	...
Argentina	8.5	2.2	40	39	56[f]	57	4	4	Above 50
Aruba	...	...	...	...	...	...	...	...	...
Bahamas	...	...	...	...	...	...	...	...	...
Barbados	...	...	...	...	...	...	...	...	...
Belize	...	...	...	...	...	...	...	...	...
Bermuda	...	...	...	...	...	...	...	...	...
Bolivia	0.8	...	22	...	74[f]	...	4	...	...
Brazil	6.4	2.0	73	68	24[f]	29	3	3	25–50
British Virgin Islands	...	...	...	...	...	...	...	...	...
Cayman Islands	...	...	...	...	...	...	...	...	...
Chile	5.7	2.3	15	17	80[f]	77	5	6	Above 50
Colombia	4.2	1.1	50	24	48[f]	71	2	5	Above 50
Costa Rica	2.7	...	70[f]	...	25	...	5	...	...
Cuba	...	...	...	...	...	...	...	...	...
Dominica	...	...	...	...	...	...	...	...	...
Dominican Republic	...	...	...	...	...	...	...	...	...
Ecuador	1.2	0.4	30	...	65[f]	...	5	...	Above 50
El Salvador	0.6	...	70[f]	...	25	...	5	...	...
Grenada	...	...	...	...	...	...	...	...	...
Guatemala	0.7	...	70[f]	...	25	...	5	...	...
Guyana	...	...	...	...	...	...	...	...	...
Haiti	...	...	...	...	...	...	...	...	...
Honduras	0.5	...	70[f]	...	25	...	5	...	...
Jamaica	...	...	...	...	...	...	...	...	...
Mexico	5.7	3.5	57	38	41[f]	59	2	3	Above 50
Montserrat	...	...	...	...	...	...	...	...	...
Netherlands Antilles	...	...	...	...	...	...	...	...	...
Nicaragua	0.1	...	70[f]	...	25	...	5	...	...
Panama	2.0	...	70[f]	...	25	...	5	...	...
Paraguay	1.3	0.3	35	...	64[f]	...	1	...	Above 50
Peru	0.7	0.1	17	...	82[f]	...	1	...	Above 50
Saint Kitts and Nevis	...	...	...	...	...	...	...	...	...
Saint Lucia	...	...	...	...	...	...	...	...	...
Saint Vincent and the Grenadines	...	...	...	...	...	...	...	...	...

Table 15. Recorded music: Sales and repertoire

Country or Territory	Retail sales[a] US$ per capita 1998[3]	2004[2]	Repertoire[b] % Domestic 1998[3]	2006[1]	% International 1998[3]	2006[1]	% Classical 1998[3]	2006[1]	Piracy level in % 2006[1]
Suriname	...	...	...	...	...	...	...	...	...
Trinidad and Tobago	...	...	...	...	...	...	...	...	...
Turks and Caicos Islands	...	...	...	...	...	...	...	...	...
Uruguay	5.1	1.4	41	...	49[f]	...	10	...	Above 50
Venezuela	4.1	0.6	69	...	28[f]	...	3	...	Above 50
Pacific									
Australia	33.0	35.7	20	35	73	59	7	6	Under 10
Cook Islands	...	...	...	...	...	...	...	...	...
Fiji	...	...	...	...	...	...	...	...	...
Kiribati	...	...	...	...	...	...	...	...	...
Marshall Islands	...	...	...	...	...	...	...	...	...
Micronesia (Fed. States)	...	...	...	...	...	...	...	...	...
Nauru	...	...	...	...	...	...	...	...	...
New Zealand	27.0	28.8	6	9	86	89	8	2	Under 10
Niue	...	...	...	...	...	...	...	...	...
Palau	...	...	...	...	...	...	...	...	...
Papua New Guinea	...	...	...	...	...	...	...	...	...
Samoa	...	...	...	...	...	...	...	...	...
Solomon Islands	...	...	...	...	...	...	...	...	...
Tokelau	...	...	...	...	...	...	...	...	...
Tonga	...	...	...	...	...	...	...	...	...
Tuvalu	...	...	...	...	...	...	...	...	...
Vanuatu	...	...	...	...	...	...	...	...	...

Sources:
1. International Federation of the Phonographic Industry, 2007. Recording Industry in Numbers 2007 (2006 figures).
2. International Federation of the Phonographic Industry, 2005. Recording Industry World Sales 2005 (2004 figures).
3. UNESCO, 2000. World Culture Report 2000 (1998 figures).

Notes:
a. Retail value of CDs, cassettes and records in US value using monthly average exchange rate from specified year; 2004 figures also include music DVD sales.
b. From physical sales only (excluding digital sales in 2006).

c. 2006 figures reported on a different basis from previous years.
d. Repertoire is based on language.
e. Jazz included in classical category.
f. Including regional popular.

... Data not available
-n Data refer to the year n years before the reference year

Table 16. International flows of selected cultural goods and services

Core cultural goods[1,a] (million USD)

	Total trade annual compound growth rate[d]	Trade coverage ratio[e] %	Total exports trade ('000)	Annual compound growth rate for exports per capita	Exports[b,c] Heritage goods	Books	Newspapers & periodicals	Other printed matter	Recorded media	Visual Arts	Audiovisual media
Country or Territory	2001–2006	2006	2006	2001–2006				Share by products % 2006			
Arab States											
Algeria	5	4	1,474	-3	0.0	14.0	81.8	0.2	1.9	2.1	0.0
Bahrain	-5[+1]	3	223	-6[+1]	0.0	39.0	13.2	1.8	0.0	46.0	0.0
Djibouti	...	...	...	...	...	...	...	...	...	...	...
Egypt	...	...	...	...	...	...	...	...	...	...	...
Iraq	...	...	...	...	...	...	...	...	...	...	...
Jordan	2	46	10,929	-3	0.0	79.5	7.1	0.8	0.5	12.1	0.0
Kuwait	...	...	...	...	...	...	...	...	...	...	...
Lebanon	...	...	...	...	...	...	...	...	...	...	...
Libyan Arab Jamahiriya	...	...	...	...	...	...	...	...	...	...	...
Mauritania	...	...	...	...	...	...	...	...	...	...	...
Morocco	-4[+1]	13	10,663	-22[+1]	7.3	14.0	1.6	6.4	0.5	70.1	0.0
Oman	-8	8	1,906	5	0.0	85.0	5.5	0.8	6.6	2.2	0.0
Palestinian A. T.	...	...	...	...	...	...	...	...	...	...	...
Qatar	6	1	247	-10	0.0	83.7	0.4	3.5	0.0	12.4	0.0
Saudi Arabia	6	9	12,104	20	1.3	53.0	34.6	2.8	5.0	2.9	0.5
Sudan	-2	1	51	-17	0.0	92.0	8.0	0.0	0.0	0.0	0.0
Syrian Arab Republic	29	444	30,352	30	0.0	6.2	1.7	88.6	0.0	3.5	0.0
Tunisia	...	...	...	...	...	...	...	...	...	...	...
United Arab Emirates	...	...	...	...	...	...	...	...	...	...	...
Yemen	-17[+3]	9	159	21[+3]	0.0	48.4	3.0	38.8	0.0	9.8	0.0
Sub-Saharan Africa											
Angola	...	...	...	...	...	...	...	...	...	...	...
Benin	...	...	...	...	...	...	...	...	...	...	...
Botswana	-1	4	1,088	3	0.0	79.4	0.0	1.6	10.7	7.0	1.2
Burkina Faso	...	...	...	...	...	...	...	...	...	...	...
Burundi	24[+2]	0	5	-33[+2]	0.0	43.3	0.0	0.0	0.0	56.7	0.0
Cameroon	7	5	986	16	0.4	60.1	10.6	8.3	0.0	20.6	0.0
Cape Verde	8	0	0	...	...	...	...	...	...	...	...
Central African Republic	...	...	...	...	...	...	...	...	...	...	...
Chad	...	...	...	...	...	...	...	...	...	...	...
Comoros	...	...	...	...	...	...	...	...	...	...	...
Congo	...	...	...	...	...	...	...	...	...	...	...
Congo (Dem. Rep.)	...	...	...	...	...	...	...	...	...	...	...
Côte d'Ivoire	1	28	4,415	3	0.0	7.3	0.1	1.1	0.1	91.3	0.0
Equatorial Guinea	...	...	...	...	...	...	...	...	...	...	...
Eritrea	...	...	...	...	...	...	...	...	...	...	...
Ethiopia	8	1	263	10	2.7	2.6	1.3	0.1	0.1	93.2	0.0
Gabon	-1	3	284	-11	1.1	47.3	0.0	3.6	0.0	48.0	0.0
Gambia	12	1	16	-1	0.0	6.7	0.0	37.8	0.0	55.5	0.0
Ghana	38[+2]	416	78,980	88[+2]	0.0	0.1	0.0	0.0	0.0	99.9	0.0
Guinea	...	...	...	...	...	...	...	...	...	...	...
Guinea-Bissau	...	...	...	...	...	...	...	...	...	...	...
Kenya	8	46	16,303	15	0.0	21.0	4.0	27.0	0.3	47.7	0.0
Lesotho	...	...	...	...	...	...	...	...	...	...	...
Liberia	...	...	...	...	...	...	...	...	...	...	...
Madagascar	4	12	1,211	3	23.4	2.1	2.0	0.5	0.1	71.9	0.0
Malawi	5	28	4,705	30	0.0	33.7	0.0	0.9	0.3	65.1	0.0
Mali	3	16	474	-3	0.1	0.0	0.0	70.1	0.0	29.9	0.0
Mauritius	10	142	29,673	16	0.1	39.6	1.3	1.5	55.0	1.8	0.7
Mozambique	10	2	404	18	9.0	3.8	5.7	8.4	3.2	68.8	1.0
Namibia	6	20	4,383	5	64.3	14.2	0.1	0.9	3.7	15.4	1.4
Niger	...	...	...	...	...	...	...	...	...	...	...
Nigeria	...	...	...	...	...	...	...	...	...	...	...
Rwanda	10	7	286	12	2.0	6.6	0.7	0.0	0.0	90.7	0.0
Saint Helena	...	...	...	...	...	...	...	...	...	...	...
Sao Tome and Principe	...	...	...	...	...	...	...	...	...	...	...
Senegal	7	13	2,441	-1	0.0	8.8	0.0	3.4	0.0	87.8	0.0
Seychelles	16	0	6	...	0.0	0.0	0.0	4.1	0.0	95.9	0.0
Sierra Leone	...	...	...	...	...	...	...	...	...	...	...
Somalia	...	...	...	...	...	...	...	...	...	...	...
South Africa	11	17	90,380	8	13.3	52.3	5.6	4.7	2.7	18.2	3.2
Swaziland	...	...	...	...	...	...	...	...	...	...	...

Total imports trade ('000)	Annual compound growth rate for imports per capita	Heritage goods	Books	Newspapers & periodicals	Other printed matter	Recorded media	Visual Arts	Audiovisual media	Exports Audiovisual services	Exports Royalties & license fees	Imports Audiovisual services	Imports Royalties & license fees	Country or Territory
2006	2001–2006				2006					2005			
													Arab States
38,867	4	0.0	73.2	6.7	1.6	7.5	7.4	3.5	...	...	...	...	Algeria
8,845	-6+1	0.2	52.9	0.6	4.8	12.6	16.2	12.7	...	...	...	...	Bahrain
...	...	...	...	...	...	...	...	...	...	...	...	...	Djibouti
...	...	...	...	...	...	...	...	...	...	...	...	...	Egypt
...	...	...	...	...	...	...	...	...	...	...	...	...	Iraq
23,797	3	0.8	76.6	1.0	4.4	2.0	11.4	3.8	...	...	...	...	Jordan
...	...	...	...	...	...	...	...	...	...	...	...	...	Kuwait
...	...	...	...	...	...	...	...	...	...	...	...	...	Lebanon
...	...	...	...	...	...	...	...	...	...	...	...	...	Libyan Arab Jamahiriya
979	0	0.0	92.2	1.4	2.8	1.6	1.6	0.4	...	...	...	...	Mauritania
79,360	6+1	0.3	64.3	21.9	1.0	0.2	11.7	0.6	...	12.72	...	45.41	Morocco
23,368	-9	0.1	42.4	13.3	2.8	8.9	30.3	2.2	...	...	...	...	Oman
...	...	...	...	...	...	...	...	...	...	...	...	...	Palestinian A. T.
36,900	4	1.3	27.5	13.1	9.2	18.2	22.8	7.9	...	...	...	...	Qatar
133,307	2	0.0	32.4	0.4	9.4	26.3	23.8	7.7	...	...	...	...	Saudi Arabia
9,426	-2	0.0	41.6	5.8	12.6	23.9	11.9	4.2	...	...	...	...	Sudan
6,830	20	0.0	88.7	1.3	2.9	0.9	5.4	0.8	...	...	...	12.00	Syrian Arab Republic
...	...	...	...	...	...	...	...	...	...	14.03	...	7.71	Tunisia
...	...	...	...	...	...	...	...	...	...	...	...	...	United Arab Emirates
1,811	-20+3	0.0	15.1	1.8	11.0	20.1	46.5	5.5	...	149.00+1	...	9.20	Yemen
													Sub-Saharan Africa
...	...	...	...	...	...	...	...	...	...	49.43	...	3.38	Angola
...	...	...	...	...	...	...	...	...	0.01-1	...	0.13	...	Benin
25,582	-2	0.0	75.8	11.0	2.5	6.3	2.6	1.6	...	0.46	...	12.33	Botswana
...	...	...	...	...	...	...	...	...	...	...	...	...	Burkina Faso
1,905	23+1	0.0	60.0	5.0	31.2	0.6	3.1	0.1	...	...	...	...	Burundi
18,590	5	0.0	69.5	25.2	2.0	0.9	2.1	0.3	...	...	...	...	Cameroon
2,738	7	0.0	44.4	6.6	11.7	13.1	21.6	2.5	0.01+1	...	0.60	...	Cape Verde
...	...	...	...	...	...	...	...	...	...	...	...	...	Central African Republic
...	...	...	...	...	...	...	...	...	...	...	...	...	Chad
...	...	...	...	...	...	...	...	...	...	...	...	...	Comoros
...	...	...	...	...	...	...	...	...	...	...	...	...	Congo
...	...	...	...	...	...	...	...	...	...	...	...	...	Congo (Dem. Rep.)
16,029	0	0.0	52.0	37.6	3.6	3.5	2.5	0.9	0.01-4	0.17-1	0.82	10.32	Côte d'Ivoire
...	...	...	...	...	...	...	...	...	...	...	...	...	Equatorial Guinea
...	...	...	...	...	...	...	...	...	...	...	...	...	Eritrea
19,017	6	1.2	85.0	3.1	4.8	0.8	3.8	1.3	0.46+1	...	0.01	...	Ethiopia
9,396	-1	0.1	43.6	40.6	6.0	3.9	5.3	0.6	...	...	...	...	Gabon
1,822	10	0.0	79.0	3.5	12.9	0.4	4.1	0.0	...	...	...	...	Gambia
19,001	6+2	0.0	88.6	2.0	3.4	3.5	2.1	0.4	...	...	...	...	Ghana
...	...	...	...	...	...	...	...	...	...	...	0.51-1	...	Guinea
...	...	...	...	...	...	...	...	...	...	...	...	0.00-1	Guinea-Bissau
35,203	4	0.0	55.1	5.1	16.6	20.2	2.5	0.4	...	...	...	...	Kenya
...	...	...	...	...	...	...	...	...	...	...	...	...	Lesotho
...	...	...	...	...	...	...	...	...	...	...	...	...	Liberia
9,950	2	1.5	67.1	17.2	2.2	8.3	3.5	0.2	0.28-2	2.32	0.11-2	4.61	Madagascar
16,684	1	0.0	94.3	1.9	2.0	0.5	1.1	0.3	...	...	0.01-3	...	Malawi
2,896	3	0.0	35.9	0.6	4.8	52.8	4.4	1.5	0.01	0.16	1.13	1.09	Mali
20,890	4	0.1	44.0	22.3	4.0	13.0	10.1	6.5	0.55	...	5.64	...	Mauritius
23,063	9	0.0	83.5	4.9	2.9	0.6	7.2	0.9	...	2.20	...	5.29	Mozambique
21,385	5	0.2	67.3	3.6	4.8	15.7	5.5	3.1	...	3.81-3	...	1.75	Namibia
...	...	...	...	...	...	...	...	...	0.01-2	...	0.43-2	...	Niger
...	...	...	...	...	...	...	...	...	...	...	...	...	Nigeria
3,910	9	0.0	76.0	13.1	6.6	1.3	2.4	0.7	0.38+1	...	3.56+1	...	Rwanda
...	...	...	...	...	...	...	...	...	...	...	...	...	Saint Helena
268	35	0.0	70.6	1.9	13.5	5.2	6.6	2.1	...	...	...	...	Sao Tome and Principe
18,366	7	0.0	43.1	21.6	29.3	2.6	3.2	0.2	0.01-2	...	0.30-1	...	Senegal
2,588	16	0.0	74.2	5.3	9.2	0.0	10.2	1.1	...	...	...	0.55	Seychelles
...	...	...	...	...	...	...	...	...	...	...	...	...	Sierra Leone
...	...	...	...	...	...	...	...	...	...	...	...	...	Somalia
543,722	11	1.1	36.9	1.7	2.1	10.3	39.3	8.6	...	...	...	...	South Africa
...	...	...	...	...	...	...	...	...	0.00	...	0.04-1	...	Swaziland

Table 16. International flows of selected cultural goods and services

Core cultural goods[1, a] (million USD)

Country or Territory	Total trade annual compound growth rate[d]	Trade coverage ratio[e] %	Total exports trade ('000)	Annual compound growth rate for exports per capita	Exports[b, c] Share by products %						
					Heritage goods	Books	Newspapers & periodicals	Other printed matter	Recorded media	Visual Arts	Audiovisual media
	2001–2006	2006	2006	2001–2006	2006						
Tanzania (United Rep.)	3	13	1,397	3	34.0	8.6	0.7	0.6	44.7	10.3	1.0
Togo	...	...	...	...	...	...	...	...	...	...	...
Uganda	1	6	553	5	1.0	31.3	0.1	17.4	0.0	50.2	0.0
Zambia	15	3	946	6	57.0	14.4	0.1	0.3	0.0	28.2	0.0
Zimbabwe	...	...	...	...	...	...	...	...	...	...	...
Central and South Asia											
Afghanistan	...	...	...	...	...	...	...	...	...	...	...
Armenia	1	4	346	27	0.0	90.6	1.6	1.6	0.1	6.2	0.0
Azerbaijan	13	5	470	13	0.0	37.2	32.7	0.9	5.9	23.0	0.3
Bangladesh	...	...	...	...	...	...	...	...	...	...	...
Bhutan	...	...	...	...	...	...	...	...	...	...	...
Georgia	20	10	1,278	18	0.2	95.5	0.0	0.9	0.1	3.2	0.1
India	3	378	831,133	11	0.0	14.7	7.4	1.5	19.8	54.4	2.2
Iran (Islamic Rep.)	-5	289	15,408	13	0.0	80.1	0.1	11.0	1.9	6.8	0.1
Kazakhstan	12	1	578	8	0.4	31.7	42.7	3.8	3.4	15.2	2.7
Kyrgyzstan	4	4	119	-20	0.0	89.1	2.7	1.1	1.5	5.7	0.0
Maldives	4	0	0	...	0.0	0.0	0.0	0.0	0.0	100.0	0.0
Nepal	...	...	...	...	...	...	...	...	...	...	...
Pakistan	3[+2]	44	21,578	-7[+2]	0.1	12.5	2.8	1.6	46.7	36.0	0.2
Sri Lanka	...	...	...	...	...	...	...	...	...	...	...
Tajikistan	...	...	...	...	...	...	...	...	...	...	...
Turkmenistan	...	...	...	...	...	...	...	...	...	...	...
Uzbekistan	...	...	...	...	...	...	...	...	...	...	...
East Asia											
Brunei Darussalam	2[+1]	4	500	131[+1]	0.0	19.6	2.0	4.2	40.1	33.5	0.5
Cambodia	...	...	...	...	...	...	...	...	...	...	...
China	11	1,644	9,646,104	12	0.0	8.9	0.1	3.3	0.3	34.7	52.6
Hong Kong (SAR China)	8	6	208,165	-1	0.0	67.1	10.4	3.1	14.2	3.7	1.4
Macao (SAR China)	7	1	68	1	0.0	75.0	0.0	0.0	0.0	25.0	0.0
Indonesia	2	345	142,972	0	0.1	18.8	1.7	4.5	1.3	73.4	0.2
Japan	2	38	912,179	-1	1.5	10.5	4.3	2.1	6.8	9.6	65.2
Korea (Dem. People's Rep.)	...	...	...	...	...	...	...	...	...	...	...
Korea (Rep.)	9	81	675,966	8	1.2	13.8	1.0	6.2	11.8	51.9	14.0
Lao (People's Dem. Rep.)	...	...	...	...	...	...	...	...	...	...	...
Malaysia	5	90	222,535	4	0.2	72.9	0.6	3.2	9.4	10.9	2.8
Mongolia	17	3	152	13	9.6	15.3	1.8	0.4	0.0	30.4	42.5
Myanmar	...	...	...	...	...	...	...	...	...	...	...
Philippines	2	151	116,818	-1	0.1	2.1	0.4	1.1	1.3	94.9	0.1
Singapore	7	135	1,086,515	7	4.6	51.0	5.0	1.9	7.0	13.2	17.2
Thailand	2	101	163,586	4	0.0	25.4	5.1	7.3	9.5	46.4	6.2
Timor-Leste	...	...	...	...	...	...	...	...	...	...	...
Viet Nam	20	74	48,303	21	0.0	6.7	0.6	3.3	9.7	79.8	0.0
Europe											
Albania	7	4	235	0	0.0	68.3	0.2	1.3	0.4	29.7	0.0
Andorra	...	...	...	...	...	...	...	...	...	...	...
Austria	5	64	798,602	5	2.1	11.1	7.6	5.4	23.7	50.0	0.1
Belarus	10	63	32,113	7	0.0	81.3	8.8	7.1	0.7	1.9	0.1
Belgium	2	76	1,154,725	2	3.5	42.5	18.6	5.8	13.0	13.5	3.2
Bosnia and Herzegovina	9[+2]	13	5,298	18[+2]	0.0	22.4	42.1	2.8	20.3	11.8	0.6
Bulgaria	13	72	22,276	14	0.0	14.1	10.1	7.7	5.3	13.0	49.8
Croatia	7	66	55,305	4	0.1	28.6	55.3	2.3	3.3	7.8	2.5
Cyprus	5	1	1,130	-3	0.0	29.5	25.7	0.5	37.7	5.8	0.7
Czech Republic	9	102	370,709	10	0.7	31.9	37.5	7.0	13.0	4.7	5.2
Denmark	2	78	419,286	-1	5.1	29.9	18.9	4.5	11.1	16.4	14.0
Estonia	8	186	45,925	15	0.4	28.7	44.7	3.8	6.5	15.9	0.1
Finland	2	101	281,971	1	0.4	18.2	56.0	9.1	3.5	10.7	2.2
France	4	92	2,971,653	4	8.7	25.6	16.4	4.0	8.2	32.9	4.1
Germany	4	174	5,881,126	6	1.9	29.8	18.5	7.2	11.5	12.0	19.2
Gibraltar	...	...	...	...	...	...	...	...	...	...	...
Greece	3	45	162,431	3	26.4	33.2	8.8	3.0	16.0	5.5	7.1
Holy See	...	...	...	...	...	...	...	...	...	...	...

Total imports trade ('000)	Annual compound growth rate for imports per capita	Heritage goods	Books	Newspapers & periodicals	Other printed matter	Recorded media	Visual Arts	Audiovisual media	Audiovisual services	Royalties & license fees	Audiovisual services	Royalties & license fees	Country or Territory
2006	2001–2006				2006						2005		
11,135	1	5.9	72.0	6.9	9.5	3.4	1.7	0.6	...	0.00[+1]	...	0.22	Tanzania (United Rep.)
...	...	...	...	...	...	...	...	...	...	...	...	...	Togo
8,517	-1	0.0	76.6	5.7	8.2	4.0	4.6	0.9	...	7.42	...	1.46	Uganda
36,600	14	0.0	91.0	4.4	1.6	1.2	1.3	0.5	...	...	...	...	Zambia
...	...	...	...	...	...	...	...	...	...	...	...	...	Zimbabwe
													Central and South Asia
...	...	...	...	...	...	...	...	...	...	...	...	...	Afghanistan
8,228	1	0.9	39.4	8.1	1.6	0.9	47.9	1.2	2.78	...	3.82	...	Armenia
9,724	13	0.0	68.1	19.1	1.4	1.0	10.3	0.1	...	0.06[+1]	...	1.21[+1]	Azerbaijan
...	...	...	...	...	...	...	...	...	1.13	0.26	0.03	2.74	Bangladesh
...	...	...	...	...	...	...	...	...	...	...	...	...	Bhutan
12,320	21	0.0	43.9	16.7	12.1	4.1	22.0	1.3	0.28	9.29	...	5.32	Georgia
219,662	-9	0.7	63.0	1.7	2.1	9.2	18.6	4.7	...	131.16	...	766.96	India
5,329	-16	0.4	55.8	1.9	2.4	0.3	33.6	5.7	...	...	...	...	Iran (Islamic Rep.)
88,526	12	0.0	61.6	23.6	4.8	4.9	3.6	1.5	0.15	0.02	15.73	30.90	Kazakhstan
3,248	10	0.0	72.2	13.0	8.3	1.4	4.9	0.2	...	1.74	...	5.98	Kyrgyzstan
5,312	3	0.0	64.6	5.2	8.6	0.1	19.6	1.8	...	...	...	...	Maldives
...	...	...	...	...	...	...	...	...	...	...	...	...	Nepal
49,027	9[+2]	0.3	33.2	0.7	1.2	60.4	3.6	0.5	1.00[-2]	15.00	8.00	109.00	Pakistan
...	...	...	...	...	...	...	...	...	...	...	...	...	Sri Lanka
...	...	...	...	...	...	...	...	...	...	...	...	...	Tajikistan
...	...	...	...	...	...	...	...	...	...	...	...	...	Turkmenistan
...	...	...	...	...	...	...	...	...	...	...	...	...	Uzbekistan
													East Asia
12,138	1[+1]	0.5	32.9	37.8	4.9	11.5	6.9	5.4	...	...	...	...	Brunei Darussalam
...	...	...	...	...	...	...	...	...	...	...	...	...	Cambodia
586,721	3	0.5	19.3	23.2	4.9	10.6	5.6	35.9	133.86	...	153.95	...	China
3,593,233	9	5.9	22.4	0.8	3.5	1.4	12.0	54.0	...	...	...	...	Hong Kong (SAR China)
9,564	7	9.3	25.8	0.3	6.9	17.7	34.3	5.7	...	...	...	...	Macao (SAR China)
41,405	7	0.0	32.6	5.6	5.8	31.8	7.3	16.9	...	...	...	...	Indonesia
2,425,627	4	1.6	12.6	5.8	3.9	8.6	24.7	42.8	81.91	...	902.52	...	Japan
...	...	...	...	...	...	...	...	...	...	...	...	...	Korea (Dem. People's Rep.)
835,947	9	2.6	21.5	2.4	2.5	13.8	28.4	28.8	127.20	1,772.00[+1]	159.20	3,636.80[+1]	Korea (Rep.)
...	...	...	...	...	...	...	...	...	...	...	...	...	Lao (People's Dem. Rep.)
248,427	4	0.1	62.4	3.6	2.3	17.6	8.2	5.8	...	27.04	...	1,369.66	Malaysia
5,018	17	0.0	18.7	1.1	1.5	2.1	75.6	0.9	...	...	...	...	Mongolia
...	...	...	...	...	...	...	...	...	...	...	...	...	Myanmar
77,295	4	0.1	80.1	4.2	1.4	2.8	7.1	4.2	19.00	...	5.00	...	Philippines
804,178	5	0.8	34.4	3.6	3.7	5.1	16.5	35.8	...	...	...	...	Singapore
161,773	-1	0.0	39.7	7.6	2.0	41.6	4.0	5.1	...	...	...	...	Thailand
...	...	...	...	...	...	...	...	...	...	...	...	...	Timor-Leste
64,978	18	0.1	57.0	4.0	4.3	21.5	4.8	8.2	...	...	...	...	Viet Nam
													Europe
5,730	7	0.1	50.2	3.2	10.3	16.0	15.7	4.5	0.01	0.51	0.73	4.20	Albania
...	...	...	...	...	...	...	...	...	...	...	...	...	Andorra
1,257,021	5	2.2	40.4	17.9	6.5	13.8	13.4	5.8	206.44[9]	...	291.00[9]	...	Austria
50,654	14	0.0	37.6	40.0	14.8	2.6	4.0	1.0	1.40	...	7.30	...	Belarus
1,511,314	2	2.5	36.2	24.0	4.7	14.4	13.6	4.7	443.86	...	397.36	...	Belgium
40,221	7[+2]	0.0	24.0	51.9	4.5	12.5	5.2	1.8	...	...	...	...	Bosnia and Herzegovina
30,996	12	0.7	49.1	20.1	8.6	4.8	12.5	4.2	8.43	4.82	9.10	71.91	Bulgaria
84,041	9	0.2	34.0	23.7	6.7	13.9	13.6	8.0	7.40	...	23.31	...	Croatia
81,867	4	0.3	27.4	46.3	3.8	6.7	11.5	4.0	6.38	14.03	15.55	34.24	Cyprus
364,144	9	0.7	43.6	32.7	7.5	4.8	4.6	6.0	46.44	38.81	46.81	452.82	Czech Republic
534,996	3	4.1	29.8	10.3	9.0	14.8	13.4	18.7	198.77[9]	1,147.59[9]	1,004.52[9]	853.94[9]	Denmark
24,721	2	0.5	46.7	11.1	7.1	18.1	13.0	3.6	1.17	4.62	0.75	22.10	Estonia
280,220	3	0.7	29.7	25.5	7.6	13.4	14.8	8.3	7.37	...	12.11	...	Finland
3,216,393	4	3.0	26.7	16.7	4.8	13.6	19.5	15.7	1,424.02	...	1,839.82	...	France
3,383,416	2	1.6	22.2	14.1	6.1	16.1	22.9	17.0	1,165.13	1,698.56	3,479.14	2,319.07	Germany
...	...	...	...	...	...	...	...	...	...	...	...	...	Gibraltar
360,326	3	0.7	29.6	6.9	4.6	34.0	13.3	10.9	885.61[-1,9]	...	59.75	...	Greece
...	...	...	...	...	...	...	...	...	...	...	...	...	Holy See

Table 16. International flows of selected cultural goods and services

Core cultural goods[1, a] (million USD)

Country or Territory	Total trade annual compound growth rate[d]	Trade coverage ratio[e] %	Total exports trade ('000)	Annual compound growth rate for exports per capita	Exports[b, c] Share by products %						
					Heritage goods	Books	Newspapers & periodicals	Other printed matter	Recorded media	Visual Arts	Audiovisual media
	2001-2006	2006	2006	2001-2006	2006						
Hungary	-6	48	80,582	-15	0.4	56.8	11.0	8.6	6.7	15.1	1.4
Iceland	6	17	5,253	6	0.0	23.8	0.3	70.4	0.8	4.2	0.6
Ireland	1	141	997,490	-2	0.3	20.9	3.2	0.3	68.6	2.4	4.3
Israel	-4	68	106,706	-3	1.6	37.1	2.0	3.1	0.0	55.2	0.9
Italy	4	109	1,709,866	3	1.1	36.8	13.7	12.3	2.6	18.7	14.8
Latvia	11	35	17,740	11	0.0	55.5	16.6	21.8	2.0	3.2	0.9
Liechtenstein	...	...	...	...	...	...	...	...	...	...	...
Lithuania	11	164	48,104	15	0.1	33.8	50.7	1.4	4.4	9.3	0.2
Luxembourg	3	26	40,859	1	0.8	33.4	34.2	1.2	24.2	4.6	1.4
Macedonia (TFYR)	8	27	2,025	19	0.0	45.7	33.6	8.2	0.1	12.3	0.1
Malta	4	40	12,593	15	0.1	80.4	1.8	0.3	12.1	1.4	3.9
Moldova (Rep.)	10	21	1,722	11	0.0	59.5	11.5	26.6	0.0	2.4	0.0
Monaco	...	...	...	...	...	...	...	...	...	...	...
Montenegro	...	...	...	...	...	...	...	...	...	...	...
Netherlands	-1	108	1,564,089	-2	1.7	26.5	11.1	5.1	35.5	13.9	6.2
Norway	3	15	78,633	-4	3.7	26.5	6.1	7.4	12.0	41.9	2.5
Poland	8	186	464,159	13	3.8	30.6	44.4	7.9	5.1	7.9	0.3
Portugal	3	36	148,871	-1	0.2	24.0	3.1	3.5	5.6	60.1	3.5
Romania	10	44	31,100	8	0.8	11.2	34.2	5.8	4.3	29.0	14.6
Russian Federation	5	69	403,462	3	0.1	46.7	22.3	10.2	3.4	16.7	0.5
San Marino	...	...	...	...	...	...	...	...	...	...	...
Serbia	...	76	36,097	...	0.0	24.6	59.7	3.7	7.6	4.0	0.3
Slovakia	6	167	171,613	6	0.0	42.1	35.6	6.1	1.5	1.9	12.8
Slovenia	8	164	110,618	9	0.0	69.5	21.4	2.2	4.6	0.7	1.6
Spain	1	98	1,349,106	0	0.2	58.6	13.5	3.1	3.4	16.5	4.9
Sweden	5	66	429,456	5	3.7	33.5	8.0	8.4	18.2	14.2	14.0
Switzerland	4	68	1,801,350	6	9.9	15.6	5.0	8.4	2.6	57.5	0.9
Turkey	0	24	25,262	-6	0.0	45.5	2.1	6.9	10.8	34.5	0.1
Ukraine	9	95	59,546	13	0.0	65.4	31.1	1.9	0.0	1.4	0.2
United Kingdom	5	118	9,753,553	4	15.6	26.2	8.1	4.2	5.3	37.6	3.1
North America											
Canada	3	36	1,402,911	0	1.4	29.4	12.9	18.0	8.5	5.9	23.9
United States of America	2	50	8,643,872	3	4.2	26.3	14.6	5.3	7.0	34.1	8.5
Latin America and the Caribbean											
Anguilla	...	...	...	...	...	...	...	...	...	...	...
Antigua and Barbuda	...	...	...	...	...	...	...	...	...	...	...
Argentina	-2	84	97,301	-1	1.3	45.9	6.3	5.6	28.0	6.9	6.0
Aruba	-3[+1]	4	574	4[+1]	0.0	2.7	0.0	4.0	0.0	93.3	0.0
Bahamas	-1	0	28	-9	0.0	77.2	0.0	1.6	0.0	21.2	0.0
Barbados	1	12	2,068	9	0.0	16.7	17.7	18.8	3.5	43.0	0.2
Belize	1	1	26	5	1.0	31.5	0.0	0.0	0.0	67.5	0.0
Bermuda	...	...	...	...	...	...	...	...	...	...	...
Bolivia	0	6	772	-1	0.0	47.2	1.3	5.6	2.2	40.4	3.3
Brazil	-1	53	64,468	6	0.0	38.1	22.3	6.2	10.5	22.4	0.4
British Virgin Islands	...	...	...	...	...	...	...	...	...	...	...
Cayman Islands	...	...	...	...	...	...	...	...	...	...	...
Chile	-2	24	25,887	-11	0.7	72.8	15.2	5.9	0.7	4.4	0.4
Colombia	2	198	181,551	1	0.0	75.2	13.6	2.3	5.8	2.9	0.1
Costa Rica	-1	22	9,321	-3	0.0	58.4	11.0	3.9	15.9	10.7	0.1
Cuba	...	...	...	...	...	...	...	...	...	...	...
Dominica	-1	0	1	...	0.0	9.5	0.0	5.2	85.3	0.0	0.0
Dominican Republic	...	...	...	...	...	...	...	...	...	...	...
Ecuador	3	6	4,275	0	0.0	69.7	4.6	4.0	3.8	17.8	0.0
El Salvador	3	18	7,031	6	0.0	54.9	3.7	23.5	5.1	12.6	0.2
Grenada	19	0	0	-17	0.0	0.0	0.0	0.0	0.0	100.0	0.0
Guatemala	3	6	3,971	-7	0.0	68.3	4.5	8.1	4.9	13.2	1.1
Guyana	7	1	106	11	0.0	14.0	0.0	0.3	0.7	85.0	0.0
Haiti	...	...	...	...	...	...	...	...	...	...	...
Honduras	17	1	269	11	0.0	43.9	2.6	31.7	6.2	12.1	3.5
Jamaica	9	4	3,532	21	0.0	9.7	5.1	0.3	74.8	10.0	0.0
Mexico	3	52	583,602	-1	0.0	26.2	6.0	17.9	8.4	15.8	25.7
Montserrat	1	0	0	...	...	...	...	...	...	...	...

Total imports trade ('000)	Annual compound growth rate for imports per capita	Heritage goods	Books	Newspapers & periodicals	Other printed matter	Recorded media	Visual Arts	Audiovisual media	Exports — Audiovisual services	Exports — Royalties & license fees	Imports — Audiovisual services	Imports — Royalties & license fees	Country or Territory
2006	2001–2006				2006						2005		
166,255	7	0.3	56.0	24.7	4.7	3.9	6.1	4.4	1,234.77	767.90	1,096.42	1,003.14	Hungary
30,850	6	0.4	50.5	8.7	5.1	14.6	13.4	7.4	...	...	...	...	Iceland
709,892	6	0.4	36.0	24.6	5.2	13.4	7.2	13.2	203.95[9]	590.71[9]	134.31[9]	19,459.78[9]	Ireland
156,214	-6	0.2	22.4	3.8	2.1	26.2	26.5	18.9	...	...	...	...	Israel
1,566,273	5	1.0	18.9	14.8	3.3	35.4	17.7	8.9	327.77	669.40	1,268.97	1,100.28	Italy
50,090	12	0.1	41.2	27.6	8.8	10.7	8.2	3.4	2.40	8.80	9.10	12.60	Latvia
...	...	...	...	...	...	...	...	...	...	...	...	...	Liechtenstein
29,346	6	0.9	54.0	7.6	8.3	6.3	20.3	2.6	2.82	1.50	0.75	18.29	Lithuania
155,959	2	0.2	30.6	26.3	7.5	14.2	14.6	6.6	230.64[9]	133.80[-1,9]	323.01[9]	132.92[-1,9]	Luxembourg
7,527	7	0.0	37.4	25.8	4.1	15.7	11.6	5.4	2.72	...	3.33	...	Macedonia (TFYR)
31,329	2	1.2	20.3	41.1	7.8	7.8	16.1	5.6	16.90	47.90	2.22	53.62	Malta
8,025	10	0.0	40.7	38.4	5.4	7.8	7.5	0.3	0.78	1.59	0.58	2.33	Moldova (Rep.)
...	...	...	...	...	...	...	...	...	...	...	...	...	Monaco
...	...	...	...	...	...	...	...	...	...	...	...	...	Montenegro
1,442,964	-1	5.3	28.6	7.4	7.9	14.5	22.4	13.8	593.62[9]	2,840.31[9]	761.38[9]	3,175.18[9]	Netherlands
516,148	4	1.9	31.3	17.6	9.6	16.5	11.0	12.2	192.15	524.04	335.20	465.25	Norway
249,408	3	1.1	48.1	11.9	12.7	5.6	15.2	5.3	36.00	61.20[9]	99.00	1,003.56[9]	Poland
416,956	5	2.9	19.9	28.1	3.1	10.6	19.0	16.4	27.78	58.62	118.15	327.64	Portugal
70,936	11	0.3	46.4	20.2	8.8	7.3	15.0	2.1	64.10	3.00[-3]	88.11	85.00[-3]	Romania
581,359	7	0.2	34.8	44.5	10.2	1.4	8.0	0.9	126.75	...	378.96	...	Russian Federation
47,222	...	0.0	46.6	18.7	2.8	20.8	8.3	2.8	...	...	...	...	San Marino
102,706	6	0.1	37.2	23.8	5.8	11.2	9.1	12.9	4.97[9]	75.18[9]	7.13[9]	93.78[9]	Serbia
67,602	6	0.0	29.2	41.4	2.6	10.4	8.8	7.6	10.80	...	23.40	...	Slovakia
1,375,697	1	0.9	22.2	15.2	9.7	9.1	20.9	21.9	461.04	...	1,141.44	...	Slovenia
651,575	5	3.3	29.8	18.1	7.3	13.6	11.3	16.6	153.27	...	129.64	...	Spain
2,651,871	3	5.6	23.2	14.5	7.9	4.0	42.4	2.4	...	...	...	...	Sweden
105,841	1	1.9	37.4	0.2	3.6	11.9	33.7	11.2	...	0.00[9]	...	439.00	Switzerland
62,481	7	0.7	44.2	19.5	7.2	1.5	18.3	8.6	...	...	...	...	Turkey
8,275,744	4	9.1	19.5	3.8	4.4	6.6	46.4	10.3	2,860.97	6,247.27[9]	1,145.51	5,805.45[9]	Ukraine / United Kingdom
													North America
3,866,277	3	1.1	34.3	26.6	8.6	4.6	6.5	18.3	1,895.53	2,639.96[9]	1,727.31	5,454.88[9]	Canada
17,160,887	1	9.9	15.0	2.0	6.4	2.2	38.6	25.8	7,037.50	57,261.00[9]	925.20	24,356.00[9]	United States of America
													Latin America and the Caribbean
...	...	...	...	...	...	...	...	...	...	...	...	...	Anguilla
...	...	...	...	...	...	...	...	...	...	...	...	...	Antigua and Barbuda
116,201	-5	0.1	64.6	7.9	4.5	2.7	10.4	9.9	183.47	...	172.70	...	Argentina
14,999	-4[+1]	1.2	23.1	0.0	21.6	0.0	54.0	0.0	...	...	...	...	Aruba
18,303	-1	3.5	56.4	2.0	15.1	1.3	20.6	1.1	...	...	2.00	16.10	Bahamas
17,917	1	0.1	52.0	11.7	5.4	16.5	11.1	3.2	0.10	1.70	0.02	29.05	Barbados
3,539	0	0.0	70.8	3.5	9.4	8.3	6.9	1.1	...	...	...	0.39	Belize
...	...	...	...	...	...	...	...	...	...	...	...	...	Bermuda
11,883	-1	0.0	69.4	5.8	5.2	12.5	4.5	2.6	1.08	...	5.39	...	Bolivia
122,023	-4	3.2	72.1	6.6	4.1	2.9	7.5	3.5	16.03	...	314.05	...	Brazil
...	...	...	...	...	...	...	...	...	...	...	...	...	British Virgin Islands
107,996	2	0.3	50.6	5.9	3.6	5.6	16.7	17.3	...	...	...	...	Cayman Islands
91,701	2	0.1	62.0	7.0	2.3	5.3	10.0	13.4	24.04	9.94	41.23	118.09	Chile
42,563	-1	0.0	55.8	14.2	5.5	10.4	12.2	1.8	0.10	...	...	...	Colombia
...	...	...	...	...	...	...	...	...	...	...	...	...	Costa Rica
1,829	...	0.0	79.7	1.4	5.6	7.0	5.6	0.7	...	...	...	...	Cuba
...	...	...	...	...	...	...	...	...	...	...	...	30.80	Dominica
66,626	3	0.0	68.5	8.8	2.7	6.1	11.6	2.2	38.54	...	106.06	42.86	Dominican Republic
39,817	2	0.1	73.6	6.6	3.9	6.4	6.0	3.4	...	...	...	...	Ecuador
23,039	19	0.0	95.5	1.1	1.3	1.4	0.8	0.1	...	...	...	...	El Salvador
61,648	2	0.0	68.7	5.6	5.2	8.1	8.0	4.4	0.25	0.10[+1]	0.04	0.00[+1]	Grenada
8,529	7	0.0	89.7	1.2	3.7	1.6	3.2	0.6	...	...	...	...	Guatemala
...	...	...	...	...	...	...	...	...	...	4.49	...	0.40	Guyana
26,875	16	0.0	65.1	10.0	7.0	6.8	9.1	2.0	...	...	5.70	...	Haiti
81,519	9	0.1	88.9	2.6	1.8	4.8	1.6	0.2	0.60[-4]	0.00[+1]	1.29	10.36[+1]	Honduras
1,125,222	4	0.2	38.3	5.3	5.3	2.8	6.9	41.1	372.90	...	275.40	...	Jamaica
231	0	0.0	52.3	1.2	13.3	29.4	2.9	0.9	...	...	...	...	Mexico / Montserrat

Table 16. International flows of selected cultural goods and services

Core cultural goods[1, a] (million USD)

Country or Territory	Total trade annual compound growth rate[d]	Trade coverage ratio[e] %	Total exports trade ('000)	Annual compound growth rate for exports per capita	Exports[b, c] Heritage goods	Books	Newspapers & periodicals	Other printed matter	Recorded media	Visual Arts	Audiovisual media
	2001–2006	2006	2006	2001–2006				2006			
Netherlands Antilles	...	...	...	...	...	...	...	...	...	...	...
Nicaragua	3	5	931	0	0.4	29.3	23.1	10.5	1.7	35.0	0.0
Panama	4	0	94	-4	0.0	38.2	13.5	9.7	0.0	38.5	0.0
Paraguay	23	1	1,021	2	0.0	72.7	0.2	2.1	2.5	8.0	14.4
Peru	2	77	40,974	3	0.4	62.4	3.3	14.5	4.0	15.3	0.1
Saint Kitts and Nevis	3	0	8	-18	0.0	38.4	0.1	35.4	2.8	23.3	0.0
Saint Lucia	4	3	186	1	0.0	16.8	44.4	0.9	1.1	36.4	0.4
Saint Vincent and the Grenadines	0	0	1	33	0.0	0.0	0.0	0.0	0.0	100.0	0.0
Suriname	...	...	...	...	...	...	...	...	...	...	...
Trinidad and Tobago	8	26	11,318	6	0.0	86.5	1.0	10.6	0.4	1.5	0.0
Turks and Caicos Islands	7	2	58	...	5.2	14.3	8.0	0.0	0.0	72.5	0.0
Uruguay	8	318	14,818	21	0.4	52.0	0.1	0.3	34.7	10.9	1.6
Venezuela	-3	1	653	-17	0.0	32.5	7.1	2.5	7.9	49.5	0.4
Pacific											
Australia	5	32	384,041	5	2.6	30.8	10.8	5.9	9.0	23.2	17.6
Cook Islands	...	...	...	...	...	...	...	...	...	...	...
Fiji	8[+1]	11	1,289	15[+1]	0.0	76.1	6.7	11.0	2.1	3.8	0.3
Kiribati	...	...	...	...	...	...	...	...	...	...	...
Marshall Islands	...	...	...	...	...	...	...	...	...	...	...
Micronesia (Fed. States)	...	...	...	...	...	...	...	...	...	...	...
Nauru	...	...	...	...	...	...	...	...	...	...	...
New Zealand	4	13	44,313	5	7.3	38.1	5.5	14.9	12.5	19.8	1.8
Niue	...	...	...	...	...	...	...	...	...	...	...
Palau	...	...	...	...	...	...	...	...	...	...	...
Papua New Guinea	...	...	...	...	...	...	...	...	...	...	...
Samoa	...	...	...	...	...	...	...	...	...	...	...
Solomon Islands	...	...	...	...	...	...	...	...	...	...	...
Tokelau	...	...	...	...	...	...	...	...	...	...	...
Tonga	...	...	...	...	...	...	...	...	...	...	...
Tuvalu	...	...	...	...	...	...	...	...	...	...	...
Vanuatu	...	...	...	...	...	...	...	...	...	...	...
World[h] (sample)	4	...	57,585,990	...	4.8	25.6	10.6	5.5	8.4	28.5	16.6
Arab States	-3	19	68,107	...	1.4	30.4	10.3	41.2	1.3	15.3	0.1
Sub-Saharan Africa	8	28	239,199	...	6.8	28.2	2.6	4.1	8.3	48.7	1.3
Central and South Asia	3	217	870,910	...	0.0	16.0	7.2	1.7	20.0	52.9	2.1
East Asia	8	149	13,223,861	...	0.6	14.9	1.1	3.3	2.5	32.4	45.2
Europe	4	103	31,652,641	...	7.2	29.2	13.7	5.7	10.9	26.1	7.2
North America	2	48	10,046,783	...	3.8	26.8	14.4	7.1	7.2	30.1	10.6
Latin America and the Caribbean	2	44	1,054,845	...	0.2	41.5	8.3	12.3	10.0	12.7	14.9
Pacific	5	27	429,642	...	3.1	31.7	10.3	6.9	9.3	22.8	16.0

Sources:

1. UNESCO Institute for Statistics, 2008 based on data from UN Comtrade database, DESA/UNSD, 2008. For details about the methodology used, please refer to UIS/UNESCO Culture Sector, 2005. International Flows of Selected Cultural Goods and Services, 1994–2003: Defining and Capturing the Flows of Global Cultural Trade.

2. International Monetary Fund, 2008. Balance of Payments Statistics — March 2008 CD-ROM. Other figures provided by OECD Statistics on International Trade in services Database, 2008.

Notes:

a. Data for cultural goods were extracted from the United Nations (UN) Comtrade database. The database covers about 160 reporting countries or areas, which cover more than 90% of world trade. Low-value transactions are not included, but in general they represent less than 1% of total global trade. Valuation is based on customs records in current United States of America dollars (USD) and the trade data are classified using the Harmonized Commodity Description and Coding System 96 (HS).

b. When data are available, re-exports have been deducted from exports data in order to measure domestic exports. It should be noted that China exports are overestimated compared to the US where re-exports are included.

c. The exports are valued at transaction value (Free on Board: F.O.B.), i.e. the price includes the cost of transportation and insurance to the border of the exporter country.

d. Average Annual Growth Rate (AAGR) is calculated by taking the arithmetic mean of the growth rate over two annual periods. In our case the AAGR is calculated as Annual Compound Growth Rate (ACGR) by taking the number root of the total percentage growth rate, where n is the number of years in the period being considered. This can be written as follows: ACGR = [(Ending Value / Beginning Value) (1 / # of years) — 1]. When 2001 data were not available, this ratio is calculated on the basis of 2001+ n.

e. (Export/Import)*100

f. The imports are recorded at transaction value (Cost Insurance Freight: C.I.F.), which means that the price includes cost of transportation and insurance to the border of the importing country.

Total imports trade ('000)	Annual compound growth rate for imports per capita	Imports[f] Share by products %							Services[2] (million USD) Exports		Imports		Country or Territory
		Heritage goods	Books	Newspapers & periodicals	Other printed matter	Recorded media	Visual Arts	Audiovisual media	Audiovisual services	Royalties & license fees	Audiovisual services	Royalties & license fees	
2006	2001–2006	2006							2005				
...	...	...	...	...	...	...	...	...	...	...	...	...	Netherlands Antilles
17,354	2	0.1	73.7	10.1	4.6	4.3	5.7	1.5	...	...	...	...	Nicaragua
54,488	3	0.0	51.5	15.8	3.5	11.9	8.5	8.9	...	...	...	...	Panama
100,633	22	0.0	11.3	0.4	0.7	2.0	1.7	83.9	...	218.70	...	0.90	Paraguay
52,928	1	0.0	73.7	6.3	2.0	4.2	8.9	5.0	...	1.79	...	81.63	Peru
2,429	3	0.0	69.8	6.7	11.3	5.0	6.6	0.5	...	...	...	...	Saint Kitts and Nevis
5,495	3	0.0	63.1	8.2	8.4	7.2	11.5	1.5	...	...	...	...	Saint Lucia
3,049	0	0.0	64.4	14.4	6.8	5.9	7.3	1.0	...	...	...	...	Saint Vincent and the Grenadines
2,928	0[+1]	0.0	57.6	6.0	14.3	9.2	11.4	1.5	...	...	...	...	Suriname
43,166	8	0.0	83.8	2.4	2.4	6.5	4.3	0.6	...	...	...	...	Trinidad and Tobago
3,024	...	0.5	51.6	21.4	10.1	0.0	15.6	0.8	...	...	...	...	Turks and Caicos Islands
4,654	-4	0.0	5.4	1.1	18.0	29.9	20.7	25.0	0.40[-2]	0.07	10.40[-2]	6.91	Uruguay
122,465	-4	0.0	70.9	13.0	1.1	4.9	6.0	4.1	4.00	...	19.00	...	Venezuela
1,217,456	**5**	**2.3**	**38.7**	**13.7**	**5.9**	**6.5**	**13.9**	**18.9**	**126.00**	**538.39[g]**	**590.54**	**1,619.74[g]**	**Pacific**
...	...	...	...	...	...	...	...	...	...	...	...	...	Australia
11,417	7[+1]	0.2	49.8	0.2	3.3	28.1	8.5	9.9	0.65	0.12	2.01	1.18	Cook Islands
...	...	...	...	...	...	...	...	...	...	...	...	...	Fiji
...	...	...	...	...	...	...	...	...	...	...	...	...	Kiribati
...	...	...	...	...	...	...	...	...	...	...	...	...	Marshall Islands
...	...	...	...	...	...	...	...	...	...	...	...	...	Micronesia (Fed. States)
340,078	3	3.2	39.7	22.0	4.9	15.2	7.5	7.4	90.14[+1,g]	...	13.62[+1,g]	...	Nauru
...	...	...	...	...	...	...	...	...	...	...	...	...	New Zealand
...	...	...	...	...	...	...	...	...	...	...	...	...	Niue
...	...	...	...	...	...	...	...	...	...	...	...	...	Palau
...	...	...	...	...	...	...	...	...	...	...	...	...	Papua New Guinea
...	...	...	...	...	...	...	...	...	...	...	...	...	Samoa
...	...	...	...	...	...	...	...	...	...	...	0.09[-4]	...	Solomon Islands
...	...	...	...	...	...	...	...	...	...	...	...	...	Tokelau
...	...	...	...	...	...	...	...	...	...	...	...	...	Tonga
...	...	...	...	...	...	...	...	...	...	...	...	...	Tuvalu
...	...	...	...	...	...	...	...	...	...	0.18[+1]	...	0.47	Vanuatu
66,247,942	**...**	**5.1**	**25.0**	**9.8**	**5.8**	**7.9**	**26.3**	**20.0**	**...**	**...**	**...**	**...**	**World[h] (sample)**
363,490	...	0.3	48.7	8.1	5.8	14.1	18.1	5.0	...	...	...	...	Arab States
869,258	...	0.8	49.3	5.2	3.9	8.9	26.0	5.8	...	...	...	...	Sub-Saharan Africa
401,376	...	0.5	58.1	7.6	3.0	13.7	14.0	3.1	...	...	...	...	Central and South Asia
8,866,303	...	3.2	22.8	4.4	3.6	7.0	16.7	42.4	...	...	...	...	East Asia
30,756,330	...	4.2	25.9	13.8	5.9	11.9	27.2	11.1	...	...	...	...	Europe
21,027,164	...	8.2	18.6	6.6	6.8	2.7	32.7	24.4	...	...	...	...	North America
2,395,071	...	0.3	51.2	6.2	4.4	4.2	7.9	25.8	...	...	...	...	Latin America and the Caribbean
1,568,951	...	2.5	39.0	15.4	5.6	8.6	12.5	16.3	...	...	...	...	Pacific

g. Data provided by OECD instead of IMF.

h. Total of available countries.

... Data not available

+n Data refer to the year n years after the reference year

-n Data refer to the year n years before the reference year

Table 17. Tourism flows[1]

Country or Territory	Outbound — Tourists departures[a] ('000)	Outbound — Expenditure in other countries (US$ per capita)	Outbound — Main destination[b]	Inbound — Tourists arrivals[c] ('000)	Inbound — Expenditure in the country (US$ Million)	Inbound — Main origin[d]
			2005			
Arab States						
Algeria	1,513	11.26	Tunisia	1,443[e]	184	France
Bahrain	...	791.96	Saudi Arabia	3,914	1,603	Saudi Arabia
Djibouti	...	17.91	Egypt	30[f]	...	...
Egypt	5,307	26.52	Saudi Arabia	8,244	7,206	Germany
Iraq	...	...	Syrian Arab Republic	127[-4,e]	...	...
Jordan	1,523	117.78	Syrian Arab Republic	2,987	1,759	Syrian Arab Republic
Kuwait	1,928[-1]	1,755.93	Saudi Arabia	3,056[-1,e]	410	Saudi Arabia[-1]
Lebanon	...	888.86	Syrian Arab Republic	1,140	5,969	Jordan
Libyan Arab Jamahiriya	...	155.45	Tunisia	149[-1]	301	Egypt[-1]
Mauritania	...	...	Senegal	30[-5]	...	...
Morocco	2,247	32.76	Nigeria	5,843	5,426	France
Oman	2,060[-3]	334.26	Saudi Arabia	1,114[f]	599	United Kingdom
Palestinian A. T.	...	...	Egypt	88[f]	...	...
Qatar	...	...	Saudi Arabia	913[f]	...	...
Saudi Arabia	4,403	176.94	Bahrain	8,037	5,626	Kuwait
Sudan	...	...	Saudi Arabia	246	...	...
Syrian Arab Republic	4,564	30.91	Jordan	3,368	2,035	Iraq
Tunisia	2,241	44.73	Algeria	6,378	2,800	Libyan Arab Jamahiriya
United Arab Emirates	...	1,507.20	Saudi Arabia	7,126[f]	3,218	United Kingdom[-1]
Yemen	...	10.62	Saudi Arabia	336[f]	...	Saudi Arabia
Sub-Saharan Africa						
Angola	...	8.39	Namibia	210	103	Portugal
Benin	...	6.83	Nigeria	176	108	Congo
Botswana	...	163.95	South Africa	1,675	561	South Africa[-1]
Burkina Faso	...	3.80	Nigeria	245[f]	45	France
Burundi	...	7.89	Tanzania	148	2	...
Cameroon	...	22.63[-1]	Nigeria	176[f]	212[-1]	France
Cape Verde	...	161.80	Brazil	198	177	Italy
Central African Republic	8	7.76[-1]	Nigeria	12	4[-1]	France
Chad	23[-3]	8.77[-3]	Nigeria	29[f]	25[-3]	France[-1]
Comoros	...	12.53	Tanzania	26	24	France[-1]
Congo	...	49.86[-1]	Benin	22[-3,f]	23[-1]	France[-3]
Congo (Dem. Rep.)	...	...	South Africa	61	...	...
Côte d'Ivoire	...	29.54	Nigeria	...	93	...
Equatorial Guinea	...	68.05[-4]	Angola	...	14[-4]	...
Eritrea	...	...	Saudi Arabia	83[e]	66	Italy
Ethiopia	...	0.77[-1]	Nigeria	227	533	USA
Gabon	236[-2]	216.51[-1]	Nigeria	222[-2]	74[-1]	United Kingdom
Gambia	387	4.33	Senegal	108	57	Nigeria
Ghana	...	20.95	Nigeria	429	867	France
Guinea	...	4.55	Senegal	45	32[-2]	Portugal
Guinea-Bissau	...	11.27	Senegal	5	2[-1]	Germany[-2]
Kenya	...	5.71[-4]	Uganda	1,536	969	South Africa
Lesotho	...	18.17	South Africa	304[e]	...	...
Liberia	...	...	Nigeria	...	...	France
Madagascar	...	4.29	Mauritius	277	290	Mozambique
Malawi	...	5.67	South Africa	438	43	France
Mali	...	11.45	Senegal	143[f]	149	France
Mauritius	183	237.68	India	761	1,189	South Africa
Mozambique	...	9.11	South Africa	578	138	Angola
Namibia	...	...	South Africa	778	363	France
Niger	...	3.17	Nigeria	60	44	Niger
Nigeria	...	9.80	United Kingdom	1,010	46	...
Rwanda	...	3.87[-4]	Uganda	113[-4]	29[-4]	...
Saint Helena	...	...	...	...	...	Portugal
Sao Tome and Principe	...	13.09[-3]	Angola	16	334	France
Senegal	...	12.23	Nigeria	769	269	France
Seychelles	52	689.80	Mauritius	129	...	...
Sierra Leone	63	6.01	Nigeria	40	...	...
Somalia	...	...	Saudi Arabia	...	8,448	Lesotho
South Africa	3,794[-3]	100.36	Zimbabwe	7,369	78	South Africa
Swaziland	1,082	53.36	South Africa	839[f]	835	Kenya
Tanzania (United Rep.)	...	15.00	Zambia	590	27	France
Togo	...	6.73	Nigeria	81[f]		

Table 17. Tourism flows[1]

	Outbound			Inbound		
Country or Territory	Tourists departures[a] ('000)	Expenditure in other countries (US$ per capita)	Main destination[b]	Tourists arrivals[c] ('000)	Expenditure in the country (US$ Million)	Main origin[d]
			2005			
Uganda	189	4.59	Tanzania	468	383	Kenya
Zambia	...	6.88	Zimbabwe	669	...	Zimbabwe
Zimbabwe	...	...	South Africa	1,559[e]	99	South Africa
Central and South Asia						
Afghanistan	...	...	Pakistan	...	...	...
Armenia	269	48.38	Russian Federation	319	161	USA
Azerbaijan	1,830	22.51	Russian Federation	1,177	100	Georgia
Bangladesh	1,767	2.45	India	208	79	India
Bhutan	...	...	Thailand	14	19	USA
Georgia	317[-3]	52.98	Azerbaijan	560[e]	287	USA
India	7,185	6.87	Singapore	3,919	7,652	United Kingdom
Iran (Islamic Rep.)	2,921[-3]	65.69	Turkey	1,659[-1]	1,364	...
Kazakhstan	3,004	61.80	Russian Federation	3,143	801	Russian Federation
Kyrgyzstan	201	13.64	Kazakhstan	315	94	Kazakhstan
Maldives	77	318.32	India	395	...	United Kingdom
Nepal	373	8.16	India	375	160	India
Pakistan	...	11.09	Saudi Arabia	798	828	United Kingdom
Sri Lanka	727	28.87	India	549	729	India
Tajikistan	...	...	Russian Federation	4[-4]	10	...
Turkmenistan	33	...	Turkey	12	...	Iran (Islamic Rep.)
Uzbekistan	455[-1]	...	Kazakhstan	262[-1]	57[-1]	...
East Asia						
Brunei Darussalam	...	...	Malaysia	119	...	Malaysia
Cambodia	427	9.89	Viet Nam	1,422	929	Korea, Republic of
China	31,026	18.82	Singapore	46,809	31,842	Korea, Republic of
Hong Kong (SAR China)	72,300	...	Thailand	14,773	13,588	USA
Macao (SAR China)	295	...	Thailand	9,014	7,757	Japan
Indonesia	4,106	20.97	Singapore	5,002	5,094	Singapore
Japan	17,404	376.10	United States	6,728[e]	15,555	Korea, Republic of
Korea (Dem. People's Rep.)	...	...	China	...	...	...
Korea (Rep.)	10,080	353.54	China	6,023[e]	8,290	Japan
Lao (People's Dem. Rep.)	...	...	Thailand	672	...	Thailand
Malaysia	30,761[-1]	169.14	Thailand	16,431	10,389	Singapore
Mongolia	...	67.04	China	338	203	China
Myanmar	...	0.71	China	232	85	Thailand
Philippines	2,144	18.29	China	2,623	2,755	USA
Singapore	5,159	...	Malaysia	7,080	...	Indonesia
Thailand	3,047	78.04	Malaysia	11,567	12,102	Malaysia
Timor-Leste	...	...	Australia	...	...	...
Viet Nam	...	...	China	3,468[e]	1,880	China
Europe						
Albania	2,097	256.20	Greece	748[e]	880	Serbia and Montenegro
Andorra	...	...	Belgium	2,418	...	...
Austria	8,206	1,538.23	Italy	19,952	19,310	Germany
Belarus	572	68.60	Ukraine	91	346	Russian Federation
Belgium	9,327	1,599.92	Spain	6,747	10,881	Netherlands
Bosnia and Herzegovina	...	40.36	Croatia	217	550	Serbia and Montenegro
Bulgaria	4,235	239.91	Turkey	4,837	3,063	Turkey
Croatia	...	172.69	Slovenia	8,467	7,625	Germany
Cyprus	781	1,196.91	Greece	2,470	2,644	United Kingdom
Czech Republic	...	255.60	Croatia	6,336	5,616	Germany
Denmark	5,469	...	Sweden[-1]	4,699	...	Germany
Estonia	2,075[-2]	400.20	Russian Federation	1,917	1,207	Finland
Finland	5,902	690.43	Russian Federation	2,080	3,070	Sweden
France	22,270	615.65	Spain	75,908	52,153	Germany
Germany	77,400	998.46	France	21,500	38,220	Netherlands
Gibraltar	...	...	United Kingdom	...	...	...
Greece	...	274.33	Bulgaria	14,765	13,453	United Kingdom
Holy See	...	...	...	...	...	...
Hungary	18,622	334.01	Ukraine	3,446	4,864	Germany
Iceland	...	3,351.01	United Kingdom	871	630	Germany
Ireland	6,113	1,493.01	United Kingdom	7,333	6,780	United Kingdom
Israel	3,687	564.85	Turkey	1,903	3,358	USA

Table 17. Tourism flows[1]

Country or Territory	Outbound			Inbound		
	Tourists departures[a] ('000)	Expenditure in other countries (US$ per capita)	Main destination[b]	Tourists arrivals[c] ('000)	Expenditure in the country (US$ Million)	Main origin[d]
			2005			
Italy	24,796	456.53	France	36,513	38,374	Germany
Latvia	2,959	284.56	Russian Federation	1,116	446	Germany
Liechtenstein	...	...	Switzerland	50[f]	...	Germany
Lithuania	3,502[-2]	221.02	Russian Federation	2,000	975	Germany
Luxembourg	...	6,520.50[-1]	Germany	913	3,880[-1]	Netherlands
Macedonia (TFYR)	...	46.22	Bulgaria	197	92	Serbia and Montenegro
Malta	225	772.45	United Kingdom	1,171	923	United Kingdom
Moldova (Rep.)	57	43.85	Ukraine	23	138	Romania
Monaco	...	...	United States	286[f]	...	Italy
Montenegro	...	...	...	272	...	Bosnia and Herzegovina
Netherlands	17,039	881.88[-3]	France	10,012	11,745[-3]	Germany
Norway	3,122	1,929.89[-1]	Spain	3,824	3,959	Sweden
Poland	40,841	122.68	Ukraine	15,200	7,127	Germany
Portugal	18,110	355.62	Spain	10,612	9,009	Spain
Romania	7,140	49.61	Bulgaria	5,839[e]	1,325	Italy
Russian Federation	28,416	127.99	Ukraine	19,940	7,806	Ukraine
San Marino	...	...	United States	2,107[e]	...	Italy
Serbia	...	26.36	...	453	308	Bosnia and Herzegovina
Slovakia	22,405	167.64[-1]	Ukraine	1,515	932[-1]	Czech Republic
Slovenia	2,660	509.65	Croatia	1,555	1,894	Italy
Spain	10,508	424.93	France	55,914	53,066	United Kingdom
Sweden	12,603	1,310.46	Norway	7,627[-2]	8,580	Germany
Switzerland	11,427[-3]	1,432.31	France	7,229[f]	11,991	Germany
Turkey	8,246	43.99	Bulgaria	20,273	19,720	Germany
Ukraine	16,454	65.60	Russian Federation	17,631	3,542	Russian Federation
United Kingdom	66,494	1,222.88	Spain	28,039	39,569	USA
North America						
Canada	21,099	709.35	United States	18,770	16,006	USA
United States of America	63,503	331.63	Canada	49,206	123,093	Canada
Latin America and the Caribbean						
Anguilla	...	...	United States	62	...	USA
Antigua and Barbuda	...	...	United States	267	...	United Kingdom
Argentina	3,894	91.57	Uruguay	3,823	3,217	Chile
Aruba	...	2,342.15	Netherland Antilles	733	1,076[+1]	USA
Bahamas	...	1,633.18	United States	1,608	2,082	USA
Barbados	...	524.09	United States	548	905	United Kingdom
Belize	...	163.31	United States	237	...	USA
Bermuda	161	3,724.25	Canada	270	429	USA
Bolivia	386	27.99	Chile	524	345	Peru
Brazil	4,667	31.61	United States	5,358	4,168	Argentina
British Virgin Islands	...	...	United States	337	437	USA[-2]
Cayman Islands	...	...	United States	168	356	USA
Chile	2,651	82.79	Peru	2,027	1,652	Argentina
Colombia	1,553	34.75	United States	933[e]	1,570	USA
Costa Rica	487	128.49	United States	1,679	1,810	USA
Cuba	162	...	United States	2,261	2,399	Canada
Dominica	...	...	United States	79	...	USA
Dominican Republic	419	53.96	United States	3,691	...	USA
Ecuador	664	49.31	United States	860[e]	488	USA
El Salvador	1,397	64.33	Guatemala	969	838	Guatemala
Grenada	...	...	Trinidad and Tobago	99	...	USA
Guatemala	982	39.34	El Salvador	1,316	883	El Salvador
Guyana	...	60.85	Trinidad and Tobago	117	37	USA
Haiti	...	18.61	United States	112	...	USA
Honduras	296	47.85	El Salvador	673	466	USA
Jamaica	...	108.11	United States	1,479	1,783	USA
Mexico	13,305	85.85	United States	21,915	12,801	USA
Montserrat	...	...	United States	10	...	United Kingdom
Netherlands Antilles	...	...	Aruba	...	...	USA
Nicaragua	740	29.66	Costa Rica	712	210	USA
Panama	285	120.07	United States	702	1,108	USA
Paraguay	188	22.02	Brazil	341	96	Argentina
Peru	1,841	35.56	Chile	1,487	1,438	Chile
Saint Kitts and Nevis	...	...	United States	128	...	USA

Table 17. Tourism flows[1]

Country or Territory	Outbound			Inbound		
	Tourists departures[a] ('000)	Expenditure in other countries (US$ per capita)	Main destination[b]	Tourists arrivals[c] ('000)	Expenditure in the country (US$ Million)	Main origin[d]
			2005			
Saint Lucia	…	…	Barbados	318	…	USA
Saint Vincent and the Grenadines	…	…	Barbados	96	…	USA
Suriname	…	207.75	United States	160	96	Netherlands
Trinidad and Tobago	…	176.77	United States	463	593	USA
Turks and Caicos Islands	…	…	United States	176	292[-3]	USA
Uruguay	658	99.53	Brazil	1,808	699	Argentina
Venezuela	1,067	68.96	United States	706	722	USA
Pacific						
Australia	4,756	767.74	United Kingdom	5,020	22,566	New Zealand
Cook Islands	13	…	New Zealand	88	91	New Zealand
Fiji	104[-2]	159.41	Australia	550	676	Australia
Kiribati	…	…	China	3	3[-4]	Australia
Marshall Islands	…	7.05	Russian Federation	9	6	USA
Micronesia (Fed. States)	…	54.52	Guam	19	17	USA
Nauru	…	…	Australia	…	…	…
New Zealand	1,872	…	Australia	2,365[e]	…	Australia
Niue	2[-1]	…	New Zealand	3	1	New Zealand
Palau	…	74.53	Guam	86	97	Taiwan (Prov. of China)
Papua New Guinea	92[-3]	9.26	Australia	69	4	Australia
Samoa	52	70.71	New Zealand	102	78	New Zealand
Solomon Islands	…	23.28	Australia	9	7	Australia
Tokelau	…	…	…	…	…	…
Tonga	…	…	New Zealand	42	…	New Zealand
Tuvalu	2	…	Korea, Republic of	1	…	Fiji
Vanuatu	14	60.36	Australia	62	95	Australia

Source:

1. World Tourism Organization, 2007. Compendium of Tourism Statistics, 2007 Edition. http://www.unwto.org/statistics

Notes:

a. Departures as recorded by origin country.

b. Arrivals of non-resident tourists at national borders, unless otherwise specified.

c. Arrivals of non-resident tourists in all types of accommodation establishments.

d. Estimations based on origin of inbound tourists as reported by receiving countries, with some of them not reporting any. Travel between mainland China, Hong Kong, SAR (China) and Macao, SAR (China) is considered as domestic tourism.

e. Arrivals of non-resident visitors at national borders.

f. Arrivals of non-resident tourists in hotels and similar establishments.

… Data not available

+n Data refer to the year n years after the reference year

-n Data refer to the year n years before the reference year

Table 18. Environment, biodiversity and habitat

Country or Territory	Population density[1] (population per sq km)	% Urban population[2]	Population growth (% annual average)[2] Urban	Rural	Forest area[3] % of total land	Average annual variation 1990/2000	2000/2005	Number of Biosphere Reserves[4]	Protected terrestrial and marine area[5, a] (%)	Biodiversity[6, b] Plant species threatened	Animal species threatened
	2005	2005	2000/2005		2005	1990/2000	2000/2005	2007	2005	2007	
Arab States											
Algeria	14	63	2.7	-0.3	1.0	1.8	1.2	6	5.0	3	71
Bahrain	1,044	97	2.0	-7.1	0.6	5.6	3.8	.	1.3	...	16
Djibouti	35	86	2.7	-1.5	0.2	...	...	.	0.0	2	28
Egypt	73	43	2.0	1.8	0.1	3.0	2.6	2	13.3	2	59
Iraq	64	67	2.5	3.3	1.9	0.2	0.1	.	0.1	.	40
Jordan	62	82	3.2	0.8	0.9	...	...	1	10.9	.	43
Kuwait	152	98	3.7	2.7	0.3	3.5	2.7	.	2.6	...	23
Lebanon	386	87	1.2	0.1	13.3	0.8	0.8	2	0.5	.	38
Libyan Arab Jamahiriya	3	85	2.4	-0.2	0.1	...	...	.	0.1	1	31
Mauritania	3	40	3.2	2.8	0.3	-2.7	-3.4	1	1.7	...	44
Morocco	68	59	2.7	-0.2	9.8	0.1	0.2	3	1.2	2	76
Oman	8	71	1.0	1.1	0.0	...	...	.	11.3	6	50
Palestinian A. T.	625	72	3.3	3.1	1.5	...	...	.	...	.	9
Qatar	72	95	6.0	3.9	0.0	...	...	1	0.6	...	13
Saudi Arabia	11	81	3.0	1.5	1.3	...	...	.	37.1	3	45
Sudan	15	41	4.4	0.4	28.4	-0.8	-0.8	2	4.7	17	47
Syrian Arab Republic	102	51	2.7	2.3	2.5	1.5	1.3	.	1.9	.	59
Tunisia	62	65	1.7	0.0	6.8	4.1	1.9	4	1.3	.	52
United Arab Emirates	49	77	6.3	7.1	3.7	2.4	0.1	1	4.0	...	27
Yemen	40	27	4.5	2.6	1.0	...	...	1	...	159	47
Sub-Saharan Africa											
Angola	13	53	4.1	1.5	47.4	-0.2	-0.2	.	12.1	26	62
Benin	75	40	4.1	2.6	21.3	-2.1	-2.5	2	23.0	14	34
Botswana	3	57	1.6	-1.7	21.1	-0.9	-1.0	.	30.2	.	18
Burkina Faso	51	18	5.2	2.7	29.0	-0.3	-0.3	2	15.4	2	13
Burundi	282	10	6.1	2.7	5.9	-3.7	-5.2	.	5.6	2	48
Cameroon	37	55	3.6	-0.1	45.6	-0.9	-1.0	3	8.9	355	157
Cape Verde	126	57	3.8	0.6	20.7	3.6	0.4	.	0.1	2	25
Central African Republic	7	38	1.6	1.2	36.5	-0.1	-0.1	2	15.7	15	17
Chad	8	25	5.0	2.9	9.5	-0.6	-0.7	.	9.3	2	21
Comoros	357	37	4.4	1.7	2.9	-4.0	-7.4	.	2.7	5	23
Congo	11	60	3.6	2.1	65.8	-0.1	-0.1	2	14.1	35	37
Congo (Dem. Rep.)	25	32	4.3	2.1	58.9	-0.4	-0.2	3	8.4	65	126
Côte d'Ivoire	58	45	2.5	0.9	32.7	0.1	0.1	2	16.4	105	73
Equatorial Guinea	17	39	2.4	2.3	58.2	-0.8	-0.9	.	14.3	63	42
Eritrea	38	19	6.0	3.9	15.4	-0.3	-0.3	.	3.2	3	38
Ethiopia	72	16	3.8	2.2	11.9	-1.0	-1.1	.	16.9	22	86
Gabon	5	84	2.5	-2.1	84.5	0	0	1	16.2	108	43
Gambia	143	54	4.7	0.9	41.7	0.4	0.4	.	4.1	4	31
Ghana	94	48	3.8	0.7	24.2	-2.0	-2.0	1	14.7	117	56
Guinea	37	33	3.4	1.6	27.4	-0.7	-0.5	4	6.1	22	61
Guinea-Bissau	44	30	2.9	3.0	73.7	-0.4	-0.5	1	7.3	4	29
Kenya	61	21	3.2	1.9	6.2	-0.3	-0.3	6	12.7	103	172
Lesotho	65	19	1.0	-0.1	0.3	3.4	2.7	.	0.2	1	11
Liberia	31	58	2.7	-0.4	32.7	-1.6	-1.8	.	12.7	46	60
Madagascar	32	27	3.4	2.6	22.1	-0.5	-0.3	3	2.6	280	262
Malawi	112	17	4.8	1.8	36.2	-0.9	-0.9	2	16.4	14	141
Mali	9	30	4.8	2.2	10.3	-0.7	-0.8	1	2.1	6	21
Mauritius	608	42	0.8	1.1	18.2	-0.3	-0.5	1	0.9	88	65
Mozambique	26	35	4.3	0.9	24.6	-0.3	-0.3	.	8.6	46	93
Namibia	2	35	3.0	0.6	9.3	-0.9	-0.9	.	14.6	24	55
Niger	10	17	4.1	3.2	1.0	-3.7	-1.0	2	6.6	2	20
Nigeria	153	48	4.1	0.7	12.2	-2.7	-3.3	1	6.1	171	79
Rwanda	351	19	9.2	1.0	19.5	0.8	6.9	1	7.6	3	49
Saint Helena	...	39	-0.2	0.0	6.5	...	...	.	...	26	33
Sao Tome and Principe	158	58	3.9	0.2	28.4	...	...	.	...	35	28
Senegal	60	42	2.8	2.1	45.0	-0.5	-0.5	4	10.8	7	55
Seychelles	...	53	1.6	0.1	88.9	...	...	.	1.0	45	48
Sierra Leone	78	41	5.9	2.9	38.5	-0.7	-0.7	.	3.9	47	48
Somalia	13	35	4.3	2.6	11.4	-1.0	-1.0	.	0.7	17	55
South Africa	39	59	1.6	-0.4	7.6	...	...	5	6.1	73	323
Swaziland	65	24	0.9	0.0	31.5	0.9	0.9	.	3.5	11	16
Tanzania (United Rep.)	41	24	3.6	1.5	39.9	-1.0	-1.1	3	38.4	240	299

Table 18. Environment, biodiversity and habitat

Country or Territory	Population density[1] (population per sq km) 2005	% Urban population[2] 2005	Population growth (% annual average)[2] Urban 2000/2005	Population growth (% annual average)[2] Rural 2000/2005	Forest area[3] % of total land 2005	Forest area[3] Average annual variation 1990/2000	Forest area[3] Average annual variation 2000/2005	Number of Biosphere Reserves[4] 2007	Protected terrestrial and marine area[5, a] (%) 2005	Biodiversity[6, b] Plant species threatened 2007	Biodiversity[6, b] Animal species threatened 2007
Togo	110	40	4.5	1.6	7.1	-3.4	-4.5	.	11.2	10	33
Uganda	120	13	4.2	3.3	18.4	-1.9	-2.2	2	26.3	38	131
Zambia	15	35	1.8	1.7	57.1	-0.9	-1.0	.	41.5	8	38
Zimbabwe	34	36	1.9	0.0	45.3	-1.5	-1.7	.	14.7	17	35
Central and South Asia											
Afghanistan	38	23	6.1	4.2	1.3	-2.5	-3.1	.	0.3	2	33
Armenia	101	64	-0.8	0.2	10.0	-1.3	-1.5	.	10.0	1	35
Azerbaijan	96	52	0.9	0.4	11.3	...	...	.	7.3	.	38
Bangladesh	1,064	25	3.5	1.4	6.7	0	-0.3	.	1.3	12	89
Bhutan	14	11	5.1	1.9	68.0	0.3	0.3	.	26.4	7	41
Georgia	64	52	-1.3	-0.9	39.7	0	0	.	4.0	.	46
India	345	29	2.3	1.3	22.8	0.6	0	4	5.4	247	313
Iran (Islamic Rep.)	42	67	1.8	-0.7	6.8	...	...	9	6.6	1	75
Kazakhstan	6	57	0.1	-0.8	1.2	-0.2	-0.2	.	2.9	16	55
Kyrgyzstan	26	36	1.4	1.1	4.5	0.3	0.3	2	3.6	14	22
Maldives	991	30	4.0	1.9	3.0	...	...	.	...	...	14
Nepal	184	16	5.3	1.6	25.4	-2.1	-1.4	.	16.3	7	72
Pakistan	199	35	3.0	1.5	2.5	-1.8	-2.1	1	9.1	2	78
Sri Lanka	291	15	0.1	1.0	29.9	-1.2	-1.5	4	17.2	280	177
Tajikistan	46	25	0.2	1.4	2.9	0	...	.	18.2	14	27
Turkmenistan	10	46	1.9	1.0	8.8	...	...	1	4.1	3	44
Uzbekistan	59	37	1.1	1.6	8.0	0.5	0.5	1	4.6	15	33
East Asia											
Brunei Darussalam	65	74	2.9	0.6	52.8	-0.8	-0.7	.	38.3	99	50
Cambodia	77	20	5.1	1.3	59.2	-1.1	-2.0	1	21.6	31	82
China	137	40	3.1	-0.9	21.2	1.2	2.2	28	14.9	446	351
Hong Kong (SAR China)	6,422	100	1.2	.	...	...	...	.	...	6	37
Macao (SAR China)	18,196	100	0.7	.	...	...	...	.	...	...	9
Indonesia	119	48	4.0	-1.0	48.8	-1.7	-2.0	6	9.1	386	464
Japan	338	66	0.4	-0.2	68.2	0	0	4	8.6	12	190
Korea (Dem. People's Rep.)	196	62	1.0	-0.2	51.4	-1.8	-1.9	2	2.4	3	44
Korea (Rep.)	481	81	0.7	-0.7	63.5	-0.1	-0.1	2	3.9	.	54
Lao (People's Dem. Rep.)	24	21	4.1	1.9	69.9	-0.5	-0.5	.	16.0	21	77
Malaysia	78	67	3.7	-1.2	63.6	-0.4	-0.7	.	17.3	686	225
Mongolia	2	57	1.2	1.1	6.5	-0.7	-0.8	6	13.9	.	38
Myanmar	71	31	2.9	0.4	49.0	-1.3	-1.4	.	4.6	38	118
Philippines	282	63	3.2	-0.3	24.0	-2.8	-2.1	2	6.5	213	253
Singapore	6,336	100	1.5	.	3.4	...	...	.	2.2	54	44
Thailand	123	32	1.6	0.5	28.4	-0.7	-0.4	4	19.0	86	157
Timor-Leste	72	26	7.0	4.9	53.7	-1.2	-1.3	.	1.2	.	11
Viet Nam	256	26	3.0	0.8	39.7	2.3	2.0	6	3.6	146	152
Europe											
Albania	110	45	2.1	-0.8	29.0	-0.3	0.6	.	2.9	.	45
Andorra	...	91	0.0	4.4	35.6	...	...	.	7.2	.	7
Austria	99	66	0.3	0.1	46.7	0.2	0.1	6	28.0	4	62
Belarus	47	72	0.1	-2.1	38.0	0.6	0.1	3	6.3	...	17
Belgium	341	97	0.2	-0.5	22.0	-0.1	...	.	3.3	1	29
Bosnia and Herzegovina	76	46	1.4	-0.6	43.1	-0.1	...	.	0.5	1	55
Bulgaria	70	70	-0.4	-1.4	32.8	0.1	1.4	16	9.5	.	47
Croatia	81	56	0.5	-0.2	38.2	0.1	0.1	1	6.5	1	78
Cyprus	90	69	1.4	0.8	18.9	0.7	0.2	.	4.0	7	23
Czech Republic	129	74	-0.2	0.3	34.3	0	0.1	6	15.8	4	39
Denmark	126	86	0.5	-0.3	11.8	0.9	0.6	1	44.0[c]	3	28
Estonia	30	69	-0.6	-0.4	53.9	0.4	0.4	1	30.9	.	14
Finland	16	61	0.3	0.3	73.9	0.1	0	2	7.8	1	19
France	111	77	0.7	-0.4	28.3	0.5	0.3	10	13.3	7	117
Germany	232	75	0.1	0.0	31.7	0.3	...	13	30.0	12	59
Gibraltar	...	100	0.2	.	...	...	...	.	...	.	15
Greece	84	59	0.3	0.2	29.1	0.9	0.8	2	2.8	11	95
Holy See	...	100	-0.1	.	...	...	...	.	...	.	.
Hungary	108	66	0.3	-1.3	21.5	0.6	0.7	5	8.9	1	55
Iceland	3	93	1.0	-0.3	0.5	4.3	3.9	.	5.6	.	17

Table 18. Environment, biodiversity and habitat

Country or Territory	Population density[1] (population per sq km)	% Urban population[2]	Population growth (% annual average)[2] Urban	Population growth (% annual average)[2] Rural	Forest area[3] % of total land	Forest area[3] Average annual variation 1990/2000	Forest area[3] Average annual variation 2000/2005	Number of Biosphere Reserves[4]	Protected terrestrial and marine area[5, a] (%)	Biodiversity[6, b] Plant species threatened	Biodiversity[6, b] Animal species threatened
	2005	2005	2000/2005	2000/2005	2005	1990/2000	2000/2005	2007	2005	2007	2007
Ireland	59	60	2.2	1.1	9.7	3.3	1.9	2	0.7	1	15
Israel	302	92	2.0	1.6	8.3	0.6	0.8	1	16.2	.	79
Italy	195	68	0.2	-0.1	33.9	1.2	1.1	8	12.5	19	119
Latvia	36	68	-0.6	-0.4	47.4	0.4	0.4	1	13.9	.	23
Liechtenstein	...	15	0.2	1.1	43.1	0.6	...	.	40.1	.	6
Lithuania	52	67	-0.5	-0.1	33.5	0.4	0.8	.	10.6	...	20
Luxembourg	177	83	1.1	2.4	33.5	0.1	...	.	17.0	.	7
Macedonia (TFYR)	79	69	1.4	-2.1	35.8	...	...	.	7.1	3	34
Malta	1,274	95	0.9	-6.3	1.1	...	...	.	1.4	.	20
Moldova (Rep.)	115	47	-0.1	-0.5	10.0	0.2	0.2	.	1.4	.	28
Monaco	...	100	1.1	.	...	...	...	.	25.5	.	10
Montenegro	44	...	...	...	...	...	...	1	14.6	.	49
Netherlands	393	80	1.4	-2.7	10.8	0.4	0.3	.	20.1[d]	2	32
Norway	12	77	0.9	-0.6	30.7	0.2	0.2	9	27.1	4	38
Poland	118	62	0.0	-0.2	30.0	0.2	0.3	3	5.0	16	147
Portugal	114	58	1.7	-0.9	41.3	1.5	1.1	3	5.1	1	64
Romania	91	54	-0.7	0.0	27.7	0	0	3	8.8	7	153
Russian Federation	8	73	-0.6	-0.2	47.9	0	0	39	...	.	...
San Marino	...	...	1.6	-16.0	1.6	...	...	.	3.8	1	42
Serbia[e]	112	52	0.2	-0.3	26.4	0.3	0.3	1	25.2	2	44
Slovakia	110	56	0.0	0.0	40.1	0	0.1	4	7.3	...	80
Slovenia	99	51	0.1	-0.1	62.8	0.4	0.4	2	7.7	3	30
Spain	86	77	1.2	0.7	35.9	2.0	1.7	38	9.2	49	170
Sweden	20	84	0.4	0.1	66.9	0	0	2	28.7	3	44
Switzerland	180	75	0.8	-1.3	30.9	0.4	0.4	2	3.9	3	121
Turkey	93	67	2.2	-0.1	13.2	0.4	0.2	1	3.4	1	58
Ukraine	78	68	-0.9	-1.5	16.5	0.3	0.1	6	3.4	13	38
United Kingdom	248	90	0.4	-0.4	11.8	0.7	0.4	9	13.2	13	38
North America											
Canada	3	80	1.2	0.3	33.6	...	...	15	6.8	1	77
United States of America	31	81	1.4	-0.7	33.1	0.1	0.1	47	23.2	242	937
Latin America and the Caribbean											
Anguilla	...	100	1.7	.	71.4	...	...	.	...	3	20
Antigua and Barbuda	...	39	2.2	0.7	21.4	...	...	.	0.9	4	22
Argentina	14	90	1.2	-0.8	12.1	-0.4	-0.4	13	6.2	42	152
Aruba	572	47	1.5	1.6	2.2	...	...	.	...	...	23
Bahamas	23	90	1.7	-1.6	51.5	...	...	.	0.9	5	37
Barbados	679	53	1.4	-0.9	4.0	...	...	.	0.1	2	20
Belize	12	48	2.4	1.9	72.5	...	...	.	30.4	30	44
Bermuda	...	100	0.4	.	20.0	...	...	.	...	4	43
Bolivia	8	64	2.7	0.7	54.2	-0.4	-0.5	3	19.8	71	80
Brazil	22	84	2.1	-2.1	57.2	-0.5	-0.6	6	18.7	382	343
British Virgin Islands	...	61	2.5	-0.2	24.4	-0.1	-0.1	.	...	10	24
Cayman Islands	...	100	2.5	.	48.4	...	...	.	...	2	22
Chile	22	88	1.5	-1.4	21.5	0.4	0.4	9	20.8	39	95
Colombia	39	73	2.0	0.5	58.5	-0.1	-0.1	5	31.6	222	382
Costa Rica	85	62	2.8	0.6	46.8	-0.8	0.1	3	23.3	111	131
Cuba	102	76	0.2	0.3	24.7	1.7	2.2	6	15.1	163	115
Dominica	...	73	0.8	-1.0	61.3	-0.5	-0.6	.	4.5	11	27
Dominican Republic	195	67	2.8	-1.0	28.4	...	...	1	32.6	30	81
Ecuador	46	63	2.3	0.2	39.2	-1.5	-1.7	4	53.5	1,838	340
El Salvador	317	60	2.3	1.2	14.4	-1.5	-1.7	2	0.9	26	29
Grenada	306	31	0.0	0.4	12.2	0	...	.	0.2	3	23
Guatemala	117	47	3.3	1.6	36.3	-1.2	-1.3	2	30.8	84	133
Guyana	3	28	-0.1	0.3	76.7	0	...	.	2.2	22	50
Haiti	335	39	3.1	0.4	3.8	-0.6	-0.7	.	0.1	29	91
Honduras	61	46	3.2	1.5	41.5	-3.0	-3.1	1	20.0	110	102
Jamaica	244	53	1.0	0.0	31.3	-0.1	-0.1	.	13.5	209	61
Mexico	53	76	1.7	0.3	33.7	-0.5	-0.4	35	8.7	261	579
Montserrat	...	14	6.9	2.2	35.0	...	...	.	...	4	23
Netherlands Antilles	233	70	1.1	0.1	1.5	...	...	.	...	2	26
Nicaragua	42	59	2.7	1.1	42.7	-1.6	-1.3	2	18.2	39	59
Panama	43	71	3.3	-1.3	57.7	-0.2	-0.1	2	24.6	194	121

Table 18. Environment, biodiversity and habitat

Country or Territory	Population density[1] (population per sq km)	% Urban population[2]	Population growth (% annual average)[2] Urban	Population growth (% annual average)[2] Rural	Forest area[3] % of total land	Forest area[3] Average annual variation 1990/2000	Forest area[3] Average annual variation 2000/2005	Number of Biosphere Reserves[4]	Protected terrestrial and marine area[5, a] (%)	Biodiversity[6, b] Plant species threatened	Biodiversity[6, b] Animal species threatened
	2005	2005	2000/2005		2005	1990/2000	2000/2005	2007	2005	2007	
Paraguay	15	58	3.5	0.9	46.5	-0.9	-0.9	2	5.8	10	39
Peru	21	73	1.8	0.8	53.7	-0.1	-0.1	3	13.3	274	238
Saint Kitts and Nevis	...	32	0.7	1.3	14.7	...	...	.	9.7	2	23
Saint Lucia	299	28	0.5	0.9	27.9	...	...	.	2.4	6	27
Saint Vincent and the Grenadines	307	46	1.2	0.0	27.4	0.8	0.8	.	1.3	5	25
Suriname	3	74	1.2	-0.7	94.7	...	...	.	11.5	26	40
Trinidad and Tobago	258	12	2.7	0.0	44.1	-0.3	-0.2	.	1.8	1	38
Turks and Caicos Islands	...	44	6.3	5.9	80.0	...	...	.	...	2	21
Uruguay	19	92	0.9	-0.8	8.6	4.5	1.3	.	0.4	1	66
Venezuela	29	93	2.3	-4.2	54.1	-0.6	-0.6	1	62.9	68	166
Pacific											
Australia	3	88	1.3	-0.6	21.3	-0.2	-0.1	14	17.5	55	568
Cook Islands	...	70	0.6	-4.2	66.5	0.4	...	.	...	1	25
Fiji	45	51	1.9	-0.1	54.7	0.2	...	.	0.3	66	35
Kiribati	...	47	4.0	0.4	3.0	...	...	.	1.5	...	13
Marshall Islands	...	67	3.7	3.0	...	...	...	.	0.7	...	15
Micronesia (Fed. States)	157	22	0.6	0.6	90.6	...	...	2	0.1	5	31
Nauru	...	100	2.2	.	...	...	...	.	...	...	7
New Zealand	15	86	1.2	0.3	31.0	0.6	0.2	.	19.6	21	124
Niue	...	37	-0.4	-3.1	54.2	-1.3	-1.4	.	...	1	15
Palau	...	70	0.7	0.6	87.6	0.4	0.4	.	0.4	4	22
Papua New Guinea	13	13	2.4	2.1	65.0	-0.5	-0.5	1	3.6	142	158
Samoa	65	22	1.3	0.7	60.4	2.8	...	.	1.8	2	20
Solomon Islands	16	17	4.2	2.3	77.6	-1.5	-1.7	.	0.2	16	61
Tokelau	...	0	.	-0.3	...	...	...	.	...	...	7
Tonga	153	24	1.1	0.2	5.0	...	...	.	27.8	4	17
Tuvalu	...	48	1.4	-0.3	33.3	...	...	.	0.1	.	10
Vanuatu	18	23	3.5	1.5	36.1	...	...	.	0.2	10	25
World	**48**	**49**	**2.0**	**0.4**	**30.3**	**-0.22**	**-0.18**	**529**	**11.6**	**8,447b**	**7,850b**

Sources:

1. United Nations, Department of Economic and Social Affairs, Population Division, 2007. World Population Prospects: The 2006 Revision.

2. United Nations, Department of Economic and Social Affairs, Population Division, 2006. World Urbanization Prospects: The 2005 Revision.

3. Food and Agriculture Organization of the United Nations, 2006. Global Forest Resources Assessment 2005. http://www.fao.org/forestry

4. UNESCO List of Biosphere Reserves: http://www.unesco.org/mab/wnbrs.shtml. Last updated October 2007.

5. United Nations, 2006. Millenium Development Goals. Target 7.A — Indicator 26: Ratio of area protected to maintain biological diversity to surface area. http://millenniumindicators.un.org. Last Updated July 2006 from UNEP-WCMC data.

6. International Union for Conservation of Nature, 2007. IUCN Red List of Threatened Species. http://www.iucn.org

Notes:

a. The World Conservation Union (IUCN) defines a protected area as an area of land and/or sea especially dedicated to the protection and maintenance of biological diversity, and of natural and associated cultural resources, and managed through legal or other effective means. The total protected area extent by country/territory is divided by total territorial area of the country/territory (includes total land area, inland waters and territorial waters up to 12 nautical miles).

b. Threatened species are those listed as Critically Endangered, Endangered or Vulnerable. Species assessed to date amount to 41,415 worldwide. The total number of species on the planet is unknown; estimates vary between 10 and 100 million, with 15 million species being the most widely accepted figure; 1.7 to 1.8 million species are known today. World total does not add up for the sum of all individual country figures since species can be threatened in multiple locations.

c. Including Greenland.

d. Including Svalbard, Jan Mayen and Bouvet Islands.

e. Data refer to Serbia and Montenegro, except for population density, number of biosphere reserves and threatened species.

... Data not available

. Not applicable

+n Data refer to the year n years after the reference year

-n Data refer to the year n years before the reference year

Table 19. Economic development and innovation

Country or Territory	GDP per capita[1,a]	ODA (Official Development Assistance)[2,b]		Life expectancy at birth[3]	Population below poverty lines (%)[4]		Income inequality[5]	Unemploy. Rate[6]	R&D expenditure[7]	Researchers in R&D[7]	Innovation[8]	Scientific articles[9,c]	
	PPP	Net receipt (US$ Million)	ODA/GNI	Years	$1.25 a day	$2 a day	richest 10% to poorest 10%[d]	%	% of GDP	per million inhabitants	Scores[cc]	per million inhabitants	% intl. co-authored
	2005	2006	2006	2000–2005		1992–2006[e]		2005	2007	2007	2008	2005	2005
Arab States													
Algeria	...	209	0.2	71.0	6.8	23.6	10[i]	15.3	0.07[-2,±]	170[-2,±]	3.48	11	...
Bahrain	27,236	...[g]	...[g]	74.8	...	...	...	5.2[-4]	...	...	4.20	...[u]	...
Djibouti	1,964	117	14.0	53.4	18.8	41.2	...	...	...	...	1.29	...[u]	...
Egypt	5,049	873	0.8	69.8	<2	18.4	8[i]	10.7[-1]	0.23[±]	654[±]	4.55	23	...
Iraq	3,200	8,661	...	57.0	...	...	11[i]	...	...	...[-4,o]	...	...	...
Jordan	4,294	580	3.9	71.3	<2	3.5	11[i]	12.4[-1]	0.34[-5]	3,052[-4,o]	5.66	50	...
Kuwait	44,947	...	...	76.9	...	...	...	1.7[-1]	0.08[-1,±]	166[±,x]	5.05	58	...
Lebanon	10,212	707	3.2	71.0	...	...	...	...	...	...	4.69	...[u]	...
Libyan Arab Jamahiriya	...	37[g]	0.1[g]	72.7	...	...	12[i]	...	...	...	1.75	...[u]	...
Mauritania	1,691	188	6.8	62.3	21.2	44.1	12[i]	...	...	...	3.67	15	...
Morocco	3,547	1,046	1.8	69.6	2.5	14.0	12[i]	11.0	0.64[-1]	910[-1,±,o]	4.95	44	...
Oman	20,334	35	...	74.2	...	...	...	...	...	...	...	...	...
Palestinian A.T.	...	1,449	34.6	72.4	...	...	...	26.8[-1]	...	...	5.77	...[u]	...
Qatar	68,696	...	...	74.3	...	...	...	3.9[-4]	...	...	4.04	24	...
Saudi Arabia	21,220	25	...	71.6	...	...	...	5.2[-3]	0.05[±]	41[±,o,x]	1.97	...[u]	...
Sudan	2,249	2,058	6.0	56.4	...	...	...	12.3[-2]	0.29[-2]	304[-2,o]	3.44	4	...
Syrian Arab Republic	4,059	27	0.1	73.0	...	...	13[i]	14.2	1.02[-2]	1,550[-1,s]	4.58	57	...
Tunisia	6,461	432	1.5	73.0	2.6	12.8	...	...	...	...	6.74	56	...
United Arab Emirates	...	...	...	77.8	...	...	...	2.3[-5]	...	...	1.68	...[u]	...
Yemen	2,276	284	1.6	60.3	17.5	46.6	9[i]	11.5[-6]	...	...	...	...	...
Sub-Saharan Africa											2.44	...[u]	
Angola	3,533	171	0.4	41.0	45.3	70.2	...	...	...	111[±]	2.33	...[u]	...
Benin	1,390	375	8.0	54.4	47.3	75.3	9[i]	23.8[-2]	0.38[-2,s]	941[-2,±,o]	4.34	...[u]	...
Botswana	12,057	65	0.7	46.6	31.2	49.4	43[j]	2.4[-7]	0.11[±,x]	12[±,x]	2.15	...[u]	...
Burkina Faso	1,140	871	14.0	50.6	56.5	81.2	12[i]	...	...	...	...	...[u]	...
Burundi	...	415	52.8	47.4	81.3	93.4	19[i]	7.5[-4]	...	26[-2,±]	2.49	7	...
Cameroon	1,995	1,684	9.3	49.9	32.8	57.7	16[i]	...	...	127[-5,±]	2.25	...[u]	...
Cape Verde	2,831	138	12.6	70.2	20.6	40.2	...	...	...	9[±]	...	...[u]	...
Central African Republic	675	134	9.0	43.3	62.4	81.9	69[i]	...	...	...	...	...[u]	...
Chad	1,749	284	5.5	50.5	61.9	83.3	...	...	...	...	...	...[u]	...
Comoros	1,063	30	7.6	63.0	46.1	65.0	...	...	...	...	...	...[u]	...
Congo	3,621	254	...	53.0	54.1	74.4	...	...	...	32[-7,±]	...	...[u]	...
Congo (Dem. Rep.)	264	2,056	25.2	45.0	59.2	79.5	...	...	0.48[-2,±,s]	177[-2,±,o]	...	...[u]	...
Côte d'Ivoire	1,575	251	1.6	46.8	23.3	46.8	17[i]	4.1[-7]	...	68[-2,±]	2.52	...[u]	...
Equatorial Guinea	11,999	27	0.5	49.4	...	...	...	...	...	...	1.56	...[u]	...
Eritrea	...	129	12.0	55.2	...	...	...	...	0.17[±]	19[±]	1.57	1	...
Ethiopia	591	1,947	14.7	50.7	39.0	77.5	7[i]	5.4	...	114[-1,±,o]	...	...[u]	...
Gabon	12,742	31	0.4	56.8	4.8	19.6	...	...	...	28[-2,±]	...	...[u]	...
Gambia	726	74	14.8	58.0	34.3	56.7	20[i]	...	...	...	2.08	4	...
Ghana	1,225	1,176	9.2	58.5	30.0	53.6	14[i]	10.1[-6]	...	258[-7,o]	...	...[u]	...
Guinea	946	164	5.0	53.7	70.1	87.2	11[i]	...	...	...	...	...[u]	...
Guinea-Bissau	569	82	27.9	45.5	48.8	77.9	19[i]	...	...	...	...	...[u]	...
Kenya	1,359	943	4.5	51.0	19.7	39.9	14[i]	9.8[-6]	...	...	3.87	6	...
Lesotho	1,415	72	4.0	44.6	43.4	62.2	105[i]	39.3[-8]	0.06[-3,±]	10[-3,±]	2.70	...[u]	...
Liberia	383	269	54.4	43.8	83.7	94.8	...	...	...	...	...	...[u]	...
Madagascar	988	754	13.9	57.3	67.8	89.6	19[i]	5.0[-2]	0.14[±]	48[±]	2.54	...[u]	...
Malawi	691	669	30.5	45.0	73.9	90.4	11[i]	0.9[-7]	...	...	2.11	...[u]	...
Mali	1,027	825	13.4	51.8	51.4	77.1	13[i]	8.8[-1]	...	43[-1,±]	1.69	...[u]	...
Mauritius	10,155	19	0.3	72.0	...	...	...	9.6	0.38[-2,s]	...	3.70	...[u]	...
Mozambique	743	1,611	23.2	44.0	74.7	90.0	19[i]	...	0.50[-5,s]	16[-1,±,o,x]	1.86	...[u]	...
Namibia	4,547	145	2.3	51.5	49.1	62.2	129	31.1[-4]	...	...	3.30	...[u]	...
Niger	613	401	11.0	54.5	65.9	85.6	46[i]	...	...	8[-2]	...	...[u]	...
Nigeria	1,892	11,434	11.1	46.6	64.4	83.9	18[i]	0.6[-9]	...	202[-2,±,o]	2.72	3	...
Rwanda	813	585	23.6	43.4	76.6	90.3	19[i]	18.0[-7]	...	...	1.47	...[u]	...
Saint Helena	...	28	...	...	...	...	...	14.4[-5]	...	...	...	...[u]	...
Sao Tome and Principe	1,460	22	17.9	64.3	...	...	...	...	0.09[-2,±,*]	265[±,*]	2.77	7	...
Senegal	1,676	825	9.3	61.6	33.5	60.3	12[i]	...	0.38[-2,±]	157[-2,±]	...	...[u]	...
Seychelles	...	14	2.0	72.7[h,k]	...	...	...	...	...	...	...	...[u]	...
Sierra Leone	790	364	25.7	41.0	53.4	76.1	87[i,j]	...	...	...	1.70	...[u]	...
Somalia	...	392	...	45.9	...	...	...	...	...	...	...	...[u]	...
South Africa	8,477	718	0.3	53.4	26.2	42.9	33[i]	26.7	0.92[-2]	361[-2]	6.92	50	36
Swaziland	4,384	35	1.3	43.9	62.9	81.0	25	25.2[-8]	...	...	4.55	...[u]	...
Tanzania (United Rep.)	1,018	1,825	14.5	49.6	88.5	96.6	9[i]	5.1[-4]	...	...	2.39	3	...
Togo	888	79	3.6	57.6	38.7	69.3	...	...	...	33[±,x]	...	...[u]	...
Uganda	991	1,551	16.9	47.8	51.5	75.6	17[i]	3.2[-2]	0.41	29[o]	2.72	3	...

Table 19. Economic development and innovation

Country or Territory	GDP per capita[1,a] PPP 2005	ODA (Official Development Assistance)[2,b] Net receipt (US$ Million) 2006	ODA/GNI 2006	Life expectancy at birth[3] Years 2000–2005	Population below poverty lines (%)[4] $1.25 a day 1992–2006[e]	Population below poverty lines (%)[4] $2 a day 1992–2006[e]	Income inequality[5] richest 10% to poorest 10%[d] 1992–2006[e]	Unemploy. Rate[6] % 2005	R&D expenditure[7] % of GDP 2007	Researchers in R&D[7] per million inhabitants 2007	Innovation[8] Scores[cc] 2008	Scientific articles[9,c] per million inhabitants 2005	Scientific articles[9,c] % intl. co-authored 2005
Zambia	1,175	1,425	14.3	39.2	64.3	81.5	32[i]	12.0[-7]	0.03[-2,±]	69[-2,±,o]	2.37	...[u]	...
Zimbabwe	538	280	...	40.0	83.0	...	22[i]	8.2[-3]			4.09	...[u]	...
Central and South Asia													
Afghanistan	...	3,000	35.7	42.1	...	...	...	8.5			...	...[u]	...
Armenia	3,903	213	3.3	71.4	10.6	43.4	8[i]	36.4[-8]	0.21[±]	1,370[±,o]	6.17	60	...
Azerbaijan	4,648	206	1.2	66.8	<2	<2	10[i]	8.6	0.18	1,332[o]	3.05	14	...
Bangladesh	1,268	1,223	1.9	62.0	49.6	81.3[aa]	8[i]	4.3[-2]	...	42[-8,o]	1.71	1	...
Bhutan	3,694	94	10.2	63.5	26.2	49.5	...	...	...	...	...	...[u]	...
Georgia	3,505	361	4.9	70.5	13.4	30.4	15[i]	13.8	0.18[-2]	1,813[-2,o]	5.38	32	...
India	2,126	1,379	0.2	62.9	41.6	75.6[bb]	9[i]	5.0[-1]	0.69[-3,*]	111[-7]	3.97	13	13
Iran (Islamic Rep.)	10,692	121	0.1	69.5	<2	8.0	17[i]	11.5	0.67[-1]	965[-1,o]	3.02	38	...
Kazakhstan	8,699	172	0.3	64.9	3.1	17.2	9[i]	8.4[-1]	0.21	747[o]	3.77	6	...
Kyrgyzstan	1,728	311	11.8	65.3	21.8	51.9	6[i]	8.5[-1]	0.25	383[o]	2.70	...[u]	...
Maldives	4,017	39	4.4	65.6	...	...	...	2.0[-5]	...	...	2.33	...[u]	...
Nepal	1,081	514	6.3	61.3	55.1	77.6	16[i]	8.8[-4]	...	59[-5,*]	2.04	...[u]	...
Pakistan	2,396	2,147	1.7	63.6	22.6	60.3	7[i]	7.7	0.67	161	2.75	3	...
Sri Lanka	3,481	796	3.0	70.8	14.0	39.7	11[i]	7.6	0.18[-3]	141[-3,x]	4.44	7	...
Tajikistan	1,413	240	8.8	65.9	21.5	50.8	8[i]	...	0.06	191[o]	2.33	...[u]	...
Turkmenistan	...	26	0.3	62.4	24.8	49.6	12[i]	...	...	...	...	...[u]	...
Uzbekistan	...	149	0.9	66.5	46.3	76.7	11[i]	...	...	...	3.51	6	...
East Asia													
Brunei Darussalam	47,465	...	...	76.3	...	...	...	...	0.04[-3,±,x]	279[-3,±,x]	...	...[u]	...
Cambodia	1,453	529	7.7	56.8	40.2	68.2	12[i]	1.7[-4]	0.05[-5,±,**]	17[-5,±,*]	...	...[u]	...
China	4,091	1,245	0.0	72.0	15.9	36.3[bb]	22	4.2	1.49	1,071	5.12	32[v]	15
Hong Kong (SAR China)	35,680	...	...	81.5	...	...	18	5.6	0.81[-1]	2,569[-1]	8.64	.[v]	...
Macao (SAR China)	37,256	...	...	80.0	...	...	...	4.1	0.11[-2,±,*]	631[-2,±,*]	...	...	...
Indonesia	3,234	1,405	0.4	68.6	21.4	53.8[bb]	8[i]	10.3	0.05[-2,±,x]	199[-6,y]	3.32	1	...
Japan	30,290	...	...	81.9	...	...	5	4.4	3.40[-1]	5,546[-1]	9.15	434	14
Korea (Dem. People's Rep.)	...	55	...	66.7	...	...	...	...	...	...	...	...[u]	...
Korea (Rep.)	21,342	...	...	77.0	...	...	8	3.7	3.22[-1,±]	4,162[-1,±]	8.47	343	17
Lao (People's Dem. Rep.)	1,811	364	12.1	61.9	44.0	76.8[aa]	8[i]	1.4	...	...	1.43	...[u]	...
Malaysia	11,466	240	0.2	73.0	<2	7.8	22	3.5[-1]	0.64[-1]	371[-1]	6.83	24	...
Mongolia	2,643	203	7.8	65.0	22.4	49.0	8[i]	14.2[-2]	0.23[±]	662[±,o]	2.06	...[u]	...
Myanmar	...	147	...	59.9	...	...	...	...	0.16[-5,±,**]	18[-5,±]	1.17	...[u]	...
Philippines	2,932	562	0.4	70.3	22.6	45.0	16[i]	7.4	0.12[-2]	82[-2]	3.63	2	...
Singapore	41,479	...	...	78.8	...	...	18	4.2	2.31[-1]	5,713[-1]	9.56	834	27
Thailand	6,869	-216	-0.1	68.6	<2	11.5	13[i]	1.3	0.25[-1,*]	325[-2]	5.98	20	...
Timor-Leste	...	210	24.7	58.3	52.9	77.5	...	...	...	...	...	...	...
Viet Nam	2,142	1,846	3.1	73.0	21.5	48.4	7[i]	2.1[-1]	0.19[-5]	115[-5]	2.83	3	...
Europe													
Albania	5,369	321	3.4	75.7	<2	7.8	7[i]	14.4[-1]	...	...	3.10	...[u]	...
Andorra	...	...	...	...	...	...	...	...	...	...	...	...[u]	...
Austria	34,108	...	...	78.9	...	...	7	5.2	2.52[*]	3,750[*]	8.90	551	47
Belarus	8,541	73[g]	0.2[g]	68.4	<2	<2	7[i]	...	0.97[p]	1,961[o]	5.54	50	...
Belgium	32,077	...	...	78.2	...	...	8	8.1	1.91[p]	3,437[p]	8.96	658	47
Bosnia and Herzegovina	6,506	494	4.2	74.1	<2	<2	5[i]	...	...	...	3.29	...	...
Bulgaria	9,353	...	...	72.4	<2	<2	7[i]	10.1	0.48	1,467	6.43	99	...
Croatia	13,232	200	0.5	74.9	<2	<2	7[i]	12.7	0.93	1,345	7.54	209	...
Cyprus	24,473	...	...	79.0	...	...	...	5.3	0.45[p]	1,021[p]	7.65	108	...
Czech Republic	20,281	...	...	75.4	<2	<2	5	7.9	1.59	2,737	7.60	311	41
Denmark	33,626	...	...	77.3	...	...	8	4.8	2.57[*]	5,434[*]	9.57	930	42
Estonia	16,654	...	...	70.9	<2	<2	11[i]	7.9	1.12[p]	2,763[p]	7.49	327	...
Finland	30,469	...	...	78.4	...	...	6	8.4	3.47	7,391	9.66	917	35
France	29,644	...	...	79.6	...	...	9	9.8	2.10[p]	3,443[-1]	8.61	497	36
Germany	30,496	...	...	78.7	...	...	7	11.1	2.54[*]	3,462[*]	9.00	534	34
Gibraltar	...	...	...	...	...	...	...	...	...	...	...	...	...
Greece	25,520	...	...	78.3	...	...	10	9.6	0.50[*]	1,868[*]	7.63	387	27
Holy See	...	...	...	...	...	...	...	...	...	...	...	...[u]	...
Hungary	17,014	...	...	72.4	<2	<2	6[i]	7.2	0.97	1,734	8.14	259	44
Iceland	35,630	...	...	81.0	...	...	...	2.6	2.78[-2]	7,287[-2]	7.98	697	...
Ireland	38,058	...	...	77.8	...	...	9	4.3	1.34[p]	2,883[-1,p]	9.04	512	39
Israel	23,845	...	...	79.7	...	...	13	9.0	4.74[r,p]	...	9.34	943	31
Italy	27,750	...	...	79.9	...	...	12	7.7	1.14[-1]	1,504[-1]	8.04	420	29
Latvia	13,218	...	...	71.3	<2	<2	12[i]	8.7	0.63	1,855	6.40	58	...

Table 19. Economic development and innovation

Country or Territory	GDP per capita[1,a] PPP	ODA (Official Development Assistance)[2,b] Net receipt (US$ Million)	ODA/ GNI	Life expectancy at birth[3] Years	Population below poverty lines (%)[4] $1.25 a day	Population below poverty lines (%)[4] $2 a day	Income inequality[5] richest 10% to poorest 10%[d]	Unemploy. Rate[6] %	R&D expenditure[7] % of GDP	Researchers in R&D[7] per million inhabitants	Innovation[8] Scores[cc]	Scientific articles[9,c] per million inhabitants	Scientific articles[9,c] % intl. co-authored
	2005	2006		2000–2005	1992–2006[e]			2005	2007	2007	2008	2005	2005
Liechtenstein	...	...	...	...	...	...	...	...	...	...	...	...[u]	...
Lithuania	14,085	...	...	72.0	<2	<2	10[i]	8.3	0.83	2,504	6.59	119	...
Luxembourg	70,014	...	...	78.2	...	...	...	4.5	1.69[p]	4,660[p]	8.91	129	...
Macedonia (TFYR)	7,393	200	3.2	73.4	<2	3.2	13[i]	37.3	0.21[-1]	522[-1]	4.76	...[u]	...
Malta	20,410	...[f]	...[f]	78.6	...	...	...	7.5	0.60[p]	1,267[p]		57	...
Moldova (Rep.)	2,362	228	6.0	67.9	8.1	28.9	8[i]	7.3	0.55[±]	689[±,o]	4.39	23	...
Monaco	...	...	...	...	...	...	...	...	...	308[±,o,**]	...	...[u]	...
Montenegro	7,833	96	4.1	74.0	...	...	...	...	1.18	1,092[o]	...	...	...
Netherlands	34,724	...	...	78.7	...	...	9	5.2	1.75[p]	2,687[p]	9.48	850	36
Norway	47,551	...	...	79.3	...	...	6	4.6	1.68	5,213[x]	9.06	786	39
Poland	13,573	...	...	74.6	<2	<2	9[i]	17.7	0.56[-1]	1,562[-1]	6.92	179	35
Portugal	20,006	...	...	77.2	...	...	15	7.6	1.19[p]	2,635[p]	7.43	276	40
Romania	9,374	...	...	71.3	<2	3.4	8[i]	7.2	0.54	877	5.66	41	...
Russian Federation	11,861	...	...	64.8	<2	<2	13[i]	7.9[-1]	1.12	3,292	6.89	100	29
San Marino	...	...	...	...	...	...	...	...	...	...	...	...[u]	...
Serbia	8,609	1,586	5.0	73.2	...	...	...	15.2[-2,z]	1.50[-1,q,±]	1,627[-1,±,o]	4.85[z]	86	...
Slovakia	15,881	...	...	73.8	<2	<2	7	16.2	0.46	2,292	6.86	171	...
Slovenia	23,004	...[f]	...[f]	76.8	<2	<2	6[i]	5.8	1.57[p]	3,223[p]	8.31	518	...
Spain	27,270	...	...	80.0	...	...	10	9.2	1.28	2,769	8.14	423	28
Sweden	31,995	...	...	80.1	...	...	6	7.7	3.71[p]	4,855[b,x]	9.79	1,108	38
Switzerland	35,520	...	...	80.7	...	...	9	4.4	2.93[-3]	3,436[-3]	9.89	1,178	50
Turkey	7,786	570	0.1	70.8	2.7	9.0	17[i]	10.3	0.58[-1]	577[-1]	5.67	107	11
Ukraine	5,583	484[g]	0.5[g]	67.6	<2	<2	6[i]	7.2	0.87	1,706[o]	5.77	45	39
United Kingdom	31,580	...	...	78.5	...	...	14	4.6	1.80[-1]	3,033[-1,w]	9.18	756	31
North America													
Canada	35,078	...	...	79.8	...	...	9	6.8	2.03[p]	4,162[-2,p,*]	9.43	801	29
United States of America	41,674	...	...	77.4	...	...	16	5.1	2.67[p,t]	4,629[-2,w]	9.45	685	16
Latin America and the Caribbean													
Anguilla	...	4	...	...	...	...	...	7.8[-3]	...	...	...	...	...
Antigua and Barbuda	...	3	0.4	73.9[h,l]	...	...	...	...	...	...	...	...[u]	...
Argentina	11,063	114	0.1	74.3	4.5	11.3	41	10.6	0.51	978	6.85	79	34
Aruba	...	...	...	73.5	...	...	...	7.5[-8]	...	...	...	...[u]	...
Bahamas	...	...	...	71.1	...	...	...	10.2	...	...	...	...[u]	...
Barbados	...	-1	...	76.0	...	...	...	9.8[-1]	...	...	7.51	...[u]	...
Belize	...	8	0.7	75.6	...	...	...	11.0	...	...	...	...[u]	...
Bermuda	...	...	...	...	...	...	...	...	0.08[-8]	...	...	...	...
Bolivia	3,618	581	5.4	63.9	19.6	30.3	168	5.4[-3]	0.28[-5]	120[-5]	3.05	...[u]	...
Brazil	8,596	82	0.0	71.0	7.8	18.3	51	8.9[-1]	1.02[-1]	625[-1]	6.07	53	22
British Virgin Islands	...	...	...	...	...	...	...	...	...	...	...	...	...
Cayman Islands	...	...	...	...	...	...	...	4.1[-8]	...	...	...	...	...
Chile	12,262	83	0.1	77.9	<2	5.3	33	6.9	0.67[-3]	833[-3]	6.81	96	...
Colombia	6,306	988	0.8	71.7	15.4	26.3	64	9.5	0.18[-1]	145[-1]	4.26	9	...
Costa Rica	...	24	0.1	78.1	2.4	8.6	38	6.6	0.37[-3]	122[-2]	6.24	24	...
Cuba	...	78	...	77.2	...	...	...	1.9[-1]	0.41[-1,**]	465[n,o]	...	23	...
Dominica	...	19	7.0	75.6[h,m]	...	...	...	10.9[-4]	...	...	3.76	...[u]	...
Dominican Republic	...	53	0.2	70.8	5.0	15.1	29	17.9	...	...	2.91	...[u]	...
Ecuador	6,533	189	0.5	74.2	9.8	20.4	45[i]	7.7	0.15	69	3.55	...[u]	...
El Salvador	...	157	0.9	70.7	14.3	25.3	58	6.8[-1]	0.08[-9]	40[o]	3.19	...[u]	...
Grenada	...	27	5.6	67.8	...	...	...	15.2[-7]	...	...	...	...[u]	...
Guatemala	...	487	1.4	69.0	12.7	23.7	48	3.4[-2]	0.05[-1]	25[-1]	2.47	...[u]	...
Guyana	...	173	20.1	63.6	7.7	16.8	...	9.1[-4]	...	...	4.47	...[u]	...
Haiti	...	581	13.4	58.1	54.9	72.1	72	7.2[-6]	...	...	1.15	...[u]	...
Honduras	...	587	6.6	68.6	22.2	34.8	34	4.2	0.04[-3]	82[-4,o]	3.30	...[u]	...
Jamaica	...	37	0.4	72.0	<2	5.8	17[i]	10.9	0.08[-5]	...	5.36	...[u]	...
Mexico	11,317	247	0.0	74.9	<2	4.8	25[i]	3.5	0.50[-2]	464[-2]	5.82	37	32
Montserrat	...	32	...	...	...	...	...	...	...	...	...	...	...
Netherlands Antilles	...	...	...	75.0	...	...	...	15.1[-2]	...	...	...	...	...
Nicaragua	...	733	13.9	70.8	15.8	31.8	16[i]	8.0[-2]	0.05[-5]	60[-3,o]	1.99	...[u]	...
Panama	...	30	0.2	74.7	9.2	18.0	58	10.3	0.25[-2]	62[-3,x]	5.45	...[u]	...
Paraguay	3,900	56	0.6	70.8	9.3	18.4	65	7.9[-2]	0.09[-2]	71[-2]	3.47	...[u]	...
Peru	6,466	468	0.5	69.9	8.2	19.4	30	11.4	0.15[-3]	184[-3,o]	3.88	5	...
Saint Kitts and Nevis	...	5	1.2	70.0[h,l]	...	...	...	...	...	...	...	...[u]	...
Saint Lucia	...	18	2.2	72.5	20.9	40.6	...	24.8[-2]	0.41[-6,s]	489[-6,o]	...	...[u]	...
Saint Vincent and the Grenadines	...	5	1.0	70.6	...	...	...	...	0.15[-5]	179[-5,o]	...	...[u]	...

Table 19. Economic development and innovation

Country or Territory	GDP per capita[1,a] PPP	ODA (Official Development Assistance)[2,b] Net receipt (US$ Million)	ODA/GNI	Life expectancy at birth[3] Years	Population below poverty lines (%)[4] $1.25 a day	$2 a day	Income inequality[5] richest 10% to poorest 10%[d]	Unemploy. Rate[6] %	R&D expenditure[7] % of GDP	Researchers in R&D[7] per million inhabitants	Innovation[8] Scores[cc]	Scientific articles[9,c] per million inhabitants	% intl. co-authored
	2005	2006		2000–2005	1992–2006[e]			2005	2007	2007	2008	2005	2005
Suriname	...	64	4.1	69.1	15.5	27.2	...	13.8[-6]	...	...	...	...u	...
Trinidad and Tobago	...	13	0.1	69.0	4.2	13.5	13	8.0	0.10[-1]	519[-1,o]	6.02	...u	...
Turks and Caicos Islands	...	0	...	...	...	...	...	...	...	...	...	...	...
Uruguay	9,266	21	0.1	75.3	<2	4.5	18	12.2	0.36[-1]	373[-5]	5.26	61	...
Venezuela	9,876	58	0.0	72.8	18.4	31.7	48	15.0[-1]	0.34[-2,s]	189[±,o]	5.73	20	...
Pacific													
Australia	32,798	...	...	80.4	...	...	13	5.1	2.17[-1]	4,251[-1]	8.72	786	28
Cook Islands	...	32	...	...	...	...	...	...	...	...	...	...u	...
Fiji	4,209	56	2.0	67.8	...	...	...	...	...	...	...	...u	...
Kiribati	...	-45	-37.6	...	...	...	...	...	...	...	...	...u	...
Marshall Islands	...	55	28.5	...	...	...	...	25.4	...	...	...	...u	...
Micronesia (Fed. States)	...	109	41.3	67.6	...	...	...	...	...	...	...	...u	...
Nauru	...	17	...	...	...	...	...	...	...	...	...	...u	...
New Zealand	24,554	...	...	79.2	...	...	13	3.7	1.17[-2]	4,207[-2]	8.65	728	35
Niue	...	9	...	...	...	...	...	...	...	...	...	...	...
Palau	...	37	23.5	...	...	...	...	...	...	...	...	...u	...
Papua New Guinea	...	279	5.5	56.6	35.8	57.4	24[j]	2.8[-5]	...	...	...	...u	...
Samoa	...	47	11.3	70.0	...	...	...	...	...	...	...	...u	...
Solomon Islands	...	205	60.6	62.3	...	...	...	...	...	...	...	...u	...
Tokelau	...	11	...	...	...	...	...	...	...	...	...	...	...
Tonga	...	21	9.6	72.3	...	...	...	...	...	...	...	...u	...
Tuvalu	...	15	...	...	...	...	...	...	...	...	...	...u	...
Vanuatu	...	49	13.6	68.4	...	...	...	...	...	...	...	...u	...
World	8,971	...	...	66.0	...	...	...	...	...	...	8.01	109	...

Sources:

1. World Bank, 2008. 2005 International Comparison Program. http://go.worldbank.org/VMCB80AB40
2. OECD, 2008. Development Co-operation Report 2007. Table 25. ODA Receipts and Selected Indicators for Developing Countries and Territories.
3. United Nations, Department of Economic and Social Affairs, Population Division, 2007. World Population Prospects: The 2006 Revision.
4. World Bank, 2008. World Development Indicators. http://siteresources.worldbank.org/DATASTATISTICS/Resources/WDI08supplement1216.pdf
5. World Bank, 2007. World Bank Indicators Database. http://www.worldbank.org/data
6. ILO (International Labour Organization), 2008. Key Indicators of the Labour Market. 5th Edition. http://www.ilo.org/kilm
7. UNESCO Institute for Statistics, Science & Technology Database, 2007.
8. World Bank Institute, Knowledge Assessment Methodology, 2009. http://www.worldbank.org/kam
9. National Science Foundation, 2008. Science and Engineering Indicators 2008 (for articles figures); UN (United Nations, 2007. World Population Prospects: The 2006 Revision (for population figures).

Notes:

a. Population estimates for 'GDP per capita' are those provided by national authorities participating in the International Comparison Program.
b. ODA receipts are total net ODA flows from DAC (Development Assistance Committee) countries, multilateral organizations and non-DAC countries.
c. Articles are counted from set of journals covered by Science Citation Index (SCI) and Social Sciences Citation Index (SSCI). Articles are classified by year of publication and assigned to region/country/economy on basis of institutional address(es) listed in the articles. For articles on fractional-count basis, i.e. for articles with collaborating institutions from multiple countries/economies, each country/territory receives fractional credit on the basis of the proportion of its participating institutions. Percentage of international co-authorship is based on the assumption that when co-authored articles involve two countries, each country has been given a 0,5 count.
d. Data show the ratio of income or expenditure share of the richest group to that of the poorest. Because the underlying household surveys differ in method and in the type of data collected, the distribution data are not strictly comparable across countries.
e. Latest available year.
f. These countries left the DAC List of ODA Recipients on 1 January 2003.
g. These countries left (no data) or joined the DAC List of ODA Recipients on 1 January 2005.
h. Data refer to a year other than that specified.
i. Data refer to expenditure by percentiles of population, ranked by expenditure per capita.
j. Refers to 1989.

k. Data are from national sources.
l. Data are from the Secretariat of the Organization of Eastern Caribbean States, based on national sources.
m. Data are from the Secretariat of the Caribbean Community, based on national sources.
n. Underestimated or based on underestimated data.
o. Based on headcount instead of full-time equivalent.
p. Provisional.
q. Data exclude Kosovo.
r. Defence excluded (all or mostly).
s. Overestimated or based on overestimated data.
t. Excludes most or entire capital expenditure.
u. This country/territory is included in the index of scientific articles, but the number of articles published is not available since it accounted for less than 0.01% of the world share.
v. Publications from Hong Kong, SAR (China) are included in China.
w. OECD estimation.
x. Break in series.
y. Based on regional publication.
z. Refers to Serbia and Montenegro combined.
aa. Adjusted by spatial consumer price index information.
bb. Weighted average of urban and rural estimates.
cc. Three variables of the innovation system are scaled by population (the weighted innovation variables).
... Data not available
* National estimation
** UIS estimation
0 Magnitude negligible (less than half the last decimal shown)
. Not applicable
± Partial data
+n Data refer to the year n years after the reference year
-n Data refer to the year n years before the reference year

Glossary

Normative and institutional framework

Table 1. Ratifications of the seven cultural conventions of UNESCO
Ratification year of Convention per Member State: Year of ratification, acceptance or accession by States to these conventions. The Director-General of UNESCO is usually appointed as the depositary for such instruments. However, this responsibility may also be vested in the Secretary-General of the United Nations. This is particularly the case when the instrument has been adopted under the joint auspices of UNESCO and of one or more other organizations.

Table 2. World Heritage sites and Intangible Cultural Heritage of Humanity
Endangered site: Property appearing in the World Heritage List for the conservation of which major operations are necessary and for which assistance has been requested under this Convention.

Intangible heritage: The practices, expressions, knowledge and skills that communities, groups and sometimes individuals recognize as part of their cultural heritage. Also called 'living cultural heritage', it is usually expressed in one of the following forms: oral traditions; performing arts; social practices, rituals and festive events; knowledge and practices concerning nature and the universe; and traditional craftsmanship.

Intangible Cultural Heritage in Need of Urgent Safeguarding: an element of intangible cultural heritage whose viability is at risk despite the efforts of the community, group or, if applicable, individuals and State(s) Party(ies) concerned or facing grave threats as a result of which it cannot be expected to survive without immediate safeguarding.

Representative List of the Intangible Cultural Heritage of Humanity: an element of intangible cultural heritage whose inscription contributes to ensuring visibility and awareness of the significance of the intangible cultural heritage and to encouraging dialogue, thus reflecting cultural diversity worldwide and testifying to human creativity. At the Third Session of the Intergovernmental Committee for the Safeguarding of the Intangible Cultural Heritage (Istanbul, 4-8 November 2008), the 90 elements that had been proclaimed 'Masterpieces of the intangible cultural heritage' on the occasion of the Proclamations of 2001, 2003 and 2005 were incorporated as the first elements of the Representative List of the Intangible Cultural Heritage of Humanity.

Tentative List: The first step a country must take is to make an 'inventory' of the important natural and cultural heritage sites located within its boundaries. This 'inventory' is known as the Tentative List and provides a forecast of the properties that a State Party may decide to submit for inscription in the next five to ten years; the inventory may be updated at any time. It is an important step since the World Heritage Committee cannot consider a nomination for inscription on the World Heritage List unless the property has already been included on the State Party's Tentative List.

World Heritage site: To be included on the World Heritage List, sites must be of outstanding universal value and meet at least one of ten selection criteria. These criteria are explained in the *Operational Guidelines for the Implementation of the World Heritage Convention*.

Cultural site: Monuments, groups of buildings, sites that are of outstanding universal value from an historical, aesthetic, ethnological or anthropological point of view.

Natural site: Natural features consisting of physical and biological formations, or groups of such formations, that are of outstanding universal value from an aesthetic or a scientific point of view or that constitute the habitat of threatened species of animals and plants of outstanding universal value from the perspective of science or conservation.

CONTEXT

Table 3. Demographic context
Age structure: Categorization of the population of communities or countries by age groups, allowing demographers to make projections of the growth or decline of the particular population.

Crude birth/death rate: The crude birth/death rate is the number of births/deaths occurring in a given time period, divided by the population of the area as estimated at the middle of the time period. The rate is usually expressed in terms of 'per 1,000 of population'.

Government's policy on emigration: *Overall level*: The government's policies on the current level of emigration from the country. It is coded into one of four categories: to raise, to maintain or to lower the level of emigration, or no intervention. *Encouraging the return of citizens*: Indicates whether the government has specific policies encouraging the return of citizens. It has two categories: yes and no.

Government's policy on fertility: *View on fertility level*: Indicates whether the government regards the national fertility level as Too Low, Too High or Satisfactory. *Policy to modify fertility*: Indicates whether policies in place are to raise, maintain, or lower fertility levels, or if there is no such intervention.

Government's policy on immigration: *Overall level*: The government's policies on the current overall level of immigration into the country. It is coded into one of four categories: to raise, to maintain or to lower the level of immigration, or no intervention. *Highly skilled workers*: The government's policies on the current level of immigration of highly skilled workers. It is coded into one of four categories: to raise, to maintain or to lower the level of immigration, or no intervention. *Integration of non-citizens*: Indicates whether the government has specific policies on the integration of non-citizens. It has two categories: yes and no.

Migrant stock: *Number*: The mid-year estimate of the number of people who are born outside the country. For countries lacking data on place of birth, it is the mid-year estimate of the number of non-citizens. In either case, the migrant stock includes refugees, some of whom may not be foreign-born.

Net migration: *Number:* Net average annual number of migrants, that is, the annual number of immigrants less the annual number of emigrants, including both citizens and non-citizens. *Rate*: The net number of migrants, divided by the average population of the receiving country over the period considered. It is expressed as the net number of migrants per 1,000 inhabitants.

Number of refugees: Persons recognized as refugees under the 1951 *Convention Relating to the Status of Refugees* and the 1967 *Protocol Relating to the Status of Refugees*, or under the Organization of African Unity's 1969 *Convention Governing the Specific Aspects of Refugee Problems in Africa*; those

granted refugee status in accordance with the *Statute of the United Nations High Commissioner for Refugees* (UNHCR); or those granted humanitarian status or temporary protection by the State in which they find themselves. Also included are Palestinian refugees registered with the United Nations Relief and Welfare Agency (UNRWA).

Percentage of gross domestic product: The percentage of the gross domestic product (GDP) attributable to remittances.

Percentage of population: The migrant stock as a percentage of the total population. Definitions of migrant may differ (*see code in table*).

Rate of natural increase: The difference between the crude birth rate and the crude death rate. The natural increase (or natural decrease) is negative when the number of deaths exceeds the number of births. This measure of population change excludes the effects of migration.

Remittances: Total remittances as reported by the World Bank include three types of transactions: workers' remittances, compensation of employees and migrants' transfers. Workers' remittances are all current transfers from migrants staying in a country for one year or longer to households in another country. Usually, they are regular transfers from members of the same family who are residing in different countries. Compensation of employees include the wages, salaries and other remuneration earned by migrants staying in a country for less than one year and who are paid by residents of that country. Migrants' transfers are the net worth of migrants who are expected to remain in the country for more than one year. They are not transactions but rather contra-entries to flows of goods and changes in financial items that arise from the migration of individuals. All data are reported in current US$.

Total annual growth rate: The sum of net migration and natural increase rates.

Total population: The total mid-year de facto population.

Table 4. Telecommunication access

Broadband (% of subscribers): Proportion of fixed broadband Internet subscribers out of total (low-speed and high-speed) subscribers.

Cost of calls: Price of a three-minute fixed/cellular telephone local call at peak rate.

Fixed lines: Number of main (fixed) telephone lines in operation, expressed in terms of 'per 1,000 inhabitants'.

International telephone traffic: This covers the effective (completed) international traffic of a given country with destinations/origin outside that country. It may not include some traffic from or to cellular phones.

Internet users: This indicator is based on nationally reported data to ITU. In some cases, surveys have been carried out that give a more precise figure for the number of Internet users. However, surveys differ across countries in the age and frequency of use they cover. The reported figure for Internet users may refer only to users above a certain age. Countries that do not have surveys generally base their estimates on derivations from reported Internet Service Provider (ISP) subscriber counts, calculated by multiplying the number of subscribers by a multiplier.

Mobile cellular subscribers: The sum of post-paid and prepaid cellular telephone subscribers in a given country, divided by its total population.

Percentage of monthly GNI per capita for 20 hours of usage: This indicator refers to the lowest price for 20 hours of dial-up Internet usage per month. It includes the tariff components of monthly line rental, line usage charges and Internet access charges, plus any taxes that may be levied (as this is a service used by both residential and business consumers). The tariff chosen for a particular country would be the package for 20 hours per month that is the cheapest, that is widely available (or, in the case of regional service providers, is available in the capital city) and is available to the general public without restriction.

Table 5. Gender
Economic activity index (1990=100): Numbers that measure the same characteristics and are all expressed relative to the same reference period. The reference period is called the base and often set at 100.

Female activity rate: Percentage of women employed (including self-employed), unemployed and actively looking for work, expressed as a proportion of men's percentage.

Gender Parity Index (GPI): Calculated by dividing the female Gross Enrolment Ratio (GER) by the male GER (see definition in Table 9) for tertiary level, that is the number of pupils or students enrolled in tertiary level divided by the population of official school age for that level. The population of the official age for tertiary education is the 5-year age-group immediately following the end of secondary education. A GPI of 1 indicates parity between the sexes; a GPI that varies between 0 and 1 typically means a disparity in favour of males; whereas a GPI greater than 1 indicates a disparity in favour of females. A GPI of less than 1 indicates that there are fewer females, in proportion to the appropriate school-age population, than males in the formal education system.

Income disparity ratio: Calculated by dividing women's earned incomes estimates (calculated using Purchasing Power Parity in US$) by that of men, based on data for the most recent year available between 1996 and 2005. For further details, see Technical note 1 from the *Human Development Report 2007/2008*.

Values and identities

Table 6. Highlights of the World Values Survey
World Values Survey: The World Values Survey is an ongoing international academic project conducted by social scientists to assess the state of socio-cultural, moral, religious and political values of different cultures around the world. All results are freely available on the website at [www.worldvaluessurvey.org]. Please refer to the notes at the end of the table for the description of each question.

Languages and education

Table 7. Languages
Indigenous/Immigrant language: An indigenous language or autochthonous language is a language that is native to a region and spoken by indigenous peoples.[1] In certain cases, especially in post-colonial contexts or in metropolitan areas where people from other countries or regions came for permanent residence, indigenous languages can coexist with or even be dominated by immigrant languages. In *Ethnologue*, the decision on whether a language should be treated as an immigrant language or as a proper language originating from the country is made on the basis of a 'primary country' for each language. According to John Paolillo (UIS, 2006), *Ethnologue* tends to retain indigenous

languages, even when they may be extinct, and to underreport immigrant languages.

International languages taught in school: This refers to instructional time allocated to non-official international or exogenous languages. IBE'S classification for official/national languages (as opposed to local/regional and international languages) does not necessarily overlap with Ethnologue's classification.

Linguistic diversity index: Derived from Greenberg's diversity index and published in the 2005 edition of *Ethnologue*, this is the probability that in a given country any two people selected at random would have different mother tongues. The highest possible value 1 indicates total diversity (i.e. no two people have the same mother tongue), whereas the lowest possible value 0 indicates no diversity at all (i.e. everyone has the same mother tongue). The computation of the diversity index is based on the population of each language as a proportion of the total population.

Local or Regional languages taught in school: This refers to time devoted to non-official indigenous languages, namely, those spoken by a significant cultural minority in the country. IBE'S classification for official/National languages (as opposed to local/regional and international languages) does not necessarily overlap with Ethnologue's classification.

Official or national languages taught in school:
Combination of all instructional time allocated to the official languages of each country. This is combined from previous estimates of instructional time for national/official languages. IBE'S classification for official/National languages (as opposed to local/regional and international languages) does not necessarily overlap with Ethnologue's classification.

Total yearly instructional hours devoted to languages: This quantity is calculated based on the data of Table 10.

Table 8. Translations
Published translations: Number of books translated and published in a country during a year.

Major languages into which translated (target language): Languages into which translations are published most in a country.

Major languages translated (original languages): Languages from which translations are published most in a country.

Most frequently translated authors: Individual authors whose books were translated the most in the country during the considered period of time. Corporate translations (established by enterprises, companies or associations) are excluded.

Table 9. Education and literacy
Adult literacy rates: Number of literate persons aged 15 and above, expressed as a percentage of the total population aged 15 and above. A person is considered to be literate if he/she can read and write, with understanding, a simple statement related to his/her life.

Compulsory education: Educational programmes that children and young people are legally obliged to attend. They are usually defined in terms of a number of grades or an age range, or both.

Legal guarantee of free education: States which legally guarantee access to free primary education.

Gender Parity Index (GPI): Calculated by dividing the female Gross Enrolment Ratio (GER) by the male GER for the given level of education. It reflects females' level of access to education compared to that of males' access. A GPI of less than 1 indicates that there are fewer females, in proportion to the appropriate school-age population, than males in the formal education system.

---

1. There is no universally accepted definition of 'indigenous peoples'. Although the UN Special Rapporteur Jose R. Martinez Cobo proposed in 1986 a working definition of indigenous peoples in his *Study on the Problem of Discrimination against Indigenous Populations* ('Indigenous communities, peoples and nations are those which, having a historical continuity with pre-invasion and pre-colonial societies that developed on their territories, consider themselves distinct from other sectors of the societies now prevailing on those territories, or parts of them. They form at present non-dominant sectors of society and are determined to preserve, develop and transmit to future generations their ancestral territories, and their ethnic identity, as the basis of their continued existence as peoples, in accordance with their own cultural patterns, social institutions and legal system'), this definition was rejected by both indigenous groups and states. Today many indigenous groups have lost their original languages and speak a different language than their mother tongue or a Creole. For this reason, some experts understand 'indigenous' to be synonymous with 'endogenous' regarding language, that is to say, they maintain that even large regional languages could be considered 'indigenous' because they originated locally and evolved to a dominant position in the course of history.

Gross Enrolment Ratio (GER): This ratio determines the population of official school age for each level of education with reference to the theoretical starting ages and durations of ISCED97 Level 0 (Pre-primary education and Early Childhood Care and Education [ECCE]), Level 1 (primary education) and Levels 2 and 3 (secondary education) as reported by the country. The population of the official age for tertiary education is the 5-year age-group immediately following the end of secondary education. It divides the number of pupils or students enrolled in each level of education by the population of official school age for that level, multiplied by 100.

Percentage of tertiary students in [Field]: Percentage of students in tertiary education in fields *Education* (teacher training and education science) and *Humanities and arts* (humanities, religion and theology, fine and applied arts).

School life expectancy: The number of years a child is expected to remain at school, or university, including years spent on repetition. It is the sum of the age-specific enrolment ratios for primary, secondary, post-secondary, non-tertiary and tertiary education.

Youth literacy rates: The percentage of the population aged 15–24 years who can both read and write, with understanding, a short simple statement on everyday life.

Private enrolment as % of total enrolment: The percentage of enrolled students who are enrolled in a private educational institution.

Pupil/teacher ratio: The expected number of students for each teacher at various educational levels.

Female teachers as % of total teachers: The percentage of female teachers as a percentage of total teachers operating at a given level.

Table 10. Education and curricula
Official school curriculum: A list of subjects to be taught, quantities of instructional time allocated to subjects, authorized textbooks to accompany classroom instruction, authorized lesson plans or syllabi delineating the topics to be taught and official directives or guidelines concerning pedagogy and assessments. The present table focuses solely on the first two components.

Intended annual hours of instruction: To calculate this quantity for each grade and country, three components were taken into account: a) the duration of the working school year; b) the number of teaching periods allocated to each subject and grade level; and c) the average duration of these afore-mentioned periods (lessons or hours), expressed in minutes.

Median yearly instructional hours: Medians are less sensitive to outliers than means; the longitudinal trends based on medians provide a more reliable and informative picture.

Percentage of tertiary students in [Field]: Percentage of students of tertiary education in fields *Education* (teacher training and education science) and *Humanities and arts* (humanities, religion and theology, fine and applied arts).

Table 11. International flows of mobile students at the tertiary level
Gross outbound enrolment ratio: Mobile students coming from a country/region as a percentage of the population of tertiary student age in their home country.

Inbound mobility rate: The number of students from abroad studying in a given country, as a percentage of the total tertiary enrolment in that country.

Mobile students: Students enrolled in an education programme in a country of which they are not permanent residents.

Outbound mobility ratio: The number of students from a given country studying abroad as a percentage of the total tertiary enrolment in that country.

Media and culture

Table 12. Newspapers
Average circulation: Total average circulation refers to the sum of the average circulation for all newspapers reported in a given category.

Community newspaper: A community newspaper is a periodic publication that is generated by and circulated primarily to a specific community, such as a village, a small town or some other limited geographical area.

Newspaper: Newspaper refers to a periodic publication intended for the general public and mainly designed to be a primary source of written information on current events related to national and international affairs, social and political issues, etc. A *daily* newspaper is a newspaper that mainly reports events that have occurred in a 24-hour period before going to press and that is published at least four times each week. A *non-daily* newspaper is any other type of newspaper, usually one that gives news covering a longer period but that, either owing to their local nature or for other reasons, provides its readers with a primary source of general information. Non-dailies are published three times per week or less frequently.

Online newspaper: An online newspaper is a free or paid version of a print newspaper or a free or paid subscription-based newspaper published only on the Internet.

RSF Press Freedom Index: This index is compiled from questionnaires with 52 criteria for assessing the state of press freedom in each country. It includes every kind of violation directly affecting journalists (e.g. murders, imprisonment, physical attacks and threats) and news media (e.g. censorship, confiscation of issues, searches and harassment). The index should in no way be taken as an indication of the quality of the press in the countries concerned.

Freedom House's Press Freedom Index: The examination of the level of press freedom in each country currently comprises 23 methodology questions divided into three broad categories: the legal environment, the political environment and the economic environment. For each methodology question, a lower number of points is allotted for a more free situation, while a higher number of points is allotted for a less free environment. Each country is rated in these three categories, with the higher numbers indicating less freedom. A country's final score is based on the total of the three categories. A score of 0–30 places the country in the Free press group; 31–60, in the Partly Free press group; and 61–100, in the Not Free press group.

IPI's Journalists Killed: When evaluating countries, IPI takes a multi-layered approach. First, IPI analyzes countries using its yearly report on the media entitled *The IPI World Press Freedom Review*. The study provides a comprehensive review of over 176 countries and territories around the world and often alerts the secretariat to countries where there are severe obstacles

to press freedom. Second, the reports are combined with the assessments of IPI members who, due to their experience, have a wealth of information on the state of the media.

CPJ's Journalists Killed: The Committee to Protect Journalists lists two categories — "confirmed" and "unconfirmed" — of journalists killed. "Confirmed" cases refer to journalists killed "because of their work as journalists," indicating that the organization has collected evidence to determine the journalists "either died in the line of duty or were deliberately targeted for assassination because of their reporting or their affiliation with a news organization," according to CPJ. "Unconfirmed" cases refer to journalists killed under circumstances where the motive remains under investigation by CPJ.

Table 13. Broadcast content

Government/Public institutions: *Government* broadcasting institutions are operated in all respects by government (e.g. central or federal, state, provincial, local) either directly or through a separate institution created by it. *Public* broadcasting institutions are created or licensed by a legislative act or regulation (e.g. central or federal, state, provincial, local) and constitute an autonomous body.

National production: Programmes produced in the country, either by its broadcasting institutions or otherwise.

Percentage of broadcasting time by programme type: This refers to programmes (reported in number of hours) broadcast on government/public channels. Types of programmes shown in tables are news and information; education and science; film and series (for television only); arts and culture; music; other entertainment; sports; religion; advertising; unclassified.

Private broadcasting institutions: Corporate or privately owned institutions operating for financial profit.

Table 14. Movies

Cinema: Place possessing its own equipment and primarily engaged in projecting cinematographic or audiovisual works. It includes indoor cinemas, outdoor cinemas, drive-ins and mobile units.

Distribution company: Establishment primarily engaged in selling, renting, lending or exchanging copies of films to cinemas on a commercial basis. They are in charge of marketing and promoting films, collecting revenues and distributing them among the parties sharing in the profit.

Feature film: Film with a running time of 60 minutes or longer intended for commercial exhibition in cinemas. Films produced for television broadcasting, as well as newsreels and publicity films, are excluded.

Multiplex: Cinema with eight screens or more.

National co-production: Feature film produced by one or more producers of national origin and one or more producers from other countries.

National production: Includes 100% nationally produced feature film and co-produtions, i.e. feature films produced for cinema release exclusively by producers of national origin.

Nationally controlled company: Complete or more than 50 percent ownership/control of a business or resource in a country by individuals who are citizens of that country or by companies whose headquarters are in that country. It excludes foreign affiliates.

Table 15. Recorded music: Sales and repertoire
Repertoire: Market share of domestic (national repertoire), international popular and classical music in country, based on origin of main artist or group.

Retail sales: Sales figures are net shipments (record company shipments to retail minus returns). All figures presented here refer to combined audio formats: singles, LPs, cassettes, CDs, DVD Audio, SACD, and Minidisk. Digital sales are not included here. Figures were collected from national IFPI members and include an estimate for non-reported sales, effectively representing 100 percent of the market.

Cultural flows

Table 16. International flows of selected cultural goods and services
Audiovisual and related services: Services and associated fees related to the production, post-production, distribution, broadcasting and projection of motion pictures (on film or videotape), radio and television programmes (live or on tape) and musical recordings.

Audiovisual media: Video games used with a television receiver; photographic and cinematographic film, exposed and developed.

Books: Printed books, brochures, leaflets, etc.; children's pictures, drawing or colouring books.

Cultural goods: Consumer goods that convey ideas, symbols and ways of life. They inform or entertain, help to build collective identity and influence cultural practices. They are the result of individual or collective creativity.

Cultural services: Consist of the overall set of measures and supporting facilities for cultural practices that government, private and semi-public institutions or companies make available to the community. Examples of such services include the promotion of performances and cultural events, as well as cultural information and preservation (libraries, documentation centres and museums). Cultural services may be offered for free or on a commercial basis.

Heritage goods: Collections and collectors' pieces; antiques of an age exceeding 100 years.

International trade in services: Trade between residents and non-residents of an economy. It also includes the value of services provided through foreign affiliates established abroad, described here as foreign affiliates trade in services (FATS). Services are also supplied by individuals located abroad, either as service suppliers themselves or employed by service suppliers, including those in the host country.

Newspapers and periodicals: Newspapers, journals or any other periodicals, whether or not they are illustrated or contain advertising material.

Other printed matter: Printed music, maps, postcards, pictures, designs, etc.

Other royalties and license fees: Include international payments and receipts for the authorized use of intangible, non-produced, non-financial assets and proprietary rights (e.g. patents, copyrights and industrial processes and designs) and with the use, through licensing agreements, of produced originals or prototypes (e.g. manuscripts, computer programs, and cinematographic works and sound recordings).

Recorded media: Gramophone records; discs for laser-reading systems for reproducing sound only; magnetic tape (recorded); other recorded media for sound.

Trade coverage ratio: Trade coverage ratio for selected categories of cultural goods. The trade coverage ratio is defined as exports value divided by imports value in current US$ multiplied by 100. It is used to identify whether a country is considered to be a net exporter or importer of cultural goods. It is not only a way of visualizing the foreign trade balance but also of measuring exports relative to imports. A value of 100 indicates that the foreign trade balance is equal for core cultural goods. When the results are higher than 100, exports are larger than imports in value terms for the category concerned.

Visual Arts: Paintings and other visual arts (statues, sculptures, lithographs, etc.).

Table 17. Tourism flows

Tourists arrivals: Persons who do not reside in the country of arrival and are admitted to that country under tourist visas (if required) for purposes of leisure, recreation, holiday, visits to friends or relatives, health or medical treatment, or religious pilgrimage. Arrivals associated with inbound tourism correspond to those arrivals by international visitors within the economic territory of the country of reference and include tourists and, in some cases, same-day non-resident visitors. Data on arrivals may be obtained from different sources, such as border statistics derived from administrative records (police, immigration, traffic or other types of control applied at national borders), completed by means of border statistical surveys. In other cases, data are obtained from different types of tourism accommodation establishments (hotels and similar establishments and/or all types of tourism accommodation establishments). Arrivals cannot be assumed to be equal to the number of persons travelling. When a person visits the same country several times in one year, an equal number of arrivals is recorded. Likewise, if a person visits several countries in the course of a single trip, his/her arrival in each country is recorded separately.

Tourists departures: Departures associated with outbound tourism correspond to the number of international departures of resident tourists outside the economic territory of the country of reference, as recorded as his/her 'origin' country. Many countries do not record their citizens' departures abroad.

Tourists expenditures: *Tourism expenditures in the country of reference* are obtained from the item 'Travel receipts' of the balance of payments of each country and corresponds to the 'expenditures of non-resident visitors (tourists and same-day visitors)' within the economic activity of the country of reference. *Tourism expenditures data in other countries* are obtained from the item 'Travel expenditures' of the balance of payments of each country and corresponds to the 'expenditures of resident visitors (tourists and same-day visitors)' outside the economic territory of the country of reference.

Culture and sustainable development

Table 18. Environment, biodiversity and habitat

Biodiversity: Also referred to as 'biological diversity', this term means the variability among living organisms from all sources, including terrestrial, marine and other aquatic ecosystems, and the ecological complexes of which they are part; this includes diversity within species, between species and of ecosystems (UNEP, CBD).

Biosphere reserves: Biosphere reserves are sites, recognized under UNESCO's Man and the Biosphere (MAB) Programme, which innovate and demonstrate approaches to conservation and sustainable development. They are under national sovereign jurisdiction, yet share their experience and ideas nationally, regionally and internationally within the World Network of Biosphere Reserves.

Forest area: Land area covered by forest as a share of total land area, where land area is the total country area excluding the area of inland water bodies (major rivers, lakes and water reservoirs). The definition of forest, as stated in the Food and Agriculture Organization's (FAO) *Global Forest Resources Assessment 2005*, is land spanning more than 0.5 hectares with trees higher than 5 meters and a canopy cover of more than 10 percent, or trees able to reach these thresholds *in situ*. It does not include land that is predominantly under agricultural or urban land use.

Population density: The number of population per unit of total land area of a country.

Population growth (urban/rural): Because of national differences in the characteristics that distinguish urban from rural areas, the distinction between urban and rural population is not amenable to a single definition that would be applicable to all countries. National definitions are most commonly based on size of locality. Population that is not urban is considered rural.

Protected terrestrial and marine area: The International Union for Conservation of Nature (IUCN) defines a protected area as an area of land and/or sea especially dedicated to the protection and maintenance of biological diversity, and of natural and associated cultural resources, and managed through legal or other effective means. The size of the protected area is that officially documented by the national authority. The total protected area by country/territory is divided by total territorial area of the country/territory (including total land area, inland waters and territorial waters up to 12 nautical miles).

Threatened species: Threatened species are those listed as critically endangered, endangered or vulnerable. Species assessed to date amount to 41,415 worldwide. The total number of species on the planet is unknown; estimates vary between 10 and 100 million, with 15 million species being the most widely accepted figure; but 1.7–1.8 million species are known today.

Urban population: Proportion of the population residing in urban areas as reported to the United Nations. Estimates are based on different national definitions of what constitutes the urban area. Cross-country comparisons should be made with caution.

Table 19. Economic development and innovation
Gross Domestic Product (GDP): Sum of gross value added by all resident producers in the economy, including distributive trades and transport, plus any product taxes and minus any subsidies not included in the value of the products.

GDP per capita: This is the total GDP divided by the number of people in the country.

Income inequality (richest 10% to poorest 10%): Ratio of income (or expenditure) share of the richest group to that of the poorest. Because the underlying household surveys differ in method and in the type of data collected, the distribution data are not strictly comparable across countries.

Innovation: According to the World Bank, the innovation system is the simple average of the normalized scores (on a scale of 0 to 10) on three key variables: a) Total Royalty and License Fees Payments and Receipts; b) Patent Applications Granted by the US Patent and Trademark Office; and c) Scientific and Technical Journal Articles. These variables are

available in two forms: scaled by population (weighted) and in absolute values (unweighted). In innovation, absolute size of resources matters, as there are strong economies of scale in the production of knowledge and because knowledge is not consumed in its use.

Life expectancy at birth: According to the World Bank, life expectancy at birth is the average number of years a newborn baby can be expected to live based on current health conditions. This indicator reflects environmental conditions in a country, the health of its people, the quality of care they receive when they are sick, and their living conditions.

ODA (Official Development Assistance): Flows of official financing administered with the primary objective of promoting the economic development and welfare of developing countries, and which are concessional in character with a grant element of at least 25 percent (using a fixed 10 percent rate of discount). By convention, ODA flows comprise contributions of donor government agencies, at all levels, to developing countries ('bilateral ODA') and to multilateral institutions. ODA receipts comprise disbursements by bilateral donors and multilateral institutions. Lending by export credit agencies, with the pure purpose of export promotion, is excluded.

Population below poverty line: The poverty lines set at US$1.25 and US$2 per day are the proportion of the population having per capita consumption of less than these amounts per day, measured in 2005 international Purchasing Power Parity terms. National estimates are based on population-weighted subgroup estimates from household surveys. The poverty line is an income level that is considered minimally sufficient to sustain a family in terms of food, housing, clothing, medical needs, etc.

Research and development (R&D): Comprise creative work undertaken on a systematic basis in order to increase the stock of knowledge, including knowledge of humanity, culture and society, and the use of this stock of knowledge to devise new applications. The term R&D covers three activities: basic research, applied research and experimental development.

Researchers in R&D: Professionals engaged in the conception or creation of new knowledge, products, processes, methods and systems, and also in the management of R&D projects. Full-time equivalent is presented, but when missing, headcount is used as an alternative.

Scientific articles: Articles are counted from set of journals covered by Science Citation Index (SCI) and Social Sciences Citation Index (SSCI). Articles are classified by year of publication and assigned to region/country/economy on the basis of institutional address(es) listed in the articles. For articles on fractional-count basis, that is, for articles with collaborating institutions from multiple countries or economies, each country or territory receives fractional credit based on the proportion of its participating institutions. *Percentage of international co-authorship* is based on the assumption that when co-authored articles involve two countries, each country has been given a 0.5 count.

Unemployment rate: The unemployed comprise all persons above a specified age who, during the reference period, were:

- without work (i.e. were not in paid employment or self-employment during the reference period);

- currently available for work (i.e. were available for paid employment or self-employment during the reference period); and

- seeking work (i.e. had taken specific steps in a specified recent period to seek paid employment or self-employment).

Unemployment rates represent unemployed persons as a percentage of the civilian labour force.

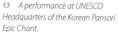 *A performance at UNESCO Headquarters of the Korean Pansori Epic Chant.*

Abbreviations

ABC	Australian Broadcasting Corporation
ACALAN	African Academy of Languages
ACHPR	African Commission on Human and People's Rights
ADG	Assistant Director General
AIDS	Acquired Immune Deficiency Syndrome
ALECSO	Arab League Educational, Cultural and Scientific Organization
AMARC	World Association of Community Radio Broadcasters
AMIDEAST	America-Mideast Educational and Training Services
AOC	Alliance of Civilizations (UN)
APTN	Aboriginal Peoples Television Network
ASEAN	Association of Southeast Asian Nations
ASPnet	UNESCO Associated Schools Network
ATLAS	Association of Tourism and Leisure Education
AU	African Union
BBC	British Broadcasting Corporation
BCE	Before Common Era
BOLD	Business Opportunities for Leadership Diversity
BRICs	Brazil, Russia, India and China
CAN	Community of Andean Nations
CBD	Convention on Biological Diversity
CD	Compact Disc
CDO	Chief Diversity Officer
CDPL	Cultural Diversity Programming Lens
CE	Common Era
CEDAW	Committee on the Elimination of Discrimination against Women
CEM	Cultural Environmental Movement
CEO	Chief Executive Officer
CERD	Committee on the Elimination of Racial Discrimination
CESCR	Committee on Economic, Social and Cultural Rights (UN)
CIHR	Cambodian Institute of Human Rights
CIMPs	Coastal Infrastructure Management Plans
CNC	Centre national de la cinématographie
CNN	Cable News Network
COP 12	12th session of the Conference of the Parties to the Climate Change Convention
COP 13	13th session of the Conference of the Parties to the Climate Change Convention
CRC	Committee on the Rights of the Child
CRIS	Communication Rights in the Information Society
CSIV	Children International Summer Village
CSR	Corporate Social Responsibility
DESD	Decade of Education for Sustainable Development (UN)
DVD	Digital Video Disc

EBU	European Broadcasting Union
ECHR	European Court of Human Rights
ECOSOC	Economic and Social Council
ECRI	European Commission against Racism and Intolerance
ECSR	European Committee of Social Rights
ECRML	European Charter of Regional and Minority Languages
EFA	Education for All
EFTA	European Fair Trade Association
EU	European Union
FAO	Food and Agriculture Organization (UN)
FGM	Female genital mutilation
FLO	Fairtrade Labelling Organizations
FRA	Agency for Fundamental Rights (EU)
GDP	Gross domestic product
GIS	Geographic Information Systems
GRTKF	Genetic Resources, Traditional Knowledge and Folklore
GSM	Global System for Mobile communications
HDI	Human Development Index
HIP-1	Human Poverty Index
HIV	Human Immunodeficiency Virus
HR	Human Resources
HRC	Human Rights Council
IAE	International Association for the Evaluation of Education Achievement
IAIPTF	International Alliance of the Indigenous and Tribal Peoples of the Tropical Forest
IAPAD	Integrated Approaches to Participatory Development
IBCD	Index of Biocultural Diversity
IBE	International Bureau of Education
ICAF	International Child Art Foundation
ICANN	Internet Corporation for Assigned Names and Numbers
ICCPR	International Covenant on Civil and Political Rights (UN)
ICESCR	International Covenant on Economic, Social and Cultural Rights
ICH	Intangible Cultural Heritage
ICOMOS	International Council on Monuments and Sites
ICPD	International Conference on Population and Development
ICSU	International Council for Science
ICTs	Information and Communication Technologies
IDN	Internationalized Domain Name
IDPs	Internally Displaced Persons
IIEP	International Institute for Educational Planning
IIFB	International Indigenous Forum on Biodiversity
ILO	International Labour Organization
IMC	International Music Council
IMF	International Monetary Fund

INCD	International Network for Cultural Diversity
IOM	International Organization for Migration
IP	Intellectual Property
IPDC	International Programme for the Development of Communication
ISCO	International Standard Classification by Occupations
ISESCO	Islamic Educational, Scientific and Cultural Organization
ISTC	International Student Travel Confederation
ITU	International Telecommunication Union
IUCN	International Union for Conservation of Nature
IUFRO	International Union of Forest Research
LDI	Linguistic Diversity Index
LEG	European Leadership Group
LINKS	Local and Indigenous Knowledge Systems
MA	Millennium Ecosystem Assessment
MAB	Man and the Biosphere (UNESCO)
MCTs	Multi-purpose community telecentres
MDG	Millennium Development Goal
MEDIACULT	International Research Institute for Media, Communication and Cultural Development
MONDIACULT	World Conference on Cultural Policies, Mexico City
MPA	Motion Picture Association of America
NAPA	National Adaptation Programme of Action (Samoa Islands)
NEPAD	New Partnership for Africa's Development
NEWS	Network of European Worldshops
NGO	Non-Governmental Organization
OAS	Organization of American States
OAU	Organization of African Unity
OCLC	Online Computer Library Center
OCWs	Overseas Contract Workers
OECD	Organisation for Economic Co-operation and Development
OEI	Organización de Estados Iberoamericanos para la Educación, la Ciencia y la Cultura
OHCHR	Office of the United Nations High Commissioner for Human Rights
P3DM	Participatory three-dimensional modelling
PIRLS	Progress in International Reading Literacy Study
PISA	Programme for International Student Assessment (OECD)
PPA	Participatory poverty assessment
PPN	Power of Peace Network (UNESCO)
PRIME	Peace Research Institute in the Middle East
PRSPs	Poverty Reduction Strategy Papers
PSB	Public service broadcasting
PTF	Poverty Task Force (Vietnam)
RIAA	Recording Industry Association of America
RIMCU	Research Institute for Mindanao Culture
SABC	South African Broadcasting Corporation

SASI	South African San Institute
SFCG	Search for Common Ground
SIL	Summer Institute of Linguistics
STI	Sexually transmitted infection
TCE	Traditional cultural expressions
TCK	Third culture kids
TGI	Target Index Group
TIMSS	Trends in International Mathematics and Science Study
TK	Traditional knowledge
UCLG	United Cities and Local Governments
UIS	UNESCO Institute for Statistics
UK	United Kingdom
UN	United Nations
UNCED	United Nations Commission on Environment and Development
UNCHR	United Nations Commission of Human Rights
UNCTAD	United Nations Conference on Trade and Development
UNDP	United Nations Development Programme
UNEP	United Nations Environment Programme
UNESCO	United Nations Educational, Scientific and Cultural Organization
UNESCOCat	UNESCO Centre of Catalunya
UNFCCC	United Nations Framework Convention on Climate Change
UNFPA	United Nations Population Fund
UNHCR	United Nations High Commissioner for Refugees
UNPFII	UN Permanent Forum on Indigenous Issues
UNWTO	World Tourism Organization (UN)
UPF	Unity Productions Foundation
US	United States of America
VALEUR	Valuing All Languages in Europe
VDCs	Village Development Committees
WFTO	World Fair Trade Organization
WHO	World Health Organization
WIPO	World Intellectual Property Organization
WOMAD	World of Music and Dance
WRTA	World Religious Travel Association
WSIS	World Summit on the Information Society
WSSD	World Summit for Sustainable Development
WTO	World Trade Organization
www	World Wide Web

Photographic credits

Page	Credits
ii	© UNESCO/Michel Ravassard
iv	© UNESCO/Nina Levinthal
ix	© UNESCO/Michel Ravassard
xii	© iStockphoto
xii	© UNESCO/Fernando Brugman
0	© Mihai-Bogdan Lazar
1	© UNESCO/Marc Soosaar
2	© Sven Torfinn
3	© UNESCO/Claude Bablin
4	© UNESCO/Michel Claude
6	© UNESCO/Ministerio de Cultura y Deportes/GMA PRO
7	© Jack Stein/Photo Edit
8	© Robert Churchill
10	© Nigel Pavitt/Alamy
11	© UNESCO/Giacome Cuticchio
12	© Jacob Silberberg
17	© UNESCO/Luiz Santoz
20	© UNESCO/Georges Malempré
22	© Penny Tweedie
23	© UNESCO/Michel Ravassard
24	© UNESCO/Philippe Bordas
27	© UNESCO/Japanese Agency for Cultural Affairs
31	© UNESCO/Michel Ravassard
35	© UNESCO/Frédéric Sampson
36	© Markus Winkel
37	© Alfredo d'Amato
38	© UNESCO/Marc Sosaar
39	© UNESCO/Luiz Santoz
40	© UNESCO/Georges Malempré
41	© UNESCO/Michel Ravassard
44	© UNESCO/Michel Ravassard
47	© UNESCO/Mairie de Douai
48a	© UNESCO/Georges Malempré
48b	© UNESCO/Wande Abimbola
50-51	© UNESCO/Philippe Bordas
53a	© UNESCO/Chimbidzikai Mapfumo
53b	© UNESCO/Moe Chiba
53c	© UNESCO/Vice Ministerio de Cultura de Bolivia
53d	© UNESCO/Chinese Academy of Arts
55	© Hasim Syah
56	© UNESCO/Jojo Unalivia
57	© UNESCO/Peter Coles
58	© UNESCO/Roya Aziz/Star Group
59	© UNESCO/Yoshihiro Higuchi
63	© UNESCO/Russian State House of the People Creativity, Ministry of Culture
64	© Jacob Silberberg

Page	Credits
66	© Chris Stowers
67	© Gary Calton
68	© UNESCO/Frédéric Sampson
74	© UNESCO/Dominique Roger
75	© UNESCO/Michel Ravassard
79	© UNESCO/Anahit Minasyan
82	© PjrFoto/studio/ Alamy
84	© UNESCO/Frédéric Sampson
86	© UNESCO/Dominique Roger
89	© UNESCO/Philippe Bordas
92	© UNESCO/Alison Clayson
94	© UNESCO/R. Taurines
95	© UNESCO/Justin Mott
96	© UNESCO/Manoocher/Webistan
97	© UNESCO/Niamh Burke
103	© UNESCO/Niamh Burke
106	© UNESCO/J. Caro Gardiner
110	© UNESCO/Katys Anis
112	© UNESCO/Vice Ministerio de Cultura de Bolivia
115	© Joseph Fisco
127	© UNESCO/Galentro Alexandra
128	© Danny Yanai/Alamy
130	© UNESCO/Sergio Santimano
135	© UNESCO/Serge Daniel
136	© Ugurhan Betin Brkovic
138	© Andrew Esson
140	© G.M.B. Akash
144	© UNESCO/Sam Dhillon
146a	© UNESCO/Dominique Roger
146b	© UNESCO/Mario Borg
149	© UNESCO/Dominique Roger
151	© UNESCO/Christophe Buffet
153	© UNESCO/Dominique Roger
155	© UNESCO/Justin Mott
158a	© UNESCO/Georges Malempré
158b	© UNESCO/Zhanat Kulenov /
158c	© UNESCO/Natanakairali
159	© UNESCO/Pierre Gaillard
160	© UNESCO/Frédéric Sampson
161	© Jeff Ulrich
162	© UNESCO/Michel Ravassard
164	© UNESCO/Michel Ravassard
168	© iStockphoto
169	© Matjaz Boncina
171	© Dieter Telemans
177	© Matjaz Boncina
179	© UNESCO/Marc Romanelli
180	© UNESCO/ WWAP/Alison Clayson

Page	Credits
182	© iStockphoto
185	© Jochem Wijnands/Alamy
186	© Klaus Claudia Dewald
188	© Alfredo d'Amato
190	© QiangBa DanZhen
191	© Alfredo d'Amato
192	© UNESCO
195	© UNESCO/Michel Ravassard
198	© UNESCO/Pierre Gaillard
201	© Randy Plett
203	© UNESCO/Adrienne Kaeppler
204a	© UNESCO/Francisco Bech
204b	© UNESCO
204c	© UNESCO/R. Greenough
207	© UNESCO/Yann Layma
209	© UNESCO/Frédéric Sampson
210	© UNESCO/Dominique Roger
214	© UNESCO/Alexis N. Vorontzoff
220	© Mikkel Ostergaard
221	© UNESCO/Moe Chiba
222	© Jocelyn Carlin
224	© Alfredo d'Amato
226	© John Woodworth
230a	© iStockphoto
230b	© UNESCO/Georges Malempré
233	© UNESCO/Françoise Pinzon Gil
236	© Gerd Ludwig
237	© UNESCO/Alexis N. Vorontzoff
238	© UNESCO/Abdelhak Senna
240	© UNESCO/Zhanat Kulenov
241	© UNESCO/Alison Clayson
245	© UNESCO/Yoshihiro Higuchi
249	© Mlenny
250	© Alex Ramsay/Alamy
251	© Rick Lord
252	© UNESCO/Henri Hiribarne
253	© Karim Hesham
254	© UNESCO/NCCA-ICH/Renato S. Rastrollo
255	© UNESCO/Olav A. Saltbones
258	© UNESCO/National Garifuna Council
259	© UNESCO/Wagner Horst
260	© UNESCO/Russian State House of the People Creativity, Ministry of Culture
273	© UNESCO/N. Burke
275	© UNESCO/Jane Wright
381	© UNESCO/Michel Ravassard
275	© UNESCO / Jane Wright
381	© Michel Ravassard / UNESCO

Index

A

Aboriginal Peoples Television Network (APTN), 148
abortion, 20
access
  to art, 30
  to cultural expressions, 31
  to cyberspace, 31
  to diverse cultures, 30
  to the Internet and new media, 135–9, 144, 149, 150, 257
  to mobile phones, 144–5
  to the public sphere via the media, 14, 146
  to scientific and technical knowledge, 30
action research, 110
advertising, 13, 173, 175
affirmative action, 107, 150, 177
  see also discrimination
Afghanistan, 46, 51, 58, 96, 104, 146, 151, 168, 191, 251
Africa(n), 23–4
  contribution to world's cultural heritage, 40
  cultural data from, 261
  cultural diversity in sub-Saharan, 234
  diaspora, 40–1
  film industry, 149
  -influenced cuisine, 40
  intangible value of products, 169
  music from/influenced by, 40
  trade in cultural goods and services, 131 (*see also* trade)
  traditional medicine, 195
African Academy of Languages (ACALAN), 24
African (Banjul) Charter on Human and Peoples' Rights, 228
African Charter on Broadcasting 2001, 152
African Commission on Human and People's Rights (ACHPR), 146

African National Congress (ANC)
African Union, 23, 87, 98, 245
Africultures, 134
Afro-Americans, 40
agriculture
  ill-conceived 'development' of, 17, 192
  intercropping, 208
  irrigation for, 243–5
  modes of subsistence, 204, 208–9
  reindeer husbandry, 227
  skills needed, 110
  slash-and-burn, 193, 208
  traditional forms being destroyed, 17
aid, 380
  international, ill conceived, 192
air travel, 170, 176–7
Al Jazeera, 134
Albania, 49, 132, 133
Algeria, 132
Algiers Declaration on the Rights of Peoples (1976), 228
Alliance of Civilizations *see under* United Nations
Alliance of the Indigenous and Tribal Peoples of the Tropical Forest (IAIPTF), 207
Amazon.com, 135
Amazon region, 208
American Convention of Human Rights, 228, 229–30
AMIDEAST programme, 46
Amman Affirmation (1996), 102
Amnesty International, 134, 230
Angola, 40, 117
Anguilla, 132, 133
Anna Lindh Euro-Mediterranean Foundation for the Dialogue Between Cultures, 59
Anni Äärelä and Jouni Näkkäläjärvi v. Finland, 227
AOL, 131
Aperian Global, 181

Apirana Mahuika et al. v. New Zealand, 227
Appadurai, Arjun, 199
Apple Computers, 72
Arab League Educational, Cultural and Scientific Organization (ALECSO), 59
Arab States, 25, 87, 166, 173
Arab identity/culture, 25, 41
archaeological sites
  underwater, 26, 29
  see also cultural sites; heritage, tangible
Argentina, 78, 83, 104, 133,134, 264,
Armenia, 79
Art Basel, 166
Article, 19, 230
arts, the
  artistic exchanges, 163–5, 180, 257
  and cultural diversity, 4, 161–85
  and education, 113–18
  exhibitions of visual, 163
  and intercultural dialogue, 257
  international market, 165–6
  as means of engagement, 241
  'primitive', 163–4
  traditional, 163
  and value transmission, 6
  visual, 163, 166, 352–9
Aruba, 133
Asian Development Bank, 53
Association of Southeast Asian Nations (ASEAN), 24, 87
Association of Tourism and Leisure Education (ATLAS), 170
astronomy, 113
Aswan Dam, 26
Atlas of the World's Languages in Danger (2009), 74, 77
audiovisual industry, 131–4, 257
  trade, 132, 352–9

and translation, 82–3
  see also cinema, media, radio, television
Auroville/Auroville Charter, 109
Australia, 13, 19, 22, 69, 71, 74, 80, 88, 104, 133, 146, 165, 220, 234, 235, 236, 261
  Aboriginal peoples, 49, 75, 78, 79, 148, 163, 208
  Australian Broadcasting Corporation Act (1983), 152
Austria, 104, 132, 133, 166, 240
AVENUE project, 83
Azerbaijan, ii

B

Bali, 168
  theatre, 165
Bali Concord II (*Declaration of ASEAN Concord II*), 24
Baku Declaration (2008), 54
Bamyan, Afghanistan, Buddhas of, 51
Bangladesh, 70, 133, 140
banks, 173, 175–6
Bantu people, 40
Barber, Benjamin, 140
Bauman, Zygmunt, 142
BBC, 134, 149
Beirut Agreements (1948), 26
Belarus, 104
Belgium, 47, 131, 133, 166, 224
belief systems, 2, 27, 81
  see also religion, values
Belize, 53
Benhamou, Françoise, 272
Benin, 40, 59, 158, 245
Berlitz Cultural Consulting, 181
Berne Convention for the Protection of Literary and Artistic Works, 29
Bhutan, 132, 133, 211, 265–6
biennial art exhibitions, 163
bio-prospecting and piracy, 195
biocultural diversity, 74

Biodiversity Target (2010), 74
biodiversity
    and cultural diversity, parallels
        between, 1, 204–5
cultural and spiritual values of, 3
    depletion of, 52
    and linguistic diversity, 74–5
    management of, 208–9, 252
    statistics, 364–7, 379
biological diversity *see*
    biodiversity
biosphere reserves, 364–7, 379
Bishkek Declaration, 58
blog(s)/blogging, 146
blues, the, 40
BMJ Ratings, 178
body ornamentation, 163
Bogatá Declaration (1978)
Bolivia, 17, 24, 52, 53–4, 78, 105,
    112, 169
Bosnia, 36, 51
Botswana, 24, 106, 194
Bouchard–Taylor
    Commission, 232
Boutros-Ghali, Boutros, 239
brands/branding, 172–5
Brazil, 17, 39, 40, 47, 74, 83, 104,
    106, 132, 133, 134, 146, 160,
    164, 165, 166, 194, 204, 245,
    264
    as emerging economy, 14,
        173–5, 180
    samba, 40
Bretton Woods, 3
BRICs (Brazil, Russia, India and
    China), 14, 173
Brundtland Report, 189
Bruno Manser Fund, 134
Bulgaria, 133
Burkina Faso, 198–9
Burundi, 4, 206
Business Opportunities for
    Leadership Diversity
    (BOLD), 177
business(es)
    craft-based, 167–9
        (*see also* handicrafts)
    and cultural diversity, 172–9
    in cultural sector, 131, 146,
        171, 262–4, 267–8, 271

sector and translations, 82
small and microfinance, 169
see also culture, corporate;
    multinational
    corporations; private
    sector; trade

C
Cairo Biennial, 163
calypso, 40
Cambodia, 46, 103, 106, 133, 241
Cameroon, 132, 133, 195
campaign-oriented
    participation, 237
Canada, 47, 104, 131, 133, 143,
    170, 179, 227, 261, 263, 271
    Aboriginal Peoples Television
        Network (APTN), 148
    economy of, 263
    immigrants to, 232, 234
    indigenous peoples, 49, 241
    language use, 71, 77, 78, 79,
        88
Canadian Translation Bureau, 84
Cannon Hill Park (Birmingham), 47
capacity-building, 45, 48
Capoeira, 40
Carneiro da Cunha, Manuela, 5
carnivals, 47
    Carnaval de Oruro (Bolivia), 17
cause-oriented activities, 237
celebrity, cult of, 142
censuses, national, 4, 42, 74, 77
Central African Republic, 75
Central Asian Women's Cultural
    Network, 48
Centre for Human Rights and
    Conflict Resolution (Skopje
    University, Macedonia), 49
Centre Georges Pompidou, 166
ceremonies, traditional, 18
Chad, 245
change
    capacity to accept and
        sustain, 3
    and cultural diversity, 5, 13,
        28, 223
    in evolving cultures, 9, 20
    in identity, culture and
        language, 76

*Charter for African Cultural
    Renaissance*, 23, 98
*Charter on the Preservation of
    Digital Heritage* (2003), 31
chat (electronic), 71, 136
chief diversity officer (CDO), 177
Children International Summer
    Village (CISV) programme, 46
children
    care solutions, 225
    Internet usage, 135–6
    killing of female, 54
    rights of, 107, 225
    street children, programmes
        for, 46
    see also education
Chile, 83, 85, 133, 261, 264
    National Corporation for
        Indigenous Development
        (CONADI), 85
China, 8, 18, 37, 49, 68, 74, 76, 84,
    87, 113, 142, 166, 190, 209
    as emerging economy, 14,
        173–5
    the four arts, 163
    language policy, 87, 104,
        131, 132, 133, 146
    media productions, 134
    traditional medicine, 195
Chocolate Route project, 57
Christianity, 18
    in central Asia, 21
    disputes involving, 19
    intolerance of other
        religions, 17
    see also religion
cinema, 131–5, 270
    access to videos, 138
    African, 149
    Bollywood, 133, 134, 149
    choice of viewing, 138
    data on, 260
    international trade in, 270
    local productions, 18, 132–3
    origin of top movies, 133
    statistics on, 344–7, 378
    UIS survey on, 262
    see also audiovisual, media
citizenship, 16, 236
civil society movements, 237

civilization(s)
    clash of, 1, 5, 39, 56
    definition, 4–5
clash of civilizations *see under*
    civilizations
climate change, 136
    and migration, 15
    responses to, 206–9
Clissold Park (northeast
    London), 47
CNN, 131, 134
Coca-Cola, 173
Coetzee, J. M., 22, 167
Coleman, James S., 101
Colombia, 74, 78, 133, 146, 162,
    167, 169, 240, 261, 264
colonialism, 234
    and education, 111
    and mass media, 141
    post-colonial states, 16, 193
    and underdevelopment, 191
colonization
    in Africa, 234
    as form of cultural
        imposition, 11, 41
    and languages, 67
    and memory, 42
    'of minds', 25, 144
Communication Rights in
    the Information Society
    (CRIS), 145
communication, 6
    barriers to, 6
    between speakers of
        different languages, 75
        (*see also* translation)
    and cultural content,
        6, 129–59, 254
        (recommendations
        regarding, 257)
    equipment, 133, 135, 154
    impacts of, 137–43
    statistics, 294–7
    traditional and new forms
        of, 18
    see also information
        and communication
        technology, media
*Communication on a European
    Agenda for Culture in a
    Globalizing World* (2007), 25

communitarianism, 48, 235, 236
Community of Andean Nations (CAN), 83
community/communities, 4, 27
    of allegiance, 22
    -based approaches, 52, 208
    -based disaster risk reduction, 208
    building, 237
    cultural, 47
    development, 111
    diasporic, 15, 134, 147 (see also diasporas)
    and diversity, 232
    educational culture of, 111
    empowerment, 6, 209, 241
    groups, 238
    heritage role of, 30
    identity, 39, 43, 89
    imagined, 140
    of interest, 241
    learning to be in a, 109
    media, 134, 146, 147, 148, 154, 201
    minority see minorities
    multicultural, 14
    networks, 48, 55
    on the periphery, 144 (see also marginalization)
    online, 147
    of origin, 54
    preservation, 266
    rights of, 221, 229
Conference of the Parties to the Climate Change Convention
    (COP12, Nairobi, 2006), 207
    (COP13, Bali, 2007), 207
conflict
    and cultural issues, 232, 253
    Israeli–Arab, 25
    resolution procedures, 226 (see also justice)
    in schools, 102
    prevention strategies, 50, 251
Congo (Dem. Rep.), 132, 133
connectivity, 136, 147
consumerism, 13
Convenio Andrés Bello, 264
Convention on Biological Diversity (CBD), 53, 74, 189

Convention against Discrimination in Education (1960), 31, 102
Convention on the Elimination of All Forms of Discrimination Against Women (CEDAW, 1979), 225
Convention on the Means of Prohibiting and Preventing the Illicit Import, Export and Transfer of Ownership of Cultural Property (1970), 29
Convention concerning the Protection of the World Cultural and Natural Heritage (1972), 27, 29, 51, 204
Convention for the Protection of Cultural Properties in the Event of Armed Conflict see Hague Convention
Convention on the Protection and Promotion of the Diversity of Cultural Expressions (2005), 19, 26, 27–8, 30, 137, 193, 262
Convention on the Protection of the Underwater Cultural Heritage (2001), 26, 29
Convention on the Rights of the Child (1989), 225, 226
Convention on the Safeguarding of the Intangible Cultural Heritage (2003), 19, 26, 27, 30, 115, 169, 204, 241
copyright, 26, 29, 132, 169, 228
    four categories and employment, 263
    see also intellectual property
corporate social responsibility, 179
Cosby Show, The, 142
cosmopolitanism, 14
Costa Rica, 86, 133
Côte d'Ivoire, 24
Council of Europe, 59, 87, 88, 106, 230
    Framework Convention for the Protection of National Minorities, 106

Council of Wise Men and the Water Court, 243–4
crafts see handicrafts
Creative Cities, 180
Creative Clusters, 180
creativity
    artistic and social, 6
    creative industries, 261 (see also cinema, communication, cultural industries/economy, literature, media, music, press, the; radio, television)
    and cultural diversity, 254
    and the marketplace, 161–85 (recommendations regarding, 257)
    as part of culture, 26–8
    stimulation of, iii, 46
creoles/creolization, 22, 40, 70, 75, 80
critical distance, 144
Croatia, 132, 252
cross-cultural management, 181
Cuba, 39, 40, 104, 132, 133, 134, 163, 245
Cultivation Theory, 140
Cultural Detective, 182
Cultural Diversity Programming Lens, 209, 211–14
Cultural Environmental Movement (CEM), 145
Cultural Liberty in Today's Diverse World (2004), 3
Cultural and Spiritual Values of Biodiversity (1999), 3
Cultural Unity and Diversity, 56
cultural borrowing(s), 14, 39, 78
cultural boundaries, porosity of, 39
cultural centres, 117
    destruction of, 207
    for minority groups, 233
    schools as, 120
cultural change and globalization, 13, 19
    see also change
cultural commercialization, 17, 165

cultural creativity see creativity
cultural decline and language loss, 76
cultural difference(s)
    at root of conflicts, 1
    awareness raising, 176
    see also cultural diversity
cultural diversity
    in the arts, 163
    as basis for dialogue, 44
    benefits of, 3, 5, 179–80
    and biodiversity, 74
    and the business world, 172–9
    challenges of, 232–4, 254–5
    core notion vs outward manifestations, 3
    definition(s) of, iii, 4–5, 26, 30, 269
    difficulties posed by, 4–5
    and economic actors, v, 176–82
    and economic performance, 178, 252
    and education, 95, 106–7
    and the environment, 203–9
    and forms of governance, 238–42
    and globalization, tensions between, 165
    and human rights, 1, 221, 223–30, 255
    and intercultural dialogue, 11, 252
    and the Internet, 137–9
    investment in, 255–7
    measurement of, 256–72
    and the media, 136, 145–8, 153
    media toolkits for, 152–5
    and national cultures, 20, 251–2
    new understanding of, 251–3
    policies on, 144–50, 253
    positive and negative perceptions of, 1
    Programming Lens (CDPL), 211–4
    proxies for, 4
    recommendations regarding, 256
    regional and international initiatives, 23–8

and social cohesion, 231–7
in sub–Saharan Africa, 234
and sustainable
    development, 189–219,
    257
threats to, 13
three-part approach for
    corporate sector, 182
tools for corporate
    audiences, 181–2
UNESCO's view of, 1–2
within and between
    nations, 270–1
cultural erosion, 13
cultural exchange, 39–41
artistic exchanges, 163–5,
    180, 257
see also intercultural
    dialogue
cultural exclusion, 132
cultural expressions
generating goods and
    services, 269
protection of, 29–30
replacement of ancient
    forms with new
    technologies, 17, 19
threats to, 17–18
see also heritage
cultural festivals, 47
cultural heritage *see* heritage
cultural homogenization and
    globalization, 9, 13, 17
cultural hybridization, 22–3, 270
cultural identity *see* identity
cultural imposition, 41
cultural indicators, 2–3
cultural industries/economy, 131,
    146, 262–4, 267–8
contribution of, 264
definition of, 263, 267
sector indicators, 271
cultural institutions, 117
cultural intelligence, 178–80, 257
cultural interaction, 39–41, 55,
    136–7, 256
three main modes of, 39
see also intercultural
    dialogue
cultural interdependency, 39
cultural isolation, 25, 129

cultural literacy, 118, 254–5
cultural manifestations *see*
    cultural expressions,
    heritage
cultural or community
    mapping, 51–3
cultural meaning of brands, 175
cultural neutrality, 192
cultural participation, 260, 265–6
as audience and
    performers, 265
cultural pluralism, 255
see also identities, multiple
    individual
cultural practices, three
    categories of, 266
cultural prescription, 138
cultural production cycle, 267, 272
cultural products
demand for, 269
non-commercial, 263
cultural property, 26, 29
cultural references, 21
cultural rights, 224, 226–30, 240
case law on, 227
individual and collective
    dimensions, 229
see also human rights
cultural satellite accounts, 264
cultural sites, 9, 29, 30–1, 372
destruction of, 207
real and virtual spaces, 55
religious sites, 170
visits to, 266, 267
see also World Heritage sites
cultural skills, 101–2
cultural stereotypes *see*
    stereotypes
cultural studies, 144, 263
cultural visas, 257
see also cultural exchanges
culturalism, 20, 26
Culture Counts (conference,
    Florence, 1999), 3
culture(s)
and alternative modes of
    development, v
and change, relationship
    of, 5, 9
commercialization of, 17

core importance of, v
corporate, 176–7, 181–2, 191
definitions, 1–2, 4, 9, 27–8,
    44, 193, 228, 262, 267–8
domains of, 268
as heritage alone, 44
interaction of, 39–40
and language use/
    vocabulary, 73 (*see also*
    language)
national, 20, 44, 179
and poverty, 191
standardization of and
    globalization, 1
traditional and modern
    manifestations, 17
value judgements on, 194
as web of significance, 193–4
Western notions of high and
    low, 269
culturization of political
    claims, 19
*Curriculum Framework for
    Romani*, 106
cyberspace
access to, 31
language use in, 70–2
see also Internet
Cyprus, 117
Czech Republic, 82, 133, 170, 234

D

Dakar Biennial, 163
Dakar Framework for Action
    (2000), 95, 97, 261
dance, 18, 165
Declaration of Belem (1988), 75,
    204
Declaration on Cultural Diversity
    (Council of Europe, 2000), 25
*Declarations on Promoting
    Independent and Pluralistic
    Media*, 153
*Declaration on Principles of
    International Cultural Co-
    operation* (1966), 26, 29
*Declaration of Principles on
    Tolerance* (1995), 31
*Declaration on Race and Racial
    Prejudice* (1978), 31

*Declaration on the Responsibilities
    of the Present Generations
    towards Future Generations*
    (1997), 31
*Declaration on the Rights of
    Indigenous Peoples* (2007), 53,
    78, 79, 107, 228, 229
*Declaration on the Rights of
    Persons Belong to National
    or Ethnic, Religious and
    Linguistic Minorities*
    (1992), 225, 229
decolonization *see* colonialism,
    colonization
deforestation
and climate change, 207
and indigenous peoples, 17,
    24
*Delhi Declaration and Framework
    for Action* (1993), 102
Delors report *see* International
    Commission on Education
    for the Twenty–First Century
dematerialization/
    deterritorialization, 14
democracy
consensus democracy, 241
democratic citizenship, 98,
    104
democratic governance *see
    under* governance
democratization in sub-
    Saharan Africa, 234
and human rights, 225
and media freedom, 146
UN attitudes to, 238–9
demographic context, statistics
    on, 286–93, 298–301, 380
see also population
Denmark, 133
dependency theories, 191
deprived or vulnerable
    individuals/groups
see excluded groups,
    marginalization, poverty,
    vulnerable groups
Descola, Philippe, 113
developing countries *see*
    emerging economies

Development of a National Strategy for the Jamaica Music Industry, 149
development
    as adaptation, 193
    approaches and cultural diversity, 251
    cultural differences in conception of, 191
    cultural dimension of, 192–3, 262
    economic *see* economic development
    ill-conceived policies for, 192–3
    sustainable *see* sustainable development
    theories of, 191–2
    see also change
Dialogue between Cultures and Civilizations, 44, 254
    see also intercultural dialogue
diasporas, 15
    African, 245
    Chinese, 134
    linguistic, 73
    and media outlets, 134
    remittances from, 286–93
Diergaardt v. Namibia, 227
difference *see* cultural difference, equality and inequality
digital communication *see* communication, media
digital convergence, 261
digital divide, 129, 138, 149, 151
digital technologies *see* information and communication technology
disasters, natural, 207
    risk reduction strategies, 208
discrimination
    and education, 98, 101, 104–5, 120
    gender-based *see under* gender
    legislation/action to prevent, 84, 107, 223, 235
    positive, 150, 177
    racial, 225
    religious, 236

see also affirmative action, equality, racism, women
Disney, 131
Diversity Toolkit for Factual Programmes in Public Service Television, 154–5
diversity
    biological and cultural, 204–5
    checklist (for public service broadcasting), 155
    cultural *see* cultural diversity
    in education, 101–2
    false, 138, 150–1
    impact of loss of linguistic, 75
    and inequality, 1
    linguistic *see* language(s), linguistic diversity/ multilingualism
    linguistic and biological, 74–5
    new forms of, 4
    theoretical model of, 272
    types of dichotomy useful to assess, 270
    in the workforce, 177–8
Djibouti, 132, 133
documentation of linguistic resources, 76–7, 79
Dora the Explorer, 102
DREAM programme, 46
Dudamel, Gustavo, 165
Dushanbe Declaration (2003), 54

E
e-mail, 71, 145
Earth Summit (Rio de Janeiro, 1992), 189
earthquakes, 207
Earthwatch, 175
Eberhard, C., 45–6
economic growth and development
    and cultural industries, 131–2
    and culture, 191
    strategies for, 203
    strategies and cultural diversity, 6, 252, 254
    theories of, 191
economy, the
    and cultural industries, 263

impact of culture on, 6
statistics, 263, 368–71, 373, 380–1
Ecuador, 17, 24, 74, 78, 105, 182, 208, 240, 241
Education for All (EFA), 97–9
    Global Monitoring Report, 3, 97, 98
Education for Intercultural Understanding and Dialogue (conference, Copenhagen, 2008), 114
education and training, 6, 31, 95–127
    of adults, 102
    African systems, 23
    and the arts *see under* arts, the
    challenges to school education, 98–100
    about cultural diversity, 240
    cultural diversity within, 6, 254, 256
    curricula, 98–101, 106–7, 119–21
    educational culture, 111
    for all, iii, 6, 95, 97–8, 106, 108, 118, 119–22
    formal, 107, 120, 192
    four pillars of, 119
    global coalition of institutions, 139
    higher, 102, 328–31
    and human rights, 223–4
    inclusive, 101
    for indigenous peoples *see under* indigenous peoples
    intercultural, 113–22
    and intercultural competencies, 45, 254
    language learning, 80, 88–9, 100, 104, 105, 121–2, 304–7, 375 (*see also* literacy)
    languages of, 75–6, 102–6, 109, 119
    in Latin America, 105
    for literacy *see* literacy
    and mass media, 140
    materials for, 116
    media literacy *see* literary, media
    of minorities, 236

multicultural, 95, 114, 234
non-formal, 107–8, 112, 114, 129
out-of-school learning, 6, 254
policy, 105, 254
recommendations regarding, 256–7
relevance of, 97–107
religious, 18, 44, 48, 89, 100, 116
right to, 95, 97, 227–8, 230, 254
statistics on, 98, 312–31, 375–6
and training for teachers, 119, 121–2, 254
teaching methods, 101–2, 119–22, 257
textbooks, 49, 57, 98, 116
those lacking, 108
traditional, 111
see also learning
Egypt, 26, 104, 163, 226, 243, 252
women's rights in, 226
emerging economies, 14, 173–5, 193
    consumer class in, 173–5
emigration *see* migration
employment *see* work
empowerment *see under* power
enculturation, reverse, 41
England *see* United Kingdom
English language
    changes in, 88
    diversity of, 73
    expansion of, 13
    as language of transaction, 70, 81–3
    as matrix language, 70, 75
    as official language, 70, 87
    plural and hybrid approaches to, 70
    used on the Web, 71–2
environment
    effects of globalization on, 17
    links with language, 73–5
    marine resource management, 208
    statistics on, 364–7
    sustainability of, 203–9
    see also biodiversity
Enwezor, Okwui, 166

equality and inequality, 223
    of cultures and
        civilizations, 5
    in education, 101, 105, 120
    gender issues, 54
    issues and debates, 235
    of participants in
        intercultural
        dialogues, 51
    reduction of socio-
        economic, 235
    statistics on, 368–71, 380
    see also poverty
Erasmus programme, 25, 46
Estonia, 1, 38, 132, 133
Ethiopia, 88, 97, 104, 105, 110,
    132, 133, 169
ethnic
    classification systems, 4
    endogamy, 232
    identity, 14, 19
    massacres, 50
    superiority and national
        identity, 20
Ethnobotanical Guide for
    Anthropological Research in
    Malaya–Oceania, 208
ethnocentrism, 163
ethnography, 41
Ethnologue, 71
Eurobarometer, 265
Europe
    changes in, 233–4
    culture of, 25
    initiatives in, 25
    tourism in, 169–70
European Agenda for Culture, 25
European Audiovisual
    Observatory, 134
European Broadcasting
    Union, 154
European Centre of Culture, 58
European Centre for Modern
    Languages, 89
European Charter of Regional and
    Minority Languages, 87
European Commission ,
    translation by, 83
European Court of Human
    Rights, 224

European Fair Trade Association
    (EFTA), 200
European Union, 84, 87, 88, 105,
    146, 230
    Charter of Fundamental
        Rights of the, 228
    Roma Summit (2008), 232
exchange programmes see
    cultural exchanges
excluded individuals/groups, 4,
    199, 232, 239–40
    and education, 98
    migrants as, 14
    reasons for exclusion, 4
    see also marginalization

F
Facebook, 18, 19, 136, 138
Fairtrade Labelling Organizations
    International (FLO), 200
families
    and education decisions,
        109
    learning within, 111, 244
    values related to, 174, 244
Faro Declaration, 59
Faro Framework Convention on
    the Value of Cultural Heritage
    for Society (2005), 228
female genital cutting/
    mutilation (FGM), 54, 194,
    226
female infanticide, 54
festivals, 30
    cultural, 47
    music, 165
Fiji, 153, 222
financial crisis (2008/09), v, 166
Finland, 39, 47, 133, 143, 146,
    227, 261
fire, use of, 208
fishing, 227
Florence Agreements (1950), 26
folklore, 31, 1689
    commercialized
        spectacles, 171
    see also under knowledge
food and drink
    convenience food, 13
    culturally appropriate, 235

foreign-cuisine
    restaurants, 16
    local vs national cuisines, 13,
        171
    for religious tourists, 170
    security, 17
    shortages, 192
    soul food, 40
    world food crisis (2008), 192
forests, statistics on, 364–7, 379
forestry, 52, 227
Forum for Historical Knowledge
    and Peace in Central Asia, 49
Framework Convention for the
    Protection for National
    Minorities (EU, 1995), 59
France, 20, 51, 104, 131, 143, 171,
    174, 205, 261, 264, 272
    cinema, 133, 138
    as colonizing nation, 234
    French-German Elysée
        Treaty, 49
    French managers, 181
    immigrants to, 232
    National Film Centre, 138
    publishing industry, 272
    visual arts, 166
France24, 150
Fribourg Declaration on Cultural
    Rights (2007), 224

G
Gabon, 52
gacacas, 50
Gambia, 132, 133
Geertz, Clifford, 193
gender
    discrimination, 54, 225
    and education, 100, 108
    equality, 223
    and indigenous people, 17
    and language, 88
    and migration, 15
    parity index, 374, 376
    statistics, 298–301
    see also women
genealogy and language, 73
General Electric, 131
genetic ancestry, 43
Geneva. University of, 48

geographic information systems
    (GIS), 52, 209
geographical belonging, 42, 73
Georgia, 133
Germany, 131, 133, 166, 174, 236
    French-German Elysée
        Treaty, 49
    German managers, 181
Ghana, 194, 195
Global Alliance for Cultural
    Diversity, 180
Global Reach (company), 71, 72
global cities, 43, 47, 173, 242,
    251, 257
globalization, 11–36, 41
    as antithesis of cultural
        diversity, 9
    and the arts, 163, 165
    beneficial effects, 16, 19
    conceptions of, 13
    and cultural diversity, 9, 16,
        150, 172, 251
    definition and scope, 14
    and dialogue of civilizations,
        58
    effects of, iii, 1, 2, 5, 9, 261
    history of, 11
    impact on languages, 67, 70,
        73
    and the media, 137
    and migration, 15
    and new media trends,
        131–7
    and possible cultural
        standardization, 1
glocalization, 142
Google, 18, 131, 135
Gospel (music), 40
governance, 2
    corporate, 172, 176–7
    definition, 238
    democratic, 2, 221, 28–42,
        251, 257
    human centred, 241
    and indigenous peoples, 17,
        241
    participatory, 6
    social, 24
Greece, 117, 133, 185, 243
Greenland, 241

Guatemala, 6, 17, 83, 105, 106, 194
Guinea, 24, 50, 89
Guqin, 18
Gwangju Biennial, 163

H

Hague Convention for the Protection of Cultural Properties in the Event of Armed Conflict (1954), 26, 29
First Protocol, 29
Second Protocol, 29
Haiti, 40, 46, 75
Hamburg Declaration on Adult Learning (1997), 102
handicrafts, 6, 24, 167–71, 180, 257
craft fairs, 167
economic role, 269
happiness indicators, 211
Harragin, Simon, 192
Havana Biennial, 163
health
campaigns, 194–5, 244–5
policies, 194–5
services, culturally appropriate, 84, 224, 235
heritage, cultural
common human, 27, 29–30, 51
digital, 31
the Earth as, 27
goods, definition, 378
intangible, 23, 26–7, 30, 39, 242, 253, 257, 267, 268, 372
intellectual and artistic, 11, 41, 88, 209
protection of, 29
role of, 228
tangible, 23, 26, 27, 267
see also culture, cultural
High-level Group for the Alliance of Civilizations (2006), 3, 115
High-level Round Table on Cultural Diversity and Biodiversity for Sustainable Development, 204
Hinduism, 19
history
education in, 115–16
historical awareness, 41

shared, 49
UNESCO publications on, 57
see also heritage, memory
HIV and AIDS prevention, 194–5
Hong Kong, 76, 103
hospitality, 46, 55
Human Development Index (HDI), 198, 211
Human Development Report 2004: *Cultural Liberty in Today's Diverse World,* 191, 231
Human Poverty Index (HIP–1), 198
human capital, 88
human development, concepts of, 199
Human Rights Watch, 230
human rights
case law on, 227
civil and political rights, 223–4
cultural dimension of, 41, 88, 226–30, 257
and cultural diversity, 221, 223–42, 257
dimension of intercultural dialogue, 44, 187
and diversity issues, 1
economic and social, 224
education as, 95, 97, 227–8, 230, 254
five core cultural, 227–8
of indigenous peoples, 17, 24
individual and group rights, 54, 229
and intercultural dialogue, 44
and peace, v, 257
poverty as denial of, 196–7
promotion of universal, 6
relativism and universalism, 223, 252–3
and social cohesion, 242
statistics on, 302–3
humility, need for, 46, 55
Hungary, 132, 133, 263
Huntingdon, Samuel P., 39, 44, 58
Hutu peoples, 50
hybridization, cultural, 270

I

Iberoamerican Cultural Charter, 24
ICBM, 182
Iceland, 85, 133
ICM Associates, 181
identity(ies), 19–22
acts of, 76
Arab, 25
backlashes, 14
'brand' or consumer–based, 19, 175
'building cultural practices, 266
collective, 9, 44
community *see under* community
complexification of, 16
construction of personal, 21, 22, 54
cultural, 19–20, 235
cultural as illusion, 20
and cultural change, 5
and cultural industry development, 146
ethnic, 14, 19, 21
hybrid, 22
issues and risks of misunderstanding, iii
language and, 67, 76
of migrants, 22
monolithic national vs. multiple, 19, 28, 251–2
multiple individual, 5, 20, 43, 44, 47, 236–7, 255
national, 14, 19, 20, 28, 43
new conceptions of, 67
overlap of individual and collective, 44
personal and the Internet, 18
range of, 19
religious *see under* religion(s)
tensions over, 1
transnational, 15
tribal and regional, 21
strain, 43
and territorial ties, 14
imagined communities, 140
immigration *see* migration
Index of ability (language assessment), 77
Index of Biocultural Diversity (IBCD), 74

Index of continuity (language assessment), 77
Index Translationum, 81
India, 18, 19, 53, 66, 70, 72, 74, 81, 83, 113, 146, 158, 165, 168, 169, 182, 194, 207, 221, 232
Bihar flooding, 208
cinema, 133, 149
education in, 103, 104, 106, 109
as emerging economy, 14, 173–5
language policy, 88
participatory governance, 241
sport, 173
indigenous peoples, 4, 24, 51, 53, 202
arts of, 163
and climate change, 207
constitutional arrangements for, 240
economy of, 78
education of, 17, 18, 97, 104–7, 112
and globalization, 17, 53
land issues, 17, 24, 53, 73–4
languages of *see under* language
management of natural resources, 208
radio stations, 148
reconciliation of differences with, 49
religions of, 117
rights of, 53, 105, 107, 226–7, 229
self-determined development for, 195
skills specific to, 106
state and critical indigenism, 105
see also individual peoples by name
Indonesia, 16, 55, 74, 81, 104, 133, 148, 168, 207, 210, 230
industrialization, 15, 168, 243
inequality *see* equality and inequality
informal sector and value transmission, 6

information and communications
technologies
  access statistics, 294–7
  deterritorialization effect
    of, 14
  impact of, 9, 14, 18, 23, 41
  language use and, 70–3, 79
  and media and information,
    134–7, 154, 251, 257,
    261–2
  need to promote skills in, 6
  policies regarding, 31
  use in education, 102
  see also communication,
    Internet, media
information overload, 18
innovation scores, 172
instruments (policy)
  binding and non-binding, 11
  of international community
    to safeguard cultural
    diversity, 25–8
  see also individual
    instruments by name
intellectual property, 23, 29, 149,
  263, 269–70
  effect of rights on diversity,
    270
  protection of traditional
    cultural expressions, 169
  see also copyright, piracy
Inter-African Film Distribution
  Consortium, 149
Inter-American Indigenous
  Congress, 105
intercultural
  awareness, 115–16
  competencies, 6, 45–6,
    114–15, 254, 255
  intercultural dialogue, 5, 25,
    37–63, 211, 223, 255
  awareness of benefits, 257
  and cultural diversity, 11, 252
  focused on difference, 44
  importance of, 2
  limited concept of, 44
  and multiculturalism, 11
  novel approaches to, 5
  obstacles to, 5, 114
  prerequisites for, 5, 45–6
  recommendations
    regarding, 256

threatened by media
  fragmentation, 138
and translation *see* translation
  what went wrong with, 44
intercultural
  differences, management of,
    115
  education, 113–22
  initiatives, 105
  management consultancy,
    181–2
interfaith dialogue *see under*
  religion(s)
intergenerational
  media usage gap, 138
  transmission, 53, 54, 110, 111
  transmission of
    languages, 69
Intergovernmental Committee
  on Intellectual Property
  and Genetic Resources,
  Traditional Knowledge and
  Folklore (GRTKF), 169
Intergovernmental Conference
  on Cultural Policies for
  Development (Stockholm,
  1998), iii, 27, 191
Intergovernmental Conference
  on Cultural Policy in Africa
  (Accra, 1975), 191
International Association for
  the Evaluation of Education
  Achievement (IAE), 99
International Capoeira Angola
  Foundation, 40
International Child Art
  Foundation (ICAF), 117
International Clearing House for
  Endangered Languages, 77
International Commission on
  Education for the Twenty–
  First Century
  report of (Delors report),
    108, 111, 116, 119
International Conference
  on Education (Geneva,
  2004), 118
International Conference
  on Population and
  Development (ICPD), 194

International Council on
  Monuments and Sites
  (ICOMOS), 23
International Council for Science
  (ICSU), 112
*International Convention on the
  Elimination of All forms of
  Racial Discrimination*, 225
*International Covenant on Civil
  and Political Rights*, 224,
  226–7, 229
*International Covenant on
  Economic, Social and Cultural
  Rights*, 106, 224, 226–7, 228,
  229–30
  Optional Protocol, 230
International Federation of
  Translators, 85
International Forum on Culture
  and Democracy (Prague,
  1991), 238–9
International Forum of
  Indigenous Peoples on
  Climate Change, 207
International Freedom of
  Expression network, 134
International Fund for Cultural
  Diversity, 137
International Indigenous Forum
  on Biodiversity (IIFB), 205
International Labour Organization
  *Convention Concerning
  Indigenous and Tribal Peoples
  in Independent Countries*, 107
International Monetary Fund
  (IMF), 197
International Music Council
  (IMC), 23
International Network for
  Cultural Diversity (INCD), 23
International Organization for
  Migration (IOM), 206
International Society of
  Ethnobiologists, 75
International Standard
  Classification by
  Occupations (ISCO), 264
International Student Travel
  Confederation (ISTC), 170
International Telecommunication
  Union (ITU), 71, 260

International Union for
  Conservation of Nature
  (IUCN), 260
International Years *see under*
  United Nations
international initiatives on
  cultural diversity, 25–8
  see also under United
    Nations, UNESCO
Internet World Stats
  (company), 71
Internet, 71–2, 134–41, 146–7,
  261, 266
  access to, 135, 137, 138,
    294–7
  artistic material on, 167
  and cultural diversity, 136–9,
    147
  and information overload
  and interactivity, 136
  and music, 166
  and news, 135, 146–7
  and personal identity, 18
  in Trinidad, 147
  usage by region, 72
  usage statistics, 135–6, 374
  use in education, 102
  user populations, 71
  see also cyberspace
Internet Archive, 135
Inuit peoples, 51, 78, 110, 241
Inuit Circumpolar Council, 205
Iran, Islamic Republic of, 58, 104,
  168, 173, 194, 207, 243
Iraq, 104
Iron Route project, 57
Isa people (Nigeria), 18
Isackson, Peter, 182
Islam, 18, 199
  the arts in, 163
  in Canada, 143
  in central Asia, 21
  disputes involving, 19
  films about, 139
  Islamic banking, 175–6
  Islamic civilization, UNESCO
    study on, 57
  Islamic law, 226
  Islamic scarf, 20
  Islamization, 21

travel to holy sites, 170–1
and women's rights, 226
Islamic Educational, Scientific
and Cultural Organization
(ISESCO), 59
Israel, 48, 49, 104, 143, 166
Israeli–Arab conflict, 25
Istanbul Biennial, 163
Italy, 11, 18, 82, 104, 131, 132,
133, 166, 167, 224
Ivan Kitok v. Sweden, 227

J

Jamaica, 18, 149
Japan, xiv, 13, 27, 47, 49, 71, 82,
83, 104, 116, 133, 142, 164,
165, 166, 173, 191, 205, 273
jazz, 40, 165
*J. G. A. Diergaardt (the late Captain
of the Rehoboth Baster
Community) et al. v. Namibia*,
227
Jodhpur Process/Initiatives, 24
Johannesburg Biennial, 163
Jomtien Declaration (1990), 95,
97, 108
journalists/journalism
broadcast, 154–5, 340–3
of diverse backgrounds, 150
innovative practices, 146
killed, 332–9, 377
and media literacy, 145
travel journalism, 142
see also media; press, the;
radio; television
justice
right to, 224
social, 257
and water rights, 243–5

K

Kawabata, Yasunari, 56
Kazakhstan, 21, 127, 158, 240
Keita, Sundiata, 244
Kenya, 2, 24, 52, 104, 144, 169,
176, 204, 207, 226, 245
Khatami, President
Mohammad, 58
Klineberg, Otto, 56

knowledge
acquisition, 108 (*see also*
education)
and cultural intelligence, 178–9
culturally specific
organization of, 81
divide, 151
diversity, 112–13
economy, 261
of environmental
management, 203
exoteric and esoteric, 51
loss and language loss, 75
non-centric approach
to, 101
sharing, 139
societies, 95, 113, 153, 252
systems, 112–14, 115, 119
tacit, 209
traditional/indigenous, 30,
74, 113, 169, 180, 195,
202, 204, 206, 207–9, 245,
251, 252, 257
transmission, 18, 95, 108, 111
transparency, 51
see also handicrafts, literacy
Korea, Republic of, ix, 16, 44, 49,
71, 82, 83, 87, 133, 163, 165,
166, 191
Kriol, 75
Kundera, Milan, 22
Kutiyattam, art of, 18
Kyrgyzstan, 17, 21

L

labour *see* work
Lakalaka system, 203
land
and indigenous people, 17,
24, 53, 73–4, 202, 227
management plans, 208
mapping of, 52
ownership systems, 197
sense of place, 14, 50, 52,
73–5, 111, 204, 207
language(s), 5–6, 67–93
academic and
conversational, 104
adaptation processes, 70, 73,
75
African, 23, 72, 78, 85, 88, 245

Apache, 73
Arabic, 13, 21, 25
Catalan, 89
Chinese, 71, 87
colonial, 78
competition among, 13
creoles *see* creoles/
creolization
and cultural diversity, 4
as cultural practice, 266
cultural specificity of, 75
culturally sensitive, 194
dialects, 70, 89
of displaced persons, 206
domains of, 89
dynamics, 69–73
of education *see under*
education
endangered, 13, 69, 77, 85,
89, 103, 251, 253
English *see* English language
extinct, 77
French, 70, 78
groupings of, 78
Hindi, 13, 72
Icelandic, 85
as identity markers, 75
indigenous tongues/
languages, 17, 24, 69, 73,
74, 75, 77–8, 80, 83, 85, 87,
102, 112, 148, 271, 375
international, 76, 85, 86, 256,
375
Inuktitut, 78, 79, 148
Kauma, 78
and knowledge, 75
language loss, 67, 69, 75,
76–7, 192
learning *see under* education
linguistic diversity, 30, 70–2,
148, 304–7, 375
linguistic erosion, 85
linguistic homogenization,
70
and migration, 103–4
minority, 88, 100, 103–4, 202,
227
monolingualism, 80, 102,
103
moribund, 69, 77
as mother tongue, 102–3
multilingualism, iii, 5, 24, 30,
31, 67, 71, 76, 80–1, 85,

89, 102, 104, 151, 253,
255
narrow-niched, 73
national or official, 70, 76, 78,
86, 87, 89, 103, 245, 256,
375
number of, 69, 74, 78
official status of, 70, 75
orthographic systems for, 88
pidgin, 70, 75–6
planning, 86–9
policy, 69, 80–1, 85, 86–9,
253, 256
prestige and esteem of, 89
reappropriated, 78–9
recommendations
regarding, 256
regional dialects, 70
requirements for
immigrants, 236
revitalization, 76, 78–9, 85,
251, 253
rights, 79, 224, 227
Russian, 21
second, 77
shifts, 76, 88
sleeping, 78
Spanish, 13, 71, 78, 83
statistics on, 304–7
Swahili, 13
translation *see* translation
under pressure, 67, 69
unwritten, 79
used in cyberspace, 71–2,
132
vehicular, 13, 70
vernacular, 13
vitality, 76–7
vulnerable, 77
Yoruba, 245
Länsman cases, 227
Latin America
audiovisual sector, 133–4
culture of, 191
economy of, 264
education in, 105
initiatives in, 24
languages in, 78, 87
Latvia, 132, 133
League of Arab States, 25
*Learning Each Other's Historical
Narratives*, 49

learning
   communities/societies,
      108–13
   environment, 108, 119–21
   lifelong, 95, 108, 118
   methods, 107
   outcomes, 121
   participatory, 114–18, 120
   passive, 137
   pathways, seven, 111
   spaces and forms, 110–11
   see also education and
      training. ;lifelong learning
Lebanon, 48, 104, 133
legislation
   cultural exceptions to, 235
   on rights of indigenous
      peoples, 53–4
Lévi-Strauss, Claude, 3, 19
Liberia, 46
Lomoncocha Association, 208
Linguistic Diversity Index (LDI),
   80–1
Linguistic Vitality and Diversity
   (questionnaire), 74
*List of Intangible Cultural
   Heritage in Need of Urgent
   Safeguarding*, 30, 281–5, 372
listening skills, 45, 55
literacy, 88–9, 111
   cultural, 118
   media and information
      literacy, 6, 129, 137,
      139, 143, 144–6, 150,
      255 (programmes in,
      145; recommendations
      regarding, 257)
   statistics, 105, 108, 312–19,
      375
   marriage and ethnic
      groups, 232
literature, 82, 131, 166–7, 272
   language of, 89
   see also media, translation
Lithuania, 132, 133
Little Mosque on the Prairie, 143
*Living Together as Equals in
   Dignity* (2008), 25
logical systems, types of, 113
long tail effect, 137, 138

López Luis Enrique, 112
Luanda National Museum of
   Anthropology, 117
Lubican Lake band v. Canada, 227

M
Macedonia, 49
Madagascar, 74
magic bullet theory, 140
Makah people, 205
Malaysia, 16, 19, 20, 24, 106, 133
   traditional medicine, 195
Mali, 103, 135, 169, 195, 198,
   237, 244
managers, typology of, 181
Mandela, Nelson, 50
Manden Charter, 244
Manifesta, 163
*Manifesto on Behalf of Cultural
   Diversity from Literary
   Translators, Publishers and
   Writers* (2002), 85
Maori, 227, 271
marginalization, 198
   circumstances in which
      suffered, 47
   education and, 100, 102,
      104–5
   globalization and, 13–14, 30
   and public sphere access,
      146
   tourism and, 16
   see also excluded
      individuals/groups,
      minority groups
markets
   in developing countries, 173
   marketing of crafts, 168
   market research, 173
   micromarketing, 169
   transnational, 13
Márquez, Gabriel García, 22, 16
mariage and ethnic group, 232
Mask Dance of the Drums
   (Drametse), 18
Mau Forest Complex (Kenya), 52
Mauritania, 133, 214
Maya peoples (Belize), 53
Maya Achi identity (Guatemala),
   17

Mead, Margaret, 56
*Media Development Indicatórs:
   A Framework for Assessing
   Media Development*, 152–4
MEDIA programme, 25
media
   access to *see under* access
   balanced representation in,
      149–50, 154
   convergence, 136–7
   cross-border flows, 131
   community *see* community
      media
   and cultural contents, 129–
      59, 254
   data on, 260
   deterritorialization effect of,
      14
   development of quality, iii
   diversity in, 31, 147–8, 153–4
   and globalization, 13–14,
      17–18
   impact of, 140–3
   interactive, 136
   and language use, 82–3
   licensing, 154
   literacy *see under* literacy
   local content initiatives,
      148–9
   major companies, 131
   mass media eclipsing older
      forms, 13, 18
   mass media used by
      formerly voiceless
      groups, 14
   multicultural requirements,
      235, 241
   new, 129, 134–44, 146
   ownership, 146, 153–4
   pluralism, 30
   printed, 131, 134–5, 152, 262
      (*see also* literature; press,
      the)
   recorded, 131 (*see also*
      audiovisual, music)
   regulation and industry
      support mechanisms,
      144, 146, 148, 153, 340–3
   statistics, 332–51, 377–8
   toolkits for cultural diversity
      in broadcasting, 152–5
   user-generated content, 146,
      150

   see also communication;
      press, the
MEDIACULT, 23
mediascapes, 140
medicine, 113, 195
megalopolises *see* global cities
Memory of the World
   programme, 31, 137
memory/ies
   collective, 42, 49
   as a main element of cultural
      encounter, 42
   national, 42
   places of, 50, 256
   reconciling conflicting, 42,
      45, 48–51
   see also knowledge
MERCOSUR, 83, 264
Messenger, 138
Mexico, 74, 77, 104, 105, 106,
   111, 133, 148, 170, 176
*Mexico City Declaration on
   Cultural Policies* (1982), 4, 27,
   191, 228
microfinance, 168–9
Micronesia, 13
Microsoft, 72
migration/migrants, 14–16, 22,
   84, 201, 231
   adaptation tactics, 14
   attitudes to, 302–3
   challenge for migrants, 14
   and education, 103–4
   feminization of, 15
   forced of indigenous
      peoples, 17, 207
   illegal, 16
   intercultural nature of
      migrants, 45
   international, 14, 15
   issue between and within
      societies, 231
   media to reach, 153
   policies, 16, 231, 236, 286–
      93, 373
   remittances, 373
   rural–urban, 15
   statistics, 286–93, 373
   of students, 328–31, 376
   see also diasporas

minority groups, 30, 42–3, 106, 235
   balanced representation of, 154
languages of *see under* language and public sphere
   access, 146
   representation in media workforces, 150
   rights of, 225–6, 227, 229, 240
   seen as consumers of resources, 232
   stereotyping of, 141
   voice heard, 232–3
   see also indigenous peoples, marginalization
mobile phones, 73, 134, 136, 144–5
   access statistics, 294–7, 374
models/modelling
   cultural cycle, 267
   three-dimensional (3D), 52, 209
modernity
   concepts of, 13
   loosened grip of, 22
modernization theories, 191
Monaco, 133
monarchs, traditional, 244–5
Mondiacult Conference, 252
Mongolia, 57, 105, 129, 132, 133
Montessori, Maria, 109
Morales, Evo, 54
Morocco, xii, 17, 23, 75, 133, 141, 167, 169, 176, 195, 226, 275
Mostar Bridge, 51
Mozambique, 130, 188
MTV, 131
multi-purpose community telecentres (MCTs), 148
Multicultural Centre Prague, 234
multicultural
   challenges, 232–4
   communities/societies, 14, 15, 42, 113, 231, 251
   education, 101, 113–14
   policies, 234–6, 255
   political multiculturalism, 235
   tensions, v

multilingualism *see under* language
multinational corporations, 176–8, 131, 142
   diversity in, 177–8
   diversification and customization, 172–3
   globalization, new media and, 131
   impact of, 13
   music industry, 165
Multitrans, 84
museification of traditional practices, 18
museography, 51
museology, 201
museums, 117, 122, 201–2
music, 40, 165
   access to digital, 138
   African-influenced, 40
   classical, 165
   data on, 260
   education in, 116, 165
   Jamaican, 149
   and learning, 111
   listening to, 266
   media, 131
   modern, 13, 18
   new technologies and, 166
   piracy, 132
   popular, 165
   recorded repertoire, 133, 348–51
   recorded sales statistics, 348–51
   sales market, 165
   statistics involving, 268, 378
   traditional, 56
Myanmar, 132, 133, 168, 171
MySpace, 18, 19, 136

N

Namibia, 133, 169, 227
nation as principle of identification, 20–1
National Corporation for Indigenous Development (CONADI), Chile
national
   boundaries in Africa, 234
   censuses *see* censuses

cultures, 20, 44, 179
   governance *see under* governance
   history texts, 42
   identities, 14, 19, 20, 28, 43
   memory, 42
   ownership of cultural property, 29
   projects, 23, 208
Native Americans, 40, 78–9, 205
   see also indigenous people
natural resources and indigenous people's rights, 17
natural sites, 11, 170, 372
Nawaz, Zarqa, 143
neoliberalism, impact of, 17
Nepal, 57, 132, 148
Nessuit (Nakuru District, Kenya), 52
Netherlands, the, 131, 133, 234, 236, 271
Netherlands Antilles, 75–6
Network of European Workshops (NEWS), 200
networks
   digital, 251 (*see also* cyberspace, Internet)
   informal, 48, 55
   media-related, 134, 145, 149
   and multiculturalism, 237
   and participatory governance, 241
   Power of Peace, 139
   of solidarities, 257
   support, 145, 237
   UN Global Compact as, 179
New Frontiers of Social Policies (conference, Arusha, 2005), 3
New Latino Spaces, 134
New Partnership for African's Development (NEPAD), 261
New Zealand, 13, 73, 106, 133, 148, 227, 265–6
   Statistics New Zealand, 271
News Corporation, 131
news services, 134, 135, 137, 141, 146–7, 150, 154
   see also press, the
Nicaragua, 105
Niger, 64, 132, 133

Nigeria, 12, 18, 19, 48, 59, 70, 81, 195, 226, 245
   home video, 133, 139
   National Policy Agenda in Education, Science and Culture, 244–5
Nike, 173
Nobel prizes, 56, 166, 169
Noh drama, 165
nomadism, 17, 21, 76, 105, 208
   and forced sedentarization, 192
   nomad technologies, 144
   nomadic spirit, 23
non-governmental organizations, 23, 74, 84, 88, 139, 205, 206, 230
   inappropriate development responses of, 192
Northern Ireland, 19
Norway, 104, 133
Nubian monuments (Egypt), 26
Nuevo Television del Sur, 134
Nyerere, Julius, 234

O

occidentalism, 42
Ogiek people (Kenya), 52
Online Computer Library Center (OCLC), 71
Opera dei Puppi (Sicily, Italy), 18
opera, 165
Operational Policy on Indigenous Peoples (World Bank, 2006)
oral
   based communication, 70
   traditions, 30, 39, 111
   see also communication, storytelling
Organization of African Unity, 230
Organization of American States (OAS), 83, 146, 230
Organization for Economic Cooperation and Development (OECD), 211, 260
   Programme for International Student Assessment (PISA), 99
   trade with, 132

Orientalism, 41–2
Oslo Accords, 49
Oslo Coalition, 48
'others', ix, 45, 46, 47, 141
Our Common Future (1987), 189
Our Creative Diversity (1996), iii, 3, 27, 161, 191
overseas contract workers (OCWs)

P
Pakistan, 104, 132, 133, 143, 168, 233
Palestine, 25, 46, 49
Panama, 204
Panikkar, Raimon, 45–6, 47
Papua New Guinea, 69, 75, 80, 81, 103, 104, 132
Paraguay, 85, 87, 102, 104, 105
Paris Act on Universal Copyright, 29
Parmenides, 48
participatory
    approaches to human development, 199, 209–10, 257
    approaches to learning, 110–11
    campaign–oriented participation, 237
    forms of governance, 6
    governance and the media, 241
    intercultural projects, 46
Peace Research Institute in the Middle East (PRIME), 49
peace
    approaches to and cultural diversity, 251
    defences of, 1
    education and information, 139
    human rights, culture and, v, 6, 30, 257
    requirements for sustainable, v
PEN World Voices Festival of International Literature, 166
Pérez de Cuéllar. Javier, iii, 3
performing arts, 27, 39, 165
    education in, 116

measurement of performance, 266–7
traditional eclipsed by new forms, 13, 17, 18
see also dance, opera, storytelling
Persian culture, 21
Peru, 17, 74, 83, 103, 105, 106, 111, 240
Petronas Towers, Kuala Lumpur, 24
Philippine Initiative, 58
Philippines, 15, 56, 74, 104, 133, 153, 254
    Indigenous Peoples' Rights Act (1997), 53
Pigott, Tony, 182
piracy
    bio-piracy, 195
    of intellectual property, 132–3, 135, 138, 139, 348–51
places *see* cultural sites, environment, land
planning, spatial/urban, 4
poetry, 167
Poland, 132, 133
Pogge, Thomas, 197
political
    activism and identity issues, 19
    rights, 223–4
    see also democracy, governance
Pop Idol, 142
population
    classification systems, 4, 372–4
    and development action programmes, 194
    growth, urban and rural, 13, 364–7
    Internet user, 71
    statistical base, 276
    statistics, 286–93, 364–7, 380
Portugal, 132, 133, 134, 224
postmodernism, 141, 144
post-conflict situations, 24, 50, 114
poverty
    definitions, 197–8
    eradication/alleviation

strategies, 195, 201–3, 251, 262
    of indigenous peoples, 24
    new forms in developing countries, 193
    perceptions of, 196–203
    Reduction Strategy Paperse (PRSPs), 202
    statistics, 196, 368–71, 380
power
    and community media, 148, 150
    empowerment of people, 6, 204, 241–2
    gender and group culture, 54
    imbalances and the media landscape, 137, 142
    and poverty, 198
    relations among refugees, 206
    sharing arrangements, 241–2
prejudice *see* discrimination, stereotypes
press, the, 135–7, 377
    freedom index, 377
    newspaper statistics, 332–9, 377
    stagnation of, 135
    statistical views on, 302–3
private sector, role of, v
Prix Médicis, 166
Progress in International Reading Literacy Study (PIRLS), 99
prostitution, 15, 17
Public Service Broadcasting: A Best Practices Sourcebook, 152–3
public service broadcasting, 146, 152–5, 377
    four factors for assessment, 152
publishing *see* literature; media; press, the

Q
Quai Branly, Musée du, 51
Qatar, 132, 133, 134
quality in education, 97
Quilombos, 40

R
Rabat Commitment, 58, 114, 117
Race and History (1952), 3
racism, 31, 101
    campaigns against, 59, 121
    see also discrimination
Radio Sagarmatha, 148
Radio Suara Perempuan, 148
radio, 132, 206, 262
    access statistics, 294–7
    content statistics, 340–3
    global community movement, 148
    institution statistics, 340–3
    public, 132, 152
Rahnema, Majid, 193
rainbow cultures, 39
Rambaldi, G., 52
rap (music), 40
Recommendation on the Development of Adult Education, 102
Recommendation concerning Education for International Understanding, Cooperation and Peace and Education relating to Human Rights and Fundamental Freedoms (1974), 31, 114
Recommendation concerning the International Exchange of Cultural Property (1976), 31
Recommendation concerning the Most Effective Means of Rendering Museums Accessible to Everyone (1960), 31
Recommendation on Participation by the People at Large in Cultural Life and Their Contribution to It (1976), 31
Recommendation concerning the Preservation of Cultural Property Endangered by Public or Private Works (1968), 31
Recommendation on the Promotion and Use of Multilingualism and Universal Access to Cyberspace (2003), 31

Recommendation for the Protection of Movable Cultural Property (1978), 31

Recommendation on the Recognition of Studies and Qualifications in Higher Education (1993), 31

Recommendation concerning the Safeguarding and Contemporary Role of Historic Areas (1976), 31

Recommendation for the Safeguarding and Preservation of Moving Images (1980), 31

Recommendation on the Safeguarding of Traditional Culture and Folklore (1989), 31, 169

Recommendation concerning the Status of the Artist (1980), 31

reconciliation (post–conflict), 24, 50

Red Book of Languages in Danger of Disappearing (1994), 77

refuge regions, 208

refugees, 15, 206, 232
    statistics, 286–93, 373

reggae, 40, 165

regional
    averages, statistical, 276
    groupings used in statistics, 276
    initiatives on cultural diversity, 23–5

religion(s), 14, 19–20, 43, 204
    accommodation of diverse, 235
    in Central Asia, 21
    and ceremonies, 18
    culture and identity, 19
    freedom of, 44, 229
    and identity, 19, 21
    of indigenous people, 117
    information on plurality of, 44
    interfaith dialogue, 48, 58, 209, 252, 257
    religious conversion, 20
    religious education *see under* education

religious institutions, working with, 194
religious intolerance, 17
religious tourism, 170–1
    and secularism, 19
    as source of potential disputes, 1, 19, 116
    state separation from, 235
    traditional African, 18
    and voodoo, 40
    see also belief systems, Christianity, Islam

Renner, Karl, 240

Reporters sans Frontières, 134

Representative List of the Intangible Cultural Heritage of Humanity, 30, 281–5, 372

reproductive health, 194

resources, natural
    allocation, 257
    consumers of, 232
    shortages, 1
    see also biodiversity, forests, land, water

Ricoeur, Paul, 39, 50

Rishi School, 109

risk-taking, 175

Riyadh Declaration (2007), 25

Robben Island prison (South Africa), 50

Roma peoples, 105–6, 232

Romania, 133

Rougemont, Denis de, 58

Routes of Al-Andalus, 57

rural
    depopulation, 206
    development, 88, 148
    distance from urban world, 24
    livelihood conditions, 207
    population growth, 13, 380

Rushdie, Salman, 22, 167

Russia/Russian Federation, 21, 63, 71, 82, 104, 106, 133, 161, 166, 173, 236, 260
    as emerging economy, 14, 173–5

Rwanda, 24, 50, 104

S

Said, Edward, 41

Saint Vincent, 133

Salamanca Declaration, 24

Sami people (Finland), 39, 227

Samoa Islands, 208

sand drawing, 18

San Marino, 132

Sao Tome and Principe, 159, 198

Sayaracu Association, 208

Schoefthaler, T., 44

Scholar Ship programme, 46

schools, 108–9
    as cultural centres, 120
    see also education

science
    in Africa, 245
    Arabic, 41
    and cultural diversity, 252
    education in, 99. 112–13
    statistics on article publication, 368–71, 381

Search for Common Ground, 143

Second Life (SL), 18, 19

secularism, 19, 21

sedentary lifestyles, 17

self-enclosure (and rejection of difference), 18

Sen, Amartya, 20–1, 197, 198

Senegal, 70, 104, 153, 163, 197

serial reproduction technique, 42

Seville Strategy for Biosphere Reserves, 204

Seychelles, 75

Shuar people, 208

Sierra Leone, 75, 106

Sijuade, Oba Okunade, 245

Silk Roads, 39, 57

Simon Fraser University, Canada, 179

Singapore, 15, 16, 103, 133, 236, 261, 263

skills
    agricultural, 110
    and cultural intelligence, 179
    learning of, 106, 109–10
    management, 181–2
    survival, 110

see also education and training, intercultural competencies, knowledge

SkyTeam Alliance, 176–7

Slave Route Project, 40, 49, 57

slavery/slave trade, 15, 40, 223, 226, 244

Slovakia, 133

Slovenia, 133, 170

social capital, 238

social codes, diversity of, 4

social cohesion
    and governance issues, 238
    and multiple identities, 236–7
    national identity and, 43

social dimension of cultural activity, 265–6

social networking, 136, 138

social relations and cultural diversity, 4

social sciences, 115–16, 203–4

software, 82, 135

Solomon Islands, 197

Solomons, Jeremy, 182

Sony, 131

soul music, 40

South Africa, 24, 50, 52, 73, 104, 133, 163, 170, 232
    language use, 84, 85, 88

Southeast Asia, initiatives in, 24

Soviet Union, former, 21

space, public and private, 4, 256

Spain, 13, 49, 71, 78, 82, 83, 89, 102, 133, 261, 264,
    Council of Wise Men and the Water Court, 243–4
    MDG Achievement Fund, 193
    Ministry of Culture of the Basque Government, 85

spiritual traditions/values, 40, 43, 48
    see also belief systems, religion

spirituals, 40

sponsorship, corporate, 173

sport, 173

Sri Lanka, 259

Stasi Commission, 232

statistics, cultural, 260–367

stereotypes/stereotyping, 6, 137, 138, 150, 254, 256
  and boycotts, 44
  counter–stereotyping, 141–2
  created/reinforced by media, 129, 140–3, 154
  cultural, 41–4
  cultural borrowings as artistic, 164
  definition
  gender–based, 54
  of managers, 181
  methods for measuring, 42
  need to escape from, 5

Stirling, Andrew, 272

Stockholm Conference on the Human Environment (1972), 27

Stoetzel, Jean, 56

storytelling, 17, 52, 102, 111, 119, 206, 266

Strengthening the East African Regional Mapping and Information Systems Network, 52

Sudan, 104, 192

Sufism, 21

Summer Institute of Linguistics, 105

Super Girl Contest, 142

sustainability of traditional societies, 192, 244

sustainable development, v, 2, 23, 27, 30, 100, 171, 257, 263
  cultural diversity as key dimension, 189–219, 251
  not limited to economic growth, 211
  sustainable tourism, 170–1
  three pillars of, 189

Sweden, 133, 170, 227, 234

Switzerland, 131, 133, 143, 166, 240

symbolic annihilation, 142

Syrian Arab Rep., 132, 133

T

taboos, 117

Tajikistan, 21

Tamerlane, 21

Tanzania, 3, 10, 67, 133, 195, 206, 234

Taonga Tuku Iho activity, 271

Target Index Group (TGI), 173–4

Tashkent Declaration, 58

Tauli-Corpuz, Victoria, 17

technology, new/modern, 39
  see also information and communication technology

Teen Second Life, 19

Telesur, 134

television, 131–4, 137, 262, 266, 271
  access statistics, 294–7
  animation, 169
  confidence in, 302–3
  content statistics, 340–3
  impact of, 140, 141
  indigenous people's network, 148, 152
  institution statistics, 340–3
  programmes, 142–3
  programming statistics, 133
  public service, 152, 154
  standardization in, 142

tension
  between cultures, 42
  and national stereotypes, 56
  racial, 43
  see also conflict

terroirs, 205

teyyam, 165

Thailand, 104, 133, 167, 180, 193, 255, 265

third culture kids (TCK), 73

Thomas, Jean, 56

thought, systems of, 4

Time Warner, 131

Timor-Leste, 117

Togo, 59, 132, 133, 169, 245

Tokelau, 132

tolerance, 59, 114
  active, 44
  principles of, 31
  statistical views on, 302–3
  varying with age, 115

Tonga, 203

Torres Strait Creole, 75

tourism, 6, 16, 17, 131, 169–70, 257
  community-based, 201
  and crafts, 167–71
  cultural, 170–1
  and cultural heritage, 29
  and travel journalism, 142
  religious, 170
  statistics, 360–3, 379
  volume of, 16, 169–70

trade
  in cultural goods and services, 131–2, 352–9
  data sources, 276
  fair trade movement, 200, 201
  as form of cultural exchange, 39–41
  statistics, 264–5, 352–9, 378–9

tradition and modernity, 19

trafficking
  of migrant workers, 15, 17
  of stolen property, 29

Traficante del Sueños, 134

trans-coding, 142–3

transcultural youth, 73

translation, 5, 80–5, 256
  audiovisual industry and, 82–3
  automatic translation systems, 83–4
  between cultures, 39
  between languages, 81–5
  from/into English, 70, 81
  methods, 82–4
  statistics on, 308–11, 375
  target languages, 81–2, 166, 308–11
  of textbooks, 49
  by UNESCO, 56, 167

Trends in International Mathematics and Science Study (TIMSS), 99

Trinidad, 40, 147

Truman, President Harry S., 191

trust
  reciprocal, 232, 237
  statistics on, 302–3

truth and reconciliation commissions, 50

Tunisia, 104, 149, 167

Turkey, 104, 133, 143, 163

Turkmenistan, 21, 104

Tutsi peoples, 50

TV5, 134

U

Uganda, 194, 195, 226, 265–6

Ukraine, 132, 133

Uma Fukun, 117

Unicode, 79

UNIDROIT Convention on Stolen or Illegally Exported Cultural Objects (1995), 29

United Arab Emirates, 143

United Cities and Local Governments (UCLG), 47

United Kingdom, 47, 70, 71, 131, 133, 146, 149, 165, 170, 174
  Arts Council England, 166, 240
  British managers, 181
  as colonizing nation, 234
  policies to foster social cohesion, 236, 240

United Nations
  Alliance of Civilizations initiative, 58, 179
  Committee on Social, Economic, and Cultural Rights (CESCR), 197, 224, 230
  Conference/Commission on Environment and Development (UNCED), 53, 189
  Conference on Trade and Development (UNCTAD), 200, 264
  conventions and declarations *listed separately by title*
  core principles, iii
  Decade of Education for Sustainable Development, 101
  Decade of Interreligious Dialogue and Cooperation for Peace, 55, 59
  Delivering as One initiative, 214

Department of Economics and Social Affairs (UNDESA), 260
Development Group Guidelines on Indigenous Peoples' Issues (2008), 210
Development Programme (UNDP), 3, 193, 197, 199, 204, 260
Educational, Scientific and Cultural Organization (UNESCO) *see separate entry below*
Environment Programme (UNEP), 3, 260
Food and Agriculture Organization (FAO), 196, 260
Framework Convention on Climate Change (UNFCC), 53, 189, 207
Global Agenda for Dialogue Among Civilizations, 58
Global Compact, 179
High Commissioner for Refugees (UNHCR), 15, 206
Human Rights Committee, 227
International Year of Astronomy (2009), 113
International Year of Languages (2008), 77
International Year for the Rapprochement of Cultures (2010), 54–5
Millennium Development Goals, v, 187, 202, 210, 253
Permanent Forum on Indigenous Issues (UNPFII), 17, 191, 205
Population Fund (UNFPA), 194
publications *listed separately by title*
statistical views on, 302–3
Statistical Division, 260
World Decade on Culture and Development (1988–1997), 3, 191
Year of Dialogue Among Civilizations (2001), 58

United Nations Educational, Scientific and Cultural Organization (UNESCO)
activities regarding the arts, 167
activities regarding biocultural diversity, 74
activities regarding biodiversity, 204
activities regarding communication, 137
activities regarding cultural diversity, 178, 211–14, 254
activities regarding traditional knowledge systems 208
Ad Hoc Expert Group on Endangered Languages, 69, 74, 77
Associated Schools Project Network (ASPnet), 101
Award of Excellence programme, 169
Biosphere Reserves, 204
Catalogue of Reproductions, 56
Coastal Marine Programme, 208
Collection of Representative Works, 56, 167
Collection of Traditional Music, 56
Comprehensive Strategy for Textbooks and Other Learning Materials (2005), 98
Constitution, 1, 20, 26, 114, 164, 238
conventions, ratification of, 26, 277–80, 372 (*see also* individual conventions by name)
Creative Content programme, 148
Expert Meeting on Cultural Diversity (2007), 260, 269
Framework for Cultural Statistics (FCS), 6, 28, 256, 260, 262–70
Guidelines for Measuring Cultural Participation, 266

Guidelines on Intercultural Education, 119–22
history of dialogue at, 56–9
Institute for Statistics (UIS), 6, 262, 265, 266

Initiative B@bel programme, 84
International Bureau of Education, 99
Interreligious Dialogue programme, 58
Intersectoral Working Group, vii–viii, 2
leading role, instruments, 23, 25–6, 79, 169
Local and Indigenous Knowledge Systems (LINKS) programme, 113, 208
Major Project on Mutual Appreciation of Eastern and Western Cultural Values, 56
Man and the Biosphere (MAB) programme, 204
Masterpieces of the Oral and Intangible Heritage of Humanity, 17, 30, 39, 372 (statistics on, 281–5)
Model Plan for the Analysis and Improvement of Textbooks and Teaching Materials as Aids to International Understanding (1949), 98
networks, 58
objectives, 1
policies and activities on education, 98, 101–2, 106, 108, 111, 116, 119–22, 196
policies and activities on poverty, 198
policy on World Reports, 2
Power of Peace Network, 139
recommendations *see separate entries by name*
role of culture for, iii, 1–2, 5
Science Agenda: Framework for Action, 112
strategies of, iii

reports and conferences, *see under* specific titles
translations at, 84
World Reports Unit, 2
United States, 15, 18, 20, 40, 49, 71, 72, 73, 77, 78, 82, 84, 103, 106, 131, 133, 139, 140, 148, 150, 165, 166, 176, 177, 180, 182, 191, 205, 208, 230, 234, 232, 241, 245, 251, 263
Act Requiring Competent Interpreter Services in the Delivery of Certain Acute Health Care Services, 84
Americans with Disabilities Act (1990), 84
demographic make-up, 84
economy, 180, 263
Library of Congress, 137, 167
marriage and ethnic groups, 232
National Endowment for the Arts, 166
Unity for Journalists of Color, 150
Unity Productions Foundation, 139
Universal Copyright Convention (1952), 26, 29, 169
Universal Declaration on Cultural Diversity (2001), 27, 30, 102, 204, 223, 228, 268
Universal Declaration of Human Rights (1948). 26, 44, 106, 119, 221, 226, 230, 238, 243
Universal Declaration on Linguistic Rights, 1996 Barcelona Draft, 79
urban issues
in developing countries, 173–4
festivals, 47
growth of, 13
sedentary lifestyles, 17
urban culture, 14
Uruguay, 134, 264
Uzbekistan, 21

V
Vachon, Robert, 45
values
carriers and creators of, 54

cultural, spiritual and religious, 43, 51
in emerging economies and Western Europe, 174–5
as a main element of cultural encounter, 42
non-centric approach to, 101
transmission of, 6, 95, 108
universally shared, 43
value of cultural heritage, 27
see also belief systems
Valuing All Languages in Europe (VALEUR), 89
Vancouver Chinese New Year's Festival, 47
Vanuatu, 18, 51, 57, 197
Venezuela, 74, 94, 104, 134, 165
Veranda, The (Helsinki), 47
video clips on YouTube, 18
see also audiovisual industry
Vienna Declaration and Programme of Action, 59, 223, 226
Viet Nam, 83, 95, 155, 201–2
village development committees, 208
Vivendi, 131
voiceless, the *see* marginalization
Voices21, 145
voodoo, 40
vulnerable groups, education of, 100

W

Wade, President Abdoulaye, 197
water
conflicts over, 17, 243–4
right to safe drinking, 224
Web *see* Internet
Web 2.0, 136, 139
Welsh Language Board, 89
West(ern)
cultural paradigm, 13, 42
as driver of globalization, 13
and the mass media, 141
model of development, 189
slow decentring of, 164
values and human rights, 226

see also occidentalism
whale hunting, 205
Windhoek Declaration on the Development of an Independent and Pluralistic African Press, 152
Wolfensohn, James, 192–3
women
as agents of cultural change, 54
as autonomous agents in the construction of their identities, 54
and craft work, 168
earnings of, 374
employment statistics, 298–301
'giraffe women', 171
political positions held by, 239, 298–301
rights of, 226
as value carriers and creators, 54
see also female genital cutting/mutilation; gender
wonder, 46, 55
Words Without Borders, 85
work and employment
by children, 109
in cultural industries, 262–4
diversified environment for, v
diversified workforce in media industries, 150
employment of migrants, 15
female-oriented jobs, 15
generation of, 202–3
labour costs, 13
labour markets, v
producing handicrafts, 167 (*see also* handicrafts)
social meanings of, 198–9
statistics on, 368–71, 381
temporary nature of, 16
World Bank, 3, 53, 172, 192, 197, 199, 260
World Commission on Culture and Development, iii, 3, 27, 161, 191, 241

World Conference on Arts Education (Lisbon, 2006), 116
World Conference on Cultural Policies (Mexico City, 1982), iii, 1, 27, 191
World Conference on Education for All, 97
World Conference on Human Rights (Vienna, 1993), 196
World Conference on Science (Budapest, 1999), 112
World Congress of Imams and Rabbis for Peace (2008), 58
World Declaration on Education for All see Jomtien Declaration
World Declaration on Higher Education for the Twenty–First Century: Vision and Action (1998), 102
World Digital Library, 137, 167
World Fair Trade Organization (WFTO), 200
World Free Press Institute, 134
World Health Organization (WHO), 195, 196
World Heritage Convention (1972) see *Convention Concerning the Protection of the World Cultural and Natural Heritage*
World Heritage sites, 29, 50, 171, 201–2, 372
statistics on, 281–5
tentative list, 372
World Intellectual Property Organization (WIPO), 169, 263
World of Music and Dance (WOMAD), 165
World Observatory on Cultural Diversity, recommended, 3, 27, 256
World Observatory on the Social Status of the Artist, 164
World Religious Travel Association (WRTA), 170
World Report on Cultural Diversity
genesis, 2
objectives, 2

purpose, 3
structure, 5–6
World Report on Knowledge Societies, 2
World Summit on the Information Society (Tunis, 2005), 2

World Summit Outcome Document (2005), 210
World Summit on Sustainable Development (Johannesburg, 2002), 189, 193, 204
World Tourism Organization (UNTWO), 170, 260
World Values Surveys, 115, 375
on geographical belonging, 42–3
statistics from, 302–3
World Wide Web (www) *see* Internet
'world culture', 18, 165
world literature, 167
world-mindedness, 116
world systems theories, 191

Y

Yemen, 194, 243
young people
cultural identities of, 14, 19, 25
dialogue between, 46, 256
linguistic usages, 73, 77, 89
literacy rates, 376
tolerance of, 115
transcultural youth, 73
and travel, 170
voice for, 145, 147, 242
YouTube, 18, 19, 136, 146
Yoruba Academy of Science, 245
Yunus, Muhammad, 169

Z

Zambia, 103, 132, 195
Záparas people (Ecuador and Peru), 17
Zimbabwe, 53, 232